The Change
in the European
Balance of Power,
1938-1939

WILLIAMSON MURRAY

The Change in the European Balance of Power, 1938-1939

The Path to Ruin

PRINCETON UNIVERSITY PRESS
PRINCETON, NEW JERSEY

Copyright © 1984 by Princeton University Press
Published by Princeton University Press,
41 William Street, Princeton, New Jersey 08540
In the United Kingdom:
Princeton University Press, Guildford, Surrey

All Rights Reserved
Library of Congress Cataloging in Publication Data
will be found on the last printed page of this book
ISBN 0-691-05413-4 / 0-691-10161-2 (pbk.)

This book has been composed in Linotron Electra
Maps and charts by Lisa T. Davis

Clothbound editions of Princeton University Press books
are printed on acid-free paper, and binding materials
are chosen for strength and durability.
Paperbacks, although satisfactory for personal collections,
are not usually suitable for library rebinding

Printed in the United States of America by
Princeton University Press
Princeton, New Jersey

To the Memory of My Friends
Georg Heiner Sell, Robert Miller
and Helen Smith

If you do not intervene, you will remain the prey of the victor without dignity and without favor. It will always be the case that the party which is unfriendly to you will seek your neutrality, while your friends will demand that you declare yourself by taking up arms. Princes who lack resolution take the path of neutralization in order to avoid a present danger and for the most part find it the path to ruin.

Machiavelli, *The Prince*

Contents

x

Contents

Maps

Charts

Tables

Acknowledgments

This manuscript is the outgrowth of both the research that led to my dissertation and thought given over the considerable period of time since to the strategic processes of the late 1930s. During that time the advice and encouragement of my advisor, Hans Gatzke, was critical in providing the criteria and sense of what historical research involved. At Yale, Professors Donald Kagan and Piotr Wandycz gave me direction, encouragement, and sensible clear-headed advice. My debt to my days in graduate school would not be complete without mention of the contributions that my friend and fellow student MacGregor Knox made to my understanding of military affairs. In the preparation of the various drafts that this work has gone through, my wife, Marjorie Murray, Mark Biddle, Albert Macchioni, Nicholas Rostow, Kent Mitchell, and Brad Meyer have all made significant contributions. Here at Ohio State I owe a considerable debt of gratitude to the late Andreas Dorpalen and to my present colleague Allan Millett. Richard Challener and Richard Ullam, of Princeton University, provided enormously helpful critiques of the several drafts of the manuscript that I submitted to the Princeton University Press. At West Point Helen Bowman, Bob Doughty, and Paul Miles all provided significant support with the final proofs. In Europe Brian Bond, of the War Studies Department, King's College, London, and Wilhelm Deist, of the Militärgeschichtliches Forschungsamt, provided critical, perceptive help. I must also thank my editors at Princeton, Miriam Brokaw and Marilyn Campbell for their help in preparing the final manuscript. Lisa Tingey Davis did an outstanding job with the maps and charts.

Finally I should also mention the help that I have received from the various archives that I have visited. George Wagner, of the Captured Records Section of the National Archives, was always helpful and friendly. In Great Britain and Germany "Pat" MacDonald, of the Air Historical Branch, the staff of the Public Record Office, and the archivists at the Militärarchiv in Freiburg played an important role in guiding me through the maze of documents dealing with the late 1930s. Joni Wood-Ward did an outstanding job with the typing of the final manuscripts.

As with all works of this nature the strengths more often than not reflect the help of others: The weaknesses, however, are mine alone.

Introduction

The origins of this study lie in the spring of 1970 when, in a research seminar, I undertook to study the military aspects of the Czech crisis of 1938. As I became familiar with the period, I came to feel that, although the 1938 crisis was of great importance in delineating the shift in the European balance of power, it formed only a part of a larger picture. To understand the historical process, the entire period from March 1938 through to the winter of 1939-1940 must be seen as a whole.

This study aims to achieve such an understanding. It looks at the strategic, economic, and military situations over the period and then considers them in relation to the actual course of events. It attempts to clarify not only the real strategic positions but the differing perceptions of them by military leaders and statesmen. Above all, this study tries to describe the impact of military and strategic factors in peace as well as in war.

Only by discussing the processes through which policy evolved, by considering the misperceptions and miscalculations that guided policy makers, and by comparing their views with the actual strategic situation can one understand what went wrong in the late thirties. As in any era, politicians and military leaders faced immense difficulties in the formation of policy. What in retrospect may seem clear and obvious was not necessarily so at the time. For nearly all the strategic missteps there were seemingly good and logical reasons for taking what in retrospect was the wrong course. Yet, in the final analysis, Hitler more often than not made correct strategic decisions, while the Allied leaders did not. That difference alone suggests that something was indeed wrong with the response of the Western Powers to the crisis occasioned by the rise of Nazi Germany.

The Change
in the European
Balance of Power,
1938-1939

I

Germany: The Strategic Problem

On January 30, 1933 Adolf Hitler assumed the chancellorship of Germany. Within five days he made clear to the state's military leaders that his diplomatic and strategic aims involved not merely changes within the framework of the Versailles treaty but the wholesale destruction of that treaty as well as of the existing balance of power in Europe. [1] As he had consistently enunciated throughout his career, his purpose was not to make war for the sake of minor alterations but to destroy the European system and to acquire the Lebensraum needed by the German people. [2] It seems likely that Hitler's military listeners paid relatively little attention to the führer's dreams of vast conquests; they were undoubtedly happy enough to hear that they now possessed a government that would unshackle the hated restrictions of Versailles and allow Germany's military forces to regain their proper place in the sun.

The course of German history over the next six and one-half years would be intimately connected with the process of rearmament and preparations, at least in Hitler's mind, for *"der Tag."* Yet rearmament would not be an easy task. Economic and strategic factors influenced its course and placed limitations on the German government that proved exceedingly difficult to overcome—particularly in the period immediately before the outbreak of war. The Germans faced problems in their rearmament effort in terms of foreign exchange, availability of resources, and overall national strategy that were entirely different in nature from those faced by the Anglo-Saxon powers or the Soviet Union. [3] It is only through an understanding of the interrelations among those economic difficulties, the strategic deficiencies, and Germany's diplomatic and rearmament policies that one can come to a full understanding of Germany's strengths as well as her very considerable weaknesses at the end of the 1930s. The ability of the Germans to overcome, or at least escape, the full implications of their economic and strategic difficulties in the first year of the Second World War (although only just barely) would play a decisive role in the catastrophes of the 1939-1941 period.

THE NATURE OF THE STRATEGIC PROBLEM: THE GERMAN ECONOMY

In the last years of the First World War, the naval blockade in the North Sea had exercised an increasing, and in the final analysis perhaps decisive, effect on the strategic position of the Central Powers. By summer 1918 the specter of starvation stalked not only the populations of Austria-Hungary and the other allies of Germany but also the Germans themselves. Moreover, the privations of the previous three years of blockade directly affected military operations. For the great spring offensive of 1918 the German high command could barely scratch together forty first-class divisions, and the remainder of the German infantry had degenerated into groups of weary, ill-equipped soldiers.[4] Even the first-class attack divisions would at times become ill-disciplined mobs, looting from Allied supplies the food and equipment so long denied them by the blockade.[5]

Germany was as dependent economically on imported raw materials in the 1930s as she had been before the First World War. In fact, her dependence had increased. German resources of every strategic raw material except coal (see Charts 1 and 2) were at best insufficient, and in most cases simply did not exist. Even Germany's agricultural production could not meet her needs.

Coal was the one raw material Germany possessed in abundance. Yet strategic and economic difficulties impinged on this sector. The western coal fields, particularly those in the Saar, lay close by the border and faced the threat of French military operations. In the east the fields of Silesia faced a similar threat from the Poles and the Czechs. The demands of the German economy for coal were enormous. The iron and steel industries were the biggest users, but the transport network, synthetic industries, and electric power plants also depended heavily on coal. Moreover, one of the most important uses of German coal was to earn foreign exchange.[6] Coal exports to Southeastern Eu-

CHART 1

Percentages of 1938 World Output of Certain Raw Materials

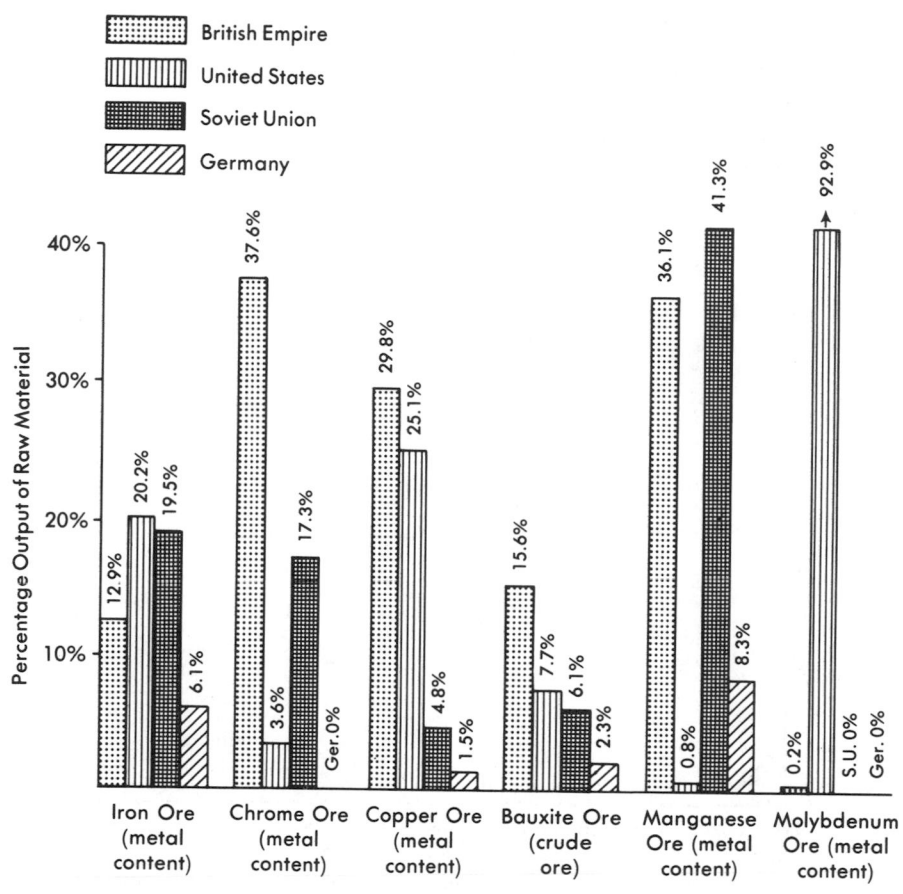

SOURCE: J. Hurstfield, *The Control of Raw Materials* (London, 1953), p. 29.

rope were of decisive importance in insuring a continuation of Balkan imports.[7] Italy was dependent on German coal and the outbreak of a European war would force the Germans to export coal to Italy over the Alps, so that deliveries to Switzerland also had to continue.[8]

Even with Germany's extensive deposits and with the inclusion of such coal-producing areas as Czechoslovakia and Poland within the German sphere of influence, coal production remained a major problem throughout the war. Increased output of synthetic oil and rubber required larger and larger amounts of coal. Because most conquered

CHART 2

Percentages of 1938 World Output of Certain Raw Materials

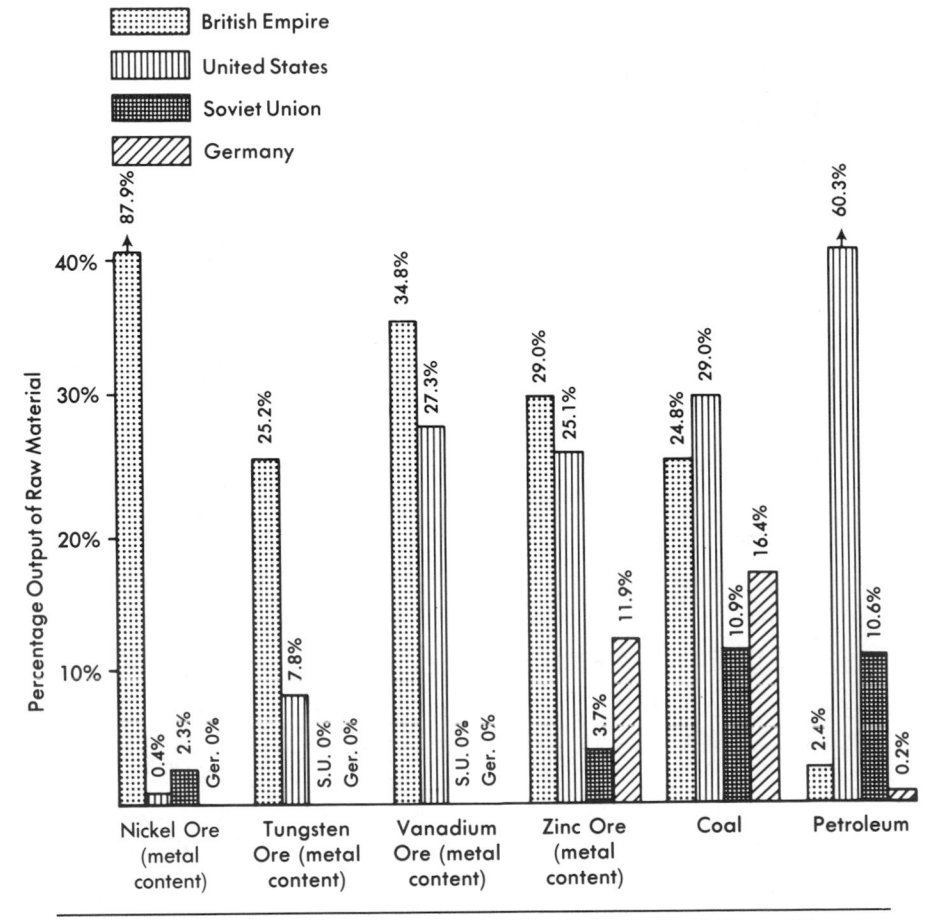

SOURCE: J. Hurstfield, *The Control of Raw Materials* (London, 1953), p. 29.

regions in Western Europe depended on Germany, demands for any increase in their production of industrial goods also required more German coal.[9]

The situation with regard to other raw materials was even less favorable. Germany's economy was particularly vulnerable in the petroleum and metals sectors. Motorization in the 1930s led to a steady growth in demand by civilian as well as military branches of the economy. By 1937 the number of vehicles in Germany equaled that in Great Britain. Demand for diesel fuel increased at an even faster rate than demand for gasoline—from 527,000 tons in 1933 to 1,312,000 tons in 1937. This was due not only to vehicular needs but to industrial demands as well.[10]

In order to maintain an increasingly motorized economy and to cut down on their external dependency, the Germans pushed construction of synthetic fuel plants (i.e., plants that used coal to make petroleum products). Nevertheless, in spite of substantial investment in the synthetic fuel industry, synthetic production never caught up with demand (see Chart 3). Although the percentage of synthetic fuel in terms of total fuel consumption steadily increased in the 1930s, Germany was importing more fuel in 1937 than she had at the beginning of the decade.[11] Demand had increased faster than synthetic production.[12] An economic study from early 1940 admitted that despite efforts to

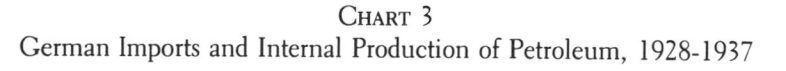

CHART 3
German Imports and Internal Production of Petroleum, 1928-1937

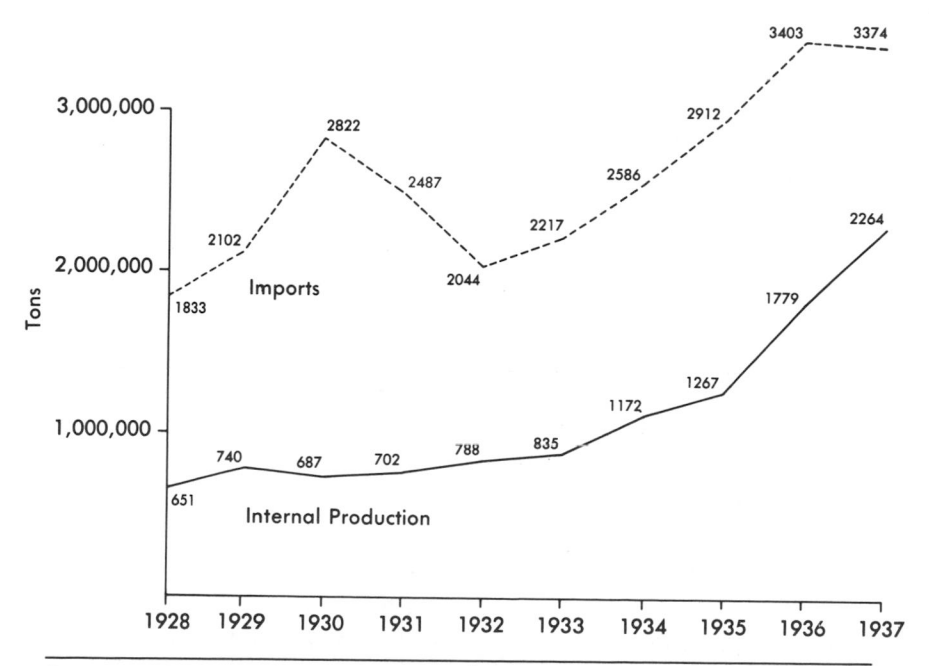

SOURCE: "Abschrift einer Aufstellung der Überwachungstelle für Mineralöl vom 3. Mai 1938: Deutschlands Mineralölbilanz nach In- und Auslandsaufkommen in den Jahren 1928-1937 in 1,000 tons" (NARS T-77, Roll 341, Frame 1179269).

free the German war economy from dependence on petroleum imports, motorization and rearmament had caused demand to rise so sharply that no decrease in oil import tonnages had occurred.[13] The fuel situation in the summer of 1938 indicates the extent of the problem. In June 1938 supplies in storage tanks could cover only 25 percent of mobilization requirements—on the average four months of full wartime needs. Supplies of aviation lubricants were as low as 6 percent of mobilization requirements.[14] This was, of course, a reflection not only of Germany's inability to meet petroleum requirements from her own resources but also of her considerable problems in earning foreign exchange to pay for imports.

The rubber industry reflected a similar picture. In the 1930s the Germans put considerable effort into the construction of synthetic rubber plants, but these investments did not begin to bear fruit until 1939; synthetic rubber plants were not in full production until 1942. Production increased from 5,000 tons in 1938 to the range of 140,000 to 150,000 tons per year in 1942, but in mid-1938 it could cover less than one-sixteenth of the economy's needs.[15]

Supplies of ferrous metal were equally precarious (see Charts 4 and 5). The Nazi regime made extensive efforts in the 1930s to reduce dependence on ore imports and managed to make some progress, but not enough to overcome a serious strategic weakness. In 1938 40 percent of the iron ore used by German heavy industry came from German sources. However, because German ore was of considerably poorer quality than French and Swedish ore, such tonnage figures give a false picture. One hundred tons of German ore produced only thirty tons of pig iron, whereas one hundred tons of Swedish ore produced fifty tons. When the iron content of the ore is taken into account, German dependence on foreign sources in 1938 was about 70 percent.[16] A replacement of all imported ores by German ore would have required 170 percent more tonnage,[17] and low-grade German ore was considerably more expensive to smelt.[18]

Of the 22 million tons of ore imported in 1938, only 12 1/2 million tons of ore from Sweden, Norway, and neutral Western Europe (Belgium) were safe from immediate blockade. War would block imports from the British and French empires, France, and Spain. Thus, German economic experts regarded Swedish ore as essential for the continued functioning of the German war machine.[19] Again using the

CHART 4

Iron Ore Supplies for the German Economy, 1936-1944

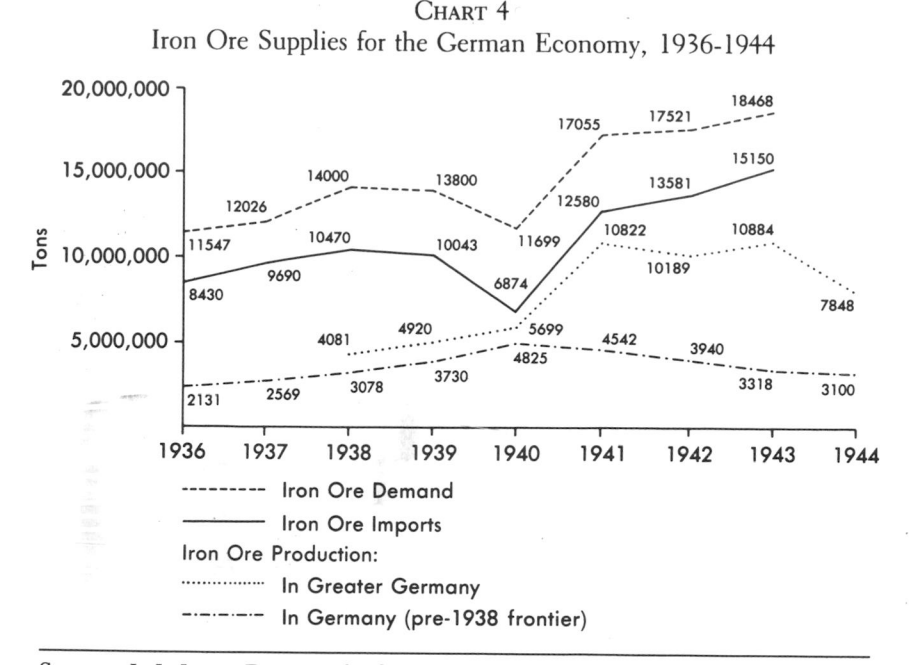

SOURCE: J. J. Jäger, *Die wirtschraftliche Abhängigkeit des Dritten Reiches vom Aus-land* (Berlin, 1969), pp. 131, 189.

year 1938, the Germans possessed stockpiles of iron ore sufficient to cover only three months of full production without recourse to Swedish deliveries.[20] Consequently, as long as access to French ore fields was denied in time of war, Swedish ore was indispensable to the German economy. Once the Germans controlled Lorraine, however, Swedish ore was no longer so critical. In 1939 one German expert warned that a continued supply of iron ore for the German economy in wartime might be a more difficult problem than pertroleum.[21]

Other strategic metals were in equally short supply. The Saar was the center of the chrome industry, and in 1939 the threat of possible French military action forced the Germans to evacuate much of this industry to the east. As a result, in spite of having on hand fifteen months' supply of chrome ore, German smelting capacity could cover chrome requirements for only eight months.[22] The German economy depended on imports of such critical metals as nickel (see Chart 6), tungsten, molybdenum, vanadium, and manganese, all used in the production of high-grade steel. In the final result, the unexpected Nazi-

In February 1938 a member of the OKW (Oberkommando der Wehrmacht, armed forces high command) economic staff warned that Germany's great weakness and Britain's strength was that the latter, with the Americans, maintained a dominant position over the world supplies of raw materials. He added that Anglo-American control over so much of the world's raw materials must make any nation pause over the risks involved in war with them.[25] Even with the bulk of the European continent under German control in World War II, it is worth noting that economic factors constrained German strategy more than Allied strategy.[26]

CONSTRAINTS ON REARMAMENT

The nature of the German victories in the first years of the Second World War led contemporaries to conclude that Germany had organized her economy for "total war" and that in September 1939 she had enjoyed overwhelming superiority in armaments, quantitatively as well as qualitatively. After the war, however, the strategic bombing surveys indicated that such was not the case. In fact, the German economy had a surprisingly low rate of production at the outbreak of war for such key items as tanks, aircraft, and ammunition. Not until the middle of the war did an enormous increase in the production of materiel occur.

From statistics in the strategic bombing survey, Burton Klein, an American economic historian, suggested that Germany could have achieved a far higher level of armament production. He argued that military output could have increased had there been lower imports of foodstuffs, higher taxes, deficit spending, and the transfer of workers from nonessential civilian industries.[27] The weakness in this thesis lies in a failure to realize that the circumstances that determined German rearmament in the 1930s and American rearmament in the 1940s were vastly different. Admittedly there were areas where Germany might have expanded armament production, but outside factors constrained German rearmament to a far greater extent than was the case with American industry. Klein's claim that the Nazi regime could have expanded military production as late as 1938 "without causing appreciable decline in the general level of civilian output," entirely ignores the difficulties the Germans faced with regard to foreign exchange (see below).[28]

Klein also ignored the political factors that influenced Hitler during rearmament. Memories of the 1923 inflation and the depression restricted the options in economic policy. Greater inflationary policies and continuation of the depression's low standard of living would have done little to improve the regime's popularity. In a real sense Hitler's political position in his first years in power depended on his ability to turn the economic crisis around.

But even had the regime been willing to take greater political risks, the question remains of how much it could have increased military production. Cuts in food imports in some cases would not have led to an increase in foreign exchange. A halt to importation of Rumanian grain, received through the barter of industrial goods, would not have increased the German balance of payments. The Rumanians could not have paid hard currency for German goods. Although in the early period of German rearmament large numbers of unemployed were available, and in the later period many Germans worked in "soft" consumer industries, the real difficulty for armament industries was the problem of finding skilled labor. As one naval expert complained in 1938, the transfer of 1,500 workers to naval dockyards would achieve almost nothing immediately because five and one-half years (including military service) were needed to produce a skilled worker.[29]

The most serious error in the Klein thesis lies in the claim that the rise in "military output which occurred from late 1942 to mid-1944 was accomplished with a relatively small increase in the resources available."[30] In 1942 Germany controlled the resources of almost the entire European continent, whereas in the 1937-1939 period the Reich was limited to the resource-scarce base of central Europe. In 1939 German industry produced 22,508,000 tons of raw steel; in 1941 production had risen to 32,039,000 tons, but only 20,836,000 tons of this were produced within the borders of the old Reich.[31] Thus, nearly 40 percent of 1941 steel production came from sources not available to Germany in 1937-1938. German success in expanding production throughout the last three years of the war did not depend to any great extent on the supposed slack within the prewar economy. Rather, it occurred because the Germans were able to exploit ruthlessly the resources of the occupied and neutral countries within their sphere of control. As Hitler in 1942 told the Bulgarian ambassador, Germany had five and one-half million prisoners of war and foreign workers at her disposal and the whole of Europe stood ready for the production of materiel.[32]

For prewar German rearmament the most critical problem was that of foreign exchange. Without hard currency to pay for imports, German industry could not produce at the levels asked for by the Wehrmacht. In fact, the course of German rearmament through the 1930s was marked by increasing difficulties in acquiring the raw materials necessary for military production, and by a series of more difficult economic crises that only the most desperate expedients could overcome.[33] Table I-1 on German trade and foreign exchange indicates the extent of the problem. As the figures underline, the decline of exports through 1934 had only recovered slightly by the beginning of the war. In addition German holdings of foreign exchange steadily dwindled. Thus, the Germans never possessed the foreign exchange in the late 1930s to raise the level of raw-material imports required by rearmament. The result was a series of increasingly grave economic crises.

As early as the fall of 1934, the German cotton industry disposed of reserves for two weeks' production, rubber plants for two months'

TABLE I-1
German Trade and Foreign-Exchange Balances, 1930-1937

Year	Exports in Million RM	Imports in Million RM	Trade Balance	Average Gold and Foreign Exchange in Million RM
1930	12,036	10,393	+ 1,643	2,806
1931	9,599	6,727	+ 2,872	1,914
1932	5,739	4,667	+ 1,072	975
1933	4,871	4,204	+ 667	530
1934	4,167	4,451	− 284	165
1935	4,270	4,159	+ 111	91
1936	4,768	4,218	+ 550	75
1937	5,911	5,468	+ 443	70 approx.

SOURCE: Hans-Erich Volkmann, "Aussenhandel und Aufrüstung in Deutschland, 1933 bis 1939," in *Wirtschaft und Rüstung am Vorabend des Zweiten Weltkrieges*, edited by Friedrich Forstmeier and Hans-Erich Volkmann (Düsseldorf, 1975), p. 85.

production, and the petroleum industry for three to three and one-half months' production. Moreover, foreign suppliers were becoming more and more doubtful about the liquidity of the German economy and as a result would not deliver on credit.[34] By 1935 this situation had caused significant portions of German industry to draw on stockpiles. From March to December 1935 stockpiles had declined as follows: iron ore, more than one-third; copper and lead, almost two-thirds; zinc, more than two-thirds; cotton, more than one-half; jute, almost two-thirds; hides, almost one-half; rubber, more than two-thirds.[35]

Lack of foreign exchange was a critical factor in limiting production both before and after the outbreak of the war. In 1937 the economy suffered severe shortages of steel because of insufficient iron and other critical ores, even though the steel industry was operating at 83 percent of capacity.[36] There was simply no foreign exchange available to pay for significant increases in imports of iron ore.[37] So low did deliveries of steel sink for the Kriegsmarine in 1937, that Admiral Erich Raeder, commander in chief of the navy, warned that shortages had reached the point where the entire naval program was threatened and that the navy would soon have to give up or postpone the construction of required dockyards, designated battleships H, J, and K, and twelve submarines. The German navy would only be able to complete two battle cruisers (the *Scharnhorst* and *Gneisenau*), and the existing level of allocations would cause shortages of ammunition for even those ships in service.[38] As an OKW report admitted in 1938, Germany possessed less than 1 percent of the world's gold and financial reserves, whereas the Americans held 54 percent and the French and British 11 percent each.[39]

The economic crisis of 1938, occasioned by the mobilizations against Austria and Czechoslovakia, increased rearmament, and construction of the Westwall, forced German industry again to draw on strategic stockpiles. In November 1938, at a meeting of the Reich Defense Committee, Hermann Göring admitted that the German economy had reached the point where no more workers were available, factories were operating at full capacity, foreign exchange was exhausted, and Germany's financial and economic situation was desperate.[40] As a result, in December the OKW made major reductions in steel and raw material allocations to armament production.[41] Continuing difficulties led Hitler to announce before the Reichstag on January 30, 1939 that Germany would have to wage an export battle (*Exportschlacht*) to raise foreign exchange. At the same time he announced further reductions in Wehrmacht allocations as follows: steel, 30 percent; copper, 20 percent; aluminum, 47 percent; rubber, 14 percent and cement, 25 to 45 percent.[42] Only the seizure of Prague in March 1939 with the Czech holdings of about 500 million RMs in gold and over 2.9 billion RMs in stockpiles of raw materials and finished goods allowed the Germans to escape their economic difficulties temporarily.[43]

Complicating German foreign-exchange and import difficulties were two other major factors. First, the recovery of the world economy from the depression in conjunction with increasing levels of armament as the 1930s drew to a close led to a steady rise in the cost of strategic raw materials. Thus, the Germans could buy less with their foreign exchange.[44] The second factor was that the increase in the production of armaments for the Wehrmacht prevented important sectors of the economy from earning foreign exchange.[45] Moreover, military contracts led many companies that normally engaged in manufacturing for export to convert to armament production.[46] The armament industry did not earn significant foreign exchange until after the seizure of Prague, because it was running at near full capacity with orders for the Wehrmacht alone. German industry was forced to turn down a proposal to build two eight-inch cruisers for Chile and three submarines for Brazil despite the support for such orders by the foreign ministry, as a step to end British influence, and by the economics ministry, as a way to earn foreign currency. The necessary dockyard capacity, steel, and skilled workers were just not available.[47]

This dependence on imports and the inability of German industry to boost foreign exchange earnings significantly was a decisive limiting factor in the prewar German economy. Overall, from September 1937 through February 1939, German industry was able to meet only 58.6 percent of its scheduled and contracted armament orders because of raw material shortages and the lack of industrial capacity.[48] Even after the conquest of Scandinavia and France in the spring of 1940, the German economics minister, Walther Funk, admitted that exports were vital (*lebenswichtig*) to securing the economy's import requirements.[49] Experts of the war ministry's economic section were gloomily to conclude in 1935 "that we are becoming poorer from day to day because of our clear internal preoccupations and that without exports we will create no foreign exchange and that without foreign exchange no rearmament is possible."[50]

THE NATURE OF THE REARMAMENT EFFORT

Upon achieving power, Hitler faced the problem of building up Germany's military forces to the level at which they could carry out his long-range political goals.[51] Even while this was being done, the military provided Hitler with a useful instrument to further his immediate diplomatic goals.[52] Nazi propaganda about Germany's military strength proved immensely effective in persuading the European powers not to oppose moves such as the unilateral announcement of rearmament or the remilitarization of the Rhineland. The gap between European perceptions of German military strength and its reality was to remain a major factor in German diplomatic successes throughout the 1930s.

During the early years of the Nazi era the German military remained shackled by the effects of Versailles' disarmament clauses. No matter how extensive the efforts of the army to prepare for rearmament in the Weimar period, the Germans could not make up immediately for the lack of industrial plant, trained workers, dockyard space, machine tools, and design facilities. As all the powers were to discover in the late 1930s, the first years of rearmament would be largely invested in the creation of the industrial base for large-scale expansion of the military. In other words the results of rearmament would not show immediately. Thus, Burton Klein's claim that rearmament through the spring of 1936 "was largely a myth"[53] ignores the fact that such weapons as tanks and aircraft have a long lead time before production could begin.[54] In fact, the Germans were hard at work expanding their military and industrial base and, in terms of naval construction, making major financial commitments by laying down the keels of the *Scharnhorst* and *Gneisenau* in 1935 and the *Bismarck* in 1936. The original design and engineering work for those ships had begun in 1933 and 1934.[55] Moreover, throughout the period, the regime made every effort to prepare the nation for full-scale rearmament and military service.

A clear indication of the rearmament effort in the 1930s appears in a comparison of the figures for production, investment, and employment in the capital-and consumer-goods industries. As the figures in Tables I-2, I-3, and I-4 indicate, the capital-goods industries (mining, steel, machine tools, armaments, etc.) realized a disproportionate share of the advances made by the German economy in the 1930s. Industrial production in the 1925-1928 period made across-the-board gains; however, increases in capital goods drastically increased from 1932 to 1936, while consumer goods made relatively modest gains. Investments in capital industries more than doubled from 1928 to 1939, although investment in consumer industries had not made it back to predepression levels. Finally, in terms of industrial employment, the number of workers in consumer-goods industry remained virtually the same,

TABLE I-2

German Industrial Production, 1925-1928 and 1932-1936

	1925	1928	increase in % 1925-1928	1932	1936	increase in % 1932-1936
Industrial production as a whole	80.0	100	+25.0%	58.7	106.7	+82%
capital goods	82.1	100	+21.8%	45.7	112.9	+147%
consumer goods	79.7	100	+25.5%	78.1	97.5	+25%

SOURCE: Anja E. Bagel-Bohlan, *Hitlers industrielle Kriegsvorbereitungen, 1936-1939* (Koblenz, 1975), p. 17.
NOTE: Base 1928 = 100.

TABLE I-3

Investment in Capital and Consumer Industry, 1928-1939
(in Million RM)

	Capital	Consumer
1928	1,717	898
1933	309	248
1936	1,637	522
1937	2,208	635
1938	2,952	739
1939	3,596	836

SOURCE: Bagel-Bohlan, *Hitlers industrielle Kriegsvorbereitungen*, p. 72.

TABLE I-4
Industrial Employment in Germany, 1929-1939

	Capital goods		Consumption goods	
	Millions of Workers	Index 1929 = 100	Millions of Workers	Index 1929 = 100
1929	6.1	100	2.9	100
1933	3.6	59	2.2	76
1938	7.6	124	2.8	98
1939	8.2	135	3.0	104

SOURCE: U.S. Strategic Bombing Survey, *The Effects of Strategic Bombing on the German War Economy* (Washington, D.C., 1945), p. 29.
NOTE: Base 1929 = 100.

whereas that in capital industries steadily increased. The disproportion between the two industries was, of course, a result of massive rearmament. It is apparent, therefore, that Hitler began a wholesale effort at rearmament from the moment he took over the reins of government. The figures in Table I-5 for military expenditures in the 1935 to 1938 period indicate the extent of the German effort both in aggregate terms as well as in terms of individual years as compared to the other European powers.

Given the above-discussed constraints on the German economy, the German rearmament effort was obviously immense—especially when compared to other European states. The slowdown in 1937 reflected the economic difficulties that the Germans experienced that year, and the large jump in 1938 led to the economic crisis of late 1938 and early 1939. To every extent possible the Nazi regime used the nation's industrial and financial resources to prepare for the coming war—a war that it fully expected to break out in the near future. The fact that certain categories of weapons production, such as tanks, remained at a low level through 1940 reflected less a lack of German effort than deliberate choices made in the fields of armament production (see below for further discussion of this point).

ORGANIZATION OF THE GERMAN ECONOMY FOR REARMAMENT

After the war General Georg Thomas, head of the OKW's economic section, described the German prewar economic system: "I can only

TABLE I-5
Military Expenditures of Major European Powers, 1935-1938

Germany (million RM)	Military Expenditure	State Expenditure	National Income	Military Expenditure as a % of State Expenditure	Military Expenditure as a % of National Expenditure	Military Expenditure in Million $
1935	6,000	14,100	74,000	42.5	8.0	2,415
1936	10,800	17,300	83,000	62.4	13.0	4,352
1937	11,700	21,400	93,000	54.7	12.6	4,704
1938	17,200	32,900	105,000	52.3	16.4	6,908
Aggregate 1935-1938	45,700	85,700	355,000	53.3	12.9	18,379
Britain (million £)						
1935	137.1	841.8	4,100	16.3	3.3	671
1936	186.0	902.2	4,400	20.6	4.2	924
1937	256.4	979.0	4,600	26.2	5.6	1,265
1938	397.5	1,033.0	4,800	38.5	8.3	1,944
Aggregate 1935-1938	977.0	3,756.0	17,900	26.0	5.5	4,804

France
(million francs)

1935	12,657	49,868	221,000 (1935)	25.4	5.7	835
1936	14,858	55,789	255,000	26.6	5.8	906
1937	21,235	68,164	304,000	31.2	7.0	1,295
1938	28,967	82,345	340,000	35.2	8.5	840
Aggregate						
1935-1938	77,716	256,166	1,120,000	30.3	6.9	3,876

Italy
(million lire)

1935-1936	12,184	66,923	(1935) 101,157	18.2	12.0	999
1936-1937	16,101	48,066	(1936) 107,367	33.5	15.0	1,175
1937-1938	12,687	40,632	(1937) 127,839	31.2	10.0	672
1938-1939	14,410	42,627	(1938) 137,877	32.8	10.5	764
Aggregate						
35/6-38/9	44,382	198,248	474,240 (1935-1938)	27.9	11.7	3,610

SOURCE: MacGregor Knox, *Mussolini Unleashed* (London, 1982) pp. 294-296.

repeat, that in Hitler's so-called Leadership State there subsisted in economic affairs a complete absence of leadership, and an indescribable duplication of effort and working at cross purposes; for Hitler shut his eyes to the need for fixed, long-range planning, Göring knew nothing of economics, and the responsible professionals had no executive powers."[56] The organization of rearmament and the various controlling and competing bodies within the rearmament effort seemingly give credence to Thomas' claim. The supreme organ for rearmament was supposedly the Reich Defense Committee, but as with most similar bodies in Nazi Germany, this committee rarely met, and real authority devolved on individuals or specific organizations.

Initially, rearmament questions as well as economic questions involved a rather loose cooperation between Hjalmar Schacht as Reichsbank president (from 1933) and Reichs economic minister (from 1934) and various staffs within the War Ministry. Interestingly, Schacht's position within the government and his relations with Hitler were such that the chief organization of big business, the Reichsverband der deutschen Industrie, avoided the process of *"Gleichschaltung."*[57] Within each military service a weapons branch received authority for the maintenance of contact with industry and the design and production of weapons. The separate organizations jealously guarded their prerogatives, and there seems to have been little cooperation between the services in terms of procurement. Within the War Ministry, and later in the OKW, an economic section (*Wehrwirtschaftsstab*) concerned itself with the larger questions of raw materials, foreign exchange, and future economic problems that might affect Germany's rearmament effort or her ability to fight a long war. As Thomas was to complain after the war, his staff had little control over the military services and even less impact on the civilian sector.

With the promulgation of the Reich Defense Law in May 1935, Schacht received authority to lead a new bureaucracy, the Plenipotentiary General for the War Economy (*Generalbevollmächtige für die Kriegswirtschaft*). Relations between Schacht's new power base and the War Ministry's economic staff almost immediately led to infighting over which authority would control the various segments of the armament industry. In October 1936 economic direction was further diffused by creation of still another bureaucracy under the leadership of Göring to run Hitler's "Four Year Plan." Following the usual practice of the Nazi regime, the relation between Göring's new office and other economic organizations was most unclear. The result was that Göring attempted to extend his influence as widely through the economy as possible, while Schacht and the economic section of the War Ministry did all in their power to oppose *"der Dicke."*[58]

The appearance made by these hostile bureaucratic organizations has given historians the impression of a chaotic, misdirected economy that severely hindered the rearmament effort.[59] Such an attitude presupposes that a centrally directed economy with only one responsible authority would have achieved greater success. The centrally planned economy of the Soviet Union and the attendant mismanagement that accompanied it raise serious questions about such a thesis. Futhermore, although the centrally controlled German economy under Speer managed to produce vast numbers of fighters in the summer of 1944, the fact that there were neither fuel nor trained pilots for those aircraft make such production totals of doubtful utility.

The diverse, decentralized German economic effort may well have been a positive factor in prewar rearmament. First of all, it prevented the Germans from overconcentrating on one weapons system to the exclusion of others. Second and most important, it allowed Hitler to manipulate the economy, for the most part with remarkable success. In the early years of the rearmament effort Hitler was able to use Schacht and his financial expertise not only to guide recovery out of the depression but to create the financial base for rearmament. Through early 1936 Schacht and Hitler largely remained in agreement, but, with increasing foreign-exchange difficulties and Hitler's grandiose plans for military expansion, the two came into conflict. Not yet prepared to remove Schacht, Hitler created the "Four Year Plan" as a method to escape foreign-exchange difficulties and the limitations on rearmament imposed by Germany's lack of raw materials as well as a means to get around the economic minister's refusal to think on a large scale. For both domestic and foreign propaganda the Nazi regime trumpeted the "Four Year Plan" as a realistic effort to free Germany from dependence on foreign trade. There was, of course, no such possibility. In fact, the plan aimed to give the German war economy strength enough to resist the immediate effects of a blockade while the German army conquered a larger economic- and raw-material base— a base from which Germany could fight a true "World War." Besides the usual remarks about "*Lebenskampf der Völker,*" Hitler stated that in four years the German army must be combat ready and the German economy prepared to meet the demands of war.[60] It was a demand that the German Wehrmacht and economy managed to fulfill.

In 1938 the critical international situation caused by the aggressive machinations of Hitler's foreign policy led to the formulation of the so-called Schnellplan. Göring singled out as pivotal certain key industries (oil, rubber, light metals, and munitions in particular) to receive increased financial and resource allocations.[61] The resulting course of the Schnellplan gives a revealing insight into what Hitler was able to achieve in the economic sphere. As usual, grandiose targets were set that were not realistic in view of conflicting demands from construction on the Westwall and armament production. The Schnellplan aimed to enlarge the capacities of the selected industries with minimum investment by expanding existing plants as well as by constructing new ones.[62] Completion of the plan depended upon the availability of steel supplies, workers, and construction material. Starting in the first quarter of the 1939 financial year, the plan required additional allocations of steel and construction material.[63] As early as August 1938 considerable difficulties had appeared. Synthetic oil plants lost valuable personnel because of military call-ups during the Czech crisis. With the low unemployment rate there was no hope of replacing reservists, and cement and steel deliveries fell behind schedule with the mounting demands of the Westwall. For the last half of August cement deliveries met only 50 percent of requirements, and in September the total was 73 percent.[64] Because of the economic difficulties, the Schnellplan received only 65 percent of scheduled material allocations in the first quarter of 1939. This delayed completion of some munition goals as much as a full year.[65]

Nevertheless, in spite of these difficulties the Schnellplan was able to bring about significant gains in production. Both synthetic fuel and rubber industries achieved important gains in 1939 over their 1938 levels of production. The munitions industry showed the most noticeable gain. In 1938 this industry was one of the more vulnerable segments of the war economy (see Charts 7 and 8). Capacity for gunpowder production was less than 40 percent of maximum First World War production, while that of the explosives industry was less than 30 percent.[66] Considering that the Second World War would see extensive

CHART 7
German Gunpowder Production, 1936-1940

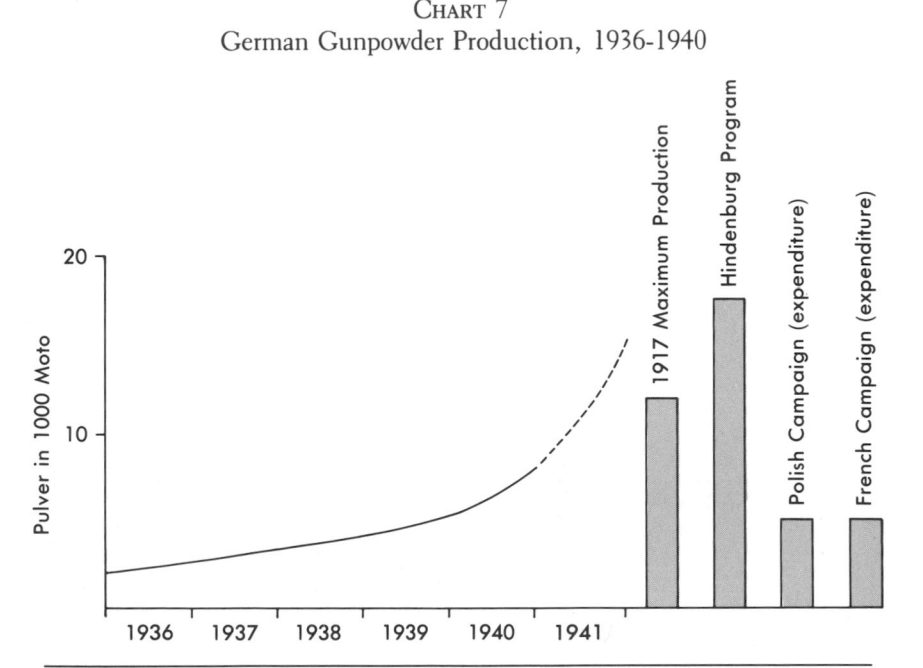

SOURCE: Bericht des Herrn Professor Dr. C. Krauch über die Lage auf dem Arbeitsgebiet der Chemie in der Sitzung des Generalrates am 24. 6. 41 (NARS T-84, Roll
217, Frame 1586749).

use of aircraft and new weapons systems, 1938 munitions capacity was
especially low.[67] The Schnellplan improved this situation considerably. By August 1939 capacity for the production of gun powder had
risen 65 percent and that of explosives 85 percent over 1938 totals.[68]
However, ammunition expenditures in the Polish campaign equaled
almost two months of production. In the 1940 campaign the Germans
used 30 percent more ammunition than in Poland, but by that time
munitions production had reached a level at which monthly output
covered campaign needs. Significantly, ammunition usage in Poland
equaled three months' production at 1938 rates.[69]

On the surface, then, the German economy gave the appearance
of many different agencies working at cross-purposes. Nevertheless,
these differences and arguments within the economic agencies can be
overemphasized. As Charles Sydnor has suggested in his work on the
SS Totenkopf division:

CHART 8
German Production of Explosives, 1936-1940

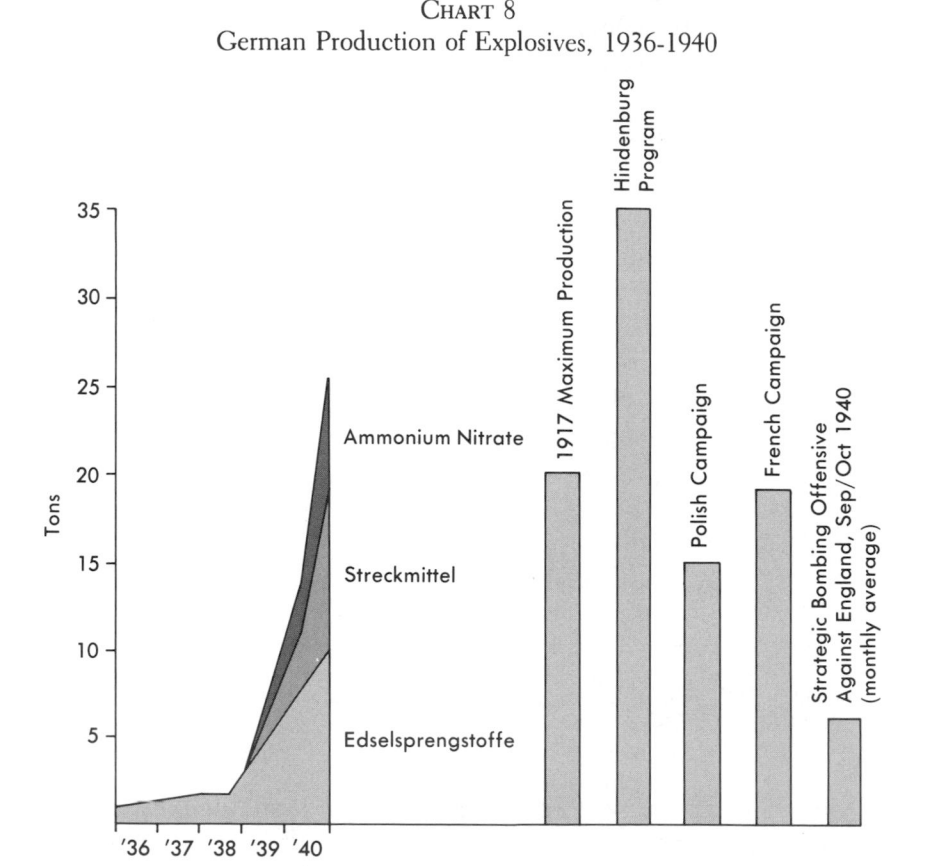

SOURCE: Bericht des Herrn Professor Dr. C. Krauch über die Lage auf dem Arbeitsgebiet der Chemie in der Sitzung des Generalrates am 24. 6. 41 (NARS T-84, Roll
217, Frame 1586749).

For a generation, one major analytical trend in studies of the
Third Reich has focused upon the internal rivalries and anarchic
divisions within the National Socialist system. . . . It may now,
however, be time to reexamine this problem from a different
perspective. The SS and the Waffen SS . . . functioned extremely well despite internal tensions and rivalries, and in the
face of extraordinary difficulties. This, it seems, would not have

been possible without a formidable degree of institutional solidity—the presence of shared assumptions and beliefs, commonly accepted norms, and the unquestioned general values that enable large numbers of people, despite individual ambitions, dislikes, and disagreements, to work together in common purpose toward definite goals.[70]

The performance of the German economy in the 1930s supports such a thesis. Although there might have been serious squabbles between Göring, Schacht, and Thomas throughout the period, it is clear that they as well as their bureaucratic organizations worked wholeheartedly toward the resurrection of German military power. Again, it is worth emphasizing that Hitler was able to use these competing organizations to further his long-range goals. The Schnellplan was an excellent example, for it enabled the Germans to cope with (though not to correct) major deficiencies within their economy. Thus, when war came the Germans disposed of sufficient (or just sufficient) supplies of fuel, rubber, and ammunition to win the first great battles.

Finally, it was impossible that Germany could have rearmed in depth, as suggested by Schacht and Thomas. Germany possessed neither the raw materials, the industrial base, nor the financial resources to have rearmed in such a manner. The only possible course, taken by Hitler, was to build German forces up as rapidly as possible and then, with that short-term military advantage, conquer the raw material and financial base for a long war. Given Germany's economic and strategic situation, it is hard to see any other possibility, at least in terms of Hitler's goals of massive territorial changes in Europe.

REARMAMENT AND THE MILITARY SERVICES

Although preparation of the Reich's military forces for an eventual conflict to realize his inordinate goals was central to Hitler's policies in the 1930s, there was a surprising lack of cohesion in the rearmament effort.[71] Given the political problems involved in placing the regime on a firm foundation, Hitler's day-to-day attention centered on other areas besides the military during his first years in power.[72] In fact, the services received carte blanche in 1933 to embark on their own independent rearmament programs. For the period from 1933 through 1936 this state of affairs did not cause serious problems because the industrial and labor resources available were sufficient to cover most needs; however, thereafter the armament programs of the three services, as they moved into high gear, came into increasing conflict over scarce resources. Despite the complications and serious economic consequences, Hitler rarely provided detailed guidance; rather, his interventions in the late 1930s seemed more often than not to set even more megalomaniacal targets for military programs (his demand for a five-fold increase in the Luftwaffe's front-line strength in late 1938, and his approval of the navy's Z plan in 1939 are cases in point). Certainly Hitler's own personality and approach to government militated against a careful examination of Germany's strategic position with regard to resources, short- and long-range goals, and financial difficulties.

There was, of course, a machinery available for the coordination of defense policy: the Defense Ministry. However, for a variety of reasons the defense minister *Generaloberst*, and later field marshal, Werner von Blomberg, was never able to gain control over the strategic decision-making process. On one side, the army, jealous of its traditional role as the premier service, refused to countenance interference by the Defense (later War) Ministry in what it regarded as its private preserve, the formulation and conduct of the Reich's ground defense. On the other hand, Göring's unique position, not only as the commander in chief of the Luftwaffe but also as a minister in his own right as well as the number-two man in the political hierarchy, insured that Blomberg would exercise even less influence over that service than he influenced over the army. The navy sailed in the lee, removed from close supervision by Admiral Erich Raeder's relationship with Hitler and by the fact that at least in the first stages of rearmament its size was so small. By 1937 that situation had changed with the shipbuilding program in full swing and major work on the first series of battleships well in hand. But naval independence in nearly all matters dealing with tactical and operational matters as well as production priorities remained unchallenged.

The most important determinant in Blomberg's failure to cast a coherent defense policy, however, was the fact that Hitler had no intention of allowing a subordinate such a concentration of power. Thus, the rearmament programs proceeded in the late 1930s independently of each other, with increasing clashes over scarce resources, and with a darkening economic outlook that made it doubtful whether any one program could succeed, much less all three. The only alternative to a drastic reduction in armaments was a diplomatic and military policy aimed at expanding Germany's financial, raw-material, and economic base. But then, Hitler had understood the alternatives from the beginning and there was no doubt which one he would choose.

There is another element in the failure of Germany's military to face satisfactorily the problems of a coherent defense policy. Although the officer corps and the general staffs of the three services would prove most competent at addressing tactical and operational matters, Germany's military leaders proved themselves less adept on the strategic level. The optimism (or naïveté) that marked the approach of most senior officers predated the Nazi regime. Blomberg, when head of the disguised general staff, had refused to accept the gloomy conclusions to the 1928 study tour in which the Reichswehr had received a battering from the Poles. His new scenario had the League of Nations intervene and force an armistice on Poland, whereupon the Soviets attacked the Poles and allied themselves with Germany. Now with Poland distracted from the east, the Reichswehr could go over to a victorious offensive.[73] Perhaps the most glaring example of this general failing on the strategic level lay in the German reaction to the fall of France in 1940 and in the completely overoptimistic appraisals marking preparations for "Barbarossa" in 1941.[74] In December 1941, Hitler, overjoyed at the Japanese success in attacking Pearl Harbor, asked his assembled military staff (army, navy, and air force) where the American naval base was located. Not one of his staff officers could find Pearl Harbor. That one incident speaks volumes on the subject of the strategic Weltanschauung of people who aimed at the conquest of the world.[75]

Nevertheless, although the strategic vision of senior generals and admirals remained limited, the three services, as suggested above, proved highly competent and innovative on the operational and tactical levels. Contributing to this state of affairs was not only a willingness to work exceedingly hard as well as realistically at the business of preparing for war, but a greater tolerance for those who lay outside the mainstream of doctrine or force structure. This later characteristic was of particular importance in the coming war. In the army the development of the panzer forces, in the navy the development of the submarine force, and in the Luftwaffe the development of close air support all lay outside the central concerns of the services' rearmament programs. Nevertheless, the success of the Germans in these areas was a result of the fact that innovators received wide latitude and freedom to develop their doctrinal and tactical conceptions. Thus, the critical element in the success of German armored divisions in 1940 was not that the German high command had devoted more resources to its armored force than had the French (which it had not) but rather that it had allowed greater freedom to those who had conceived and were developing those forces. On the other hand the French high command maintained a stranglehold over the operational and tactical development of the mechanized forces in the 1930s. Unable itself to define a role for such forces, it made sure that others could not as well (see Chapter III).

THE ARMY

Within the framework of the rise of German military power in the 1930s, the initial development of the German army into a viable force in European diplomacy and subsequently into a force of conquest was of momentous importance. Both in terms of doctrine and in terms of combat effectiveness (but not necessarily in terms of its weapons) the army would have a decisive impact on the course of European history. It would prove, in the campaigns of 1939 through 1941, to be a potent instrument capable of destroying the existing balance of power. The roots of this success lay in the lessons of the First World War and in the army's conscious and open-minded (at least in tactical and operational terms) examination of recent military history. Moreover, the Germans combined this diligence with a mental flexibility and receptiveness to new ideas that was not present in other European armies.[76]

With victory in 1918, the Allies imposed seemingly crushing terms on the new Weimar Republic. Among other provisions, the victorious powers forced the Germans to limit their army to 100,000 men with a proportionately small officer corps, to eliminate the general staff, to demilitarize a zone fifty kilometers to the east of the Rhine, and to remove tanks and aircraft from their armories. Most students of the German army have cited these limitations on the army's size as the major reason for German military competence in the interwar period. [77] These restrictions admittedly provided the Germans with a small coherent officer corps. Defeat did make the German army more receptive to new ideas. What such an argument ignores, however, is the fact that the German army had already proven the most innovative and competent of the military forces engaged in the Great War. It had developed the tactical concept of defense in depth and the tactics of breakthrough operations such as at Caporetto and in the spring 1918 offensives. By and large throughout that war the operations and performance of the German army had remained superior to those of its opponents. [78]

The new, restricted army faced considerable difficulties. With a long-service (twelve-year) military force, the Germans could no longer depend on numbers to defend their frontiers. The large trained reserve of the French army in the west and Germany's extensive frontiers to the east compounded the problem. To their credit, General Hans von Seeckt and his Reichswehr planners seized on mobility and elastic defense as Germany's only hope for military survival.

This deliberate German emphasis on mobile defense was far in advance of its time. As early as 1922 the Germans would experiment in the Harz mountains with motorized formations. Seeckt then ordered that the "after-action" report of these experiments be disseminated as widely as possible throughout the army because "we must recognize that mobility is an important substitute for our weak military power." [79]

With little money for new weapons, and severely restricted by the Treaty of Versailles, progress came slowly. However, the German army did not have to train large batches of recruits each year and could focus upon the theoretical and, as far as possible, the practical development of new tactics. Concentration on study, combined with the dictum *"Operation ist Bewegung"* was Seeckt's legacy to the Reichswehr, while the emphasis on mobility, whether defensive or offensive, represented a distinct break with the experiences of the western front. This was to be a major advantage that the German army would possess against its enemies in the first years of the Second World War. [80] Moreover, army commanders were not saddled with obsolete equipment that limited their vision. Thus, they could think in terms of a weapon's future possibilities rather than in terms of a weapon's immediate capability.[81]

Speculation and theoretical musings changed to reality once Hitler became chancellor. The appointment of Blomberg as defense minister and Colonel Walther von Reichenau as his chief assistant suggested that innovators now controlled the military establishment, for both men were interested in the British military writers, J.F.C. Fuller and B. H. Liddell Hart, and were receptive to new ideas. Nevertheless, the strong opposition of the army high command (Oberkommando des Heeres, OKH) to outside interference denied the Defense Ministry any important say in the development and organization of Germany's land forces. Although Hitler also showed an interest in new military developments, he too remained in the background until the Fritsch-Blomberg crisis of January 1938.[82] In fact, the führer played little or no role in the development of army doctrine in the tactical and operational fields. Rather, he provided the OKH with the funds and resources to produce the military forces that he would need in the future and trusted in its competence to provide such an instrument. This is not to say that Hitler was unwilling to overrule the military on strategic or diplomatic issues. On the question of the pace of rearmament, Hitler forced the army to move faster than its leaders would have liked, and he remilitarized the Rhineland against the advice of his military and diplomatic advisers. However, in the tactical, doctrinal, and operational fields the OKH remained entirely free from outside interference through the end of 1937.

Three men were to determine the shape of the new army. They were Generals Freiherr Werner von Fritsch, commander in chief, Ludwig Beck, Chief of the General Staff, and Erich von Manstein, Beck's precocious assistant. The leadership of the army faced enormous problems in planning rearmament: how to expand the 100,000 man army into a vast conscripted force while still maintaining the standards of training, doctrine, and military competence that the Reichswehr had reached. What is so remarkable is that within six years the army leadership managed to do precisely that.

Since the Second World War the chief of staff, Beck, has come under fire, especially from the tank pioneer Heinz Guderian, as an out and out opponent of armored warfare. Such criticism is most unfair and begs not only Beck's real contribution to the creation of an armored force but the serious strategic questions that such a force raised in 1934-1935. Both Beck and Fritsch willingly allowed experimentation and allotted considerable resources to this relatively unproved doctrine. However, the *emphasis* of German rearmament through the French campaign of 1940 was on the creation of an army closely resembling the forces of World War I. In September 1939 only 6 out of 106 active and reserve divisions were armored, 4 were motorized infantry, and 4 were light. In percentages this works out to barely 13 percent of the army motorized, and less than 6 percent armored. At the time of the French campaign, 10 out of 155 infantry divisions were armored, and 7 were motorized infantry; 11 percent of the army being motorized and approximately 6 percent armored.[83]

There were important economic, strategic, and military considerations that led the OKH to push army development within such a conservative framework.[84] Without the benefit of hindsight, the army leadership felt that the creation of an overly motorized and mechanized force carried serious risks. First of all, in terms of weapons production steel was in short supply, and only the inadequate Mark I tank was ready for production. Second, and perhaps more important, armored and motorized forces consumed large amounts of imported fuels. In peacetime, would funds be available to import such fuel and in war would the German military have access to sufficient supplies of fuel? Given the shortages of petroleum in Germany, these were crucial questions. Finally, in the near future with the obvious beginning of a vast rearmament program, Germany might well face the possibility of a preventive war launched by her neighbors.[85] Infantry divisions would be ready in the immediate future; no one knew how long it would take to develop armored divisions and panzer doctrine.

Beck's role in the development of Germany's mechanized and motorized forces has not generally received proper recognition, largely because of Guderian's bitter postwar attacks. Yet the chief of staff played an important part in convincing Fritsch and Blomberg that the army should establish panzer divisions. In the spring of 1935, he conducted a general staff tour on the use of a panzer corps, although the army had not yet formed the first panzer divisions (the following year the study tour examined the operations of a hypothetical panzer army).[86] The performance of the armored test units in the 1935 maneuvers impressed Beck and Fritsch sufficiently for the OKH to establish three armored divisions.[87] At the end of the year the chief of staff underlined the use of armored divisions against long-range objectives and suggested their operational use as an independent force "in association with other motorized weapons."[88] In fact, Beck's ideas on the use of armored forces at this time do not seem all that different from Guderian's. Nevertheless, in the military confrontation of 1938 Beck proved unwilling to believe that Germany should risk her national fate on an unproved operational doctrine and opposed war against Czechoslovakia. This was in part because he doubted whether the armored forces could achieve a decisive enough operational success to overcome the inherent strategic weaknesses of Germany's position.

Thus, in the fall of 1935 the Germans established three panzer divisions along with three independent tank brigades to work with the infantry and three light divisions.[89] The formation of these various motorized and mechanized units appears on the surface somewhat similar to what the French army was doing at the same time. However, unlike the French, who never managed to make up their minds on the questions of doctrine or organization, the Germans really did experiment with these forces. By the end of the Polish campaign, the army had narrowed down its mechanized and motorized forces to panzer and motorized infantry divisions.

The development of the armored force reached back into the First World War with the experience gained from being on the receiving end of Allied tank attacks.[90] Seeckt's emphasis on mobility undoubtedly spurred experimentation with motorization, but Seeckt himself never was fully won over to the concept of a wholly motorized army. In 1928 he wrote: "Many prophets already see the whole army equipped with armored vehicles and the complete replacement of the horseman by the motorized soldier. We have not yet advanced that far."[91] In the 1920s, as has often been pointed out, many Germans read the writings of Fuller and Liddell Hart. Moreover, the Germans managed to get hold of the then current British field manual on the employment of armored fighting vehicles and to use it as a theoretical framework for the study of tank warfare.[92] As important, however, to the development of German tank doctrine was the fact that the army received accurate reports on the progress that the British were making with their experimental armored force. Detailed, carefully worked out studies of the 1926, 1929, and 1934 British maneuvers warned the Germans that improvements in speed and maneuverability had broadened the role of the tank: armored vehicles were no longer tied to the pace of infantry but could now strike out on their own. Interestingly, the commentary on the 1926 maneuvers pointed out that such changes in the capability of tanks offered the possibility of rapid exploitation of a breakthrough. As late as 1934, an extensive report on the British maneuvers of that year circulated widely through the army with a detailed covering letter from Beck.[93] Not surprisingly, General Oswald Lutz, the German armor pioneer, "with some pride" told Sir John Dill during the latter's visit to Germany in 1935 "that the German tank corps had been modelled on the British."[94]

The actual course of development of the panzer force in the 1930s showed the same high level of competence that marked the rest of the German army in this period. Both Lutz and Guderian emphasized that the panzer division should be a combined-arms force of motorized infantry, artillery, engineers, and signal troops, as well as tanks.[95] Panzer doctrine stressed the use of these components in a close and explosive cooperation.[96] A key element in the development of this doctrine would be the emphasis on flexibility and speed. Above all Lutz and Guderian would demand a ruthless, mobile, and rapid exploitation of a breakthrough.[97] By 1939 the Third Reich possessed an armored force that could gain not only operational, but also strategic freedom—something that the other European armies could neither duplicate nor counter.

It is worth noting that the advocates of armor in the German army did run into serious opposition from officers in other branches. General Otto von Stülpnagel remarked to Guderian that his ideas were utopian and that large armored units were militarily impossible. General Gerd von Rundstedt pithily commented after one maneuver: "All nonsense, my dear Guderian, all nonsense (*Alles Unsinn, mein lieber Guderian, alles Unsinn*)."[98] Yet opposition within the army to armored warfare took a significantly different turn from that within the British army. German doubts mainly concerned deep penetration tactics—not whether the tank would prove to be a useful weapon. Moreover, many opponents of tank warfare proved themselves to be surprisingly adaptable to armored warfare once they had seen what tanks could do in Poland. Erwin Rommel, who would prove such a devastatingly effective armored-force commander in the Second World War, remained a steadfast infantryman, dubious about the prospect of large-scale armored operations through to the outbreak of war. Three weeks in Poland sufficed to convince him that he had been wrong. Despite his inexperience, he asked for and received command of the 7th Panzer Division. Rundstedt was so convinced by what he had seen in Poland that he would become a leading proponent of Manstein's plan for a great armored push through the Ardennes in 1940.

A major factor accounting for the flexibility and adaptability to the new system of armored warfare was the fact that German doctrine as as whole, and not just tank doctrine, emphasized speed, surprise, mobility, decentralization, and exploitation. Therefore, the transition from an infantry doctrine emphasizing those factors to an armored doctrine did not represent an insurmountable hurdle. For the officers in the British and French armies where such principles were not the basis of operations the transition proved far more difficult.

The general performance of the other branches of the German army reached a level similar to that of the panzer forces. The preparation of the Wehrmacht in the 1930s underlines several important points. First, and perhaps foremost, was the fact that the army high command, albeit within the limited sphere of its military authority, possessed the competence and intellectual honesty to recognize the major flaws and weaknesses within its organization. From the Anschluss through the French campaign it was never willing to use operational success as a standard. No matter how stunning the Polish campaign might have appeared to outsiders, most participating units had not come up to the standards of the OKH, and the high command was most dissatisfied. As a result the army introduced a drastic, thorough training program to correct the perceived deficiencies.[99] Moreover, the German army was willing to learn from experience. In terms of evaluating combat potential, an implicit trust existed between the different levels of command. The OKH, army group, army, corps, and divisional commanders, and so on down the line expected subordinates to give accurate reports on the status and capabilities of their troops. If a unit were substandard, then its commander was expected to say so. Of course, it was taken for granted that he would do all in his power to correct those deficiencies. Even more interesting is the fact that the higher the level of command the more critical of performance and the higher the expectations were. Besides its realism and toughness, German military training also seems to have given the German soldier a high sense of unit identification and a belief that he could depend on the soldier next to him. Finally, the OKH and general staff proved capable of imposing their high standards and expectations on their officers and men.

In recent historical literature certain writers, particularly economic historians, have argued that Germany's strategic and political situation led her leaders to devise a "Blitzkrieg strategy."[100] They postulate that Hitler and the high command recognized that Germany could not fight a long war and as a result developed a special strategy and tactical organization aimed at gaining quick, decisive victories. Because of a weak economic base, the Germans supposedly planned for short campaigns followed by periods of recuperation, and structured panzer divisions and close air support to carry out this strategy. This theory seems to have some basis in fact until one looks closely at the course of German rearmament. There was almost no connection between Germany's economic problems and the development of tactical doctrine. The condition of the German economy certainly constrained rearmament and limited the size and productivity of the war industry. But as we have seen, development of armor was not the central concern of the army's leadership. Rather, the army placed the emphasis in rearmament on World War I style, that is, on infantry divisions. Furthermore, the length of time that elapsed between the Polish and French campaigns was accidental rather than deliberate. Initially, because of the desperate economic situation Hitler demanded an immediate offensive in the west after the fall of Poland. That this historical fact seems to fit the Blitzkrieg thesis was the result of chance rather than deliberate German planning.

There is, moreover, a semantic problem in what is meant by "Blitzkrieg." In the traditional sense it has been present in German strategy from the time of the elder Moltke: Germany must win quickly before the weight of a two-front war could crush her. In this sense Blitzkrieg strategy was not a new concept. However, its more modern and specialized tactical definition as a particular kind of mechanized warfare—cooperation of tanks, aircraft, dive bombers, and motorized infantry and artillery—was a revolutionary change in military operations. That the broader definitions had always been present in German strategy is not proof that Hitler and the OKH pushed the development of a new tactical doctrine as the answer to Germany's traditional need to conduct a *"blitzschnell"* war. The skepticism of many within the OKH and of most senior generals conclusively underlines the fact that armored tactics were not developed to meet strategic needs.

THE LUFTWAFFE

The general historical view on the Luftwaffe's preparations for the coming war has been that the German air force was "in effect the hand maiden of the army."[101] This simplistic view of prewar developments misses both the constraints on German air strategy as well as the significant body of thought within the Luftwaffe's officer corps that looked toward the creation of a "strategic" bombing capability. It also misses the extraordinary difficulties that the Germans faced in 1933 in creating an air force from a military structure that contained a minuscule flying section within the body of the Reichswehr and an aircraft industry that employed only 4,000 workers.[102]

The initial thrust of argumentation within the new Air Ministry and the results of the first efforts at air rearmament reflected the above factors. In May 1933, the state secretary in the new Air Ministry, the future field marshal, Erhard Milch, received a major study from one of his Lufthansa subordinates, Dr. Robert Knauss, on the latter's strategic conception for the new air force.[103] Knauss's memorandum reflected elements of Douhet's "strategic" bombing philosophy, Tirpitz's "risk theory," and what today would pass for "deterrence" doctrine. To begin with, he articulated the purpose of the new Nazi regime as "the restoration of Germany's great power position in Europe." Since he believed that Poland and France would not accept such an alteration in the balance of power and would fight to preserve the status quo, Knauss argued that the Reich must build up a strong air force as soon as possible. The key element within this new force should be a deterrent fleet of 400 four-engine bombers. Knauss argued not only that modern industrialized society offered targets that when destroyed would halt an enemy's economic life, but that population centers offered the possibility of attacking morale directly.

Knauss's proposal failed due to factors that plagued the Luftwaffe's expansion throughout the 1930s; the technological and industrial base was simply not capable of meeting the requirements that such a force demanded. Over the summer and fall of 1933 Milch and his planners found that they could barely squeeze 1,000 aircraft out of Germany's tiny industry for the 1933-1934 production years, while most of that effort had to go toward production of training aircraft to expand the flying base.[104] What few "combat" aircraft industry managed to produce hardly deserved that characterization.

While Milch played the central role in creating the administrative and industrial base for the Luftwaffe, others created the operational capabilities. Blomberg insured that the army made available to the new air force not only those few officers who had worked with airpower issues in the prerearmament period, but also a number of outstanding staff officers. As he made clear from the first, the officers transferring to the Luftwaffe should represent "the best of the best."[105] The Luftwaffe's first chief of staff, General Walther Wever, reflected Blomberg's attitude, for the war minister offered Göring a choice between Wever and the future field marshal, Erich von Manstein, for the position.[106] Wever is one of the more fascinating prewar theorists on air power. He was not an unabashed champion of "strategic" bombing as some have claimed, but rather until his death in 1936 articulated a broadly based approach to the issue of the role of aircraft in future wars. He did not believe that the Luftwaffe's status as a separate service meant that its employment would be entirely independent of the army and navy. Thus, he argued that the Luftwaffe's wartime contribution could involve attacks on an enemy's air forces, his army, his fleet, or even his industrial base and armaments industry. The goals and purposes of national strategy would govern the course of a future air war.[107]

Wever's clearest formulation of a broadly based approach to the question of air doctrine came in 1936 with a manual entitled, "The Conduct of the Air War (*Die Luftkriegführung*)." The underlying theme was that "the nature of the enemy, the time of year, the structure of his land, the character of his people as well as one's own military capabilities" would determine how one should employ air power.[108] Unlike most air-power theorists, Wever showed a ready understanding for the fact that air superiority would be a most elusive goal. Changing technology and a steady replacement of losses through new production would allow an enemy to fight another day. Although Wever felt that "strategic" bombing might have an absolute impact, he warned that such an offensive might take too long to be decisive. Moreover, he argued that an air war against an enemy's industrial base should only occur 1) when an opportunity existed to affect quickly the war's course, 2) when land and naval action had prepared the way, 3) when a stalemate had occurred, or 4) when one could achieve a decisive impact solely through the destruction of the enemy's economy.

Besides Wever's articulation of a broad approach toward air-power doctrine, a significant number of senior officers in the Luftwaffe argued that "strategic" bombing should be the German air force's central mission. Knauss's memorandum had in fact gone so far as to suggest that "the terrorizing of the enemy's chief cities and industrial regions through bombing would lead that much more quickly to a collapse of morale, the weaker the national character of his people and the more that social and political rifts cleave his society." He obviously believed that a totalitarian society like Nazi Germany would prove more capable of enduring such attacks than the fractured societies of democratic nations like Britain and France. [109] Knauss himself went from the Air Ministry to head up the Air War College at Gatow, where the emphasis down to the outbreak of the war remained on "strategic" bombing rather than on tactical cooperation with the army. [110] An examination of the military literature throughout the period suggests a pervasive belief within Luftwaffe circles that "strategic" bombing would play a critical role in future warfare and that this would be the primary mission. [111]

The failure of the Luftwaffe to possess a true "strategic" bombing force at the outbreak of the war should not be particularly surprising. None of the airmen of any nation in the prewar period foresaw the magnitude of the industrial and military effort that "strategic" bombing would require. On the technological side severe developmental constraints affected the types of aircraft that German industry was able to produce. The second generation of bombers had gone into production in 1936 in considerable haste. The Germans considered none of these (the He 111, Do 17, and Ju 86) fully satisfactory and were already in 1936 engaged in developmental work on what they considered to be a true "strategic" bomber. Here the capabilities of Germany's engine manufacturers came into play. Due to the restrictions of Versailles on the development of military aircraft the Germans were seriously behind British and American power-plant development, particularly in the higher horse-power range, and the long lead time for engine development constrained German aircraft design throughout the 1930s. As a result the Germans had to cancel their first two four-engine bombers, the Ju 89 and Do 19, because these aircraft were so underpowered as to make them obsolete before they went into production. Heinkel's engineers believed that they had found a way around the power-plant problem with their He 177 design. They proposed to place four engines within two nacelles. By thus reducing the drag they believed that the Luftwaffe would possess a bomber comparable to four-engine aircraft equipped with more powerful engines. Unfortunately for the Luftwaffe, the Heinkel firm was never able to overcome the difficulties inherent in the design. The failure of the program, therefore, reflected the failure of engineering and not a lack of interest in "strategic" bombing.[112]

Interestingly, the dive bomber craze that grasped some Luftwaffe officers in the late 1930s also reflected industrial difficulties rather than an emphasis on "tactical" over "strategic" bombing. The low level of munitions production and capacity was a serious problem for German military planners in the late 1930s,[113] and experience in Spain underlined the difficulties involved in bombing accurately from high altitudes. However, the Ju 87, the "Stuka," proved itself able in Spain to hit targets accurately with a minimum expenditure of ammunition. Extrapolating from that example, the new head of the Luftwaffe's design and engineering department, Ernst Udet, decided that every future bomber should possess a dive bombing capability. Such a technical specification was manifestly impractical if not impossible, and the decision had a serious impact on German bomber design in the late 1930s. In the case of the Ju 88 prototype, Udet's demand that it possess a dive bombing capability along with 50,000 other design changes led to an increase in that aircraft's weight from seven to twelve tons and a decrease in speed from 500 km/h to 300 km/h.[114] The additional requirement for the He 177 came in the middle of program development and virtually insured that, given the inherently complex engine design, the model would never evolve into an effective heavy bomber.[115]

The war in Spain had an important impact on the doctrine as well as the equipment of the Luftwaffe. In fact, the development of close air support for the army came directly out of the civil war. The critical figure in the doctrinal evolution was Wolfram von Richthofen, the cousin of the great ace Manfred. He arrived in Spain somewhat out of favor with the German Air Ministry and with a conception of air war not substantially different from most of his fellow officers: in other words, close air support ranked at the bottom of his priorities. However, once in his position as chief of staff to the Condor Legion, Richthofen recognized that the theories of air power and the realities of the war did not have much in common. The stalemate on the ground, the lack of suitable "strategic" targets, and the great weakness of Nationalist artillery led him to consider the use of air power in direct support of Franco's offensive against Bilbao. [116]

Against considerable opposition and without official sanction, Richthofen developed the technique and tactics of close air support for ground forces in offensive operations. [117] None of the tactical elements required for such operations existed before the Bilbao offensive, and the technical expertise for communications between ground and air units (particularly radio) had not yet been fully developed. By the time that Richthofen was through developing the concept and tactics, the Germans had developed a system to insure close planning between ground and air units, had designed communication links and recognition devices, and had detailed Luftwaffe officers to serve directly with front-line units. The concept as well as its development was almost entirely due to Richthofen's drive and imagination. Significantly, there was little interest or enthusiasm in Berlin for what he was developing in Spain. [118]

On the "strategic" bombing side of the Spanish Civil War the lessons were somewhat muted. As one Luftwaffe journal noted, the particular political conditions as well as the size of the opposing air forces in war were such that "strategic" air war had never occurred. [119] On the other hand an "after-action" report on the war emphasized the impact on working-class morale of the bombing of Republican cities. The report suggested that continuous attacks even by small bombing units against a single city had "deeply impressed and depressed" the population. [120] Whatever the direct lessons, the air war in Spain did point out to the Germans not only how difficult accurate bombing from high altitude would be, but also the considerable problems involved in finding and hitting targets at night and in bad weather. As a result, only the Luftwaffe of the world's air forces, nearly all of which found the concept of "strategic" bombing an attractive role, had developed a navigational means to carry out night and bad weather bombing at the beginning of the war. The *"Knickebein"* system of using radio beams for navigational and bombing purposes, first used in the Battle of Britain (a system more advanced than anything the RAF would possess until 1943), is a clear reflection of the interest in "strategic" bombing within the prewar Luftwaffe.

One of the critical factors involved in estimating the capabilities and performance of any military organization is its leadership. In the first three years of the Luftwaffe's existence Milch, on the administrative and productive sides, and Wever, on the operational and doctrinal sides, provided solid guidance, while Göring, largely concerned with the establishment of the regime's political stability, remained in the background. The situation changed considerably with Wever's death in 1936. None of Wever's successors as chief of staff possessed his breadth of vision or strategic sense. By 1939 Göring had chosen the young and arrogant Hans Jeschonnek as chief of staff—a man who although first in his class at the Kriegsakademie proved himself to be one of the many German officers who would betray their training and embrace the belief that the führer was the greatest military leader in human history.

On the other side, Göring became increasingly jealous of his state secretary's authority and reputation, and Milch found himself shunted outside of the production and research and development process, as Göring placed Ernst Udet in charge of the technical departments. No matter what his claim to fame as a World War I ace Udet was a dreadful administrator. At one time he had no fewer than twenty-six separate departments reporting directly to him.[121] Göring's own abilities did not equip him to provide the guidance that the rapidly expanding air force required. The future Reichsmarschall's mental framework remained that of a World War I squadron commander, and throughout his tenure as Luftwaffe commander he remained largely ignorant of supply, logistics, strategy, aircraft capabilities, technology, and engineering—in other words just about everything having to do with air power. Compounding his ignorance was the fact that even before the war Göring took a rather loose view on the subject of hard work. In July 1938 during an address to manufacturers, he even admitted that he saw Udet at most once a week.[122]

Exacerbating the leadership problem was the fact that the Luftwaffe's officer corps expanded from the tiny nucleus of less than 300 officers who transferred from the army in 1933 to 15,000 officers on active duty on the outbreak of war.[123] The result was a lack of homogeneity among the officer corps. Moreover, given the demands for technical knowledge and the shortness of the Luftwaffe's lifespan, most generals and staff officers had little time and less enthusiasm for the wider issues involved in the role of air power in national strategy. Even issues directly relating to the employment of air forces, such as maintenance, logistics, and supply, did not receive adequate attention from an officer corps that emphasized operational matters above all else.[124]

Several features of the Luftwaffe's preparation for the coming war need additional emphasis. The first and most obvious is that the prevailing historical picture of the Luftwaffe closely tied to the army's doctrine is no longer tenable.[125] Most Luftwaffe leaders believed, as did their counterparts in Britain and the United States, that "strategic" bombing was the chief mission of an air force and that in such a role they would win the next war. They did not believe the twin-engine aircraft at their disposal in 1937 and 1938 adequate for a campaign against Britain, Russia, or the United States, but within the context of Central Europe were not such aircraft adequate for attacking Warsaw, Prague, and Paris? Most Germans thought so, and certainly the leaders of the French and British air forces agreed with them. Like most of their contemporaries in other air forces, Luftwaffe leaders considerably overestimated the possibilities and potential of "strategic" air war. This was not surprising since there was so little empirical evidence on which to base predictions. The prevalence of such attitudes within the Luftwaffe's officer corps does help to explain Rotterdam as well as the seemingly casual shift from an air superiority strategy to a direct attack on London during the Battle of Britain.

Nevertheless, there were factors pushing the Germans toward a broader conception of air power than was the case in Britain and America. Above all, there was Germany's strategic position on the heart of the European continent. Unlike British and American air forces, German air strategists confronted the fact that Germany would face a great land battle the minute that war occurred. No matter what "strategic" successes the Luftwaffe might achieve in the first days of a war, the loss of Silesia, Pomerania, and the Rhineland due to the ground battle would spell defeat for the Reich. In effect German air doctrine at the outbreak of war was a mixture of these divergent trends.

Unfortunately for the Western Powers, the broader strategic approach enunciated by Wever and the greater flexibility in Luftwaffe doctrine caused by the above-mentioned trends corresponded more closely with aircraft capabilities than did the almost exclusive "strategic" bombing doctrines of the RAF and the US Army Air Corps. Accordingly, the Luftwaffe was in a position in the initial stages of the Second World War to have a direct and immediate impact on the field of battle.

THE NAVY

In many respects the German navy's position in the German military hierarchy was analogous to that of the British army in Britain. Few in Germany, including those in the navy, had any sense of what an effective naval strategy for the Reich might be. Early in the twentieth century Grand Admiral Alfred von Tirpitz, the father of the modern German navy, had coined the doctrine of a "risk fleet." If Germany possessed a fleet strong enough to sink a substantial part of the Royal Navy, Tirpitz argued, the British would not dare oppose the Reich for fear of damaging their overall strategic situation.[126] To say the least, the theory proved itself inadequate in the period from 1900 to 1918. Nothing shows the paucity of strategic thinking on the part of the German navy more than the fact that in the 1930s the naval staff resurrected the "risk theory" as a justification for once again building a large fleet.[127] While the Germans were able to build ships that may well have been the finest in the world in terms of construction, the navy was consistently unable to formulate a coherent doctrine suited to the Reich's strategic situation.

In terms of doctrine and shipbuilding programs, the German navy was one of the most backward among prewar naval powers. The prohibition of submarines by Versailles resulted in few admirals possessing U-boat experience, while the creation of the "pocket" battleships in the 1920s gave many officers a vested interest in surface raiders. Shipbuilding programs consistently emphasized surface ships and, significantly, minimized carrier construction.[128] Admiral Erich Raeder, commander in chief of the navy, characterized aircraft carriers before the war as "only gasoline tankers,"[129] and his assistant, Admiral Rolf Carls, remarked casually that land-based aircraft could do everything that carrier-based aircraft could do.[130] Meanwhile, the Luftwaffe offered minimal cooperation in terms of air support and resolutely opposed every effort the navy made to acquire its own air assets.[131]

In terms of submarine warfare, the naval staff grossly underestimated the role that submarines could and would play in the coming war. This fact is especially ironic, considering how close the submarine force came to winning the Battle of the Atlantic and the war in the great convoy battles of 1942-1943. In a prewar study the Flottenabteilung went so far as to predict that submarines in a future war would not attack merchant shipping as they had in the First World War but would perform other tasks such as scouting for the battlefleet.[132]

The failure to estimate highly submarine prospects as commerce raiders resulted from the illusion, shared by the British, that the Royal Navy had solved the submarine problem. An OKM (Oberkommando der Kriegsmarine, naval high command) study of October 1938 remarked that a submarine offensive against Britain could not expect any significant successes because British antisubmarine tactics and technical gear were at such a high level.[133] A 1939 study of the naval situation reported that "the importance of U-boats has considerably declined compared to 1915. One can assume that England has good submarine detection gear, which makes torpedo attacks on a secured unit or convoy impossible."[134] For the naval staff, the submarine's role now became reconnaissance for the battle fleet and attacks against enemy surface forces—missions that German submarines had performed with a notable lack of success in World War I.[135]

As a result of the above lack of interest and priority, the German navy possessed only twenty-six ocean-going submarines at the outbreak of war. In the first year only thirty-five boats capable of use in the Atlantic entered service, while twenty-eight were lost at sea.[136] This slow rise in U-boat totals was a direct reflection of this failure to grasp the submarine's importance. Yet in terms of doctrine, training, and leadership, the submarine force was admirably prepared for war. Admiral Karl Dönitz, commander of submarines, was a first-class trainer and leader who recognized the limitations as well as the advantages of his weapon.

Thus, the German navy that entered the war of September 1, 1939 was a force that had almost completely concentrated on the construction of a battleship fleet. It possessed no carriers, and although one carrier was being built, further work on it halted at the outbreak of the war. As Admiral Raeder gloomily noted on Britain's declaration of war:

> Today the war against England and France broke out. . . . It is self-evident that the navy is in no manner sufficiently equipped in the fall of 1939 to embark on a great struggle with England. It is true in the short time since 1935 . . . we have created a well-trained submarine force which at the present time has twenty-six boats capable of use in the Atlantic, but which is, nevertheless, much too weak to be decisive in war. Surface forces, however, are still so few in numbers and strength compared to the English fleet that they . . . can only show that they know how to die with honor and thus, create the basis for the recreation of a future fleet. [137]

Raeder's prediction proved largely correct. With the exception of the Norwegian campaign in the spring of 1940, the German surface fleet exercised almost no influence on the course of the war. On the other hand the submarines came dangerously close to winning control over Atlantic trade routes, but because of minimal investment in men and material before the war, it would take the German submarine force almost two years to exercise full pressure. By then it was too late.

The above failings reflected a refusal by Raeder and his staff to pay the slightest attention to the economic constraints and the strategic commitments that Germany as a great continental power had to face. One can not escape the conclusion that the naval staff aimed, as had Tirpitz, to build a great fleet to meet and defeat the Royal Navy on the high seas in a great clash of battleships—a goal that was manifestly unrealistic. Perhaps the most revealing comment on the navy's strategic incompetence occurred in the late spring of 1940. In early June, afraid that the war would end before its two battlecruisers, the *Gneisenau* and *Scharnhorst*, had engaged enemy naval forces, the naval staff risked these ships in a pointless operation in northern waters to insure that it could support its claims for the allocations of financial and industrial resources in the postwar debate over the defense budget. The result was that both ships were damaged and were not available for operational use until December 1940. [138] Considering that Raeder had already broached the possibility of invading Britain with Hitler as early as May 20, such a misuse of naval resources is surprising, to say the least. [139]

Conclusion: The Strategic Window

The victories from 1939 to 1941 underline the success of the Nazi rearmament effort. Unfortunately, historians have in many cases distorted the impact that Germany's strategic situation and her lack of raw materials and foreign exchange had on this process. By examining selected topics within the large framework of rearmament or by making assumptions (such as a connection between the development of armor doctrine and Germany's lack of raw materials) that the documents do not support, they have created a series of myths about Germany's prewar economy and strategic situation.[140]

After his takeover, Hitler faced political, economic, and strategic constraints in his rearmament effort. First of all, the immediate pragmatic problem facing the Nazis was how to bring Germany out of the depression. Rearmament, at least for the first years, could not provide the necessary impetus for recovery—production capabilities were just too low. Nevertheless, even in the early period the regime restrained the civilian economy, while rearmament received an increasing and eventually disproportionate share of resources in terms of investments, industrial capacity, and employment. The rearmament effort itself suffered throughout the 1933-1939 period from the twin problems of foreign-exchange and raw-material difficulties and from a lack of *skilled* workers.

Even so, as the tables in the economic section of this chapter indicate, the Germans keyed their rearmament at a far higher level than did their future opponents. Despite their economic difficulties the Germans maximized their rearmament potential, at the same time that the British and French minimized theirs. This is not to say that the Germans could not have done more—obviously no society is totally efficient. Rather, the important point is that the Germans were willing and able to do *far* more than their neighbors.

One cannot emphasize enough that German rearmament reflected Hitler's goals. In the long run, Hitler faced the problem of when exactly Germany would gain a sufficient military advantage over her opponents to be able to risk war. When, in other words, would Germany enter the strategic window between her inferiority of the present, caused by the restrictions of Versailles, and the point at which British and French rearmament would catch up to the initial German spurt? This was the crucial decision that Hitler faced in the 1930s. Risk war too soon and the German military and economy would not withstand the military superiority built up by her neighbors through 1932. Wait too long, and the lead would be lost.

There are two corollaries to this point. Germany did not rearm in depth because she possessed neither the resources nor the economic capability for such an effort to achieve access to the strategic window. Had Germany rearmed in depth and followed the prescription of General Thomas and OKW economic planners, Germany would never have caught up to her possible opponents. Similarly, when General Beck in 1938 raised serious questions not only about the economy, but also about the readiness of the army, Hitler objected that the important question was not whether the army was fully prepared. Instead, it was whether the army was superior to its opponents at *that* time. To wait until the army was fully prepared would only mean that Germany's opponents would also be prepared. As Hitler realized, Germany must pick the time when she enjoyed maximum advantage. In fact, Hitler almost jumped too soon in 1938. When Germany did go to war in September 1939 she still faced immense economic and strategic difficulties, but she did possess the basic minimum of resources and military strength necessary to overcome those problems (admittedly with considerable help from the Allies). The story of how the Germans managed to escape the full consequences of their economic and strategic position and how the Western Powers would fritter away every strategic advantage will be considered in succeeding chapters.

II

Britain

As did the other European powers, Great Britain embarked on the First World War with the lighthearted belief that her soldiers and fleet would return victorious before the gales of fall had subsided. The effect of the war, however, is best summed up by the title of Arthur Marwick's work, *The Deluge*.[1] Victory only came after four years of brutal, bitter fighting in the mud of the western front, in the Middle East, in the Atlantic, and after the deaths of over 700,000 British and Commonwealth servicemen. Considering the costs, the fruits of victory seemed none too sweet. By the middle of the 1920s, Britain's elite, as well as the great majority of her population, had concluded that victory in the First World War had gained nothing and that little separated the lot of the losers from that of the victors. These feelings failed to strike a similar chord in Britain's neighbor across the North Sea.

With some justification, the British believed that the Great War had strained their economic foundation to the breaking point. Not only did the Americans and Japanese now threaten their position in world trade but New York now contested London's position dominating world finance. Nevertheless, the relative calm of the 1920s, both domestically and internationally, allowed the British to settle into the comfortable assumption that the world could and would return to the nineteenth century. Moreover, the seemingly stable international situation permitted the British the luxury of almost entirely disarming and viewing questions such as armaments, strategic options, and defense requirements as irrelevant in a world protected by "collective security."[2] The thirties proved a harder and tougher period for such assumptions. Britain faced economic, diplomatic, and strategic challenges that neither her leaders nor her people recognized until too late. When they did, the substance of Britain's position and power in the world had collapsed. Yet, one cannot ignore the fact that the British political leadership faced complex problems in scarcity of resources, strategic challenges, and diplomatic assessments. This chapter will examine the nature of the problem; succeeding chapters, the response.

The Strategic Problem

At the end of the 1920s, Britain seemingly faced only one potential enemy, a power at the end of long and tenuous lines of communications to the Far East. Events in Manchuria in 1931 contributed to British feelings that Japan represented not only an economic and political danger to Britain's interests in that region but a hostile power as well that might undertake military operations against British dependencies in Asia. Further Japanese involvement against China, especially the invasion beginning in 1937, reinforced such apprehensions. Nevertheless, British leaders, especially in the military, ignored the fact that the growing quagmire in China made it unlikely that Japan could or would be willing to follow an aggressive military policy toward British dependencies in Southeast Asia.[3]

Almost immediately after Hitler's assumption of power in January 1933 it became clear that the Nazi government represented a distinct challenge to the existing European balance of power. Those who pushed initially for rearmament in Whitehall did so in response to the German danger. For the most part, these men cast their perceptions of this threat in terms of the peril of "strategic" bombing attacks on the British Isles. Although a few recognized that the Germans represented more of a threat to the European balance of power on land,[4] the misapprehension of a Germany preparing to strike a "knock-out" blow from the air continued right up to the war's outbreak. In any event, a German enemy called for different strategic commitments from Britain than did Japan, no matter in what manner the threat materialized. The air threat demanded major investment in the Royal Air Force, while the War Office argued the need for land forces to reinforce the French. Consequently, the emergence of Germany as a potential enemy demanded a different orientation for rearmament than did the preparations required to meet a Japanese threat.

Further complicating Britain's strategic situation in the thirties was the disastrous misfiring of British policy during the Abyssinian crisis. Caught between those who argued that Italy represented a major support against Germany and those who argued that Britain's foreign policy must stand on the League and "collective security," the prime minister, Stanley Baldwin, and his Cabinet thoroughly bungled British policy.[5] The result of the Ethiopian mess was that British military planners had to consider the possibility that Italy might cut the lines of communication to the Far East at the onset of war with Japan. The threat of cooperation between Fascist Italy, Nazi Germany, and Japan seemed all too real.

Thus, from the mid-1930s British planners faced a strategic threat in the Far East to the Empire's far-flung, almost indefensible possessions, while an increasingly hostile Italy threatened the supply and communication lines to that region running through the Mediterranean. Finally, Germany was carrying out a massive program of rearmament that menaced the European land balance of power and in the air seemed to pose a direct threat to the British Isles.

ECONOMIC CONSTRAINTS

In economic terms Britain faced a set of strategic problems differing from those confronting the Third Reich. Unlike the Germans, the British had access both in times of peace and more importantly in war to the raw materials required by the massive production effort of war in the industrial age. Like the Germans, however, the British faced the problem of how to pay for imports of raw materials. Throughout the 1930s the British economy balanced precariously on the need to pay for imports with foreign exchange earned by exports of finished goods. After the economic disaster of 1931, Britain faced a balance of trade that proved favorable in only one year (1935) (see Table II-1). More depressing was the fact that the actual balance of trade, not including income from overseas investments, was even less favorable. Compounding these gloomy figures was the fact that in 1931 Britain's economic plight had reached the point where it threatened to cause the collapse of the sterling bloc. Throughout the late 1930s worries over the state of the British economy and the possibility that overexpenditure on defense might lead to economic catastrophe dominated arguments over rearmament policies at the highest level. In December

TABLE II-1
British Balance of Payments, 1933-1938 (Not Including Gold)

Year	million £s	Year	million £s
1928	+ 123	1934	− 7
1929	+ 103	1935	+ 32
1930	+ 28	1936	− 18
1931	− 104	1937	− 56
1932	− 51	1938	− 55
1933	0		

SOURCE: R. S. Sayers, *The Bank of England, 1891-1944*, Vol. III (London, 1976), appendix 32, table A, pp. 308-309.

TABLE II-2
British Balance of Trade, 1929-1938 (in Million £)

	1929	1930	1931	1932	1933	1934
Imports	1,117	953	786	641	619	683
Exports	854	670	464	425	427	463
Balance	− 263	− 283	− 322	− 216	− 192	− 220

	1935	1936	1937	1938
	724	786	950	849
	541	523	614	564
	− 183	− 263	− 336	− 285

SOURCE: Sayers, *The Bank of England, 1891-1944*, Vol. III, Table C, pp. 312-313.

1937 Prime Minister Neville Chamberlain fully supported arguments "that the maintenance of Britain's economic stability represented an essential element in the maintenance of her defensive strength."[6] Thus, he argued, Britain's staying power was of decisive importance. Although such sentiments made sense, what was questionable was the consistent effort of the British government in the 1930s to follow a course of "business as usual." Chamberlain noted to the Cabinet in February 1937 that rearmament was "placing a heavy strain on our resources. Any additional strain might put our present programmes in jeopardy."[7] The fundamental assumption was that rearmament *must* not interfere with the normal course of British business. The Defense Requirements Committee argued that Britain need only build up sufficient reserves in peace to reach the point in wartime where her industry had converted to full military production. Such a rearmament effort should not interfere with civil or export trade. "From the production point of view this greatly complicates the matter, but any such interference would adversely affect the general prosperity of the country."[8] From a different perspective some British soldiers argued that the government was following a policy of preparing to pay the indemnity when Great Britain lost the coming war.[9]

What one must also stress is that arguments within the various British governments in the 1930s over the cost of rearmament involved the level of defense spending for future years. Through 1938, British military expenditures remained at a minuscule percentage of national income. Only in 1937 did British spending exceed that of Fascist Italy as a proportion of national income. In 1935 and 1936 British expenditures on the military reached barely one-quarter of Germany's percentage rate, and in 1937 and 1938 the effort only approached 30 percent of Germany's. Finally, in 1938 British defense spending reached 8 percent of GNP—a rate that the Germans had reached in 1935.[10] Thus, with real justification Winston Churchill characterized the middle 1930s as the "locust years."

It is also worth noting that from 1931 through 1937 Britain's gold holdings and currency reserves underwent a steady upswing as gold fled an unsettled continent (see Table II-3). Thus, in the short run Britain never faced the exchange difficulties that so plagued the German rearmament effort. Nonetheless, throughout the 1930s worries

TABLE II-3

Gold and Convertible Current Reserves in Britain, 1931-1938
(in Million £ at End of Financial Year)

1931	121
1932	206
1933	372
1934	415
1935	493
1936	703
1937	825
1938	615

SOURCE: G. C. Peden, *British Rearmament and the Treasury, 1932-1939* (Edinburgh, 1979), pp. 96, 208.

about the impact of rearmament on the stability of the pound remained a major consideration in Cabinet discussions.

THE STRUCTURE OF GOVERNMENT

The British government in the 1930s represented a highly organized bureaucratic system in which a series of committees guided and determined the course of rearmament. At the top of the pyramid sat the prime minister who possessed both the executive power of an American president and the legislative power of the party leaders in the Senate and House of Representatives.[11] The most important committee was the Cabinet, in which the leading ministers sat, for it made the final decisions on defense policy. Underneath the Cabinet were a number of key committees that debated the critical issues involved in the rearmament process. The Committee of Imperial Defense (CID) consisted of the chief service ministers, the chancellor of the exchequer, the prime minister, the foreign minister, and the minister for the coordination of defense. Underneath the CID in a direct advisory role was the Chiefs of Staff Sub-Committee, while a whole host of other committees tendered their advice in a well-orchestrated upward flow of papers and memoranda. Of key importance in military recommendations was the Joint Planning Committee, consisting of the chief planning officers of the three services.[12] On the diplomatic side the Foreign Policy Committee provided a major forum for the determination of British diplomacy.

The Cabinet held the final say in the decision-making process. Yet, it is worth noting that the strategic background and estimates were usually worked out well ahead of time by those serving within the committee system. On a particular strategic issue the Cabinet or prime minister could request a study from the Chiefs of Staff. They in turn would ask the Joint Planning Committee for a position paper. The three members of the Joint Planning Committee would then draw on their own services and on MI 6 (known also as the Secret Intelligence Service). The role of the latter remains unclear because virtually *all* of the intelligence estimates from this period remain classified. After the Joint Planning Committee had deliberated, its staff study would go directly to the Chiefs of Staff. In almost every case that body would forward to the Committee of Imperial Defense (CID) the Joint Planning

Committee's paper under their own signature with few substantive changes. Very rarely were the military willing to step beyond the "terms of reference" that they received from the Cabinet or the Committee of Imperial Defense. Once a strategic issue had reached the floor of the CID, the Treasury and Foreign Office entered the argument. More often than not they were willing to continue the argument at the Cabinet level, if unsatisfied with decisions reached by the CID. The whole system is, in fact, a historian's dream; there was a logical progression of ideas up and down the committee levels with few power centers existing outside of the structure. Unfortunately, the system proved only as good as those who ran it.

Civil servants of formidable stature like Robert Vansittart in the Foreign Office, Warren Fisher in the Treasury, and Maurice Hankey, the secretary of the Cabinet and of the Committee of Imperial Defense, were essential figures in the functioning of the bureaucratic system. These three civil servants played a key role in prodding the government to consider rearmament in the early 1930s.[13] In fact, the system of government by committee, particularly in defense matters, owed much to Hankey's bureaucratic skills. Hankey's biographer has praised the system created by his subject as a major factor in Britain's survival in the Second World War.[14] But this begs the issue; for if military and strategic planning worked smoothly during the war, the system took maximum time to produce minimum results before the war. With little leadership from above (especially before Chamberlain's assumption of power in 1937) committees rarely reached swift decisions but at the same time generated innumerable studies, "strategic appreciations," and recommendations. An exasperated Vansittart noted in February 1938: "The other point which I wish to make is that relating to procedure. . . . It seems clear that all the machinery here contemplated will involve the maximum delay and accumulation of papers. We surely do not want any more written 'European Appreciations.' We have been snowed under with papers from the Committee of Imperial Defense for years. Moreover, this procedure by stages implies a certain leisureliness which is not what we want at the present moment."[15]

The initial impetus for rearmament in the early 1930s is an excellent example of the system's inability to come to rapid decisions. Beginning in November 1933, Vansittart, Hankey, and Fisher formed with the Chiefs of Staff the Defense Requirements Committee.[16] After numerous wranglings and arguments the committee recommended in March 1934 that Great Britain spend approximately £71 million over the next five years to correct deficiencies in the military services.[17] The Cabinet then ignored the report for a month before referring the recommendations to another committee, the Committee on the Disarmament Conference. After considerable infighting that involved not only the services but the Treasury as well, the Cabinet agreed to the amended recommendations on July 31, 1934.[18] The whole process had taken eight months, countless discussions, and vast amounts of paperwork to reach what at best was a rather modest increase in defense spending.

On a smaller scale, an arms purchase requested by Belgium in the late 1930s provides another example of the system's inertia. In May 1936 the Belgians expressed a desire to buy arms from Britain. The British failed to respond, so the Belgians tried again in July. The Foreign Office passed the request to the War Office, which suggested that the diplomats control the negotiations. The Foreign Office then referred the matter to the Committee of Imperial Defense. Not until January 1937 did the Belgians receive an affirmative reply and they immediately requested permission to make extensive purchases. However, the War Office suggested that the government should examine the political implications before the technical experts dealt with the Belgian requests. Here the matter rested until the Cabinet authorized a response in February 1938. The Belgian ambassador did not receive this answer until July 1938.[19] Unfortunately, such governmental lethargy seems to have been the rule rather than the exception.

THE NATURE OF BRITISH POLICY

Fundamental to understanding Britain's response to the diplomatic and military crisis of the thirties is a firm grasp of the general philosophy and personalities of those who controlled British policy in the 1938-1939 period. Neville Chamberlain, as the prime minister, has quite rightly received considerable criticism for the course that he pursued. L. S. Amery described the prime minister in his memoirs in the following terms:

> Inflexibly dedicated to his self-imposed mission at all costs to avert the risk of a world war he ignored the warnings of the Foreign Office, dominated his colleagues, over-rode wavering French

Ministers, brushing aside their moral compunctions as lacking realism, and, to the last moment, refused to acknowledge failure. . . . It was only in that fixed determination that he could persuade himself, in face of all evidence to the contrary, that Hitler's pledges were sincere, or shut his eyes to the dishonorable aspects of his treatment of the Czechs. . . . He claimed for himself, as against the 'illusionists' of collective security, that he was a realist. But 'appeasement', as he pursued it, was no less of an illusion, and his passionate pursuit of peace and horror of war, in themselves noble, blinded him to the practical realities. . . .[20]

As Amery suggests, Chamberlain's abhorrence of war, undoubtedly deepened by a cousin's death in the First World War, was of major importance in his approach to foreign policy.[21] By nature he was incapable of understanding and dealing with men like Hitler and Mussolini. Nor could Chamberlain believe that his opponents did not regard war with horror and that they might willingly court military confrontation and world war in order to achieve *Weltmacht*. He remarked to his foreign minister, Lord Halifax, that the dictators "were men of moods—catch them in the right mood and they will give you anything you ask for."[22] In July 1937 he told Russian Ambassador Ivan Maisky that "if only we could sit down at a table with the Germans and run through all their complaints and claims with a pencil, this would greatly relieve all tension."[23] Inherent in Chamberlain's approach was a belief that a "modern" statesman could safely ignore considerations of balance of power, strategic requirements, and power politics. In a real sense Chamberlain's approach to diplomacy and questions of national security represented a nineteenth-century liberal *Weltanschauung*.[24]

The result of such attitudes was that while British strategic policy rested on a "worst case analysis," Chamberlain based his foreign policy on the most optimistic interpretation of German motives and aims. On the one hand the prime minister received advice that Britain should avoid war at all costs because of a desperate military situation. On the other hand he believed that relatively minor concessions would guarantee peace and world order. In this light it is not hard to understand his course.

It is also worth noting that Chamberlain as the chancellor of the exchequer before May 1937 and as prime minister thereafter played a major role in efforts to keep defense spending at the lowest possible level. He not only represented the Treasury view but at times placed himself even more than did his Treasury advisers on the side of financial stringency. In a May 1937 Cabinet meeting shortly before becoming prime minister, Chamberlain commented in a discussion on defense expenditure that "he could not accept the question at issue as being a purely military matter. Other considerations entered into it. He himself definitely did challenge the policy of their military advisers. The country was being asked to maintain a larger army than had been the case for very many years: a great air force, which was a new arm altogether: and, in addition, an army for use on the Continent; as well as facilities for producing munitions which would be required not only for our forces but also for our Allies."[25]

Within the Cabinet there existed a spectrum of beliefs and attitudes toward questions of international affairs similar to those within British society. For the most part Chamberlain maintained a strong hold over his colleagues, although in the September 1938 crisis he faced Cabinet opposition that severely limited his options. At the beginning of his term as prime minister in May 1937, Chamberlain enjoyed significantly more support than he would in his last year. Lord Halifax was one of the prime minister's chief adherents and, after Anthony Eden's resignation, was the government's spokesman for foreign policy during the critical years of 1938 through 1940. Halifax consistently supported the prime minister, although at times he showed a greater sense of the German danger. Moreover, in 1939 he played a major role in guiding British policy into the path of firmness toward Germany. Sir John Simon, chancellor of the exchequer, was closest to the attitudes and beliefs of the prime minister. As the representative of the Treasury, he waged a relentless battle against almost every increase in defense expenditure through to the outbreak of war.[26] Simon naturally proved one of the strongest supporters of appeasement. Sir Samuel Hoare, the home secretary, was also a member of the prime minister's inner circle and both within and outside the Cabinet remained a steadfast adherent of appeasement. Hoare could not discuss the strategic situation without constant, repetitive utterances about the possible horrors of aerial warfare. Also firmly within the Chamberlain camp was Sir Thomas Inskip, the minister for the coordination of defense. Baldwin, Chamberlain's predecessor, had created Inskip's position in 1936 in response to parliamentary demands but had given the new minister little real authority. Inskip had been selected precisely because he would not challenge either the government or the defense establishments. His lack of knowledge and background in defense matters insured that he would provide only a buffer between the government and defense ministries and that he would consistently support the Treasury attitude toward rearmament. In his last months in office, he seems to have taken a more independent line and this may explain his removal in winter 1939.[27]

On the other side of the Cabinet, Alfred Duff Cooper, first lord of the admiralty, and Oliver Stanley, president of the Board of Trade, advocated a hard line against Germany. Duff Cooper's arguments proved a constant nuisance to Chamberlain, and his resignation after Munich ended a situation that had become untenable. Oliver Stanley held on to his position longer and during the Munich crisis proved himself the Cabinet minister most willing to ask hard, searching questions. Neither man was within Chamberlain's inner circle of advisers and, although the prime minister allowed them to air their views within the Cabinet, they exercised little influence over the decision-making process.

Outside of the Cabinet Sir Nevile Henderson, ambassador to Berlin, affected British policy out of all proportion to his rank. Ironically, Vansittart played a major role in Henderson's appointment to Berlin with the typically British reasoning that Henderson was a "good shot" and deserved a good post after yeoman service in Argentina. Vansittart could not have made a worse selection. Henderson fell for Nazi propaganda hook, line, and sinker. He pictured the Nazi leaders and particularly Hitler as moderates with limited aims and argued right to the end that they were men with whom Britain could achieve a lasting settlement. There were, however, Henderson believed, certain radicals within the Nazi party: in particular Heinrich Himmler and Joachim von Ribbentrop, who were eager to push Hitler into desperate action if the British government did not grant his relatively modest demands.[28] Henderson seems to have gone so far as to tamper with the instructions of his government and either to ignore them or to tone down their implications. The historian Lewis Namier quite accurately summed up Henderson's career. "Conceited, vain, self opinionated, rigidly adhering to his preconceived ideas, he [Henderson] poured out telegrams, dispatches and letters in unbelievable numbers and of formidable length, repeating a hundred times the same ill-founded views and ideas. Obtuse enough to be a menace, and not stupid enough to be innocuous he proved *un homme néfaste*—important, because he echoed and reinforced Chamberlain's opinions and policy."[29] Henderson had no special relationship with Chamberlain, but his reports from Berlin helped to confirm the prime minister in his course. More than once, Chamberlain pointed to Henderson's dispatches in order to contradict reports from unofficial sources on the German danger.

Chamberlain's foreign policy, supported by the great majority of his Cabinet and, for that matter, by the British people, aimed to achieve a general easement of European difficulties through the removal of points of dispute between nations. Although appeasement in the context of the pre-Munich period meant something very different from the abject surrender of Czechoslovakia, it is clear that Chamberlain and his chief supporters believed that questions of strategic interest and war were not the first priority of statesmen. They believed that morality in terms of righting past wrongs and of supporting minority rights, national aspirations, and the like should receive special consideration in the determination of foreign policy. Lewis Namier has commented on the *Documents on British Foreign Policy* as follows: "[i]n the 1250 large pages of the British pre-Munich documents, the question of Europe's political and strategic configuration after Czechoslovakia had been obliterated is nowhere dealt with: amazing mental reticence. . . . [O]n the British side a blind wall is raised against the future, at least by those vocal in the documents. All they know is that war must be averted."[30]

Two quotations from the documents best capture this mixture of morality and hope that a future built on such an approach would bring better days. In July 1938 Halifax told the Cabinet that he had debated "whether it was worthwhile to draft an appeal to the contending sides in Spain to stop the war. Such an appeal would, of course, be based on grounds of humanity, Christianity, the peace of the world and so forth. He feared that it would not be likely to succeed, but it would strengthen the moral position of His Majesty's Government and might put them in a position to take helpful action later on."[31] Henderson in his own inimitable fashion wrote Halifax in the summer of 1938. "Personally I just sit and pray for one thing, namely that Lord Runciman will live up to the role of impartial British liberal statesman. I cannot believe that he will allow himself to be influenced by ancient history or even arguments about strategic frontiers and economics in preference to high moral principles. The great and courageous game which you and the Prime Minister are playing will be lost in my humble opinion if he does not come out on this side of the higher principles for which in fact the British Empire really stands."[32]

THE CONTRIBUTION OF STRATEGIC PLANNING TO APPEASEMENT

One cannot grasp British diplomatic policy and its response to the crisis of the late 1930s without a full understanding of the effect that military planning and advice had on the formulation of decisions. As mentioned above, the chief committee involved in discussion of strategic issues was the Committee of Imperial Defense. The chief military adviser of the government and in particular the CID was the Chiefs of Staff Sub-Committee, although the Joint Planning Committee enjoyed great latitude in formulating strategic surveys that the Chiefs of Staff submitted to the CID and Cabinet.

The Abyssinian crisis had come as a great shock to government and public opinion in Great Britain. Collective security and the League—those concepts that had seemingly guaranteed security without armaments—had failed. In an uncertain present, with Japan preparing to march on China, with Italy actively hostile to British interests in the Mediterranean,[33] and with Germany rearming *"ohne hast, ohne rast"* (sic),[34] the future looked particularly grim to British military planners. The central theme running through British strategic planning in the late 1930s was the belief that Britain was not and would not be able to face war against those three powers, should they move simultaneously or even singly. As the basic premise of military planning, the British used the "worst case" hypothesis. From Abyssinia through to the start of World War II, the Chiefs of Staff and the Joint Planning Committee maximized the number of enemies and hostile neutrals and minimized the number of powers that might be allied or benevolently neutral. Unfortunately, there was almost no cooperation between the Foreign Office and the military services in the drawing up of strategic surveys. Hankey complained shortly before retirement that he "had for a long time felt strongly that it would be of great value, if when the Foreign Office were asked to draw up appreciations as to the possibility of wars and the circumstance in which they might break out, they should in the first instance discuss the matter with the COS Sub-Committee. One reason why this was so important was that a decision to make war was affected not only by political but at least as much by military considerations in which the COS were the constitutional advisers. It was essential that foreign policy and military policy should go hand in hand."[35] Hankey was complaining that the system did not allow the military sufficient influence over Foreign Office reports and policies; but in general this lack of communication worked both ways. For if the military had few direct opportunities to guide diplomatic policy, the Foreign Office had even less say in framing strategic appreciations. This partly explains the unreality pervading so many strategic surveys prepared in the late 1930s.

Use of "worst case" analysis is not surprising—nearly all military organizations follow similar procedures. Unfortunately, the Joint Planning Committee rarely made clear that this was the basis of their reports, and civilian ministers often read strategic surveys as defining the only possibility. In late 1936 the Deputy Chiefs of Staff, discussing a Joint Planning Committee report, did admit that a German staff officer studying the same material might well come to a conclusion that differed from the Joint Planning Committee's assumption that "Germany has great superiority in land and air forces."[36] But this was an isolated case. In strategic terms, the "worst case" syndrome produced the belief that from the beginning of war Britain would face Germany, Italy, and Japan acting in unison.[37]

In other, more specific areas, strategic reports were no less misleading. Military appreciations almost uniformly exaggerated Italian military capacity.[38] Intelligence estimates of German aircraft production were quite accurate, but Air Staff descriptions of Luftwaffe combat capabilities erred wildly.[39] Similarly, estimates on the size of the regular German army were accurate, but those on reserve forces and armament production were excessive.[40] Interestingly, British reports on the number of divisions that the French could maintain in the field remained low until British foreign policy underwent a fundamental change toward increased reliance on France in early 1939.[41] There was an element of self-fulfilling prophecy in the advice tendered by the Chiefs of Staff. As Britain capitulated to each Axis move because of the supposedly impossible strategic situation, she found herself closer and closer to facing an imposing coalition alone.

In calculations dealing with war against Germany and Italy, military and civilian experts underrated Axis vulnerability to economic pressure. The British seem to have believed claims that Germany had achieved self-sufficiency in synthetic fuel and rubber production.[42] Admittedly, there was some recognition that Germany by herself lacked raw materials. But economic planners claimed that the excellence of the distributive system radiating from Vienna into Southeastern Europe—a questionable claim—and German control of the Baltic would "facilitate the replacement of the desired commodities from accessible sources."[43] Economic analyses mentioned neither Russian pressure in the Baltic nor the attitude of Balkan nations toward a German invasion of Czechoslovakia. Moreover, the British defined economic pressure in terms of their experience in the First World War, despite the increasing dependency of European economies on raw-material imports.[44]

BRITISH FOREIGN POLICY

The contradictions between the strategic requirements of empire versus defense of the British Isles, the self-imposed limitations on defense spending, as well as the dislikes, prejudices, and predilections of policy makers, presented British politicians and diplomats with increasingly unpleasant choices in the thirties. Limitations on defense spending discouraged military planners faced with Britain's worldwide commitments. In early 1938 Lord Chatfield, Chief of Naval Staff, justifiably complained that after a brief period of major rearmament, money had again become tight. In view of the steadily worsening international situation, he found the pendulum's swing back to financial stringency inexplicable and indefensible.[45] Similarly, Vansittart bitingly commented on opposition to increased defense spending that "the Treasury are always preoccupied with the problem of how we are going to live five years hence and not whether we shall be alive one year hence."[46]

The responses of the diplomatic and military advisers were, however, quite different from one another. The military proved far more willing to support appeasement. Their emphasis that Britain in war would face a unified coalition of Japan, Germany, and Italy consistently colored British strategic assessments. The next stage was to step from assumption to certainty. At the end of 1937 the Chiefs of Staff would underline their fears by commenting that "[w]e cannot, therefore, exaggerate the importance, from the point of view of Imperial defense, of any political or international action that can be taken to reduce the number of our own potential enemies. . . ."[47] In January 1938 Chatfield warned that Britain was drifting into a position where she would face these three powers in conflict, and that there had been no diminution of Britain's imperial responsibilities. Thus, Chatfield argued, there were only two alternatives: either rapprochement with one or more of the possible opponents, or "else the whole tempo of our rearmament program ought to be accelerated at all costs."[48] The Joint Intelligence Center argued in late 1938 that these three powers would not risk war unless in concert with each other.[49]

Only the Foreign Office challenged such appreciations. In late January 1938, shortly before his removal, Anthony Eden wrote Chamberlain that an alliance of Germany, Japan, and Italy did not exist, and would not exist unless Great Britain "gravely mishandled the international situation." France's guarantee to Belgium, as well as French strategic interests there, made it doubtful whether she would remain neutral in an Anglo-German war. Moreover, in view of Italian failures in Spain, Eden questioned whether Britain need take Mussolini seriously. In conclusion, he warned that Britain must avoid overestimating the capabilities of her enemies and weaknesses of her friends.[50] Both Eden and the professionals within the Foreign Office consistently offered support for an increased defense budget. In late 1937 Eden argued that:

> [i]f our own safety has been insured so far, and if the position in Europe has hitherto been held, and has not suffered catastrophic disturbance, this may be attributed in great measure to the German army's present unreadiness, and to Germany's financial and economic weakness, on the one hand, and on the other, to the closeness of the Anglo-French connection, to the mere announcement of our program of rearmament, to the lingering doubts in the minds of some governments whether in fact Great Britain would refrain from armed intervention if trouble arose, and to the influence of our still powerful prestige in the world. But some of these are wasting assets and if we are obviously

outstripped in the race for material strength, the forces of diplomacy, however prudently and resourcefully used, cannot be relied on to generate our safety except at the cost of deep national humiliation.[51]

There were two major areas in which the conflicting views of the diplomatic and military advisers came into friction: Britain's relations with Eastern Europe and in particular the Anglo-French association. For the Chiefs of Staff, Eastern Europe, excluding the Soviet Union, was a conglomeration of small states of no particular military significance. Through 1939, they saw these states only as a possible highway for the deployment of Russian troops against Germany.[52] After Stalin's purges of the Russian army, British planners were justifiably suspicious of Russian military capabilities. Generally the British regarded Eastern Europe as an area more remote from their interest than India or Hong Kong. The prime minister would echo such sentiments in his famous radio speech at the height of the Munich crisis. "How horrible, fantastic, incredible it is that we should be digging trenches and trying on gas masks here, because of a quarrel in a far away country between people of whom we know nothing!"[53]

In January 1936 the First Lord of the Admiralty, Viscount Monsell, warned the French that a Japanese move against Britain's Far Eastern territories was of greater concern than any German action in Eastern Europe.[54] In a February 1937 meeting of the Chiefs of Staff, Chatfield suggested that it might be a good thing to let the Germans entangle themselves in Eastern Europe. He expressed skepticism that Germany would emerge from such an enterprise militarily strengthened, and doubted claims that Germany would dominate Europe after absorbing Czechoslovakia.[55] Among the military only Hankey recognized the possible importance of Eastern Europe to Britain's strategic interests. In 1936 he observed that one of the chief dangers to the Reich was the threat of aircraft from bases in Czechoslovakia and Poland.[56] In the following year he warned that "if Germany were to absorb Czechoslovakia she might then go on from strength to strength, and might ultimately reach a stage when she would be in a position to demand from us the return of her colonies." Chatfield immediately retorted that by the time Germany could present an ultimatum to Great Britain her military power might be exhausted in Eastern Europe.[57]

The Foreign Office held a more balanced view. In January 1937

Sir Orme Sargent, an undersecretary in the Foreign Office and one of the most perceptive observers on the European situation, argued that German domination of Central and Eastern Europe would result in the eclipse of France unless she received British support. Such a success in establishing German hegemony throughout Europe could lead to a clash between the British and German empires—empires no longer separated by smaller powers.[58] One of the most damning indicators of the low level of British strategic thinking during the Czech crisis is the fact that not until September 16 did a British official think that it would be worthwhile to analyze the implications of a peaceful absorption of Czechoslovakia by Germany.[59]

There is no sadder tale in the 1930s than the tangled misperceptions, prejudices, and disagreements that marked Anglo-French relations.[60] English biases about the flighty French, about the supposed French drive to dominate Europe, or simply about "frogs" met French disbelief at the British performance in the Ethiopian crisis, dislike of British arrogance or simply unhappiness with "perfidious Albion." Such attitudes led to Vichy France on one hand and on the other to the English sense of relief on the defeat of France summed up so well by the King's comment: "Personally I feel happier now that we have no allies to be polite to and pamper."[61] Few in 1940 and even fewer earlier would have understood the import of General Sir Edmund Ironside's reaction to the crushing German victory on the Meuse: "This is the end of the British Empire."[62] What is so surprising about the prewar period is the general distaste and unwillingness of most British politicians and military leaders to recognize the community of interest between the two great western democracies or to realize that Anglo-French strategic interests were closely intertwined. Throughout the period there was much *Schadenfreude* on the part of the British toward French problems with rearmament and strategic difficulties in Eastern Europe. Not until the great scare of early 1939 over supposed German plans for a surprise air attack on the British Isles did the British finally awake to the possibility that France might be as important for Britain as Britain was for France.[63]

The Abyssinian crisis severely strained the relations between the two powers. Caught in the web of their belief that moral pressure and the League would exercise an influence on international affairs, the British faced the possibility of war with Italy. They found the French bewildered by the direction that British policy had taken and none too enthusiastic about a military commitment to Great Britain should war break out. French hesitations outraged the British who were all too willing to forget their own hesitations about guaranteeing the security of France and Belgium against German aggression.[64] The British re-action to German rearmament did nothing to reassure the French. While the British moralized that the French should accept German equality in land armaments (and of course refused to promise any support on land), they assiduously sought agreements limiting Ger-many's air and naval forces. Only with naval forces were the British successful, although it is worth noting that the 35 percent figure in the Anglo-German Naval Treaty granted the German navy equivalency with its French counterpart.

The key question in relations with France was the problem of whether Great Britain should commit her army to the defense of France.[65] With such a contribution came the problem of staff conversations to determine where and to what purpose a British Expeditionary Force would be used on the continent. In April 1937 Duff Cooper, still the secretary of state for war, stressed that an expeditionary force was a necessity, as the French had hinted that they would not send forces into the Low Countries without British support.[66] On the other hand there was real fear that any commitment of an expeditionary force to the continent, no matter how small, would grow to a force similar in size to the BEF in World War I.[67]

Opposition to a continental force was not limited to civilian circles. In January 1938 Sir Cyril Newall, Chief of Air Staff, suggested that the undersea cable between England and Jersey be extended to France in order to improve wartime communications. Chatfield wished to have no part of such a dangerous expedient and suggested that the proposal savored of staff conversations with the French. Such an action, Chatfield feared, might sabotage negotiations that he assumed were in progress for reaching détente with Germany.[68] As a result, the Chiefs of Staff paper on the extension of the cable system from Jersey to France admitted the military need but argued that conversations with the French would not remain quiet and that "the consequent effect on any political advances towards a better understanding with Germany would be serious." Sargent noted that this was incredible and observed that surely it was not too much to request the Chiefs of Staff to rewrite their paper.[69] At a CID meeting in February, Inskip for once placed things in proper perspective by commenting that the whole affair was too trivial to have any significance.[70]

By early 1938 the Foreign Office had become justifiably suspicious of military attitudes toward staff talks with the French. Sargent was alarmed that the Chiefs of Staff Sub-Committee, with no Foreign Office representation, rather than the CID, which did have a diplomatic adviser, was about to discuss the subject of staff talks with the French. Sir Alexander Cadogan, permanent undersecretary of state for foreign affairs, thought that the military were hanging back on "political grounds" and thus "should not have the last word in the matter." Vansittart remarked on the scale of Britain's military preparations and the unwillingness of the military to begin staff talks with the French in the following terms:

> At present our position is briefly this. We are proceeding on two assumptions both of which I am sure will be falsified: first that France can hold out on two or perhaps three frontiers [German, Italian, and Spanish] with no expeditionary force from us. . . . Secondly we are assuming that the war, if it comes, will be a long one and we must therefore lay great stress on conserving our staying power. This really means spending less in the crucial years ahead. . . . If, in addition to these two main conceptions, . . . we add the third error of making no preparations at all with the French even when we might be able to help . . . the cumulative effect may well prove fatal to us.[71]

The Chiefs of Staff more than lived up to Foreign Office fears. On February 4, they produced a paper arguing that "the very term 'staff conversations' has a sinister purport and gives an impression . . . of mutually assumed military collaboration." Although the chiefs admitted that staff conversations with the French might have some military utility, they argued that French leaks would upset and so alarm the Germans that there would be no possibility of reaching a "detente" with Germany. They concluded by observing that they had no objection to a proposal that "information should continue to be transmitted through the channel of the naval, military, and air attachés."[72]

This was too much even for Chamberlain. In April he told the Cabinet that the government would be in an anomalous position in accepting obligations, while refusing to act to fulfill them. "He could not reconcile the acceptance of such obligations with the frequent rejection of French approaches which only meant that our action would not be decided until the emergency arose."[73] On April 13, the Cabinet agreed that only naval and air force conversations would be necessary, because it would not be practicable for Britain to send an expeditionary force of ground troops. They did think that the French would have to be handled delicately on this question and that the Foreign Office and the military should avoid the impression that Britain would not at some stage in the war contribute ground forces.[74]

On the following day Halifax wrote Chamberlain that this approach would not work. To inform the French that Britain would not make any contribution on the ground might upset the French needlessly. Moreover, Britain needed French help to solve the Czech problem, and such a wounding might lead them to refuse cooperation.[75] In a Cabinet meeting on April 27, Chamberlain partly reversed the Cabinet's decision of April 13 by authorizing limited staff conversations concerning a continental force of two divisions. Nevertheless, some Cabinet members worried that the French might assume other forces would follow as had been the case in the First World War. Others fretted that the prospect of Anglo-French staff talks would unnecessarily alarm the Germans.[76] Still, it was hardly a major commitment. A letter from Hankey to the prime minister typified the British approach. Hankey recommended British negotiators stress that the Channel ports were of great strategic importance for France and that it would be a "strong French interest to cover them by an extension of the Maginot Line." He then added that it was also a vital British interest, but that "it would be advisable *not* to say so, or else the French might ask us to pay!"[77] At the end of April the subject of possible conversations on Anglo-French economic strategy in case of war came up. This thoroughly upset some in the Cabinet who felt that the French would assume that Britain stood behind France and that they would then pursue past policies, such as encircling Germany.[78]

The course of staff conversations over the summer followed none too easy a path. By July naval conversations were on the point of considering redistributions of major fleet units. The naval staff warned that if fleet locations changed, Britain would have a difficult time remaining neutral once France became involved in war. However, if conversations were not to discuss the redistribution of fleet units, there would be little purpose in holding staff talks.[79] The suggestion appalled William Strang, a senior Foreign Office bureaucrat, who recalled that redistribution of naval forces in 1912 had included an explicit agreement that discussions did "not constitute an engagement that commits either government to action in a contingency that has not yet arisen and may never arise." As in 1914, however, Strang suggested such an agreement would involve a moral commitment that Britain could not escape.[80]

The general unwillingness of British diplomats, politicians, and military leaders to recognize the importance of giving effective military and diplomatic support to the French is striking. Not until 1939 did the British finally admit that they could not escape sending a significant expeditionary force to the continent. Such a realization was, however, a direct result of the abandonment of Czechoslovakia and the resulting subtraction of Czech military forces from the French side.

In a larger sense the Chamberlain government's basic failure lay in its inability to recognize the nature of the European world in which it made policy. In December 1937 Lord Halifax had seen the making of "further progress in improving relations with Germany" as the only alternative to massive rearmament.[81] Showing less cynicism but no more realism, Chamberlain stated to the Cabinet that same month that there would be no deliberate policy of making concessions to one of the three hostile powers—rather Great Britain would attempt to appease all three together.[82] Yet as he was soon to find out, there was no alternative to that of the ancient Roman proverb: "If you wish peace, prepare for war."

THE COURSE OF REARMAMENT

As discussed above, the British rearmament effort had hardly gotten off to a flying start. The attitude of the Cabinet toward matters of national defense is suggested by the fact that at the very time at which the minimal suggestions of the Defense Requirement Committee were trimmed, the Cabinet provided £24 million in subsidies to a new Cunard liner and to various agricultural sectors of the economy (including £5 million to beet-sugar farmers).[83] In the period through 1937 Prime Ministers Ramsay MacDonald and Stanley Baldwin provided almost no guidance to the increasingly bitter conflict between Treasury and service ministries. The Abyssinian crisis did almost nothing to shake the government out of its profound apathy.

If the MacDonald-Baldwin coalition governments were reluctant to push rearmament, the opposition provided no alternative. The Labour party opposed every major initiative for increased defense funding right through to the introduction of conscription in the spring of 1939. The general approach of the Left to international affairs is best represented by Kingsley Martin's remarks in the *New Statesman* shortly after the Anschluss: "Today if Mr. Chamberlain would come forward and tell us that his policy was really one not only of isolation but also of Little Englandism in which the Empire was to be given up because it could not be defended and in which military defense was to be abandoned because war would totally end civilization, we for our part would wholeheartedly support him."[84]

The advent of Neville Chamberlain in late spring 1937 to the prime ministership of Great Britain ended the drift in defense policy. In his last months as chancellor of the exchequer, Chamberlain initiated a comprehensive study of rearmament. This survey focused on the question of how large an arms budget Britain could sustain without suffering economic damage or without introducing economic and financial controls. The Treasury predicated its report on two principles that served to diminish the final estimate of Britain's capacity to rearm. First, there should be no major dislocation of industry, such as conscription of skilled workers for armament factories.[85] Second, the burden of defense spending would be borne by limited borrowing, not by increased taxation.[86]

In July 1937 the new chancellor of the exchequer, Simon, reported the Treasury findings to the Cabinet. He advocated the imposition of a £1,500,000,000 ceiling on defense spending for the five-year period from 1938 to 1942, as the maximum that Britain could bear. If foreign trade declined or prosperity diminished, the sum would have to be decreased.[87] The full details of the evolution of this policy have been discussed elsewhere,[88] but there are several important points worth noting. First, although the Treasury would supply support, Chamberlain as prime minister consistently sought to keep defense expenditures at a minimum. The Treasury policy was in effect *his* policy. In 1937 he enjoyed the general support of his Cabinet but after 1938, as tensions on the international scene threatened to explode, Chamberlain faced increasing opposition from his colleagues. Until the German occupation of Prague in March 1939 Chamberlain refused to alter his course.[89] Yet, even within the Treasury there were those who argued that Britain could do significantly more in its defense effort. An October 1938 Economic Advisory Council paper argued that the government could raise expenditure on defense £400 to 500 million per year by putting the unemployed to work, diverting investment from the civil to military sectors, increasing taxes and price controls, and limiting dividends.[90] Such a policy demanded active intervention in the economy—something that the government was not willing to countenance until the outbreak of war. Significantly, the government did not stop the steady hemorrhage of Britain's currency reserves until August 22, 1939—an outward flow that saw Britain's reserves fall from £800 million in March 1938 to barely £600 million in September 1939.[91]

The impact of these financial limitations varied from service to service. Both the Royal Navy and the RAF suffered to a certain extent: the navy could not build up to a two-power standard, and the Royal Air Force did not receive production funding for a four-engine bomber force until well into 1939. The army suffered considerably more. Throughout the long rearmament debate, the army remained in limbo. Not until February 1939 did the government provide the financial support for a serious commitment of British forces to the continent. The unwillingness of the Chamberlain government to provide the needed financial support severely retarded the efforts of all three services. Nevertheless, there is a nagging doubt, which the last section of this chapter will address: Would Britain's military forces have been better prepared even had they received more financial support?

THE NAVY

Of the three services, the Royal Navy was best prepared to face the kind of war that it thought would occur. And when conditions in the Second World War proved quite different from what had been expected, the navy would adapt. In fact, it can be argued that the Royal Navy's victory in the Battle of the Atlantic would be the decisive element in the contribution of the Western Powers to the defeat of Nazi Germany.[92]

In many respects the Great War had been as trying and expensive for the Royal Navy as it had been for the British army. Admittedly, the High Seas Fleet had surrendered, but Jutland had been anything but a tactical success, and the German submarine campaign had almost brought Britain to her knees. Only the intervention of the War Cabinet had forced the Admiralty to introduce convoys. Moreover, the appearance of aircraft during World War I threatened to change many of the premises of naval warfare.[93]

In the 1930s the British enjoyed considerable superiority over potential opponents in European waters, especially when the French navy was included in Allied naval strength. The two forces had such superiority that they dominated the Atlantic trade routes and most of the Mediterranean.[94] Furthermore, geography endowed Britain with certain important advantages, for the British Isles dominated the North Sea, and control of Suez and Gibraltar effectively locked the Italians in the Mediterranean.

Naval rearmament after the Abyssinian fiasco was considerable. There was, however, great difficulty in starting the shipbuilding program because of the hiatus in warship construction in the early thirties. In 1933 new warship tonnage was only 10,665. In the period from 1930 to 1935, annual building averaged only slightly in excess of 30,000 tons.[95] Even so, once naval rearmament began, it rapidly accelerated. On January 1, 1935, warship tonnage under construction was 139,300; by January 1, 1936, it had reached 291,000; on January 1, 1937, it was 375,000; on January 1, 1938, 547,000; on January 1, 1939, 544,000; and on March 31, 1939, 659,000.[96]

However, there were several major deficiencies in the naval program, for no capital ships would be ready until 1941, and the first new aircraft carriers would not enter service until 1940.[97] In addition, the program concentrated on major fleet units to the exclusion of smaller ships. By 1938 the British had already laid down or authorized seven battleships, twenty-nine cruisers, and five carriers, but had begun work on only thirty-three destroyers and authorized only an additional eighteen.[98] Not until 1939, with a proposal for sixteen destroyers, twenty fast escort vessels, and three normal escort vessels, did the Admiralty substantially increase the strength of its antisubmarine forces.

One aspect of British shipbuilding remained beyond Admiralty control but was to have an immense effect on the war's course. British merchant shipping had fallen on hard days, and shipyard capacity had decreased from World War I levels. In 1933 merchant-ship construction totalled less than 140,000 tons, which partly explains the great shortage of ships at the war's outbreak.[99] Significantly, no landing craft appeared in naval programs until summer 1939.[100]

The failure to prepare adequately for submarine warfare was clearly the Admiralty's greatest error. One naval expert warned in 1938 that the shipbuilding program was dangerously distorted and that it threatened the security of trade routes:

> The great amount of battleship and heavy cruiser tonnage that has been laid down since rearmament started has been much in excess of our requirements in European waters and was, therefore, clearly designed for Far Eastern use as part of Sir Samuel Hoare's two-hemisphere fleet. At the same time we have been left seriously short of small ships for anti-submarine and anti-aircraft work in home waters. The Admiralty, therefore, seem to have been committing the grave error of preparing for ambitious operations in a far distant theater without first taking steps to ensure the safety of the home base.[101]

The basic reason for this distortion lay in the Admiralty's underestimation of the submarine threat. In 1935 Samuel Hoare, still First Lord of the Admiralty, told the Cabinet that the Royal Navy was "rather less apprehensive of submarines today than they had been during the war."[102] In 1937 the Admiralty claimed in regard to the World War I submarine campaign that "our defeat was in reality not quite so near as it appeared then."[103] Supposedly, techniques of antisubmarine warfare had reached the point where Britain could "face the future with confidence . . . ," and where "it can be stated that in future warfare submarines will have to face a form of defense which to a large extent robbed them of their chief advantage, i.e., their invisibility."[104] Because asdic (sonar) had advanced the ability to locate submerged submarines, the Admiralty felt that it had a weapon that had solved the submarine problem.[105]

However, the Royal Navy was not close to ending the submarine menace. It had tested antisubmarine tactics in daytime, in good weather, in limited areas, and for only short periods of time.[106] Exercises dealt almost exclusively with battlefleet protection and did not study the problem of protecting slow-moving merchant convoys.[107] Most optimism on antisubmarine warfare resulted from the mistaken belief that submarines would attack while submerged. A study of German tactics late in the First World War would have shown this to be incorrect, as the Germans were already perfecting night surface tactics for submarines. In 1918 the British replied by fitting aircraft with searchlights and using them over convoys. Coastal Command, the maritime wing of the RAF, did not possess similar aircraft until 1942.[108]

The Admiralty also made the mistake of basing its estimates of escort requirements on the number of submarines that potentially hostile powers possessed—rather than on the number that would be required to protect British shipping.[109] Shortly before the outbreak of the war, Russell Grenfell, a commentator on naval affairs, pointed out that battleships should not be a measure of Britain's naval strength: "Against what many people regard as the two most dangerous threats to our merchant shipping, namely submarines and air attack, they are no test of strength. . . ."[110] It proved an accurate forecast.

In the late 1930s the Royal Navy fell behind the Japanese and American navies in the development of naval air power. In the prewar period there were four basic schools of thought on this subject. The Douhet-Mitchell-Trenchard view held that air power made navies obsolete; therefore there was no need for naval aircraft. On the other hand, the Japanese and American navies relied on air power along with the fleet to extend range and striking power. The Royal Navy treated aircraft as an auxiliary that would aid the battlefleet in coming to grips with the enemy. Finally, the German and Italian navies viewed naval tactics as strictly a matter of gunnery.

The more extreme view of air-power advocates as well as the organizational structure of the British military, which gave the RAF control of the Fleet Air Arm for most of the interwar period, distorted the development of a naval air force. In July 1918 the carrier *Furious* had launched seven Sopwith Camels that destroyed the zeppelins L54 and L60 in their hangars.[111] This striking start to naval air power aborted. The Admiralty put up little opposition to the transfer of its air arm to the new RAF and in 1918 turned over its 2,500 aircraft and 55,000 men to the new service.[112] In the early interwar period the RAF and the navy reached a temporary compromise in which the Admiralty established aircraft requirements while the RAF was responsible for aircraft construction, personnel training, and tactics of Fleet Air Arm. Seventy percent of aircrews were naval, but were "attached" and not "seconded" to the RAF. Thus, they received only equivalent RAF rank.[113] This compromise did much to stunt the growth of naval air power. At this time the United States navy was training and promoting naval officers who had a solid grasp of aircraft potential. In the Royal Navy during the interwar period, ignorance of aircraft in senior ranks led to underestimation of the capabilities of the air weapon.[114] The Royal Navy paid dearly for this, especially against the Japanese.

Returning Fleet Air Arm to the Admiralty in 1937 could not correct basic deficiencies, as the Royal Air Force retained control of research and development. Considering its doctrine and rearmament effort, the RAF had neither time nor money to develop specialized naval aircraft.[115] Moreover, the transfer of Fleet Air Arm did not include landbased aircraft. Not until 1936 did the RAF establish Coastal Command as an independent command, and it remained a poor second compared to other major commands well into the war.[116] The Admiralty also misjudged the effectiveness of anti-aircraft fire. In introducing the 1937 estimates, Hoare went so far as to claim that anti-aircraft guns made the fleet the most costly target that the enemy could select.[117] The loss of the *Repulse* and *Prince of Wales* was a direct result of such thinking.

Nevertheless, despite the weaknesses discussed above, the Royal Navy was an effective force. The training and combat effectiveness of surface units was high. Fleet performance against superior Italian forces in 1940 and 1941 (the victory off Calabria, the destruction of the Italian fleet at Taranto, and the victory off Cape Matapan) indicates a higher standard in the navy than in the other services when war broke out. In the great Battle of the Atlantic the navy showed flexibility and adaptability in meeting the desperate threat once it realized that its antisubmarine doctrine was faulty.[118] Certainly, the leadership of admirals like Cunningham, Mountbatten, and Vian points to a generally higher level of competence in the naval officer corps than was the case in either army or air force. In 1938 and 1939 the Royal Navy could meet whatever enemies it might encounter in a European struggle with some hope of success. It could quickly clamp a blockade on German and, if necessary, Italian commerce. It could run down and destroy German raiders and commerce on the high seas. Finally, although it was not fully prepared to master the submarine threat to

Britain's life lines, the Germans were not yet in a position to launch an effective campaign.

THE ROYAL AIR FORCE

The Royal Air Force was the first independent air force. It owed its creation in 1917 largely to the public outcry in Britain over the bombing of London by German aircraft based in Belgium. Interestingly, the political rationale behind its creation seems more to have been the launching of reprisal raids than the defense of British territory. As one recent commentator has noted: "Indeed, an essential, continuing characteristic of the RAF was established in its very creation; it was an offensive service arm which was created to deal with defensive needs."[119]

By 1918 the British were strongly advocating the creation of an Allied independent "strategic" bombing force. RAF representatives at the Inter-Allied Aviation Committee suggested that a "strategic" bombing campaign "must be conducted in pursuance of a carefully conceived policy and with a thorough elaboration of detail." Attacks on enemy railroads and air bases in the enemy's immediate rear areas should be the task of units assigned to cooperate with ground forces. The "special long range striking force" would have a more important task: "the dislocation of the enemy's key industries." The British representatives argued further that the launching of such attacks would force the Germans to divert significant resources from the western front to home defense. In conclusion, they noted that: "if the Allies are to reap the full benefit of the reaction in Germany due to the failure of the German effort in 1918, it is essential that no time shall be lost in developing coordinated and widespread strategic air attacks to synchronize with a period of acute popular depression."[120]

An Air Ministry paper of October 1918 on the air raids against German cities suggests further interest in the articulation of a "strategic" bombing doctrine before the First World War had ended. The authors of the paper argued that "in the period August-October evidence has accumulated as to the immense moral effect of our air raids into Germany." The deduction that the paper then drew was that the enemy's fighting capacity decreased "as the number of raids increased. . . . Though material damage is as yet slight when compared with moral effect, it is certain that the destruction of 'morale' will start before the destruction of factories and, consequently, loss of production will precede material damage."[121]

With the coming of peace the British government made wholesale cuts in military expenditures and for a period of time seriously considered doing away with an independent air force. Churchill's appointment in December 1918 to both the War Office and to the Air Ministry did not appear advantageous to the future existence of the RAF; however, not only did Churchill vigorously defend the new service, but he was instrumental in bringing back Sir Hugh Trenchard as the RAF's Chief of Air Staff.[122] And Trenchard through force of personality as well as skillful political maneuvering insured the continued existence of the fledgling service. In addition, he reinforced the interest in and the emphasis on "strategic" bombing already apparent before the end of the war. One must note that this trend in RAF doctrine seems to have occurred entirely independently of outside influence.[123]

Trenchard's doctrine postulated that air power alone could defend Britain and that, properly used, its massive striking power could destroy her enemies at the onset of war. In conference with his staff in 1923 the Chief of Air Staff underlined his faith in "strategic" bombing and his belief that the British people would exhibit greater staying power in an air war between Britain and France: "I would like to make this point again. I feel that although there would be an outcry, the French in a bombing duel would probably squeal before we did. That was really the first thing. The nation that would stand being bombed longest would win in the end."[124]

In March 1924 the Air Staff presented its case in a memorandum on the proper objectives of an air offensive. It argued that air forces "can either bomb military objectives in populated areas from the beginning of the war, with the objective of obtaining a decision by moral effect which such attacks will produce, and by the serious dislocation of the normal life of the country; or, alternatively, they can be used in the first instance to attack enemy aerodromes with a view to gaining some measure of air superiority and, when this has been gained, can be changed over to the direct attack on the nation. The latter alternative is the method which the lessons of military history seem to recommend, but the Air Staff are convinced that the former is the correct one."[125] For the conduct of the air offensive against an enemy power (the belligerent countries, not named, would be "separated by twenty or thirty miles of sea"), the Air Staff suggested that fighters would play almost no role. The distances involved, the staff suggested, would make it impossible to build a fighter that would have sufficient range and efficiency. Thus, the conclusion was that "as a principle . . . the bombing squadrons should be as numerous as possible and the fighters as few as popular opinion and the necessity for defending vital objectives will permit."[126]

If Trenchard can be accused of taking a too single-minded approach to the question of air power, his accomplishment in defending the independence of the Royal Air Force is his greatest monument. Moreover, he identified and supported such strong personalities in the RAF's officer corps as Hugh Dowding, Arthur Tedder, Charles Portal, and John Slessor among others. They and their service would be Trenchard's contribution toward the winning of the Second World War. One should also note that throughout the 1920s when Trenchard and the Air Staff were creating their doctrine of "strategic" bombing, RAF officers serving in the world of colonial pacification, police actions, and border skirmishes were actively engaged in air operations that had little to do with "strategic" bombing. Their experience and the flexibility of mind that such tasks demanded proved of vital importance once the war had begun.

Unfortunately, such experience had little impact on the higher levels of the Air Staff. Trenchard's persuasive influence endured long after he had relinquished his position. Even Slessor, for the most part a perceptive thinker on military matters before the war, could not avoid arguing in his book *Air Power and Armies* in 1936 that the coming war would involve mainly aerial warfare and that Britain could only gain and maintain air superiority through a "resolute bombing offensive" against an enemy's cities and industries. Such a strategy would force the enemy to use his air strength in a passive, defensive role and would divert strength away from the primary task of "strategic" bombing, which alone could be decisive. Air operations would fall heaviest on the poorer and more unreliable segments of the population and would force the enemy to divert further strength from his strategic effort. Ground operations would rarely occur, and armies would mostly serve as frontier guards while the bombers flew overhead.[127] Slessor's position as chief of plans in the Air Staff underlines the widespread currency of such beliefs in the higher levels of RAF leadership.

Considering that "strategic" bombing represented the raison d'être for the RAF, surprisingly little was done to prepare it for this task. Prewar doctrine had called for trained aircrews to precede the bomber force and mark the targets for following aircraft. In the late 1920s, when asked how trained aircrews would find their targets, Tedder replied, "You tell me!"[128] Regrettably, most of the RAF's top commanders would not face up to this problem until 1941, when analysis of mission photography revealed that a sizeable percentage of the bombs dropped on Germany was landing in the countryside.[129]

Admittedly, in the late 1930s there was no clear conception of the parameters involved in the coming air war in terms of either weapons or tactics. There was enormous difficulty in estimating capabilities with so little experience on which to draw. In 1938 the Joint Planning Committee conceded: "In considering air attack we are faced with the difficulty that we lack the guidance of past experience in almost all the factors which affect it, and consequently the detailed methods of application and their effects are almost a matter for conjecture. We do not know the degree of intensity at which a German air offensive could be sustained in the face of heavy casualties. We do not know the extent to which the civilian population will stand up to the continued heavy losses of life and property."[130] Yet the general tenor of arguments paid little attention to the problems involved in navigation in bad weather, target identification, and bombing accuracy. As Slessor admitted after the war, the prewar belief in the bomber had been "a matter of faith."[131]

This emphasis on "strategic" bombing as *the* doctrine seriously affected the development of other aspects of air power in Britain during the interwar period. Even air defense received little recognition or interest from the Air Staff in the 1920s and early 1930s. After all, as Trenchard had argued, the best defense was a good offensive. In October 1938 Sir Warren Fisher of the Treasury commented on the early CID meetings, in which the government determined to spend more on air defense: "When I insisted on the insertion in the report of passages such as these [on the need to build up Britain's air defense system] the representative of the Air Staff acquiesced with a shrug of his shoulders. The Air Staff proposals were, of course, again quite insufficient."[132] Air Staff strategic assessments consistently overstated the Luftwaffe's capabilities, while underestimating the defensive potential of an air defense system.[133] In terms of British fighter production, only Sir Hugh Dowding's spirited objections in June 1938 kept the emphasis of British fighter production on Spitfires and Hurricanes and away from the ill-fated, two-seated Defiant.[134]

It is worth underlining that the creation of Fighter Command as an effective defense force and the articulation and conception of an air defense system was due almost entirely to Dowding. In charge of RAF research in the early 1930s, he provided critical support for the development of radar as well as the single-seater fighter. As the leader of Fighter Command in the late thirties he waged a lonely fight with the Air Staff to build an integrated air defense system based on the Spitfire and the Hurricane.[135] He then conducted and won the Battle of Britain with the force and strategy that he had created—surely as great a conceptual triumph as the creation of the German panzer force.

The refusal of the Chamberlain government to buy a large bomber air force considerably aided Dowding's efforts to build up an air defense system. Although the Chamberlain government was willing to give priority to the production of fighter aircraft, it showed less interest in the other aspects of air power. Thus, the RAF met no serious challenge to its refusal to provide close air support to ground forces. Admittedly the government's refusal to commit the army to the continent until February 1939 provided the RAF with an excuse to ignore the close-support mission, but that excuse only shielded a deeply held inclination. After a 1939 combined exercise, General Sir Archibald Wavell commented that the RAF had obviously not given any thought to supporting ground operations and thus its pilots were incapable of performing that mission.[136] As late as November 1939, when considerable evidence existed as to what the Germans had done in Poland, the Air Staff dourly commented on the value of close air support for the army: "Briefly the Air Staff view—which is based on a close study of the subject over many years—is as follows: The true function of bomber aircraft in support of an army is to isolate the battlefield from reinforcement and supply, to block or delay the movement of reserves, and generally to create disorganization and confusion behind the enemy front. . . . But neither in attack nor in defense should bombers be used on the battlefield itself, save in exceptional circumstances. . . . All experience of war proves that such action is not only very costly in casualties, but is normally uneconomical and ineffective. . . ."[137] This is indeed a somewhat surprising document when one considers that the Polish campaign had just ended. In France in 1940 the support extended to units of the First Armored Division confirmed the above Air Staff doctrine. Requests by that command for close air support met the objections that such calls were impracticable and unnecessary.[138] In July 1938 the Chiefs of Staff at the urging of the Air Ministry dismissed the employment of parachute troops with the argument that such a task would divert aircraft from a more useful employment as bombers.[139] Thus, as a result of an overriding belief in "strategic" bombing on the highest levels, when war broke out in 1939 the RAF possessed almost no capability in terms of aircraft and no capability in terms of training to carry out interdiction, close air support, or transport missions. Only at great cost in aircraft and crews would the RAF develop these capabilities in North Africa.[140] One must also note that the RAF was most unwilling to tender or even recognize the considerable needs that the Royal Navy would have for air support in a future war.[141]

The RAF's heavy emphasis on "strategic" bombing had a definite impact on British foreign policy in the late 1930s. By overemphasizing the effects that bombing would produce, the Air Staff contributed to the mood supporting the appeasement of Germany, and the belief in RAF circles that the Luftwaffe was preparing to launch a bolt from the blue played a major role in framing the gloomy strategic surveys that Chamberlain used to such effect in persuading his Cabinet to surrender Czechoslovakia.[142] As Hoare argued to his colleagues in the Cabinet over an army report on the commitment of troops to the defense of France: "The impression made . . . by the report was that it did not envisage the kind of war that seemed most probable. In a war against Germany our own home defenses would be the crucial problem. . . . The problem was to win the war over London! . . . We should need in the initial stages all our available troops to assist in the defense of this country."[143]

In summation, the myopia of the Air Staff hindered the development of a broadly based conception of air power in Great Britain. Admittedly Trenchard's devotion to his service and advocacy of air power saved the Royal Air Force as an independent service. Moreover, one must admit that the evidence from the First World War did not provide clear, unambiguous evidence on the impact of air power. But when all is said and done, too many of those in the higher positions of the

RAF between the wars allowed doctrine to become dogma and refused to examine the assumptions on which they based their air strategy in the light of current capability and the difficulties that had emerged even in peacetime flying. The result was that outside of air defense—and the Air Staff's role there was somewhat ambiguous—the RAF had prepared only for "strategic" bombing; in all the other aspects of air power (close air support, interdiction, airborne operations, long-range reconnaissance, and maritime support) the RAF had done little to anticipate the requirements of the coming war.

THE BRITISH ARMY

Since the days of Cromwell, the British have been skeptical of their army. The horror of the Somme and the mud of Flanders in the First World War only served to accentuate innate suspicions. In the interwar period the feeling that the youth of Great Britain was too precious to entrust to generals who had proved themselves "brilliant to the top of their boots" became ingrained in British society. Furthermore, the failure in the 1930s to define a strategic role for the army played a major role in its dismal showing in the first years of the Second World War. As one commentator noted: "Here is of course the salient difference between us and Germany that they know what army they will use and, broadly, how they will use it and can thus, prepare . . . in peace for such an event. . . . In contrast we here do not even know yet what size of army we are to contemplate for purposes of supply preparation between now and April 1939."[144]

With peace in 1919 the British army faced comprehensive reductions in men and material. Stretched between the demands of Ireland, India, and other parts of the empire, and with a steadily diminishing defense budget, the War Office had little money for experimentation; but to its credit it did establish an independent tank corps that made it possible to develop tank tactics in the interwar period.[145] Nevertheless, there was a definite effort to escape the horrors of the Great War by returning to "peacetime" soldiering. Not until 1932 did the army establish a committee to study the war's lessons—much too late to have any effect on either doctrine or training.[146]

During the interwar period two British military thinkers, J.F.C. Fuller and B. H. Liddell Hart, stand out as extraordinary prophets of future warfare. They so influenced military thought and experimentation that by 1935 true armored warfare was already a possibility. Moreover, their partnership with officers like Charles Broad, George Lindsay, Percy Hobart, and Giffard Martel was of great importance in transforming ideas into reality. In the end, however, both angered the military establishment to the point where their views no longer received proper attention. The Germans, rather than the British, received maximum benefit from British theorizing and experimentation with armor.

Fuller was the foremost exponent of the operational use of tanks. He argued that only the tank could restore mobility to the battlefield. As early as 1920 he wrote that "the tank can replace infantry and cavalry, can supplement artillery, can reduce the present number of field engines, and can accentuate the value of machine gunners, and that the cross-country tractor can practically abolish the horse."[147] Armor dominated his thoughts during the interwar period to the exclusion of the older branches, and Fuller never saw future armored divisions as a combination of weapons. He saw the tank as an operational and tactical, rather than a strategic, weapon.

Liddell Hart's initial works after the war concerned infantry. His studies of German tactics in the 1918 battles had great influence on his thinking. From these studies he developed the idea of the "expanding torrent," and after reading Fuller's early work, he combined this concept with the armored mobility of the tank. Unlike Fuller, Liddell Hart realized that armor could transpose the German tactics from the operational to the strategic level of warfare. By the mid-1920s his work had pointed out the strategic potential of armored mobility.[148]

The period from 1925 through 1933 was of great importance in experimentation with armor. The Chief of the Imperial General Staff (CIGS), Field Marshal Lord Milne, proved to be an important element in these developments. Milne has remained an enigmatic figure. On the one hand he seemed to favor experimentation with mechanization and in 1927 went so far as to predict that someday the British army would be a completely armored force. On the other hand, Milne obviously believed that such a day was far in the future and for the present proved most unwilling to disturb the troglodytes in the War Office. Nevertheless, Fuller's and Liddell Hart's after the fact criticism is most unfair. Given the financial stringencies that bound the army in the late twenties and early thirties, it is to Milne's credit that he provided financial support to the experiments. In addition, until the development of the German threat in the middle 1930s it is hard to see the utility of an armored force since it was hardly suitable to the Indian frontier or the jungles of Malaya.

The maneuvers with the experimental armored force from 1926 on played an extraordinarily important part in the conversion of theory to doctrine.[149] By 1931 experiments were studying the techniques of deep-penetration tactics,[150] and the 1934 maneuvers pointed the way toward future tank tactics. Throughout the 1934 maneuver period, the flexibility, mobility, and fire power of the armored force consistently proved superior to conventional infantry and cavalry forces. Unfortunately, the final portion of the 1934 maneuvers in front of Britain's leading military figures was not as successful, because the mechanized force worked within a narrow framework that made it difficult to utilize armor's superior speed and flexibility. Thus, many senior officers came away from the exercise with the impression that the tank arm had not lived up to the claims of its advocates.[151]

There was to be a striking set of contradictions in Liddell Hart's thinking in the 1930s. While urging the army to mechanize, he argued against a conscript army and the commitment of large forces to the continent. In works such as *The British Way in Warfare*, he recommended that Britain return to a strategy that had supposedly conquered the empire in the eighteenth century—a strategy that Liddell Hart termed "limited liability." In past wars naval superiority had allowed the army's use in theaters where the enemy was weak rather than strong, while allies pinned down the enemy's main forces. However, as Michael Howard has pointed out, there were problems with the analogy: "It was . . . precisely the failure of German power to find an outlet and its consequent concentration in Europe, its lack of any significant possessions overseas, that made it so particularly menacing to the sprawling British Empire in two world wars and which make so misleading all arguments about 'traditional' British strategy drawn from earlier conflicts against the Spanish and French Empires, with all the colonial hostages they had offered to fortune and the Royal Navy."[152]

Moreover, in previous world wars—the revolt in the Netherlands, the War of Spanish Succession, the Seven Years' War, and the Napoleonic Wars—Britain had sent large expeditionary forces to the continent to help her allies with the conduct of military operations. Liddell

Hart did, however, argue that a strategy of "limited liability" depended on the maintenance of alliances not only in Western Europe but in Eastern Europe as well.[153]

Liddell Hart's strategic arguments proved most useful to the Chamberlain government with its efforts to cap military spending. The prime minister and other Cabinet ministers used the "limited liability" strategy against War Office requests for funds to prepare the army for a continental role. As a result, many in the army tended to react paranoiacly when Liddell Hart's name came up. The British army's leadership felt with some justification that Liddell Hart's influence on the Cabinet and particularly on the secretary of state for war, Leslie Hore-Belisha, short-circuited normal channels. The bitter feelings on both sides confused the real issue—the need for modernization. Liddell Hart's arguments allowed the government to delay this decision on the future role of the army until too late, and the army's reaction to Liddell Hart's opposition to a sizeable continental commitment prevented the military from coming to grips with the critical tactical and doctrinal questions he had raised.

The period 1934 to 1939 is one of the most depressing in the British army's history. The War Office did almost nothing to build on the framework of earlier experiments with tanks. Although one can argue that lack of money made it difficult to do more about mechanization before 1935, progress between 1935 and 1939 leaves the army open to criticism.

Only with great reluctance did the army motorize its cavalry. Duff Cooper, at that time at the War Office, announced in the House that asking the cavalry to give up horses for trucks "was like asking a great musical performer to throw away his violin and devote himself in the future to the gramophone."[154]

Immediately before he became prime minister, Chamberlain had served notice that he would not support plans for a significant expeditionary force. In a May 1937 Cabinet meeting he attacked proposals to increase funding for the Territorial Army: "He did not believe that we could, or ought, or, in the event, would be allowed by the country, to enter a Continental war with the intention of fighting on the same line as in the last war. We ought to make up our minds to do something different. Our contribution by land should be on a limited scale. It was wrong to assume that the next war would be fought by ourselves alone against Germany. If we had to fight we should have allies who must . . . maintain large armies. He did not accept that we also must send a large army."[155] Unlike Liddell Hart, however, Chamberlain did not recognize that to escape the burden of a land war Britain had to depend on allies in the east as well as in the west. Nor was the Cabinet any more willing than Liddell Hart to see that a failure to supply land forces might have serious political and diplomatic repercussions on the continent. It would be difficult to build any European coalition without British support, and for Europe, support meant ground forces. The Belgian retreat into neutrality after the German remilitarization of the Rhineland was almost as much a result of Britain's unwillingness to offer support as of internal political pressures.[156] After Munich, even the French began to hesitate in helping Britain unless they received British ground support.[157]

The Chamberlain government established four roles for the army: 1) to protect the British Isles, 2) to help guard the trade routes, 3) to provide garrisons for the empire, and 4) to cooperate in the defense of Britain's allies—but only after the first commitments had been met.[158] While Hore-Belisha, sacking the CIGS and most of the Army Council, cleaned house in the War Office, progress in the rearming of the army ground to a halt. The 1937 limit on defense spending discussed above cut £70 million from the army budget.[159] Military reforms in terms of tactics did no more than put the infantry in trucks, and industrial preparation for the medium tank halted.[160] The new motorized division was in no sense a mechanized force and possessed fewer antitank guns and artillery than equivalent German motorized infantry divisions. The army paid no attention to Liddell Hart's criticism that "to maintain mobility when one comes under fire, one needs armored mobility."[161]

The new policy defined the army as "general purpose." This nebulous formula made it difficult to request supplies or equipment for particular theaters.[162] In March 1938 Lord Gort, the new CIGS, warned that the field force had no howitzers comparable to those of foreign armies. He told the Committee of Imperial Defense that "in the circumstances it would be murder to send our forces overseas to fight against a first class power."[163]

The obvious role for the army, if not on the continent, was as an amphibious force. Chamberlain, Hore-Belisha, and Liddell Hart were thinking along these lines, but none showed comprehension of the complexities of combined operations. The services had no interest in such operations. Their attitudes ranged from a smug belief that amphibious operations had worked well in the last war to a confidence that amphibious operations would never again occur.[164] One of the Deputy Chiefs announced in 1938 that the landings at Gallipoli indicated that nothing was wrong with British amphibious techniques except for a few minor breaks in communications.[165] Suggestions that the navy prepare for combined operations met a stone wall. The Deputy Chief of Naval Staff, Andrew Cunningham, reported that the Admiralty "at the present time could not visualize any particular combined operation taking place and they were, therefore, not prepared to devote any considerable sum of money to equipment for combined training."[166] The army was no more forthcoming. In January 1939 Gort announced at a meeting of the Chiefs of Staff that railroads would always allow land-based power to concentrate more rapidly than sea-based power. Thus, the strategic mobility conferred by sea power, although politically an attractive idea, no longer worked in favor of naval power.[167]

Consequently, despite the decision that the army should be a force capable of using Britain's naval superiority, nothing was done to prepare for such a contingency. Had the services examined the possibilities with more care, the costs would have proven far higher than the government would have been willing to pay. As it was, the failure to study the problem contributed directly to the disaster in Norway.

It is clear that civilian pusillanimity and the failure to define a clear role for the army until 1939 directly affected its preparedness. Some writers have gone so far as to suggest that, had the bulk of rearmament funds been spent on the army rather than the navy and RAF, the 1940 campaign would have had a different outcome.[168] The general performance of the army in the prewar period, however, makes this a doubtful proposition. As Michael Howard has suggested, "[t]he evidence is strong that the army was still as firmly geared to the pace and perspective of regimental soldiering as it had been before 1914; that too many of its members looked on soldiering as an agreeable and honorable occupation rather than as a serious profession demanding no less intellectual dedication than that of the doctor, the lawyer or the engineer."[169]

The army response to rearmament was anything but forward looking. In 1937 the War Office cast its rearmament program to equip a field force similar in most respects to the 1914 BEF. The only significant difference was its motorization. In 1937 the War Office argued against establishing armored divisions: "Various proposals were considered including one for an army of a more highly mechanized nature than that decided upon for the Regular Army. . . . The Chiefs of Staff have stated that in their opinion the present would be a most unfortunate moment to disturb an organization which has valuable traditions and has survived the lean years through which it has passed since the war."[170] Similarly, Gort suggested to Liddell Hart that "we musn't upset the people in the clubs by moving too fast. . . ."[171]

The British military journals serve as a barometer for the intellectual atmosphere in the army during the interwar period. Although the journals had been fairly responsive to new ideas in the twenties, in the thirties they sank into a studied conservatism. From 1937 to 1940, thirty-three articles or editorials in the *Journal of the Royal United Services Institute* and the *Army Quarterly* discussed some aspect of mechanization and/or armored warfare. Twenty-four of these showed a distinctly antediluvian approach. In February 1939 one writer in the *JRUSI* asserted that "tanks themselves . . . will never achieve any permanent results."[172] In April 1940 another commentator argued that German success in Poland was strictly an isolated case due to flat terrain, and that conditions in the west would remain static. Supposedly "the delaying power of modern means of warfare are so great" that mobile operations would never occur.[173]

One need not rely on the journals to complete a depressing picture of the army in the period before the war. Its priorities were clearly askew. In 1937 the equitation school at Weedon had a budget of £20,000 to train thirty-eight pupils, while the tank corps school of 550 students had to exist on a budget of £46,000.[174] The 1938 army budget provided £772,000 for petroleum and £400,000 for forage.[175] The treatment that Britain's only mechanized division received on the outbreak of war indicates the army's perception of the future for armored warfare. In September 1939 the divisional artillery was sent to France to support other units. As the division did not go to France, it received a low priority on supply requisitions. Its requests for increased allocations for a force operating on a wider front and in greater depth than infantry divisions met with the response that "[i]t was strenuously urged from the technical standpoint that the divisional commander should restrict the frontage and, thus, refrain from presenting the Ordnance Service with an abnormal problem."[176]

What is also clear is that many of the best minds within the army remained closed to the possibilities of mechanized warfare. In a 1925 discussion with the tank pioneers Broad and Lindsay, Lord Alanbrooke, the future CIGS under Churchill, argued for distributing tanks in small packets among the infantry and for massive barrages with carefully laid timetables.[177] As late as 1944 he announced to a gathering of American and British generals that warfare had returned to 1918 and that lightning drives such as the German push through the Ardennes in 1940 were no longer possible.[178] There is no doubt that the British army was completely unprepared for the pace and fluidity of German mobile operations. In 1938 the Chiefs of Staff commented that a German advance through Belgium and Holland "despite mechanized forces, would be considerably slower than in the last war."[179] So closely tied to the conditions of the last war was the army that intelligence documents had stamped on them the command: "Not to be taken into the trenches."[180]

Part of the explanation for this failure to realize the value of armor lay in the army's compartmentalization. For artillerymen like Alanbrooke, the howitzer remained the chief weapon, while infantrymen like the future Field Marshal Bernard Montgomery remained tied to the pace of the ground forces throughout their careers. But in a larger sense the British failed to adapt to the conditions of modern mechanized warfare because nowhere did their tactical doctrine emphasize speed, aggressive exploitation, initiative, and drive. With the emphasis on careful preparation and on a minimum willingness to take risks, British commanders did not adjust to the fluid, swift conditions of modern mechanized warfare. Their German counterparts did.

CONCLUSION

Neither in her diplomacy nor in her rearmament policies did Great Britain meet the challenges of the 1930s. A major part of the blame lies squarely on the shoulders of Neville Chamberlain. Chamberlain's policy both as chancellor of the exchequer and as prime minister minimized the potential of British rearmament. But there is more than enough blame to share, for Chamberlain's approach to rearmament enjoyed the wholehearted approval of the British people, and a substantial minority believed that no rearmament was necessary. Thus, in 1938 the British faced the possibility of war with their military services in a most inadequate state of preparation, while the "worst case analysis" of the government's military advisers made a difficult strategic situation appear even worse. This, combined with Chamberlain's "best case" analysis of the motives of Britain's opponents on the international scene, predetermined the course of appeasement. There is, however, a larger issue. Nearly every decision made by the British in this period in terms of rearmament, diplomacy, and military doctrine appears in the harsh light of May 1940 to have been disastrous.[181] Somehow British society in the widest sense failed to meet the challenges of the 1930s.

III

The Rest of Europe

FRANCE

No other combatant, except possibly Russia, had felt more the full fury of the First World War than had France. She had lost a million and a half men, and war had devastated her countryside from the Channel to Switzerland. These events led to the reaction of the French nation and political leadership that war must never happen again. At the same time, both the French people and their government feared, and feared desperately, that a revived and recovered German nation would try it all again. As Winston Churchill commented in his memoirs: "Worn down, doubly decimated, but undisputed masters of the hour, the French nation peered into the future in thankful wonder and haunting dread. Where then was that SECURITY without which all that had been gained seemed valueless, and life itself, even amid the rejoicings of victory, was almost unendurable? The mortal need was Security. . . ."[1] The hard-line policy followed by French statesmen immediately after the war collapsed in the debacle of the Ruhr crisis. More moderate positions succeeded it in the late 1920s and proved less than successful in achieving rapprochement with Germany. With the establishment of the Nazi regime in 1933, the French faced the challenge that they had seen in their nightmares. They were no more ready for it than were the British.

France's military and political leaders had had few illusions about the permanency of peace on the signing of the Versailles treaty in 1919. Marshal Ferdinand Foch remarked shortly afterwards that Versailles represented no more than a twenty years' truce. It is in this light that French policy toward Weimar Germany must be seen. The great concern of French foreign and military policy was not the weak German republic but, rather, a revitalized and remilitarized Germany of the future. To meet this latent threat, the French followed divergent and contradictory courses. In the years immediately following the war Foch and Premier Georges Clemenceau molded the direction of a French grand strategy that would remain fundamentally intact until 1938. They operated from the sound premise that France, with a smaller population and economic potential than Germany, needed allies. Therefore, as French leaders had done before 1914, they looked to the east to redress the disparity. Because of their antipathy to the successful Bolshevik revolution in Russia, they sought allies against Germany among the smaller successor states of Eastern Europe— Poland, Czechoslovakia, Yugoslavia, and Rumania. Alliances with these states served, moreover, as a barrier to Soviet influence in Central Europe.

The second, and perhaps the most important, influence on French strategy was a strong desire for British military and diplomatic support. The experience of the Ruhr occupation taught the French that without British support they could not impose their will even on the strife-torn Weimar regime. The response of French military authorities to the Rhineland occupation in March 1936 emphasized the extent of French dependence on Britain. With overwhelming superiority at his disposal, the French commander in chief, General Maurice Gamelin, reported to his ministers that France could not hope to win a decisive success against Germany unless she waged war within the framework of a coalition, that is, alongside England.[2] There was, of course, a contradiction between maintaining an alliance system with eastern European states and desiring the support of a British government that often regarded the defense of France herself as an optional obligation.

What is more, there was a dangerous weakness inherent in French strategy. The French feared, and on the basis of their First World War experiences had every reason to fear, that Germany's military forces would repeat the crushing invasion of August 1914. Therefore, the French molded their doctrine and strategy to meet such a threat. Under the direction of Marshal Philippe Pétain, the hero of Verdun, and other generals with wartime experience, the French army established a tactical doctrine that emphasized the defense and in a strategic sense sought to insure that the mistakes of 1914 would not be repeated.[3] The alliances with Poland and Czechoslovakia were an integral part of this approach and, as the Russians had done in 1914, the eastern allies were supposed to invade the Reich upon the outbreak of war.

This combination of strategy and doctrine would be fine if the Germans were to follow the pattern of 1914. Should Germany move first against France's eastern allies, such a strategy and diplomatic position would possess serious weaknesses. Would France move to support her allies in the east without British diplomatic and military backing? What aid could France render Eastern Europe when her tactical doctrine stressed the powers of the defense? These were questions that the French were neither politically nor morally prepared to answer.

THE STRUCTURE OF GOVERNMENT AND REARMAMENT IN FRANCE

Although other works have examined in detail the French response to the crisis of the late 1930s,[4] it is necessary to note here several features in the French system that directly affected not only rearmament policies but the formulation of policy in civilian and military departments. Unfortunately for the French, their governmental structure proved incapable of casting or articulating strong policies in either the military or diplomatic spheres. The Third Republic did not grant its premier either the powers or the political base that were given the British prime minister. Admittedly, neither the MacDonald nor Baldwin governments had provided strong leadership for Britain; that, however, was a result more of personality than of system. Chamberlain, both in terms of his diplomatic as well as his rearmament policies, showed the extent to which the British system permitted strong leadership.[5]

The French government was very different. Whereas in the British system, the prime minister could rely on the discipline of his party in the House, French politics forced premiers to base their cabinets on the shifting sands of innumerable parties within the Chamber of Deputies. Between 1930 and 1940 there were twenty-four changes of ministry.[6] Even the relatively long ministry of Edouard Daladier, April 1938 to March 1940, reflected the weaknesses of the system. Neither by inclination nor by the prerogatives of his office was Daladier able to exert dynamic, bold leadership. Had he done so the political parties that tolerated his ministry would have quickly forced his downfall.

The result was not government, but the absence of government. Drift, not decision, characterized France in the 1930s.

Moreover, the French system did not provide the premier with the Cabinet secretariat that was the keystone of the British system. In a real sense the French premier was no more than the first minister among his colleagues. Thus, to control political events, a French premier not only had continually to patch together his weak coalition of disparate political interests but often had to serve also as the head of a key ministry such as Defense or Foreign Affairs. Daladier at the beginning of his premiership in 1938 held on to the post of war minister and toward the end of his term added the Quai d'Orsay. Because of the tasks and demands he faced as premier, Daladier spent relatively little time managing the civilian side of the War Ministry.

These political instabilities and weaknesses directly affected the course of French rearmament. What is astonishing about the French effort over the period from 1935 through 1938 is the fact that in terms of dollars the French were outspent by the British and barely spent more than the Italians.[7] Considering the fact that the French consistently overestimated the state of German rearmament and the size of the Reich's military forces throughout the period, the low level of French rearmament is surprising. Only in 1938 did the French devote 8 percent of their national income to defense expenditures—a level reached by the Germans in 1935. This failure to move quickly resulted from the French government's inability to get the rearmament effort off dead center. The leadership for a stronger rearmament response to the German danger in the late 1930s simply did not exist.

On the military side, the committee system mirrored many of the weaknesses and few of the strengths present in the British government. The Conseil Supérieur de la Défense Nationale had played an important role in the First World War and with its specialist subcommittees should have played a role similar to that of the Committee of Imperial Defense in Britain. It did not and fell into disuse in the interwar period. In the late 1930s the Comité Permanent de la Défense Nationale played an important role in formulating French strategy. Its members consisted of the premier, the service ministers, the Chiefs of Staff, and the aged Pétain.[8] In no sense were the French chiefs willing, as were the British chiefs, to act as one body. The failure to establish effective coordination between the services resulted from the army's dominant position within the French military establishment and its unwillingness to surrender any of its prerogatives.

THE FRENCH ARMY

To a great extent the French army reflected the paralysis and crisis in leadership that seems to have gripped French society in the 1930s. The structure of the army contributed to an unwillingness to make decisions. Theoretically the general staff was in command of the entire army, but in fact it had no control over finances, personnel, or administration. The secretary general of the army controlled the administration but had no command responsibility. This bureaucratic nightmare further contributed to the unfortunate proclivities of the army's commander in the thirties, General Maurice Gamelin. Gamelin delighted in creating committees and in adding layers of administration between the army high command and its combat units. His basic purpose seems to have aimed at providing an alibi for a future disaster rather than guidance for his civilian superiors or his subordinates. His reply to Daladier's surprise at a report on the size of the German armored force indicates his basic approach: "The bulletin is what one might call a smoke screen in case things turn out badly."[9] Furthermore, Gamelin consistently overestimated the size of the German threat and, as we shall see, cast his strategic estimates in the darkest colors. He was not alone; the army, especially the intelligence branch, echoed his pessimistic estimates on German capabilities.[10]

As had been its tradition since Napoleon, the French army managed to learn all the wrong lessons from its experiences in World War I. In seeking to avoid the errors of those years, it insured that the defeat of 1940 would reach catastrophic proportions.[11] The war of movement in 1918 had been of short duration. As a result, in their "lessons learned" analysis, the French drew their tactical doctrine from the first three years of the war when they had been mired in the mud of northern France.[12] They concluded that future offensive operations would be extremely difficult and could only succeed after careful preparation and massive artillery bombardments.[13] Whereas prewar doctrine had emphasized morale and the offensive as the most important factors in war, material strength now became the basic principle of French strategy. In the coming war France would stand on the defensive and wait for the Germans to attack. Only after she had gathered her resources and the Germans had exhausted theirs would the French army go over to the offensive. Such a strategy depended, it should be noted, on maintaining overseas imports for the French economy and on the financial as well as the military resources of the British Empire.[14]

Ironically, the French army had had relatively limited experience with defensive warfare on the western front and, as the heirs of Napoleon, displayed little interest in learning from the Germans. Verdun and the spring 1918 battles constituted possible precedents for French theorists. Because so much of the army had fought at Verdun, many military thinkers selected it as the paradigm for future defensive warfare and believed that the battle on the Meuse had established the invulnerability and utility of large fortresses for the future. Unfortunately, the French absorbed few of the important lessons from the 1918 battles; the most important of which were the need for a flexible defensive system and the importance of strategic reserves. French doctrine between the wars thus underestimated the value of a defense in depth and refused to recognize the importance of tactical and strategic reserves for counterattacking enemy penetrations. The French also did not understand that with mechanization the Germans could now exploit breakthroughs far more quickly. Believing that they would be able to transfer reserves by railroad faster than German infantry could move forward, the French were surprised by the speed of the German thrust across the Meuse in May 1940 and incapable of countering it.

The French faced and failed to answer the most important strategic question confronting them in the interwar period: how to counter a German swing through the Low Countries and around the Maginot line. Clearly, the French general staff aimed to avoid a repetition of 1914 when the initial German rush had occupied so much of northern France. French strategy counted on establishing a main line of resistance as far away from French territory as possible. During the 1936 Rhineland crisis Gamelin remarked that, as the French army barely equalled the German in strength, he could only hope to meet the Germans deep in Belgian territory.[15] This effectively ruled out offensive operations against Germany. The rapid Allied move into Belgium in 1940 reflected Gamelin's strategic approach. Once the Allies had established a front line on the Dyle, Gamelin believed that the Germans would suffer heavy and perhaps prohibitive casualties as they pushed toward French territory.[16] But this whole maneuver, swinging the Allied armies deep into Belgium in a long line, completely neglected the importance of both tactical and strategic reserves. According to the French, the coming campaign would replay 1914, and the line where German and Allied armies first clashed would result in a static battle-front for the duration. As a result of this rush into Belgium, the French high command did not recognize the direction of the main German thrust until they had committed Allied armies. Once the direction of the German offensive became clear it was too late: nearly all Allied reserves were in Belgium.

Although preaching the superiority of the defense, French doctrine paid little attention to the problems of defensive warfare. On the small-unit level French training stressed offensive operations, although admittedly in a highly stylized form—with lengthy artillery preparations—and paid no attention to exploitation, speed, or surprise. The results became clear on the western front in the fall of 1939 when the Germans found French troops largely unskilled in the tactics and demands of defensive warfare.[17] France's leading advocate of the superiority of the defense, General Narcisse Chauvineau, wrote in 1940 that the attacker must possess a three-to-one superiority over the defender in infantry, a six-to-one superiority in artillery, and a fifteen-to-one superiority in ammunition in order to be successful.[18] Although emphasizing the difficulty of offensive operations, Chauvineau indicated little understanding of the need for flexible defensive tactics or the requirement for operational and strategic reserves. As with the RAF's belief in "strategic" bombing, French defensive doctrine was largely intuitive. Such beliefs in the powers of the defense may help to explain why the French generals did not demand higher military budgets as German military expenditures rapidly outdistanced their own in the mid-1930s. If the defense were so strong, then France standing on the defensive need not match the Wehrmacht's rate of expansion.

The shattering experience of Verdun had contributed to the construction of the great frontier fortifications on the German border. Whereas the Germans constructed the Westwall in the 1930s with their three years' experience of defensive warfare on the western front in mind, the French chose a six-month battle, atypical of most other World War I battles, as their model. In 1937 the British military attaché reported a discussion on recent French maneuvers that he had recently had with General Billotte of the general staff. The Frenchman reported that five infantry divisions had carried out an exercise to study a possible German attack on the Maginot line. Supposedly the attacking force had received whatever weapons it required, and all the decisions of the referees went in its favor. Nevertheless, Billotte claimed, "not withstanding these extremely favorable conditions, successful penetration of the line would not have been achieved."[19] After the fall of France the Germans had the chance to examine the Maginot line in detail. They did not rate it highly. German analysts believed it important because it allowed the French to complete an undisturbed mobilization and closed the Belfort gap, thus freeing French reserves to meet German flanking moves through either Belgium or Switzerland. They did not believe that it possessed either sufficient depth or the prepared positions necessary for reserves.[20]

In a strategic sense, of course, the Maginot line achieved its purpose. It closed off one of the traditional invasion routes to the heart of France and forced the Germans to go elsewhere. The basic problem remaining, however, for French strategy was what to do about the northern frontier with the Low Countries. The best military solution to this problem would have involved a continuation of the Maginot line into Luxembourg and Belgium along the German border. The Franco-Belgian tensions that eventually led to Belgium's retreat into neutrality in 1936 negated such a possibility. The other military option was to extend the line of fortifications to the English Channel. Politically and diplomatically such an effort might well have proved disastrous. It would have clearly signaled the Belgians that, when the Germans came west, Belgium could expect little comfort and less aid from France. As a result, significant French fortifications ceased on the frontier with Luxembourg, and the Belgian fortifications on the German frontier proved unimaginative and unsuccessful.

The Maginot line both reflected and helped reinforce the stultification of French military thought. With such a large percentage of the military budgets devoted to fortifications in the late twenties and early thirties it is not surprising that the French high command came to feel that it had a vested interest in the Maginot line. In March 1935 the minister of war, General Joseph Maurin, asked the Chamber of Deputies: "How could anyone believe that we contemplate the offensive when we have spent billions to establish a fortified barrier? Would we be mad enough to go beyond this barrier to I don't know what kind of adventure?"[21] Given French belief in the strength of the Maginot line, it became most unlikely that they would initiate an offensive against the Reich once the Germans had begun to construct their Westwall.

French offensive doctrine limited attacks to short bounds, or leaps forward, after intensive artillery preparation; it paid little attention to close air support. French manuals stressed that "firepower had given a remarkable strength of resistance to improved fortifications." As a result the French army would only go over to the offensive "in favorable conditions after the assembling of powerful material means, artillery, tanks, munitions, etc. . . . Thus the attack is preceded by a more or less lengthy period of preparation, employed in gathering together this matérial and utilizing it."[22] The length of the preparatory process limited surprise, and the stylized nature of the attack eliminated the possibility of mobile operations. In 1936 a special military commission under General Joseph Georges evaluated the 1921 army instructions that were still in force and concluded that the doctrine had remained basically sound. Even though a great number of technical innovations had occurred in the intervening period, it argued that a corresponding development of defensive capability had canceled out each offensive innovation.[23]

Since the Second World War it has become clear that the Germans possessed neither quantitative nor qualitative superiority in armored fighting vehicles. In addition, they did not even have superiority in the number of mobile and mechanized divisions.[24] French tanks were fully equal in their armor, weaponry, and speed to the best German tanks.[25] It was in its doctrine, in the "tank time sense," as Liddell Hart called it, that the French army failed at all levels of command. Unlike their British counterparts, the French recognized that the tank was a useful weapon, but for the most part they refused to see its possibilities beyond infantry support. There were a few tank advocates in the French army in the immediate post-World War I period, but they did not receive the widespread publicity that Fuller and Liddell Hart received in Great Britain.[26] Although the French made some progress toward motorization in the late 1920s and early 1930s, they proved unwilling to establish an effective armored force with an independent role. Liddell Hart's criticism of Joffre and Foch during this period insured that the French high command would make every effort to exclude his influence from the army.[27]

In 1934 the future general, Charles de Gaulle, published his *Vers l'armée de métier*, a book that advocated the establishment of a specialized, professional armored force to guard the frontiers against a sudden German strike and to give the French army a powerful offensive striking force. On the tactical side the work offered little that was new. De Gaulle showed little realization of the importance of a combination of arms to the success of mechanized warfare. In most respects his arguments were a rehash of Fuller's pleas for an all-tank army.

The political consequences of de Gaulle's book, however, were significant. De Gaulle's proposals had reopened the old conflicts between the Left and the military; as a result, the conflict over his arguments was, unfortunately, fought out on political rather than on military grounds. For those on the Left, like Leon Blum, de Gaulle's ideas "for the army of the future" sounded suspiciously like an effort to wrest control of the army from the Republic and to turn it into a professional force in the hands of the military.[28] Blum went so far as to accuse the military of having Napoleonic ambitions and of trying to create a shock army for aggressive purposes. If Germany were to attack France, he argued, the working class would rise as one man to defend the country.[29]

In the critical last five years before the war the French army made little progress to speak of toward establishing an armored force. Nevertheless, there existed, especially among the lower ranking officers, a willingness to experiment with new forms of warfare and at least a partial recognition of armored warfare's possibilities. A 1936 general-staff memorandum suggested that in the future armored divisions would have a mission analogous to that of the cavalry, but would have the additional advantage of being constituted as a shock force capable of rupturing the enemy's front. Armor, with its strategic and tactical mobility, offered the possibility of swift and far-reaching operations.[30]

Neither Gamelin nor the high command, however, could decide on what role tanks should play in actual French planning. Decisions within the army's Conseil Supérieur de la Guerre evaded broad questions of doctrinal reform and designed experiments with mechanized and motorized forces to solve limited technical questions. Gamelin was at his best in equivocating the issue. A 1937 meeting of the Council suggested establishing an inspector of tanks to study exercises with armored forces the following summer.[31] The minutes of a Council meeting held in December of the following year indicates that little progress occurred. Gamelin admitted that mobilization for the Czech crisis upset plans to study proposals for the composition of an armored division and claimed that it would be impossible to establish a complete tank division in peacetime. General Georges added that only on rare occasions could armored divisions be employed to exploit battlefield conditions. Thereupon Gamelin showed his complete failure to understand mechanized warfare by discussing armored exploitation in classic First World War terms of "bounds" forward. The meeting concluded by authorizing two armored divisions, restricted to a table of organization of four tank battalions. Their final composition would be decided at a future date.[32] The army's unwieldy staff system combined with Gamelin's procrastination to make the implementation of decisions as difficult and as lengthy as the taking of them. On the outbreak of war nine months later, the army had done almost nothing to set up the two armored divisions.[33]

Nothing indicates the high command's confusion about the future of mobile warfare more clearly than the proliferation of motorized and mechanized divisions within the French army in the years preceding the Second World War. At the time of the collapse in May 1940 France possessed three armored divisions, three light mechanized divisions, five light cavalry divisions, seven motorized infantry divisions and thirty-three independent tank battalions.[34] By this time the German army had reduced the types of mobile formations to two: panzer and motorized infantry divisions. Although the Germans possessed a well-defined doctrine for the utilization of mobile forces, the French did not.

The French high command and senior officers constituted the army's most glaring weakness. Gamelin not only reflected, he as much as caused the incapacities of the top echelons. As commander in chief of the army, he must bear a major share of responsibility for the disaster. Although Gamelin understood the politics of the Third Republic and remained on the best side of most politicians, he possessed few qualities of leadership. His pervasive fumbling accentuated all the wrong trends in the army. As one staff officer accurately put it: "the general has no guts."[35] In 1935 Gamelin froze French military thought by establishing the high command as the sole arbiter of army doctrine. Henceforth, all articles, lectures, and books had to receive approval before publication. As one officer recalls, "[e]veryone got the message, and a profound silence reigned until the awakening of 1940."[36]

Other areas were as frozen as French doctrine. By 1938 the average age for army commanders was sixty-five, for corps commanders sixty, and for division commanders fifty-nine.[37] Marc Bloch's portrait of an officer in the 1940 defeat may be atypical but not by much: "Weighed down, I do not doubt, by years spent in office work and conditioned by a purely academic training, this regular soldier had lost every quality of leadership—and of the self-control and ruthlessness which the word implies."[38] Another officer serving with the army in Algeria recollected: "Under the pressure of punctilious administration with next to nothing to provide, the shambles was complete; the troops were occupied in guard duties and trivial chores, instruction was reduced to a useless routine quite out of touch with what I had been taught at Saint Cyr. I tried in vain to introduce a few indispensable reforms (for instance, dividing the company into platoons). But the company commander, who never got out of his office, said it was hopeless because the sergeant-major was against it."[39] The best epitaph for the defeat of 1940 and the responsibility of those at the top levels of the army was Bloch's, written shortly after the catastrophe:

> Our leaders, or those who acted for them, were incapable of thinking in terms of a *new* war. . . . The ruling idea of the Germans in the conduct of this war was speed. We, on the other hand, did our thinking in terms of yesterday or the day before. Worse still: faced by the undisputed evidence of Germany's new tactics, we ignored, or wholly failed to understand, the quickened rhythm of the times. . . . Our own rate of progress was too slow and our minds too inelastic for us ever to admit the possibility that the enemy might move with the speed which he actually achieved.[40]

The French Navy and Air Force

Considering France's strategic position and the probable participation of the Royal Navy in any war in which France would be involved, the French fleet was the best prepared of the military services and provided an invaluable augmentation to Allied naval strength. Two new battle cruisers, the *Dunkerque* and the *Strasbourg*, equalled the speed and firepower of their new German counterparts. Moreover, they were combat ready in 1938, whereas neither German ship would enter service until 1939. Combined with the aircraft carrier *Bearn*, these battle cruisers represented a serious threat to any raiding force the Germans might send out into the Atlantic. Three reconditioned and two unreconditioned First World War battleships balanced the Italian battle fleet in the Mediterranean. Seven heavy cruisers, eleven light cruisers, and seventy modern destroyers (including thirty-two heavy destroyers) gave the French a dominant position in the western Mediterranean and represented a significant enhancement of Allied strength in the Atlantic.[41] Two new battleships were scheduled for completion in 1940 and 1941.[42]

Thus, the French fleet represented a powerful, well-equipped force, which in cooperation with the Royal Navy would allow the Allies to dominate the Mediterranean and guarantee the Atlantic trade routes. British and French Mediterranean fleets were in a position to eliminate Italian seaborne trade, to blockade Libya, and to raid Sicily and the northwest Italian coast—in other words, to put Italy in a desperate military situation from the moment that she entered a war.

In historical literature the French air force has seemingly provided an unhappy contrast with the navy. In the mid-1930s it lacked modern aircraft, and its putative doctrine bore little relation to its equipment and capabilities. As early as October 1935 the British Committee of Imperial Defense was warning that

> . . . the French aircraft industry was in no state to meet the accelerated program. After years of comparative stagnation and subjection to a policy which refused to allow foreign inventions to be adopted, design was backward, and prototypes of new aircraft ordered in 1933 were only just beginning to appear. The majority of these were of a type to which French aircraft designers had paid little attention in the past and were not even up-to-date, but they were the only types which showed any advance on the obsolescent types in service. Obsessed by the German threat the French air staff was unwilling to delay placing orders and felt that they must re-equip with a type of airplane which would fulfill

their immediate needs. Once committed to a program, however, there was no turning back for grave delays would follow before other and more suitable and up-to-date types could be evolved.[43]

An official in the British Air Ministry commented in September 1938 that not only was the French air force inferior to the Luftwaffe, but that it was also weak "in the state of its organization, tactical training and technical efficiency."[44]

Not surprising, the results of the 1940 campaign have led most Anglo-American historians to agree with these contemporary British assessments. They have imputed to the French air force the same dismal level of performance that led the army and eventually the nation to collapse with such stunning suddenness in spring 1940. Nevertheless, there is evidence available that the French put up a better show in the air than historians have allowed and that the French air force was able to make the Luftwaffe pay a heavy price throughout combat operations in the west. Moreover, for the combat and logistic deficiencies that hampered French air operations throughout the campaign there are simple and direct explanations that have not received enough attention in historical literature.

To begin with, the Luftwaffe lost more aircraft in three weeks in May 1940 than in any other month of that year, including August and September when the Battle of Britain reached its height.[45] In May 1940, largely as a result of the three-week campaign in the west the Germans lost no less than 20.2 percent of their total force structure and 27.4 percent of the bombers present in flying units at the beginning of the month. The losses for the whole campaign in the west suggest the level of opposition that the Germans met (see Table III-1). Because the data in the table comes from the Luftwaffe quartermaster general (the data on the operational side of the house was largely lost at the end of the war), one cannot determine what causes were directly responsible for German aircraft losses (the RAF and ground anti-aircraft fire undoubtedly played a role). Nevertheless, the level of German losses does suggest that the French put up serious resistance in the air.

Unfortunately, it was not enough to arrest materially the rapidly escalating collapse. There are several explanations for the weaknesses of the French air force, but the most satisfactory lies in the fact that the French government refused until 1938 to provide the necessary level of funding to its air force and aircraft industry to allow timely

TABLE III-1
German Aircraft Losses, May-June 1940

Type	Strength 4.5.40	Destroyed	Losses as Percent of Initial Strength	Damaged
Close-Recce	345	78	23%	18
Long-Range Recce	321	88	27%	21
Single-Engine Fighters	1,369	257	19%	150
Twin Engine Fighters	367	110	30%	29
Bombers	1,758	521	30%	203
Dive Bombers	417	122	30%	28
Transports	531	213	40%	27
Coastal	241	39	16%	12
Total	5,349	1,428	28%	488

SOURCE: Williamson Murray, *Strategy for Defeat, The Luftwaffe 1933-1945* (Montgomery, 1983), p. 40.

rearmament. As a result the French were not able to match their opponent either quantitatively or qualitatively. They did not miss by much. By spring of 1940, following a considerable infusion of financial support beginning in 1938, France's aircraft industry was producing two excellent fighter aircraft, the Morane-Saulnier, M.S. 406 and the Dewoitine, D.520. The former's performance level was close to the Hawker Hurricane, whereas the latter was close to the performance capabilities of the Spitfire and the Bf 109.[46] It is, of course, difficult to judge how good these aircraft were since the French produced so few. Nevertheless, both aircraft possessed considerable potential, and in larger numbers they could have given the Germans serious difficulties. The problem was that these aircraft entered service during the last months of peace and during the "Phony" War. As a result, French fighter squadrons, with their new high-performance aircraft, went through the same teething troubles in maintenance, supply, and training that had plagued the Luftwaffe with the introduction of the Bf 109 in 1937 and the RAF in 1938 and early 1939 with the Spitfire and Hurricane. Unfortunately for the French, this critical period occurred during the campaign of May 1940. Thus, a substantial number of French squadrons ran operationally ready rates of 40 percent in early 1940 and even lower rates under the pressures of the air battle over northern France.[47] Thus, one has a convincing explanation for the fact the RAF pilots saw their French counterparts flying so many fewer missions in May and June of 1940: Most French aircraft were out of commission during the campaign.

The French did possess one important advantage over their German opponents. Most French pilots had been around longer and had far greater experience than German pilots. As a result some French fighter squadrons equipped with obsolete aircraft such as the Curtis Hawk 75 did surprisingly well against the Luftwaffe.[48] With better aircraft, they would have given the Germans even greater problems.

If the French did not miss by much, their air force was nevertheless unable to affect the course of the 1940 campaign. The consistently low level of funding that the French gave their rearmament efforts through to 1938 probably had the greatest impact on the air force. With the army receiving the lion's share of the budget, with the navy protected by the large colonial lobby, the air force came last in defense allocations. These budgeting trends in the early 1930s received added impetus with the election of the Popular Front in 1936. The Blum government with its ideological preconceptions could hardly wax enthusiastic about a service whose doctrine aimed at blasting the working class in enemy cities. At the end of 1937 Pierre Cot, the air minister, admitted to the Comité Permanent de la Défense Nationale that Germany was producing 500 aircraft per month, England 175 to 200, but France only 50. Cot argued that the problem was not wholly one of industrial capacity; the French air force was receiving only one-third the funding that the RAF received. Increased budgetary allocations, he thought, would allow the French aircraft industry to produce 60 percent more aircraft in the near future.[49]

The top military leadership explained away the air force's weaknesses with idle hopes. As late as the fall of 1937, the French were telling the British that, although they might be unable to match the Luftwaffe in production of numbers of aircraft, they believed that with "a veritable forest of guns" over the Maginot line they could prevent German aircraft from intervening in the land battle.[50] French army officers assured the visiting British CIGS that they planned to strengthen the Maginot line to counter the German air superiority and that they believed an "enemy would require an unrealizable supremacy of machines to get over the anti-aircraft defences. . . ."[51] On such comforting assumptions was the disaster of 1940 built.

The real problem, therefore, was not the antiquated state of the French aircraft industry with old-fashioned manufacturing processes, but rather that the aircraft manufacturers, starved for research and development resources and denied large production contracts, could neither modernize their plant nor produce up-to-date models in the late 1930s. In fairness to the French, one must also note that the German aircraft industry in the late thirties and in the first years of the Second World War was hardly modern and innovative in its manufacturing procedures—and it had received a far higher level of support in the 1930s than had the French.[52]

Further exacerbating French difficulties was the fact that no one, except perhaps those in the air force (and their views bore no correlation to their capabilities), possessed a clear conception of what the role of aircraft would be in the next war. The army seems to have foreseen a role for spotter aircraft with perhaps some support from "tactical" bombers. And only in the last years of the 1930s did the politicians awake to what an enemy air force could do to French cities. Since the German army had in the last seventy years done a fair job of smashing up the French countryside, one should not be surprised that their awakening came later than had that of British leaders across the Channel. Unfortunately, the French political system did not possess the power to force a build-up in fighter strength such as the Chamberlain government was able to impose on the RAF in 1938.

Without a clear push from above, French airmen continued to place considerable emphasis on their antiquated bomber force. Not surprisingly, many officers in the French air force (established in April 1933), found, as did their contemporaries in Britain, Germany, and the United States, the role of "strategic" bombing attractive. As one historian noted in the early 1930s, they "saw that a healthy share of [their] rather unhealthy credit allocations was devoted to the construction of machines which could carry out strategic bombing missions."[53] When the awakening came in 1938, the French made desperate efforts to catch up. The air staff, however, could not give up its dream of "strategic" bombing; therefore much effort remained directed toward the manufacture of bombers.[54] Although increased emphasis was given to the fighter force in the last plans before the war, it was not enough to overcome the severe constraints that the earlier lack of research and development had imposed on the air industry. Doctrinally, the French air force seems to have dreamed of Douhet and of "strategic" bombing while doing little to prepare to help the army on the ground. Further accentuating the weaknesses in the air was the fact that no French airman emerged who possessed the vision and grasp of reality of Dowding in Great Britain. Thus, the French air force, although it was beginning to acquire modern up-to-date fighter aircraft in early 1940, was unable to affect in any real sense the course of the campaign on the ground; its sacrifices in May 1940 did, however, materially contribute to the RAF's victory in the Battle of Britain. [55]

THE ITALIAN STRATEGIC SITUATION

In retrospect it is hard to see how any knowledgeable military expert took the Italians seriously in the prewar period. [56] Italy's geographic position and almost total economic dependency on imports of raw materials meant that her strategic situation was extremely weak. British control of Suez and Gibraltar effectively bottled up Italian forces in the Mediterranean. Only imports from Germany, Yugoslavia, and Hungary were secure in wartime and none of those three powers could cover Italian requirements except in coal.

To a greater extent than Germany, Italy had to import raw materials in order to produce finished goods. This dependency on trade and on the need to earn hard currency set off a vicious cycle. The conquest of Abyssinia, partly motivated by a desire to broaden the country's raw-material base, used up what little surplus foreign exchange Italy possessed in the 1930s, a shortage that, in turn, prevented exploitation of whatever raw materials Abyssinia might possess. [57] Capital shortage made it difficult to expand arms production at a time when wars in Abyssinia and Spain drained weapon and munition stocks. [58] The Italians were so dependent on raw material imports that they urged the Germans not to embark on a European war until the 1942 World's Fair in Rome had earned enough hard currency to increase raw material stockpiles. [59]

Italy's need for imports made German economic officials dubious about how useful the Italians would prove in a general European war. Discussions between the German air and naval staffs concluded that, in a war involving both Axis powers, Italy might divert some Allied forces to the Mediterranean, but Italian raw material requirements would strain the German economy to the breaking point.[60] Lacking significant coal deposits, the Italians would have to import one and one-half million tons of German coal per month in order to keep their economy running once the British imposed a blockade. Petroleum supplies were even more vulnerable to blockade, and Italy had neither cracking facilities nor coal to produce synthetic fuels.[61] War between Italy and the Western Powers would block seaborne deliveries of Rumanian oil and force the Italians to import the oil through the Balkans.[62] This depressing picture led the German naval staff to conclude that it would be more advantageous for Italy to be neutral than belligerent.[63] As late as February 1940 the German naval attaché in Rome warned that Italian participation in the war as an ally would undermine Germany's strategic position, economically as well as militarily.[64] Underlining the general weakness of Italy's war economy, steel production barely reached a level of 2.4 million tons in 1939 compared to 22.5 million tons for Germany and 13.4 million tons for Great Britain.[65]

Given these difficulties and economic deficiencies, it is surprising to discover that Italian expenditures on the military came close to the levels of Britain and France for the period 1935 to 1938 (see Table I-5, Chapter I). This effort to build up the military strength of Fascist Italy is one among many indications of the aggressive, expansionist nature of Benito Mussolini's foreign policy.[66] At the least Mussolini seems to have aimed at gaining control of Nice (to the Var), Tunis, Corsica, Albania, Switzerland up to the St. Gotthard pass, and Jibuti in the Red Sea.[67] The duce was more than willing to act ruthlessly to expand Italy's power and recoiled from any squeamishness. Crushing Arab rebels in Libya, using mustard gas in Abyssinia, massacring Yugoslav villagers were characteristic actions.[68] Perhaps only a higher level of civilization among the people, combined with a general level of inefficiency, kept the Italians from reaching the mendaciousness and callous disregard for life exhibited by the Germans and the Russians in this period.

A major share of the blame for the general unpreparedness of Fascist Italy must fall on the shoulders of Benito Mussolini. Conceited and vain, albeit with considerable powers as a politician and propagandist, Mussolini remained a dilettante in military matters throughout his career. Aside from the pomp and propaganda displays of Italian military might, he had small interest in the nuts and bolts of either weapons or training and doctrine. While he was pushing Italy toward the disasters of the war years, the duce did little to prepare Italy economically and militarily for the conflict. Compounding his general lack of military knowledge was his preference for nonentities and sycophants. Those few competent individuals in either the party or the military were either removed or shuffled out to the distant provinces.[69]

THE ITALIAN ARMY

Yet Mussolini was not solely responsible for the Italian disasters of the Second World War, as so many of his countrymen later suggested. As one commentator has noted:

> Mussolini did not invent his generals. He had to take them as he found them. Nor could incompetents simply be dismissed. The rigidity of the Italian Armed Forces' seniority system insured that replacements would have to be drawn from the topmost ranks of the services. There was no guarantee that such men would be any improvement over the incumbents. The *Duce*'s problem— which, admittedly, he was slow to recognize and unable to remedy—lay in what one might term the Italian general staff tradition: Custoza, Lissa, Adua, Caporetto. On those occasions the military, as yet uncontaminated by contact with fascism, distinguished itself by the lack of the sort of diligent study, careful planning, and scrupulous attention to detail which characterized the Germans, and by a tendency to confusion of responsibilities and of incessant intrigue among senior officers.[70]

The career of Marshal Pietro Badoglio reflects the extraordinary survivability of some high-ranking Italian officers. He was a corps commander at the Battle of Caporetto, where his corps distinguished itself by the rapidity of its collapse. This signal failure did nothing to hinder his career and during the interwar period he commanded the forces that conquered Abyssinia and served as commander in chief of the army. The entrance of Italy into the war in June 1940 found Badoglio serving as the highest officer in the Italian armed forces, the head of Commando Supremo. The disastrous defeats in the fall of 1940 only temporarily sidetracked his career; he succeeded Mussolini as head of state in July 1943.[71]

In 1937 Blomberg visited Italy and watched a series of maneuvers. What he saw made him seriously doubt Italian military capabilities. At an exercise of three infantry, two fascist militia, and three artillery battalions, he noted the shoddy appearance, the lack of leadership, and a general absence of tactical skill.[72] The military attaché in Rome reported in 1937 that Italian failings were general. Recruit training was insufficient, a lack of noncommissioned officers hindered unit training, and the officer corps lacked a tradition of leadership. Finally, most staff officers were incompetent.[73]

The Italian performance in Spain underlined these inadequacies. The disaster at Guadalajara, accurately described by Lloyd George as "the Italian skedaddle," reflected inadequate staff planning, poorly trained troops, and a complete indifference to weather conditions in central Spain during the winter. The chain of command collapsed because troop commanders from platoon to division had received little training in their combat responsibilities.[74] The officer in charge had drawn up his operational plan on the basis of a 1:400,000 Michelin road map. Significantly, the disaster had no discernible effect on his career.[75]

The Italian army surprisingly had received considerable financial support for its rearmament efforts. Yet, only nineteen of the seventy-seven divisions mobilized in 1939 had a full complement of weapons and men. Division TO & E (table of organization and equipment) called for 10 percent of the antitank weapons allocated to German divisions, and almost all divisions were equipped with First World War artillery pieces. Italian infantry divisions had fewer battalions than their French and German counterparts and 60 percent of the battery strength of a German division. The two armored divisions possessed a few three-ton tanks with machine guns. There were no medium or heavy tanks, and mobile artillery did not exist.[76] After visiting the Italian summer maneuvers in August 1939 a German officer noted that Italian armored forces and doctrine were still in "children's shoes."[77] Supplies of all munitions were insufficient for a major war. The army itself possessed no modern anti-aircraft guns and even clothing was in short supply.[78]

Italian military thought was as backward as that of the aged generals in France or the Colonel Blimps in London. Some Italians went so far as to base military strength exclusively on the size of a nation's population: "With the army, man is the decisive element: use of weapons is dependent on the number of men who can be called up. This principle has not changed by the fact that weapons have acquired a greater significance in ground war through mechanization than was the case earlier."[79] Such opinions, minimizing the importance of the industrial base or natural resources of European powers, struck a responsive chord in the duce. In March 1939 he proclaimed that war potential was equivalent to a country's population.[80]

As was the case in most of Europe, the army underestimated motorized and mechanized warfare. In May 1939 General Pariani, the army's commander in chief, doubted whether tanks would play an important role because of antitank weapons.[81] At the time he seems to have been pushing a concept of "Blitzkrieg warfare" with truck-borne infantry. The fact that Italy had no tanks to speak of undoubtedly colored his perceptions. As late as May 16, 1940 Admiral Cavagnari, commander in chief of the navy, remarked in a speech that little movement would take place on the western front because of the strong fortifications.[82] In July 1940 Badoglio received an army intelligence report on the nature of the armored tactics that had brought the Germans such an overwhelming victory in France. He noted in the margin: "We'll study it when the war is over."[83]

The general deficiencies of the army and the weaknesses of Italy's overall strategic situation were reflected by the situation in Libya. During a visit by Heinrich Himmler to North Africa in 1937, a table-top exercise showed the German SS leader that the Italian position in Libya and Abyssinia was almost impossible.[84] Shortly before Italy entered the war, Marshal Balbo told a German liaison officer: "My situation [in Libya] between two future fronts in east and west is almost hopeless, if Italy really enters this war. Fortifications on the western frontier are illusory. You are not an accurate observer if you have not noticed that my bunkerline is not equipped with the necessary anti-tank and machine guns." Balbo further complained of his lack of motorized artillery, tanks, and anti-aircraft guns, and most of his aircraft were obsolete.[85] As one commentator has accurately summed up the sorry state of affairs in the army: "The Regio Escercito's deficiencies in armament, doctrine, organization, staff work, training, and leadership were concurrent, interrelated, and mutually reinforcing."[86]

THE ITALIAN NAVY

The Italians regarded the navy as the strongest and best prepared of their three military services.[87] In 1934 naval weakness led the duce to authorize a major building and refitting program. Italian shipyards almost immediately began to rebuild Italy's four World War I battleships on a gradual basis. By September 1938 the navy possessed two rebuilt battleships with the other two still in dockyard. Not until the spring of 1939 did Italian battleship strength again reach four. Of the two new battleships authorized in 1934, shipyards did not complete the first until 1939 and the second until 1940. In 1939 the remainder of the Italian navy consisted of 7 heavy cruisers, 12 light cruisers, 65 destroyers, and 106 submarines. Italian battleships appear to have been competently constructed, but there were serious problems with lighter units. Cruisers were exceedingly fast but achieved speed at the cost of armor, underwater protection, and accuracy of main armament. The Italians designed some of their ships almost exclusively for operations in light seas.[88] Moreover, as a result of sacrificing armor for speed, many Italian cruisers had the habit of disintegrating "suddenly and spectacularly under fire." Though in numbers Italian submarines represented a serious threat, their tendency to give off poisonous gases when under depth charge attack was a serious deficiency.[89]

The real problem with the navy lay in its training, doctrine, and morale. From the first the Italians exhibited a deep-seated inferiority complex vis-à-vis the Royal Navy.[90] As was true of the other Italian services, tactical skill and training left much to be desired. In 1937 the German naval attaché reported that, although the Italians could parade their ships, they had much to learn about training.[91] In August 1938 he succinctly pointed out: "It is clear that the Italian navy either has little war experience or has not successfully utilized it. There is no similarity between their training for war and ours; they do not create difficult circumstances in their maneuvers, as we consciously seek to do in our exercises. The Italian navy can learn much from us in the tactical sphere in order to escape its rigidity." He added that Italian reconnaissance was weak both by day and night, and cruiser and destroyer tactical training was almost nonexistent.[92] The 1938 summer naval maneuvers made a particularly bad impression. To German observers Italian tactics appeared rigid and unimaginative: for example, cruisers remained tied to the main battlefleet and thus the Italian fleet received no reconnaissance. The participating units made no differentiation between moonlit and dark nights, and the fleet took no evasive action to avoid submarines. Subordinate commanders neither displayed nor were encouraged to display initiative. Finally, even the radio direction finders were inaccurate.[93]

The Italian navy possessed no aircraft carriers. The navy had wanted an aircraft carrier in its building program but had been overruled by Mussolini.[94] The duce's position seems to have been caused by a fear that construction of carriers might diminish the role of the air force.[95] Air force opposition to a carrier and confidence in its ability to control the surrounding seas were not reflected in preparations. The air force not only turned down the aerial torpedo developed by the Whitehead firm at Fiume,[96] but at the outbreak of war, it possessed no armorpiercing bombs to use against enemy ships.[97]

Though it possessed over one hundred boats, the Italian submarine force had almost no impact on the Mediterranean naval war. The difficulty of waging submarine warfare in an enclosed area like the Mediterranean played a role in this failure.[98] Engineering defects were another important factor, but the generally indifferent level of tactical training played an equally important role. In 1937 the German naval attaché observed a submarine practice in which the target ship sailed by four stationary submarines that did not maneuver.[99] A 1939 report on submarine maneuvers indicated that little had changed. The submarine involved had only waited for the target ship in the exercise area without maneuvering for position. The "after action" discussion offered no criticism or suggestions about the conduct of submarine operations.[100] Incredibly, Italian submarines possessed no attack computers and had to carry out their attacks on plotting tables.[101]

Italian naval strategy and war plans reflected fears of British sea power. The fundamental missions of the navy were 1) to keep Britain's Gibraltar and eastern Mediterranean fleets from joining, 2) to avoid meeting superior enemy forces, 3) to wear the enemy down with submarines, 4) to protect lines of communication, and 5) to engage enemy fleet units close to Italian bases. At the Friedrichshafen conference between commanders of the German and Italian naval staffs in 1939, the Italians described their basic strategy in terms of blocking the central Mediterranean between Sicily and Libya with aircraft, mine fields, and naval forces.[102] They minimized Malta's threat to communication between the Italian mainland and North Africa.[103]

Right from the beginning of the war the Italian navy showed that it could not adequately fulfill the minimum expectations with which it had entered the war. In early July 1940 the Italian and British fleets met off the coast of Sicily. The action took place close to Italian shores, and by means of cryptographic intelligence the Italians possessed a clear picture of British strength and intentions; they had superiority in speed; and the moonless night offered an opportunity for combined U-boat-torpedo-boat operations.[104] The senior German observer with the Italian command acidly summed up the results. "Since one cannot always calculate that one will be lucky in war, it is very questionable whether the Italian navy will again be offered such a favorable set of circumstances. So far as one can make a judgment from existing reports, the Italian navy on July 9 and 10 has probably missed its decisive hour."[105]

THE ITALIAN AIR FORCE

The Regia Aeronautica faced considerable strategic problems. Air bases in southern France threatened the industrial districts of northern Italy. Corsica represented a threat to Italian control of the central Mediterranean, and French aircraft based on Corsica could attack central Italy. Despite the vulnerability of Italy and her colonial possessions, the Italians seem to have had a thoroughly unjustified faith that the Regia Aeronautica could play a major role in achieving a quick victory.

With the shift in Italian foreign policy after Abyssinia, the emphasis of the air force shifted from the north to the south. Unfortunately, the slowness of base construction hindered this move and made it difficult for the Italians to implement their new strategy.[106] Nevertheless, the air force had the responsibility of 1) threatening the transport lines between France and North Africa, 2) controlling the area between Sicily and Tunisia, and 3) attacking French Tunisia and Egypt.[107]

Air Force tactical training was almost nonexistent. Because line aircraft had inadequate instrumentation, regular units received little training in blind navigation, and thus training took place almost exclusively in good weather. In early 1939 German air intelligence reported: "On the basis of their backward tactics, Italian air units will suffer setbacks at the beginning of a war against an opponent with strong fighter and air defense. It is questionable, considering the Italian mentality, whether the Italian air force possesses the inner strength to overcome such weakness."[108]

As early as 1937 the Germans had indications that the Italian air defenses were badly organized.[109] The official responsible for home defense was an assistant of the army undersecretary. Each corps district contained a territorial defense office that controlled military zones in each divisional command. These military zones held responsibility for preparing the air and coastal defenses, and the air force and navy were supposed to place the necessary defense forces at the disposal of these relatively minor army commands. In practice nothing of the kind occurred.[110] In December 1938 the German air attaché pointed out that the extension of the Italian Empire had worsened the prospects for a successful air defense of Italy, that the Regia Aeronautica had neither the equipment nor training to launch air attacks on southern France, and finally that "time works more for opponents than for Italy. France and Britain are carrying out long-term rearmament and defense measures for equality in air power and for cooperation of their air power and fleets in a struggle against Italy." In no sense, the attaché continued, were the Italians ready to meet such challenges.[111] So disorganized and dishonest were those who were in charge of the Italian air force that the Foreign Minister, Count Galeazzo Ciano, suggested to Mussolini that civilian prefects count the aircraft in hangars and on airfields to establish exactly how many aircraft the air force really possessed.[112] Thus, given the technical weaknesses of the Italian air industry and the general inefficiencies of its staff and organization, the Regia Aeronautica neither was a threat to Italy's possible opponents nor was it capable of effectively defending Italian air space.

EASTERN EUROPE

The strategic and diplomatic situation in Eastern Europe is harder to assess, both because of gaps in the sources and because of the problem of weighing intentions. Obviously the collapse of Austria-Hungary, Germany, and Russia in the First World War had fundamentally altered the balance of power in Eastern Europe. The emergence of the new states, all divisive, dissatisfied, and mutually suspicious, created instability and provided both the Soviet Union and Germany with an area open to external as well as internal subversion. None of these so-called successor states possessed the economic, industrial, or social strength individually to resist outside pressure, and few of them were willing to embark on even the most modest schemes of cooperation.

Polish-Czech relations provide a characteristic example. Although Germany represented a clear threat to both states, their widely differing attitudes toward the Soviet Union, as well as the Czech seizure of the Teschen district in 1919, made cooperation between the two powers almost impossible.[113] The French had hoped to use the Eastern European states, and Poland and Czechoslovakia in particular, to balance off the German superiority over France. Unfortunately, they were no more willing to give these states long-term economic aid than they were to give them a hard guarantee that France would actively respond to a German attack on Eastern Europe. Not only had the loss of the Tsarist loans made French investors wary of investing in the region but the economies of the Eastern European states were more compatible with the economy of Germany than with that of France.

CZECHOSLOVAKIA

Czechoslovakia and her leaders in the interwar period hardly deserve the martyred status they have been accorded since Munich. Their seizure of the Teschen district in 1919 had at best been high-handed, and their behavior toward Poland during the Soviet offensive against Warsaw in 1920 was hostile. The Czechs handled their minorities relatively well by Eastern European standards; however, over one-third of the population of Czechoslovakia consisted of nationalities that had no desire to be included within the new Czech state.

Both in terms of her location and her industrial and economic strength, Czechoslovakia was of immense importance to the security of Eastern Europe. Napoleon had once commented that the power controlling Prague controlled Central Europe. In strategic terms, as a French ally Czechoslovakia represented a direct threat to Silesia and to central and southern Germany. Conversely, mastery over Czechoslovakia offered the Germans important advantages. Command of Czech territory would allow Germany to surround Poland on three sides and isolate her. It would give the Germans a corridor that reached deep into the Balkans and provide them with a frontier with Hungary and Rumania. In effect, with Czechoslovakia under their control they would be only three hundred rather than one thousand kilometers away from Rumanian oil.[114] Czechoslovakia was, in addition, the only highly industrialized nation in Eastern Europe. The Skoda works were one of the great armament centers in the world, and control of these works would be of great importance in the German prosecution of the Second World War.

The German seizure of Austria in March 1938 surrounded Czechoslovakia on three sides, and the Germans were now in a position to put severe economic pressure on the Czech state. In long-range terms Czechoslovakia was in a hopeless strategic position. In tactical terms, however, geography offered the Czechs the possibility of putting up a sustained and costly opposition to any German invasion. High mountains and rugged terrain on the Bavarian, Saxon, and Silesian borders offered significant obstacles to military operations. Only along the old Austro-Czech frontier did the Germans face terrain favorable to offensive military operations.

At the beginning of 1938 the Czech army consisted of seventeen active-duty divisions. As the crisis in the spring of 1938 exploded, the Czechs established an additional two regular divisions.[115] In their mobilization plans they had planned to have a reserve unit available for every active formation, but because the crisis came before their preparations were complete, they could only mobilize eleven reserve divisions in September 1938.[116] At that time, German intelligence estimated that the active-duty Czech army possessed a manpower strength of 350,000, whereas the fully mobilized army would have 750,000 men.[117]

Most of the Czech army consisted of infantry units, either field or fortress. It seems to have been well armed and equipped, although patterned after the rather cumbersome French structure. In addition, there were four semimechanized divisions, which the Germans characterized as "Schnelldivisionen." These latter units contained a cavalry brigade of two regiments, each possessing machine and antitank guns, a motorized brigade of two infantry battalions, a motorcycle battalion, motorized artillery, and one tank battalion. The tank battalion possessed the T-38 tank, which in 1938 was the equal of anything in the German inventory.[118] Arbeitsstab Leeb, the planning staff designated to lead the Twelfth Army in the invasion of Czechoslovakia, estimated that although the Czech Schnelldivisionen could concentrate or shift direction quickly, they could not support sustained combat nor did they possess much offensive punch.[119] In general, their organization does not reflect the influence of a particularly perceptive military doctrine.

On the whole, Czech military equipment was excellent. Yet, in the summer of 1938 the Czechs were still in the process of reequipping active duty and reserve units. They had almost completed reequipment of regular divisions, but reserve formations were only beginning to receive new hardware. The Skoda works gave Czechoslovakia one of the better equipped European armies both in terms of quantity as well as quality. In June 1938 Colonel Kurt Zeitzler of the OKW staff and future chief of staff of the German army reported to the führer that Czechoslovakia's armaments were of high quality and reequipping was proceeding rapidly because of the productive capacity of her industry. Regular units had already received new medium artillery, but much of their heavy artillery was left over from the days of the Austro-Hungarian Empire. Infantry divisions had received new rifles, light machine guns, and an improved heavy machine gun. Overall, Zeitzler emphasized the quality of Czechoslovakia's matériel.

A German intelligence evaluation, written after Munich, confirms Zeitzler's impression. By September 1938 the Czechs had almost completed reequipping their regular units. The only major deficiencies remained with the heavy artillery and with the reserves, although mobilization indicated serious shortages in weapons and clothing for reserve troops.[120] In 1938 this was not, it should be noted, a problem unique to the Czech army.

Fortifications formed a significant element in Czechoslovakia's defense policy, partly because of the influence of the French general staff.[121] Given the long, exposed borders of Czechoslovakia, especially along the German frontier, the Czechs were incapable of building a fortified system on the scale of the Maginot line. As it was, Czechoslovakia's geography made such a system unnecessary, since the high mountains and rough terrain of the areas on the Bavarian and Saxon frontiers provided significant natural obstacles. In those regions where geography did not offer significant protection, the Czechs had embarked on a major construction effort. Particularly along the eastern Silesian frontier, the Czechs had managed to build a major system of fortifications that would have represented a serious hindrance to a German invasion.[122]

The Germans did not have a high opinion of Czech military leadership. Their intelligence pictured General Jan Syrový, commander in chief of the Czech army, as possessing neither the personality nor military qualities required for a position of high military responsibility. They attributed his position to political influences among veterans of the Czech Legion. Outside of a few corps commanders, the Germans gave the other senior officers of the army similarly low marks, although they did feel that regimental and company-grade leadership was quite good.[123] German reports on the whole acknowledged that the Czechs could have put up strong resistance behind their fortifications but tended to doubt whether Czech troops could have matched German soldiers in the open.[124]

The reports of the British military attaché in Prague agreed with most of the German estimates. Lt. Col. Stronge reported that leadership in the Czech army varied even more than in most armies. The higher commanders were not impressive, but many regimental commanders were outstanding soldiers.[125] After a tour of the old Austrian border in March 1938 he reported that fortification work in this region was insufficient to offer much of an obstacle.[126] Six months later, however, he noted that work on fortifications was so advanced that even weak sections had some defensive value.[127] His final reports at the height of the crisis emphasized that the key to Czech resistance would be the morale of the people, and from what he had seen it would remain high.[128]

THE POLISH STRATEGIC SITUATION

Poland is a factor that many historians have ignored, especially with regard to the strategic situation in 1938. The rather murky nature of Polish foreign policy throughout the period, as well as the country's dismal showing in 1939, undoubtedly have contributed to this attitude. The Poles had scant liking for the Czechs and no desire to sacrifice their national interests to preserve Czechoslovakia unless the possibility existed that substantial foreign aid would be forthcoming. As one Czech writer somewhat morosely but aptly noted, the Poles were prepared to march against Czechoslovakia if England and France remained neutral, to maintain their neutrality if only France intervened, but to join a war against Germany if Britain came in.[129] Such a policy reflected a certain realism, though the Poles never understood the enormity of the German threat or the extent to which the security of their nation

was intertwined with that of Czechoslovakia.[130] Polish frontiers after
1921 were difficult enough to defend, but German control over Czechoslovakia would surround Poland. Unlike Czechoslovakia, Poland had
no significant geographic or strategic features on either side of the
frontier with Germany.

The Polish army itself did not equal the standards and matériel of
the Czech army. In early 1939 Poland possessed thirty active divisions,
ten reserve divisions, eleven cavalry brigades, and one armored brigade.
Almost the whole of the army was dependent on horse-drawn transport,
and most of the equipment, especially in heavy weapons, was outdated.[131] In December 1937 a German intelligence report noted that
without strong tank forces and heavy artillery the Polish army would
not be able to wage an offensive war against an enemy that possessed
modern equipment.[132] The Poles trained their military forces along
lines similar to those of the French, although they emphasized maneuver to a greater extent than did their allies. Experiences in the
1920 campaign against the Soviets as well as insufficient matériel and
industrial production to fight a war of matériel on the scale demanded
by French doctrine undoubtedly played a major role in Polish thinking.

There is something gallant in the manner with which the Poles
faced the crisis of 1939. A British delegation to Poland in 1939 reported:
"[t]hey [the Poles] are thus dealing with their own problem in the most
menacing aspect and the one which presents the greatest difficulties.
They are under no delusion that this will cause them tremendous
losses, involve the abandonment of a large part of their country, the
loss of their Silesian industrial resources and perhaps of others further
inland, but they face the catastrophe with a certain admirable confidence."[133] Such "admirable confidence" amounted in fact to overconfidence, and in both foreign and strategic policies the Poles displayed a consistent tendency to ignore their considerable weaknesses.
In 1939 it led them to conclude that they could bring a German
offensive to a standstill and then launch a counteroffensive.[134] Yet in
1938, what would become overconfidence by 1939 would have offered
prospects of success against a Germany preoccupied with Czechoslovakia. In 1938 Poland was not only one of the few countries with the
potential of attacking the Reich but was perhaps the only one with the
will to do so should she become embroiled in a war with Germany.
The problem, of course, was whether she would intervene.

THE SOVIET UNION

If historians have tended to ignore the Poles in calculating the strategic balance in the late 1930s, they have been far too willing to accord the Soviet Union a strategic significance that her military capabilities and her geographic position simply do not justify. In geographic terms alone, it would have been almost impossible for the Soviet Union to exert any important military pressure in Central Europe in 1938. She had frontiers with neither Czechoslovakia nor Germany and was thus unable to bring direct military pressure on the Germans or to supply the Czechs with matériel or reinforcements unless either the Poles or the Rumanians would allow the Red Army to cross their territories. Throughout the 1938 crisis, both governments justifiably made clear their opposition to allowing Soviet soldiers on their soil. Only in the Baltic could the USSR exert pressure on Germany. German trade with Scandinavia, especially the iron-ore supplies, was vulnerable to blockade and other forms of interference by the Soviet navy.

Stalin's internal policy gives little reason to suggest that he was actively preparing for war with Germany. Admittedly, the Soviets strenuously denounced fascism both in Germany and Italy, but the catastrophic purges of their military establishment beginning in 1937 hardly suggest that Stalin feared that he would face a military confrontation with Germany in the near future. The effects of these purges, moreover, cast serious doubt on the utility or capability of Soviet military assistance.

On paper the Soviet Union possessed a formidable military instrument in the late 1930s. In the spring of 1939 the British Chiefs of Staff estimated that the USSR could mobilize the following forces in Europe as shown in Table III-2. In addition, the British calculated

TABLE III-2
Russian Mobilization Strength

	Z + 7	Z + 14	Z + 21	Z + 36	Z + 40
Armored Divisions	4	4	4	4	4
Cavalry Divisions	26	26	30	30	30
Infantry Divisions	61	61	85	85	138

NOTE: In British terminology the letter Z was equivalent to the letter D in American terminology.

that the Soviets could mobilize one armored division, five cavalry divisions, and twenty-five infantry divisions in the Far East at the start of any conflict.[135] At this time the USSR was building up a vast tank park that by 1941 would contain somewhere between 17,000 and 24,000 armored vehicles and that in 1938 already contained well in excess of 7,000 tanks.[136]

In the early thirties Soviet military doctrine had been one of the most progressive in Europe. The Russians established their first armored division in 1931, four years ahead of the Germans, and Russian paratroopers made the first large-scale drop in history during the 1936 maneuvers.[137] Combined with the extensive production of Soviet industry, the Red Army was well on the way toward becoming the most formidable military force in Europe by the mid-1930s. There were of course major weaknesses. Small-unit commanders exhibited little flexibility and less initiative during maneuvers. Generally the junior officers and NCO corps needed tactical upgrading and advanced training to deal with the technological complexities of modern warfare.

The Red Army's leadership was well aware of weaknesses in these domains. Marshal Tukhachevsky, commander in chief of the army, was particularly perceptive on the subject of military doctrine and realistic about the difficulties that the Soviet Union would face in a coming war. He argued that a major war between Russia and Germany would see mobile operations occurring over hundreds of kilometers and lasting months on end and might well begin with the Germans enjoying an initial superiority that would enable them to conquer large areas of the Soviet Union.[138] Such admirable realism was intolerable in Stalin's Russia. By 1937 the military alone had yet to be purged.[139]

Beginning in May 1937 the heavy and ruthless hand of the Soviet secret police attacked the Soviet military. Some writers have argued that these purges allowed Stalin to promote bright young men more quickly.[140] Nothing could be farther from the truth. These purges almost led to the destruction of the Soviet Union. The "liquidation" of the Red Army's officer corps in the period from 1937 through 1939 was directly responsible for the crushing defeats that the Soviet Union suffered in the Winter War against Finland and for the catastrophes of Minsk, Smolensk, Kiev, Vyazma, and Bryansk in 1941. The pernicious effect of the purge on the stability and combat capabilities of the Russian army cannot be overemphasized. By the time the purges ended, Stalin had had well over half of the officer corps either shot or sent to concentration camps—approximately 35,000 out of 70,000. The NKVD liquidated three out of five marshals of the Soviet Union, thirteen out of fifteen army commanders, fifty-seven out of eighty-five corps commanders, one hundred ten out of one hundred ninety-five division commanders, two hundred twenty out of four hundred six brigade commanders, all eleven vice commissars of war, and seventy-five out of eighty members of the Supreme Military Council. By rank, Stalin removed 90 percent of all generals and 80 percent of the colonels.[141]

Some talented officers like Zhukov survived, more by luck than deliberate policy. The fiascos of the Winter War and the first months of the German invasion in 1941 reveal the capabilities of most officers promoted by the purge. In 1938 the German military attaché in Moscow informed his British colleague that the German army had regarded the Red Army under Tukhachevsky as a menace to Germany, but with the purges this was no longer the case. Had the whole Soviet command not been eliminated, he claimed, Germany would not have dared to move against Austria.[142]

The twisted logic of the Stalinist regime demanded that Tukhachevsky's doctrine as well as the man must go. Because he had played a major role in the establishment of mechanized divisions, his "treason" had tainted these formations and the doctrine on which their use was based. Moreover, as did the French, the Red Army drew the wrong lessons from Spain. The chief Soviet adviser to the Spanish Republic, General Pavlov, returned from Spain in 1938 and persuaded Stalin that the doctrine of distributing tanks among the infantry divisions was the wave of the future. At the end of 1938 the Red Army therefore began to break up their armored divisions and distribute tanks from the seven mechanized corps to the infantry.[143] The positional fighting in the Winter War, especially along the Mannerheim line, further reinforced the Soviet belief that they were on the right track. Not until the collapse of France did they begin to grasp the extent of their error. By that time it was too late, and as a result catastrophe would overtake Soviet armies the following year.

Soviet naval strength was considerable, although split between three major fleets—the Baltic, the Black Sea, and the Far East. British intelligence estimated that the Soviet submarine strength presented a real threat to Germany's strategic and economic position in the Baltic, where the Soviet navy would be able to contain considerable German naval forces and interfere with the supply of Swedish iron ore.[144] The Kriegsmarine had similar fears. However, the purges hit the navy as hard as the army, and throughout the war the navy would display consistent incompetence. Even with the coasts of the Baltic Republics at its disposal, it managed to achieve nothing. Thus, its precipitous retreat to Leningrad in 1941 makes doubtful whether Soviet naval forces were ever a significant threat at any time after the purges began.

The Russian air force was an even more doubtful factor. German commanders have described Soviet air units floundering in impossible formations in obsolete aircraft in the slaughter of June 1941—a slaughter that possesses many similarities to the Marianas' turkey shoot.[145] Most Russian aircraft were obsolete even as early as 1938, and the Russians had neither the technology nor the aircraft to wage an air offensive from their territory.[146] In 1938 it was doubtful, given the superiority of the Luftwaffe, whether Soviet air units could have established air bases on Czech soil after fighting had begun.

CONCLUSION

The basic fact of the European strategic situation in 1938 was that *not* a single one of the powers was prepared to wage even a limited war not to mention a long drawn out conflict. There were, of course, a variety of explanations for this state of affairs. On the one hand Germany, although clearly aiming to overthrow the entire European balance of power, never possessed the economic and strategic preconditions necessary to rearm in depth. Moreover, her rearmament had not yet progressed to the point where her armed forces had much prospect of winning anything more than a conflict with one of the smaller European nations. To Germany's east the smaller nations, given their fundamental hostility to each other, had little prospect of forming any sort of united front—the one possible foundation on which their fragile independence might have rested.

For the other powers, the difficulties that faced the formulation of national security policies in the diplomatic as well as in the military and strategic realms were equally daunting. The Italians had none of the attributes, industrial, intellectual, economic, or geographic, required by the pretentions of their ruler and by the nationalists of the upper and middle classes. The French were for the short term relatively secure behind their fortifications. In the long run, without either the morale or strategic courage to support their allies in Eastern Europe, they could only huddle behind their artificial barriers and wait for *"der Tag"*—a day that would come only at a time chosen by the Germans.

In the European strategic equation of the late 1930s the Soviet Union still remains the great enigma. Without the documents (if they exist and, given the nature of Stalin's tyranny, their existence is much in doubt), one can only guess at the motivations and purposes of Soviet foreign policy. Nevertheless, the purges of Soviet military forces that had begun in 1937 and had continued in full fury throughout 1938 make it likely that Stalin perceived internal dangers as of far greater importance than any external threat. The absence of a frontier with either Germany or Czechoslovakia undoubtedly reinforced such feelings and perhaps induced Stalin to hope that a great military crisis in Central Europe would enable him to make gains on the border marches of the USSR at the expense of Poland and Rumania. The wholesale execution then ravaging the Red Army hardly suggests, however, that Stalin viewed a great military confrontation in the immediate future as a real possibility.

In conclusion, the potential of European powers to resist the German threat was less than the sum of the parts. Most of the European nations hated and feared the Germans, but that was not sufficient to force any degree of cooperation between the smaller or even the greater powers to meet the growing danger. Those faced with the most immediate peril, Poland and Czechoslovakia, could not find common ground to resist. Complicating this fragmented situation was the fact that few politicians or generals were capable of forming a balanced view not only of their own strengths and weaknesses but also of the very great difficulties that confronted the Third Reich. Nevertheless, considerable powers of resistance did exist on the continent to meet the German danger. Unfortunately, Europe's leadership in the 1930s was not capable of mustering the continent's strength.

IV

The Line of Departure:
European Background to the Anschluss

Most historians view the events they record sequentially. Quite naturally, they attribute relationships to those events that follow on others. Such an approach, however, distorts as much as it enlightens, for in reality events often have very different associations than their sequence suggests. In fact, they may have no connections at all. The 1930s are a case in point. Historians have seen a direct, unbroken path leading from Hitler's appointment as chancellor, to the announcement of German rearmament, to Abyssinia, to Spain, to the Anschluss, to Munich, and eventually to the Second World War. In March 1938 Winston Churchill suggested just such a progression: "For five years I have talked to this House on these matters—not with very great success. I have watched this famous island descending incontinently, fecklessly, the stairway which leads to a dark gulf. It is a fine broad stairway at the beginning, but after a bit the carpet ends. A little farther on there are only flagstones, and a little farther on still these break beneath your feet. . . ."[1] Although there may be much truth in Churchill's comments, the path to the outbreak of war was far from distinct to those who made policy. In fact, some of the great crises of the decade, such as Abyssinia and the Spanish Civil War, distracted Europe from the critical danger of a rearmed Germany; they undoubtedly aided the forward thrust of Nazi foreign policy, but indirectly rather than directly. As Hitler pointed out in November 1937, a continuation of the Spanish Civil War, rather than a quick victory by Nationalist forces, best served German interests.[2]

Most European diplomats recognized that Hitler's accession to power

MAP I *Europe in 1937*

in January 1933 heralded a radicalization of German foreign policy.[3] The question was how extreme would be the Nazi break with the past. A few, such as the British ambassador in Berlin, recognized the danger from the beginning.[4] However, most Europeans, including at times even the French, hoped to avoid a confrontation by redressing the supposed inequities of Versailles. As noted in the first chapter, such an approach had no hope of success. Hitler had no intention of settling for anything less than German mastery over Europe from the Urals to Spain.[5]

Skillfully maneuvering between European hopes and fears, Hitler achieved a revolution in Germany's diplomatic and strategic position in the period from 1933 to 1937. In 1933 Germany withdrew from the League; in 1934 she signed a nonaggression pact with Poland that alleviated tensions on her eastern frontier; in 1935 the Saar returned to the Reich after an overwhelmingly favorable vote in the plebiscite, Hitler announced introduction of rearmament and conscription, and the Reich concluded a naval agreement with Great Britain; finally, in March 1936 Hitler denounced the last restriction of Versailles and remilitarized the Rhineland. In the last case strong French protests were rendered meaningless by a cabinet crisis in France, French military incompetence and impotence, and loose British talk about the Germans returning to their backyards.[6] It is worth stressing that none of the above successes was due to German military might.

The basic problem facing European statesmen was that the only possible method of upsetting these German probes was with military force and, quite likely, war. Only once did Hitler stumble. In summer 1934, shortly after the Röhm purge, a Nazi-sponsored coup in Austria badly misfired. The Italians threatened mobilization and warned the Germans not to attempt to recoup their losses. They thus forced Hitler to drop his associates in Vienna and to abandon hopes of incorporating Austria for the immediate future. The key feature of the 1934 Austrian crisis was that Mussolini had appeared willing to use military force to maintain the status quo. In no other crisis between 1933 and 1937 did Hitler's diplomatic opponents seriously consider force to resist a German initiative.

As a result of the Austrian adventure, the German announcement of rearmament in March 1935, and the general intransigence of Nazi diplomacy, Britain, France, and Italy established the so-called Stresa front in April 1935. From the beginning, diplomatic cooperation between the three powers was minimal. Moreover, the British formula referring only to the maintenance of peace in Europe gave Mussolini the green light to begin the Abyssinian adventure. In June the British turned around and signed the Anglo-German Naval Agreement recognizing Germany's right to build up to 35 percent of the Royal Navy's tonnage. As a result, the British not only broke the Stresa front and legitimized Germany's disregard of treaties limiting her military forces but also conceded a fleet ratio similar to that between the French and British navies.[7] This egregious slap at France seems to have been motivated by an idle hope that the agreement could prevent a naval race between Britain and Germany. Ironically, it accomplished nothing of the sort: the Germans could not have built up their fleet more quickly than they managed under the provisions of the agreement.[8]

Whatever remained of Stresa collapsed in the wreckage of Abyssinia. The Italian invasion of Ethiopia forced the British to face the question of whether they wished to honor their obligations under the League covenant. Publicly they took a strong stand, but privately their efforts at compromise only further encouraged Mussolini. Once military operations commenced, events in Africa forced Britain to brand fascist Italy as an aggressor and ask the League to impose sanctions. None of the sanctions requested seriously threatened the Italian military effort, and the League powers refused to impose the oil sanctions that might have led to an Italian collapse. Retarding the British government's efforts throughout the crisis were the dark warnings of its military advisers, who preached caution, warned of Italian military power, and underlined the weaknesses of Britain's military establishment.[9] Fortified by such advice, Baldwin and his ministers sought a compromise with the help of the French, but the ill-fated Hoare-Laval Agreement made a bad situation worse. Throughout the crisis the French, worried by the Germans, attempted to prevent the diplomatic confrontation from turning into a Mediterranean war. Despite an unwillingness to commit themselves to France, the British were outraged that the French were less than enthusiastic about supporting strategically unimportant Ethiopia. The denouement came in March 1936. On the brink of the imposition of oil sanctions on Italy, the Germans remilitarized the Rhineland. The resulting crisis led to a postponement of the oil sanction question, while the Western Powers floundered in an attempt to respond to the German move. When the dust settled, Abyssinia had collapsed and the German army was in the Rhineland.

The result of the Abyssinian crisis was clear. Italy had been driven into the arms of Germany, and by November 1936 Mussolini referred publicly to the Rome-Berlin "Axis." Although Italy's move into the German camp was not a disaster for the Western Powers, frictions between France and Great Britain during the crisis seriously affected Franco-British relations throughout the remainder of the 1930s. At the same time, the Abyssinian crisis did nothing to disabuse the Left in England of the notion that arms and rearmament were unnecessary and that all Britain need do for her defense was to rely on the League covenant.

While Europe absorbed the lessons of Ethiopia, a new crisis exploded in Spain. In July 1936 much of the Spanish army, aided and abetted by right-wing parties, revolted and attempted to otherthrow the Republic. The result led to civil war between contending political factions. In strategic terms the vicious, prolonged conflict between Right and Left caused so much destruction and devastation that Spain was to be of little significance in the coming European war. The uprising led both Hitler and Mussolini to intervene independently of each other. [10] Both dictators readily supplied aircraft to bring the Spanish Moroccan army from Africa. Nevertheless, their response indicated significant differences in approach. The Italians soon supplied not only aircraft and armaments but also large numbers of troops. The Germans, on the other hand, kept their contributions to the civil war at a rather low level. Certainly Hitler was willing to supply aircraft and weapons and, at times, even advisers to the rebels, but he never gave the Spanish an open-ended commitment. In December 1936 he flatly refused a Spanish request for three German divisions. Significantly, he commented to his advisers that it was in the German interest if Franco did not win quickly so that European attention would remain centered on Spain. Moreover, he added, victory in Spain should not be gained at the expense of Germany's own rearmament program. [11]

The Spanish Civil War's impact on European diplomacy lived up to Hitler's expectations. Through 1937 western interest remained centered on the Mediterranean. Britain and France sought to dampen the civil war or at least avoid a direct confrontation between the powers. Despite the efforts of the Non-Intervention Committee, they could not prevent the Italians and Germans from giving considerable aid to Franco, nor the Russians from similarly helping the Republic. What was particularly damaging was that the diplomatic and political problems of the Spanish Civil War removed the German danger from immediate European focus throughout 1936 and 1937. The civil war and travails with Italians in the Mediterranean led many conservatives in Britain to conclude that German quiescence as rearmament proceeded indicated that the Reich represented the least bellicose of England's putative enemies.

The Left in Britain and France, also influenced by events in Spain, misperceived the German danger. The ideological nature of the Spanish conflict and its origins resulted in a feeling that fascism represented an internal rather than an external danger. After all, had not Mussolini and Hitler come to power in their respective nations as a result of internal politics? Was not Franco following in their footsteps? Consequently, the Left often perceived fascism as an internal threat while it minimized the external danger of German military power. There was little that was consistent in left-wing attitudes. The Labour party in Britain strongly urged support for the Spanish Loyalists, while attacking every minimal step taken by conservative governments to speed rearmament. As a "critic" noted in the *New Statesman* in 1936: "I see no intellectual difficulty in at once working for the victory of the Spanish people and in being glad of the growing pacifist movement in England."[12] In France, Blum's remark that his nation could rely on the working class to defeat a German invasion, rather than on a politically dangerous elite tank force, reflected a similar attitude.[13] Hugh Dalton, a leading Labour M.P., and one of the few in his party with much sense on defense matters, remarked that the Left regarded collective security as something to which Britain should make little contribution "except to sponge on the Red Army."[14]

HITLER'S STRATEGY: 1937

With the exception of military aid to Spain, 1937 was a quiet year for German diplomacy. On the other hand, it represented a year in which the Wehrmacht began to reap the benefits of the rearmament effort that had begun in 1933. Late summer maneuvers indicated that the army was firmly in control of the massive expansion program that had increased its forces from ten to well over forty regular divisions. Foreign observers, including Mussolini, were most impressed with the proficiency, competence, and drive that army units displayed.[15] Although serious weaknesses appeared in 1938, the army was well on the road to mastering the problems caused by precipitate expansion. Similarly, the Luftwaffe, acquiring a new generation of aircraft, had already become a significant military factor, although it was not close to possessing the capabilities that Nazi propaganda claimed for it or that foreign military experts attributed to it.[16]

On the other hand, the German economic situation indicated that the Nazi regime had run into major difficulties in maintaining the tempo of rearmament. The economic and foreign exchange difficulties discussed in Chapter I were the basis of the problem. The shortfall in steel production over the course of 1937 and the resulting effect on military production had a definite impact on rearmament plans. In September 1937 Raeder warned that, unless steel allocations rose, the navy would have to abandon or postpone much of its battleship program and construction of submarines and dockyards would halt. Moreover, steel allocations at current levels would cause ammunition shortages for ships already in service.[17] At the same time, Blomberg warned Göring that steel shortages were delaying completion of ships under construction up to six months and would cause a full year's delay in stockpiling ammunition reserves. Turning to the Reichsminister's own preserve, Blomberg estimated that the shortfall would delay reequipping the Luftwaffe by one and one-half years.[18] Earlier in 1937 the OKH economic staff had reported: "The major difficulty at the moment lies in supplying iron and steel. Here an extraordinary bottleneck has occurred that will have still greater effect, by the fact that ore availability will be more difficult. Serious stoppages have occurred in delivery of iron and steel production for Wehrmacht purposes that have already led to great difficulties in the completion of assembly programs."[19]

These two factors, Germany's growing military strength and her increasing economic difficulties, probably played a major role in Hitler's decision to meet with his chief diplomatic and military advisers in November 1937. Although there has been much controversy among historians over the meeting, several factors underline the motives and purposes behind the conference.[20] First and most obvious is the fact that the first half of the meeting discussed the diplomatic and strategic opportunities for Germany in the coming years. As Hitler noted, the German military would soon be able to tip the diplomatic scales. German foreign policy no longer had to lead from weakness or rely on bluff. The Wehrmacht could and would play a decisive role. In contrast, fully half of the meeting—not transcribed—considered economic and rearmament problems. Obviously the difficulties cited above were at the heart of the discussion. Economic problems and the possibility of using Germany's growing military power on the international scene must not be separated. Intertwined throughout Hitler's discussion of Germany's strategic options was an emphasis that Germany must move before her enemies completed their own preparations.

The discussion itself did not go as Hitler had planned. Instead of meeting the approval of his diplomatic and military advisers, the führer ran into substantial opposition. Present at the meeting on the military side were Blomberg, Fritsch, Raeder, and Göring, with the foreign minister, Konstantin von Neurath, representing the German foreign office. Hitler's hypotheses and prognostications did not lay out a rigid blueprint but rather the general direction of German policy for the immediate future. As one writer has noted, "even if it were not a timetable for aggression, it was a ticket for the journey: and the first stops Prague and Vienna were clearly marked."[21] Hitler warned his listeners that only through military pressure could Germany satisfy her long-term needs. The first stage would involve settlement of the Austrian and Czech "problems." Although the circumstances that Hitler foresaw were quite far-fetched, he indicated that he would grasp whatever opportunities offered themselves. To achieve his dreams of German domination over Europe, he remarked, Germany would have to take the same great risks that the Romans and British had taken in acquiring their empires.

Both Blomberg and Fritsch, and to a lesser extent Neurath, raised serious objections. They warned that for the present Germany could not face war with England and France. Italian participation at Germany's side would only draw off about twenty French divisions, so that the French army would still possess overwhelming superiority on the western front. The general lack of fortifications made the strategic situation there even more threatening. Finally, Blomberg warned that in the east, Czech fortifications, in some areas as strong as the Maginot line, would make German offensive operations most difficult.[22]

In this meeting Hitler emphasized his long-range goals along with his willingness to act expediently as events developed. As a statesman, the führer operated on two distinct planes: the tactical level of day-to-day decision making and the strategic level of long-term goals. Yet no matter what action the current situation might demand, Hitler never abandoned or changed his long-range aims. The concurrence between his constantly expressed dream of a Europe from the Urals to Spain, a Europe *"judenfrei,"* dominated by Germany, and the actual course of events is too close to require comment.[23] As Hitler once explained to his generals, one could not see the future clearly enough to predict the exact course of events.

> It was clear to me that a conflict with Poland had to come sooner or later. I had already made this decision in the spring, but I thought that I would first turn against the West in a few years, and only after that against the East. But the sequences of these things cannot be fixed. Nor should one close one's eyes to threatening situations. I wanted first of all to establish a tolerable relationship with Poland in order to fight against the West. But this plan, which appealed to me, could not be executed, as fundamental parts had changed.[24]

After the November meeting, Hitler's military advisers drew the correct conclusions from the discussions. Fritsch, in fact, asked whether he should give up a proposed vacation trip to Egypt scheduled to begin only a few days later. Hitler replied that a European crisis was not yet so imminent. Nevertheless, Blomberg immediately set about recasting German deployment plans. The 1937 directives for *Fall Rot* (deployment against the west) and for *Fall Grün* (deployment against the east) had admitted that "the general political situation justifies the supposition that Germany does not have to calculate on an attack from any quarter."[25] Within a month of the above meeting, the War Ministry issued two important amendments to deployment orders, giving German plans a more aggressive character.

THE FRITSCH-BLOMBERG CRISIS

The new year brought with it a major internal crisis that would thoroughly unsettle the Generalität. Combined with these internal difficulties came the first stages of a diplomatic confrontation with Austria that led to the Anschluss. The Fritsch-Blomberg crisis that exploded at the end of January began with the mésalliance between Field Marshal von Blomberg and a woman who, as one party official euphemistically put it, "had a past." Present evidence indicates that suggestions that the SS arranged the romance are incorrect.[26] However, once presented with an opportunity, Himmler, Göring, and Heydrich not only supported the dismissal of Blomberg but also launched an attack on Fritsch. Hitler seized on the situation to carry out a purge of senior military and diplomatic officials who opposed a more aggressive, risky foreign policy. It is no coincidence that the three who had voiced serious misgivings about the plans of the führer on November 5 now found themselves removed from office. Despite Blomberg's considerable services to the Nazi regime, Hitler does not seem to have found it difficult to remove the war minister. As he told his army adjutant in April, Blomberg had shown neither political nor strategic judgment in a difficult situation, an obvious reference to the war minister's faintheartedness during the Rhineland crisis.[27]

The naming of Blomberg's successor represented a serious problem for Hitler. He could hardly jump another general over Fritsch, and if he assumed the position of war minister himself, he would have the stubborn, independent Fritsch as his immediate subordinate. Furthermore, Fritsch had resisted Nazi influence in the army to a greater extent than had Blomberg, and his forcefully expressed views on German foreign policy made clear that he would be a formidable opponent of a policy of military confrontation. Thus, the obvious solution was to remove Fritsch as well as Blomberg. However, the method chosen to remove Fritsch, a trumped-up charge of homosexuality manufactured by Heydrich's minions, created serious political difficulties.[28] Not only had the SS manufactured the case by deliberately misidentifying Fritsch and suborning witnesses, but it did a most incompetent job of covering its tracks. The result was that, although the initial charge seemed convincing to the officer corps, the SS case came apart at the seams during February. Unfortunately, the military involved in defending Fritsch did not grasp the nature of Hitler's role until the very end of the case. For a time there seemed to be a real possibility, especially to Heydrich, that the army might settle accounts with the SS.[29]

As usual, the führer at the center of the storm managed events with consummate political skill. Hitler used the crisis to carry out a wholesale purge of the top ranks of the military and foreign service. He himself assumed Blomberg's powers.[30] With Blomberg's advice he selected General Wilhelm Keitel to act as his military secretary. Keitel's standards and capabilities are best summed up by the nickname given him by his fellow officers: *"Lakeitel"* (a play on *"Lakai,"* the German word for lackey). The choice of a new commander in chief proved more difficult. Hitler moved quickly in order to insure that, no matter what the outcome of the Fritsch case, he would not have to reappoint the army's old commander. He initially pushed Reichenau for Fritsch's position but, after almost universal opposition from top generals, settled on General Walther von Brauchitsch. The irony of the appointment and army opposition to Reichenau was that Brauchitsch proved himself a thoroughly servile commander in chief who consistently bent to the führer's will. Not only was this due to personality but also to the fact that Hitler provided his new commander in chief with a substantial sum of money so that he could divorce his first wife and remarry. As a result, Brauchitsch was never able to stand up to the führer at critical moments, nor was he capable of defending the army's interests.[31]

The housecleaning within the military, of course, went a good deal further. The War Ministry was now renamed the Oberkommando der Wehrmacht (OKW, the armed forces high command). Hitler replaced von Neurath at the Foreign Office with Joachim von Ribbentrop and recalled the ambassadors from Tokyo, Rome, and Austria. Within the ranks of the military, seven army and six Luftwaffe generals went into retirement. Manstein, Beck's brilliant cohort, was transferred from the OKH. More important in the long run was that, as a condition of appointment, Hitler forced the new commander in chief to replace General Viktor von Schwedler in the army personnel office with Keitel's younger brother, Bodewin Keitel, another weak-willed, pro-Nazi officer.[32]

The reorganization considerably strengthened Hitler's position and power. As the oberster Befehlshaber der Wehrmacht, Hitler enjoyed direct command authority over the military forces of the Reich. The commanders in chief of the three services now reported directly to the führer and not through an intermediary. The key figure in the purge was Fritsch, not Blomberg, for the army chief had enjoyed great respect throughout the officer corps. Because of his prestige and authority, Fritsch had been in a position to speak for the whole army. His successor, Brauchitsch, however, never held the same high level of respect from his fellow officers, and was thus never able to speak with the same authority. All this helped Hitler to force the military to fall in step behind his foreign policy.

On the fourth of February, in front of his senior generals and admirals, Hitler announced the reasons that had caused him to take such drastic action. He stressed an overwhelming sense of betrayal at Blomberg's mésalliance and declared that Blomberg had displayed neither spine nor courage on critical occasions. The attack on Fritsch was less direct but no less successful. Hitler emphasized his supposed unwillingness to use the SS file on Fritsch until the removal of Blomberg made it necessary to consider the army commander in chief for the vacated post in the Kriegsministerium. The führer argued that the identification of Fritsch by his accuser made it impossible to keep Fritsch in his present post until judicial procedures had resolved the charges. Therefore, Brauchitsch was assuming the post of army commander in chief.[33] For the moment Hitler succeeded in persuading his listeners that all was in order and that the services must rally behind their new supreme commander in chief.

Within four days the result of this conference had filtered down to division level. The operations officer of the 10th Division at Regensburg described the situation for his fellow officers in the following terms: Blomberg had drawn the conclusion from his mésalliance and retired. Hitler had taken up command authority over the army—something foreseen in his program but only sometime in the future. Fritsch also had retired since in the circumstances he could not succeed Blomberg. Interestingly, there was no mention of the charges against the army's former commander. The separation of other generals had not been as a result of their political or military beliefs but simply to make room for younger commanders in top ranks. The operations officer stressed that these changes were not the result of party or SS attacks on the army. The führer would protect the army from any outside attacks. "His heart belonged to the army."[34]

Unfortunately for the SS, the Fritsch case now unraveled both because of its inherent weaknesses and because of gross incompetence by the SD.[35] By the beginning of March, shortly before Fritsch's court-martial began, the SS case was in shreds and Hitler faced the danger of a direct confrontation with his generals. It is worth noting that in summer 1938 Hitler's continued refusal to rehabilitate Fritsch led the pro-Nazi general, Eugene von Schobert, to contemplate resigning because of the shabby treatment the former army commander had received.[36] The situation in March was even more threatening to Hitler's standing with the Generalität. However, on the very morning on which the Fritsch court-martial opened, the Austrian crisis burst. Göring gladly postponed the trial until after the führer had gained his greatest foreign policy achievement to date—a triumph that placed him in an unassailable political position.

THE ANSCHLUSS

In retrospect, one of the most surprising elements of the Fritsch-Blomberg crisis is the fact that at the same time that he purged senior officials, Hitler also set in motion the diplomatic confrontation with Austria. Actually, the two series of events are inseparable. As early as January 31, the future General Alfred Jodl noted that Hitler wished to divert attention from the Wehrmacht, disturb Europe, and by shifting a number of offices, give the impression of strength rather than weakness. "Schuschnigg [Kurt Schuschnigg, chancellor of Austria] should not receive encouragement but should shudder."[37]

An opportunity immediately presented itself at a meeting between the führer and the Austrian chancellor on February 12. Hitler was at his worst. He thoroughly browbeat his Austrian guest and conveniently had available Keitel, Reichenau, and the Air Fleet 3 commander from Munich, General Hugo Sperrle, to back up threats of military force unless the Austrians bowed to his demands. Schuschnigg collapsed and agreed not only to turn the Austrian Ministry of Interior over to a Nazi but also to provisions severely limiting Austria's independence.[38] Undoubtedly Hitler was delighted with the results, for they continued the process of subversion that the Austro-German accord of July 1936 had begun and that the German ambassador in Vienna had so assiduously fostered.[39] Nevertheless, even though the Austrian government confirmed Schuschnigg's agreement, the Germans kept up considerable pressure. Throughout the latter half of February and the beginning of March, the German military, at the instigation of Keitel, Jodl, and

Admiral Wilhelm Canaris, chief of intelligence, alarmed the Austrians with reports of troop movements, phony radio traffic, and rumors about cancellation of leave in Bavarian garrisons.[40]

The Germans seemed to have aimed at insuring that Austria would live up to the February agreements, but the false alarms led the Austrians to believe that their independence was being directly threatened. Of course, in the long run it was, but Schuschnigg precipitated an immediate crisis on March 9, 1938 by announcing a plebiscite to determine whether the Austrian people were for a "free, independent, social, and Christian Austria." After recovering from his surprise, Hitler was outraged, especially since he knew Schuschnigg would probably win. The crisis caught the German military completely by surprise with Brauchitsch not even in Berlin.[41] Hitler conferred with Keitel early on March 10 and then summoned Beck to the chancellery. The chief of staff, accompanied by Manstein, received a long lecture on the political necessity of moving into Austria. Hitler stated that Britain and France would not lift a finger to defend Austria. At the end of his monologue the führer asked what proposals the generals had and what formations the army would assign to an invasion. The initial discussion between Hitler and Beck assigned the following units to the operation: the VII Army Corps (Munich) with the 7th and 27th Infantry Divisions and the 1st Mountain Division, and the XIII Army Corps (Nürnberg) with the 10th and 17th Infantry Divisions and the 2nd Panzer Division (Würzburg). The XVI Panzer Corps and SS Leibstandarte (part of the future Waffen SS) were added later in the day.[42] Manstein and Beck returned to army headquarters in the Bendlerstrasse to draw up mobilization orders and establish an army command to supervise the movement.

While the army made an intensive effort to improvise plans for the Austrian venture, the crisis enabled Göring, presiding officer at the Fritsch court-martial, to postpone proceedings in view of the critical international situation. The fact that the newly promoted field marshal was a major driving force behind the Anschluss probably indicates his desire to escape the consequences of the rather dubious role he had played in the Fritsch-Blomberg proceedings.[43] Thus, right from the start of the crisis there would be a major effort at the top of the Nazi regime to utilize the Austrian crisis to defuse the Fritsch situation.

Meanwhile, Beck and Manstein had little advanced planning with which to work. During the previous summer, Blomberg had issued a broad directive aimed at preventing a Hapsburg restoration in Austria, but the OKH (Oberkommando des Heeres, or army high command) had done little to draft plans for a march into Austria. The army had made some preparation for "Case Otto" should the Hapsburg claimant attempt to seize the vacant throne. Background planning suggested a two-corps operation into the Republic, but the army had initiated almost no detailed planning.[44] On the morning of March 10 Beck admitted to Keitel that "we have prepared nothing; nothing has been done, nothing at all."[45] After the war Manstein acknowledged that, on returning from the chancellery, he sat and drafted the orders for the Anschluss in a four- to five-hour period.[46]

At 16:30 hours on March 10, Brauchitsch and Beck received General Fedor von Bock, commander of Heeresgruppenkommando 3, Dresden, and appointed him commander of the Eighth Army to form up on the Austrian frontier. Bock emphasized that the swift occupation of Vienna was essential. He expected little resistance in border areas, and only in industrial centers did he foresee possible light resistance. At 19:00 hours Hitler gave permission to mobilize units assigned to the Eighth Army.[47]

Bock immediately left Berlin to assemble his staff, while OKH controlled the mobilization of assigned units. There were major difficulties in deploying large numbers of troops on the Austro-German frontier. The transportation network in the border region was most inadequate, and the Eighth Army reported "initial deployment . . . led down the Danube valley between the Alps and the Austro-Czech border—an area from Linz on where there was only one fully operational railroad system and a single highway suitable for motorized units; the question of utilizing Danube shipping was still not clarified. Deep snow lay in some sections, around Salzburg, Steiermark, Kärten, Tirol, Voralberg; and roads were icy."[48] There were other problems. Most army units had recently received their yearly quota of recruits who had not yet completed basic, much less small-unit, training. Moreover, the army had no plans for a partial mobilization of military districts (*Wehrkreise*), while the invading force was to be on the Austrian frontier within thirty-six hours.[49]

The actual course of military operations against Austria gives a clear picture of the Wehrmacht's very considerable weaknesses in spring

1938. The mobilization came at a bad time of day. At 19:00 hours many soldiers had departed their posts but had still not arrived home. Therefore, the telephone recall did not work, and most offices had closed. Although there was no state of alert, the OKH demanded that units be ready to move in four and three-quarters hours. The 1914 mobilization had gone more smoothly, not only because of better preparation but also because of a lack of surprise. Furthermore, in 1914 the army allowed six days for unit mobilization; the 1938 schedule demanded a two-day mobilization.[50]

For the most part, the mobilization of regular formations took place without difficulty, as 80 to 90 percent of their personnel were already serving.[51] Even so, the 27th Infantry Division reported that it was only partly ready because it lacked the required matériel and weapons.[52] The 7th Infantry Division indicated that previous practice mobilizations enabled it to bring its units to full strength with little delay.[53] Although cooperation with civil and policy organizations was excellent, relations between army and SS were strained. Mobilized SS units (*Verfügungstruppen*) were not part of mobilization plans; nonetheless, they seized trucks and other vehicles scheduled for army use. Wehrkreis XIII (Military District Thirteen) reported that the number of trucks within its area was insufficient to meet army needs and that fortunately Luftwaffe ground forces and Landwehr units mobilized in the region had not required additional vehicles.[54]

The Nürnberg army authorities characterized the truck situation as catastrophic.[55] Most civilian vehicles mobilized by the army were not appropriate for military tasks, many were in dreadful mechanical condition, and the multiplicity of types made supply and maintenance almost unmanageable.[56] Regular units all shared the serious problem that support units were drawn from the untrained reserves. One unit argued the army could not fully realize its potential until combat units comprised only active-duty personnel and support troops consisted of trained reservists. Such a state of affairs did not yet exist.[57]

The mobilization of the reserves and Landwehr revealed greater shortcomings. Most reservists received mobilization assignments for which they had received no training. Even units called up the previous summer for training had major weaknesses, for up to 70 percent of their personnel were newly assigned. Most Landwehr soldiers held their First World War rank and did not possess knowledge commensurate with their duties. The 97th Landwehr Division lacked ninety of the officers, twenty-four of the civilian technicians, and 718 of the NCOs authorized by its table of organization. As a result NCOs filled junior officer slots and untrained personnel served as NCOs. Officers who had never ridden a horse commanded horse-drawn supply columns; soldiers with cavalry experience received assignment to motorized units, and reservists who had never worked a radio reported to signal and communication units.[58] The division's final report concluded that, although it had been ready to march after five days, it would have required a much longer period to prepare its middle-aged veterans for combat.[59] The 119th Landwehr regiment reported a severe shortage of NCOs and trained personnel.[60] Out of 120 reservists assigned to a cavalry regiment, only seventeen had ever ridden.[61] Heavy Artillery Battery 611 did not complete mobilization until D + 6 because most of its gun tractors were in repair shops and replacement vehicles from the civilian economy could not drag its cannons.[62]

The morale of those mobilized differed from unit to unit. Reservists called to service with combat units displayed an excellent attitude, but those serving with support units were generally less enthusiastic.[63] The 27th Division reported that Landwehr veterans from the First World War possessed high morale in spite of their age, but that those who had completed short reserve training courses were dissatisfied and unhappy.[64] One artillery regiment reported that Landwehr personnel were zealous, but their ages (many over 50) and physical condition did not correspond to the demands they would meet in combat.[65] On the other hand the 7th Division noted that reservists and Landwehr personnel mobilized for support tasks did not give a favorable picture of *"Wehrfreudigkeit und Einsatzbereitschaft."*[66] A less serious problem arose because the army allocated uniforms to the reserves in the same proportion of sizes as that for recruits. As a result, 50 to 60 percent of the men did not fit into their uniforms.[67]

While mobilization proceeded in fitful fashion, Bock and his staff journeyed from Dresden to Mühldorf, where they assumed command of the Eighth Army at 22:00 hours on March 11. Intelligence reports emphasized that German soldiers would face little resistance. At 05:30 hours the following morning, German troops crossed into Austria. Almost immediately Eighth Army units ran into difficulty. The 2nd Panzer Division tried to enter Austria through Scharding but discovered

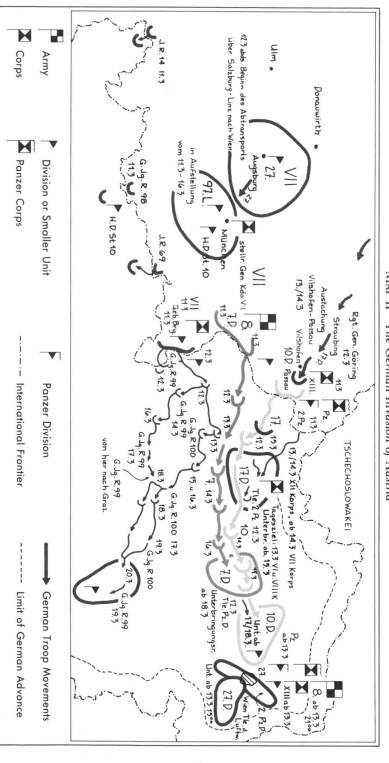

MAP II *The German Invasion of Austria*

Legend:

- ⊞ Army
- ⊠ Corps
- ⊠ Panzer Corps
- ▼ Division or Smaller Unit
- ▼ Panzer Division
- → German Troop Movements
- — — International Frontier
- – – – Limit of German Advance

too late that the bridges there could not support armored vehicles. In response, the division was rerouted through Passau, causing considerable loss of time for both it and the 10th Infantry Division through which the tanks now moved.[68] The resulting traffic jam in Passau completely undermined the operation's schedule. Moreover, the 2nd Panzer Division faced special difficulties because it had completed a two hundred-mile deployment from Würzburg with some units arriving at midnight the previous night. With the primary goal Vienna, Guderian, commander of the panzer corps, hustled his vehicles down the road toward the Austrian capital with orders to arrive by March 13. As the first divisions marched into Austria, Eighth Army headquarters arranged to send the 17th and 27th Infantry Divisions to Vienna by railroad.

The next few days continued in a similar fashion. Within two days much of the panzer corps—2nd Panzer Division, General Göring Regiment, and SS Leibstandarte Adolf Hitler—lay scattered along three hundred kilometers from Straubing (in Bavaria) to St. Pölten (in Austria). March discipline did not come up to expectations, and heavy traffic led to long delays. The fact that Luftwaffe, SS, and police units had not taken part in large-scale troop maneuvers further complicated the movement.[69] These nonarmy forces consistently ignored movement orders, used roads assigned to others, and deployed themselves at areas reserved for the army.[70] Fuel scarcity added to the confusion. The Eighth Army admitted that "the supply of the panzer troops with gasoline was a very difficult proposition; without use of private gas stations, the Panzer Corps would have had to come to a halt by noon on this day. . . ."[71] Bock's final report pointed out that a lack of reconnaissance, faulty march discipline (partly due to poor training of Landwehr and reserve officers), the numerous vehicles clogging official fuel-supply points, and poor traffic control at crossroads created most of the traffic jams.[72]

Foreign observers almost immediately noted that the Germans were experiencing difficulties. The British military attaché reported vehicle breakdowns on the Berlin to Leipzig road.[73] A fellow countryman recorded shortly before the war that numerous tanks and heavy artillery tractors had broken down in Austria and that petrol shortages plagued the whole invasion.[74] Guderian, however, was to claim in his memoirs that traffic jams were infrequent, that few tanks broke down on the road from Linz to Vienna, and that the performance of motorized units did not disturb Hitler.[75] But, as usual, the tank commander was being less than completely honest. In 1942 Hitler recalled that "[o]n the stretch from Linz to Vienna we saw over eighty tanks immobilized by the side of the road—and yet what an easy road it was! Our men hadn't enough experience. A year later we went into Czechoslovakia and nothing of the sort happened."[76] Guderian is not even correct in the claim that his units suffered relatively few breakdowns on the road to Vienna. However, the 25th Panzer Regiment, assigned to VII Army Corps and not to Guderian's panzer corps, suffered the majority of tank breakdowns. This unit was equipped with early model Pzkw I and Pzkw II tanks that by 1938 were in bad mechanical shape. The Eighth Army reported this regiment should not be utilized in combat for reasons of: "Incomplete training. Inadequate peace and wartime armament. Insufficient combat readiness of the mass tanks due to heavy use, faulty replacement parts, and bad maintenance. The latter due to the lack of a local workshop and trained technicians."[77] The 7th Division's evaluation was even harsher: "the tanks of this regiment proved themselves unsuitable for combat and even for propaganda purposes."[78]

In the first three days of the move into Austria lead formations of the Eighth Army—the 7th and 10th Infantry Divisions, and the 2nd Panzer Division—suffered numerous breakdowns of major equipment; approximately 300 vehicles from these three divisions alone became incapacitated within this period of time.[79] These breakdowns also contributed to many of the traffic jams, and infantry columns frequently had to halt to move disabled vehicles.[80]

A lack of march discipline hindered German movements throughout the Austrian operation.[81] This was partly caused by the motorized, nonarmy units that took part in the invasion.[82] Still, the numerous reports on bad march discipline indicate this problem was endemic to the army as well as to SS, police, and Luftwaffe units,[83] and the frequency of accidents supports criticism by higher commanders about the general lack of discipline.[84] The accident rate led Bock to warn that the situation was inexcusable and resulted from careless driving by soldiers who showed an unsoldierly and undisciplined attitude.[85] The XIII Army Corps argued that the cause lay not with drivers but with the failure of NCOs and officers to understand the need for an *"eiserne Fahrdisziplin."*[86]

The discipline problem was not limited to those driving or marching. General Schobert, commanding the VII Army Corps, was so angry with what he considered a cavalier attitude toward orders that he issued a special memorandum to his troops. "I had to remark with surprise, that many leaders apparently could not even read simple clear orders. . . . Without unequivocal, unconditional obedience, no leadership! . . . 'Know-it-alls' and fault-finders are not soldiers! Before Tannenberg many orders were also not understood by the troops. Unconditional obedience, which did not ask why, brought one of the most beautiful of victories."[87]

Nevertheless, the performance of many army units met the Wehrmacht's high standards. The marching ability of infantry matched the performance of the Kaiser's troops. The 10th Division covered 260 kilometers in six days for an average of forty-three kilometers per day. The 2nd Panzer Division's 5th Reconnaissance Battalion covered 680 kilometers from Stuttgart to Vienna in thirty-eight hours, and the 2nd Motorcycle Battalion covered 750 kilometers from Kissingen to Vienna in forty hours. The 7th Motorized Reconnaissance Battalion covered the 600 kilometers from Munich to Vienna in thirty-one hours without accident or breakdown.[88]

Units of the 2nd Panzer Division reached Vienna by morning of March 13, and by nightfall Eighth Army headquarters established itself in Vienna. On the following day the 7th Reconnaissance Battalion (motorized) reached Graz. Most infantry divisions continued the march until they reached assigned deployment areas. The 27th Infantry Division moved to Vienna by rail, and its first units arrived in the Austrian capital on March 13.

On March 14, the Eighth Army held a major parade for Hitler's benefit, consisting of units from the 27th Division, the 2nd Panzer Division, the SS Leibstandarte, and the former Austrian army. Millions of Austrians cheered the parading units and their new führer. On March 17, with euphoria somewhat abated, German troops returned to serious business and resumed training throughout Austria.[89]

THE ANSCHLUSS: THE STRATEGIC RESULT

The joyous, enthusiastic crowds that greeted the führer in his journeys throughout his homeland led Hitler to announce a union between the two German states. In every respect Austria represented a significant addition to the "old" Reich. However, the seizure of Austria did not alter Germany's long-range economic or strategic situation. In effect, Austria represented no more than important short-range help to overcome current difficulties.

In a strategic sense the Anschluss did give the Germans a stranglehold over Czechoslovakia. German territory now surrounded the Bohemian plateau on three sides. Thus, the Czechs were in an impossible strategic situation. There could be no chance of a protracted, strategic defense of the Czech state. The best that the Czechs could hope for was that their defense would be tenacious enough to deny the Germans a quick victory, allowing time for other European states to intervene against the Reich.

Besides the immediate strategic advantage gained against the Czechs, the Anschluss spread German influence into the Balkans. The new greater German state possessed boundaries with Hungary and Yugoslavia and could thus exert more direct pressure on those two nations. The economic advantages of having access to the raw materials of the Balkans were obvious. Finally, Germany now possessed a frontier with Italy. Hitler was profuse in his assurances to Mussolini that Germany regarded the frontier between the two Axis powers as inviolable and that he renounced claims to Alto Adige forever.[90]

The immediate impact of the Anschluss on the German economy was of great importance. Of particular value was the fact that the government, individuals, and banks of Austria possessed considerable reserves of hard currencies. Immediately available from the Austrian Central Bank and other accounts was nearly $200 million in gold and foreign exchange reserves. Moreover, the Anschluss seems to have restored Austrian confidence in the strength of their economy within the expanded Reich. Over the months that followed, substantial sums flowed back from abroad. German estimates placed the inflow of such funds as high as $466 million.[91] Given the Reich's lack of hard currency and its foreign exchange difficulties in 1937, these sums represented a godsend. One authority estimated that the positive financial balance of the Austrian economy could support the raw-material and foreign exchange requirements of German rearmament for at least 1938 and perhaps for the first half of the Four Year Plan.[92]

Austria's high unemployment, coupled with a low rate of industrial utilization, also represented valuable assets—especially considering the fact that Germany had almost exhausted her unemployed rolls and now possessed no ready source to meet increasing manpower needs.[93] Although the process of enlisting these Austrian assets proved no easy task, within a year and a half the Third Reich had realized important economic advantages. By the end of 1939 Austrian factories were turning out Bf 109s, and the Austrian metal industry had contributed 16.3 percent of Germany's refined-steel production for the year. Austrian iron-ore production rose from 1,880,000 tons in 1937 to 2,660,000 tons in 1938 and 2,971,000 tons in 1939. Crude-oil production increased 350 percent from 32,900 to 144,300 tons in the same period. One historian has noted that "[i]n practice the ruthless and successful exploitation of all resources of the land [Austria] for the armament of the Third Reich proved that the military-political expectations that led to March 13 were widely fulfilled."[94]

Yet in the long run, Austria would be a considerable burden to the Third Reich. Outside of iron ore and a rather small amount of oil, she possessed few raw materials to improve overall German deficiencies. As with Germany, Austrian industry had to export in order to earn the foreign exchange necessary to pay for imports. Furthermore, Austria did not produce enough food to feed her own population. Although the Austrian unemployed would be of significant help to the German economy, there were also problems. Many Austrians had been out of work throughout the depression and needed considerable retraining to work in new industries. In addition, Austria possessed little armament industry and, to be fully utilized, Austrian labor would have to move to Germany to work in armament factories.[95] Lastly, the Austrian railroad system was in even worse shape than the German system.[96]

THE MILITARY BENEFITS

The Germans incorporated the Austrian army directly into the Wehrmacht. The OKH ordered the establishment of Heeresgruppen Kommando 5 (Army Group 5) in Vienna, Wehrkreis XVII (military district and corps headquarters) in Vienna, and Wehrkreis XVIII in Salzburg to control the southern and western sections of what was now called the *Ostmark*. They established the 44th Infantry Division in Vienna, the 45th Infantry Division in Linz, the 2nd Mountain Division in

Graz, the 3rd Mountain Division in Innsbruck, and the 4th Light Division in Vienna.[97] All of the above units came from the old Austrian army. The British military attaché estimated that the addition of the Austrian army had increased the peacetime strength of the Wehrmacht by approximately 100,000 regular soldiers.[98] Nevertheless, the Austrian army was considerably lower in quality and overall training than the Wehrmacht, and it would take much time to bring these new units up to the standards of the German army. As late as the following fall, General Ritter von Leeb noted that the difference between German and Austrian units was the difference between day and night.[99] In fact, the Austrian army would not reach the high standards of the Wehrmacht until 1939. Finally, in an overall reorganization of units as a result of the Anschluss the 2nd Panzer Division remained in Vienna to keep an eye on the Austrians.[100]

A drastic purge of the Austrian officer corps accompanied its incorporation into the Wehrmacht. A commission, chaired by a German general, passed on the political reliability of Austrian officers and by the time it had completed its work had removed half of the Austrian generals and colonels from active duty along with 20 percent of the junior officers. Thirty senior officers of the Austrian army soon found themselves in Dachau, and the Gestapo murdered General Wilhelm Zehner, secretary of war in Schuschnigg's cabinet, on the same day that Austrians voted on whether or not they approved of the Anschluss.[101]

In the largest sense, the Anschluss proved an excellent training ground for the Germany army. The mobilization of both regular and reserve units had shown gross deficiencies and inadequate procedures. Manstein records in his memoirs that the mobilization was of great value in pointing out weak areas and that the army was lucky the mobilization had occurred in peacetime.[102] The XIII Army Corps noted in its "after-action" report that military operations in Austria "for commanders, troops, military districts, administrative, matériel, campaign and economic offices, as well as civil and party offices, had brought plenty of experience that would be most instructive and therefore profitable to weigh for future operations."[103]

Overall, the army's reaction to the conduct and success of its move into Austria underlines several important points and indicates why the Wehrmacht would prove consistently superior to its opponents in the first years of the Second World War. First, it was willing to learn from experience. Second, the army high command, within the limited sphere of its military responsibilities, possessed the integrity to recognize that, no matter how successful the Anschluss operation had appeared on the surface, it revealed major deficiencies and weaknesses. This ability to criticize itself ruthlessly would remain a key feature of the German military up to and including the first years of the Second World War. The utilization of the experience gained in the Anschluss was the first stage in a process that would see the German army turn itself into one of the most fearsome instruments in military history. In March 1938 it still had much to learn, but it was on the right path.

CONCLUSION

The Anschluss was Hitler's greatest success up to that time. He had achieved Austria's incorporation within the Third Reich without bloodshed. As a result, the political stability of the Nazi regime was significantly strengthened, and at the same time Hitler was able to divert attention away from the explosive court-martial of Fritsch. When the trial resumed after the Anschluss, it no longer represented a danger. Not only did events in Austria hold the army's attention, but Hitler's achievement seemed one more confirmation that the führer was an extraordinary individual deserving unconditional obedience. Even Fritsch later remarked that Hitler was Germany's fate.

The success reinforced Hitler's high opinion of himself and his self-appointed mission. Although Fritsch and Blomberg had expressed serious doubts the previous fall as to whether the West would allow Germany to move into Eastern Europe, Hitler had achieved the Anschluss with scarcely a protest. The wildly cheering crowds, the whole ambiance of the Blumenkrieg confirmed the führer's growing belief that the Western Powers would react in similar fashion when he tightened the screws on Czechoslovakia. Certainly when he confronted his generals in summer 1938 on the issue of whether or not Germany could invade and destroy Czechoslovakia without facing British and French intervention, he argued with justification that, on almost every key foreign policy issue from the withdrawal from the League to the Anschluss, events had proven him correct and his military advisers wrong.

153

The reaction of the other powers, of course, contributed to Hitler's elation. The British largely ignored the event, while placing the responsibility for Germany's high-handed action on everyone but the deserving. Henderson, in delivering his government's protest, added his own view that it was all Schuschnigg's folly and fault.[104] The reaction of the French, as so often in the midst of a cabinet crisis, was hardly stronger. The Italians, most directly affected by the German move, swallowed the first bitter medicine of the Axis and dreamt of close political cooperation with Yugoslavia.[105]

The seemingly overwhelming approval of the Austrian people that accompanied the German invasion undoubtedly affected the European reaction. It was hard to argue that a great crime had occurred when so many Austrians expressed their joy at the prospect of joining the Third Reich. Schuschnigg had initially thought of resisting the German invasion, and the initial deployment difficulties of the German army suggest that the Austrians might have caused the Germans some trouble. The outcome, however, would never have been in doubt. On the other hand, any Austrian resistance, no matter how brief, would have made it more difficult for other European governments to ignore the nature of Hitler's move. Yet, with a thoroughly divided nation, a weak military position, and no foreign support, it is difficult to fault Schuschnigg for his capitulation to Nazi demands.

V

From Austria to Czechoslovakia

The ruthless, swift annexation of Austria indicated the fundamental unwillingness of the Western Powers to confront the German drive into Eastern Europe. On the whole, the British were the most honest about their lack of interest in the area. After all, they had no alliances or treaty obligations to the states in Eastern Europe. By mid-February, events in Austria had sufficiently disturbed Chamberlain that he expressed doubts as to whether the Berchtesgaden conversations between Hitler and Schuschnigg were the last stop. Moreover, he warned the Cabinet that the consequences of an eventual Anschluss could be worrisome.[1] They were not worrisome enough, however, to prevent the prime minister from proposing two weeks later a wholesale redistribution of African colonies from the Sahara to the former German colony of Southwest Africa—a redistribution that would of course include Germany.[2]

The French understood better Austria's strategic importance. They faced, however, an impossible task in persuading their British colleagues of the danger. On March 2, the French foreign minister asked his ambassador in London to argue that Europe's stability depended on the independence of Austria and Czechoslovakia, and a failure of Britain and France to stand behind Austria would only confirm the Germans in the methods that they had used since 1935.[3] In reality, the French were no more eager to confront the Third Reich. On the day the Austrian crisis exploded, the French prime minister, Camille Chautemps, resigned—a move that Daladier characterized as "running away from office."[4] Thus, as had been the case during the Rhineland crisis, France had no government. Blum's appointment as premier further weakened the West's position. Not only did the Right in France despise the new government, but the British were almost as unhappy. Some within the Foreign Office went so far as to suggest that their government do all in its power to weaken the new regime.[5] Not until April when Daladier replaced Blum did relations between Britain and France return to some semblance of normality.

Neither of the Western Powers had had the will or the inclination to make an issue out of the Anschluss. Czechoslovakia, however, was a different matter, for France had a direct alliance with the Czech state. In March 1938, in response to the Austrian crisis, the British and French governments carefully reviewed the strategic situation and their options, military as well as diplomatic, should a crisis occur over Czechoslavakia. In fact, the Western Powers formulated the policies that they would pursue through to the dismemberment of Czechoslovakia the following September.

On the other side of the hill, the Germans were not yet determined on the immediate course that they should follow after the Anschluss. Not until May did Hitler come down solidly in favor of a military as opposed to a chemical solution to the Czech problem. Although all senior officials in the German government were agreed on the desirability of destroying Czechoslovakia, Hitler's aggressive policy and seemingly firm decision in May to attack the Czechs in the fall sparked perhaps the only serious debate over strategic policy to occur in the annals of the Third Reich. The nature and course as well as the results of that strategic debate make an interesting contrast to the discussions that occurred in the West. As with the Western Powers, Germany in the months after the Anschluss would chart her course toward the diplomatic and strategic confrontation over Czechoslovakia in September.

THE BRITISH RESPONSE

The sudden German invasion of Austria occurred at the same time that the new German foreign minister and former ambassador to the Court of St. James, Joachim von Ribbentrop, was paying his farewell calls in London. From Chamberlain as well as Halifax, Ribbentrop received an earful of criticism for the unilateral manner with which Germany had carried out the Anschluss. Their criticisms, however, made little impact for as usual British leaders were more concerned with Germany's bad form than with the actual event. At a Cabinet meeting on the first day of the German invasion of Austria, Chamberlain admitted that German methods had shocked and distressed the world "as a typical illustration of power politics," while unfortunately making international appeasement more difficult.[6] Whatever initial impression the Anschluss made, it was short-lived. On March 15, Chamberlain told the Foreign Policy Committee that the Anschluss had not caused him to alter his policy—rather the German invasion of Austria had only confirmed that it was the right one.[7]

With the burial of Austria, attention turned toward Czechoslovakia. For the British the real concern about Czechoslovakia was that a military confrontation between the Czechs and Germans would draw the French in and cause a general European war. These worries about the prospect of war led to an enormous flurry of activity in policy-making sectors of the British government in the last half of March. Not only did decision makers draw up important position papers on the strategic situation, but almost continuous meetings of critical committees like the Cabinet, Foreign Policy Committee, and Chiefs of Staff Committee occurred.

On March 16, Chamberlain asked the Chiefs of Staff to examine the general strategic situation should war break out over Czechoslovakia.[8] He did not, however, give his military advisers any latitude in how they examined the balance of power.[9] The prime minister's "terms of reference" are an interesting comment on his Weltanschauung: He automatically assumed Russia to be neutral; gave Poland no role even though the Poles shared a long frontier and a history of bad relations with the Germans; and assumed that the United States would put the neutrality legislation into operation "at the outset" and *would not* provide any significant help. Instead of using either Poland or Russia to counterbalance Germany in the east, he asked that Rumania and Yugoslavia as well as Turkey and Greece be studied as to the help that they could render Czechoslovakia. The "terms of reference" assumed that Britain would fight Germany with the help of only France and Czechoslovakia, although both had alliances with Russia. Moreover, Chamberlain's assumption of Poland's neutrality flew in the face of the fact that Poland and France had a direct alliance that the Poles considered a cornerstone of their foreign policy. Chamberlain did not solicit Foreign Office views on any of these "terms of reference."

The results were a foregone conclusion. The Chiefs of Staff presented a draft on March 21 and their final report on March 28. They admitted the Western Powers possessed overwhelming superiority at sea, although they suggested that Germany's "pocket battleships" were "a serious potential danger" to trade routes. The British army with two divisions would contribute little to the ground war.[10] The chiefs calculated that France could mobilize an army of fifty-three divisions but felt the French economy could only maintain thirty to forty divisions in the field. In Eastern Europe they estimated the Czech army at seventeen infantry and four cavalry divisions.[11] According to the chiefs then, these three powers could barely maintain fifty divisions in the field at the initiation of hostilities. On the other side they assessed Germany as capable of doubling her peacetime army on mobilization, although conscription had only begun in 1935. Supposedly the Wehrmacht possessed eighteen reserve and twenty-four Landwehr divisions. Added to thirty-nine regular divisions and nine [sic] divisions of the old Austrian army, the Germans could field nearly ninety divisions against fifty Allied.[12] The chiefs emphasized that Germany would dominate the air. Quoting an earlier paper, they reiterated that the whole Luftwaffe might concentrate on Britain as the most promising method of winning a war. In addition, they warned that their earlier study had considered a possible air attack in 1939 and that an air offensive in 1938 would cause far more damage because few defensive measures yet existed. Thus, they warned: "[i]n point of fact, the scale of attack which Germany could direct upon us in April this year (1938) is unlikely to be less than 400 tons per day, but, so far from our defense preparations being similarly advanced, they are, in fact, very far from complete. The danger to this country must, therefore be considered as correspondingly greater than we thought it would be when we recorded the above opinion [for 1939]." Finally, they concluded that Germany would not launch a war "unless her responsible statesmen believed that she could win."[13]

Not content with this disagreeable picture, the chiefs proceeded to outline the military situation should Japan and Italy join Germany. Italian armed strength was sufficient "to cause considerable diversion of Allied forces from the main theater and to add immeasurably to our military anxieties."[14] The addition of Japan as well as Italy to Germany would make opposing naval strengths almost equal. The chiefs reached this conclusion by counting three German "pocket battleships" as battleships, by including a German battle cruiser that would not be ready until 1939, and by considering two Italian battleships undergoing major refit.[15] In their summary the chiefs cautioned:

[w]e conclude that no pressure that we and our possible allies can bring to bear, either by sea, on land or in the air could prevent Germany from invading and overrunning Bohemia and from inflicting a decisive defeat on the Czechoslovakian army. We should then be faced with the necessity of undertaking a war against Germany for the purpose of restoring Czechoslovakia's lost integrity and this object would only be achieved by the defeat of Germany and as the outcome of a prolonged struggle. In the world situation today it seems to us. . . . Italy and Japan would seize the opportunity to further their own ends and that in consequence the problem we have to envisage is not that of a limited European war only, but of a World War. On this situation we reported as follows some four months ago:—"Without overlooking the assistance we should hope to obtain from France and possibly other allies, we cannot foresee the time when our defense forces will be strong enough to safeguard our territory, trade and vital interests against Germany, Italy, and Japan simultaneously."[16]

As was the case with so many strategic estimates that the Chiefs of Staff and the Joint Planning Committee provided in 1938, this survey heavily overestimated the military forces of Britain's opponents while it minimized the potential of her friends. The calculations of ground forces reflected such an approach. Not only did the chiefs minimize the mobilized strength of the French army but they also doubted whether the French could maintain even this low estimate. On the other hand they wildly overestimated the strength of the German reserve and Landwehr forces. The naval estimate was no more accurate, and estimates of the German air threat in 1939 were brought forward as having the same validity in 1938—an amazing assumption.

Nevertheless, the weakest element in the analysis lay on the strategic level. The warning that "if Germany could be certain of Italian support, this would appreciably enhance her prospects of a rapid success and still further minimize the deterrent effect of our undertaking" could be considered ridiculous were it not to become the basis of British strategic policy toward Italy through the late thirties. Even more damaging to a balancing of strategic risks was the fact that nowhere in this report did the chiefs consider the implications of abandoning Czechoslovakia without a struggle. In other words, what would the strategic balance be if Britain and France faced Germany in 1939 after the Reich had seized Czechoslovakia, her arms dumps, and the Skoda works? That, of course, was the essence of the Czech problem, but it was a question that British policy makers ignored throughout 1938. Finally, the chiefs failed to recognize that the war in China had so hamstrung the Japanese that there was little chance of Japan's intervention unless her strategic position became endangered.

There was a mild recognition that Germany's economy represented a serious threat to her strategic situation. The government's military advisers admitted that Germany could not face the prospect of a long war with confidence but argued that German control of "Central and East Europe would, as in the Great War, alleviate the economic situation."[17] The analysis, therefore, missed Germany's extraordinary economic weaknesses. As mentioned in Chapter I, Germany possessed almost no stocks of raw materials in 1938, and control of Eastern Europe could not possibly "alleviate the economic situation" as the chiefs suggested. Furthermore, there was an inherent contradiction between the argument that Czechoslovakia could not be defended and the suggestion that only "supremacy in Central and East Europe" would allow Germany to escape the economic consequences of a long war.

The report's effect was immediately discernible. On March 18, Inskip observed to the Committee on Foreign Policy that the chiefs were studying military aspects of the Czech problem, and it seemed Czechoslovakia would fall in less than a week (the chiefs' memorandum had not gone that far). Britain's only means of pressure would be blockade, but that would take at least two to three years before it would seriously hurt the German economy. Halifax added that France would not be able to aid Czechoslovakia effectively, and offensive operations against Germany would be dangerous and formidable. Chamberlain then broke in to comment that the more he studied the map of Central Europe, the more he became convinced it was hopeless to think that Czechoslovakia could receive significant help. However, he ended on the optimistic note that "it would be rash to forecast what Germany would do, but at the same time the seizure of the whole of Czechoslovakia would not be in accordance with Herr Hitler's policy which was to include all Germans in the Reich, but not to include other nationalities."[18]

Two important committees met shortly after completion of the Chiefs of Staff's draft report. The Committee on Foreign Policy met on March 21, and the full Cabinet discussed the report the following day. As already mentioned, Chamberlain had established the strategic criteria for the chiefs. His "terms of reference" had isolated Czechoslovakia against Germany and entirely ignored Poland and Russia as significant factors. Consequently, the chiefs' strategic survey described Czechoslovakia's hopeless situation and emphasized that Britain and France would face serious and possibly impossible difficulties in war against Germany. The prime minister and his supporters now used this report to convince doubters that since military prospects were hopeless the government should make no effort to improve the strategic situation and should avoid a military confrontation at *all* costs. Thus, Britain should not make approaches to either Russia or Poland.

In Cabinet and committee meetings those who raised objections met categorical statements that the chiefs had conclusively proved the hopelessness of Czechoslovakia's strategic position. On March 21 Halifax told Oliver Stanley, president of the Board of Trade, that the Chiefs of Staff believed it was impossible to prevent a German conquest of Czechoslovakia. He added that it "accordingly behooved us to take every step that we could, and to use every argument that we could think of, to dissuade the French from going to the aid of Czechoslovakia."[19]

The Cabinet minutes from March 22 are even more explicit. Halifax began by reading appropriate passages from the chiefs' report on Czechoslovakia. Initially, there was some skepticism—one Cabinet member actually mentioned that the report had not considered Russia in the calculations—but the minutes make clear that doubts appeared less and less frequently as the meeting proceeded:

> The view that was accepted more generally and increasingly as the discussions continued was that the policy proposed by the Foreign Secretary [with the niceties stripped away to tell the French not to honor their commitments to the Czechs] and supported by the Prime Minister was the best available in the circumstances.

Several members of the Cabinet, including the Prime Minister, and the Foreign Secretary, admitted that they had approached the question with a bias in favor of some kind of guarantee to Czechoslovakia, but that the investigation at the Committee on Foreign Policy had changed their views.[20]

Throughout the coming period this report buttressed the arguments of those who felt that England could not and should not support Czechoslovakia.[21]

THE FRENCH RESPONSE

Surprisingly, there was little difference between the British and French strategic view. In fact in some critical areas such as evaluation of land forces, the French military gave an even gloomier prognostication than had their British counterparts. The great difference, of course, between the two nations was the fact that France had alliances with many Eastern European nations, and her frontier with the Third Reich made her considerably less phlegmatic about a collapse in the east.

French concern for the strategic situation in Eastern Europe predated that of the British. On February 8, the secretariat of the National Defense Council reported that the Little Entente's exclusive concern with Hungary meant that Czechoslovakia would have to face German pressure alone. Furthermore, Russia was going through an internal crisis and had fixed her attention on the Far East. As a consequence, help from the Soviet Union would be slow in developing and dependent, moreover, on the attitude of Poland and Rumania since Russia did not border on Germany. If war were to break out, Britain could supply relatively few troops. Military forces of other nations would protect their own territory, so that there would be little to spare against Germany. As a result, only Poland could undertake offensive operations against Germany. In these depressing circumstances the French army would have to defend France and her empire. If Italy entered a war on the side of Germany, French forces could launch attacks across the Alpine and African frontiers. Finally, if possible, the army would attack Germany at an opportune moment. Thus, by February 1938 the French military had decided that there was little it could do to keep the Germans from destroying France's allies in Eastern Europe.[22]

French intelligence reported that Germany could attack Czechoslovakia, defend herself against a Polish attack, and still dispose of sufficient divisions to equal French forces in the west.[23] As early as June 1936, the Deuxième Bureau (French military intelligence) reported a German active and reserve division strength in excess of one hundred divisions.[24]

In early March, an extensive study on European attitudes offered few bright prospects. The French felt Britain would declare war if Germany attacked France and violated Swiss, Belgian, or Dutch territory; would probably declare war if either Germany or Italy or both attacked France without violating neutral territory; and would remain passive if Italy were neutral and France came to the aid of Czechoslovakia in response to a German attack. They accurately concluded that the British were preoccupied with the defense of the British Isles and empire, so that ground support for Europe would be symbolic—at best two infantry divisions. If Italy entered the war, the British would concentrate their forces in the Mediterranean to secure Suez and act against Libya. In Central Europe, Czechoslovakia would defend herself against a German attack and would aid France if Germany struck in the west. The Czechs would have to concentrate the bulk of their forces against Germany and only cover the Hungarian frontier. Their strategy aimed to hold Prague and the narrow neck between Silesia and Austria to prevent German armies from cutting Czechoslovakia in half. Eventually the Czechs would maintain a last-ditch resistance from Moravia and Slovakia. Poland would support France if Germany attacked France directly, but because of Polish-Czech hostility would probably remain neutral if France came to Czechoslovakia's aid. The Soviet Union would honor her obligations if Germany attacked France or France supported Czechoslovakia. However, as the Soviet Union had no common frontier with Germany, its active military support would require that Poland and Rumania allow Russian troops to cross their territory. As these states were hostile to communist ideology, Russian intervention not only risked their support but might actually drive them into the opposing camp.[25] In addition, French intelligence reported the following weaknesses of a Polish army threatened from both east and west: unknown value of the high command, insufficient training of NCOs, antiquated doctrine, insufficient matériel and munitions, and a weak war industry.[26]

On March 14, Gamelin reacted to the Anschluss with more pessimism. He predicted that the Anschluss would have grave consequences if Germany fully exploited the new strategic situation. Germany now almost entirely surrounded Czechoslovakia, and German territorial gains had outflanked Czech fortifications. Offensives from Silesia and Vienna would cut Czechoslovakia in half, and a Hungarian attack on Slovakia would lead to a quick collapse of Czech resistance. Incorporation of the Austrian army into the Wehrmacht would increase German fighting strength from 40 peacetime and 120 wartime divisions to 60 peacetime and 180 wartime divisions (a gross overestimation). Gamelin's report concluded by noting the danger of a conflagration, because success had exhilarated Germany, whereas England was reconstructing her military forces, and French military power possessed considerable weaknesses—especially in the air.[27]

On the following day (March 15) a meeting of the Permanent Defense Council came to the same doleful conclusions. According to Daladier, France could not aid Czechoslovakia directly; the most that she could do would be to mobilize and tie down the maximum number of German troops in the west. Gamelin thought that the army could launch some attacks, but as any offensive would take place in a fortified zone (despite the fact that major construction on the Westwall had not as yet begun), it would take a long time to achieve success. When Blum mentioned Russia, Gamelin discoursed on the problems of getting Soviet troops across Rumania and Poland. General Joseph Vuillemin, chief of the French air force, believed that it would be difficult for the Russian air force to help the Czechs. Finally, Gamelin pointed out that the French army had only 400,000 active duty soldiers, compared to the German total of more than 900,000. As a result, there appeared little that France could do to help Czechoslovakia. It is worth noting that a substantial portion of this meeting was spent discussing the situation in Spain. In fact the minutes suggest that some felt that events in the Spanish Civil War were of greater significance to French security than the threatening situation in Eastern Europe.[28]

On April 6, Gamelin presented the French Cabinet with a breakdown of opposing land forces should France face a German-Italian coalition in the near future. Again he warned that the Austrian venture had accelerated the whole program of German rearmament. Thus, Germany would soon be capable of launching an attack against either

Czechoslovakia or France from a standing start. Czechoslovakia, faced with considerable internal difficulties as well as possible offensives from Austria and German Silesia, no longer represented the serious problem for the German military that she had before the Anschluss. Disunity within the "Little Entente" naturally multiplied German opportunities. In the south Italy could concentrate the bulk of her forces on the Alpine and Tunisian frontiers while leaving weak covering forces on the Yugoslav border. Gamelin did admit that the dictators' political prestige as well as the precarious nature of their financial and economic situation demanded that they seek a quick victory. Specifically, Gamelin stated that in 1939 the Germans would possess 126 divisions while the Italians would mobilize 66 (not counting forces in North Africa). The Axis would dispose of its forces as shown in Table V-1. Thus, Gamelin estimated that France's opponents could concentrate 120 divisions against her and rapidly increase the number to 142 after the destruction of Czechoslovakia. The message was clear: in the immediate future France would confront an overwhelmingly powerful land coalition in a major European war.[29]

The conclusion of the new premier, Daladier, and especially of his

TABLE V-1
1938 French Estimate of German Strength for 1939

Germany:		
Against Czechoslovakia	25	(initially, rapidly
Facing Poland	12	declining to 12)
Facing Yugoslavia	2	
Reserve in the East	9	
	48	(decreasing to 26)
Initially mobilized against France	78	
With divisions transfrd from Czech	13	
Transferred from reserve	9	
Total facing France	100	
Italy:		
Facing Yugoslavia	10	
Defending the Southern Coasts	10	
Over-seas expeditionary force	4	
	24	
Available against France	42	

foreign minister, Georges Bonnet, was that France must not allow events to draw her into a major European war over Czechoslovakia. Therefore, throughout the spring and summer the French cooperated with British efforts to push the Czechs into making significant concessions to the Sudeten Germans before frictions within Czechoslovakia led to a military confrontation. Since France was allied to the Czech state, the French could not easily follow a cold-blooded policy of dumping Czechoslovakia. Accordingly their course over summer 1938 aimed to avoid war and to allow the British to undertake the major initiatives both as a means of entangling Britain in Eastern Europe as well as a convenient cover to escape the implications and responsibilities of their alliance system.

FRANCE AND BRITAIN: THE RESPONSE, APRIL AND MAY

Although Western soldiers and politicians generally depicted the strategic situation in the same bleak colors, Britain and France approached the Czech question from differing points of view. As a result, differences in approach caused considerable friction throughout the summer as the Czech crisis expanded from a local disturbance to a major international confrontation. Complicating relations and causing hard feelings in France was a dogged determination by the British, politicians as well as military, not to initiate substantive staff talks on military cooperation should war occur.[30]

Almost immediately after the Anschluss, the British were eager to get back to dealing with the Germans. On March 12, Chamberlain remarked that at any rate the Austrian "question was now out of the way."[31] By the eighteenth, the prime minister was noting that Hitler had done nothing in the past few days to provoke Britain, and German officials had shown consideration in matters such as exchange facilities and passports for returning British subjects.[32] Alexander Cadogan, permanent undersecretary in the Foreign Office, wrote Henderson in April: "Thank goodness Austria's out of the way. I can't help thinking that we were badly informed about opinion in that country. . . . I can't work up much moral indignation until Hitler interferes with other nationalities."[33] Halifax told the Cabinet he differentiated between "Germany's racial efforts and a lust for conquest on a Napoleonic scale which he did not credit."[34]

From Berlin Henderson continued to assure his government that Germany did not represent a serious threat. Britain, he argued, should recognize Germany's moral right to self-determination, and Germany would fit peacefully into a new European order. On April 17, he wrote Halifax:

> [w]hat is defeatism? Is it to say that war sooner or later between Great Britain and Germany is inevitable? Or is it to say that peace can only be preserved if Germany is allowed to become one of the satisfied angels? I believe the latter, she may never be satisfied but that is the risk we have got to face. I do not mean, when one talks of satisfying Germany, giving her a free hand, but I do mean basing one's policy towards her on moral grounds and not allowing oneself to be influenced by consideration about the balance of power or even the Versailles Treaty. We cannot win the battle for the rule of right versus might unless and until our moral position is unassailable. I feel this very strongly about the Sudeten question.[35]

The British ambassador in Paris, Sir Eric Phipps, fully seconded Henderson's efforts. Phipps gave a clearly prejudiced picture of the French political scene. He based his reports on conversations with defeatists like Joseph Caillaux and Georges Bonnet, rarely discussing the views of those such as Alex Leger, Georges Mandel or Joseph Paul-Boncour, and then only in the most disparaging terms.[36] Moreover, Phipps apparently was willing to intervene directly in French politics against those advocating a strong line.[37]

On April 27, Halifax suggested that the British government adopt the following position: "At the moment the danger to peace lay in Czechoslovakia. On that matter he thought that we ought to be brutally frank and make clear that nothing was to be gained by military action. Having made that solid contribution towards European peace, it was important not to impair the cordiality of the French though it was equally important not to antagonize Germany."[38] One week later Halifax emphasized His Majesty's Government's desire to avoid anything that resembled a commitment to Czechoslovakia. Britain should say to Czechoslovakia that she must go far toward meeting German demands and to Germany that it required two for a settlement. At the end of negotiations, then, Britain could say to Germany that 75 percent of her demands had been met and that it would be folly to wage war for the full 100 hundred percent.[39] There were admittedly strong pressures on the British government to take a soft line. Conservative members of Parliament reported to the Foreign Office the worries of their constituents that the Sudeten-German quarrel would draw Britain into a European war.[40] The dominions were even less eager to support France and Eastern Europe.[41] Nevertheless, although the British government would occasionally refer to popular dominion opinion, Chamberlain by and large cast the direction of his foreign policy with little reference to the state of the public mind.

Nothing underlines more clearly the ambiguities in Anglo-French relations than the inter-governmental meeting in London at the end of April.[42] Not only did the British carefully guide the conversations, but they consistently emphasized their lack of interest in Eastern Europe. The initial phase of the conversations dealt with Spain. Before turning to Czechoslovakia and Eastern Europe, the British brought up the issue of staff talks, but only in terms of conversations between the air staffs. Halifax suggested that Britain's wartime contribution would largely be limited to the sea and the air. Since he ruled out Italian cooperation with Germany, there was no need to begin naval talks. On land Britain could only provide two ill-equipped divisions. There was no mention of staff talks on where these divisions would be used. Daladier and his colleagues were naturally upset and the French premier argued persuasively and logically that the international situation demanded a more detailed examination of strategic policies and possible military cooperation in all fields. The British remained adamant and Chamberlain went so far as to suggest that his government could not even commit its two understrength and underequipped divisions to the defense of France.

Discussions about Czechoslovakia followed a similar direction. The British used all the gloomy advice provided by their military advisers to argue that Czechoslovakia's position was hopeless. Halifax further argued that purges and unrest in Russia made it doubtful whether that country could make a significant military contribution and even whether "she could make any contribution at all." In addition, he dismissed Poland as an uncertain factor. Interestingly, in view of the gloomy analyses of the French military over the past months, Daladier argued that the military situation was not hopeless. The Czech army possessed considerable powers of resistance; it was large, well armed and well equipped, and although the Russian army had suffered considerably in the purges, the Soviet Union still possessed the largest air force in Europe with approximately 5,000 combat aircraft.

In retrospect, there is an explanation for the apparent difference between Daladier's strong statements in London and the pessimistic estimates he had received in Paris. The French premier appears to have hoped that a strong stand in London would enable him to force concessions from the British. Having presented arguments on the importance of Eastern Europe for the security of France, he could then wring a military commitment from Britain should France have to surrender her eastern allies. Such a policy required that the British apply the pressure on Czechoslovakia against the apparent wishes of France. Underlining this aspect of French policy is the fact that Daladier had selected Bonnet, an advocate of appeasement, as foreign minister over the hard-line Joseph Paul-Boncour.[43] In fairness to the French, one must note that since the Ruhr crisis they had felt that British support was essential to France's defense. If France became involved in war over Czechoslovakia and did not receive British backing, her leaders believed the results would be catastrophic: France *must not fight* a war against Germany without British support.

The ministerial discussions led to an innocuous communiqué and the decision that both nations would undertake a simultaneous *démarche* in Prague to pressure Beneš into making significant concessions to the Sudeten Germans. For the French the conversations were eye-opening and depressing. Considering their own estimate of the strategic situation, they must have found British intransigence on staff conversations and military support more upsetting than the British lack of interest in Eastern Europe.

Both governments now proceeded to pressure Czechoslovakia. His Majesty's minister in Prague warned the Czechs in language taken directly from the strategic surveys of the British Chiefs of Staff that Czechoslovakia's position was hopeless and only a protracted war would lead to restoration of the Czech state. Moreover, he added, it was doubtful whether Czechoslovakia would reappear in its present form after such a war.[44] The French were more circumspect in what they told their allies, but the message was clear: France regarded her relations with Britain as paramount.[45]

It is worth noting that not all within the British policy-making structure were happy with the government's course. In late May the advocates of a stronger policy in the Foreign Office persuaded Halifax to present a forceful memorandum to the Cabinet. In it they warned that if Germany gained control of Southeast Europe, the Reich would be well on the way to gaining hegemony over the continent. They then asked: "Are we prepared to stand by and allow these vast districts to pass completely under German domination? . . . This process if it were allowed to continue would mean that Central and South-East Europe would tend to become to Germany what . . . the Dominions are to the United Kingdom. One of the main differences would be perhaps to the advantage of Germany, namely that the area would be a geographically compact one."[46] Strategically such an eventuality could satisfy Germany's raw material and foodstuff needs, strengthen her economy, and allow her to dominate Central and Southeastern Europe. If war broke out, Germany would be able to rely on most, if not all, of these nations. Not only British traditions, but British self-interest argued against such a state of affairs.

Chamberlain's response underlined the basic drift of his policy. He assailed the assumptions at the heart of the argument: first, that these areas would fall under German control; and second, that Britain could prevent this from happening. The prime minister denounced both points and doubted whether the strengthening of Germany's economy would be a bad thing. A better economic situation might result in fewer political adventures. The Foreign Policy Committee whole-heartedly echoed the prime minister's sentiments, with Inskip and Simon once again dragging out the Chiefs of Staff's March report. Halifax wilted under the assault and admitted that the memorandum had been ill-conceived.[47]

GERMANY AND CZECHOSLOVAKIA

The weak reaction of Britain and France to the Anschluss did not escape Hitler's notice. In fact, their response fully confirmed his impression that the West would not stand behind the Eastern European nations.[48] What had only been an impression before Austria now became a firm conviction to which Hitler would hold until the last days of September. Although Hitler did not seek an immediate confrontation with Czechoslovakia, certainly the Czechs were much on his mind.

Even before political tensions increased, the Germans initiated preparations for a possible military confrontation with Czechoslovakia. As early as March 28, the OKW began work on extending the road networks and strengthening the bridges in northern and northeastern Austria to facilitate movement of large military vehicles up to the former Austro-Czech frontier.[49] In April, work was well under way for new deployment orders against Czechoslovakia that would exploit the Austrian territory now available to the Wehrmacht.[50] By mid-May, the OKW had completed a new *Fall Grün* directive for Hitler's signature. The covering page included the interesting statement that "it is not my intention to crush Czechoslovakia militarily in the immediate future." However, Hitler added that developments in Czechoslovakia or a favorable situation in Europe might make an early move against the Czechs possible.[51]

In mid-May Hitler journeyed to Rome to reconfirm the special relationship between the two fascist powers. He seems to have undertaken the journey particularly to sound out Mussolini on Italy's willingness to pursue an aggressive, expansionist foreign policy. Were the Italians satisfied with just expansion in Ethiopia, then the Czech question might have to be shelved for the present. Hitler, however, discovered that Mussolini's ambitions rivaled his own, and with Italian support the führer believed that Britain and France would not dare to fight.[52] Thus, there is a direct connection between Germany's aggressive policy over the summer and the support that Hitler received from Mussolini during the May visit. Basking in the glow of his Rome triumph, Hitler returned to Berlin to face a crisis that for one of the few times in the 1930s did not result from German actions. The führer molded his response to unfolding events with Italian support much in mind. Hitler's desire for Italian support is somewhat surprising in light of German military estimates about the considerable weaknesses of Italy's military forces. It seems, though, that Hitler never fully accepted the cold, rational staff judgments of Italian capabilities; the ideological affinity between Nazism and Fascism led him into self-deception and an overestimation of Italian military competence. Not until the fall of 1940 was he to be fully disabused of the notion that fascist Italy could offer significant help to the German effort.

Hitler's return to Germany was followed almost immediately by a major diplomatic crisis. Alarmed perhaps by intelligence information that the Germans were now rapidly preparing for military operations and misinterpreting the redistribution of military forces after the Anschluss, the Czechs felt they faced a direct challenge. In response they mobilized a portion of their reserves and occupied the frontier districts. That latter action immediately improved their military situation; whether it improved their overall situation is another matter. Nevertheless, fearing that Germany was about to move against Czechoslovakia, both Britain and France warned the Germans against taking precipitous action such as they had taken against Austria.

The May crisis was a critical factor in pushing Hitler toward a military confrontation over Czechoslovakia. This should not suggest that he was not already moving in that direction, nor, as we have suggested above, can one ignore the Rome visit. Nevertheless, the Czech mobilization enraged the führer. It angered him for two reasons: the Czech mobilization made it easier for them to maintain order in the Sudeten districts during local elections, and it allowed them to occupy their fortifications in some strength. As a result, the Germans could not seize the Czech fortifications by a surprise attack—something that Hitler was already turning to in mid-May.[53]

The impression of strength that the initial Anglo-French reaction to the crisis had given was misleading. Beneath the exterior of stern warnings to Berlin, the British and French felt that they had been on the brink of war, and they determined not to allow the Czech problem to explode into another crisis. On May 22, two days after the crisis had broken, Halifax ordered Phipps to warn the French that Britain's attitude toward Czechoslovakia had not undergone a change of heart.[54] Within a week, the Foreign Office sounded out its embassy in Prague on the advisability of a plebiscite in the Sudetenland and a neutralization of Czechoslovakia.[55] The French were equally concerned. Bonnet expressed to the German ambassador in Paris "the thanks of the French government for the dignified calm and the restraint that the Germans had shown" during the crisis.[56] Yet even among the appeasers there remained a lack of understanding as to what had occurred. At the end of July, Halifax told the Cabinet that the war party in Germany had received a setback during the May crisis.[57]

German perceptions were, of course, quite different. The prospect of war had not frightened Hitler; he just was not prepared for war at that precise moment. He was, however, furious at what he regarded as a blow to Nazi prestige. Suggestions in the Western press of a "diplomatic victory" for the Western Powers further intensified his anger.[58] Nine days after the Czech mobilization, Hitler signed a new directive for *Fall Grün* with several significant changes from the May 20 version. The covering letter to the directive, signed by Keitel, demanded the completion of preparations for an invasion of Czechoslovakia by October 1. The preamble now ominously read: "[i]t is my unalterable decision to smash Czechoslovakia by military action in the near future."[59]

On the same date that the OKW issued the new *Fall Grün* directive, Major Rudolf Schmundt, Hitler's chief military aide, noted the führer's demand that construction work on the Westwall move forward with all possible speed.[60] The decision to begin massive construction of fortifications on the Franco-German frontier underlines Hitler's desire to frighten the French out of honoring their alliance with Czechoslovakia. In June the Germans also began major projects to increase production in certain strategically critical sectors of the economy, such as the synthetic fuels, light metals, and munitions industries. Moreover, as a result of the May crisis Hitler finally seems to have concluded that a collision with Britain was inevitable. On May 29 Hitler discussed with Raeder a program to build the navy up to a level where it could challenge the British at some future date.[61] As such naval measures were long-term projects, they, of course, did not contribute to planning for military operations in the fall against Czechoslovakia. They do indicate, however, the future direction of German policy.

For the time being in 1938, Hitler believed that he could isolate Czechoslovakia and wage a limited war. He envisaged a campaign that by its suddenness would smash Czechoslovakia and present the West with a fait accompli. A quick victory, Hitler felt, would insure that war would not spread.[62] Both of the *Fall Grün* directives stressed the decisive nature of the first few days—the directive of May 20, the first four days of the campaign; the directive of May 30, the first two to three days. Within this period German successes had to be on a scale to discourage Western intervention because of the hopelessness of the Czech situation, while encouraging Poland and Hungary to join the attack.[63] What Hitler's directives did not spell out was how the Wehrmacht was to accomplish this task. The reaction of a significant body of senior officers within the German military to Hitler's scenario and to the prospect of war in 1938 underlines both the weaknesses of Germany's strategic position as well as the doubts in the German high command as to how such a war could be waged.

THE GENERAL STAFF'S APPRECIATION

Leading those in the German military who had serious qualms about the Reich's strategic position was the Chief of the General Staff, Ludwig Beck. As early as the end of April, Beck had become alarmed at Hitler's aggressive foreign policy, and from May until his resignation in August, he pressed the argument that Germany was not prepared to face a military conflict of any sort.[64] Furthermore, Beck took issue with the basic assumption of Hitler's diplomacy and strategy: that Britain and France would not fight if war broke out over Czechoslovakia.

In their general tone Beck's memoranda possess striking similarities in style and approach, if not in content, to British and French papers written at the same time. As with Western military analysts, he based his studies on a "worst case" analysis. He depicted the European situation in gloomy terms for Germany. Thus, Beck's Europe bears little resemblance to the Europe described by British and French military planners. Neither picture was entirely accurate, but in retrospect Beck's analyses seem closer to reality.[65]

Beck's first strategic evaluation, dated May 5, discussed three aspects of the strategic situation: the international balance, the military position of the West, and Germany's military situation.[66] Unlike British experts, Beck recognized the advantages of Britain's position as a world power. He saw no possibility that Japan and Italy would act in concert with Germany in a world war. The Sino-Japanese War and its resulting drain on Japanese resources eliminated that threat to Britain's position in the Far East. Once again Britain and France had initiated staff conversations and, as in the First World War, both would act together in any European military confrontation. Germany would have to consider Russia an enemy in any war. Although Rumania, Yugoslavia, and Poland might initially adopt a tentative attitude, they would intervene on the Allied side if the war should last or go against Germany.

Turning to the strategy of the Western Powers, Beck believed that

England would seek to prevent the outbreak of war in Central Europe. Nevertheless, the Sino-Japanese War and lessening tensions in the Mediterranean now made it easier for Britain to devote full attention to Europe. The English, Beck felt, understood that German rearmament was not complete and that the German economy was in serious trouble. He argued that Britain had undergone a decided change in her attitude toward Germany in February and March 1938. He recognized that France did not desire war, but that there were limits beyond which even the French would not permit Germany to go. Some circles in France, he argued, already regarded the Anschluss as another Sadowa. Moreover, Beck believed the French army was still the best in Europe. Czechoslovakia would be a point of honor for France, and should France come to Czechoslovakia's defense, England would follow suit.

As for Allied strategy, Beck believed that Britain and France would pursue a limited war, at least on the ground. There might be a restricted offensive into the Rhineland, but for the most part, the Western Powers would be content to wage war by air and sea. Admittedly, such an approach would not immediately help the Czechs, but as with Serbia in the First World War, the war's outcome would determine Czechoslovakia's final fate. Beck had no doubts as to who would win. Germany's military position had improved over that of the 1920s and early 1930s but was not equal to that of 1914. The Reich had neither the economic nor military base to fight a major war, much less a world war, with any prospect of success. The German economic situation was bad—worse, Beck argued, than in 1917-1918. The Czech problem could not be solved without the agreement of Britain and France, and there seemed little chance they would allow Germany a free hand in Czechoslovakia. Beck thought that if Germany attempted to force a solution against Britain's will, the Reich would face a coalition of overwhelming strength—France, Britain, and Russia. America would certainly support these powers economically. In addition, once England had turned against Germany, the smaller powers would follow, whether from inclination or necessity.

Beck's memorandum of May 5 indicates the basic approach he would use in other position papers written in the summer of 1938. On May 29, one day after Hitler's "unalterable decision" to smash Czechoslovakia in the autumn, he completed another study.[67] His argument was similar to that of May 5 and directly contradicted Hitler's assumption that Germany could stage a limited war against Czechoslovakia. Beck stressed that Germany could not yet wage war on Britain and France. The Czech army was a serious military factor, and as a result the Wehrmacht could not overrun Bohemia and Moravia quickly. Beck thought that destruction of the Czech army would require at least three weeks and perhaps more. Should, as was probable, Britain and France intervene, the outcome of the war would not depend on the first clash of arms, but on a whole series of factors over which Germany had no control. Time and space, as well as Allied superiority in men and material, would work against Germany and Britain's great prestige would affect the attitudes of the neutral powers.

Beck's evaluations of the overall strategic situation are an interesting contrast to the British and French studies discussed at the beginning of this chapter. Beck made, of course, faulty judgements, particularly in the realm of high policy. His belief that Britain and France recognized the importance of Czechoslovakia was wrong. In fact, both Hitler and Beck misjudged Western policy; if Germany had attacked Czechoslovakia, then Beck was probably correct in his estimation that Britain and France would declare war on Germany. But Beck failed to see that the Western Powers would be so foolish as to deliver the Czechs to the Reich without a struggle. On the other hand, Hitler's actions over summer 1938 indicate that the führer believed he could get away with a military invasion of Czechoslovakia without Western intervention. On other aspects of the military situation, Beck was close to the mark in his evaluation of Germany's strategic position. As we shall see in succeeding chapters, Germany's economic, strategic, and diplomatic situations were at best precarious. In 1938 the Third Reich presented the world with an imposing facade of military and political power. However, the reality behind that facade contained great weaknesses.

The strategic assessments by the major European powers in response to the Anschluss underline one of the major factors involved in the 1938 crisis. Not one of the major powers was prepared to face the prospect of a major war. All confronted considerable difficulties and strategic deficiencies, and the military forces of Germany did not possess the striking or the staying power for a long conflict. Notwithstanding, Hitler was pushing the Czech problem into a direct military confrontation in a belief that the other European nations, in particular the Western Powers, would allow him a "short" war against Czechoslovakia. Ironically, the more the British urged a diplomatic settlement of the Czech problem, the surer Hitler became that he could get away with a short, brutal attack on Czechoslovakia.

In the period between the Anschluss and the end of May, the strategic and diplomatic policies of the powers crystallized. For the British, Chamberlain's "best case" analysis of German motivation combined with the "worst case" analysis of his strategic advisers to set British diplomacy on the road to appeasement and Munich. On the other side of the Channel, the French were more realistic about the nature of the German danger, but their unwillingness to follow an independent foreign policy and their belief in the necessity of British support as a sine qua non effectively hamstrung their policy. They, too, received the most dismal and gloomy assessments of the strategic situation and German might from their military.

For the rest of Europe, the increasing pressure on Czechoslovakia was most distressing but there appeared little that could be done. Poland's view was hopelessly clouded by an overestimation of her own power. With no frontier with either Czechoslovakia or Germany the Russians were undoubtedly more worried that the Western Powers were encouraging the Germans to move east against the Soviet Union than about the possibility of war over Czechoslovakia.[68]

THE EXPLODING CRISIS: GERMAN POLICY, SUMMER 1938

In June 1938 the pace of German military planning quickened. At the beginning of the month Hitler requested information on key questions such as the progress of fortifications in the west and Czech military equipment.[69] Initially, German planners proposed a surprise attack on Czechoslovakia in order to break through her fortifications before the Czech army could occupy them in strength. The bulk of the Wehrmacht would then deploy to the east to complete the military conquest, while a screening force remained in the west. German strategy also aimed at preventing the Czechs from retreating into Slovakia. As summer continued, the Czech army demobilized those called up in May but discreetly mobilized other reservists to serve in the fortified zones. This decision insured that the Czechs could hold the fortifications against a surprise attack and allow time for reserves to mobilize. Even the British recognized the importance of the fortifications and gave tacit approval for the manning of fortified districts, although Henderson in Berlin opposed such support as provocative.[70] Through most of the summer Czech regular units remained on a war footing.[71]

Occupation of the fortified districts changed the tactical problem for the Germans, making it more difficult to achieve a quick and decisive victory. As a result, German planners turned from a surprise attack to a phased mobilization that would gradually bring the Wehrmacht to a wartime footing by the end of September. Beginning in September, units designated for the invasion would participate in maneuvers designed to simulate the coming offensive.[72] Then, at the end of the month, the army would move to its final jump-off positions and invade Czechoslovakia. The summer maneuvers fit German plans fortuitously, for on May 20 the OKH had ordered training to emphasize attacks against fortifications.[73]

In early June the general staff carried out a *Generalstabsreise* to study ramifications of war with Czechoslovakia. At the evaluation afterward, Beck indicated that Germany would have little difficulty in crushing Czechoslovakia, but, he thought, within this period France would intervene. With western Germany denuded of troops for the invasion of Bohemia, the French could push into the Rhineland and perhaps even over the Rhine.[74]

Beck's campaign against a military adventure received little support from Brauchitsch. In July the new commander in chief wrote to General Wilhelm Adam, commander of forces in the west, that creation of a favorable situation for mobilization was a political task.[75] Since politics were not his responsibility, Brauchitsch offered only nominal opposition in spite of evidence that Hitler was pushing Germany toward a war she was not prepared to fight economically, militarily, or politically. Ulrich von Hassel, former ambassador to Rome, noted in late summer that when presented with evidence on German weaknesses Brauchitsch hitched his collar up a notch and remarked, "I am a soldier; it is my duty to obey."[76]

By mid-July Beck had become convinced that his studies had had little effect. Nevertheless, he wrote one last statement, dated July 15, which once again argued that *Fall Grün* would lead to a major European war that the German people did not want and that could only end in catastrophe.[77] Victory over Czechoslovakia would not come before France had intervened, and the western front would then collapse. Beck argued that only Germany's military leaders could prevent disaster by presenting a united front against war.

Two important members of the naval staff were thinking along similar lines. Captain Hellmuth Heye of the Seekriegsleitung noted that it was common knowledge Germany intended to invade Czechoslovakia in the fall. Thus, the Czechs had clear warning of what was coming. England, Heye admitted, was doing everything possible to prevent a military confrontation, but present British diplomacy would make intervention more likely if Germany were responsible for war. Heye then argued that the prevailing attitude in Europe was strongly anti-German. This sentiment was not so much due to pro-Czech feeling as to antipathy toward Germany, her treatment of the Jews, and her handling of church questions. Substantial numbers of Europeans regarded Germany as another Soviet Russia, but more of a threat because of her aggressive instincts. They abhorred Nazi political methods. As a result Germany was the most disliked nation in Europe. Heye warned that an invasion of Czechoslovakia would have the same effect as the invasion of Belgium in 1914, except that in 1914 the invasion had called forth anti-German hostility, whereas in 1938 that attitude was already present. Britain and France, and possibly also the United States and Russia, would use an attack on Czechoslovakia as an excuse to settle the German problem permanently. Neutrals who feared Germany and considered themselves future targets of Nazi aggression would pursue a pro-English policy. "In this situation a war against England and France means, militarily speaking, a lost war for Germany with all its consequences." British and French statesmen would have no difficulty in persuading their nations to intervene. Therefore, Heye suggested "that it is the duty of the military to speak their judgment even of the most unfavorable situation for the political leadership, so that that leadership recognizes the extent of their responsibility and does not make decisions based on incomplete reports."[78]

Within a few days of Heye's memorandum, Admiral Günther Guse, also of the Seekriegsleitung, completed a short study on the strategic situation. Guse argued that preparations for the invasion of Czechoslovakia were such common knowledge that surprise was now impossible, and that even if the invasion succeeded, Germany could not count on a speedy victory. Hitler, however, still held the fate of Europe in his hands and a pacific speech would prove Germany's good intentions. Most officers in the Wehrmacht, Guse observed, believed that an invasion of Czechoslovakia would cause a major war. Although it was doubtful that Göring would bring his influence to bear, the commanders in chief of the army and navy should warn Hitler, with all the weight and prestige of their positions, as to how dangerous the situation had become.[79]

Shortly after presenting his last memorandum, Beck urged Brauchitsch to gain the cooperation of leading figures in the Reich for a general housecleaning. Beck did not propose to overthrow the regime, but rather suggested that the better, more responsible party leaders with military assistance should eliminate SS and party radicals, restore justice, and establish Prussian standards in government. Hitler would remain as head of state. Beck received no cooperation from Brauchitsch. Admittedly, the scheme was most unrealistic.[80]

On August 4, the OKH ordered leading generals to Berlin, ostensibly to discuss plans for invading Czechoslovakia. Actually, Brauchitsch was to deliver a speech prepared by Beck on the dangerous military situation. At the last moment, however, the commander in chief backed away, although he did allow Beck to read from his July 15 memorandum. Except for two avowedly pro-Nazi generals the consensus was that Germany would face quick defeat in case of Western intervention.[81] Adam, selected to lead German forces against the French, characterized an invasion of Czechoslovakia as a "war of desperation" and argued that Germany's strategic position in the west was almost hopeless. The Westwall offered no serious obstacle and with the Wehrmacht concentrated against Czechoslovakia, the forces assigned for the defense of the western frontier consisted of only five regular and four reserve divisions. Adam concluded by warning, "I paint a black picture, but it is the truth."[82] Though Kluge did suggest that if Hitler pushed things to the brink the generals should all resign, most senior officers despite their seeming agreement on the seriousness of the strategic situation were unwilling to make even a symbolic gesture.[83] At the end of July, Manstein, now a division commander, wrote a long letter to Beck urging the chief of staff to remain at his post. Manstein's letter is a revealing comment on weaknesses in the officer corps' opposition to war. Manstein had no doubt that the Wehrmacht would overwhelm the Czechs. On the larger issue as to whether the West would intervene, Manstein argued that final responsibility was Hitler's. The military should attempt to avoid such an eventuality and make clear the risks. And, added Manstein, "Hitler has so far always estimated the political situation correctly."[84] Interestingly, Manstein spent much of the letter arguing that the OKH insure that the OKW did not supplant the army's traditional role as the chief strategic adviser to the government. Manstein's refusal to face the critical issues that had led to Beck's confrontation suggests why so large a part of the Generalität refused to consider taking action against Hitler's drive for war.

Adding to the ambivalence of those generals who were doubtful about the course of Hitler's policy of confrontation but unwilling to support Beck's open break were several factors. First was the information provided by the military attachés in Paris and London that the Western Powers were most unwilling to engage the Third Reich in a war. Second, and of greater importance, intelligence evaluators in the general staff cast considerable doubt on how quickly the French would be able or willing to launch an attack on Germany's western frontier. Moreover, the general staff map exercise in June indicated that the war against Czechoslovakia could be a relatively quick affair. The study suggested that by the twelfth day the German forces would have broken the back of the Czech army. Within seven days the Germans could begin withdrawing the first units from the front for transfer to the west.[85] Nevertheless, although such indications cast a more favorable light on the specific military problem of the first days of a conflict with Czechoslovakia, in no manner did they contradict Beck's fundamental argument that Germany's strategic and economic position rendered her incapable of fighting a prolonged war.

As it became clear that Hitler was pushing for a major military confrontation, worry over the prospect of war rose in other circles. Throughout the summer, the state secretary in the Foreign Ministry, Ernst von Weizsäcker, attempted to convince Ribbentrop that a military invasion of Czechoslovakia would be folly. It would involve the Western Powers and the Soviet Union, whereas Germany would have no allies. On June 8, Weizsäcker argued that, although France was Germany's most implacable enemy, England was her "most dangerous foe." Should a conflict develop, Germany would face both or neither. In a major war Germany would find Russia and the United States associated with Britain and France. Such a constellation of power required Germany to avoid conflict with the West. Even in Eastern Europe the Reich could achieve its goals only with the sufferance of these powers. Blocking the West (through construction of the Westwall) and conquest in the East would not decide the issue. To win, Germany must dictate peace in London and Paris and she lacked the military means to do it. Germany could only inflict superficial damage on Britain. Even with Japanese and Italian help she could not strike the heart of the British Empire. Weizsäcker believed that the Rome-Berlin-Tokyo Axis could serve as a preventive measure but lacked the necessary power to deter. He did think that the West had no real interest in Czechoslovakia, yet that Germany must proceed with care. The Czech situation was not ripe for a surprise attack. Any such action would bring Western intervention. The Germans could only hope that through diplomatic pressure and claims for self-determination they could gain the Sudetenland and dissolve the Czech state. It would have to be a gradual, long-term project.[86]

Weizsäcker's arguments had no success. Attuned to what Hitler wished to hear, Ribbentrop pressed for war on Czechoslovakia and assured the führer that the West would not intervene.[87] In early August the foreign minister cabled his embassies that the German nation would rise to a man in the event of war. Germany was militarily better prepared than ever; the Westwall was almost completed; and Czechoslovakia represented no serious problem.[88] Urged on by such support, Hitler pursued his dream of a military confrontation.

As a result relations between Hitler and the army went from bad to worse. If Hitler found Fritsch opposed to Nazi influence in the army, he had at least respected Fritsch. The führer had almost no respect for the new commander in chief. He launched a series of reproaches, outbursts, and accusations at the army both for its conservatism in rearmament and for its opposition to a limited war with Czechoslovakia. As early as May 22 Hitler told his army adjutant that although he respected Beck for his role in the Ulm trials,[89] the chief of staff's point of view was that of an officer in the 100,000-man Reichswehr.[90] In mid-June, Hitler's adjutant Gerhard Engel noted that a conference between Hitler and Brauchitsch had been most unsatisfactory. Hitler had characterized the officer corps as reactionary and denounced the army ordnance authorities for their incompetent development of the 210mm howitzer and armament for the new Pzkw IV tank.[91]

Sometime during mid-July Brauchitsch and Keitel showed Hitler the last half of Beck's May 5 memorandum.[92] The chief of staff's comments infuriated the führer who expressed special contempt for its estimates of French superiority in ground forces. He characterized Beck's comparison as *"kindische Kräfteberechnungen"* (childish calculations) and announced that he would make his own calculations, including SS, SA, and police formations, and then "hold it in front of the noses of the gentlemen" responsible for such estimates.[93] On July 24, Hitler discussed Beck's memorandum with Brauchitsch and, as Engel remarks, put the commander in chief completely on the defensive. Hitler also criticized the army's armament program and calmed down only after Brauchitsch complained that the army was not getting the steel it required.[94]

By August Hitler was well aware that preparations for war had aroused widespread opposition. Brauchitsch screwed up enough courage to show the führer Beck's July 15 study and to inform him that it had been read to an assemblage of senior generals.[95] Hitler responded by appealing to the younger generals. On August 10, before senior army and Luftwaffe staff officers, Hitler lectured for three hours on his military and foreign policy.[96] He refuted Beck's depiction of the international situation and claimed that England's state of disarmament and France's internal difficulties made it doubtful that those powers would intervene to save Czechoslovakia.[97] The purges had removed Russia as a military factor, and Poland, moreover, would never allow Russian troops to cross her territory to aid Czechoslovakia. That afternoon a question period took place, during which a major row erupted over the condition of the Westwall. General Alfred Jodl, head of the OKW's Führungsstab, was as disappointed as Hitler in the reaction to the führer's speech. He blamed the lack of faith on the general staff's failure to limit itself to military matters. Fundamentally, Jodl thought, senior generals did not believe in the führer's genius. He feared that their defeatism not only might have political consequences, but could endanger troop morale as well.[98] By the end of August the OKW was debating the timing for a staged incident to justify the coming invasion. Jodl noted that the moment picked for the incident was of critical importance to maximize the effect of a surprise attack.[99]

As the summer passed, Beck had become increasingly isolated. The aversion of almost all senior generals to confronting Hitler, as well as Brauchitsch's lack of support, led him to the conclusion that his position was untenable. He resigned as chief of the general staff on August 18 and took his leave on August 27. Hitler and Brauchitsch immediately accepted his resignation, although Hitler insisted on no public announcement until after resolution of the crisis. Due to a misplaced sense of patriotism, Beck agreed to this arrangement. It emasculated whatever protest value his resignation might have had.[100]

Halder replaced Beck as chief of the general staff. Hitler appears to have had a good initial impression of Halder. As early as May he had remarked that as Halder was a modern general, he would be easier to work with than Beck. On August 20, he told his army adjutant that he trusted Halder because as a Bavarian he was more receptive to National Socialism than a member of the Prussian officer corps would be.[101]

By summer 1938 Hitler was well on the way to a direct confrontation with a significant number of his generals. Although his opponents certainly accepted the proposition that the existence of Czechoslovakia was "unbearable,"[102] they could not accept his argument that Germany could avoid the detrimental consequences of an invasion of Czechoslovakia. Faced with opposition, Hitler exploded: "what do I have for generals, when I as chief of state must drive them to war? . . . I demand not that my generals understand my orders, but that they obey them."[103] On the other hand, and equally frustrating to Hitler, was the fact that the Western Powers, particularly the British, were involving themselves increasingly in Czech affairs. In May the German ambassador in London made Hitler's position clear to Halifax. Germany did not wish to join negotiations over the Sudeten question and would not guarantee the results.[104] Unfortunately for the führer this message had not discouraged the British from seeking a peaceful, negotiated settlement to what from the German point of view was an insoluble problem. British interference made it more difficult for the Germans to pretend that the crisis was entirely the fault of a Czech government that refused to deal with the Sudeten Germans.

THE BRITISH RESPONSE: SUMMER 1938

Over the summer the British and French governments sought to escape an increasingly dangerous situation. Because they were allied to Czechoslovakia, the French generally seconded British actions. The Chamberlain government initially believed in the viability of a solution to the crisis within the framework of the Czech state. A June paper drawn up for the Committee on Foreign Policy strongly attacked a *Times* proposal suggesting that the Sudeten Germans choose their future through a plebiscite. The Foreign Office argued that a separation of Czechoslovakia into ethnic parts would destroy the state.[105]

If the British hesitated on the subject of a plebiscite, they showed no reluctance in pushing for the neutralization of Czechoslovakia. On June 1, Halifax suggested to Czech ambassador Jan Masaryk that a declaration of neutrality by his government might end German hostility.[106] The real benefit in British eyes to such an arrangement would have been the end of the Franco-Czech alliance. In early June Halifax telegraphed Phipps that Czech neutrality, the "readjustment of Czechoslovakia's external relations," would reduce the provocative elements in Czech foreign policy and "should tend to promote stability in Central Europe and lessen the chances of France being called upon to fulfil her obligation to Czechoslovakia in possibly unfavorable circumstances."[107] On June 16, Halifax told the Committee on Foreign Policy that as long as France remained allied to Czechoslovakia she would face the dilemma of "dishonor or war." He thought that France would not be sorry to be relieved of "the fear of having to fulfil an obligation in regard to Czechoslovakia."[108] Throughout the summer Henderson pressed for abrogation of the Soviet-Czech alliance and reported that the Germans would regard such an action "as an earnest of sincere neutralization, and [it] would constitute such a success for Herr Hitler that he could probably afford to waive any claim for the total severance of Czechoslovakia's ties with France."[109] The strategic naïveté of such attitudes needs little emphasis.

Because negotiations between the Czechs and Sudeten Germans were at an impasse, the British pressed a supposedly neutral mediator on Prague: the choice, Lord Runciman, was a man thoroughly ignorant of diplomatic and military affairs as well as of Eastern Europe. The British government, moreover, disowned responsibility for the mission because of fear that the mediated solution might not be acceptable to Berlin.[110] Runciman himself accurately characterized his position as being put out "in a dinghy in mid-Atlantic."[111] Given the fact that the Sudeten-German party was a front manipulated by the Nazis, there was, of course, no chance of achieving a mediated solution to Czech-German differences.[112]

In early summer the British believed that Germany was not fully prepared for war and thus would not resort to a military solution to the Sudeten problem. They received confirmation from German sources not only of German unpreparedness but also of growing opposition in the Reich to Hitler's policy of military confrontation. On returning from a visit to Berlin and Prague a Foreign Office observer reported that the German army was urging a prudent course because of its weaknesses. He also pointed out that the Germans were not so conscious of Britain's weaknesses as were the British, but rather were more concerned with their own difficulties.[113] General Kurt von Tippelskirch, head of the OKH attaché group, observed to the British military attaché "how unreasonable it was to imagine that from the military point of view Germany should wish to risk a general conflagration at the present moment."[114] Even Henderson reported in August that one officer had expressed the hope that Germany would be let down lightly if as a result of war the army overthrew the Nazi regime. He further added that Admiral Canaris was "very outspoken against war."[115]

Nevertheless, in July the Joint Planning Committee produced another pessimistic analysis of the strategic situation. The committee warned that, although Britain might have the diplomatic and political initiative, the military initiative lay in German hands. The report greatly exaggerated the Wehrmacht's capacity to expand on the outbreak of war and estimated that Germany could field seventy-five divisions along with thirty-six Landwehr divisions.[116]

By late July the first indications began to filter through British intelligence that Germany planned war on Czechoslovakia in the early fall. On July 18, the British received information that the Germans had recalled pilots from Spain.[117] On August 3, an observer reported that Germany had selected September 28 for an attack on Czechoslovakia.[118] The next day, Hastings Ismay told Inskip that signs pointed to a German military move around October 1. German buyers had received orders to make extensive new material purchases before that date.[119] In early August the Germans warned the British about a coming "practice" mobilization in September. The OKH attaché group indicated that the Wehrmacht would conduct a limited call-up of reservists in August and September and that reservists would serve until the end of the latter month. The British military attaché reported that this represented a "most dangerous and provocative announcement." It was, he noted, without question a partial mobilization, announced ahead of time to mitigate diplomatic consequences.[120] Militarily it would give the Germans a head start on the rest of Europe in case war occurred. On August 17, the military attaché conversed with a German who possessed good army connections. His informant indicated that Hitler was an inveterate liar and was determined to invade Czechoslovakia. The only hope for Europe, the German argued, lay in Franco-British intervention. Such an action would lead to conditions in which the army would "be able to bring about the overthrow of Hitler and the party."[121]

There remained considerable differences within the Foreign Office. It was clear, however, who held the upper hand. Vansittart, with the help of his considerable personal sources within Nazi Germany, presented the most accurate picture of German intentions.[122] The government, nevertheless, had little interest in the permanent secretary's gloomy forecasts. Rather, as R. A. Butler, undersecretary of state for foreign affairs, wrote Halifax at the end of July, the main concern was to minimize Vansittart's influence among hard-line members in Parliament.[123]

On the other hand, Henderson's reiterative emphasis on Czechoslovakia's unreasonableness and Germany's moderation had a definite impact on British policy. As the ambassador admitted to Cadogan, "one of my crosses is to have to represent the German point of view."[124] The real importance of the mountain of dispatches and letters that poured forth from his pen was the fact that they provided Chamberlain with an important tool to support appeasement. In mid-July the prime minister issued a "caveat against too much credence to unchecked reports from nonofficial sources. He himself had seen His Majesty's ambassador to Berlin, who gave an account of the attitude of the Nazi government that was not discouraging."[125]

Henderson's opinions also played an important role in shaping the government's attitudes toward the stirrings of opposition in Germany.[126] The Berlin embassy consistently downplayed reports that Hitler's policy disturbed many Germans, and Henderson even went so far as to characterize one anti-Nazi German as "one whose pronouncements are clearly biased and largely propaganda."[127] In late summer Henderson urged the government not to receive the German general staff's informal emissary, Major Ewald von Kleist-Schmenzin.[128] Von Kleist did see Vansittart and Churchill, and his warnings, passed through Vansittart, seem to have made some impression on Chamberlain. Even so, Henderson's influence was more substantial on the prime minister, who, while admitting that perhaps something ought to be done, confessed to Halifax that the German opposition reminded him "of the Jacobites at the Court of France in King William's time."[129]

In spite of the threatening situation, most of the British Cabinet went on holiday in August. Not until the end of the month did Chamberlain summon leading ministers back to London to discuss the increasingly serious crisis.[130] Halifax began their meeting with a detailed explanation of recent developments and listed German military preparations. He reported that the Foreign Office had appealed to Germany to delay military measures but had received a most inadequate response. Even more disturbing indications of trouble had appeared. The German ministers in Belgrade and Bucharest had warned that Germany would soon intervene in the Sudeten question, if necessary with force. If France responded, there would be a general European war. The only bright spot, the foreign secretary suggested, appeared to be the Czech willingness to make concessions. Beneš had offered three autonomous German districts, removal of the Czech police from German districts, and exchanges between German and Czech officials.[131]

Halifax then turned to German intentions. There were two possible explanations, he suggested, for the military preparations. The first—admittedly with a good deal of supporting evidence—was that Hitler, against the advice of "the army and the moderate party," had determined to intervene militarily in the Sudeten question. The second possibility was that, although Hitler had determined to solve the Sudeten problem in 1938, he had not yet decided to use military force. Explanations for the first case focused on Hitler's desire to avenge the May crisis, his need for a spectacular success, and his belief that only force could solve the question. Those who supported this position felt that Hitler believed that France would not intervene and that Britain would do everything possible to avoid war. If this were Hitler's policy, the only deterrent, Halifax commented, would be a declaration that invasion of Czechoslovakia would immediately bring Britain into the war. The difficulty, however, was that such a declaration might split the empire. If deterrence failed, it was hard to see what Britain, France, and Russia could do to aid Czechoslovakia. "It would, of course, be possible to fight a war to make Germany give up Czechoslovakia, but he thought that it was unlikely that any peace reached at the end of such a war would recreate Czechoslovakia as it existed today. It might, therefore, be said that there was not much use in fighting a war for an object that one could not secure. . . . We were, in effect, concerned with the attempt of the dictator countries to attain their ends by force. But he asked himself whether it was justifiable to fight a certain war now in order to forestall a possible war later."[132]

At this moment Henderson, recalled to London, broke into the discussion and argued that the thousands of workers on the Westwall proved that Germany had no hostile intentions toward France. As he had done so often in dispatches, Henderson now depicted Hitler as a moderate surrounded by extremists and discounted military preparations as being defensive.[133] Halifax observed that, if the second possibility were correct and Hitler had not made up his mind, Britain must follow her current policy. A strong stand might push Hitler into moving irrevocably toward war.

Chamberlain then declared that Germany appeared divided into camps, extremists and moderates, and a diplomatic warning would consolidate the extremist position. He admitted that he had toyed with a warning but had always come to the conclusion that "no democratic state ought to make a threat of war unless it was both ready to carry it out and prepared to do so." Events might force war on Great Britain, and she would do her best, but there was little to recommend present military prospects.[134]

The discussion divided the ministers into two distinct groups. Led by Simon and Hoare, most ministers wholeheartedly agreed with the prime minister. They stressed the desperate military situation, London's vulnerability to German bombers, and Czechoslovakia's exposed position. In fact, they used every argument that they could marshal against resisting German demands. Lord Maugham, lord chancellor, suggested that Britain might not come to the aid of France if Germany attacked the French for intervening in a Czech-German conflict. Inskip thought that a German conquest of Czechoslovakia would only increase their internal difficulties, and Henderson argued that Hitler had not yet decided on war: the führer was not an extremist; and threats would only strengthen the radicals in Germany.[135]

A minority of the ministers, particularly Stanley and Duff Cooper, emphasized the European implications of the Czech problem and argued that the military situation was not so desperate as it had been painted. Duff Cooper noted that the German officer corps opposed a military adventure, and Stanley argued that if Britain were unprepared, Germany was no more ready to fight a major war. He accurately warned that "in a year or so Germany would be in an immeasurably stronger position for fighting a long war than at the present time." The majority remained unpersuaded by strategic arguments. Significantly there was no discussion of what might happen if Czechoslovakia fell into German hands without a struggle.

At the conclusion of the meeting the ministers decided that they would: 1) give no warning to the Germans; 2) keep the Germans guessing as to their policy; 3) press the Czechs to proceed with negotiations; 4) refuse to consider until later the question of aiding France if she went to the aid of Czechoslovakia; 5) press the French not to take any action that might lead to war without consulting Britain; and 6) make no approach to the opposition. [136]

THE FRENCH RESPONSE: SUMMER 1938

The period from May to September does not represent one of the better moments in Franco-British relations. The British had the correct impression at the beginning of summer that the French were not overly enthusiastic about pressuring the Czechs to make major concessions to the Sudeten Germans. It was not so much a disagreement with British policy, as a preference for Britain to apply the strong measures. Unfortunately for Bonnet, the French minister in Prague gave away his instructions to his British colleague. The resulting squabble between London and Paris set the tone for coming months. [137] Even the visit of the King and Queen to Paris in July did not clear the air.

The Germans themselves played a game in Paris similar to the one they were playing in London. On the one hand they went to great lengths to assure their continental neighbor that Germany had no claim on France. In late June the French air attaché, Captain Paul Stehlin, held a long conversation with General Karl Bodenschatz, a top Göring aide. The German emphasized that the Reich had no aggressive designs on France, but that the Czech situation had become intolerable. The Czech state was a permanent danger to Germany's security, and communist subversion from Prague menaced internal peace. The West's attitude during the May crisis, Bodenschatz pointed out, had profoundly irritated Hitler. Because of the possibility of another confrontation with the Czechs, he added, Germany had begun work on a massive system of fortifications on her western frontier. François-Poncet noted that these conversations confirmed the remark of police and SS chief Heinrich Himmler that Czechoslovakia must disappear from the map of Europe. Bodenschatz had implied that Hitler believed that Czechoslovakia was condemned to perish.[138] In early July Hitler assured a visiting French general that Germany desired a rapprochement with France. The only existing question between them, the Saar, had been settled satisfactorily in 1935. Nevertheless, the führer warned his guest, Czech behavior in May had been unacceptable and intolerable. Germany would not allow further provocations. The Czechs must end their persecution of the Sudeten Germans as well as their procommunist line.[139]

Although François-Poncet indicated to Paris the seriousness of German propaganda attacks on Prague,[140] he followed a path in his analyses similar to that followed by his British colleague in Berlin. At the beginning of August, he reported that Hitler, isolated in Berchtesgaden, had not yet decided on a final course of action but was vacillating between alternatives.[141]

In Paris Bonnet followed the apparently irreconcilable policies of publicly standing by Czechoslovakia while dumping the Czech alliance. Halifax's proposal that Czechoslovakia surrender her alliance with France and declare neutrality was too obvious and dishonest even for Bonnet. So, he warmly accepted the Runciman mission. Although there was no French representative with Runciman, Bonnet warned the Czechs that they must accept this mediation effort. On July 20, the French foreign minister told the Czech ambassador that France would not go to war over the Sudetenland. France would give public support to the Czechs in order to facilitate an honorable solution, but if war came Czechoslovakia should not expect to find France at her side.[142] Unfortunately for his future reputation, Bonnet became increasingly defeatist. In early September, after warning the German ambassador that an attack on Czechoslovakia could lead to war between France and Germany, Bonnet begged that Germany spare France from having to honor her obligations and promised that France would meet all Germany's demands so long as the Reich kept the peace.[143] Bonnet's attitude was typical of a wide sector of French public opinion that wished to avoid war at any cost. In early August the annual Congress of the National Syndicate of Teachers proclaimed "the necessity of a campaign against the development of militaristic feeling in France and particularly against the two years' service law and obligatory preparations."[144]

The French made fitful efforts to enlist Eastern European support, but, at best, such efforts were halfhearted. In July Bonnet attempted to enlist Polish support for Czechoslovakia, but the Poles declined. They believed the French aimed at gaining diplomatic leverage with Berlin rather than at meeting the coming confrontation and refused to commit themselves without a guarantee of French military support. Bonnet brushed aside indications that Poland might support a hard line against Germany—that was the last thing he wished.[145] The Poles themselves showed nothing but disdain for the Czechs and argued that the present Czech state was impossible to maintain.[146] There was also French interest in Hungary's joining the "Little Entente,"[147] but such an idea foundered on Eastern European antagonisms as well as Hungarian expectations of sweepings from Germany's table.

Daladier wavered between strength and weakness. In late June he told the American ambassador, William Bullitt, that if the Czechs honestly attempted to meet Sudeten demands, and if in response the Germans spurned their offer and began military operations, then France would honor her obligations.[148] But in summer 1938, Daladier faced more than just a crisis over Czechoslovakia. For the fourth time in three years, the franc was under pressure. Already in May the French had had to devalue the currency. Now with uncertainty over Czechoslovakia as well as economic instability endemic in French industry, French gold again fled the continent. From Berlin François-Poncet warned that French financial difficulties were further encouraging those Germans who wished to pursue an aggressive policy.[149] The British provided nothing more than sympathy and not much of that. Daladier did manage to restore financial confidence by scrapping most of the Popular Front's social reforms, including the forty-hour workweek that had, in particular, hurt aircraft production. His move resulted from the darkening international scene as much as the franc's difficulties. Nevertheless, two socialist ministers resigned; in response Daladier appointed two ultra-appeasers.[150] These moves, one strong, the other weak, typified the premier's approach to the republic's difficulties.

In some respects the prospects of war and the strategic situation alarmed the French even more than had been the case in the spring. The defects in the air force and the threat of German air attacks on major population centers created close to a panic in Paris. In mid-August General Joseph Vuillemin, chief of staff of the French air force, paid a courtesy visit to the Luftwaffe. His hosts treated him with great respect and appeared willing to show him everything. In fact, they presented him with a gigantic Potemkin village. Luftwaffe authorities declared aircraft not beyond prototype stage to be in full production; displays of German bomber accuracy were frightening, and Luftwaffe strength figures were out of all proportion to reality. Vuillemin indicated to his hosts that France would honor her commitment to Czechoslovakia. Göring had the bad form to explode at this assertion and, interestingly, gave away one of the incidents that the Germans had proposed among themselves as the spark to begin war—the murder of their own ambassador in Prague.[151] The Germans, nevertheless, had achieved their purpose. Vuillemin returned to Paris thoroughly frightened and his gloomy forecasts that the Luftwaffe could destroy the French air force in two weeks provided ammunition for those in France who advocated the surrender of Czechoslovakia.[152] By the end of August, French intelligence had sniffed out the target date for "Case Green" as sometime after the twenty-fifth of September.[153] All the French could do now was wait and hope that either they could buy off the Germans or gain a more substantial British commitment. There seemed little chance of either possibility.

CONCLUSION

As August ended, Adolf Hitler, against the advice of nearly all his diplomatic and military advisers, had almost single-handedly, and certainly single-mindedly, set the stage for a crisis that would bring Europe to the brink of war. Outside Germany and a narrow circle of those concerned with diplomacy, surprisingly few Europeans sensed what was coming. Certainly few even within the governments on either the political or the military sides were aware of the issues. In an editorial at the beginning of August, Kingsley Martin of the *New Statesman*, who had for so long demanded resistance to fascism, urged that "the question of frontier revision, difficult though it is, should at once be tackled. The strategical value of the Bohemian frontier should not be made the occasion of a world war."[154]

VI

Munich: The Diplomatic Crisis

In September the Sudeten crisis reached its peak. In spite of military advice, Hitler directed German policy toward an invasion of Czechoslovakia and until the end of the month remained convinced that the West would not intervene. Nevertheless, the führer had a sharper understanding of Western attitudes than did those in Germany who opposed war. Beck, Halder, and other opposition leaders believed that, in view of Czechoslovakia's strategic importance, Britain and France would not abandon her. But, although Hitler correctly gauged Western reluctance to fight for Czechoslovakia, he miscalculated in his belief that the West would stand aside if Germany used force. As with his generals, Hitler's appreciation did not fully correspond to reality. Yet there was logic to his calculation that the West would remain inactive. After all, why should Britain and France go to war to prevent what they had already accepted in principle?

For the British and French, September was a terrifying ride toward the deadline at September's end. By that time the Germans would finish military preparations. Hustled from one position to another, the Western Powers accepted conditions that had been objectionable the previous week. By the end of September, Chamberlain and his government, whose policy had aimed at avoiding any commitment, found themselves mired in Eastern European affairs, with British public opinion incensed at Nazi behavior.[1] Ironically, British involvement as a "mediator" had created a climate where intervention in a war caused by Germany became a probability, rather than a possibility.

As the crisis mounted, the British found themselves in an increasingly awkward position. Lord Strang noted later: "In diplomacy, the word soon gets passed around; and the ambivalence of our policy of trying to deter the Germans from armed action by pointing to the probability of British intervention, and to discourage the Czechs from fighting by hinting at its improbability was not long concealed."² By the end of August the British received clear warning that a military crisis was imminent.³ Nevertheless, even in early September they failed to realize the importance of Sudeten areas to Czech security. Not until September 2, when a dispatch from Prague pointed out the consequences of granting the Sudeten Germans autonomy, did the Foreign Office consider the strategic aspects of the question.⁴ On September 8, Halifax minuted on this dispatch that up to that moment he had not known that Czech fortifications lay inside the Sudeten areas and had informed the Cabinet that morning that Czech fortifications were outside the Sudetenland.⁵

On September 7, the *Times* published its well-known editorial claiming that Czechoslovakia's position would improve with separation of the Sudetenland through a plebiscite. Although Foreign Office representatives denied that the British government had originated the idea, official thinking in most circles found such a solution increasingly attractive. By the ninth, Halifax was remarking to the French ambassador that a plebiscite in Sudeten districts was not a bad idea.⁶

On the same day, the British notified the Germans that they had begun precautionary measures because of massive preparations under way in the Reich. Admiral J. A. G. Troup, director of naval intelligence, warned the German naval attaché that once war commenced "it would be quite impossible to say where it might end." Revealingly, the attaché replied that no one in Germany believed there was the slightest chance that Britain would involve herself in a continental conflict. "He had not believed it possible *until the present moment*."⁷ At the September 12 Cabinet meeting, Halifax made much of the attaché's reaction. Unfortunately, what had alarmed the German and impressed the foreign secretary—mobilization of mine sweeper flotillas—was not likely to impress the führer.

In this Cabinet meeting the ministers again discussed Hitler's personality. Halifax admitted that the führer might be quite mad, and that "this view . . . was supported by a good deal of information from responsible quarters [in Germany]." Even so, a firm stand would destroy the chance of bringing Hitler back to sanity. Moreover, Halifax added, "to say without qualification that we were prepared to go to war to defend Czechoslovakia, would, in fact, put the decision of peace or war in the hands of others than ourselves."[8]

Although Halifax, on the whole, had supported Henderson's analysis, Duff Cooper strongly criticized his government's molding of foreign policy on the advice of one man, Nevile Henderson. Chamberlain replied that some Germans warned that a strong message would not change Hitler's mind if he had already made it up, and would drive him over the edge if he had not. Still, the prime minister did not mention anyone besides Henderson who agreed with this view. Lord Maugham thought there might be a third solution to the problem of whether or not to support France. In case of conflict, the government should not intervene at first and tell the French they were not yet ready for war; then, once British defenses were in order, they would help. Britain would not stand by if French security were endangered, but meanwhile the French should do no more than hold the Maginot line. At the end of discussions, the Cabinet asked the Chiefs of Staff for an updated assessment of the strategic situation.[9]

THE FRENCH

As August drew to a close, mounting German preparations were all too obvious to the French. War with Germany over Czechoslovakia was no longer a possibility; it was close to reality. François-Poncet reported in early September that German military preparations were proceeding relentlessly.[10] At the same time the French consul in Munich noted that German officers were predicting that they would need only ten days to destroy Czechoslovakia; France would only mobilize, England would make diplomatic protests, and Russia was incapable of military action.[11] On September 6, the French military attaché estimated that Hitler had firmly committed himself to an attack on Czechoslovakia.[12] On the following day François-Poncet indicated that his information suggested a massive German attack on Czechoslovakia at the end of the month in combination with a ruthless aerial bombardment of Prague.[13] Unfortunately, François-Poncet did not indicate to his government the full extent of German opposition to war. After the crisis he admitted that he had never informed Paris of messages "from emissaries of the army and . . . officers, urging France to be firm and unyielding. . . ." He claimed that "their origin made them suspect and that they might [have] unduly strengthened the hands of the warmongers in France and Beneš and Company."[14]

Nevertheless, the French embassy did indicate to a greater extent than did its British counterparts that all was not well in the Reich. On September 7, a cable reported that Hitler's August visit to the western front had resulted in a major crisis between the führer and the army's chief of staff.[15] On the same date French intelligence disclosed that Beck had resigned and that Halder had replaced him.[16] In addition, the economic attaché indicated that Germany would enter a European war, if it occurred in the near future, without gold, foreign exchange, raw materials, or foodstuffs.[17]

Although there was conflicting information from Berlin, Bonnet grasped the gloomiest news as confirmation of his desperate belief that France must avoid war at *any* cost.[18] There were many who echoed his view. Horror stories about Luftwaffe capabilities, already current after Vuillemin's visit, received further impetus with Colonel Charles Lindbergh's arrival in Paris. Bonnet told Phipps that Lindbergh had returned from Germany "horrified at the overwhelming strength of Germany in the air . . ." and convinced that peace must be preserved at all cost.[19] On the sixteenth Phipps reported that the French air minister described the air threat to the Chamber of Deputies as "quite catastrophic."[20] At the end of the month, Dentz told the British military attaché that in war "French cities would be laid in ruins and that they had no means of defense. They were now paying the price of years of neglect of their air force."[21] Gamelin was as gloomy as ever. In mid-September he warned Daladier that an offensive against the Westwall would lead to another Somme.[22]

In a real sense France looked to Britain for an escape from the crisis and wholeheartedly supported Chamberlain's efforts to achieve a peaceful settlement. Unlike the British, however, most French had few illusions about a general appeasement of Europe. Yet some diplomats seem to have believed well into September that a radical restructuring of the Czech state would satisfy German demands and could leave a Czechoslovakia able to help in blocking the German *"Drang nach Osten."*[23] Certainly the French had little cause for satisfaction with British attitudes. On September 7, Halifax cautioned that although His Majesty's Government might feel an obligation to support France, it would not automatically declare war on Germany if France became involved in war as a result of her treaties.[24] Two days later he warned the French ambassador that Britain was not prepared to go to war "on account of an aggression by Germany on Czechoslovakia."[25]

BERCHTESGADEN

Hitler's long-awaited speech concluded the Nürnberg Party Congress on September 12. A convenient incident occurred, and Conrad Henlein, Sudeten German leader, broke off negotiations. Thus, Hitler's Nürnberg speech was the signal for widespread disturbance. Henlein immediately demanded that the Czechs withdraw their police from German areas; the Czechs refused and the Czech military quickly suppressed the violence, while Henlein fled into Germany.[26] Events, however, had moved beyond Czech control.

Chamberlain now decided that only a dramatic gesture could save peace. On September 13, with the agreement of his inner circle, Chamberlain ordered Henderson to inform the Germans that he wished to visit the Reich and solve the Czech problem with the führer's help. Before leaving, Chamberlain suggested to the Cabinet that, if Hitler demanded a Sudeten plebiscite, Britain must accede. He admitted that there were serious difficulties with a plebiscite, but "it would be difficult for the democratic countries to go to war to prevent the Sudeten Germans from saying what form of government they wanted." He commented that he recognized strategic and economic factors as of importance and promised the Cabinet to make an effort to safeguard them. Nonetheless, Czechoslovakia might refuse to cede her territory and strategic frontiers. As a result, he argued that Britain would have to join in guaranteeing the integrity of the new Czech state.[27]

Perhaps nothing else reveals so clearly Chamberlain's naïveté. To guarantee what one has rendered indefensible is, indeed, eccentric. Among the ministers, only Duff Cooper attacked the premises of appeasement. He warned that the choice was not between plebiscite and war, but between war now or war later. "He had never been optimistic about our catching up on Germany in our rearmament program. . . . He was quite confident that if we went to war we should win." On the other hand, Inskip held that Britain could not prevent the Wehrmacht from overrunning Czechoslovakia. Since British foreign policy did not wish to encircle Germany or to deny her dominant position in Southeast Europe, he objected to the use of threats and force.[28]

On September 14, the Joint Planning Committee completed its study updating the March strategic assessments. In most respects the results followed the March 28 study, "COS 698 (Revise), Military Implications of German Aggression against Czechoslovakia." The planners argued that Italy and Japan would probably join Germany and that the Soviet Union was an incalculable factor. On the economic side, they suggested that Germany was vulnerable to a blockade, but that Nazi control of Austria and Austrian connections to the Balkans would help to make up much of the Reich's raw-material shortages. They stressed that the major threat for the Western Powers lay in German air power. The report predicted that the Luftwaffe could launch a sustained bombing offensive of 500 to 600 tons per day against Britain. Paraphrasing the chiefs' March report, the planners argued in conclusion that the intervention of either of the other Axis powers would present Britain's military services with commitments "which neither the present nor the projected strength of our defense forces is designed to meet, even if we were in alliance with France and Russia and which would, therefore, place a dangerous strain on the resouces of the Empire. . . ."[29]

The Berchtesgaden conversations have received the attention of numerous historical works. It is sufficient to note that Chamberlain agreed to Hitler's major demands, which in effect separated the Sudetenland from Czechoslovakia and rendered the Czechs defenseless. Upon his return, the prime minister set out to convince his colleagues, the French, and finally the Czechs, that Hitler's demands, if met, would produce a lasting peace. Tragically, Chamberlain believed not only that war would end civilization but also that Hitler could be trusted. Immediately on landing in London he reported to his ministers his belief that Germany would have no further demands on Czechoslovakia after a plebiscite and would be satisfied once the Sudeten Germans were in the Reich.[30]

At a Cabinet meeting on September 17, the prime minister described Hitler as an excitable but rational man with strictly limited aims. The "impression left on him was that Herr Hitler meant what he said." Yet Chamberlain did not find unanimous support. Duff Cooper thought the premise that Britain should not intervene without overwhelming superiority unrealistic. Britain, he argued, was unlikely ever to achieve such a condition. Moreover, he doubted whether the Sudetenland constituted Hitler's last demand. Earl De La Warr, lord privy seal, thought that, although "it was impossible to object to the principle of self-determination," it was also impossible to agree to the German demands. He pointed out that "these concessions would be unfair to the Czechs and dishonorable to ourselves after all that we had done in the last two months." Stanley argued that the present was the best time to fight. He had no doubt that the Cabinet would find itself six months hence discussing the same points with regard to the Polish Corridor or Memel. A plebiscite under the guns of one and a half million soldiers was surrender. Lord Winterton, chancellor of the duchy of Lancaster, felt there was no profit in war, but sometimes one must face war since otherwise "the alternative was to become a vassal state."[31]

Nevertheless, most of the Cabinet still supported the prime minister. Like Chamberlain, some believed Hitler was a difficult but reasonable man. Others shrank from war. Lord president of the council Viscount Hailsham announced that "it was in our interests to prevent any single power from dominating Europe; but that had come to pass and he thought we had no alternative but to submit to what the Lord Privy Seal regarded as humiliation."[32]

The French proved no harder to convince. Daladier and Bonnet arrived in London on September 18. The deliberations between British and French took place in an atmosphere of unreality. The minutes report discussions of guarantees, population distribution in different districts, and strategic considerations; these topics appear, are debated, and recede unresolved. Chamberlain began discussions by describing Berchtesgaden and with much solemnity acceded to a French demand that Britain guarantee the new Czech frontier.[33] At the conclusion of discussions both sides agreed to demand Czech capitulation to German demands.[34]

For the Czechs, Anglo-French pressure was a crushing blow. They had based their foreign policy on Western support and a belief that Britain and France would recognize Czechoslovakia's strategic importance and the spurious nature of German claims. They had done their best to convince the British and French that a plebiscite would destroy their state and damage the balance of power. On September

16, Beneš argued that abandoning frontier areas would make a satis-factory relationship between Czechs and Germans impossible. Czech-oslovakia would continue to exist, but as a mutilated remnant at the mercy of hostile neighbors.[35] Under Allied pressure the Czechs finally collapsed. Faced with abandonment, the Czechs could not conceive of anything but surrender and as a result refused to stand alone or call upon the Soviet Union.[36] A new Czech government under General Syrový took power to underline the army's suppport for the policy of not fighting alone. On September 19, the British military attaché reported that the Czech army would obey whatever decision the gov-ernment made.[37]

Having obtained French and Czech agreement, Chamberlain pre-pared to return to Germany. But the hard liners did prevail on their colleagues to attempt to limit the prime minister's freedom of action. On September 21, the Cabinet decided that 1) if Hitler refused to make a settlement until Hungarian and Polish demands were met, the prime minister should return immediately; 2) the proposed guarantee should be joint and not several; 3) Germany should sign a nonaggres-sion pact with Czechoslovakia; and 4) an international force should be created to monitor territorial exchange.[38] Some ministers urged Chamberlain to get German concessions as a sign of good faith. At the least they felt that Germany should demobilize her army, withdraw military units from the frontier, and disband Henlein's Freikorps.[39]

GODESBERG

The Godesberg meetings were most difficult. Hitler replied to Cham-berlain's efforts with a curt comment that such concessions no longer sufficed. Instead of ending discussions in accordance with his Cabinet instructions, Chamberlain remained in an attempt to patch things up. As it became apparent that Chamberlain had encountered a serious snag, the Cabinet cabled their Prime Minister:

> It may help you if we give you some indication of what seems predominant public opinion as expressed in [the] press and else-where. While mistrustful of our plan, but prepared perhaps to accept it with reluctance as [an] alternative to war, [the] great mass of public opinion seems to be hardening in sense of feeling that we have gone the limit of concession and that it is up to the

Chancellor to make some contribution. We, of course, can imagine [the] immense difficulties with which you are confronted, but from point of view of your own position, that of the government, and of the country, it seems to your colleagues of vital importance that you should not leave without making it clear to the Chancellor, if possible by [a] special interview, that, after the great concessions made by Czechoslovak Government, for him to reject [the] opportunity of [a] peaceful solution in favor of one that must involve war would be an unpardonable crime against humanity. [40]

Unfortunately, Chamberlain made no effort to impress the Germans with the extent to which both Cabinet and British public opinion had hardened. After achieving nothing the prime minister returned with only a memorandum from Hitler, setting forth Germany's increased demands. It was, in effect, an ultimatum. [41]

As Chamberlain and Hitler met, the situation from London appeared more threatening. Intelligence reports indicated an increased build-up of German troops along the Czech frontier and Sudeten German Freikorps raids into Czechoslovakia. With the failure at Godesberg the inequity of preventing Czech mobilization, while Germany openly prepared, became clear. Vansittart bitterly commented:

> We have got a bad enough name over this whole business anyhow and I cannot contemplate what it would be if it were realized that we know firstly, as we do, that the Czechs are going to fight if pushed too far or attacked and secondly that it is we who have prevented them from defending themselves effectively. That would indeed produce a comprehensible explosion. So may we please remove a bar that is in my opinion so unfair as to be iniquitous unless in the next couple of hours we receive from Godesberg any solid reason for believing that the Germans are not playing with us. It is almost universal opinion that they are. And that lays us open to even more disastrous criticism if we end up being duped. The criticism will be that our action has been entirely one-sided, and that, I find, is the interpretation generally put on the Prime Minister's communiqué of last night urging *Czechoslovakia* to "maintain a state of orderliness and to refrain from action of any kind that would be likely to lead to incidents." I

---

could see no reason at the time for such a communiqué and I
cannot see any now.[42]

THE CRISIS IN GERMANY

Hitler's maniacal drive toward confrontation led to increasing opposition as *Fall Grün* approached. Even Jodl, who normally slavishly
supported the führer, had troubling doubts. Stülpnagel warned Jodl
that Hitler's fundamental preconception—that the West would not
intervene—did not correspond with the facts. In recording this conversation in his diary, Jodl admitted that even he was beginning to
worry.[43] Reports of military opposition reached Hitler and led him to
make a violent attack on the officer corps; Keitel passed the führer's
views along to the OKW staff. With his spine stiffened, Jodl noted on
September 13 that the whole German nation stood behind Hitler except
for leading members of the officer corps.[44]

The officer corps' concern about Germany's prospects in a European
war was well known in the West. As early as June, the German air
attaché in Paris told his British counterpart that the German military
"wholeheartedly" opposed war.[45] In early August the acting head of
the attaché group in the German high command informed the British
military attaché "that the army was now being called upon to undertake
much that the General Staff considered undesirable or unwise, but
that it was obligated to do so, as unless the army cooperated sufficiently
with the government there was always the possibility that control of
the army might be taken out of the army's hands."[46] By early September
the British government knew that Beck had resigned but did not cir-
culate the news widely. Had the reports become public, the government would have had a more difficult time in maintaining its position
that Germany possessed overwhelming strength.[47]

The German officer corps had reason to be upset.[48] In retrospect
there is no doubt that Hitler aimed to invade Czechoslovakia. Diplomatic maneuvers and military preparations were not, as some historians have suggested, designed to extract maximum advantage from
the crisis.[49] Hitler strove to isolate the Czechs, so that the German
military could destroy Czechoslovakia in a quick campaign. A clear
indication of Hitler's policy was his performance at Godesberg. The
führer had already gained, as a result of the Berchtesgaden talks,

concessions that encompassed the eventual destruction of the Czech Republic and a strategic position that made the Czechs his vassals. Yet, at Godesberg he added Polish and Hungarian claims to those of Germany. He did not want Chamberlain's peaceful solution. The most conclusive proof of Hitler's desire for war, however, was his interference in military planning.[50] If military preparations were merely intended to support diplomatic pressure, deployment of the Wehrmacht scarcely mattered as long as it made a credible threat. The initial OKH plan certainly served such a purpose, but Hitler's changes indicate that the führer envisaged an actual, though limited war. Finally, after Munich, Hitler was most unhappy at having lost the opportunity to crush Czechoslovakia by military action. As early as September 21, Hitler informed the Hungarians that the only danger was that Czechoslovakia would submit to every demand.[51] During the Polish crisis the next year he remarked: "I only fear that at the last moment some swine will lay a plan of negotiations before me."[52]

To many in the officer corps such a course seemed disastrous. Among other military and civilian figures, General Erwin von Witzleben, commander of the Berlin military district, and General Erich Hoepner, a panzer division commander, organized a rather loose plot to remove Hitler and prevent war. With little available documentation it is hard to estimate the conspiracy's extent or chances. Since the war, some Germans have claimed that the plot was organized to the last detail and that only Munich saved the Nazi regime.[53] It seems more likely, however, that the plotters hoped to remove Hitler if the war against Czechoslovakia went badly and if the West intervened decisively. With some justification, the German historian Gerhard Ritter concludes that the proposed coup represented an enormous gamble.[54] Another German has gone so far as to claim that the plot was a guaranteed form of suicide.[55] Existing evidence suggests that the plotters did not have a much greater chance of success in 1938 than those involved in the 1944 effort. At the least, Halder's plan to arrest Hitler and place the führer on trial was dangerously naïve.[56]

The success of any coup depended on the active support of the whole army. The plotters needed to overpower Hitler's SS bodyguards and to maintain control over key points in Berlin. Thus, the key element would have been the attitude nor only of senior officers but also of the troops, NCOs, and junior officers. Without the cooperation of the ranks a coup had little chance of success. It was precisely the attitude of the younger officers and soldiers that was doubtful, for these were men who for the most part believed in the führer's genius.[57] Most "after-action" reports on the Czech crisis speak of excellent morale among the troops. Although there was widespread disaffection among civilians, younger officers and NCOs largely supported the regime.[58] Even had war gone against Germany, one can still doubt whether a coup would have had a much greater chance. A desperate military situation might well have rallied the population to the regime in defense of "the Fatherland."

CABINET REVOLT

Although the mounting crisis gravely concerned leading members of Germany's officer corps, Chamberlain remained unruffled by the new demands. At Berchtesgaden the prime minister had agreed to German proposals in the belief that Hitler was an honest and reasonable man. Chamberlain should have realized at Godesberg that this was not the case. Unwilling to recognize that he was being duped, the prime minister concluded that the difference between Berchtesgaden and Godesberg was one only of degree. However, he discovered that a considerable faction within the Cabinet saw the situation in a different light.

Upon his return from Germany on the twenty-fourth, Chamberlain held two major meetings with his ministers and advisers. After meeting with Halifax, Vansittart, Wilson, Cadogan, and Strang in the afternoon,[59] Chamberlain reiterated the same message to the full Cabinet. He told his colleagues that "[i]n his view Herr Hitler had certain standards. (He spoke now with greater confidence on this point than after his first visit.) Herr Hitler had a narrow mind and was violently prejudiced on certain subjects; but he would not deliberately deceive a man whom he respected and with whom he had been in negotiation, and he was sure that Herr Hitler now felt some respect for him. When Herr Hitler announced that he meant to do something it was certain that he would do it."[60] Chamberlain attempted to obscure the real issues by asking the ministers to compare the Godesberg and Berchtesgaden terms and to decide whether the difference justified war. He had just flown up the Thames and had imagined German bombers taking the same course. "He felt that we were in no position to justify waging a war to prevent a war hereafter."

The prime minister then turned to larger prospects. Hitler had assured him that with the Czech difficulty out of the way Anglo-German relations would reach a turning point. Chamberlain felt that an opportunity existed to reach "an understanding with Germany on all points of difference between the two countries." Moreover, he felt he had achieved solid influence over the German chancellor and "that the latter trusted him and was willing to work with him. If this was [*sic*] so, it was a wonderful opportunity to put an end to the horrible nightmare of the armament race."[61] Chamberlain's fanciful portrayal of a meeting that one can at best describe as a diplomatic disaster is astonishing. At both meetings on September 24, Halifax supported the prime minister. Because of the late hour the Cabinet meeting adjourned before other ministers could voice their opinions.

After a night's discussion with Cadogan, Halifax changed his position.[62] The foreign secretary began Cabinet dicussions on the morning of the twenty-fifth by arguing that the Godesberg terms were unacceptable. Halifax's turnabout signaled a general revolt that split the Cabinet. Eight ministers opposed the prime minister, four leaned toward further appeasement, but only eight gave Chamberlain their wholehearted support.[63] Hailsham pointed out that Hitler had given the same promises after the introduction of conscription, the Rhineland, and the Anschluss. Duff Cooper and Stanley argued that war now was better than war later. Their position was bolstered by Liddell Hart's efforts to bring Czechoslovakia's strategic importance to the attention of those in power.[64] De La Warr pointed to the great concessions that Czechoslovakia had made. Germany was leading Britain on and His Majesty's government was "slowly abandoning the moral basis of [its] cause." Walter Elliot agreed with Halifax that the differences between Godesberg and Berchtesgaden were not merely of degree but of principle.[65]

There were, of course, those who still clung to Chamberlain's recommendation that the government accept the Godesberg proposals. But few thought Britain should press Czechoslovakia to accept additional demands. Inskip now admitted that if France threw her whole military weight against Germany, the situation was "more favorable than we had previously thought." He added that the latest intelligence indicated that "Germany had only a thin couverture of troops on her western frontier." The previous evening Inskip had substantially undermined the argument that the Luftwaffe would strike from the blue when he admitted that Germany could not undertake a heavy bombing attack "on this country unless she either concentrated her bombing squadrons in N.W. Germany or flew over Holland or Belgium. The latter case would involve an infringement of neutrality while the former concentration would involve some delay."[66]

Nevertheless, some still based their position on a hopeless military situation, a horror of war, and the openness of British cities to German air attack. William Morrison, arguing both sides of the issue, commented that "if war is declared now, there would be no doubt, in Sir Horace Walpole's phrase, a ringing of bells on the part of the bellicose, but before long there would no doubt be a wringing of hands on the part of the same people."[67] The gulf between opposing points of view complicated Chamberlain's course and hampered his freedom of maneuver. The threat of a political crisis was grave. After the Cabinet meeting Stanley indicated to American ambassador Joseph Kennedy the gulf between opposing views. He told the American that the morning meeting had gone badly and that seven ministers might resign before evening if Chamberlain pursued his efforts to force Czechoslovakia to bow to the Godesberg demands.[68]

For the meeting that afternoon with Daladier and French ministers the Cabinet could only agree on the following instructions: "1) We should not say that if the proposals were rejected we undertook to declare war on Germany. 2) Equally we should not say that if the proposals were rejected we should in no circumstances declare war on Germany. 3) We should put before the representatives of the French and Czech Governments the full facts of the situation, as we saw them, in their true light."[69] This last instruction enabled Chamberlain to press the French to surrender. Significantly, the prime minister packed the British delegation with leading appeasers.

In the afternoon conversations with the French, Chamberlain, and particularly Simon, launched a barrage of questions, all designed to show the visitors the hopelessness of defending Czechoslovakia. What did France intend to do? Would she declare war? How would she fight Germany? How could she defend her cities against German air attacks? Daladier's replies were dignified but not altogether honest. Once again the French presented a stronger front than their real views justified.[70] That evening Duff Cooper angrily attacked the conduct of discussions. He charged that "judging by the account that had been given to the Cabinet, the British Ministers appeared to have contested the French at every point and to have allowed it to appear that they disagree with the French government's suggestions without making any positive contributions themselves." An angry exchange between the prime minister and the First Lord of the Admiralty then took place.[71]

FINAL MILITARY EVALUATIONS

In these circumstances British military and intelligence organizations contributed their last assessment of the strategic situation. On September 18, the Secret Intelligence Service urged that the West force Czechoslovakia to surrender the Sudetenland and calculated that 1938 was not an advantageous time for a stand. They also recommended that Britain inject "resisting power" into those Southeastern European states that Germany threatened—making "them realize that we and the French are strong and united; encouraging them as far as possible to look to us short of committing ourselves to supporting them actively." Britain should not count on the Soviet Union but "to keep on the right side of this devil we must sup with him to some extent adapting the length of our spoon to circumstances at any given moment."[72]

On September 23, the Joint Planning Committee of the Chiefs of Staff warned that air attacks against Germany could have serious results. "To attempt to take offensive action against Germany until we have had time to bring our military, naval, and air forces, and also our passive defense services onto a war footing would be to place ourselves in the position of a man who tries to show how brave he is by twisting the tail of a tiger which is preparing to spring before he has loaded his gun."[73] On the following day the planners argued that Britain and France could not help Czechoslovakia on the ground, although they admitted that the Wehrmacht had only weak forces in the west.[74]

On the same day the Chiefs of Staff produced a far more optimistic memorandum that broke significantly with their past pessimism. They pointed out that their assumption that Germany could man her western front in strength was wrong. The Germans possessed only eight or nine divisions in the west, and, unless they took steps to correct this weakness, there was a significant opportunity for the French. Only a transfer of troops from east to west would correct this imbalance. "Whether the German General Staff have yet had sufficient experience to carry out these movements is open to doubt." They made no direct mention of a German air menace and concluded on a note totally divergent from previous estimates: ". . . until such time as we can build up our fighting potential we cannot hope for quick results. Nevertheless, the latent resources of the Empire and the doubtful morale of our opponents under the stress of war *give us confidence as to the ultimate outcome* [my emphasis]."[75] Unfortunately the change came too late. Earlier memoranda had provided appeasers with arguments that Britain could not face war under any circumstance. Admittedly Chamberlain and his supporters were more influenced by revulsion against war than by fears about the strategic situation, but the chiefs had consistently provided ammunition against a strong policy.

Curiously the Chiefs of Staff never addressed the question of what the military balance might be should Germany absorb Czechoslovakia without a fight. Stanley first raised this question in the Cabinet on September 16. As a result Inskip asked the chiefs to prepare an appreciation on this point.[76] The chiefs did not complete the study before Munich, but Hastings Ismay, secretary of the Chiefs of Staff Committee, finished a draft on September 20. Ismay warned that no matter what Britain and France did in the next six to twelve months, Germany would strengthen her land superiority. The Germans would have time to complete the Westwall and to correct many defects in training. More important, British prestige might suffer a severe blow. But Ismay believed the critical question lay in comparative air strengths. It is significant that a military mind as perceptive as Ismay's accepted the argument that Germany could launch a successful "strategic" air offensive against the British Isles. He thus argued that six to twelve months would enable Britain to strengthen her air defenses to meet a German bombing offensive. He concluded that "it follows, therefore, that, from the military point of view, time is in our favor, and that, if war with Germany has to come, it would be better to fight her in say six to twelve months' time than to accept the present challenge."[77]

The French military were as gloomy over the strategic situation as their British counterparts. Furthermore, there was no switch from pessimism in French strategic evaluations as was the case in Britain.

At a meeting with the British in late September Gamelin gave a most discouraging picture. Although he admitted that the Wehrmacht had weak forces in the west, he suggested that the French army would have to wait until the government had evacuated major cities before beginning military operations.[78] Gamelin's pretense that he would then move swiftly was undercut when he suggested that his forces would retreat behind the Maginot line once the Germans appeared in strength. Gamelin's discourse gave his hosts the clear impression that the French would do little on the outbreak of war.

Gamelin's fellow chiefs of staff were even more outspoken on Allied weaknesses. Vuillemin reported that the French air force possessed 250 fighters, 320 bombers, and 130 reconnaissance aircraft available for service. Compared to the Luftwaffe the disproportion of forces was "extremely acute." The French air force was inferior not only in numbers, but also in quality. "The losses on the ground and in the air suffered by the French air force in the first weeks would be very heavy and could not be made good"; by the end of the first month the French would lose 40 percent of their strength; by the end of the first two months 64 percent. As a result, the French army would not receive air intelligence on German troop movements, whereas the Luftwaffe could intervene against French ground forces almost at will. Finally, and most dangerously, weakness in the air would allow the enemy to launch massive and repetitive attacks against the great population centers of France without effective French retaliation.[79]

Admiral Jean Darlan, Chief of Naval Staff, was equally pessimistic. The lines of trade and communication that supported the British and French Empires were everywhere open to interdiction. Ethiopia, Franco's Spain, political trouble in French North Africa, Egypt, and Palestine, he suggested, represented serious threats to sea lines. Darlan warned that the German fleet was far better prepared to conduct operations over the distant oceans than the High Seas Fleet in the First World War (a great exaggeration of the pitifully small German navy). The past five years had allowed the Germans to accumulate the material and defenses that now made it impossible for the French army to launch a successful offensive. Nevertheless, he did admit that if the Western Powers could maintain their lines of communications and close off the Atlantic to the Germans, they would win. As in 1918, Germany would succumb, asphyxiated.[80] Nowhere in the available documentation does it appear that the French considered what the impact would be on the general strategic situation should Germany gain Czechoslovakia without a fight.

THE COLLAPSE

The crisis now approached its denouement. On September 25, the Czech minister in London, Jan Masaryk, rejected the Godesberg terms in a dignified manner. He noted that Hitler's demands constituted "a *de facto* ultimatum of the sort usually presented to a vanquished nation and not a proposition to a sovereign state which has shown the greatest possible readiness to make sacrifices for the appeasement of Europe."[81] Hitler's reply was a vituperative public attack on Beneš, described by the *Times* "as a rather offensive statement of a perfectly reasonable case."[82]

As Europe drifted toward war, Anglo-French relations remained surprisingly far apart in view of the seriousness of the situation. This state of affairs was largely the result of conscious British policy. Halifax's statement of British intentions, made on September 12, perhaps best sums up the ambivalence of the British position. The foreign secretary informed the French that although His Majesty's government would never allow France's security to be threatened, "they were unable to make precise statements on the character of their future action, or the time at which it would be taken in circumstances that they cannot at present foresee."[83] Typical of the shabby treatment of the French was Gamelin's experience on the twenty-sixth. Having given a long, detailed exposé of French strategy to British ministers and the Chiefs of Staff, Gamelin asked his opposite numbers about their strategy, should war occur. With evident embarrassment they answered that they had no authorization to discuss their strategic plans.[84] Similarly, after his return to Paris that day, Bonnet requested a British reply to the following questions: If France became involved in war over Czechoslovakia, would Britain mobilize; would she introduce conscription; and would she combine her economic and financial resources with those of France?[85] Halifax's reply was not encouraging. British help would be mostly confined to the sea and air; at best Britain could send two understrength and underequipped divisions to the continent. On conscription and combining of resources, Halifax gave no answer; only Parliament could decide such issues.[86]

In the last days before Munich, Chamberlain continued his efforts to convince his colleagues of Czechoslovakia's hopeless strategic position. On the basis of a one-day tour of frontier districts, the military attaché in Berlin, Colonel Mason-MacFarlane, had reported that Czech morale was low and Czech defenses would not stop a German invasion.[87] Despite an immediate response from the military attaché in Prague that morale was high and that Czechs would fight bravely,[88] Chamberlain recalled Mason-MacFarlane to give his observations on Czechoslovakia.[89] That evening, September 27, Chamberlain used this testimony before the Cabinet to prove that the Czechs would not fight well.[90]

There is a strange irony in Chamberlain's peacemaking efforts. He had hoped to keep Britain out of war by preventing a European conflict. But appeasement had not worked. The efforts to mediate between Czechs and Germans had increasingly involved Britain in the crisis. Chamberlain's peacemaking flights served above all to underline the mendaciousness of Nazi diplomacy. Hitler's brusque dismissal of the British efforts at Godesberg had revealed the real purposes of Nazi Germany. By the end of September, appeasement and the German reaction had persuaded much of the British public that Germany was again a menace that must be stopped—by war if necessary.

Chamberlain's policy also stiffened dominion attitudes.[91] Except for South Africa, which believed it could remain neutral and still allow the Royal Navy to use port facilities on the Cape,[92] the dominions had begun to recognize the German threat. Even De Valera made a small overture to support Inskip when both were in Geneva.[93] At the end of September, Australian prime minister Joseph Lyons telegraphed that the precise method of population transfer seemed hardly to warrant war.[94] Within a day, however, the Australian high commissioner reported that Lyons had sent his message before additional information had arrived, and that "I feel bound to record my considered view that Mr. Lyons' message is very far from representing the core of Australian majority opinion . . . and that it would be condemned by public sentiment here as an insulting underestimation of their appreciation of immediate and ultimate issues involved."[95] On September 28, the British received a report that Canadian public opinion strongly supported Britain and that Canada would fight if war occurred.[96] The dominions had wholeheartedly supported appeasement, but, as with British public opinion, the cynicism of German policy altered attitudes. With the exception of South Africa and Eire, the dominions indicated that they would stand with Britain if the Sudeten crisis resulted in war.

CONCLUSION

The essence of Chamberlain's tragedy was that, having pursued a course that revealed the nature of Nazi policy, he refused to recognize that reality. From the Anschluss on, he rejected a strong, anti-German line. He was quite correct in his belief that a forceful policy would split the British nation and certainly the Conservative party, not to mention the dominions. The weakness in Churchill's argument lies in the fact that a vigorous hard line would not have convinced the British people of the Nazi danger. Ironically, the conciliatory nature of appeasement and the blatant, cynical Nazi response convinced most British that Hitler and his regime were malicious and dangerous. At Godesberg appeasement reached a dead end. Had Chamberlain recognized that fact, he would have had little difficulty in persuading his ministers and the country to resist. He did not and, in the end, threw everything away on the gamble that Hitler was trustworthy, that war would not come, and that Britain had no strategic interest in either Czechoslovakia or Southeastern Europe.

The French government was for the most part relieved not to fight for Czechoslovakia. Georges Mandel, Clemenceau's old associate, urged the Czechs to resist Munich and commented that only moderate fighting would force France to honor her obligations.[97] His reaction, as Churchill's in Britain, was a clear exception. The Czechs, of course, collapsed, and their surrender to overwhelming odds was in marked contrast to the behavior of the Poles and the Finns in 1939.

In Germany, preparations continued on a massive scale up to Hitler's acceptance of the four-power conference. As late as the evening of September 27, Hitler remarked that he could now destroy Czechoslovakia. As only Ribbentrop and Weizsäcker were present, the führer was clearly giving vent to his feelings and purpose.[98] In spite of this, at the last moment Hitler did pull back from the abyss. It was a decision he regretted almost immediately. The reasons for his acceptance of a peaceful solution have never been entirely clear. Most probably a combination of factors served to change his course. The serious doubts of German military leaders as to whether the Reich could face a major European war combined with Hitler's realization that the West was going to intervene. Indications of a Royal Navy mobilization also helped to convince the führer that he could not wage a limited war against Czechoslovakia. He later told Göring that the naval mobilization was the decisive event that changed his mind.[99] Equally convincing must have been the dismal reception that Berliners gave troops moving toward Czechoslovakia on the twenty-seventh.[100] The German people had no desire to fight for the Sudetenland and plainly showed it. Finally, the Italian attitude and Mussolini's strong support for a peaceful solution played a significant role. All of these factors in combination helped to drag Germany back from a desperate gamble, the nature of which we will examine in the next chapter.

Of all who have attempted to sum up Munich and its results, none has done so more accurately or more eloquently than Winston Churchill. In a speech before a hostile House of Commons on October 4, 1938, Churchill forewarned:

> All is over. Silent, mournful, abandoned, broken Czechoslovakia recedes into the darkness. She has suffered in every respect by her associations with France, under whose guidance and policy she has been actuated for so long. . . . Every position has been successively undermined and abandoned on specious and plausible excuses.
>
> I do not grudge our loyal, brave people, who were ready to do their duty no matter what the cost, who never flinched under the strain of last week, the natural, spontaneous outburst of joy and relief when they learned that the hard ordeal would no longer be required of them at the moment; but they should know the truth. . . . They should know that we have sustained a defeat without a war, the consequences of which will travel far with us along our road; they should know that we have passed an awful milestone in our history, when the whole equilibrium of Europe has been deranged, and that the terrible words have for the time being been pronounced against the Western Democracies: "Thou art weighed in the balance and found wanting." And do not suppose that this is the end. This is only the beginning of the reckoning. This is only the first sip, the first foretaste of a bitter cup. . . .[101]

MAP III   *The Munich Agreement*

VII

Munich: The Military Confrontation

The possible outcome of a war over Czechoslovakia in 1938 has intrigued historians since Munich, particularly those interested in either condemning or justifying Chamberlain's diplomatic and strategic policies. Unfortunately, most students of Munich have regarded the 1938 military situation as a peripheral issue. Few have studied the strategic situation objectively; most have been content to look for factors supporting a particular point of view and to overlook other contradictory elements. As a result, arguments about the military situation have centered on two issues. Those condemning Munich as a strategic disaster point to Germany's lack of ground strength, and her weakness in the west. They suggest that war in 1938 would have led to the relatively swift collapse of Nazi Germany.[1] On the other hand, some argue that Britain's air defenses were desperately weak and that as a result Chamberlain saved Britain at Munich from defeat at the hands of the Luftwaffe.[2] The problem is, however, far more complex than either view suggests.

In fact, the latter argument is based on considerable ex post facto reasoning. Those in power in Britain in 1938 fought against war not because they feared Britain might lose, but because of possible damage to Britain's world position (both in terms of her economic standing and control of her colonies) and a moral aversion to the use of force. Even Henderson admitted that Germany might not last more than "a certain number of months."[3] Halifax told the Cabinet in mid-September that "he had no doubt that if we were involved in war now we should win it after a long time," but added that he "could not feel we were justified in embarking on an action which would result in such untold suffering."[4] As has been noted, the Chiefs of Staff viewed the outcome of a military confrontation with some optimism by the end of September.[5]

To evaluate the historical circumstances, one must analyze 1) the actual military situation in 1938, 2) German and Allied operational planning, and 3) the probable course that a war would have taken. The first element in the complex strategic situation would have been the military confrontation and outcome of war between Germany and Czechoslovakia. The second factor would have been the consequent strategic environment in Eastern Europe and its effect on German prospects. Third would be the western front in 1938: not only weaknesses of the Westwall but also French willingness to take advantage of German shortcomings; and fourth, the naval situation in September 1938 must be considered. The fifth factor, of great importance in settling one of the historiographical arguments on the Czech crisis, would be the possibility of a "strategic" bombing offensive against the British Isles. The sixth element would involve Germany's diplomatic and economic situation in a major European war. Seventh and last, this chapter will discuss the probable course that a war in 1938 would have followed.

The German-Czech Military Confrontation

In dealing with the German army of the thirties it is difficult to ignore the great victories won early in the Second World War. In 1938, however, the army was a very different organization from the one that invaded Poland in 1939 or France in 1940. Although the Wehrmacht had made vast progress in rearmament, there was still a considerable gap between propaganda and reality. Both the Anschluss and the Czech crisis indicated that there were serious weaknesses. To crush Czechoslovakia and free Germany from her limited economic and strategic base, mechanized and motorized divisions would have to carry the burden. These formations were later to win the great victories of 1939 through 1941, but in 1938 critical deficiencies existed in the mobile forces. There were, moreover, deficiencies in equipment for reserve units, and it was unlikely that German industry could replace combat wastage at the same time as it was equipping those reserve forces.[6]

At the time of the Czech crisis, the German army consisted of forty-eight active-duty divisions. Of these, only three were panzer;[7] four were motorized infantry; thirty-four were infantry; four were light motorized; and three were mountain divisions. This total includes two infantry, one light motorized, and two mountain divisions that the Wehrmacht inherited from the old Austrian army.[8] The Wehrmacht had not yet fully integrated these divisions, and some Austrian units were of lower quality than their German counterparts. Of the total, less than one quarter of the army consisted of motorized or mechanized divisions. The great bulk was thus infantry divisions that were organized and equipped almost exactly as World War I infantry. With horse-drawn artillery and transport, these thirty-seven divisions were no more modern than contemporary infantry in the French army. Unlike 1914, there were few trained reserves, a factor that hindered mobilization of even the regular army.

The three panzer divisions were weak compared to those that broke through the Ardennes in 1940. Their equipment consisted entirely of Pzkw I and II models, for the Pzkw IIIs and IVs were not yet in production, although a few prototypes did exist.[9] The Pzkw I weighed less than six tons and carried two machine guns; the Pzkw II weighed ten tons and possessed one 20mm gun as its main armament.[10] Surprisingly, these two tanks formed the majority of German tanks through the French campaign. Even in May 1940, Pzkw Is and IIs numbered 1,478 out of the 2,339 tanks on the western front.[11] In 1938, however, without the hitting power and armored protection of heavier tanks, the light tanks would have had difficulty in gaining and maintaining the freedom necessary for mobile operations. After the war Halder admitted that only by spring 1940 had the Wehrmacht brought its armored equipment up to date.[12]

In the period from 1933 to 1937 the German army had expanded fourfold from the 100,000-man Reichswehr and had split each formation at least twice to create new units.[13] This rapid expansion, with accompanying shortages of officers and NCOs, led to a serious decline in the level of performance.[14] As a result, throughout summer 1938 the Wehrmacht worked to improve training and combat effectiveness at basic company level.

Active-duty divisions possessed one significant deficiency. Although their combat units consisted entirely of active-duty soldiers, most support personnel were reservists. This hampered effectiveness and the capability to respond quickly. One after-action report on the Czech crisis complained that the army still organized itself on a defensive philosophy and urged that the Wehrmacht expand support services so that regular units would reach a higher level of readiness. [15]

Another serious problem the Wehrmacht faced was that of expanding to meet its strategic commitments should a major war break out over Czechoslovakia. This represented the twofold problem of finding trained personnel and of acquiring equipment to arm the reserves. Still, in 1938 the Versailles treaty's 100,000-man limit represented an indirect constraint. No ready reserve existed. Reserve classes from 1919 through 1934 had received little military training, and only in 1939 did the army have the resources to address this problem. Since the 1935 conscripts had only finished training the previous fall (1937), only one class of trained reservists was available. Until such time as additional conscript classes had received training, the Wehrmacht had to bridge the gap between available reservists and army needs by a series of expedients. Where possible, World War I veterans fleshed out support units, while the army relied on Landwehr divisions, consisting almost entirely of World War I veterans, to act in place of reserve divisions.

The 1938 situation revealed how little depth German rearmament had achieved. At mobilization the army could call up eight reserve and twenty-one Landwehr divisions. [16] In other words, it could only mobilize 500,000 reservists for a regular army numbering slightly over 500,000 men. Nearly all reservists were World War I veterans with little training in the intervening twenty years. Serious organizational problems existed: reservists who had just completed service received assignment to support units while reserve combat units, such as antitank and infantry companies, possessed only one-third of their required trained personnel. [18] Many Landwehr officers and NCOs did not measure up to their duties and responsibilities. Most were too old. [19] In July 1938 Brauchitsch pointed out that the training of Landwehr and reserve units indicated that most reserve officers and NCOs were below army standards. [20] In one Landwehr division mobilized in 1939 the average age of officers was forty-five, and one regimental commander was sixty-seven. [21] Another Landwehr division, mobilized at the same time, took ten days to assemble instead of the four demanded by plans. Its artillery could not move even after the tenth day because it had not yet received saddles. In spite of the availability of

Czech equipment, the division possessed only three batteries of artillery and World War I machine guns.[22] The situation was even worse in 1938.

There were shortcomings in the regular army as well. Manstein, a division commander after March 1938, discovered that his division was short one infantry battalion and possessed no heavy artillery.[23] In 1938 there was barely enough ammunition for six weeks of heavy fighting,[24] and German industry was not ready to replace heavy munition expenditures.[25] Heavy artillery was almost nonexistent, and there were shortages of medium-caliber guns.[26] Hitler was especially angry at the Heereswaffenamt because the heaviest caliber weapon was a 210mm howitzer, and regular units had received only twenty-three of these howitzers (eight in East Prussia).[27] Support vehicles, such as trucks, came largely from the civilian sector; most were not designed for military use and performed badly in combat conditions.[28]

In 1938, the German army faced strategic demands that it was not yet ready to meet. Three infantry divisions remained in East Prussia, because the Germans could not trust the Poles. The army detailed thirty-seven regular divisions, including nearly all mechanized and motorized units, for the invasion of Czechoslovakia. This left the OKH with eight regular divisions for deployment elsewhere. Five received assignment to the western front.[29] Thus, only three remained to act as a strategic reserve or as a screen along the Pomeranian and Silesian frontiers. In an August conference with Adam, Hitler claimed that twenty reserve divisions would be immediately available for the west on mobilization. Brauchitsch, however, corrected the führer and warned that only eight would be ready within three weeks of mobilization. The other twelve would take considerably longer to establish.[30] At the end of September OKW admitted that there would be only fourteen reserve and Landwehr divisions available for eventual duty in the west.[31] September's mobilization did proceed more smoothly than had that for the Anschluss. There were two fundamental reasons. First, the lengthy call-up, spread out and prepared in advance, eased the process. Second, the Germans had learned from their Austrian experiences. Thanks to the Anschluss, traffic as well as march discipline was considerably improved.[32]

Throughout the crisis, troop morale was excellent. Some units even expressed disappointment at the invasion's cancellation after long months of preparation.³³ At the same time, the 7th Division reported that civilian morale had been low throughout the crisis.³⁴ This lack of enthusiasm for war outraged one army corps: it urged the Nazi party to "reawaken the popular instincts" for honor and duty "after years of pacifist teaching."³⁵

Many troop units, detailed for *Fall Grün*, were dissatisfied with their state of readiness. The 25th Panzer Regiment, which had performed so poorly in March, warned that, if it participated in September maneuvers, it would not be ready for the invasion of Czechoslovakia.³⁶ The 7th Division reported that its support elements were weak and that it needed three days after mobilization to reach full readiness.³⁷ Reserve and Landwehr divisions were in an unsatisfactory state. A special "training" division, consisting of Landwehr personnel, mobilized along with the regular army in September. Although the army had prepared its mobilization beforehand, the division encountered major difficulties. The "after-action" report indicated that troop units could not have fought for at least two weeks after mobilization. Soldiers lacked knowledge of their weapons; the division lacked trained officers and NCOs; reserve officers and NCOs were too old, too fat, and rarely met Wehrmacht standards.³⁸

In nearly every respect, the Wehrmacht was not ready in 1938. It did not possess an armored force capable of winning decisive victories. It could not fight simultaneously in the east and the west. Germany possessed neither trained reserves nor the industrial capacity to put substantial reserve forces in the field. Industry would have faced considerable difficulty in meeting wartime demands for fuel, ammunition, and weapons just for the regular army. Thus, it is hard to see exactly what major military operations the Germans could have mounted after the conquest of Bohemia.

On the other hand the Anschluss and the looming crisis over the Sudeten borderlands came before the Czechs were ready. They had made progress in correcting deficiencies in the regular army, but work on fortifications had advanced haltingly. In some areas the Czechs had nearly completed the defensive system, but in other districts work had hardly begun. In April 1938 the British military attaché reported that, if the Czechs completed their fortification program, their resistance would surprise not only their enemies, "but all those whose judgment of their capacity for defense was based on a glance at the map." He added:

A sudden attack in great strength, carried out at the present moment against any portion of the line of fortifications except that which covers Ostrava, would be likely to get through after prolonged and heavy fighting, but if the present intensified construction program is fulfilled, those sectors in the north which otherwise offer the best facilities for penetration on a large scale could be closed by the autumn of this year. . . . My most abiding general impression is that, whereas I had expected to find a comparatively weak line in an advanced state of preparation, I found in fact a very strong one far from ready.[39]

Even along the old Austrian border some fortification work had begun. The attaché disclosed that although these defenses except near Bratislava could not hold the Germans for "more than quite a temporary period, a matter of a day or two," they were strong enough to "prevent anything in the nature of a clear run through and to force the enemy to give battle seriously."[40]

The strongest fortifications lay opposite Silesia, where barely one hundred miles separated Austria from German Silesia. A successful German offensive across this narrow neck would slice Czechoslovakia in half. Because of the Anschluss the Germans could now launch a two-pronged assault to split the Czech state. A German strategic study, written after Munich, reported that Czech fortifications along the Silesian frontier represented a solid system of mutually supporting strong points. In view of mountainous terrain along the Saxon frontier, Czech fortifications were limited, and the system on the Bavarian frontier consisted of a mixture of field works and strong points with the valleys heavily fortified. An additional line of field fortifications stood before Prague. Finally, the fortification work opposite Austria was the weakest in the Czech system.[41]

Throughout the summer the Czechs extensively pushed construction work on their defensive system. At the end of July the British assistant military attaché reported that "[t]he Czech military authorities were undoubtedly increasing their frontier defenses daily and extensively. With every day therefore the *Spaziergang* (stroll) into Czechoslovakia of which Bavarian officers who had marched into Austria talked after the *Anschluss* becomes more difficult to make."[42] A September OKH intelligence summary warned that Czech fortification work had advanced so far that a defensive system now existed along the entire German frontier, although it still had gaps and insufficient

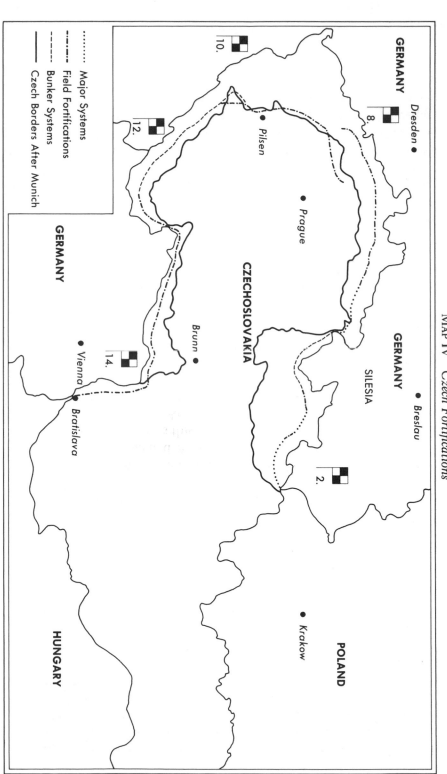

MAP IV *Czech Fortifications*

Legend:
.... Major Systems
-·-·-·- Field Fortifications
-·-·- Bunker Systems
―――― Czech Borders After Munich

GERMANY

● Dresden

● Pilsen

● Prague

CZECHOSLOVAKIA

● Brunn

● Vienna

● Bratislava

GERMANY

SILESIA

● Breslau

GERMANY

POLAND

● Krakow

HUNGARY

depth.[43] After occupation of Sudeten districts German viewers were generally impressed with what they saw. The VII Corps recorded: "During a visit to troop units the operations officer had the occasion to visit the Czech bunkers near Hintring. Fortification work made a quite solid impression; they were cleverly laid out and would have been able to support each other well, if it had come to war. One could not escape the impression that the attack through the Moldau valley would not have been simple."[44]

Arbeitsstab (working staff) Leeb reported that its forces would have suffered light casualties in overrunning fortified areas that possessed no depth but would have suffered both delays and heavy casualties where the Czech system was organized in depth.[45] Opposite Bavaria, the Czechs had done relatively less work than elsewhere. *Arbeitsstab* Leeb commented that the deployment of large German infantry forces there had been correct. Czech fortifications were weak in many places, and attacking divisions would not have taken long to overwhelm frontier defenses. In some valleys the Czechs had built only one bunker line, and in others they had not completed critical work such as camouflaging new positions.[46] A more thorough study indicated that Czech fortifications in this region did not have the depth to hinder offensive operations. The XIII Corps reported that its troops would have needed one day to break down the defenses.[47]

At the beginning of September OKH completed invasion planning. Halder, as chief of staff, was responsible for *Fall Grün*, and on September 3, he and Brauchitsch presented Hitler with the plans. OKH proposed a swift transition for the invading forces from training in maneuver areas to jump-off positions on the Czech frontier. Reserve and Landwehr mobilization would not occur until the last moment in order to increase Czech uncertainty.[48] The army detailed thirty-seven out of forty-eight regular divisions and almost all armored and motorized strength for the Czech operation. Twenty-three infantry, four motorized infantry, three mountain, four light, and three armored divisions would participate in the invasion. These divisions would form up in five armies distributed around Czechoslovakia: Fourteenth Army under General Wilhelm List north of Vienna; Twelfth Army under General Wilhelm Ritter von Leeb northwest of the old Austro-German frontier; Tenth Army under General Walther von Reichenau east of Marienbad; Eighth Army under General Fedor von Bock in Saxony;

and Second Army under General Gerd von Rundstedt in the Silesian salient.[49]

Halder proposed having the Second and Fourteenth Armies drive across Czechoslovakia's narrow neck and cut Bohemia and Moravia from Slovakia. This move would prevent a retreat into Slovakia and allow German forces to defeat the Czechs in detail. In strictly military terms it was the best strategy, but Hitler raised legitimate objections at the initial planning session. First, the plan was obvious. Second, strong Czech fortifications lay opposite the Second Army in Silesia. Third, the road system in Austria was inadequate and would hinder the Fourteenth Army, whereas the Czechs would station strong forces in the region to compensate for weak fortifications. And fourth, Hitler objected, the plan failed to consider political realities. The Wehrmacht had to win a striking success in the campaign's first days to forestall western intervention. Hitler feared that a concentration of strength on the pincer arm driving from Silesia might lead to a repetition of Verdun. He then demanded that the OKH concentrate the motorized and armored strength in Reichenau's Tenth Army in Bavaria and predicted that the massive armored force could capture Prague in the campaign's first days. Such a success, he suggested, might well result in the collapse of Czech resistance, while undermining Western willingness to intervene.[50]

After discussions, Hitler departed for the Nazi party congress at Nürnberg. The argument had not been resolved and the OKH made no significant changes. Halder and Brauchitsch, however, were soon disabused of the notion that they could safely ignore the führer. On the evening of September 9, they again conferred with Hitler, who now made clear that German strategy *would* change. Engel characterized the meeting as a disaster.[51] Hitler demanded that the OKH transfer motorized divisions from the Second and Fourteenth Armies to the Tenth Army. The führer accepted the necessity for pincer movements from Austria and Silesia but argued that, since the distance between armies was so little, infantry supported by a few motorized and armored divisions could close the gap. Moreover, mechanized forces assigned to List could also drive into Slovakia and prevent establishment of a firm front there. Hitler now told Halder: "There is no doubt that the planned pincer operation is the most desirable solution and should take place. Its success, nevertheless, is too uncertain

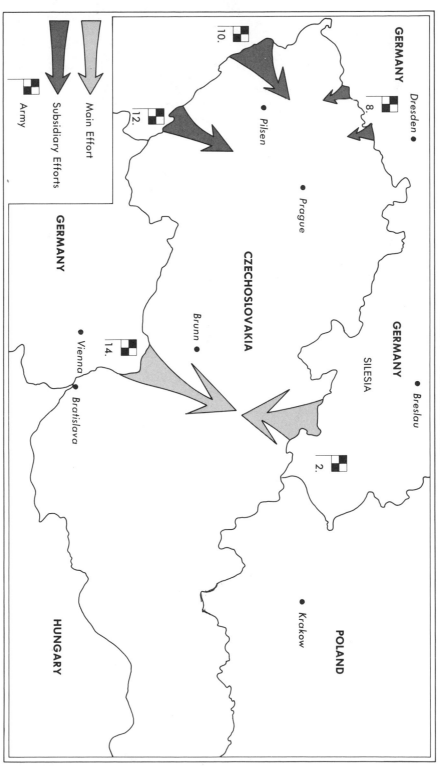

Map V The Halder Plan

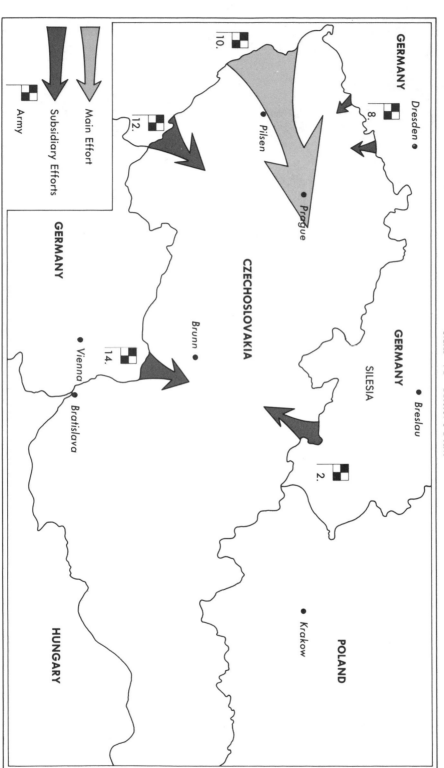

MAP VI *Hitler's Plan*

to depend on. Especially, as politically, a rapid success is necessary. The first eight days are politically decisive, in which period of time we must achieve far-reaching territorial gains. Our heavy artillery is not adequate against the fortifications. Surprise is not possible where attack is expected."[52] At the conclusion of the meeting Brauchitsch gave the führer an unexpected expression of the army's loyalty. Engel noted that the adjutants of other services were still present, and Hitler responded with a long monologue on how much the army had disappointed him.[53]

Thus, final German plans compromised between Halder's and Hitler's conceptions. The Tenth Army was strengthened and would strike at Prague. The Twelfth Army with its infantry divisions would act as a lever against Czech fortifications and threaten Prague from the south. Bock's Eighth Army would pin down Czech forces opposite Saxony, while List's Fourteenth Army and a somewhat weakened Second Army would split Czechoslovakia. The pincers movement would prevent retreat into Slovakia and a protracted Czech defense. List's army would also push into Slovakia to dislocate Czech defenses there.

As with most compromises, the final plan was weaker than either initial conception. Politically as well as militarily, Hitler's plan was better. It was more daring and risky because it would have launched armored and motorized forces across difficult terrain, but for that reason it would have been unexpected. The final plan did strengthen Reichenau sufficiently to capture Prague—eventually. Rundstedt's and List's armies also had the forces to carry out their missions. Nevertheless, it seems doubtful whether the compromise plan could have achieved a swift enough success to keep France from having to honor her obligations. And that was the key.

Czech mobilization for the crisis occurred without serious difficulty. However, somewhere between 60 and 70 percent of the Sudeten Germans refused to report.[54] Originally the Czechs had designed their mobilization plans for an eight-day period but as a result of work over the summer they completed the September call-up within five days.[55] "My personal opinion," the British military attaché reported,

is that the morale of the Czech army and nation is high. Morale, or courage, depends mainly on two factors: the "cause" and staying power. No one can say that from the Czech point of view the cause is not a good one. . . . Everything points to the fact that

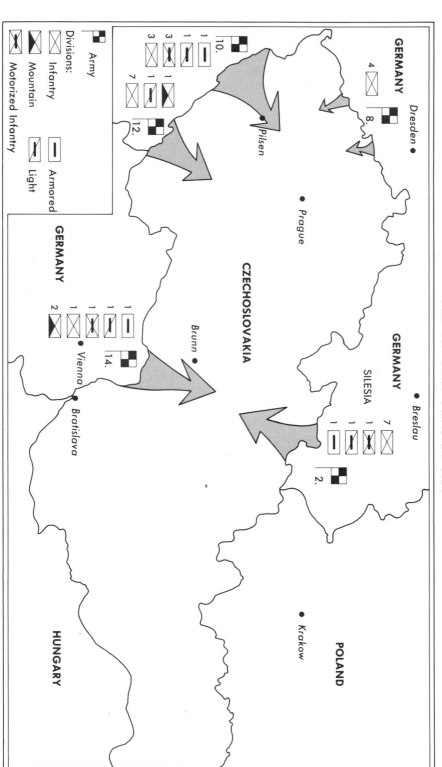

Map VII Final "Fall Grün" Plan

they have staying power as well. . . . The morale of the German army is no doubt very fine and is actuated by a great ideological impulse, but one wonders whether the "cause" in so far as it affects the individual is not somewhat thinner than in the case of the Czech soldier, the existence of whose country is at stake. To sum up, there are no shortcomings in the Czech army, as far as I have been able to observe, which are of sufficient consequence to warrant a belief that it cannot give a good account of itself. . . . In my view, therefore, there is no material reason why they should not put up a really protracted resistance single-handed. It all depends on their morale. If that gives way, the war cannot last more than a week or two. If it holds, it may drag on for months. The fall of Prague should not be vital. [56]

Numerically the Germans mustered thirty-seven divisions against approximately thirty Czech divisions. [57] The near equality is deceiving, however, since all German divisions were regular units, whereas a sizeable proportion of Czech forces was reserve. The defense of their long frontier presented the Czechs with a difficult strategic problem. Strategically the best solution was to screen Bohemia and western Moravia and concentrate the bulk of the army in eastern Moravia and western Slovakia. But politically the Czechs felt they could not abandon Prague and their industrial regions before the campaign began. Even so, unlike the Poles who defended everything in 1939, the Czechs did not distribute all their forces along the frontier. They established two significant reserve groupings. The first, centered on Prague, consisted of two mobile (*schnell*) divisions, one infantry division, and four reserve infantry divisions. A number of reserve infantry regiments also stood in the field fortifications before Prague. The Czechs established a second reserve grouping near the frontier between Moravia and Slovakia. This force consisted of two mobile divisions, one motorized infantry division, part of one regular infantry division, and five reserve divisions. [58]

Czech defenses and forces in front of Prague would have inflicted serious casualties on the German drives from Bavaria, although they could not have prevented the capture of the city. The period during which they could have held the Germans is impossible to determine, but the combination of difficult terrain and forces in the area would have prevented a quick, decisive defeat. On the other key front, facing

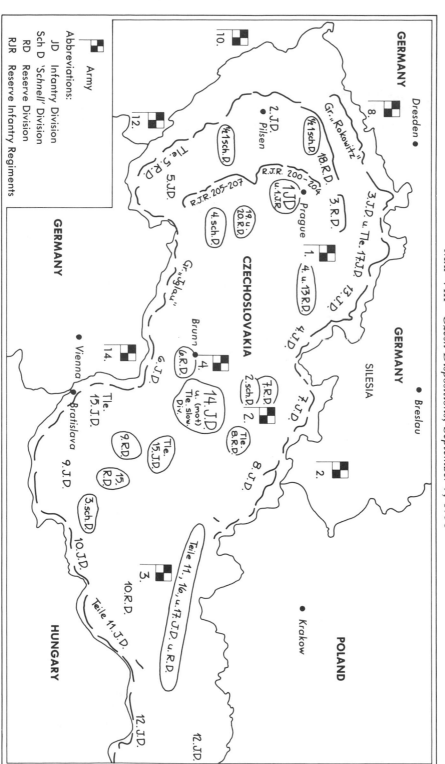

Map VIII *Czech Dispositions, September 9, 1938*

the Second and Fourteenth German armies, Czech reserves and fortifications would also have presented the Germans with difficulties. Rundstedt's forces faced an especially difficult task. Fortifications and Czech reserve forces would probably have prevented a Second Army breakthrough until List's advance unhinged Czech defenses. If Rundstedt had pushed the Silesian offensive to gain quick results, his army would have suffered heavy casualties. List's army would have had difficulty in achieving strategic freedom, but it was the most serious threat to the Czech defenses. Unlike the Second Army it could move in two directions, either east into Slovakia or north toward Silesia, and could thus unbalance the defending forces. Nevertheless, the Fourteenth Army faced major forces to the north and was the second weakest of the German armies.

The final factor in evaluating the Czech-German military confrontation is the air situation. Later we will evaluate air power's wider impact on the military balance, but it is necessary here to discuss the Luftwaffe and its possible effect on the Czech-German battle. Weather over Czechoslovakia during the projected invasion period was not good. In the twelve days from September 30 to October 11, it rained on six days with eight days of fog.[59] During the critical first five days, the weather was worse.[60] This was not the sort of weather that a young and inexperienced air force could face without serious losses—especially in view of the fact that many Luftwaffe pilots did not yet possess instrument ratings.[61]

The Third Air Force, assigned to support the advance from Bavaria and Austria, reported that it would have faced considerable difficulty in conducting air operations. German mobilization had fully alerted the Czechs. The Czech air force had, as a result, deployed its squadrons from peacetime to satellite fields and had thus robbed the Luftwaffe of the opportunity of catching its aircraft with a sudden strike. The Third Air Force felt that attacks on the Czech ground organization and supply system would have eventually crippled Czech air power, but bad weather would have seriously restricted operations. A commitment of aircraft in bad weather would have resulted in unsupportable losses through accidents, crashes, and midair collisions. Only operations using single, highly trained aircrews rather than massed formations would have been possible during bad weather, and such actions could not have had a decisive effect.[62] The First Air Force, deployed in Saxony and Silesia, reported that, although the Czechs were inferior in air power, they could have caused serious difficulties by attacking airfields in Silesia and the transportation network radiating southward from Breslau.[63] Moreover, they expected to meet a strong, well-organized anti-aircraft defense system over fortifications and important industrial centers.[64] In retrospect, the Luftwaffe would undoubtedly have played a major role in the conquest of Czechoslovakia but because of bad weather and its own weaknesses would have suffered serious losses that would have crippled its ability to meet the demands of a European war.

Czech resistance, without outside support, would probably have lasted as long as Polish resistance lasted in 1939. However, because of Czech terrain and the inadequacies of German tank forces, the Czechs would have inflicted higher casualties on the Wehrmacht, and the generally bad weather prevailing during the invasion period would have limited Luftwaffe operations. A victory over Czechoslovakia with heavy losses in men and equipment would not have provided the same boost that victory over Poland provided a year later. Furthermore, the panzer divisions did not have the same opportunity to prove themselves in Czechoslovakia that they were to have in Poland. Czech terrain was not as suitable for armored operations, and there were only three armored divisions, distributed among the infantry rather than concentrated as a powerful striking force. A failure to achieve dramatic success with these mechanized forces would have provided arguments for the conservatives within the army who doubted whether armored units should have an independent role. Finally, a campaign against Czechoslovakia would have destroyed most of the Czech matériel and possibly damaged the arms industry—both of which the Germans received intact the following March.

Doubts within the officer corps as to how swiftly they could defeat the Czechs help to explain part of the opposition to war. General Ewald von Kleist remarked that had the Czech crisis led to war, the only alternative to catastrophe would have been to arrest the political leadership.[65] General Günther Kluge commented that the army was completely unprepared for war.[66] In Belgrade the German military attaché told his British colleague that "[h]e thought that war might have dragged on for years if it had started. The German General Staff had not underrated the value of the defense which the Czechs were expected to put up. On the contrary, they thought highly of the Czech army and as regards to the fortifications, the German artillery had subjected some of them to bombardment with 24cm guns without any result."[67]

THE STRATEGIC SITUATION IN EASTERN EUROPE

The basic strategic problem for Germany was that an attack on Czechoslovakia would not have remained a limited war, and the more the war spread, the more critical Germany's strategic position would have become. In any evaluation of the 1938 military balance, the attitudes of Poland and Russia are of great significance. Although many historians have stressed Russia's importance in the crisis, Poland was the only nation in Eastern Europe that could render direct, immediate, and significant aid to Czechoslovakia.

Polish military intervention could trap Rundstedt's Silesian army, as the Germans had few forces and defenses on their Polish frontier. A Polish offensive against Breslau would have jeopardized the Second Army's supply and communication links and placed Rundstedt's forces between two enemy armies within a constricted theater of operations. Loss of Silesia, coupled with a defeat of the Second Army, might have had a decisive impact on German morale. Such a Polish intervention would have greatly changed the Czech strategic situation and enabled Czech resistance to last into the winter.

The critical question is, would Poland have intervened? Poland had few options. Józef Beck, the Polish foreign minister, believed that the Czechs would not fight, that the West would not stand, and that Poland must remain implacably hostile to Russia. Nevertheless, Beck did hint to the British that Poland might modify her policy and would never actively side with Germany.[68] Still, so tortuous was the course of Polish diplomacy that some Polish officers bemoaned that a conflict over Czechoslovakia might find Poland in the German camp.[69]

Complicating Polish diplomacy was a fundamental hostility toward Germany and the Soviet Union and a dislike and contempt for the Czechs. The Germans recognized fully the ambiguity of Polish policy. In November 1937, Hitler remarked that "our agreement with Poland will remain valid as long as Germany's strength remains unshakable. Should Germany have any setbacks, then an attack by Poland against East Prussia, perhaps against Pomerania and Silesia, must be taken into account."[70] Weizsäcker warned in late August that "Poland lies in wait and wishes to keep all roads open."[71] As usual, Polish-German relations were tense throughout the summer of 1938, and in reaction to the Czech crisis Polish public opinion became increasingly hostile to the Reich.[72] The British ambassador reported that the Poles would endeavor to remain neutral as long as possible in the event of war between Czechoslovakia and Germany. Nonetheless, it would prove difficult for them to remain on the fence should Britain and France intervene, but the government's "position is such that they can hardly take a more decided line without knowing what France, Great Britain and Russia intend to do."[73] The Poles looked to Britain for guidance as the crisis deepened. On September 13, the Polish ambassador told Halifax that "[h]is country would desire, if they could, to keep out of it. He himself thought, however, that they would probably end by being drawn in, and he knew, as had been the sense of the message that he had conveyed to the Prime Minister not long ago, that it was one of the fixed points of Mr. Beck's policy . . . to wish to orientate the policy of Poland as closely as possible with that of London."[74] In late September Gamelin claimed that the Polish commander in chief had assured him that Poland would strike west or southward into Silesia if France supported Czechoslovakia.[75]

Yet Polish diplomacy was anything but consistent. The Poles' blindness to the strategic effect of Czechoslovakia's dismemberment and openly expressed contempt for both the Czechs and French did not make them a reliable factor. In late September the Polish ambassador in Paris went so far as to claim in conversation with the American ambassador that

> Poland did not need to have the Teschen District handed to her by France or anyone else. She could and would take the Teschen District when she wished. There were five divisions on the Polish frontier opposite the Teschen District for that purpose. Any gift of Teschen to Poland would mean something only if it were . . . a gift which would be a part of the reorganization of real peace in Eastern Europe. I asked him what he meant by this. He said that it was clear that there could be no peace in Eastern Europe until Poland and Hungary had a common frontier, and Poland was encouraged by France and England to build up a bloc con-

sisting of Poland, Hungary, and Rumania to resist further German advances eastward.[76]

An additional factor complicating the situation was the state of Russo-Polish relations. The British ambassador in Warsaw warned that Poland's intervention at the side of the Western Powers depended on Soviet actions.[77] He argued that Poland would probably aid Czechoslovakia if Czech resistance proved substantial, as long as Russia did not confuse the situation. The one certainty in Polish policy was an adamant refusal to allow Russian forces to cross Poland to support Czechoslovakia.[78] This difficulty alone substantially negates post-Munich claims that Russian military forces could have played a significant role in a war. Russian troops could only have reached Czech or German territory by crossing Poland, and any attempt to force the Polish frontier would have resulted in a Polish-Soviet military confrontation.

An evaluation of Russia's possible role in 1938 must weigh the diplomatic as well as military situation. Since Munich the Russians have claimed the status of being the only European power untarnished by the events of 1938. The argument runs that Russia unselfishly supported Czechoslovakia against Germany, whereas Britain and France refused to stand with the Soviet Union in the misguided hope that they could push Germany east.[79] On the opposite side, Vansittart reflected a clear skepticism of Soviet policy: "On only one point have I changed my mind since 1938. I was an advocate of Anglo-Russian cooperation to prevent war. In the light of all subsequent Soviet conduct I have long been convinced that we should have been double-crossed, as indeed we were in 1939. Stalin's infamous deal with Hitler, whereby he got the Baltic states and half of Poland—and plotted to divide the world with his fellow dictator—made plain his real motive, which was to precipitate the war and get a maximum profit from it."[80] Throughout the crisis the Soviets displayed no eagerness to place themselves in the forefront of an antifascist crusade. In fact, throughout they insisted they would live up to the precise terms of their alliances with Czechoslovakia and France—no more, no less. In early September, Russian Foreign Minister Maxim Litvinov asked his ambassador in Prague to inform Beneš that in accordance with treaties the Soviet Union would render immediate aid if France also honored her obligations.[81] Such an attitude scarcely displayed a willingness to undertake additional risks on Czechoslovakia's behalf.[82] Above all, Stalin feared that Britain and France were dealing with Germany at Russia's expense. As a result the Soviets pushed for a strong western stand and expressed outrage at their exclusion from Munich. They certainly had no desire to bear the brunt of the fighting, nor in view of geography would they have had to.

Russia's strategic position made it difficult for her to confront Germany except in the Baltic. Poland and Rumania objected to suggestions that Soviet troops cross their territory to help the Czechs, although the Rumanians hinted that they would not interfere with aircraft flights to Czechoslovakia. It was therefore, not dangerous for Stalin to support Czechoslovakia, since there was little chance that Russia would become more than peripherally involved in a military struggle. For the West, Stalin's purges of the party, and especially the army, raised doubts as to Soviet military capabilities.[83] As one member of the House of Commons pointed out: "there must be something wrong in Russia; otherwise there would not be so many people shot."[84] Thus, there were good reasons to doubt whether Russia could bring her full weight onto the scales of a European military conflict. What is clear today is that the Soviet role in a possible war over Czechoslovakia has been exaggerated. In view of Rumanian and Polish hostility, it would have been difficult for the Russians to attack Germany or to send substantial military aid to the Czechs. Moreover, and this is a crucial point, Stalin was still in the process of purging the Red Army's officer corps.[85] The shoddy level of performance that characterized occupation of eastern Poland, the attack on Finland, and the first months of "Barbarossa" suggest that the Red Army could not have played a significant part in a 1938 war. Moreover, there are indications that Stalin hoped to use a war between the West and Nazi Germany as an excuse to settle accounts with the Poles. The bitter exchanges between Poland and Russia at the end of September suggest that both powers were more interested in renewing the 1920 war than in meeting the German threat.[86]

Yet in spite of all this, the strategic situation in Eastern Europe and the Balkans was less favorable to Germany in 1938 than in 1939-1940. To begin with, no matter what Russia's military capabilities, she could not have aided the Nazi war economy with the flow of raw materials that supported Germany after the signing of the nonaggression treaty in August 1939.[87] In addition, in 1938 Germany had not yet completely overawed the Eastern European nations. Yugoslavia and Rumania gave tacit support to Czechoslovakia in the crisis, and the Rumanians went so far as to warn the Germans that they were about to cut off delivery of oil.[88] Even the Hungarians, who had every reason to dislike the Czechs, refused to commit themselves in spite of considerable German pressure.[89]

THE WESTERN FRONT

The third factor in Germany's strategic position was the military situation in the west. Weaknesses there more than anything else alarmed the German army. Surprisingly, in spite of the fact that the Germans remilitarized the Rhineland in 1936, they did not begin extensive work on a fortified system along the French frontier until 1938.[90] In 1936 funds were not available, and in 1937 Blomberg denied requests for the steel allocations necessary to start.[91] As a result only minor preparatory work occurred. In 1936-1937 army engineers completed 540 fortified positions and began survey work for the rest of the line.[92]

In March 1938 the situation changed sharply. Hitler ordered a complete fortification of the most exposed frontier sector from Saarburg through Saarbrücken to Karlsruhe by spring 1939. The army was to complete a fortified zone along the borders of Luxembourg, Belgium, and Holland by spring 1940.[93] The May crisis altered Hitler's directive. He ordered a speedup of fortification construction in the west, especially along the French frontier. Organisation Todt received responsibility to construct major strong points, and the army was now responsible only for field fortifications. The army was ordered to supply eleven divisions in August to aid construction and the Reichsarbeitsdienst was to contribute fifty thousand workers.[94]

The construction of the Westwall underlines that political rather than military considerations motivated the führer's decision. After the war, one German officer argued that construction of an effective fortified system involved a long, slow, and complex process.[95] Instead, according to Keitel, construction of the Westwall "was a vast bluff."[96] Hitler placed his emphasis on tons of steel used and concrete poured as the basic criteria for progress.[97] His fascination with numbers was so strong that in late September he ordered Todt to ignore all considerations except completion of concrete works, although the time it takes concrete to set rendered strongpoints built at that time indefensible for most of October.[98]

Construction progress over the summer underlines the weakness of the Westwall system. By mid-September, Todt had started 5,148 bunkers but had completed only 517.[99] Squabbling between organizations was endemic, and relations between army and Organisation Todt were especially strained. The army accused Todt of more concern with impressive statistics than with the completion of a defensible line, whereas the Todt organization often found army officers offensive and arrogant.[100] So sharp did this conflict become that Adam, in charge of the western defenses, had to order subordinates to cooperate with Todt.[101] His final 1938 report recommended that Organisation Todt be completely eliminated from construction work on the Westwall because of deficiencies that appeared in its summer work.[102]

In the west the fortifications possessed none of the requirements for static or flexible defense. At its best the Westwall in 1938 was a single line of bunkers with no depth. Because of this weakness, the Germans needed large ground forces to defend the west against a possible French attack,[103] and they did not have sufficient forces available to occupy even the front line in strength. As a result, the main line of resistance, the army felt, could not hold up the French long enough to allow deployment of reserves. And there were almost no reserves. Those few available were Landwehr divisions scheduled for mobilization only after the war's outbreak.

What particularly frightened the western command was the comparative strengths of opposing forces in the west. The OKH had to assign so much strength to *Fall Grün* that only one Landwehr, four reserve, and five regular divisions remained for immediate defensive employment.[104] Opposite them the Germans estimated that the French would have fifty-six divisions available by the fifth day of mobilization—fifty infantry divisions, three mechanized divisions, and three cavalry divisions. Besides having a five-to-one superiority in divisions, the French would have a margin of five-to-one in light and nine-to-one in heavy artillery. The western command further argued that German defenses were weak compared to World War I defensive systems. In the First World War experienced divisions defended narrow sectors supported by heavy artillery and strong reserves. In 1938, inexperienced, ill-equipped divisions were responsible for much wider sectors and possessed little artillery.[105] Equally worrisome was the fact that an invasion of Czechoslovakia without mobilization would expose the western positions at a time when there were only five regular divisions, work battalions, and frontier guards available. This might result in the loss of important sections of the Westwall before reserve divisions could deploy.[106]

The unfavorable situation in the west seriously alarmed many of the senior generals in summer 1938. Considering German weaknesses, it is difficult to fathom Hitler's cavalier attitude. At an August conference of chiefs of staff with the führer, General von Wietersheim argued that current German forces in the west could not hold the fortifications for more than three weeks against a determined French attack. Hitler retorted, "I assure you, general, the position will not only be held for three weeks but for three years."[107] Late in August, in conference with Adam during a tour of western fortifications, Hitler played down French military strength, their willingness to declare war, and their army's ability to concentrate quickly. The führer promised Adam twenty reserve divisions for the west. Brauchitsch interrupted to point out that only eight could deploy within three weeks of mobilization. The other twelve would take considerably longer to form. Nevertheless, Hitler remarked that the French could not force German troops out of the Westwall.[108] Such exchanges resemble Hitler's performance six years later, when he let his fingers drift across situation maps, decreeing fortresses in every town—fortresses where neither men, equipment, trenches, nor bunkers existed. He now dismissed the preponderate French strength with a wave of the hand, ignored the incompleteness of the western defensive system, and created twenty reserve divisions from nothing.

On the Upper Rhine, difficulties in making a river crossing and the nature of terrain on the German side gave the Reich a measure of security. The region between the Moselle and Rhine along the axis of Saarburg, Saarbrücken, Karlsruhe was the most exposed. Considering the above-mentioned weaknesses, the Germans would have had difficulty here in offering anything more than a delaying action to a major French offensive. Without reinforcements the Germans could have lost the Saar and possibly the Rhineland, and a determined French thrust might have reached the Ruhr.

Thus, with even moderately aggressive military leadership, France could have waged her own *Blumenkrieg* in the Rhineland; but in 1938 such leadership was not available. At this time de Gaulle, discussing French military intentions with Blum, sarcastically commented that "[i]t's quite simple. . . . Depending on actual circumstances, we will recall the 'disponibles' or mobilize the reserves. Then, looking through the loopholes of our fortifications, we will passively witness the enslavement of Europe."[109] De Gaulle had correctly sized up the situation.

On September 26, Gamelin visited London to discuss strategic possibilities and French plans. His comments give a clear picture of the high command's intentions. Gamelin first emphasized France's strengths to his British listeners. France could mobilize 5,500,000 men in one hundred divisions, sixty of which would face Germany. As only four divisions were needed to support the Maginot line, fifty-six were free for operations elsewhere. On the other side Gamelin estimated that Germany could mobilize sixty-six divisions in the first weeks of war, and that thirty-four were then on the Czech frontier, with only eight in the west. Gamelin claimed that the French army would not sit behind its fortifications. As soon as he received permission from his government, he would attack. But although immediate action had advantages, Gamelin thought that one might better wait until Paris was evacuated. He then acknowledged that the Luftwaffe had deployed its bombers against Czechoslovakia. How soon the Germans could transfer forces from the east to help their western defenses would depend on the campaign against Czechoslovakia and Poland's attitude. When the Germans did transfer troops to the west and the French faced a major German concentration, they "would retreat strategically in the manner of Hindenburg in 1917 to their fortifications in the Maginot line devastating their territory as they went." With this statement Gamelin admitted that in spite of a seven-to-one superiority (fifty-six divisions to eight) he did not feel he could achieve significant military success. Later Gamelin returned to this point and suggested that after the initial offensive the French would be compelled to retreat to the Maginot line by winter. Here he raised the question of eventual support by the British army and stressed that he hoped for active British assistance during the winter after his forces had returned to the Maginot line. Gamelin's comments fully suggest that a French offensive in 1938 would have resembled the sorry performance of 1939. He emphasized that blockade would be the weapon that would defeat Germany. He gave the Czech army, its armament, and fortifications high marks, but to be on the safe side he remarked that as a soldier "he was only prepared to say that she [Czechoslovakia] could hold out certainly for a few weeks, but perhaps not for a few months; the whole question depended on the attitude of Poland."[110]

Other high-ranking French officers were less optimistic. In a conversation with the British military attaché, General Dentz pointed out that if war came, the Luftwaffe would destroy France's defenseless cities. He left the British officer with the impression that the French regarded German annexation of Czechoslovakia as a certainty.[111] On the same day, Colonel Ferdinand Gauche, chief of military intelligence, commented that "of course there will not be a European war since we are not going to fight."[112]

The British did nothing to encourage the French. As early as September 12, the Chief of Air Staff warned that the French army might attack the "greatly" strengthened fortifications in the west. He suggested that the Chiefs of Staff be allowed to initiate staff conversations in order to persuade the French of the folly of such action.[113] The chiefs told a meeting of ministers at the end of September that they "feared that France might start some offensive action against Germany that would not be likely to achieve any effective result. They thought that it was important to impress on the French government that they should not take any offensive action until they had consulted with the British government."[114]

THE NAVAL SITUATION

German naval inferiority was even more marked in 1938 than at the outbreak of the Second World War. Neither the *Scharnhorst* nor *Gneisenau* was ready for action, and the *Bismarck*-class battleships were two years from completion. The three largest ships in service, the so-called "pocket battleships," were glorified commerce raiders. There were no heavy cruisers, no aircraft carriers, only six light cruisers and seven destroyers, and submarine strength was minimal. In February 1938 the navy possessed twelve submarines suitable for service in the Atlantic with a further twenty-four small U-boats (*kleine Unterseeboote*) capable of only working in shallow seas.[115]

Such a small force had restricted strategic capabilities. The most obvious strategic task would be to defend ore shipments from Sweden and Norway. Alarmed by naval weaknesses, Raeder had earlier in the year pressed Hitler for a rapid increase in naval strength to guarantee ore supplies.[116] Naval strength was not sufficient to insure even this limited objective. War with England would immediately threaten the ore route from Narvik,[117] and Germany's Baltic position was similarly uncertain. In October 1938 Admiral Rolf Carls, Baltic commander, suggested that Germany must seize Denmark to protect that sea.[118] Marine Gruppenkommando Ost warned in late 1938 that if England entered a war against Germany, the strategic situation in the Baltic would change decisively. One could no longer expect imports across the North Sea, and protection of the Swedish ore trade would be the chief task of the fleet.[119]

Considering the Baltic fleet's size, even that task seemed beyond its capacity, especially considering Soviet naval forces. In July 1938 Baltic fleet command doubted whether its strength could protect ore ships from Lulea from Russian interference. The best strategy, it suggested, would aim to block the Gulf of Finland at the onset of war with mines, submarines, and surface units, thus bottling up the Russians.[120] But such strategy was beyond German means. Against a Russian submarine force of twenty 500-ton boats and numerous smaller craft, Baltic antisubmarine forces consisted of fishing boats requisitioned in August. Obviously the technical equipment was not first class. The German submarine school observed that, with exception of the flotilla chief (who had received a one-day instruction course), Baltic officers on antisubmarine duty had no experience in their assigned work. There were few reconnaissance aircraft and no major fleet units except for two predreadnought battleships. After the crisis, the Baltic command warned that it could have performed its reconnaissance and combat tasks only in a limited fashion and that if Germany had faced Russia, the Baltic fleet could not have met its responsibilities without substantial reinforcement.[121] Minesweeper flotillas were in no better condition than antisubmarine forces. Their vessels came entirely from the fishing fleet, and their personnel were all civilians. The few assigned sailors had never worked with mines.[122] The OKM commented that its forces could only have established a partial minefield in the southern Baltic that would have hindered, but not prevented, Soviet naval operations. Moreover, it could not have guaranteed the security of the ore route, with or without minefields. [123]

THE AIR SITUATION

One of the most persistent myths in postwar historical literature has been that Chamberlain saved Britain at Munich from defeat at the hands of the Luftwaffe and won time for the RAF to win the "Battle of Britain." Supposedly the year's grace allowed the RAF to equip fighter squadrons with Hurricanes and Spitfires and to extend the radar network to cover the whole of the British Isles. The key question that such commentators do not address is whether Germany could actually have launched a "strategic" bombing offensive in 1938. To answer this question one must establish the actual balance of air power in 1938 by comparing the RAF and the Luftwaffe, and discuss in detail Luftwaffe training and support services as well as strategic and tactical planning.

There are striking similarities in the development of the British and German air forces in the late thirties. Both air staffs had to grapple with rapid expansion, a new generation of aircraft, crew training, supply and maintenance—all on a scale far exceeding anything previously experienced. These problems were so great as to make the respective air forces barely fit for combat for much of the late 1930s. In 1937 the British Air Staff reported that

> [t]he above picture of our state of readiness for war discloses many unsatisfactory circumstances, but it must be realized that the RAF is now in the midst of a most difficult stage of transition. We are in the process of expanding from a small force which mainly consists of light single-engined aircraft to a large force equipped with aircraft which are in many cases multi-engined and all of which have a high performance and completely different characteristics from those on which the bulk of the air force has been trained. Our squadrons are manned largely by personnel who—though enthusiastic and efficient—are yet lacking in experience and higher training. [124]

A German "after-action" report on the Czech crisis reflects a similar state of affairs in the Luftwaffe of 1938:

In the last months the following special measures have had to be carried through at the same time: 1) equipment of many new units, 2) rearmament of numerous units, 3) early overhaul of about 60 percent of the frontline aircraft, 4) replacement of spare parts, 5) rebuilding of numerous aircraft in the supply depots, 6) rearmament of many aircraft, 7) accelerated introduction of over-hauled motor models . . . 8) establishment of four new air groups and one new airfield . . . 10) preparation and resupply of mo-bilization supplies, corresponding to the newly established units, rearmed units, and transferred units. . . . The compression of these tasks into a very short time span has once more and in clear fashion pointed out the known lack of readiness in maintenance of flying equipment as well as in technical personnel.[125]

Neither air arm was prepared for the war that would come. The RAF saw a future war as a rapier-like surgical operation carried out by opposing air forces on populations hundreds of miles distant. For the Luftwaffe, air war involved more interservice cooperation, but it also believed in a short war with "strategic" bombing playing a major role.

The reality in the Second World War was, of course, quite different. Air war resembled the strategy of the First World War, although at-trition was in terms of aircraft, bombs, crews, training programs, fuel supplies, and munitions production. Month after month, year after year, crews climbed into aircraft to fly over a darkened continent. Success was measured in drops of percentage points in bomber losses rather than yards gained. As one commentator has pointed out: "De-spite the visions of its protagonists of prewar days, the air war during the Second World War . . . was attrition war. It did not supplant the operations of conventional forces; it complemented them. Victory went to the air forces with the greatest depth, the greatest balance, the greatest flexibility in employment. The result was an air strategy completely unforeseen by air commanders."[126] Neither air force was ready to fight anything resembling such a war in the late 1930s, when the skills, tactical training, and required depth were not yet at hand.

After the Second World War certain leading air marshals argued that Munich saved Britain from destruction. Sholto Douglas claimed that "without any reservations . . . we followed the only course that we could in the circumstances of the time."[127] Slessor, chief of coastal command during the war, writes, "the question has been discussed whether we also over-estimated the dangers of an attack on England; I can only record my own feelings of profound relief that we were not called upon to answer that question in September 1938."[128] If one considers only the British point of view there is some justification for such claims, but considering actual Luftwaffe capabilities, such a position cannot be defended.

Admittedly the Royal Air Force was not ready for war in September 1938. Its rearmament program had made little progress. Reequipment of fighter squadrons was only beginning, and Bomber Command had no modern aircraft in production. Considerable delay would occur before the great four-engined bombers that ravaged Germany came off assembly lines. As a contemporary pointed out, "in a word, expansion caught the Air Ministry napping, and the attempt to expand, side by side with getting up-to-date technically, resulted in confusion and muddle so that no expansion program—and they succeeded each other rapidly—was ever punctually or completely carried out."[129] When Bomber Command mobilized in September, only ten out of forty-two squadrons possessed what at the time passed for heavy bombers. Reserve aircraft numbered only 10 percent of front-line aircraft, and barely 200 out of 2,500 pilots were fully "operationally ready." Many aircraft had no turrets, and parts were in such short supply that Bomber Command had to cannibalize some squadrons to provide spares. By peacetime standards less than 50 percent of the force was combat-ready.[130]

Fighter Command was in scarcely better shape. Instead of the fifty squadrons considered the minimum for Britain's air defense, twenty-nine existed.[131] Only five of those possessed Hurricanes and none Spitfires. The Hurricanes could not operate at high altitudes because their guns did not have required warmers. The remaining squadrons possessed obsolete Gladiators, Furys, Gauntlets, and Demons.[132] As of October 1, British first-line strength was 1,606 machines with only 412 aircraft in reserve. British estimates for France were 1,454 first-line aircraft with 730 in reserve; and for Germany 3,200 first-line with 2,400 in reserve.[133] In fact the Germans had 3,307 aircraft, including transports, but almost no aircraft in reserve.[134] The British anti-aircraft situation was even less encouraging. The War Office provided the figures in Table VII-1 in its post-Munich review.[135]

Surprisingly, the situation in Germany did not differ substantially from that in Britain. For most of 1938 the Luftwaffe was involved in

TABLE VII-1
British Anti-Aircraft Guns, Fall 1938

Type	Approved Program	Available	Actually Deployed
3 in.	320	298	269
3.7 in.	352	44	44
2 pdr barrels	992	50	49
Naval 3 in.	—	96	95
Search Lights	4,128	1,430	1,280

exchanging first generation aircraft for those with which it would fight World War II. Fighter squadrons received Bf 109s for their biplane Arado Ar 68s, but by fall 1938 there were no more than 500 Bf 109s in regular fighter squadrons.[136] Furthermore, transition to Bf 109s led to a high accident rate in newly converted squadrons.[137] The two bombers in production, the Do 17 and He 111, were twin-engined aircraft that possessed neither the range nor bomb-carrying capacity to act as real "strategic" bombers, and their defensive armament was insignificant. He 111s carried a bomb load of 500 kilograms, and although London was within their range, they could barely reach industrial regions in the midlands from bases in western Germany. The Do 17 had an even shorter range. Early production models could barely reach London with a 500-kilogram bomb load.[138] Moreover, bombing attacks launched from Germany would not have had fighter escort, for even when based on Pas de Calais in 1940, Bf 109s hardly had sufficient range to stay with the bombers over London. The Ju 88, supposedly a significant advance in bomber construction, would not begin initial production until April 1939 and would not reach full production until 1940.[139] In August 1938 most ground attack squadrons still possessed Hs 123s that carried four 50-kilogram bombs and He 45s that carried eighteen to twenty-four 10-kilogram bombs.[140] In view of raw-material scarcities, German industry would have found it difficult to maintain its rate of aircraft production if war had broken out over Czechoslovakia. On the other hand, once production restraints imposed by the Chamberlain government disappeared because of war, British production would have risen much faster than was actually the case in late 1938 and early 1939.

In numbers, the Luftwaffe mustered just over 3,000 aircraft at the end of September. These consisted of 1,128 bombers, none of which were Ju 88s, 773 fighters, 513 reconnaissance aircraft, 226 dive bombers, 195 ground attack aircraft, 164 naval support aircraft, and 308 transports. In May 1940 shortly before the invasion of France Luftwaffe strength was in excess of 5,000: 666 reconnaissance aircraft, 1,736 fighters, 1,758 bombers, 417 dive bombers, 49 ground attack aircraft, 241 coastal aircraft, and 531 transport aircraft.[141] Differences in strength and quality were striking.

Introduction of a new generation of aircraft brought with it problems in aircrew training, maintenance, and supply. The high accident rate during the summer of 1938 resulted from aircrew training in models that were more sophisticated than anything pilots had up to then handled. The Bf 109 with its narrow undercarriage presented fighter pilots with an especially difficult transition problem. Table VII-2 on crew training status indicates the Luftwaffe's lack of readiness in 1938 to fight any sort of air war, much less a "strategic" air campaign. The Third Air Force reported that two factors contributed to the large number of partly operational crews: bomber crews that were not fully operational lacked required training in instrument flying, and Stuka crews did not possess fully trained radio operators and gunners.[142]

The Luftwaffe's "in commission" rate for the period August 1 to

TABLE VII-2
German Aircrew State of Readiness, August 1938

Type of Aircraft	Authorized Number of Crews	Crew Training Status:	
		Fully Operational	Partly Operational
Strat Recon	228	84	57
Tac Recon	297	183	128
Fighter	938	537	364
Bomber	1,409	378	411
Dive Bomber	300	80	123
Ground Attack	195	89	11
Transport	117	10	17
Coastal and Navy	230	71	23
Total	3,714	1,432	1,145

SOURCE: Air Ministry, *The Rise and Fall of the German Air Force, 1933-1945*, Air Ministry Pamphlet No. 248 (London, 1948), pp. 19-20.

December 8 indicates the extent of supply and maintenance problems. There was a significant improvement in September percentages, but this resulted from a deliberate reduction of flying and training time as *Fall Grün* approached. The Third Air Force admitted that it had brought its "in commission" rate up to a high level by carefully planned measures, but that losses, as well as the heavy demands of combat operations, would have quickly lowered these rates. Additionally, its units did not possess adequate reserves of spare parts to support even normal flying. [143] By December 1938 "in commission" rates had fallen considerably. Although it is hard to estimate how much strain the Luftwaffe could have sustained before combat effectiveness suffered, August "in commission" rates could not have given German commanders encouragement. As already mentioned, the high September percentages do not indicate that the Luftwaffe had solved its maintenance problems. The chief of supply services warned that the Luftwaffe was in an impossible situation in late 1938: "[t]he consequence of these circumstances was: a) a constant and, for first line aircraft, complete lack of reserves both as accident replacements and for mobilization; b) a weakening of the aircraft inventory in the training schools in favor of regular units; c) a lack of necessary reserve engines, supplies for the timely equipment of airfields, supply services, and depots both for peacetime needs as well as for mobilization."[144]

In September 1938 the Luftwaffe faced a complicated strategic situation beyond its capabilities. Contrary to what many pro-appeasement historians and contemporary RAF officers have supposed, the Luftwaffe's first strategic task was to support the destruction of Czechoslovakia. Other tasks, such as the disruption of French mobilization, the protection of North Sea trade, and the bombing of Britain were strictly peripheral to the central mission. In fact, the Second Air Force

TABLE VII-3
Luftwaffe "In Commission" Rates (in Percentages)

	1 Aug	15 Aug	5 Sep	12 Sep	19 Sep	26 Sep	8 Oct	8 Dec
Bombers	49	58	76	84	89	90	90	78
Fighters	70	78	89	88	93	95	90	78
Overall	57	64	79	83	90	94	92	79

SOURCE: Air Historical Branch, Air Ministry, Vol. VII, Translations: Luftwaffe Strength and Serviceability Statistics, G 302694/AR/9/51/50.

admitted in September that it was completely unprepared to launch air operations against the British Isles. [145] Even the French in their less panicky moments recognized that the Germans had deployed their bombers to the east. On September 26, Gamelin conceded that most German bombers were on airfields in the vicinity of Czechoslovakia. [146] German planning for both *Fall Rot* and *Fall Grün* deployed the mass of the Luftwaffe against Czechoslovakia. Only after a decisive air and land attack had destroyed Czechoslovakia would the Luftwaffe shift to the west. Air operations and the losses suffered in attacking the Czechs would have seriously affected the Luftwaffe's capacity to launch attacks against Britain later in the year. Moreover, German planning for *Fall Grün* indicates that the Germans expected serious French air attacks against targets in western Germany. Luftwaffe planners especially feared that the French air force would hinder deployment of German forces along the Westwall, thus facilitating a successful French offensive against the Rhineland. [147]

Expecting a major war against Britain well in the future and committed to supporting the attack on Czechoslovakia, the Luftwaffe was unprepared to launch bombing attacks against the British Isles and had only just begun to plan for such an eventuality. [148] In August 1938 one member of Second Air Force staff—which had responsibility for operations over the North Sea and against the British Isles—characterized his command's capability as no more than the capacity to inflict pinpricks. [149] The Second Air Force emphasized that the Wehrmacht would have to seize Belgium and Holland before the Luftwaffe could hope to inflict serious damage on Britain. [150] Any offensive operation to capture the Low Countries would have required extensive Luftwaffe support. Disregarding the question of whether the army could have launched such a campaign, one can only wonder about the Luftwaffe's condition after supporting major offensives against Czechoslovakia and the west. As the Luftwaffe discovered after the beginning of the war, it could not undertake air operations against Britain until completion of the land campaign in the west. It did not possess the resources for both, and the ground situation ranked first in German priorities. [151]

General Helmuth Felmy, commander of the Second Air Force, warned the Luftwaffe high command in late September that "given the means at his disposal a war of destruction against England seemed to be excluded."[152] In May 1939 Felmy concluded a command planning meeting with an address pointing out how unprepared the Luftwaffe was, both in 1938 and 1939, to support a "strategic" bombing offensive against Britain. First of all, the Second Air Force did not possess the supply and maintenance organization to support such an undertaking. Even by 1940 Felmy felt that the Luftwaffe could only achieve partial success against England. He admitted that his command would not have even one air division fully trained and prepared to attack Britain in summer 1939. Considering the Second Air Force's equipment, preparations for attacks on Britain were completely inadequate (*völlig ungenügend*). Finally, Felmy declared that supplies of fuel and ammunition were not yet ready on forward operating fields.[153] One week later, the Luftwaffe staff admitted that "in 1939 equipment, training, and strength of the Second Air Force could not lead to a decisive success against England within a short period of time."[154]

In September 1938 the Luftwaffe found itself facing a series of problems that severely restricted its effectiveness against the British Isles. In order to frame weather predictions, the German weather service depended on, 1) reports from England, Iceland, Norway, and Greenland, 2) ship reports from the Atlantic, and 3) reports from France, Spain, and Portugal. At the end of September the Luftwaffe discovered, much to its consternation, that no alternative sources were available. Once the above reporting stations were lost, the Germans could not forecast weather over England and would have had difficulty in making long-range continental predictions.[155]

Even with well-trained aircrews, the Luftwaffe did not yet have the capacity to bomb accurately in bad weather. The future Field Marshal Albert Kesselring, admitted in 1939 that his excellent all-weather aircraft would still not enable his air crews to hit targets effectively in bad weather.[156] Moreover, in 1938 the Luftwaffe did not possess the radio technology necessary for long-distance navigation and bombing,[157] and navigation equipment in Germany was designed to aid aircraft operating over the North Sea rather than over England.[158]

Considering that air war has proven itself to be the most scientific, precise form of war man has waged, the technical, as well as the operational, inadequacies of the Luftwaffe in 1938 define its weaknesses. In nearly every respect it was unprepared to launch a "strategic" bombing offensive and so could not have significantly damaged Britain's war effort in spite of weaknesses in British air defenses. In addition, the Luftwaffe would have had difficulty just in fulfilling its operational commitments to support ground forces operating against Czechoslovakia and the west.

THE AXIS AS A MILITARY FACTOR, SEPTEMBER 1938

Adding to German difficulties was the nature of their diplomatic position. The Rome-Berlin-Tokyo combination that British defense planners had so feared throughout the late thirties remained no more than a loose combination of overlapping interests with little community of either ideology or goals. Nevertheless, in 1938 the Italians appear to have placed themselves in a situation where they would have had difficulty in remaining neutral despite their almost total unpreparedness.

The initial, and probably correct, Western estimate was that the "Italian government neither desire nor expect it [the crisis] to be settled by force of arms."[159] However, Italian blustering, especially at the end of September, committed Mussolini closely to Germany. On September 15, the British received an account of a conversation between the Belgian ambassador and Ciano, in which the foreign minister claimed: "I can only reaffirm our position in this matter. Everybody knows that we are bound by no treaty, alliance or military agreement; but we are convinced that every hour that passes strengthens our bond with Germany and that the Rome-Berlin Axis has been reinforced in an absolute and definite sense in the course of events."[160] On September 26, Ciano told the Belgian that the Italian government had always recognized that Russia and France might honor their obligations to Czechoslovakia and did not regard such an intervention as entailing a general conflict. "If, however, Great Britain came in then Italy would be compelled to do the same."[161] On September 28, Ciano directly informed the British minister "that Italy's interests, honor, and pledged word required she should actively and fully side with Germany."[162]

Although the Italians could easily have denied such nonpublic statements, in late September Mussolini placed his government in a dangerous political position. In a series of public speeches beginning at Trieste on September 18 and continuing through the 28th, Mussolini reiterated that, although Italy hoped for peace, the outbreak of war over Czechoslovakia would find Italy at Germany's side. Such precise public statements would have been difficult to disavow.[163] They seem to have, moreover, reflected Mussolini's thought at the time. At the end of September he told Hitler's special emissary, Prince Philipp of Hesse, that "France will not march, because England will not fall in behind her. Should the conflict, however, become general we will place ourselves by the side of Germany immediately after the entry of England into the war. Not before, in order not to give her justification for war. The Duce too reaffirmed his full conviction of our victory— force of arms and irresistible force of spirit."[164] Of course, it is entirely conceivable that Mussolini would have drawn back from the edge as he was to do in 1939 when confronted with the extent of Italian deficiencies. Even so, this was less likely in 1938 both because of Mussolini's public statements, as well as the fact that those of his advisers who opposed war were less organized than they would be in 1939.

Italian participation in a war at Germany's side would have harmed the German strategic situation in several important respects.[165] First, and most important, it would have increased the effectiveness of the Allied blockade. The burden of supplying Italy with raw materials from the limited available sources might have strained the Nazi economy to the breaking point.[166] Considering British and French command of the Mediterranean, there is no doubt that Allied navies could have quickly cut supply lines to Libya and bombarded Italian coasts. The French were optimistic about prospects both in the Alps and Libya. A French general staff officer commented that the Allies would be able to score major successes against Italy within two months of hostilities.[167]

A senior Italian officer warned a German colleague in Rome that there was no prospect of a quick victory over Czechoslovakia. As a result, he argued, there was a serious possibility of a world war for which the Axis was not ready. Italy was prepared neither militarily nor politically for war and only the connection between Mussolini and Hitler tied the two countries together. He suggested that it was necessary to build a real alliance before the two powers embarked on war. Everything was against the Axis if the Czech crisis resulted in war.[168] The German naval attaché reported in November that reorganization of the Italian army, weaknesses in the air force, and matériel and training deficiencies in the navy severely limited Italian capabilities. Moreover, he suggested, the dependency on imports placed Italy in a dangerous situation. Thus, throughout the crisis the Italian military had had no desire to fight, and most Italians saw no reason for war over Czechoslovakia.[169]

British strategic planners as usual confused the issue by casting Mediterranean estimates in the worst possible light. Further complicating matters was a serious difference of opinion between planners and intelligence services over Italian capabilities. This disagreement surfaced in an August meeting of the Joint Planning Committee in discussion of a memorandum by the Industrial Intelligence Center on "The number of divisions that Italian industry might maintain in the Field": "Mr. Morton pointed out that the memorandum . . . stated that Italian industry could not maintain more than fifteen to sixteen divisions in the field. . . . Col. Allen said the War Office view was that Italy would not maintain in peacetime an army of say thirty-six divisions unless she had satisfied herself that she could maintain them in the field for a short war."[170] In late September the Chiefs of Staff recommended that it was of the "highest importance" that Italy be kept out of the war so that Britain could strengthen her military position in the Middle East.[171] But the War Office and the Chiefs of Staff ignored the long war and economic premises upon which they based Anglo-French strategy. Halifax hinted at an opposing conception when he telegraphed Roosevelt "that a neutral Italy might be more valuable to Germany as an avenue of supply, than Italy as an ally in arms."[172]

Conflict with Italy would have involved the Allied naval forces that would remain in the Mediterranean regardless of whether Italy were neutral or joined the Reich. Italian land forces, such as they were, had little outlet: Abyssinia was an internment camp with no strategic possibilities; Libya, cut off from the mother country because of overwhelming Allied naval superiority, could only support minimal forces from its scanty resources. Only along the inhospitable Alpine frontier with France could the Italians deploy their army. Thus, the Italians represented no greater a threat in 1938 than in 1940. Their participation would have drained German military and economic resources, and the Germans could not have afforded any significant aid to bolster Italy in 1938.

The Japanese attitude throughout the mounting European crisis was ambivalent. Although they were not sorry to see troubles in Europe that would divert attention from the Far East, they had their hands full with the war in China.[173] In September they launched a major campaign to capture Hankow, and thus the Japanese military were too heavily involved in military operations against the Chinese to wish an expanded war.[174] Reports from Tokyo indicated that the Japanese had no desire to participate in a European conflict or to extend their commitments. In August the Japanese ambassador in Paris remarked that the armistice with Russia in Manchuria resulted from his government's wish to avoid a second military confrontation, as China had already caused sufficient difficulties.[175] On September 15, the British ambassador in Tokyo reported: "[t]he French ambassador considers it most unlikely that Japan will take any precipitate step if war were to break out in Europe. He thinks and I agree that the present campaign in China would be intensified regardless of feeling and rights of third countries, but he does not believe in an immediate attack on Soviet Russia. He is inclined to think [that the] Japanese army is now sufficiently exhausted (particularly through losses of junior officers, noncommissioned officers and war matériel) to need respite before embarking on further large enterprises."[176]

The Admiralty reported that propaganda for a drive to the south had diminished during the course of 1938. It concluded: "Compared with 1937, when anti-British feeling was widespread, the anti-foreign element in propaganda has been toned down. . . . 1938 has been a year of unusual political calm . . . and outwardly the country has given an impression of unity and concentration upon the war in China."[177] The American ambassador to Tokyo came to the same conclusion. On October 6, he commented: "Nor is there any warrant whatever for assuming that the army has any intention of becoming embroiled in troubles in Europe under anything short of the most compelling reasons."[178] Such reasons were not present in 1938.

The Impact of Economic Factors

All of the above factors underline the extent of German weaknesses in 1938. As dangerous as military shortcomings and diplomatic isolation was the state of the German economy in 1938. Although the Anschluss and seizure of Austrian gold and foreign exchange had temporarily improved the economic situation, these gains had proven to be wasting assets. Over the summer of 1938 a combination of massive armament programs, construction of the Westwall, initiation of the Schnellplan, and mobilization of hundreds of thousands of soldiers created a serious economic situation. Authorities of the Four Year Plan admitted that in the last half of 1938 the German economy had faced "undreamt of difficulties. The strong box was empty; industrial capacity was committed for years to come."[179]

The Schnellplan goals of raising synthetic fuel production by 450 percent, synthetic rubber by 2,300 percent, gun powder by 261 percent, and explosives by 215 percent indicate the extent of the effort.[180] Starting in the first quarter of the 1939 financial year, the plan required additional allocations of steel and construction material.[181] As early as August 1938 considerable difficulties appeared in allocations due to competition from other sectors of the economy. For the last half of August cement deliveries met only 50 percent of requirements, and in September the total reached only 73 percent of needs.[182] Because of economic strains, the Schnellplan received only 65 percent of scheduled material allocations in the first quarter of 1939. The delays put off completion of some munition goals by as much as a full year.[183]

The construction of the Westwall compounded all the economic problems. In its first year of major construction (1938) the Westwall consumed 900,000 tons of steel, 292,000 of wood, 2,140,000 of cement, and 11,580,000 of building material. In percentages this represents 5 percent of steel, 8 percent of wood, and 20 percent of the cement used by the German economy in 1938.[184] This massive commitment led directly to delays in the effort to expand munitions and synthetics production.[185] In addition, work on the Westwall drained significant labor from other segments of the economy.[186]

The raw-material situation was catastrophic. Throughout the 1930s the Germans had not possessed sufficient foreign exchange to build up stocks of raw material.[187] In October 1938 foreign exchange shortages forced many industries to begin using their meager stockpiles to maintain existing rates of production.[188] Nowhere was the effect of the German lack of raw materials shown more clearly than in the petroleum sector. In 1938 the Germans could cover only 2.6 million tons from their own sources to meet a projected wartime demand of 7.6 million tons. Because of the foreign exchange shortages the Germans possessed almost no petroleum stocks.[189] In June petroleum stockpiles could only cover 25 percent of mobilization requirements—on the average, four months of full wartime needs. Supplies of aviation lubricants were as low as 6 percent of mobilization requirements.[190] Supplies from Rumania were doubtful, and unlike 1939, the Germans could not have drawn oil supplies from the Soviet Union.

German rubber supplies were similarly vulnerable. In the 1930s the Germans had put considerable resources into constructing synthetic rubber plants, but the investment did not bear fruit until 1941. Only then could the Reich cover economic and military requirements from domestic production.[191] Stockpiles, captured war booty, and imports across the Trans-Siberian railroad covered the gap between demand and production in the first two years of the Second World War.[192] In mid-1938, however, synthetic rubber production covered less than one-sixteenth of German needs.[193] The German situation with other key raw materials such as iron, copper, nickel, and so forth, was scarcely better,[194] and the capacity of the munitions industry gave scant comfort. Industrial capacity for gun-powder production was less than 40 percent of maximum World War I production, and the capacity of the explosives industry was less than 30 percent of the World War I maximum.[195]

Signs of economic collapse appeared in the fall of 1938. The economy seemed to have reached a breaking point. There were few unemployed from whom to draw, and mobilization for the Anschluss and the Czech crisis added to shortages of skilled and unskilled workers.[196] Shortages of workers existed in almost every segment, particularly in the coal, munitions, and aircraft industries. In December the Reichsarbeitsminister estimated that the economy was short one million workers.[197]

In fact, the economic strain was so bad in October that the Reich Defense Committee reported that in early October "in consequence of Wehrmacht demands (occupation of the Sudetenland) and unlimited construction on the Westwall so tense a situation in the economic sector occurred (coal, supplies for industries, harvest of potatoes and turnips, food supplies) that continuation of the tension past October 10 would have made a catastrophe inevitable."[198] At a sitting of the Reich Defense Committee in November, Göring admitted that economic strain had reached the point where no more workers were available, factories were at full capacity, foreign exchange was completely exhausted, and Germany's economic situation was desperate.[199] Problems in the transportation network further reflected troubles besetting the economy. In mid-October an economic official warned that the railroads could only transport a fraction of agricultural production to market and that a lack of freight cars endangered coal supplies for the population and prevented steamers and fishing trawlers from leaving port because of coal shortages.[200] Only 20,000 railroad cars were available to transport coal, although 43,000 were needed to meet fall demands.[201]

Especially worrisome to the Germans as the Czech crisis reached its climax was the clear warning the British had given that they intended to clamp down on German trade with a stringent blockade.[202] From September 15, British shippers demanded payment in full before delivering copper, lead, zinc, or tin. From September 18, they offered Germany no further metal sales. On September 24, the Admiralty ordered all British ships to leave German harbors and diverted the tanker *Invershannon* with 8,600 tons of gasoline from Hamburg to England. At the same time Britain suspended all hard coal exports to Germany. According to the OKW economic staff, "[w]ith regard to England, the general picture shows that all measures had been prepared for a long time and all concerned authorities had received orders by September 24 to put these measures into motion. Most of these measures are aimed less to protect Britain's wartime security than to economically injure Germany."[203] Measures by other European countries, both presumed participants in a 1938 war and probable neutrals, equally alarmed the Germans. On September 16, France blocked export of iron and steel scrap. On September 28, Belgium blocked all exports including iron ore and scrap metal. But the most threatening actions to Germany came from Rumania and Yugoslavia. Both undertook blocking measures that would have cut Germany off from Rumanian oil and grain, and Yugoslav bauxite and other minerals.[204] A naval staff report of early September 1938 warned that although Rumania desired neutrality, she would intervene against Germany if 1) the League declared Germany the aggressor, 2) England and France imposed sanctions or declared war, 3) Hungary attacked Czechoslovakia. Only a quick German success would insure that Rumania would not block oil exports.[205] Rumania confirmed German fears on September 28, when she warned that as of October 3 Germany could expect no further deliveries of oil.[206]

Further complicating the difficulties that a blockade would have caused is the fact that German lines of trade were vulnerable to Allied naval action. As suggested above, the weaknesses of the German navy in 1938 were such that it could not have protected German trade within the Baltic, much less have launched an invasion of Norway. Supply lines to Rumania were similarly exposed. In 1938 the Rumanians exported 74 percent of their petroleum products through the Black Sea and Mediterranean, 21 percent up the Danube, and 5 percent by railroad.[207] In wartime British sea power excluded the first route, except for a few camouflaged exports to Yugoslavia and Italy, and the Danube was a doubtful supply route if extensive fighting broke out in the Balkans. Balkan railroads had enough trouble transporting ores and grain to the Reich. In August 1938 the OKM, which would have responsibility for guarding Germany's exposed trade routes warned: "The tasks of the buildup, the unfavorable military geographic situation, and the still undiminished dependency on foreign trade make a military confrontation of Germany with other strong powers undesirable. The basic will to maintain peace as long as it stands in our power and corresponds with our honor grows in the same direction. . . . In this our relationship with England is of decisive importance."[208]

In view of the economic situation described above, it is questionable whether the German economy in 1938 possessed the strength to support a breakout from Germany's constrained economic base. Not only was the production of synthetics and munitions substantially lower than in 1939, but no help could be expected from Russia and little from the Balkan states. In reality the problem was not so much with the shortage of workers, because great numbers of German workers were engaged in, and would continue up until 1942 to be engaged in, tasks that were peripheral to the German war economy. Rather, in 1938 the German economy simply did not have access to the sources of raw materials that it needed for a rapid increase in armament production. In 1942 the Germans would have the resources of most of the European continent at their disposal; in 1938 they had only the meager prospects of German territory and what few areas the German army could conquer on which to draw.

Most probably the German economy would not have suffered a

cataclysmic collapse had war broken out in fall 1938. Instead, the situation would have resembled the slow, steady disintegration that took place in the Italian economy in the years from 1940 to 1942. The Germans would have had to resort to a series of expedients to meet present demands at the expense of future requirements. As production decreased and as raw materials became in shorter and shorter supply, the Wehrmacht's fighting capability would have suffered a corresponding decline. Once this vicious cycle had begun, there would have been little chance that Germany could have escaped the inevitable consequences: military defeat.

Conclusion: War in 1938

The striking feature of the 1938 military situation was the relative unpreparedness of *all* the European nations to fight even a limited, much less a major, war. For the Germans the problem was compounded not only by their military unpreparedness, but by their economic vulnerability. Thus, German strategy had to be predicated on winning a war quickly, or at least if that were not possible, on the conquest of an economic and strategic base from which a long war could be prosecuted. For the Germans, the central question was not whether their army could conquer Czechoslovakia. There was no doubt about that and in retrospect it seems likely that the Wehrmacht could have completed the task in one to two months. Such a campaign, however, because of the nature of the terrain, the equipment of the Czech army, Czech fortifications, and the general state of unpreparedness of the German armored force, would have involved significantly higher casualties than the campaign against Poland in 1939. Moreover, such a campaign would have destroyed most of the Czech stocks of armaments that the Germans found so useful the following spring and might well have led to the destruction of the Czech armament industry.

But the conquest of Czechoslovakia would have had only a small impact on the strategic situation of a Germany involved in a world war. The inclusion of Czechoslovakia within the German economic orbit would have done little to alleviate shortages of raw materials. The central problem for the Nazi regime after the conquest of Czechoslovakia would have been, what next? Germany would have embarked on a world war with an unprepared military and an almost desperate economic situation. She might well have had the Italians as allies, which would have added to her economic and military burdens without bringing any corresponding advantages. The Axis economic area would have been limited to Germany, Italy, Hungary, a damaged Czechoslovakia, perhaps Yugoslavia, and the vulnerable ore trade with Sweden. Military operations against Rumania to conquer vital oil would have met a Soviet response and probably would have led to the destruction of the wells and refineries as had occurred in the First World War.

Earlier in this chapter we have pointed out that France possessed overwhelming superiority on Germany's western frontier, but that the French appeared unwilling and unable to take advantage of their superiority should war break out. Nevertheless, if the French were unwilling to attack Germany's western frontier, the Germans were in no position to win a strategic victory in the west. This does not mean that after the conquest of Czechoslovakia Germany would not have tried. As in 1940 the Germans would have had no other choice but to attack through Belgium and Holland in order to acquire the resources necessary for further prosecution of the war. But it is hard to see how the Germans could have gained the stunning strategic victories of 1940. There were few paratroopers for missions such as seizing Belgian and Dutch forts and bridges. The armored force certainly could not have undertaken the offensive that the Germans launched so successfully through the Ardennes in 1940. Moreover, in view of the shortage of fuel and munitions as well as its internal weaknesses, the Luftwaffe could not have intervened as decisively in a land campaign as it did in 1940. Thus, although the Germans might have won tactical victories in the west in 1938 or early 1939, it is most unlikely that they could have won a strategic victory and knocked France out of the war. The Germans might also have gained peripheral victories, such as the conquest of Denmark, in order to stave off economic collapse, but each military operation the Germans could launch during this period would have had the counterproductive result of using up scarce resources without supplying compensatory long-range gains for the war economy.

As a result, the war would have turned, as had the First World War, and as the Second World War would, on the economic strength and staying power of the opposing sides. In terms of numbers of divisions, economic resources, industrial capacity, and naval forces, Germany would have faced overwhelming Allied superiority in 1938 whether she faced only Britain and France, or an enlarged coalition that included Russia and perhaps Poland. Even so, the war against Germany would not have been easy, nor would it have been quickly won. But the results would have been inevitable and would have led to the eventual collapse of the Nazi regime at considerably less cost than the war that broke out the following September.

VIII

The Aftermath of Munich

The September crisis had been a shattering experience for nearly all involved. With the possible exception of Mussolini, none of the Munich participants savored their diplomatic success for long. Hitler was perhaps the most dissatisfied with the settlement. Munich, no matter how great a diplomatic triumph, represented the failure of his efforts to isolate Czechoslovakia diplomatically and then destroy her militarily. The crisis had revealed, moreover, cracks in the imposing facade of Nazi Germany. The German people had remained apathetic and in some cases hostile to the idea of war with Czechoslovakia, and opposition within the officer corps had led to a confrontation between Hitler and his generals. Chamberlain was ambivalent about the meaning of Munich and now faced substantial pressure at home to speed up British rearmament. Furthermore, the prime minister's hopes for an Anglo-German detente soon collapsed in the readily apparent German bad faith of the post-Munich period. For the French, who had few illusions about Munich, the post-Munich period was particularly depressing. France had surrendered the linchpin of her alliance system and had gained no compensatory commitment from Britain. In the east, the Russians saw Munich as the first step toward a coalition of capitalist states aimed at destroying the Soviet Union. Diplomatically Munich accentuated further Russia's exclusion from the European mainstream. Yet in retrospect they along with the Germans had the most to gain from the collapse of Eastern Europe.

Munich did not, however, make the disasters of 1939 and 1940 inevitable, for it was a symptom rather than a cause. Moreover, although its impact was devastating for Czechoslovakia and damaging to Eastern Europe, it did not destroy the European balance of power.

Its effect was more limited: it destroyed the equilibrium of Eastern Europe and made Germany the dominant power in the region—a diplomatic triumph of the first order. Nevertheless, even though Germany was now the most powerful nation in Europe, her financial resources, her economic strength, and her military power were still seriously flawed.

The German occupation of the Sudetenland rendered Czechoslovakia indefensible and stripped the Czech state of fortifications on all its frontiers. Only thirty miles now separated Silesia from Austria, and Polish occupation of Teschen cut a major east-west railroad. The economic results were catastrophic. Czechoslovakia lost 27 percent of her heavy industry, 32 percent of her lumber industry, 30 percent of her chemicals, and 53 percent of her paper industry. Loss of the Sudeten brown coal effectively placed the Czech electrical industry under German control.[1] The continued existence of the Czech state depended on an active, pro-German policy. On October 5, 1938 a Czech military writer commented: "German policy has succeeded in paralyzing us completely from a military point of view. Do not let us have any illusions about that reality. That is why our policy must, whether we like it or not, find means of bringing about good relations with Germany. . . ."[2]

In a larger sense Munich rendered Eastern Europe defenseless. Its psychological effect was as devastating as the strategic gains that Germany made at the expense of Czechoslovakia. Eastern Europe hastened to make peace with the Reich. Among others the Rumanians were impressed with "the resounding victory that Germany gained by the process of intimidation."[3] Following a trip through Eastern Europe a British businessman reported to the Foreign Office that "[m]y chief impression was one of impending change and fears. Fear: individual, racial, national, and economic. Munich has withdrawn the linchpin which held Eastern Europe together and the fragments are preparing to resort themselves. Everyone is apprehensive as to how this process will affect him individually. . . . Everywhere there is a pathetic hope in the breasts of these ignorant people that England will somehow save them from the fate which she did nothing to avert from Czechoslovakia. . . ."[4]

The Poles largely missed the implications of Munich for their position. If France had not been willing to stand by the Czechs, how could Poland expect any stronger support? In addition, the ambivalence of Polish policy over the summer and their occupation of Teschen in October gave them a dubious reputation. A junior Foreign Office official summed up British attitudes: "The regime in Poland is truly remarkable. Despised and disliked by every decent Pole, supported by no political party and with continual dissension in its ranks, having at its head no one with the slightest glimmering of political leadership, . . . it yet manages to maintain a complete stranglehold on the political life of the country."[5] A more senior official commented that no matter what foreign policy Britain might pursue she should "avoid any commitments in Poland."[6]

GERMANY

Hitler was furious at losing his opportunity to destroy Czechoslovakia. Despite Munich, his impulse had been to occupy almost immediately the remainder of Czechoslovakia. He eventually held back in the belief that such callous disregard for international form might be too much even for the British. Yet within three weeks of Chamberlain's departure from Munich, Hitler ordered Keitel to begin preparation of deployment orders for seizing the rest of Czechoslovakia. Further directives followed in November and December.[7]

Hitler's anger at the military opposition during the crisis is clear from a memorandum prepared by the Wehrmachtführungsamt on October 19. OKW stated:

> The basis for a state's political as well as military success is obedience—faith and belief in its leadership. Without this—as every officer knows—any troop is worthless—to underestimate one's own strength while overestimating that of the enemy is unmilitary and the mark of a weak military education. The calculation of military and strategic factors in establishing political goals is the task of the statesman alone. Should he wish to wait until his military forces are completely combat ready, he could not act, for military preparations are never, and cannot ever be, finished.[8]

Hitler underlined his point by insisting that Beck permanently retire from military service (Beck had commanded an army in September). The emerging army leadership, typified by generals like Guderian and Manstein, were technocrats with a narrower point of view than either

Fritsch or Beck. Brauchitsch was thoroughly cowed, and Halder would not again toy with rebellion. Munich's impact on the army, as well as the German people, cannot be overemphasized. Once again, contrary to all doubts and doubters, the führer had proved right. Britain and France had not fought for Czechoslovakia.[9] Even those who had opposed war warmed to the sight of a British prime minister humbling himself not once, but thrice before the führer. One German officer told a visiting South African "that the army would have made difficulties for Hitler last autumn, but his success would place them solidly behind him in the crisis expected *next autumn.*"[10]

On the morning following Munich Hitler and Chamberlain agreed "that the question of Anglo-German relations is of the first importance for the two countries and for Europe" and pledged themselves to work "to remove possible sources of difference and thus to contribute to assure the peace of Europe."[11] Yet as early as mid-October in a speech at Saarbrücken Hitler assailed those in England who had attacked Munich and who had urged war instead of surrender. He warned that Germany would not tolerate interference with her goals in Southeastern Europe. At the same time the propaganda minister, Joseph Goebbels, launched a virulent attack on Britain's rearmament program. German propaganda claimed that British preparations had assumed "a scale which far exceeds the security requirements of the Island Kingdom and cannot remain without serious repercussions upon the powers against whom the main British armament efforts are directed."[12]

In spite of his disappointment with Munich's peaceful solution, even Hitler could not refrain from expressing amazement at the results. In November he declared that he had fully realized the magnitude of his success when he viewed the Czech fortifications—2,000 kilometers of bunkers had fallen without a shot.[13] In a later moment of euphoria he told the Hungarian foreign minister that "[a]mazing things had been achieved. 'Do you think,' he asked, 'that I myself would have thought it possible half a year ago that Czechoslovakia would be served up to me, so to speak, by her friends? I did not believe that England and France would go to war, but I was convinced that Czechoslovakia would have to be destroyed by a war. The way in which everything happened is historically unique. We can offer each other heartfelt congratulations.' "[14]

Nevertheless, the Reich faced serious, if not desperate, problems

---

with the economy in the post-Munich period. Unlike the Anschluss where welcomed financial assistance accompanied the German triumph, the Sudetenland did not bring significant economic gains. Although the economic difficulties in the region had made the Sudetenland susceptible to Nazi subversion, they made it a mixed blessing for the German economy. Admittedly, Sudeten coal deposits helped to increase synthetic rubber and fuel production, electrical output, and chemical production, but on the whole occupation of the Sudetenland added little to the German economic situation.[15]

As discussed previously, massive economic projects, like rearmament, the Schnellplan, and construction on the Westwall contributed to the dangerous economic situation. So bad had circumstances become that the Reich's Defense Committee estimated that the German economy would have faced catastrophe in October if pressure had continued.[16] In November Göring admitted that the economic and financial situation had reached serious straits.[17] Thus, Nazi leaders had to face up to economic reality. Something had to give; what gave were major elements of the rearmament program. In December economic difficulties forced Keitel to make reductions in steel and raw-material allocations to armament industries.[18] Continuing trouble led Hitler to announce in January 1939 a great "export battle" to increase Germany's hard-currency holdings. That announcement served as a smoke screen for the more disagreeable task of reducing Wehrmacht steel allocations 30 percent, copper 20 percent, aluminum 47 percent, rubber 14 percent, and cement 25 to 45 percent.[19] The message was clear: the economic cupboard was empty.

These economic troubles were a major incentive to seize the remainder of Czechoslovakia and its considerable economic and military assets. Although German foreign policy flirted with far-fetched schemes of using Ruthenia to support a Ukrainian nationalist movement against Poland and Russia, Hitler's interest continually returned to Bohemia. In a speech shortly before the final destruction of Czechoslovakia, Hitler argued that Germany's chief aim must be to secure the raw materials necessary for its population's well-being. The occupation of Prague, he argued, would end the efforts of "Jews, democrats, and international powers" to use rump Czechoslovakia as a dam to German aspirations and open the way to "the expansion of German living space into the east." With control of Prague, Germany could bring Hungary,

Yugoslavia, and Rumania within the German sphere of influence and gain "complete economic domination over their agricultural and petroleum resources."[20] As a result, the first major political crisis in rump Czechoslovakia provided Hitler with a welcome excuse to intervene and complete what Munich had begun. By seizing Prague, Hitler gained control of Czechoslovakia's substantial resources, her industry, and military establishment and escaped the immediate economic and rearmament difficulties that faced the Reich. The next chapter will address the extent of this aid.

THE BRITISH RESPONSE TO MUNICH

Interestingly, a number of British diplomats recognized that Munich had saved the Nazis. Henderson suggested that "war would rid Germany of Hitler," and an official in the Foreign Office noted that the one risk the Nazi regime had faced "was a World War which would almost certainly have resulted in a revolution in Germany and the overthrow of the Nazi Party."[21] Nevertheless, the prime minister and his supporters had so often raised the issue of Britain's unpreparedness to face war that they could not now escape public outcry for more rearmament. Unfortunately, although the rearmament issue was a constant topic in Cabinet discussions from October 1938 through March 1939, Chamberlain insured that the rearmament program received only a minimal boost. The prime minister was more concerned with dampening political criticism than expediting programs to prepare for a possible war. Thus, as so often had been the case in the 1930s, British policy fell between two stools. On the one hand it provided useful propaganda for Goebbels, while on the other it allowed Britain to fall further behind in military strength.

In Chamberlain's eyes Munich represented the fruition of his efforts to reach an accommodation with the dictators. The conference had successfully changed frontiers established at Versailles without a resort to war. On the afternoon of September 30, the prime minister told the Cabinet that diplomacy had triumphed at Munich; representatives of the four major powers had met and settled the Sudeten matter peacefully.[22]

Despite the acclamation at home and abroad, Chamberlain faced serious political problems. Duff Cooper decided that the Munich

Agreement did not significantly differ from the Godesberg terms and resigned. Stanley wavered, but finally decided to remain. He, nonetheless, warned Chamberlain that

> I am afraid that I remain profoundly skeptical of Nazi promises and shall do so until I see peaceful words accompanied by pacific deeds. I, therefore, can only regard the present situation not "as peace in our time," but as an uneasy truce, which can only be converted into lasting peace if the interval is used drastically and energetically for the increase of our power. . . . So strongly do I feel the necessity for an intensification of our rearmament, and so much do I fear the effect on such a policy of any lulling of public opinion that I should feel bound publicly to express my skepticism of Nazi promises and my fears as to Nazi policy.[23]

The government, moreover, fared badly in the House of Commons debate over Munich. Chamberlain's speech of October 3, as well as supporting speeches by Simon and Inskip, did not constitute an inspiring defense of their diplomacy. On the other side, an imposing series of orations lashed appeasement and Munich. On the left, Labour leaders, including Clement Attlee, denounced Munich on moral, more than strategic, grounds.[24] Among rebel Conservatives, Duff Cooper, having resigned from the Cabinet, stressed the strategic results and warned that Munich had only postponed, but not prevented, war. That would now take place under more difficult conditions. He contrasted Chamberlain's reasonableness with what he believed to be the language Hitler understood—the mailed fist.[25] Amery pointed out that the West had yielded not to "superior strength nor to insuperable geographical difficulties" but to a strong will that had correctly estimated Western cowardice. Whatever military advantages Germany possessed in September, her overall strategic situation would have led inevitably to defeat.[26] But it was left to Churchill to deliver the most blistering attack on the government's lack of preparedness, its ignorance of strategic factors, and its unwillingness to recognize the Nazis for what they were.[27] Even so, attacks on Chamberlain's policy received little support from the Conservative majority. In fact, the reception of Churchill's speech might be characterized as one of sullen hostility.

For Chamberlain the problem became, what next? Attacks in the House forced the government to announce that although a formal guarantee of Czechoslovakia did not yet exist, "His Majesty's Government, however, feel under a moral obligation to Czechoslovakia to treat the guarantee as being now in force."[28] Within two weeks of Munich disturbing signs had issued from Germany to suggest that the government's hope for an appeasement of European differences was sadly misplaced. In Berlin the Germans, aided and abetted by the British and French ambassadors, displayed consistent bad faith on the commission delineating the new Czech frontiers.[29] Meanwhile, Hitler's Saarbrücken speech with its attack on British rearmament as well as Britain's press and opposition leaders had underlined the fragility of the prime minister's policies. Continuing tensions led Halifax to urge Chamberlain to form a government of national unity that would include Labour.[30] The prime minister, however, had no intention of approaching a Labour party that he despised. Rather, in late October through an informal messenger he asked Hitler for a gesture or moderation of German policy to take the pressure off the British government from those who criticized appeasement.[31]

In arguing for its policy over the summer, the government had stressed how unprepared for war the country was. Despite some attempts during the Munich debate to suggest that Britain had embarked on a "great program of rearmament," Chamberlain was caught in a web of his own making.[32] If Britain was so ill-prepared, then the government must speed rearmament to repair the deficiencies, and, all protestations to the contrary, such a policy could only imply mistrust of German intentions. Sir Horace Wilson laid great stress on that fact in arguing that Britain should make no changes in her defense policy.[33]

In fact, Chamberlain had no intention of altering British rearmament policy. He indicated his real approach in linking British rearmament to a program of general European disarmament.[34] On October 3, he told the Cabinet that ever since his term as chancellor of the exchequer he had felt that "the burden of armaments might break our back." Because of this he had embarked on a foreign policy of appeasement to resolve the conflicts that had caused the armaments race.[35]

On October 6, acting in his official capacity, Inskip asked the services to report "candidly on the extent" to which mobilization had fallen "short of requirements and the steps" needed "to repair the gaps." The measures taken, however, suggest that Chamberlain aimed more at defusing public outcry than at speeding preparations for war. From the onset of discussions on specific changes in defense policy, Simon urged a minimal increase in the defense budget. In late October Inskip, again following the prime minister's lead, attacked service requests for new programs and more funds. Such proposals, he claimed, raised two major issues. Did Munich call for revision of the scope of authorized programs? And did "the financial implications even of the present programs . . . threaten that stability which is, after all, in our experience probably our strongest weapon of war?"[36]

This rehash of arguments that had led to impotence did not satisfy most ministers.[37] The Cabinet established a special committee, the Committee on Defense Programs and Their Acceleration, to study the problem of speeding rearmament. At its second meeting Simon vigorously attacked new spending proposals—he saw no reason to build large bombers and thought that Britain had sufficient aircraft reserves. Once again he warned that "far-reaching proposals now under consideration might have literally stupendous results on the financial stability of the country."[38] At the third meeting Simon reiterated the old arguments on expense. He warned that most proposals under consideration would only reach fruition after 1940 and asked whether Britain's finances could support such greatly expanded forces.[39]

Evading its responsibility, the special committee decided that army requests did not come within its term of reference; a restructuring of land forces involved a major change in defense policy that only the Cabinet or Committee of Imperial Defense could determine. Kingsley Wood argued that "since the United Kingdom could not be equally strong all around, it followed logically that the committee ought to concentrate on first priorities."[40] The recommendations were a classic example of a mountain producing a mouse. Major questions such as army appropriations passed to the Committee of Imperial Defense, and the air program remained undecided, pending further discussions between the Air Ministry and Treasury.[41]

Even the relatively mild proposals of the Committee on Defense Programs and Their Acceleration alarmed some ministers. Chamberlain argued that the Cabinet must weigh defense needs against the possible effect of any increases on Germany. He thought new heavy bombers would result in higher defense costs without a corresponding increase in security, as had been the case with the *Dreadnought*. Simon again worried about defense expenses.[42] In the end the Cabinet approved a list of limited increases. These minimal expenditures reflected Chamberlain's continued support for a policy of "business as usual." The Cabinet authorized construction of twenty escort vessels and twelve small minesweepers, the dredging of Dover and Rosyth, an aerodrome at Scapa Flow for the fleet air arm, and orders for armor plate from Czechoslovakia. The War Office received a small increase in anti-aircraft guns and equipment, and an army study on "The role of the Army in Light of the Czechoslovakian Crisis" ended up in the Committee of Imperial Defense. The Cabinet ordered the RAF to emphasize fighter production. The bomber program would continue, but only at the minimal level necessary to prevent a deterioration in production facilities.[43] The Cabinet dealt with the obvious weaknesses of the air defense system through the dubious expedient of increasing the numbers of fighters on order by extending the number of months in each contract without increasing the number of fighters produced each month. Thus, there was *no* effort to increase monthly fighter production. That Spitfire and Hurricane production was marginally exceeding production targets throughout the post-Munich period suggests that production could have increased almost immediately and certainly within six months.[44] It did not.

Perhaps nothing better indicates the government's attempt to ride out the storm, while keeping the lid on defense, than arguments over preparing the army for a continental role. The War Office produced a memorandum at the end of October calling for fundamental changes in the government's army policy. Although the study advocated neither conscription nor forces on a World War I scale, it did warn that the September crisis had revealed glaring deficiencies in the army. Britain had possessed only two divisions, equipped for defensive but not for offensive combat. Quite correctly the War Office emphasized that "our soldiers would be put to unjustifiable and avoidable risks if adequate arrangements are not authorized for their proper equipment." The army further argued that the Czech crisis indicated that Britain must possess an adequately equipped field force for use on the continent.[45]

In a meeting of the Committee on Defense Programs and Their Acceleration, Hore-Belisha defended War Office recommendations. He argued that although there was no intention of creating a continental army, units in Britain should receive the equipment necessary to fight anywhere in the world. Hore-Belisha pointed out that Britain had sent an army to the continent in all of her previous wars. Such arguments made little impression. Simon immediately interposed that "circumstances had radically changed." Germany was unlikely to violate Belgium's neutrality and the Maginot line was the strongest system of fortifications the world had ever seen.[46] For at least the fall and early winter the prime minister continued to resist pressure to equip Britain's few divisions adequately and to regard the army as an unpleasant necessity.

ANGLO-FRENCH RELATIONS

Pressure for an increase in the readiness of the British army was building from another source. Munich had done little to improve already strained Anglo-French relations. Moreover, it had destroyed the foundation of France's alliance system in Eastern Europe. In November the British ambassador in Paris pointed out that "[a]s a result of these various developments France finds herself in a position where her efforts of twenty years to assure her peace and security are in ruins. The League of Nations and her continental alliances have collapsed. Her one remaining standby is her entente with Great Britain."[47] In a mid-October appreciation, Gamelin argued that France must rely on a close association with Britain for Mediterranean defense. Although he suggested that the defense of Eastern Europe was of some importance for French security, he felt that Russia was an unknown factor and that Poland's activities in September might have already placed her in the German camp. Above all Gamelin stressed that France must increase her armament production and military strength to face the Axis threat.[48] The air force chief of staff gave an even more pessimistic picture at the end of October. Vuillemin emphasized, as he had throughout the Czech crisis, that the French air force could not for the foreseeable future face the Luftwaffe and the Italian air force. He urged that Italian neutrality should be the first priority of French diplomacy. Finally, he entered into the realm of politics and suggested that France break entirely with the Soviet Union. Such action, he thought, would bring Poland back to the fold, and a Germany faced with Britain, France, and Poland along with the defection of Fascist

Italy would be less willing to embark on an adventure in Eastern Europe.[49]

The basic thrust of French policy after Munich was an effort to force Britain to make a reasonable commitment to the defense of the continent. Not surprisingly, the French faced a British refusal to recognize how much the surrender of Czechoslovakia undercut France's strategic position. In a Foreign Office memorandum Sargent suggested that Britain force France into abandoning the Russian treaty since "it can in the future only constitute a dangerous liability for France, all the more dangerous because, if they did get involved in a war with Germany in defence of Russia, they clearly could not count upon the collaboration of Great Britain."[50] Nevertheless, in the fall of 1938 British attitudes toward France began to undergo a subtle change. With the help of French warnings about growing pacifist sentiment in France,[51] the Foreign Office and the government's military advisers now became worried that France might not be willing to support Britain in a European war.[52] Moreover, there was a growing recognition as to how much Munich had undercut France's security.[53]

On an intergovernmental level the British were not yet willing to admit as much. In a November meeting of ministers, Daladier pushed for a hard commitment from Britain because of Munich's impact on his nation's security. Chamberlain demurred; not only did he deny that Germany would strike first against France on land but he argued that Britain would be Germany's first target from the air. Thus Britain must emphasize, he suggested, the construction of fighters and anti-aircraft defenses (although in fact she was doing no such thing).[54] Despite the prime minister's assertion, there was growing worry within the foreign policy establishment that the government's policy toward France was leading in a dangerous direction.[55]

Chamberlain unfortunately was no more tactful in public in his treatment of the French. In December he replied to a question in the House by announcing that Britain would not necessarily aid France if Italy attacked her.[56] What makes this declaration of nonsupport so surprising is the fact that at that moment France faced a direct Italian challenge in the Mediterranean. This December crisis between Italy and France has received little attention from historians, but evidence now available suggests that Mussolini considered courting a military as well as diplomatic confrontation.[57] The French were more forthcoming than their British colleagues. On December 19, Bonnet informed the Chamber of Deputies that the Republic would stand by Great Britain no matter who attacked her.[58] Yet in January Chamberlain questioned whether Britain should

> . . . enter into a binding undertaking to go to France's assistance if she were attacked by any power seeing that France had undertaken to come to our assistance if we were attacked? One obvious point was that France might be attacked from more than one quarter, whereas we were only liable to be attacked by Germany and that the obligations of mutual assistance in the event of attack would not, therefore, be equal. We had already made a statement that our obligations to France passed beyond specific treaty obligations, but he would deprecate any attempt to define the position more narrowly.[59]

THE ARMY ISSUE AND GRAND STRATEGY

For British military planners the crucial issue in early winter no longer was the strengthening of the expeditionary force but conscription. Although the prime minister had not yet even agreed to reequip the regular army, by the beginning of January army circles were already arguing that conscription was perhaps the only method to prop up the French. Chatfield admitted that although the British public and government might not like national service, France's strategic position might demand such a stand.[60]

Despite the fall rebuff the army continued efforts for greater funding. In late 1938 the CIGS, Lord Gort, pointed out that 1937 cutbacks in the army rested on the hypothesis that France "did not look to Great Britain to provide an expeditionary force on the scale hitherto proposed [five divisions]." This was no longer the case. Moreover, Gort argued, the assumption that Germany would not again violate Belgian neutrality seemed doubtful—especially in view of the strength of the Maginot line. Elimination of Czechoslovakia, he felt, now enabled Germany to concentrate her strength against France and the Low Countries. In this situation Britain must have a creditable expeditionary force. If Britain did not, France might not help Belgium and Holland, enabling Germany to seize the Low Countries, the possession of which would directly threaten Britain's security. Gort concluded with the warning that "there are certain interests in Western Europe which are vital to our existence and, if we cannot rule out the possibility that a future government may be forced to intervene on land to protect them, it is necessary to make adequate preparations in peace."[61]

The CIGS's insistence on the strategic threat to the Low Countries and his fear that France would not aid them unless she were in turn aided, was well taken. The British now began worrying that Germany planned to seize Belgium and Holland and to use bases in those countries for an air offensive against the British Isles. French intelligence reinforced these anxieties. In January the Committee of Imperial Defense circulated a series of dispatches from Paris that, besides noting Munich's impact on the military balance, communicated a French belief that Germany planned a strike at Holland. Having seized the Netherlands, the Reich would stand behind the Rhine and launch an air and submarine campaign to destroy Britain.[62]

Simon found these reports alarming enough to request a study of France's strategic situation now that she could no longer rely on Czechoslovakia "and provided that no more substantial British help would be available."[63] The Foreign Office also emphasized the strategic threat to the Low Countries. On January 19, Halifax suggested to his colleagues that Germany would strike either in the east or west, but that in any case she would strike soon.[64] On January 25, he gloomily summarized for the Cabinet the past four month's intelligence on German attitudes and plans. The foreign secretary commented that Munich had infuriated Hitler; that economic difficulties might force Germany to take drastic action; that the Germans were preparing a massive strike against Britain; and finally that current reports indicated Germany would attack Holland in the spring.[65] Halifax admitted there was no direct proof supporting these reports. As a result the Cabinet still refused to go beyond the commitments already made to the French (virtually none) because "if war broke out between Italy and France it might well be in the French interest that we should keep out of the war in order to avoid bringing Germany in on Italy's side."[66]

By the end of January the Cabinet had swung toward a recognition that Britain must prepare a continental commitment. Nevertheless, Chamberlain resisted to the last. He told the Foreign Policy Committee on January 23 "that whatever might eventually transpire, it must be clear that at the outset there could be, in fact, no possibility of Britain landing a large army on the continent."[67] On February 2, he argued strongly against higher funding for the army, and added that when "the French knew the whole position, they would appreciate not only what a gigantic effort we had made, but also that in the common interest the best course might be that we should not attempt to expand our land forces."[68] By the end of January Halifax, however, admitted that although he had long believed in a British strategy of "limited liability," he now concluded that Britain must immediately prepare not only an expeditionary force but additional industrial capacity as well.[69]

The above attacks on the prime minister's army policy culminated in a paper presented by Halifax to the CID on February 17. The foreign secretary underlined that Britain held vital interests in the defense of Western Europe and because Britain could not hold out if France fell, the government must "reach a decision on the ways and means of coming to the assistance of France on land on a larger scale and within a shorter time than has hitherto been contemplated."[70] In response Chamberlain finally capitulated and agreed to substantial increases in the army. On February 22, he conceded that Munich had altered the strategic balance and the British must help France with larger ground forces. Therefore they must have an army for continental as well as colonial use. "The Prime Minister added that while he came to this conclusion with some reluctance, he saw no alternative." The Cabinet agreed to a modest proposal for two divisions prepared to serve on the continent within twenty-one days of war, and a further two within sixty days. It authorized two colonial divisions and permitted the army to split the mobile division in half. Furthermore, Territorial Army units would prepare for continental service within six months of mobilization.[71] This decision was a belated, but nevertheless, significant change from previous policies.

RUN UP TO PRAGUE

What little public confidence in detente with Germany that remained after the September crisis eroded between Munich and the occupation of Prague. The British felt particularly frustrated in that their moves occasioned no corresponding response in Berlin. As late as November 7, Halifax urged Chamberlain "to prevent the Munich wax from setting too hard before we had taken some further action toward implementing our policy of appeasement."[72] The savage Nazi attack on German Jews in mid-November made any such move impossible. There was little moral outrage in the Cabinet at German behavior.[73] The attack on the Jews led Halifax to worry more that Germany might declare war on Britain because of British support for the Jews than about the nature of the Nazi regime, and Hoare warned his colleagues that British backing for German Jews might increase anti-Semitism in Britain. Chamberlain's response to the atrocities was that Britain should refuse settlement of colonial claims.[74]

Significantly, Henderson's October departure from Germany for medical treatment resulted in far more accurate reporting from Berlin. In December the embassy warned that Hitler had broken his word every time that he announced Germany had no further demands on Europe.[75] Chamberlain naturally regarded such reports with suspicion.[76] As late as the end of January the Berlin embassy warned that Germany was preparing to move, probably toward the southeast. The report concluded: "Such action might not necessarily entail military action but military measures would certainly be employed to further economic demands."[77] Henderson's return to his post in mid-February changed the tone. Upon his return, he proceeded to tell the Germans that Britain had no interest in Southeastern Europe and to send a series of optimistic messages to London. On February 16, he told Ribbentrop that Chamberlain's position was stronger than ever and that Germany should not allow the "noisy outcry of a section of London opinion" to influence her policy.[78] On February 18, Henderson cabled, "[m]y definite impression since my return here is that H. Hitler does not contemplate any adventures at the moment and that all the stories and rumors to the contrary are completely without foundation." He suggested his belief that Memel and Danzig would sooner or later revert to Germany and that the Germans might apply pressure on Czechoslovakia. But no major adventure would occur in the near future unless the West forced Hitler's hand. Henderson concluded: "I believe in fact that he [Hitler] would now like in his heart to return to the fold of comparative respectability. . . . I regard and always have regarded it as a bad mistake to attribute excessive importance to stories spread generally with intention either by those who regard war as the only weapon with which the Nazi regime can be overthrown or by those Nazis themselves who desire war for their own satisfaction or aggrandizement."[79]

Henderson pressed this view on a number of people in Britain. On February 22, he wrote the King that "Hitler has for the moment definitely come down on the side of peace."[80] The Germans would not make a move in the immediate future and contrary rumors were false. Hitler was all in favor of improved Anglo-German relations.[81] On February 28, Henderson assured Halifax that a period of calm was at hand and that there was little chance the Germans would undermine the peace of Europe.[82] As late as March 9, he again wrote Halifax that although there were "wild stories of attacks in various directions," he did not believe a word of such rumors. As long as Britain continued defensive preparations all would be well. Germany badly wanted peace.[83]

These efforts arguing Berlin's pacific intentions elicited various responses. Henderson's soothing words outraged Vansittart and Sargent in the Foreign Office.[84] Unfortunately, Henderson's soothing words did calm others who should have known better. On February 26, Cadogan criticized Vansittart for his forecast that Germany would engulf Czechoslovakia by May.[85] Two weeks later he noted that there had been a general improvement in the situation. Rumors and scares had died down, and it did not seem as if the Germans were planning any mischief.[86]

Only on March 10 did Henderson notice that the Germans were about to move against Czechoslovakia. By then it was too late for diplomatic warnings. Sargent underlined the importance of Henderson's performance and his influence in a bitter minute on March 16 after the German occupation of Prague:

> Sir N. Henderson here recognizes [10 March 1939] the possibility that H. Hitler may seek adventures and if so the most obvious form it would be likely to take would be some *coup* in Czechoslovakia. I can not refrain from contrasting this very accurate forecast with the one he gave in his telegram No. 64 [and the various letters and reports which Sargent did not have access to]. . . . This misleading forecast was particularly unfortunate if, as I suppose, it was one of the factors which decided the Prime Minister to issue the press last week the *mot d'ordre* to the effect that the international position could now be viewed with confidence and optimism.[87]

CONCLUSION

On March 15, 1939 the Germans completed what Munich had begun. On Hitler's order the Wehrmacht occupied the remainder of Czechoslovakia. A domestic political crisis within the Czech state, fomented and abetted by the Germans, provided the opportunity. In retrospect, this German move can be considered a diplomatic mistake, for it precipitated a violent political reaction in Britain and to a lesser extent in France. Public pressure now led the British to turn to a policy of diplomatic confrontation in Eastern Europe and to begin the series of moves that would culminate in the German invasion of Poland the following September. Yet in economic and strategic terms Hitler's move against Prague made sense. In particular it eased the serious difficulties that Germany faced with foreign exchange, the purchase of raw materials, and with maintaining the tempo of rearmament. As with the Anschluss the previous year, the occupation of Czechoslovakia gave a major boost to the rearmament effort. Thus, economic problems as well as long-range goals led Hitler to make this move.

The period between Munich and Prague had been one of frustration for the führer. The Munich Agreement had denied him the satisfaction of war against Czechoslovakia, and opposition to war within Germany and serious economic difficulties in the post-Munich period did little to improve his humor. One major factor should be underlined. The Nazi regime not only made every effort to maintain its rearmament program; it also began a major propaganda campaign to correct those deficiencies in German morale that had appeared in September. Hitler wished to insure that in the next great crisis there would be no backsliding. Moreover, the next time he would not allow himself to be tricked into a compromise; Germany would have the satisfaction at the least of a limited war.

The French faced the bleakest dilemmas in the post-Munich period. On the one hand they had abandoned Eastern Europe at Munich, and few placed the slightest reliance on Russia. On the other hand, the British showed no great willingness to help France in her hour of darkness. At times the French pretended that Munich had not destroyed their alliance system. However, Bonnet's comment to his ambassador in Warsaw indicated the reality. He stated that France did not have to revise her 1921 treaty with Poland because the protocols "contained enough loopholes" to keep France out of war.[88] It was

---

certainly not France's finest hour, but considering French strategic difficulties one can not help but feel some sympathy.

There is little good that one can find to say about British policy in the post-Munich period. The British did nothing to reassure their French partner; in fact most British moves had precisely the opposite effect. At best the British attitude toward France and French security can be termed as cavalier. No major changes were made in rearmament. Accordingly, the six months after Munich were "locust months" to be added to the locust years. Not until late February did a reluctant Chamberlain commit a minuscule British force to the continent. Finally and perhaps most damningly, the prime minister resolutely pursued his policy of appeasement. The German occupation of Prague made a shambles of the prime minister's diplomacy.

IX

The Reaction to Prague:
Diplomatic Prelude

The German occupation of Prague on March 15, 1939 precipitated a
European crisis that would not only lead to the outbreak of the Second
World War, but would also directly determine the course of the first
years of that war. In other words, the strategic decisions of the next
five months, taken in response to the occupation of Bohemia and
Moravia, would play a decisive role in creating the conditions for the
European disaster of May 1940.

Although Hitler obviously began the Second World War, Britain,
and to a lesser extent France, made a series of strategic and diplomatic
blunders that allowed Germany to escape the full consequences of her
considerable weaknesses. British diplomacy committed the West to the
defense of Poland while it spurned the Soviet Union. As had been the
case throughout the thirties, Allied planners saw danger in every course,
concentrated on the minutiae of their military problems while ignoring
the larger picture, and came down firmly on the side of inaction and
against the assumption of any risk.

The German occupation of Czechoslovakia in blatant disregard of
the Munich Agreement caused a substantial change in British diplomatic, rearmament, and strategic policies. Unfortunately, the substance of the response remained fundamentally unrealistic. At heart,
Chamberlain refused to acknowledge the inevitability of war with Germany. He, thus, sought a diplomatic rather than military containment
of the Third Reich. Hitler's willingness to risk a major European war
in his desire to humiliate Poland doomed such an approach from the
start. In fact, Chamberlain's response to the seizure of Prague resulted

as much from domestic political stimuli as from a recognition of the Nazi danger. After pledging to help defend the independence of Poland when it seemed that Germany might move east, Chamberlain became enamored by the illusion that diplomacy could deter Germany. As a result, dilatory negotiations ruined what little chance might have existed to reach agreement with Russia and the only chance to build an eastern front of any lasting military or economic value. Yet given Germany's weaknesses, especially in the economic sphere, the Western Powers did not face a hopeless situation. The real failure of Western policy lay in the inability of Britain and France to weigh the European balance of power in the cold, clear light of strategic reality.

POLAND

After the occupation of Bohemia and Moravia, Hitler announced a protectorate from the Hradschin Castle in Prague, while the Slovaks were prodded into establishing a puppet regime under German domination. The British reaction was one of sorrow, not anger. Henderson expressed the attitude best when he wrote Halifax that the most distressing aspect of the German move was the handle that the occupation of Prague would give to those who had criticized Munich.[1] The Cabinet mood was similar. Halifax observed that the conflict between Czechs and Slovaks indicated that Britain had almost gone to war in September in behalf of a state that was not "viable." He suggested that the government argue that it had guaranteed Czechoslovakia the previous October only as "a means of steadying the position during what was thought to be a purely transitory situation," but that "we had, however, never intended permanently to assume responsibility for this guarantee."[2] Chamberlain stressed that "the state whose frontiers we had undertaken to guarantee against unprovoked aggression had now completely broken up." The prime minister added that, although Germany had engineered the disruption of Czechoslovakia, the British guarantee was not proof against exercise of moral pressure. The Cabinet then decided that it should cancel Stanley's Berlin visit but that a recall of Henderson from his post represented too drastic a measure. Chamberlain suggested that Hitler had acted because of his disappointment at not having achieved a triumph the previous autumn. "He thought therefore that military occupation was symbolic more than perhaps appeared on the surface." Nevertheless, both Halifax and Hore-Belisha admitted that Germany now occupied territory where non-Germans lived and that the action was inconsistent with Munich. "Germany had preferred naked force to the methods of consultation and discussion."[3] Simon stressed that the government's statement should make clear that Britain no longer had either moral or legal obligations to Czechoslovakia.[4]

Chamberlain's statement to the House of Commons that evening gave no indication that the government had any intention of changing its policy of appeasement. After referring to Inskip's October assurance of a British guarantee for the new Czech state, the prime minister told the House:

> In our opinion the situation has radically altered since the Slovak diet declared the independence of Slovakia. The effect of this declaration put an end by internal disruption to the State whose frontiers we had prepared to guarantee and, accordingly, the conditions of affairs [the British guarantee of rump Czechoslovakia in October] described by the right honorable friend the Secretary of State for the Dominions [at the time of Munich minister for the coordination of defense] which was always regarded by us as being only of a transitory nature, has now ceased to exist and His Majesty's Government cannot hold themselves any longer bound by this obligation. . . . It is natural, therefore, that I should bitterly regret what has now occurred. But do not let us on that account be deflected from our course.[5]

The indignation in the House that evening, however, equalled the anger in the country. The *Times* denounced the German action, and even Lady Astor, a notorious appeaser, asked Chamberlain whether he would "lose no time in letting the German Government know with what horror the whole of the country regards Germany's action."[6] To the storm of public opinion the government had to react; the change, reflected in Chamberlain's famous speech at Birmingham, was one of style not substance. In pained disappointment to the occupation of Prague, the prime minister could only ask whether the German move was a "step in the direction of an attempt to dominate the world by force?"

In addition to internal public opinion, the British government had to contend with a fluid diplomatic situation in Eastern Europe. The destruction of Czechoslovakia had sent shock waves throughout the region, and the Rumanians in particular seem to have worried that they were next on someone's list. In fact, their real worry was Hungary rather than Germany. Knowing that there was little prospect of British aid to meet that threat, it seems that they reported the supposed Hungarian threat as a German one.[7] These repetitious reports of German threats and troop movements on a scale far larger than "warranted by recent events" exacerbated the problems of a British government not wishing to appear weak, indecisive, and unable to anticipate Hitler's moves before an outraged public.[8]

In a crisis atmosphere and in reaction to intense domestic and external pressures, the British government recast fundamentally its strategic and diplomatic policies. Unfortunately, at no time did the Chamberlain government base its new approach on an accurate appraisal of the strategic situation. The Cabinet meeting of March 18 reflected how fast events were forcing the government to adjust its policies. Halifax told his colleagues that a German move against Rumania would probably force Britain to intervene. Chatfield, the new minister for coordination of defense, noted that German control of Rumania could undermine the effectiveness of a blockade,[9] but warned that there was little Britain could do to prevent Rumania's occupation. If, however, Britain could secure Polish and Russian support, "the position would be entirely changed." Hore-Belisha warned his colleagues that Germany had seized the equipment for thirty-eight infantry and eight mobile divisions by occupying Prague. Britain must therefore take immediate steps to increase her own armaments. Chatfield and Earl Stanhope, First Lord of the Admiralty, emphasized that Russian and Polish help was essential to force a two-front war on Germany. Yet, the Cabinet minutes make clear that Stanhope believed that the mere threat of a two-front conflict would suffice to deter war. This attitude would become a fundamental misconception of British policy. The British government would seek diplomatic connections to deter Hitler, rather than the strongest possible strategic combination to fight the coming war. The inclination to support Poland is clear in Chamberlain's statement that she was essential to the defense of Rumania and that Britain must go further in conversations with her than with any other country.[10] Two days later, the prime minister underlined his unwillingness to recognize that the fundamental problem was to prepare for an inevitable war. He announced to his colleagues that Britain should "not . . . guarantee . . . existing frontiers and . . . the indefinite maintenance of the *status quo*." The real issue was the "security and political independence of European states against German domination."[11]

Contributing to a misevaluation of the strategic situation was a belief in Germany's military weakness and in the political instability of the Nazi regime. On March 18, Halifax told the Cabinet that if Germany did not achieve an immediate and decisive success in war, internal reaction against the Nazis might occur.[12] The military attaché in Berlin accurately reported that the Wehrmacht was not yet prepared for a major war and that it would take considerable time before the army could absorb Czech equipment.[13] On March 25, he stressed that Germany risked defeat only if she faced a two-front war and concluded that at that time Germany's ability to wage a two-front war "involving fighting for and holding essential economic areas was doubtful."[14] In a limited and immediate sense, this evaluation was correct. Unfortunately, such observations contributed to a belief that if the Reich were not ready militarily, Hitler must be bluffing. If the führer were bluffing, then a strong diplomatic coalition could deter Germany. Reflecting such hopes was Simon's argument to his colleagues that it was important that "the attitude which we took be . . . known in Germany before Germany's act of aggression took place." If this were done soon enough, the impact on the German public might "prevent the war from starting."[15]

Such reasoning contributed to a feeling that Britain and France could safely dabble with the Soviet Union. Although there was little chance in ever reaching a substantive agreement with Russia, given the nature and goals of Stalin's regime, the West's hesitant approach did little to commend Anglo-French strategic sense.[16] In the final analysis only the Soviet Union possessed the strength to establish an eastern front of any real value; the failure to understand this would underline the lack of reality in British policy throughout the coming months. Admittedly, considering the government's avowed policy of defending the independence of the small nations in Eastern Europe, there was little to recommend Russian support, and from the change in policy after Prague British ambassadors reported on the anti-Soviet attitudes of these countries.[17]

Interestingly in view of their later attitude, the French reinforced the British disinclination to deal with Russia. On March 20, French Ambassador Roger Cambon told Sargent that Poland's cooperation was more important than Russia's. Given the distance between Russia and Germany, the West should consider the Soviet Union as a second line of defense "to be called up only if and when the first has collapsed."[18] On the following day Bonnet emphasized that Polish help was essential, for Russia could only bring its power to bear with Poland's collaboration.[19] The French would change their attitude more quickly than would their British colleagues, but the damage had already been done. Eastern European attitudes caused the British to draw back from their diplomatic initiative of March 22 suggesting a joint declaration by Britain, France, Russia, and Poland that they would "immediately consult together as to what steps should be taken to offer joint resistance to any action which constituted a threat to political independence of any European state."[20] By March 27 Halifax was admitting that British diplomacy could not proceed without considerable modification in the proposed Four Power Declaration.[21] That evening he cabled the Warsaw and Bucharest embassies that "although possible variants of the original scheme have been discussed it is becoming clear that our attempt to consolidate the situation will be frustrated if the Soviet Union is openly associated with the initiation of the schemes."[22]

While the British were attempting to figure out what could be done with Russia, the German seizure of the Lithuanian port of Memel on March 22 had further contributed to a sense of impending catastrophe. Although the German action had little strategic significance, it further intensified an atmosphere in which every rumor of Nazi expansionist plans gained acceptance. On March 27, Halifax warned the Foreign Policy Committee that Rumania was next on Germany's list. Her petroleum and agricultural products would allow Germany to escape the effects of a blockade. "Poland herself would be well nigh encircled and the moral effect on smaller states, like Greece and Bulgaria, would be far-reaching." Although Rumania was directly threatened, Poland's inclusion in any plan of action was vital "because Germany's weak point was her inability at present to conduct war on two fronts, and unless Poland was with us Germany would be able to avoid this contingency." Chamberlain agreed and suggested that Germany would strike first at Rumania. Once she controlled that state she would be in a stronger position to overrun Poland. One minister, however, with more common sense, doubted whether Rumania was next, because the Germans had just signed a trade agreement with her.[23]

The worries over Rumania and the sense that Poland was the linch-pin in Eastern Europe now received a new focus at the end of the month. On March 30 the Cabinet received an unverified report that Hitler would move in the immediate future against the Poles.[24] Halifax urged his colleagues that Britain must immediately act to forestall such a move. Britain should declare support for Poland if the Germans attacked. Such a declaration might deter Hitler, and, although such a declaration might prove provocative, the foreign secretary noted that he had "no particular objection to a provocative statement provided that it did not land us in an unpleasant situation."[25] Simon and Run-ciman questioned whether a guarantee should include Danzig, but Halifax replied that "it was difficult to find any better test than the decision by Poland whether to regard such an attack as a threat to her independence which she must resist by force."[26] The discussion then turned to strategic aspects of the Polish question. Chamberlain ad-mitted that as a result of Munich there was no Czech army to help, and Czech resources were now available to the Wehrmacht. The prime minister stressed that it would be dangerous to allow the same thing to happen to Poland. Chatfield supported Chamberlain's position. The Chiefs of Staff were undertaking a preliminary study of the strategic situation and had tentatively concluded that if Britain were to fight Germany, it would be better to do so with Poland as an ally than to allow Germany to absorb her.[27] The chiefs did not believe that Poland would last more than two or three months. She had no fortifications, no natural frontiers, and was surrounded on three sides by Germany or German-controlled territory. They nonetheless believed that Britain should support Poland. The Poles had fifty divisions and 230 bombers that could bomb Berlin and force the Germans to use a considerable portion of their fighters to defend the capital. Moreover, any attack on Poland would result in substantial casualties, and the Germans would have to garrison conquered Polish territory.[28]

The following day, the Cabinet decided to pledge help to Poland in defense of her independence. Significantly, the pledge did not mention Russia. During a conference with opposition leaders that morning, Chamberlain explained that he would not mention the So-viet Union because "the present arrangement was only intended to cover the interim period and . . . the position in regard to Russia would no doubt be cleared up during Col. Beck's visit to this country."[29] That afternoon in the House, Chamberlain announced that His Majesty's government had consistently advocated negotiations when national differences arose. After suggesting that there was no question between nations that peaceful means could not settle, the prime minister informed the M.P.s that although negotiations were taking place, "in the event of any action which clearly threatened Polish independence, and which the Polish government accordingly considered vital to resist with their national forces. His Majesty's Government would feel themselves bound at once to lend the Polish government all support in their power."[30]

This statement was indeed a startling *volte-face* from previous British policy. What was particularly significant is that the British undertook this obligation with such a casual look at the strategic issues. They issued their guarantee, furthermore, in response to a nonexistent crisis and as an interim arrangement until something more final could be worked out with Russia, Poland, and Rumania. Churchill summed up the lack of realism in his memoirs:

> When every one of these aids and advantages has been squandered and thrown away, Great Britain advances, leading France by the hand, to guarantee the integrity of Poland. . . . There was sense in fighting for Czechoslovakia in 1938 when the German army could scarcely put half a dozen trained divisions on the Western Front. . . . But this had been judged unreasonable, rash, below the level of modern intellectual thought and morality. Yet now at last the two Western Democracies declared themselves ready to stake their lives upon the territorial integrity of Poland. History, which we are told is mainly the record of the crimes, follies, and miseries of mankind, may be scoured and ransacked to find a parallel to this sudden and complete reversal of five or six years' policy of easy-going placatory appeasement, and its transformation almost overnight into a readiness to accept an obviously imminent war on far worse conditions and on the greatest scale.[31]

The German Response

At this time the Germans were fully occupied in absorbing the military and economic resources that they had seized in Czechoslovakia. In every respect the booty exceeded that gained the previous year in the Anschluss. In fact, the seizure of Prague helped the Germans to overcome their economic difficulties for the immediate future and paid for resumption of full armament production by German industry.

Despite the freezing of Czech assets, the Germans were able to force the Czech national bank to transfer $28,349,440 worth of gold from London to Berlin in summer 1939. Other Czech foreign currency and gold holdings soon found their way from Prague to the Reichsbank.[32] But of even greater importance was the potential of Czech industry. With inclusion of Austria and Czechoslovakia within the Reich's economic system, Germany's percentage of world industrial production reached 15 percent of the total and equalled that of the United States. The Germans found Czech industry in excellent shape. The Czechs had not overextended their industrial plant to the same extent as had been the case in Germany for rearmament. Moreover, most Czech firms possessed substantial supplies of raw materials such as copper, lead, nickel, aluminum, zinc, and tin. The Czech steel works held sufficient supplies of ore for ten months of production. Because they found it relatively easy to incorporate Czech industry into the framework of German industrial production, the Germans left most raw-material supplies in Czechoslovakia to maintain the tempo of production. The production, it is worth noting, not only aided German armament, but earned substantial foreign exchange up to the outbreak of war.[33]

The occupation brought two great armament complexes under German control. The most famous, the Skoda works, had long been world renowned for the quality and quantity of their weapons production. The second major works, built up by the Czech government during the interwar period, were also centered in the city of Brünn. By 1937 the Brünn works employed 25,000 workers and 1,800 salaried employees.[34] As a whole, Czechoslovakia occupied fourth place among arms-exporting nations and dominated the Eastern European arms market. Two contrary opinions existed within the German government as to how the Reich could best use this armament potential: the military authorities wished to use the production immediately for the Wehrmacht, whereas economists wished to use production to earn foreign exchange. By and large the economists won out, and by insuring that Czech firms earned sufficient foreign exchange to pay for raw materials, they made certain that Czech industry could maintain full production well into the war's first winter.[35] They also assured that substantial production from the armament factories would be available to the Wehrmacht throughout the period, and that Czech exports would earn foreign exchange useful to other sectors of the German economy.

The booty from Czech arms dumps was enormous. In April 1939 an average of twenty-three trains per day, filled with ammunition and weapons, left Czechoslovakia for the Reich.[36] Hitler claimed in an April speech to the Reichstag that the Wehrmacht had seized over 1,502 aircraft, 469 tanks, 500 anti-aircraft guns, 43,000 machine guns, a million rifles, a billion rounds of rifle ammunition, and three million rounds of artillery ammunition.[37] Czech sources support Hitler's claims in general, although there are some numerical differences: 1,231 aircraft (with material for the construction of a further 240), 1,966 antitank guns, 2,254 pieces of field artillery, 810 tanks, 57,000 machine guns, and 630,000 rifles. The general estimate was that this booty was worth somewhere around 77 million marks.[38] The equipment was sufficient to equip nearly thirty divisions. However, one cannot draw the conclusion that the Wehrmacht directly added thirty divisions to its order of battle.[39] Rather, seizure of Czech dumps meant that Germany acquired large amounts of armaments to use for a variety of purposes. The Germans sold some weapons to Balkan and Middle Eastern countries to earn foreign exchange; Czech arms proved especially useful in bartering for Rumanian grain and oil.[40] Armed SS regiments, which by the 1940 campaign would expand into divisions, received Czech infantry and artillery weapons and found these arms fully as good as their German counterparts.[41] Czech factories provided a portion of the tanks in three of ten panzer divisions that invaded France in 1940 and turned out motorized assault guns for the Wehrmacht through May 1945.[42] In May 1939 Thomas admitted that Czech arms had proven qualitatively superior to expectations.[43] Moreover, a proportion of reserve divisions mobilized and trained after the outbreak of war received Czech arms. An OKH directive from November 1939 establishes that four divisions, the 81st, 82nd, 83rd, and 88th, received Czech weapons.[44] As a result, it would seem that approximately ten German divisions received either a portion or all of their arms as a direct result of the occupation of Czechoslovakia. Finally, the Germans used construction material from Czech fortifications for work on the Westwall and, after the fall of France, for the Atlantic defenses.

All in all, occupation of Czechoslovakia provided extensive military and economic help to the Reich. It enabled Germany to overcome for the time being serious economic difficulties. It provided the Wehrmacht for the first time since the beginning of rearmament with a substantial arms surplus that could either earn foreign exchange or be devoted to equipping reserve units. Lastly, the seizure of Czechoslovakia and domination of the Slovakian puppet state gave the Germans an important jumping-off position for attacking Poland.

Hitler's foreign policy in the period after Munich had as its immediate objective the destruction of what remained of the Czech state. The larger picture, however, was opaque and it seems likely that Hitler was examining the alternatives over the winter. Shortly before the outbreak of war, he told his generals that he had originally hoped to establish tolerable relations with Poland in order to fight the West. He then added: "But this plan which appealed to me could not be executed as fundamental parts had changed."[45]

German feelers extended to the Poles in October 1938 and January 1939 substantiate at least a portion of Hitler's claim.[46] The basic thrust of the German suggestion was that in return for an extraterritorial railroad across the Corridor and the return of Danzig to the Reich they would recognize the Polish-German frontier, guarantee Polish markets in Danzig, and extend the Non-Aggression Pact between the two countries. In addition the Germans extended veiled hints that the Poles should join the Anti-Comintern Pact. In January Hitler even went so far as to suggest to the Polish foreign minister, Józef Beck, that Poland and Germany might cooperate militarily against the Soviet Union.[47] Despite considerable firmness on the part of the Poles in rejecting those German overtures, the Germans remained remarkably calm.

However, once they had occupied Prague, the Germans changed the tone but not the substance of their Polish policy. On March 21 Ribbentrop received the Polish ambassador and demanded what he had hitherto proposed. He emphasized to the Pole that any agreement must contain specific anti-Soviet provisions.[48] Apparently, Hitler, although pressing the Poles hard, was still thinking in terms of an anti-Soviet agreement. Meeting with Brauchitsch on March 25, Hitler underlined his desire to avoid force against Poland—at least for the time being.[49] Events soon changed his mind.

Warsaw returned a negative reply, although Beck indicated a willingness to negotiate further. Ribbentrop conducted the next interview on March 26 in even stronger terms than the one on the twenty-first. He remarked that the Polish attitude reminded him of actions the Czechs had taken the previous May.[50] On March 28, Beck saw the German ambassador and warned that Poland would regard a seizure of Danzig or an attempt to alter the Free City's status as an act of aggression by Germany. When the incensed German declared, "You want to negotiate at the point of a bayonet," Beck coolly replied that that was Germany's mode of operation.[51]

The British guarantee now made up Hitler's mind and eliminated the German hope that Poland would cooperate. This is not to say that the Germans would not have come to the same conclusion, given Polish attitudes. But Hitler's fury at Britain precipitated an immediate decision. Canaris heard the führer shout that he would cook the British a stew on which they would choke.[52] By April 3, Hitler had ordered the OKW to draw up plans for an invasion of Poland under the code name *Fall Weiss*. The Wehrmacht would make its preparations with a target date of September 1 in mind.[53] Thus, the Poles had categorically refused to bow to German pressure, and the English guarantee threatened a European war if the Polish-German confrontation exploded. From this time, the führer sought to isolate Poland and, if that were not possible, to isolate Britain, France, and Poland. Since Poland would not join the anti-Communist crusade, he would postpone the crusade and settle accounts first with Poland and the West.

THE BRITISH REARMAMENT EFFORT

The occupation of Prague ended Chamberlain's resistance to a massive rearmament program. All three services now put forward proposals that in some cases doubled spending levels. By July the British had added nearly £1,000,000,000 to the defense budget for the next three years. In February 1938 the government had limited defense spending to £1,000,000,000 for the period 1939-1941. By fall 1938 this figure had risen to £1,100,000,000 and by July 1939 forecast expenditures reached £2,100,000,000.[54] Service proposals still did not, however, receive a clear run. Treasury resistance remained throughout summer 1939, and the labyrinth of committees made it difficult to accelerate

production. The Committee on Defense Programs and Their Acceleration refused to act on long-term projects lying within Cabinet prove-
nance. It even refused to order the second destroyer flotilla in the 1939-
1940 program, although the Cabinet had allocated funding. Approval
to begin construction would have advanced the destroyers' availability
by ten months, but as Chatfield and Simon pointed out, "this was a
long-term project."[55]

Almost from the start of discussions on altering rearmament policy,
the Treasury objected to increasing spending levels. On April 6, Sir
Alan Barlow, undersecretary of the Treasury, warned that an underlying
assumption of British strategy was the belief that Britain could support
a long war. This was not the case for "the position had radically changed
for the worse from 1914." Britain's internal financial stability was not
as great nor did she possess the foreign resources to make the same
purchases that she had made early in the First World War.[56] What
Barlow neglected to mention was that Germany's position had also
deteriorated when compared to 1914. In mid-April, Chatfield warned
Simon that "terrible criticism might fall upon us if war actually broke
out and it was said that lack of preparedness had resulted from financial
considerations." Simon replied that Britain must insure that military
efforts did not so impinge on economic resources as to render her
powerless "through incapacity to command vital imports to bring a
long war, or indeed any war, to a successful conclusion."[57]

Similar efforts to slow the pace of rearmament continued into the
summer. On July 5, Sir Richard Hopkins, the Treasury's chief civil
servant, testified before the Cabinet on the impact of massive rearmament on Britain's capacity to wage a long war. Unlike previous
Treasury arguments, his report distorted, rather than ignored, Germany's economic difficulties. After stressing the erosion of Britain's
financial position due to rearmament, Hopkins highlighted the supposed strengths of Germany's military, economic, and financial situation. Hore-Belisha immediately contrasted the Treasury analysis with
one by the Industrial Intelligence Center. The latter report had estimated that Germany could not stand the stress of war for more than
a year. Hore-Belisha also referred to a study that the director of the
Industrial Intelligence Center had read to the Imperial Defense College. This paper suggested that Germany must increase armament
production by a factor of seven in order to maintain one hundred

divisions in the field. Hopkins dismissed such estimates: Although he was "not qualified to speak on the capacity of Germany to wage war," Germany could only expect to import limited supplies from adjacent countries in case of war. Therefore, "[h]er plans had . . . been laid on the basis of self-sufficiency." He further asserted that Germany had not relaxed her armament effort and that she could indefinitely maintain her military expenditures. Such a claim was too much for Halifax, who pointed out that if Britain had serious problems with rearmament, it was likely that the situation was more difficult in Germany.[58]

There was some basis for Treasury arguments. Britain was not as strong as she had been in 1914. Nevertheless, this unwillingness to recognize that war was inevitable and that Britain must repair her deficiencies—deficiencies for which the Treasury bore so much responsibility—indicates a considerable lack of vision. The Treasury's ignorance of the strain on Germany is perhaps understandable, although the Industrial Intelligence Center was well aware of the situation. The blind distortion of Germany's economic situation, however, was inexcusable. Such Treasury arguments represented a last-ditch effort to limit rearmament regardless of strategic considerations. In 1938 such arguments had the support of the prime minister and Cabinet, but in 1939 the pressure of public opinion and a change in mood within the Cabinet made possible significant increases in rearmament despite Treasury objections.

The most dramatic alteration in rearmament policy came in the army. After Prague Chamberlain rejected conscription but raised the peacetime strength of territorial units and doubled the Territorial Army at a cost of 80 to 100 million pounds.[59] The French naturally pressed for more ground forces. General Albert Lelong, head of the French delegation at joint staff talks, warned that, although the Allies could initially match Germany's one hundred divisions, Czech arms dumps would enable the Wehrmacht to increase its size by thirty to forty divisions.[60] French representatives underlined that they would bear the brunt of fighting; "while the British divisions were assembling . . . [t]hey regarded the [size of the] British program with the greatest anxiety." The British still held to the line that they had committed only the regular army and not the Territorial Army to the continent.[61]

On April 19, Chatfield urged the Cabinet to fund full war equipment, reserves, and industrial potential for a field army of sixteen divisions. The remaining sixteen territorial divisions would receive equipment to allow a complete training program.[62] But Chamberlain was moving beyond such a proposal and by April 24 had concluded that Britain must introduce conscription. Nevertheless, a Cabinet paper pointed out that "it was not proposed either that the scheme for Compulsory Military Training should supersede our traditional methods of voluntary service or that it should become a permanent feature of our system."[63]

Conscription completely reversed the government's position on the army. Unfortunately, the hurried expansion that now took place created a conservative force organized much like the French army. It was not an army that could cope with new German tactics. Moreover, introduction of conscription had no immediate effect on the strategic balance, although it certainly represented an important commitment to the defense of France and the continent.

POLAND OR RUSSIA? THE STRATEGIC QUESTION

The guarantee to Poland had fundamentally altered Britain's orientation. The diplomatic problem was how to bolster Poland; the strategic problem was how to create a stable eastern front. The failure of British policy in coming months lay in its unwillingness to realize that the latter problem was of overriding importance. Thus, what had been an initial reluctance to deal with the Soviets hardened into a belief that Russia was not essential to establishment of an eastern front.

Regrettably, the guarantee to Poland had substantially strengthened Stalin's bargaining position. Secure in the knowledge that Britain had already committed herself to the defense of Eastern Europe, Russia could negotiate with Germany and fall back on the West if contacts with the Nazis failed. More important, the Germans were in a better bargaining position in negotiations with Russia than were the Allies. Germany could offer Stalin the Baltic States, parts of Poland and Rumania, and, if necessary, Finland. Having committed themselves to the defense of the small nations of Eastern Europe against German aggression, the Western Powers could hardly toss those nations to the Soviets. Moreover, Germany could promise Russia one thing the West could not—Russian neutrality, at least at the start of a European war.[64]

Yet the one factor that Allied statesmen excluded was the possibility that Russia and Germany might reach an accommodation.

The British military had been initially doubtful as to the utility of a guarantee to Poland. The Joint Planning Committee suggested that such a pledge would make Poland intransigent and lead to war before Britain had completed her military preparations. Nevertheless, British planners rated the Polish army highly and argued that Polish military forces would stoutly defend their own territory. With imports of iron ore, coke, and coal from the Soviet Union, Poland could maintain a lengthy defense.[65] On the importance of Russia, the military gave an accurate appraisal of her weaknesses as well as her strategic importance. On March 6, the military attachés in Moscow had warned that the purges had damaged the Russian army so much that it was incapable of undertaking offensive operations. Only in defending Soviet territory would the Red Army be a formidable opponent—as much because of the inherent difficulties of conducting operations in Russia as because of its efficiency. The Soviet air force received no higher marks: its aircraft were obsolete and it lacked support facilities necessary to sustain extensive operations.[66] On March 18, the chiefs drew up a hurried estimate on the respective values of Poland and Russia. Analyzing the strategic situation they concluded that Russia would be more valuable than Poland. The Soviets had brighter prospects for prolonged resistance and could prove a strong deterrent to Japan. Furthermore, the Russian navy could threaten the Baltic ore trade between Germany and Sweden.[67] On the whole the analysis was quite accurate, but the chiefs failed to maintain their position with sufficient vigor over the coming months.

In early April Beck journeyed to London to cement the new relation with Britain. In the British capital the Polish foreign minister showed the same hard-nosed approach to negotiations that he had displayed with the Germans. About all that Chamberlain and Halifax could extract was a promise of reciprocity: if Germany attacked Britain, Poland would declare war. Beck refused even to extend the Polish-Rumanian treaty to Germany as well as Russia because of his fear of driving Hungary into the Nazi camp. He expressed vigorous opposition to the idea of cooperating with the Russians and warned the British that an association between Poland and Russia would cause a violent German reaction. He assured his listeners that he anticipated no serious difficulties over Danzig.[68]

In a technical sense, Beck's conduct of these talks was masterful. He managed to give little in return for a British guarantee and had reinforced British impulses to avoid serious negotiations with Russia. Following discussion with Beck, Chamberlain told the Cabinet that he distrusted Russia and doubted that in case of war Britain could obtain real support from that quarter. Apparently Beck also had convinced the prime minister that any arrangement that included Russia would spark an immediate explosion. Thus, "the question of making any arrangement with Russia was obviously one which required a great deal of further consideration." Chamberlain concluded that he believed the best course was to negotiate a two-power pact with Poland. "After all, Poland was the key to the situation," he assured his listeners, "and an alliance with Poland would insure that Germany would be engaged in a war on two fronts."[69]

On April 7, the Italians occupied Albania. Halifax quite accurately told a meeting of ministers on the eighth that the Italians had timed their move for the Easter recess.[70] The Strategic Appreciations Sub-Committee typified British reaction when it urged: "We must, if possible, anticipate and not follow the next move of the Axis Powers."[71] For many Allied statesmen, the Italian action appeared as one more step toward an Axis domination of Europe by diplomatic and, if that failed, by military means. In response the Western Powers now proceeded to distribute guarantees throughout Southeastern Europe. They mistakenly believed that such action could persuade these states to cooperate and that diplomatic guarantees would deter Germany from further aggression. Moreover, they argued that a bloc of Rumania, Greece, and Turkey would deny Germany the resources of the Balkans.[72] Unfortunately, the Anglo-French guarantees ended what little chance the Western Powers had to pressure these nations into some cooperative system against the German threat. The British especially felt that by their diplomatic guarantees they had denied the Germans room for maneuver.[73] Even the military were to overestimate the efficacy of the diplomatic constraints that such "offensive diplomacy" could impose on Germany.[74] At the end of May the British chiefs went so far as to suggest that "Up to now, Germany has followed a methodical plan which consists in demolishing one after another each of the key parts of the barrier which might contain her or threaten her in Eastern Europe. The entry of Poland into a pact with Great Britain and France means the failure of this plan."[75]

French support for this active and risky policy of diplomatic confrontation with Germany needs some explanation. Two factors undoubtedly contributed to French acquiescence. The first was the fact that Great Britain now had committed herself to the defense of France, even should war break out in Eastern Europe. This after all had been a *major* goal of French policy throughout the interwar period. The second element, although of less significance, was that continued tensions in the Mediterranean led the French to feel a need for British support in that region: thus, a willingness to support the new, ambitious British diplomacy in Eastern Europe as a quid pro quo.

Particularly strong arguments took place in the Cabinet and Foreign Policy Committee in April and May over the Russian question. The guarantee of Poland had initially represented an interim measure to avert what the Cabinet believed to be an impending German invasion of Poland. Chamberlain and Halifax had assured both their colleagues and opposition leaders that the Foreign Office would work out more permanent arrangements including Soviet Russia as soon as the immediate crisis ended. But as Europe quieted and as the threat seemed less immediate, the pressure for agreement with Russia receded. The belief in the fundamental hostility between the Soviet and Nazi regimes led many in Britain to conclude that those powers could never reach even a tactical accommodation. From this perspective, Cadogan noted that not only was there little military gain in associating with Russia but that politically and diplomatically any agreement would derange relations with other nations.[76]

Chamberlain and his supporters in the Cabinet now firmly set themselves against hurrying into agreement with the Soviets. On April 19, the prime minister suggested that an alliance of Russia, Britain, and France was unnecessary. Inskip commented that the Russian proposals were an attempt to entangle the West. If Russia really wished to restrain Germany, she could supply munitions to Eastern Europe whether there were an alliance or not. Significantly, Chamberlain indicated that his attitude toward the Polish guarantee had fundamentally changed. He no longer considered the guarantee as an interim measure but a fundamental principle of British diplomacy. The prime minister urged that Britain should attach great importance to maintaining Polish morale and that "the first essential was to get Poland into a firm, confident, and self-reliant state." Thus, Britain should do nothing that might shake Poland's confidence, such as concluding an agreement with Russia. In conclusion the Foreign Policy Committee decided not to accept the Russian proposals. Halifax commented that they "would give little additional security: it would arouse the suspicion of our friends and aggravate the hostility of our enemies."[77]

As the British became more dubious about an alliance with the Soviet Union, the French moved in the opposite direction. It was not so much that they rated Soviet military assistance higher than the British. Their pressure for agreement with Russia reflected a grave concern that war lay in the near future. Daladier, especially, believed that Germany, perhaps with Italian support, planned war as soon as possible. The French saw agreement between Russia and the West as a basic strategic necessity for the coming struggle, whereas the British believed that such an agreement would precipitate war when the European situation was calming down. Consequently, the French believed the West should accept Soviet proposals for a tripartite alliance.[78] Also pushing the French toward support for an agreement with Russia was their exaggerated estimate of Western military weakness. Shortly after the Italian occupation of Albania the French general staff estimated that the Axis powers could mobilize 250 divisions against 120 Western and 110 Eastern European divisions. But the military forces of Eastern Europe, the French believed, were of doubtful utility, and Poland and Rumania both required Soviet help to maintain their resistance for any length of time.[79] By May rumors were circulating in Paris of a Russo-German deal to divide Eastern Europe.[80] Both factors provided additional impetus to French efforts to include Russia within the Western alliance system. Yet the French still found it virtually impossible to move the British from their complacent attitude.

Finally, in mid-April the arguments within the Cabinet led the ministers to request a more thorough study of Russia's military capabilities than the chiefs had produced on March 18. Interestingly, in casting the terms of reference, Chamberlain attempted to restrict their field of survey and directly ordered them not to discuss the military arguments for or against accepting Russian proposals.[81] On April 25, the Chiefs of Staff reported. They warned that Russian equipment was more remarkable for quantity than quality. Whereas Russia possessed a large tank park of high-quality armored vehicles, most of the army remained on a "horsed basis." The purges, they suggested, had shattered the army's nervous system. Erroneously, they argued that Soviet industry could not support a great war effort. Although Russia had attempted to create a war economy that could support one hundred divisions, "the new great factories built with foreign help and the plant in them have been allowed to deteriorate; insufficient skilled labor is available to increase output above the normal rate; administration is hopelessly inefficient and has been made worse by the purges which still continue." The indifferent state of internal communications would magnify Russian difficulties. Because railroads were already working at full capacity, the transportation system would only support two to three weeks of mobilization before it "would have to be suspended or at least held up to avoid a complete breakdown in industry and national life." Remarkably, for the first time in the late thirties, the chiefs went outside their "terms of reference"—not to argue the need for an alliance with the Soviet Union—but to "draw attention to the fact that the various countries in which we visualize in this report that Russian forces might be used may themselves be most unwilling to admit the entry of Russians into their territory."[82]

On the positive side, the chiefs pointed out that a Russian alliance could provide munitions to Poland and Rumania and would deny Germany raw materials and foodstuffs if the Soviet navy threatened Germany's Baltic supply lines. Finally, they warned of "the grave military dangers inherent in the possibility of any agreement between Germany and Russia," but this important point was lost among negative comments on Soviet military capabilities.[83] On the whole, the chiefs apparently favored agreement with the Soviets, but their penchant for "worst case analysis" was hardly calculated to encourage the waverers to support an alliance with Russia.

The lines of argumentation were now clearly set. On one side Chamberlain and Halifax feared that until Britain had completed an alliance system with the states of Eastern Europe she should do nothing "to impair the confidence of those states."[84] Halifax, influenced by his talks with the Rumanian foreign minister at the end of April, went so far as to suggest that "Closer relations between Rumania and the Soviet Union were likely to make war certain."[85] In response to serious criticism within the Cabinet Chamberlain was able to sidetrack the basic issue by noting that "no decision was called for at the present time."[86]

There was increasing opposition both within and outside of the government to the prime minister's unwillingness to deal with the

Russians. In the Cabinet Malcolm MacDonald argued on several occasions that a neutral Russia could supply Germany with raw materials and foodstuffs and thus undermine Britain's strategy of blockade.[87] Hore-Belisha warned that a refusal to deal with Russia might drive her into the arms of Germany.[88] The secretary of state for war's position was not surprising in view of the paper that the chiefs produced five days later on May 10. They argued that Soviet assistance would be "of great value, particularly in containing enemy forces and in supplying war material to other allies in Eastern Europe." Underlying their argument even more than their estimates of the benefits of Soviet help was a fear of a deal between Russia and the Axis powers. Now, unlike their paper in May which had worried over the impact of a Russian alliance on the Eastern European nations, they warned that they could not overlook the "danger which would result from rapprochement between Germany and Russia—an aim which has been on the minds of the German General Staff for many years. A combination of the German capacity for organization with the material and manpower resources of Russia would not only eliminate all hope of saving Poland and Rumania but would have repercussions throughout Europe and in India, the serious nature of which would be hard to exaggerate."[89]

Chamberlain and Halifax remained unconvinced. Underlining the prime minister's unwillingness to give strategic factors pride of place was his comment to the Foreign Policy Committee that there were political as well as strategic considerations and the former pointed in other directions.[90] Reinforcing the disinclination to deal with the Russians was the general sense in the Foreign Office that an agreement between Germany and the Soviet Union was "inherently improbable."[91]

Not until the end of May did the prime minister and foreign secretary alter their substantial opposition to further serious negotiations with the Russians. By that time opposition was becoming overwhelming. Not only were serious questions being asked in the House of Commons, but embarrassing opposition was appearing in the Cabinet and not just among the hard liners. On May 16, Hoare admitted that at first he had opposed any pact because it might precipitate war; he had now changed his mind both because of Russia's military value and because of the possibility of Russo-German collaboration.[92]

The conversion was hardly enthusiastic. Chamberlain admitted to his colleagues at the decisive Cabinet meeting on May 24 that unless Britain negotiated along the lines suggested by the Russians, diplomatic connections might collapse. He still mistrusted Russia and thought an alliance would result in objections throughout Europe, but a break-down of negotiations could have even worse consequences.[93] Thus, the British government embarked on its half-hearted approach to the Russians. Remarkable overconfidence, as well as substantial misconceptions, marked the negotiations that now began with the Soviets. On June 5, Chamberlain told the Foreign Policy Committee that unless Britain drove a hard bargain she "should necessarily get the worst of the bargain. . . ."[94] Despite continuing reports of Russo-German contacts,[95] Halifax and Chamberlain still did not believe that Russia and Germany might get together. On July 19, Halifax told the Cabinet that a failure of negotiations with Russia "would not cause him very great anxiety, since he felt that whatever formal agreement was [sic] signed, the Soviet government would probably take such action as best suited them, if war broke out." In reply to questions he admitted that there was evidence that the Russians and Germans were talking, but "it seemed likely these discussions related to industrial matters." Chamberlain added that he did not believe that a Russo-German alliance was a real possibility.[96] Even after first word of the Nazi-Soviet Non-Aggression Pact arrived in London, Halifax discounted the agreement as of little strategic importance, although its moral effect would be enormous.[97]

The Anglo-French negotiations with the Russians over the summer and the ill-fated military mission to Moscow in August were a fitting end to Allied approaches to the Soviet Union. Sent by slow boat to Leningrad, the British delegation did not even possess the proper credentials to negotiate. Although one can certainly doubt the sincerity of Stalin's government, the Western Powers were hardly more forthcoming. In fact, it is clear that they hoped that Russia would carry a major share of the fighting to support Eastern European governments that had thus far refused even to discuss possible military cooperation with the Soviet Union. By August the West and Russia had reached a complete impasse. On the Russian side, any Russian government, no matter how idealistic, required major concessions from the Eastern European governments for its own security. On the other hand the West, having pledged itself to defend the small nations of Eastern

Europe, could not now ignore the objections of these small states to the entrance of Russian troops onto their territory. Further muddying the inherent hostilities between the Eastern European nationalities was the ideological nature of Russia's communist regime. No one was particularly eager to deal with the Soviet regime, and even Hitler after his triumph over Poland would express surprise that one of his generals would enthusiastically endorse the Nazi-Soviet Non-Aggression Pact.[98]

The failure to reach an agreement with the Soviet Union and the resulting Nazi-Soviet pact decisively affected the course of the Second World War. The pact helped Germany to defeat Poland and concentrate against the West. Soviet supplies of raw materials were a significant help to the German war economy and to the victory over France that destroyed the possibility of a western front until 1944. As suggested above, cooperation between the West and Russia would have been a difficult task in the best of circumstances. Germany could and did offer Stalin concessions that no democracy could match, while Eastern Europe refused to consider Soviet help, even when threatened by Germany. Yet, despite these difficulties, the Chamberlain government showed a lamentable lack of strategic sense. It obviously believed that the West held the best cards while the Russians held none. In fact, the situation was the opposite; and Stalin proved more than willing to accept a gamble that the capitalist powers would fight themselves to exhaustion. Unfortunately for the Soviet people the events of May 1940 proved him disastrously wrong.

BRITAIN AND GERMANY

As the European situation quieted at the end of April, Chamberlain faced the problem of Anglo-German relations. Given the political climate in the nation, the prime minister had little room for maneuver. Nevertheless, his German policy up to the beginning of war reflected as much an attempt to bribe Germany to behave herself, as an effort to prepare for war if she should not. On May 19, Chamberlain told the Foreign Policy Committee that moderates were an important and viable segment of German society and that Britain should do all in its power to encourage them. He "greatly feared that an alliance with Russia would drive the moderate elements into Hitler's camp and Hitler would then be able with some justification to say that he had a united

Germany behind him and could proceed with his aggressive policies without fear of any internal dissensions."[99]

On April 28, in a maliciously clever speech Hitler denounced the Anglo-German Naval Agreement and the 1934 Non-Aggression Pact with Poland. Shortly thereafter Halifax commented that the speech was not as bellicose as had initially appeared. Britain's reply, he argued, should address only Germany's denunciation of the naval agreement. The foreign secretary added that Hitler "had spoken of his readiness for a clear and practical understanding." Britain should perhaps ask him what he had in mind.[100] Reinforcing the inclination within the British government to hope that things were not as bad as they appeared were the dispatches that Henderson was sending from Berlin. Typical of Henderson's reports was his assertion on May 17 that the settlement of the Danzig and Corridor issues was the only alternative to war. Once these questions had been solved " 'butter is better than guns' might really become the insistent popular German cry and the Nazi extremist regime might not be able to resist it."[101] Although Henderson's standing had declined, his illusions were shared to a point by many in higher circles. Halifax reported to the Foreign Policy Committee a conversation with the German ambassador "who had . . . referred to Herr Hitler as a reasonable and sensible man." The German had added "that no reasonable and sensible man would think of making war against the forces which Great Britain had (unjustifiably in German eyes) mobilized against Germany."[102] Halifax and Chamberlain proved no less susceptible than their military advisers to the impression that the West now held the initiative. On May 20, the foreign secretary told the French ministers in Paris that

> [i]t should be remembered that the position of France and Great Britain is quite different than it was six months ago. They had embarked upon a policy which was both decisive and firm and which had had great effect upon the psychology of the whole world. Great Britain, France, Poland, Turkey, and it was hoped, Russia, had been rallied together and the United States was very close to them. Our industrial output, particularly in the area of aircraft, had grown faster than at one time we had dared to expect. Conscription had been introduced. The general effect of this was to place our partnership in a position of evident strength.[103]

Chamberlain was unable to conceive the real nature of the Nazi threat. He told the Foreign Policy Committee in June that Britain did not propose to protect the smaller states but rather to prevent Germany from achieving continental domination—certainly a sensible goal. But he added that, although control of Poland and Rumania would increase Germany's military strength, German domination of Denmark would not. "Therefore this was not a case in which we should be bound to intervene forcibly to restore the *status quo.*"[104]

Nothing better underlines Chamberlain's real attitude than the ill-fated, secret July negotiations between Helmuth Wohlthat, an official of the Four Year Plan, and on the British side, Sir Horace Wilson, Sir Joseph Ball, and Robert Hudson. Wilson suggested to Wohlthat that wide-ranging negotiations between their countries discuss the points raised by the führer in his April 28 speech. Included in Wilson's suggested list were proposals for a joint Anglo-German declaration against aggression, "mutual declarations of non-interference, by Germany in respect of the British Commonwealth of Nations, and by Great Britain in respect of Greater Germany," a settlement of the colonial and/or mandates questions, and "a German-British declaration on the limitation of armaments and a common policy towards third countries" that would include a naval, air, and army agreement. The British also offered their good services to obtain a peaceful settlement of the Danzig and Corridor questions. Wilson implied that, not only was Britain willing to embark on wide-scale economic cooperation but was also willing to secure financial aid for German industry. Wilson assured Wohlthat that "if the führer would agree to conversations, this would be regarded as a sign of returning confidence."[105] The proposed negotiations collapsed before they began when the proposals leaked to the British press. The resulting furor led to charges in Britain that the Chamberlain government was bribing Nazi Germany. The Germans reacted sarcastically to suggestions that they would consider taking a bribe and angrily to innuendoes that Germany would disarm in exchange for "peace loans."[106]

The issue of war and peace was entirely out of British hands. The last days before war still saw many of the same illusions that had characterized British diplomacy throughout the thirties. On August 26, Henderson, recalled for consultations, assured Cabinet ministers that he "doubted whether there was any agreement to partition Poland.

. . . He thought that there was a good deal of indignation among the German people against the Russo-German alliance. His own butler (a German) had said to him with indignation that Germany had made an agreement with her one enemy. . . . There was nothing in Berlin today to indicate the likelihood of war."[107] On the morning of September 1, Chamberlain told his colleagues that they met under grave circumstances. "The event against which we had fought so long and so earnestly had come upon us. . . ." One minister went so far as to suggest that Britain should avoid a formal declaration of war. [108] Small wonder then that it required a political revolt to force a declaration of war two days after the Germans had invaded Poland, or that Britain waged the coming war in such a dilatory and half-hearted fashion.

CONCLUSION

Allied diplomacy and strategic planning did not, of course, precipitate the Second World War. Hitler's long-range goals insured that at some stage in his career a major European conflict would occur. In 1939 he once again hoped to isolate his intended victim and create the conditions conducive to a limited war. Nothing in British policy over the summer gave Hitler the impression that this was not a viable course of action. The diplomatic guarantees and efforts to speed rearmament were more than counterbalanced by the efforts at economic appeasement and the dilatory approach to Soviet Russia. The Nazi-Soviet Non-Aggression Pact reinforced Hitler's opinion that the West would not act. His appraisal of Allied leadership may not have been wide of the mark, as the refusal to support Poland on the 1st and 2nd of September indicated. But he seriously miscalculated the nature of Western public opinion; Chamberlain and Daladier no longer enjoyed the public support for a further appeasement of Nazi Germany. Still, in the final analysis, Hitler did not care; if the West chose war, then he would accommodate them.

On the other side Britain and France faced difficult diplomatic and strategic questions. What is surprising is the fact that, although they had glibly dropped the Czechs the previous year, the Western Powers now proved so solicitous of Polish sensibilities and so unwilling to deal with Russia. In a larger sense their policy of diplomatic confrontation missed the fact that Germany might not shrink from war no matter what the conditions. In dealing with the German problem, the West showed no willingness to take risks, and Western statesmen and generals failed to see the forest for the trees. Unfortunately, as we shall see in the next chapter, the Anglo-French response to the other strategic factors that they faced would be no better. One can perhaps sympathize with Chamberlain's revulsion against what another great war would mean for Europe. That does not excuse, however, the prime minister for his flawed execution of the terrible responsibilities that were his.

X

Grand Strategy and the War's Beginning

On September 1, 1939 Adolf Hitler launched the Wehrmacht against Poland. This military adventure capped a chain of events that stretched back to the previous April. From that time, Hitler had attempted to isolate Poland and create the diplomatic and military conditions necessary to enable Germany to destroy Poland in a limited war. In some respects Hitler's diplomacy was more successful than it had been the year before. This time there were no states in Eastern Europe capable or willing to help the intended victim, and the Nazi-Soviet Non-Aggression Pact not only meant that Russia would stand aside but that she would actively participate in Poland's destruction.

Hitler had no intention of settling for anything less than the military conquest of Poland. This time he would not allow the other European powers to dissuade him from his war. As for the Western Powers, Hitler apparently believed that after his agreement with the Soviet Union, they would not intervene. But if they should fight, then the führer was willing to accept the challenge and settle accounts now.

The outbreak of war marked the final collapse of Neville Chamberlain's policies and hopes. The waffling that led to Allied declarations of war more than forty-eight hours after the invasion of Poland reflected not only the diplomatic and political indecision of the Western Powers but their complete misjudgment of Hitler's drive to war. The inability of the British and French to weigh the strategic factors accurately, however, would be the greatest contributing factor to the disaster of May 1940. Hitler had seriously miscalculated in his belief that the Western Powers would not intervene after he attacked Poland, and the severe difficulties that the Germans faced upon the completion of the Polish campaign presented the Allies with major opportunities. Unfortunately, the conduct of Allied grand strategy proved seriously in error, both before and after the war had begun. The faulty strategic decisions, in fact, allowed the Germans to escape the full extent of their strategic and economic predicament. The result was that Germany was able to husband her economic resources for one great effort in the spring, prepare, as only her army could prepare, for *"der Tag,"* and in effect maximize her limited potential.

Western Strategy: Its Genesis

Allied strategic planning for 1939 followed the same paths that planners had first laid out during the previous year. Given the strategic situation, this strategy was a clearheaded, rational approach to the difficulties that the West would face in war against Nazi Germany. Unfortunately, almost from the first Allied planners diluted their grand strategy in framing responses to particular military and strategic problems. Thus, by failing to address individual issues in terms of overall strategy they insured that Germany would escape the full impact of her difficulties. Allied military planning and foreign policy often worked at cross purposes to grand strategy. The compartmentalization of planning, along with an unwillingness to ask uncompromising questions, led to an emasculated version of Western strategy and eventually to the disaster of May 1940.

The key element in Western strategy would lie in the ability of Allied economic, diplomatic, and military measures to disrupt and unbalance the German war economy. The Advisory Committee on Trade Questions in Time of War, part of the network of the Committee of Imperial Defense, molded the initial economic strategy. Because of wider departmental representation, the committee's reports were less pessimistic than the military studies. In July 1938 it presented a study that articulated the basic economic strategy against Germany and the foundation of British strategy. The committee pointed out that, in spite of her efforts to attain self-sufficiency, Germany still needed to import many commodities essential for war. Among the more important were foodstuffs, iron ore, manganese, nearly all ferrous metals, ferro-alloys, cotton, wool, and fuels. Accordingly, the stockpiles that Germany possessed at the initiation of hostilities would form an important element in Germany's capacity to resist blockade. Moreover, Germany's financial weaknesses could make a blockade of exports that earned foreign exchange critical. Shortages of funds would "render it increasingly difficult, as the war proceeds, for her to pay for imports on the scale required in war." The report recommended that in a war against Germany, Britain should take the most vigorous possible action to prevent her from receiving imports vital to the continued functioning of the economy and to force her to use up stockpiles as quickly as possible.

> Our aim should, therefore, be:
> 1) The maximum interruption of supplies of these goods in all cases where it is practicable . . . to create a shortage of them in Germany.
> 2) Any diminution of Germany's economic resources as a whole. With regard to the former the necessary conditions will be:
> a) that Germany cannot obtain adequate supplies except with the assistance of supplies, direct or indirect, coming from overseas or otherwise within our control.
> b) that steps can be taken to prevent neutrals from constituting a channel for such supplies.
> With regard to the latter, it may be that, even where there is no prospect of causing any special shortage in Germany, some measure of economic pressure may yet cause her substantial loss.[1]

In January 1939 the Joint Planning Committee presented in broad outline the strategy that the Western Powers would follow the following September. The planners pointed out that Axis preparations were further advanced, and thus Germany would try to exploit her military superiority. Britain and France must establish their defensive strength in order to deny Germany success. Then, as war continued, the Allies would increase their offensive strength while using the blockade to strangle the German economy. "It is, therefore, extremely important," they concluded, "that from the outset we should adopt every recognized means of denying supplies of all kinds to the enemy."[2]

However, the chiefs' "European Appreciation," submitted the following month, minimized Germany's economic difficulties. Supposedly the Reich's Four Year Plan had significantly reduced reliance on imports, but they admitted that Germany still required regular imports of raw materials such as foodstuffs, iron ore, manganese, nonferrous metals, fuels, and fats. Although Italy was self-sufficient in foodstuffs, she lacked most industrial raw materials. The chiefs argued that so long as Italy could carry on her Mediterranean trade, she could maintain her "naval and air operations at maximum intensity for a considerable period."[3] Growing control of Southeastern Europe would enable the Germans to make up most of their deficiencies. The chiefs did admit that Balkan supplies were limited and that the Axis powers would compete for them.[4] Two distinct trends that would dominate strategic thinking throughout 1939 appeared in this document: the former recognizing the Axis' economic difficulties; the latter minimizing the possible damage of blockade.

The occupation of Prague led to preparation of strategic estimates for Anglo-French staff conversations. One paper, entitled "The Broad Strategic Problem," stressed that ground and air inferiority would force the West to remain on the defensive. The study emphasized that stringent economic measures adopted by Germany and Italy in peace indicated that their only hope rested on a short war.[5] While planners sketched their first tentative conclusions, the military attaché in Berlin, Mason-MacFarlane, recommended immediate action against Germany. He warned that the longer Britain waited, the more difficult the strategic situation would become as Germany utilized Czech arms and munitions. At the present time the Wehrmacht was less capable, he argued, than in fall 1938, because recruit training had just begun. Moreover, the army did not have the flying start on mobilization that it possessed in September 1938 and would undoubtedly acquire again in fall 1939.[6] Regrettably, there was no chance that such a "risky" course of action would appeal to his government or its military advisers.

Emphasis on an economic strategy remained the focal point of Western planning. In late April the chiefs reported that recent Axis territorial acquisitions would not solve basic raw-material shortages. These remained as pressing as ever. Although Germany might increase land and air forces at the onset of war, raw-material demands would correspondingly increase. Rumania could cover Axis petroleum needs for at least a year, but the chiefs doubted whether transport facilities existed for delivering the fuel.[7]

Therefore, by spring 1939 the broad outline of Allied strategy was clear. With the economic vulnerability of Germany and Italy, this emphasis on an economic strategy made excellent sense. Such an approach demanded that the Allies deny Germany all sources of supply. It involved not only inclusion of Italy within the blockade, but also active operations against the Italians, denial of Southeastern Europe's economic resources as much as possible, and Soviet cooperation in blockade measures. Since the German economy was already short of raw materials, economic isolation would soon have led to a diminution of the Reich's striking power. British economic strategists placed the problem in proper perspective by emphasizing that the West should aim for the "maximum interruption of supplies of . . . goods in all cases where it was practicable."[8] This strategy, while allowing Britain and France to maintain a strategic defense, also required that the West undertake all possible military operations. By hitting Germany in peripheral areas and by pressuring Germany where possible, the Allies could force the Wehrmacht to expend scarce resources in theaters that were not decisive.

If the basis of Allied strategy were correct, as this argument suggests, why then did it fail? In the broadest sense, it failed because of the consistent Allied disinclination to aim for the "maximum interruption of supplies of . . . goods in all cases where it was practicable." In both diplomatic and strategic sectors Western leaders failed to implement basic strategy. No matter what the chances were to gain Soviet aid, the dilatory approach to Russia reflected a complete failure to understand the basic, critical demand of Allied strategy: cut Germany off from all possible sources of supply. In three other critical areas, the Italian question, the Norwegian leads, and the western front, Allied political and military leaders would show the same lamentable unwillingness to draw the correct conclusions from their grand strategy.

THE ITALIAN QUESTION

In spring 1939 the Cabinet Preparedness Committee underlined the connection between applying maximum pressure on Germany and waging war against Italy:

> Whatever military assistance Germany might gain from Italy's entry into the war, she will lose all possibility of using a neutral, but friendly, Italy as a base for import trade, while after her stocks

of arms, foodstuffs, or industrial trade have been used up, Italy herself will become an economic liability for Germany just as Austro-Hungary was in the last war. This is largely recognised in Germany. . . . Though holding relatively large stocks of most armaments, Italy is deficient in other war stores and retains but small reserves of the majority of strategic raw materials. Moreover, since German and Italian deficiencies are much the same in kind, the two countries will be competing for replacement supplies in the same, limited, continental markets. [9]

This claim that the Germans recognized that Italy represented a severe liability is substantiated by German documents. Italian vulnerability in economic sectors, not to mention their military incompetence, thoroughly alarmed the Germans. In April 1938 the naval high command reported that: "In our opinion, in a war with England, Italy, as an ally, would be a burden of the first order, especially in regards to the war's economic prosecution, while Italy would not be able to provide effective military support in districts of strategic importance to Germany (except in the Mediterranean). On this basis the OKM recommends that Italy for the time being (if war breaks out) act as a benevolent neutral."[10] As late as February 1940, the German naval attaché in Rome warned that Italian participation in the war would undermine Germany's military position, economically as well as militarily.[11]

Thus, in a European conflict, Italy offered the Western Powers the possibility of increasing economic pressure on the Reich without adding seriously to their military commitments. If anything, should war break out in Eastern Europe, the Allies would have the opportunity to better their strategic situation in the Mediterranean at Italy's expense while Germany remained fully occupied. Any aid the Germans gave Italy, whether economic or military, to bolster the position in the Mediterranean would detract from resources available for the western front.

Unfortunately, Britain's Italian strategy in the 1938-1939 period was rarely discussed within the framework of grand strategy. As a result, the tendency of the military to examine every issue in terms of "worst case" analysis combined with the strategic ignorance of most ministers to weaken Allied strategy by ignoring the possibilities that Italy offered. As early as March 1, Sir Roger Backhouse, Chief of Naval Staff, suggested that a series of hard blows against Italy at the start of hostilities could turn "the whole course of the war in Britain's favor."[12] Nevertheless, on March 20, the Joint Planning Committee submitted a pessimistic appreciation. The planners warned that there was no chance of knocking Italy out of any war quickly. Naval pressure could only affect the issue in the long run, and neither a land offensive against Abyssinia nor one on Libya "would be likely to achieve a knockout blow." Finally, Britain could not supply the bombers for a decisive attack against Italy.[13] All this was true; but, given Western strategy, it was irrelevant. In fact, it was all to the advantage of the Western Powers that a militarily crippled and battered Italian state remain at Germany's side. Allied strategy aimed to strangle Germany economically. The essential question was the effect Italian participation in the war would have on the Reich's economic and strategic situation. Yet, British planners failed to address the problem in such terms. Thus, throughout spring and summer 1939 they argued out Britain's Italian strategy on whether the West could quickly knock Italy out of a war and not on how Italy's participation in a war might affect the general position of the Axis.

A more thorough study of the Mediterranean strategic situation appeared at the end of March. The Joint Planning Committee reported that "it was anxious that the government not assume that to 'knock Italy out of the war at the outset' is a course of action which we consider to be feasible in the conditions with which we are now faced." Because of German air superiority, the planners argued, Italy could concentrate preponderant forces in the Mediterranean. They nonetheless admitted that the Royal Navy faced relatively little difficulty in blockading Italy and attacking her shores.[14] On the following day, the Joint Planning Committee asserted that "on the other hand, Italy's intervention against us would add immeasurably to our military anxieties, and greatly increase the effectiveness of German attacks on our seaborne trade."[15]

The Anglo-French staff talks beginning at the end of March showed a similar clash between fear of military complications in the Mediterranean and a belief that Italy was an easy target. The April 3 conversations suggested that Allied domination of communications to East Africa would result in a quick success in that theater.[16] On May 3, the chief French representative argued that Italian cooperation with Germany would complicate Allied naval strategy in the Mediterranean, but also admitted that Italy was the weak point in the Axis against which the Allies had "good hope of success."[17] However, on the same day Lelong reported that as long as the possibility of a German attack existed, France did not have forces available for operations against Italy.[18] On May 30, the French delegation argued outright that Italy's neutrality would aid the West and enable the Allies to concentrate against Germany. Thus, the Western Powers could launch an offensive sooner in the critical theater.[19]

While these staff talks took place on the highest level, local theater commanders also conferred. Admiral Cunningham, commander in chief of the Mediterranean fleet, and his French opposite number decided on an aggressive strategy against Italy. Their fleets would blockade Italy, bombard her ports, hunt her submarines down, and conquer Italian East Africa and Libya. If the Italian fleet dared to come out and give battle, so much the better.[20] The Mediterranean commanders apparently felt none of the fears that gripped the senior officers in London and Paris.

In June the Cabinet turned to the subject of Italy. From the first, many ministers grasped the importance of fighting Italy as well as Germany. Chatfield suggested that, when faced with several enemies, sound strategic policy dictated an attack on the weakest. Unfortunately, he argued the Italian issue in terms of knocking Italy out rather than its implications for Germany's economic position.[21] On June 22, Chamberlain argued in a meeting of the Foreign Policy Committee that there were important advantages in having the Italians at Germany's side during any war. Hoare suggested that an early offensive against Italy would force Germany to divert forces from Poland, while Stanhope underlined that Italy was more valuable to the Axis as a neutral. Hore-Belisha agreed, as did Inskip. At the conclusion of discussions, Chatfield, with the Prime Minister's support, suggested that Britain should insure that Italy did not remain neutral in a future war.[22]

In this period, when Western policy would determine whether Italy joined Germany or remained neutral, British military advisers strongly advocated a soft line toward the Italians. They consistently refused to place the Italian issue within the framework of Allied grand strategy. On July 12, the Joint Planning Committee recommended that the West should not send an ultimatum to Italy on the outbreak of war, because no one knew whether Italian intervention at Germany's side "appeared inevitable." An ultimatum, therefore, would only accelerate Italy's participation and place the Western Powers in the position of aggressors. In addition, the planners argued against a rigorous rationing control of Italy or the inclusion of Italy within the framework of economic measures adopted against Germany. Such measures could be considered acts of war. The Joint Planning Committee tendered this advice while admitting that Italy would throw "every obstacle in the way of our policy of impeding German imports" and would aid Germany in the dispatch of her exports. The report concluded that the Allies could undertake no decisive measures against Italy and added, even more questionably, that Italy might "be in a position to hit us more effectively at the outset than we can hit her. . . ."[23]

A revision of this report appeared six days later under the signature of the Chiefs of Staff. The argument now ran that, although Allied capital ships must remain in the Mediterranean even if Italy were neutral, "they would not run the risks inseparable from operations of war." With Italy neutral, there would be no threat to British operations in the Red Sea. The only disadvantage, the chiefs admitted, was that the West would find it more difficult to impose economic pressure on Germany, and Germany would not have to support the Italian economy and military effort from her own limited resources. Although such pressure on the German economy was the basic principle of Allied strategy, they concluded that "Italian neutrality, if it could by any means be assured, would be decidedly preferable to her active hostility."[24]

Central to the above analysis was the argument that Italian neutrality was preferable "if it could . . . be *assured*" [my emphasis]. There was, of course, no way to insure Italian neutrality, especially if things went badly. Surely the time to begin the struggle against Italy was at the beginning of hostilities when the Wehrmacht was occupied with Poland, not when the Allies faced a massive German assault with few resources to spare for the Mediterranean.

At the end of July, Hore-Belisha attacked the military's position on Italy before the Cabinet. Allied military leaders, he asserted, had decided that the West should do nothing in the Mediterranean and must remain inactive on the western front, while Germany destroyed Poland. He warned that if this were to be Allied strategy, the war would be lost and that "even if Italy remained neutral, we still had to leave our forces in the Mediterranean to watch her. It would be preferable to devise means to smash Italy and thus release these forces for action elsewhere. As a neutral, Italy would sustain Germany whereas as an ally, she would constitute a drain on German resources."[25]

The French military, however, proved no more optimistic than their British counterparts. In the spring they had suggested that the French army would immediately attack Tripoli from Tunisia on the outbreak of war with Italy. In late July, they indicated that they would have to wait at least two months before attacking Libya. Moreover, they argued that it would take considerable time before Tripoli fell, even though Allied naval superiority would cut Libya from the Italian mainland at the beginning of hostilities.[26] In May the French delegation at the Anglo-French staff talks went so far as to suggest that Italy's neutrality represented a positive advantage for the West. In September the French gave their rationale for appeasing Italy. Meeting Chamberlain at Brighton on September 22, Daladier argued that the Allies make every effort to maintain Italian neutrality so that their forces could recreate the Balkan front of the last war at Salonika. Where the troops would come for this replay of one of the previous war's less than successful strategies, Daladier did not suggest.[27]

In the final weeks before war, the British military continued to advocate actively further appeasement of Italy. On August 24, Sir Cyril Newall, Chief of Air Staff, suggested that France allow the Italians a free zone at Jibuti. Sir Dudley Pound, now Chief of Naval Staff, thought that offering the Italians a seat on the Suez Canal Board would not be too much.[28] In a paper that appeared the same day, the chiefs argued that if Italy desired neutrality, the Allies should undertake no measure that might lead her to join Germany. "On the contrary, it would be worth our while to pay the high price which she would doubtless demand in order to avoid this contingency."[29]

There were those within the government who still advocated a strong stand against Italy. At this time, the Defense Preparedness Committee prepared a detailed study of the economic situation and Western strategy against the Axis. They stressed that whatever military assistance Germany gained from Italy's entrance into a war, she would lose the possibility of using Italy as a base to evade the blockade. Once Italy had exhausted her stocks of munitions, raw materials, and foodstuffs, she would become as great a drain on Germany as Austria-Hungary had been in the First World War. Even the Germans recognized this, and, as the committee pointed out, regarded their Italian military alliance with alarm except perhaps "for purposes of bluff." Finally, German and Italian deficiencies were such that both countries would compete for economic resources in the limited area not controlled by the Allied blockade.[30] One member of the Foreign Office noted the following on the question of Italy's reliability: "We know that Italy is actuated solely by self-interest and it would be odd indeed if she had not made plans for every eventuality. If she now feels that for internal and other reasons she cannot risk coming in on Germany's side at the outset of a war and remains neutral, she has surely considered when and in what circumstances she will abandon her neutrality. . . . If she is convinced that Germany is going to win, she will, of course, have no hesitation whatever in coming in on her side and attempting to share the spoils."[31]

Unfortunately, the military advice proved decisive in altering the bellicose attitude that the Cabinet had displayed toward Italy in June. Now, after constant harpings on the strategic advantages of Italian neutrality by the military, Cabinet attitudes shifted to a belief that Italian neutrality would be more advantageous than her presence in war. This was of great importance, considering that in late August, Mussolini was delicately balanced between feelings that Italy must not dishonor herself by again abandoning Germany, and the urgings of Ciano and the Italian military that Italy could not face a European war in view of her grave strategic deficiencies.[32] Only the most vigorous efforts by Ciano and other Italians and the appeasement of the West kept Mussolini on the fence. The British ambassador in Rome warned that even incautious statements in the press about Italian neutrality might propel Mussolini into war.[33] Thus, faced with the issue of Italian neutrality with war in the offing, the Chamberlain government decided to follow a course of appeasement.[34] Although their policy kept Mussolini out of the war for the moment, it only insured that Italy would join the war at her own convenience and at the worst possible moment for the West. That Italy affected the war's course so much to the detriment of the Axis despite Britain's desperate situation in 1940 reflects the true capabilities of Fascist Italy.

A final issue worth considering is the advantages that the West might have gained from inclusion of Italy in the war of September 1939. The most obvious aid is that a vigorous naval campaign, planned by theater commanders, would have closed supply lines to Libya and probably led to the collapse of Italy's position in that province. Such a victory, combined perhaps with one over the Italian fleet, would have dispelled the growing myth of Axis invulnerability and offset the German victory in Poland. In strategic terms the Allies, and particularly the British, possessed an opportunity to clean up the Mediterranean before Germany could devote substantial forces to that theater.

The intriguing possibility exists that a series of humiliating Italian defeats in the Mediterranean might have forced Hitler, for reasons of prestige, to launch an offensive against northern France in late fall, an offensive that would have been guided by a pedestrian replay of the Schlieffen plan rather than by the thrust through the Ardennes. Although such a possibility may be speculation, Italy's entrance into the war in September would have increased economic pressure on Germany (the basis of Allied strategy), while offering the Allies the chance to gain victories at the expense of an ill-prepared enemy. Accordingly, appeasement of Italy in August 1939 and the resulting Italian neutrality did not, as one commentator suggests, "pay off."[35] Rather it is one more sad commentary on a British leadership, military as well as civilian, that saw danger in every policy, that preached caution at every turn, and that was unwilling to take the slightest risk in defense of its far-flung interests.

THE CAMPAIGN IN POLAND

Operational planning for the attack on Poland began in April under the code name of *Fall Weiss* (Case White).[36] The initial plan that formed the basis for subsequent planning suggested two massive blows aimed at the heart of the Polish state. The first, led by the southern army group, would jump off from Silesia and drive toward the northeast and Warsaw. Meanwhile, Army Group North would first close the gap created by the Polish Corridor between Pomerania and East Prussia and then swing to the southeast, also in the direction of the Polish capital. Army Group South would control three armies. On its left flank the Eighth Army would provide cover for the center army, the Tenth. This latter army would contain a substantial portion of armored and motorized forces, and its offensive would carry the decisive weight for the planned entrapment of Polish forces in front of the Vistula. The Fourteenth Army would cover the army group's right flank while driving toward the east and the city of Cracow to prevent a last-ditch defense by the Poles in southeastern Poland. Army Group North would control two armies, the Fourth and Third, but its forces would jump off from opposite sides of the Corridor. The former army would strike from Pomerania toward East Prussia and would then join its sister army in a drive on the Polish capital. The initial OKH conception of Army Group North's drive was that it would aim directly for Warsaw. Bock, appointed commander of the army group, argued, and eventually got his way, that motorized portions of the Fourth Army after crossing the Corridor and linking up with East Prussia would move to the left flank of the Third Army and conduct a drive to the east of Warsaw.[37] Underlying all German planning for the campaign was a firm belief that the Wehrmacht *must* carry out these operations with speed and ruthlessness.[38] The army must never allow the Poles time to recover their balance once the invasion had begun.

The strength of the forces deployed against Poland indicate the extensive augmentation of the Wehrmacht that had occurred since Munich. For the attack on Poland the Germans assembled somewhere over fifty-four divisions—a significant increase over the thirty-seven that they had concentrated against Czechoslovakia. Altogether the two army groups controlled six panzer divisions, four light divisions, and four motorized infantry divisions. The remainder of the divisions were either mountain, regular infantry, or reserve divisions.[39] Army Group North contained 630,000 men, and Army Group South possessed 886,000 men.[40] Distribution of motorized and mechanized forces naturally followed the conception of German planning. Army Group North held the 10th Panzer Division in reserve, while Guderian's XIX Corps controlled one panzer and two motorized infantry divisions for the drive across the Corridor and the eventual swing behind Warsaw. In Army Group South the Tenth Army held two panzer divisions, three light divisions, and two motorized infantry divisions for the offensive on Warsaw. Meanwhile, the Fourteenth Army held one light and two panzer divisions for the push toward Cracow.

The Germans carefully disguised their eastern deployment, so that the Poles would not be able to discern the exact attack date.[41] There was, of course, no possibility of disguising the movement to the east, and from the beginning of August the Poles knew that the Germans were preparing a massive offensive. Nor did they have any misconception as to where the major German drives would develop. What they were completely unprepared to handle was the speed and ruthlessness of German mechanized warfare.

Poland was simply in an impossible strategic situation. Unlike the Czechs the year before, the Poles possessed no natural barriers to protect their exposed frontiers. Their most valuable industrial regions lay immediately adjacent to Germany. German territory surrounded Poland on three sides, and in the east the Russians were at best a hostile and truculent neighbor. Finally, Polish terrain with the exception of the Carpathian Mountains in the far southeast was ideal for armored operations.[42]

In 1939 the Polish army consisted of thirty infantry divisions (two of which were mountain), seven horse cavalry brigades, one mechanized cavalry brigade and two air divisions. Unlike the Czechs the previous year, the Poles maintained their active duty units on a much reduced scale, necessitating full mobilization before even regular units reached full strength. A mobilization of reserves would add a further fifteen divisions and supporting units to the army's deployable strength. Polish NCOs were of high quality, but the officer corps, particularly in the senior ranks with diverse backgrounds of service in the German, Russian, and Austro-Hungarian armies, varied widely in capability.[43] The army was well trained, tough, and highly motivated but suffered considerably from a lack of equipment. Polish infantry divisions matched equivalent German formations only in manpower. In other respects—communications gear, heavy artillery, fire support weapons, supply support—the Germans held enormous advantages. In addition, the Poles possessed no equivalent to German mechanized and motorized forces, and the slow moving infantry had neither the weapons nor the doctrine to hold German armored forces. Given the nature of the terrain the Poles had no hope of catching German forces once they broke into the open. Completing the disparity in forces, the Luftwaffe enjoyed overwhelming superiority, and September's weather conditions proved perfect for tactical cooperation between advancing motorized units and aircraft. In every aspect, the Polish theater of operations was ideal for testing mechanized and motorized doctrine and its coordination with air power.

Polish dispositions made a difficult situation impossible. The Poles refused to abandon the most valuable and highly industrialized regions at the outset of operations. Unfortunately, as those regions lay near the frontier, they thus committed their army to defend areas that were virtually indefensible. Particularly in the Corridor and around Posen, Polish troops deployed where the Wehrmacht could easily cut them off from the main body of forces. Further adding to the Polish tragedy was a failure to carry out an expeditious mobilization. Here the West and the Poles were equally at fault. As they had with the Czechs in September 1938, the Western Powers applied considerable pressure on the Poles to delay mobilization in order not to offend the Germans, and the Poles hesitated as well because of their generally weak economic and financial position. A partial mobilization in March had used up considerable funds, and the Poles were reluctant to promulgate a full mobilization until they were sure that war was at hand. Although they accelerated defensive measures throughout August, the storm broke before the army completed mobilization. As a result, only about one-third of the first-line units had completed mobilization and were fully combat ready. The remainder were still in the process of integrating reservists, and reserve divisions were only in the first stages of working up.[44]

Under such circumstances, the Germans not surprisingly won an overwhelming victory over the Polish armed forces. Within the first week Army Group North's Fourth Army had cut across the Corridor, thus joining East Prussia and the Reich, and the Third Army threatened Warsaw from the north. Meanwhile, Army Group South had gained even more stunning successes. The Tenth Army, led by Reichenau and possessing the bulk of motorized forces in the south (two panzer, three light, and two motorized infantry divisions), achieved operational freedom in the first days of the campaign and broke out into the open. Some units advanced as much as fifteen miles in the first day of the campaign.[45] By September 6, tank units from the Tenth Army were halfway to Warsaw and had destroyed the Polish forces lying in front of them. The Poles to the north soon found German troops between them and the capital and their supplies. In the far south the Fourteenth Army occupied Cracow, and Polish forces to the north of the Carpathians were close to collapse. In a strategic sense, the Germans had already won.[46] By September 11, troops from both army groups had reached the vicinity of Warsaw, and the advance had

MAP IX   *The Invasion of Poland*

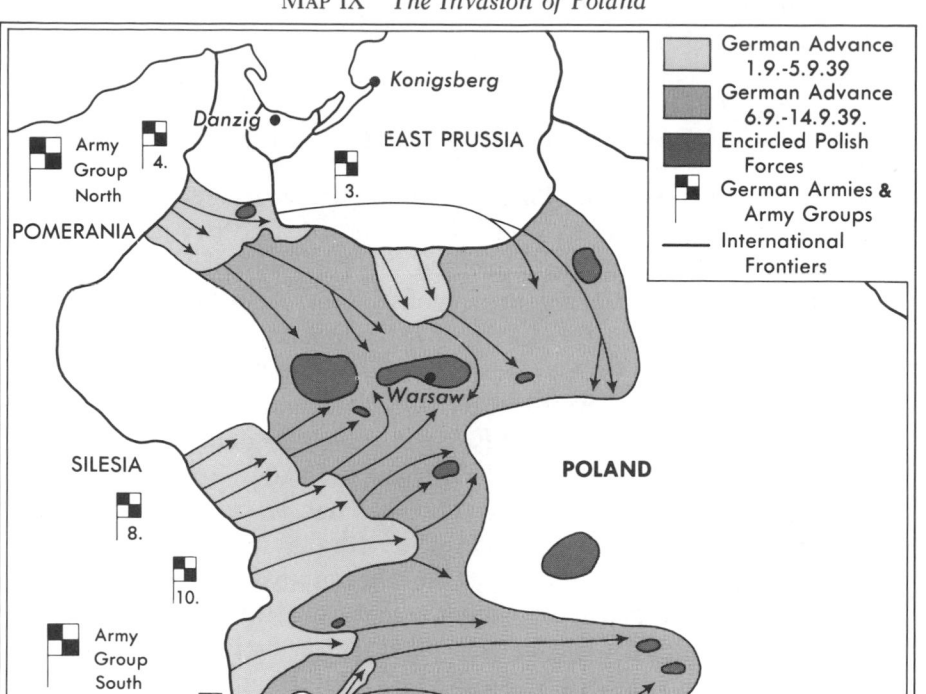

isolated Polish forces in a number of encirclement cauldrons. To the west of Warsaw the Wehrmacht destroyed the Posen and Pomeranian armies along the Bzura; to the east, Guderian's tank and motorized forces sliced to the southeast along the Bug to capture the great fortress city of Brest-Litovsk.[47] The final act occurred with the Soviet intervention on September 17; as Russian armies rolled into eastern Poland, any remaining chance of prolonging resistance into late fall disappeared. On September 29 Warsaw surrendered and on October 1 the Polish garrison of Hela gave up, ending organized Polish resistance in exactly one month.

A comparison of Polish and German casualties underlies the extent of the Nazi victory. The Poles lost 70,000 dead, 133,000 wounded, and 700,000 prisoners; 50,000 more died fighting the Russians. German casualties were 11,000 dead, 30,000 wounded, and 3,400 missing.[48] In one month's time the Polish army of one and a quarter million men had ceased to exist.

ECONOMIC AND POLITICAL DIFFICULTIES

When he embarked on his Polish adventure, Hitler apparently believed it unlikely that the West would intervene. Should they do so, the führer was not particularly concerned. Shortly before the outbreak of the war, he suggested to a gathering of senior generals that a blockade posed no serious threat to Germany's strategic situation. He calmly assured his listeners that a blockade would "be ineffective due to our autarchy and because we have economic resources in the East. We need have no worry. . . . The East will deliver us grain, cattle, coal, lead, and zinc."[49] Hitler could not have been more incorrect. The Allied blockade severely damaged the German economy in the first months of the war and was responsible for a drastic decrease in German trade. Import tonnage dropped 57 percent from base 1938, while the value of imports dropped 45 percent, a figure distorted by a drastic rise in the price of those raw materials still available. By January 1940 the value of German imports fell to RM 186 million in contrast to RM 472 million the previous January. Exports stood at RM 256 in contrast to RM 441 million in January 1939. Imports fell from 4,445,000 tons to 1,122,000, while exports fell from 4,293,000 to 1,957,000 for the same period. In terms of raw-material imports, using a base 100 for 1938, January 1940 imports fell to 17 and March 1940 imports to 13.[50] (See Charts 9, 10, and 11.)

An even more revealing indicator of economic difficulties was the fact that despite an almost complete absence of military operations between the end of September 1939 and the beginning of April 1940 fuel stocks steadily declined. At the beginning of war fuel supplies had stood at 2,400,000 tons; by the beginning of May 1940 they had shrunk to 1,600,000 tons—a decrease of 33 percent.[51] (See Chart 12.) This critical fuel situation over winter 1939-1940 caused serious economic difficulties and hampered military operations.[52] German supplies of gasoline fell from 300,000 tons on the outbreak of war to 110,000 in April 1940; diesel fuel fell from 220,000 tons to 73,000; bunker fuel for the navy from 350,000 tons to 255,000. Only aviation-fuel supplies showed no substantial decrease over the period.[53]

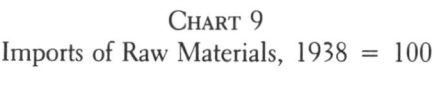

CHART 9
Imports of Raw Materials, 1938 = 100

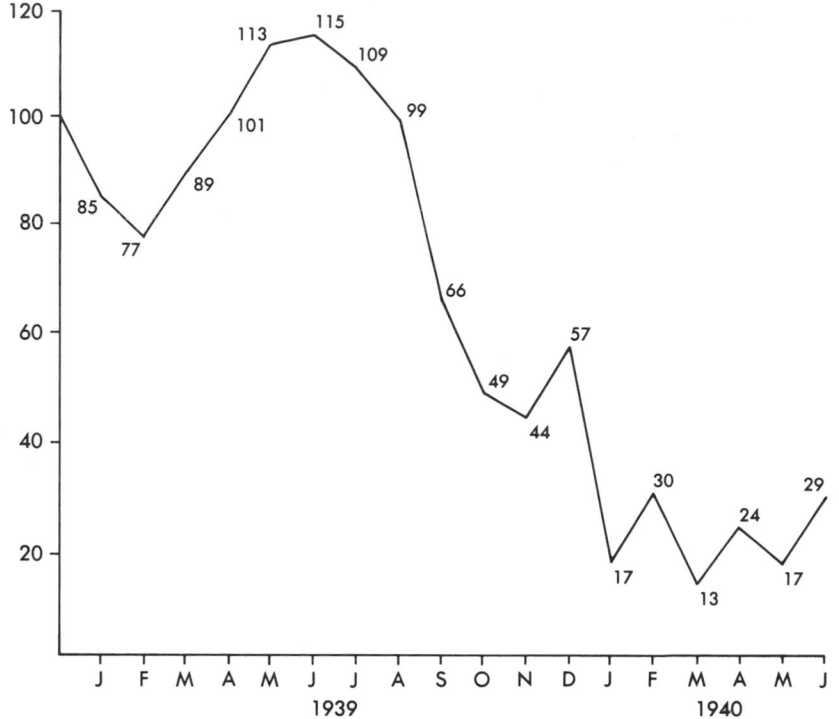

SOURCE: "Zahlen zur Entwicklung des deutschen Aussenhandels seit Kriegsbeginn." Im schlesischen Institut für Wirtschafts- und Konjunkturforschung, Breslau, Aug. 1940 (NARS T-84, Roll 195, Frame 1560551).

Contributing to this set of circumstances was the British blockade of sea routes from Rumania. Imports from Rumania declined enormously over the fall and winter, and the freezing of the Danube added to German transportation difficulties.[54] In addition, the British chartered both barge and railroad tankers available in Rumania and the Balkans, making it even more difficult to transport Rumanian oil to the Reich.[55] Allied financial control of most Rumanian refineries hindered German efforts to increase deliveries of refined petroleum, and the low refining capacity of Germany's petroleum industry did not allow a drastic increase in crude oil imports. A combination of the above factors in January 1940 resulted in the shipment of only 10,000

CHART 10
Tonnage of German Imports and Exports, 1939-1940

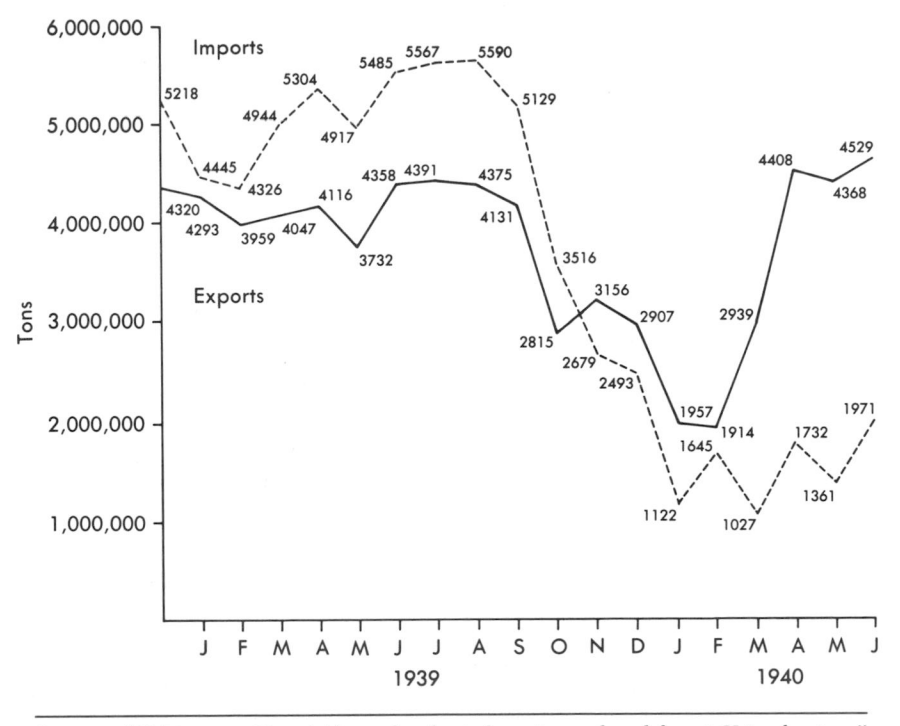

SOURCE: "Zahlen zur Entwicklung des deutschen Aussenhandels seit Kriegsbeginn." Im schlesischen Institut für Wirtschafts- und Konjunkturforschung, Breslau, Aug. 1940 (NARS T-84, Roll 195, Frame 1560551).

tons of finished petroleum products from Rumania to Germany, while 255,000 tons went to England and 106,000 tons to France.[56] Bidding between the rival sides tripled the price of Rumanian oil in the war's first six months.[57] Germany only escaped the full consequences of her petroleum difficulties by minimal oil imports from Russia and Rumania and because Allied passivity allowed the Wehrmacht to stretch out limited supplies.

In 1938 German estimates of the oil requirements of the armed forces for the first year of a war ranged from eight to ten million tons. As it turned out, the Germans underestimated the capacity of their own synthetic fuel industry.[58] In 1940, instead of producing 2.5 to 3 million tons, German industry produced 3,233,265 tons. Oil produc-

CHART 11
Value of German Exports and Imports, 1939-1940, in million RM

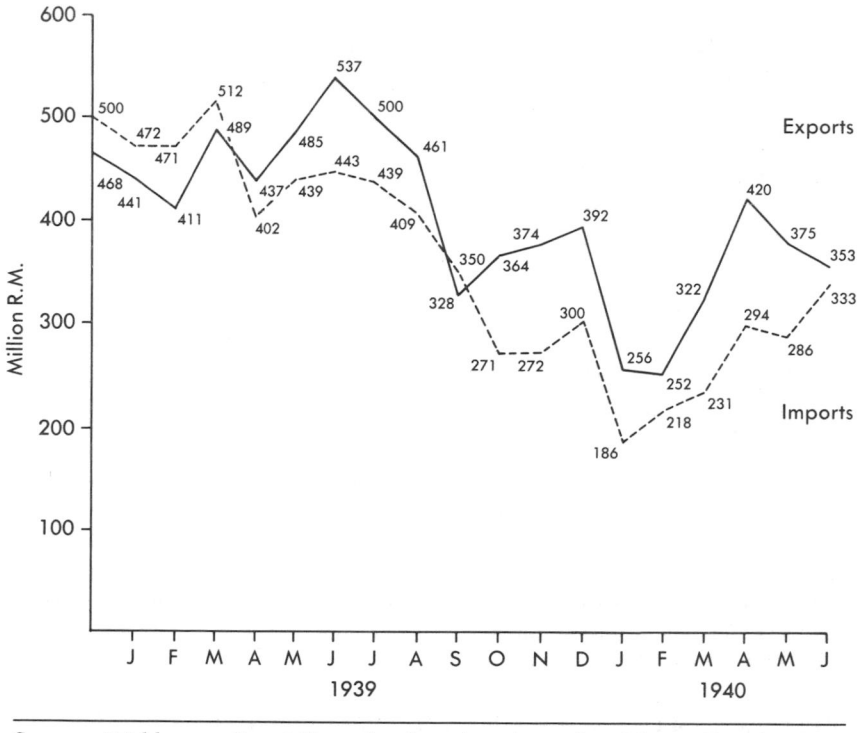

SOURCE: "Zahlen zur Entwicklung des deutschen Aussenhandels seit Kriegsbeginn."
Im schlesischen Institut für Wirtschafts- und Konjunkturforschung, Breslau, Aug.
1940 (NARS T-84, Roll 195, Frame 1560551).

tion from areas under German control reached 1,488,941 tons. Thus,
with the booty captured in the western campaigns, the Germans met
66 percent of requirements from their own resources and so were able
to cope, although imports from Russia and Rumania combined remained under 3 million tons.[59]

The situation with other raw materials presented a similarly depressing picture. Before the war, German economic officials had worried about iron-ore imports. In 1938 Germany had imported 22 million
tons of iron ore. With the outbreak of war the Germans immediately
lost 9.5 million tons from suppliers who either lay in Allied countries
or whose trade routes ran through waters controlled by the Royal
Navy.[60] With the elimination of ore supplies from Lorraine, Swedish

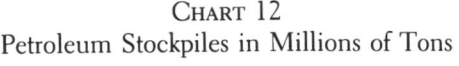

CHART 12
Petroleum Stockpiles in Millions of Tons

SOURCE: Bericht des Herrn Professor Dr. C. Krauch über die Lage auf dem Arbeits-gebiet der Chemie in der Sitzung des Generalrates am 24. 6. 41 (NARS T-84, Roll 217, Frame 1586749).

ore became of critical importance for the continued functioning of the German economy. Sweden supplied Germany with approximately 9 million tons of high-grade ore. Because the best Swedish ore fields lay in the far north, only a relatively small percentage of the ore moved through the Baltic (which froze in the winter); most of the trade was carried on through the Norwegian port of Narvik. Table X-1 gives an indication of the extent of this trade.

The Swedish railroad network lacked the capacity for large-scale transshipment of ore from the northern mine fields to the southern Swedish ports. Thus, Narvik was of crucial importance for the export of ore to Germany. Denied its facilities, the German economy could lose up to 3 million tons of high-grade ore. The OKW suggested that a shortfall of that extent for a period longer than half a year could have a decisive impact on the war economy.[61]

Other economic sectors showed similar vulnerabilities. Although 45 percent of her trade went to Germany, Yugoslavia sold most of her

TABLE X-1
Swedish Ore Exports

Harbor	Total Ore Export	To Germany	To Britain
Narvik	7,580,000	4,889,000	1,611,000
Lulea	3,102,000	1,877,000	217,000
Other Swedish Harbors	3,086,000	2,310,000	343,000

SOURCE: Maier et al., *Das Deutsche Reich und der Zweite Weltkrieg*, Vol. II, p. 195.

copper to France over the winter of 1939-1940.[62] because the German chrome industry lay in the Saar within reach of French artillery, the Germans evacuated the industry. As a result, despite a fifteen months' supply of ore, the remaining smelting capacity for chromium could only cover economic requirements for eight months.[63] Other ores crucial to the making of high-grade steels were also in short supply.[64]

Despite the gloomy economic picture, the German economy possessed substantial advantages over its situation during the Sudeten crisis of 1938. In particular the Nazi-Soviet Non-Aggression Pact played a major role in the period from September 1939 to June 1941 in supplying the war economy with substantial aid. In 1940 Soviet supplies made up 66 percent of phosphorous imports, 63 percent of chrome imports, 55 percent of manganese imports, 33 percent of petroleum imports, and 60 percent of platinum imports.[65] The major problem of Russian trade was the fact that it took so long to develop. Only after long tortuous negotiations did Russo-German commercial exchanges begin a rapid rise. Imports from Russia increased from RM 30,000,000 in 1939 to RM 390,000,000 in 1940, while German exports to Russia rose from RM 30,000,000 to 216,000,000 in the same period.[66] The Nazi-Soviet Non-Aggression Pact also helped by allowing Germany to evade the blockade through use of the Trans-Siberian railroad.[67]

Particular sectors within the German war economy showed significant improvement from the previous year. Investments in the Schnellplan paid back important dividends. Production of synthetic fuels exceeded estimates by nearly a quarter of a million tons.[68] By August 1939 capacity for gunpowder production had risen 65 percent and explosive capacity 85 percent above 1938 totals.[69] Nevertheless, ammunition expenditures in Poland almost equalled two months of full production. By spring 1940 capacity had increased to the point where it met campaign needs from monthly production, even though the Wehrmacht used 30 percent more ammunition than in Poland. Significantly, ammunition expenditure in Poland equalled nearly three months of production at the 1938 rate.[70] (See Charts 7 and 8, Chapter I.) Synthetic rubber production also had made substantial gains in the period since Munich. Late 1939 production was nearly five times what it had been in 1938.[71] Although this production rate was still not sufficient to meet German demand, it was sufficient to meet demand with the help of stockpiles and imports carried across the Trans-Siberian railroad.[72]

The conquest of Poland also provided the Germans with economic help. The swiftness of the campaign enabled the Germans to seize Upper Silesia's coal fields and Teschen's steel industry in undamaged condition. The Germans then traded Silesian coal for Swedish iron ore without using German resources.[73] Inclusion of this region within Germany's economic sphere added 2.14 million tons to annual capacity for raw steel production—a 9 percent increase.[74]

On the whole, what emerges from documents dealing with the economic situation in the first months of war is the impression that Germany faced extraordinary difficulties under the pressures of blockade. Although the economic stress did not yet interfere with military operations, it did limit options and obviously threatened long-term plans. These economic difficulties help to explain Hitler's demand after the Polish campaign that the Wehrmacht undertake an immediate military campaign in the west before the onset of winter. As an OKW paper signed by the führer in October warned, time worked more in favor of Germany's enemies than in her favor. The memorandum pointed out that "the danger in case of a prolonged war lies in the difficulty of securing from a limited food and raw-material base for a population while at the same time securing the means for the prosecution of the war."[75]

Because of this critical economic situation, Hitler demanded an immediate offensive in the west. This pressure from above resulted in a major confrontation with his generals. For the most part historians have taken the army's side in the argument.[76] As we shall see, there was justification to army claims that it could not be ready for a major western campaign until the spring. Nevertheless, the historians' one-sided approach to the argument is unfair to Hitler's intuitive judgment.

MAP X   *German Proposed Offensive (Fall 1939)*

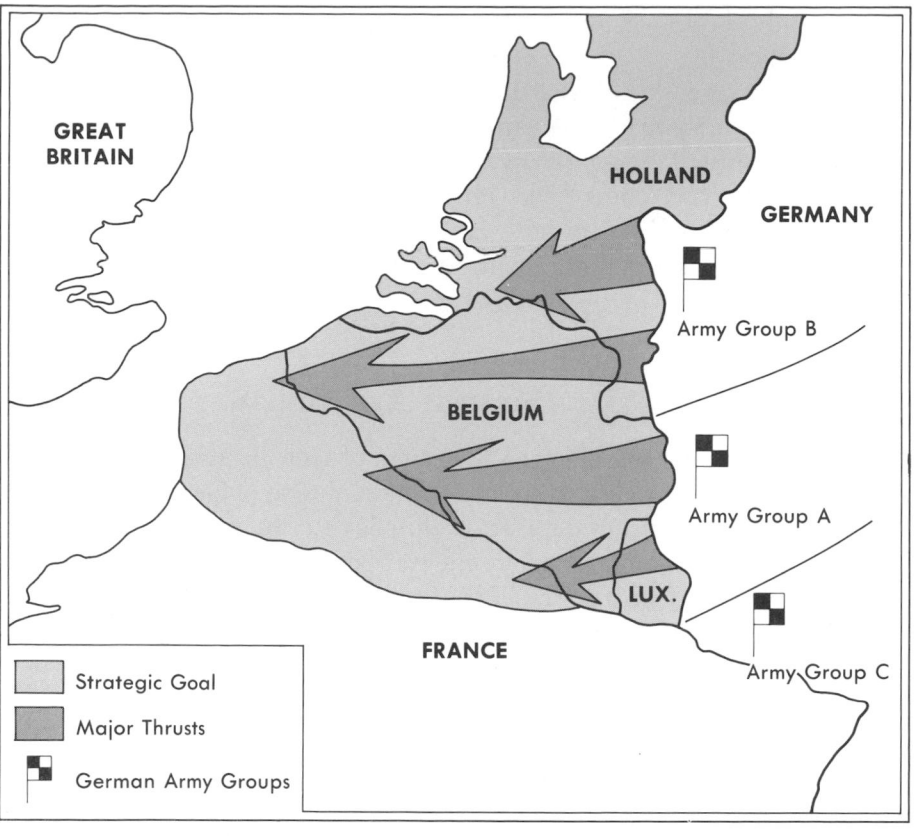

GREAT
BRITAIN

HOLLAND

GERMANY

Army Group B

BELGIUM

Army Group A

LUX.

FRANCE

Army Group C

Strategic Goal

Major Thrusts

German Army Groups

The führer was on excellent grounds when he argued that the economic situation demanded that Germany seek a decision before spring. In the end the generals proved correct, but largely because of the unwillingness of the Reich's opponents to act with any decisiveness. In fact, and this is perhaps the key to Hitler's postponement of the offensive until spring, the pressure on the economy, although serious, never reached sufficient gravity to threaten Germany's immediate economic and strategic stability.[77]

If the economic difficulties that the Reich faced gave Hitler a nasty shock, the political reception that the German people accorded the outbreak of the war could hardly have added to the führer's peace of mind. Returning from the Reichstag on September 1st after his declaration of war on Poland, Hitler faced nothing but empty streets. The contrast between the sullen mood of the German people in 1939 and the enthusiastic reception that millions of Germans had greeted the declaration of war in 1914 could not have been clearer to Hitler, especially since he himself had been a part of the joyous crowd in Munich twenty-five years earlier. As a political animal Hitler could not have missed the significance of the empty streets: undoubtedly that political unease, combined with his sense of the Reich's economic difficulties, led Hitler to push for a fall offensive, which he believed would solve his economic, political, and strategic problems before the onset of winter.

German Strategy: The Problem

If the economic data indicates the extent of Hitler's miscalculation, it does not provide a clear answer as to the evolution of German strategy in the early months of the war. A close look at the discussions in the German high command before the war began as well as the strategic arguments that took place after the completion of the Polish campaign, however, suggests certain critical elements in German strategy through to the winter of 1940 that historians have by and large missed. To begin with, the Luftwaffe was urging a far wider role for itself than the limited role of a "tactical" air force that historical literature has assigned to it. In May 1939 General Felmy, commander of Luftflotte 2, speculated at the completion of a war game on the moral pressure that a terror-bombing campaign against London could bring to bear on the British population. He emphasized the high degree of war hysteria that existed in Britain during the Munich crisis and suggested to his listeners that in contrast to the hesitant behavior of Germany's World War I government the Third Reich should take full advantage of such a state of affairs in the next war.[78]

That same month the Fifth Section (intelligence) of the Luftwaffe's general staff echoed the argument. It reported that in every respect the Luftwaffe was the best prepared air force in Europe for a major war. It argued that Germany was the only state that with respect to equipment, organization, tactics, and leadership possessed a conception of how to carry out an "offensive" air war. The intelligence section then referred to the panic in London and Paris the previous autumn before arguing that the parliamentary systems of the Western Powers gave them considerably less flexibility in "strategic" air power than Nazi Germany possessed. The dangerous conclusion that this line of reasoning led to was the suggestion that it was "quite possible that in spite of the pacts and promises to Eastern Europe, a conflict in that region would remain localized."[79]

In early July Hitler and Göring visited the Luftwaffe's test station at Rechlin to examine the latest in aircraft research, and the technical experts did a thorough job of implying that the aircraft and equipment in design and test stages were close to production. Of course they were not, but the demonstration provided one more confirmation to Hitler that the Luftwaffe not only possessed current superiority over its opponents but would maintain that superiority for the foreseeable future. In 1942 Göring was to bemoan the decisions that Hitler had taken on the basis of what he had seen that day.[80] One should minimize neither the impact of this visit on Hitler's conception of the coming war nor the general role that the Luftwaffe played in Hitler's thinking in the late 1930s. Five days before the outbreak of the war Hitler summed up his general evaluation of the strategic situation in a letter to Mussolini: "As neither France nor Britain can achieve any decisive successes in the west, and as Germany, as a result of the agreement with Russia, will have all her forces free in the east after the defeat of Poland, and as air superiority is undoubtedly on our side, I do not shrink from solving the eastern question even at the risk of complications with the West."[81] What is interesting in the above calculation of risks is the fact that the Luftwaffe played a role in two out of the three factors that Hitler cited. The belief in the short war against Poland, of course, rested on the army as well as the air force, but clearly the Luftwaffe contributed to Hitler's estimation that Poland would not take long to destroy. The emphasis on air superiority undoubtedly represented a miscalculation that the Luftwaffe could deter the West by the mere threat of major air attacks against its population centers. Nevertheless, Hitler's comment indicates a belief not only in the deterrence value of the air force but in its independent war-fighting capability.

German strategy in the first months of the war also suggests that the Luftwaffe was playing a more important role in German calculations than the historical literature admits. The campaign against Poland was supposed to begin with a massive strike against the military installations and armament factories in Warsaw to paralyze Polish resistance. Bad weather prevented the launching of such a "knock-out" blow, and by the time the weather had cleared, the interdiction and close-air-support side of operations were going sufficiently well that the Luftwaffe general staff hesitated to shift the emphasis of German air attacks.[82]

The Polish campaign provided Hitler with his first opportunity to play warlord, a role that he found most congenial. However, the end of that campaign brought Hitler face to face with a number of unpleasant realities. Chief among those were 1) the fact that Germany was now embroiled in a major European war and 2) that her economy was in catastrophic shape. On the same day that Hitler was underlining the economic factors that lay behind his demand for an immediate offensive in the west, he issued "Directive No. 6 for the Conduct of the War." In this directive he underlined the territorial goals of the coming campaign as well as its strategic purposes:

> a) An offensive will be planned on the northern flanks of the Western front, through Luxembourg, Belgium, and Holland. This offensive must be launched at the earliest possible moment and in the greatest possible strength.
> b) The purpose of this offensive will be to defeat as much as possible of the French Army and of the forces of the allies fighting on their side, and at the same time to win as much territory as possible in Holland, Belgium, and Northern France, to serve as a base for the successful prosecution of the air and sea war against England and as a wide protective area for the economically vital Ruhr.[83]

There are several interesting aspects to this directive. Historians, as well as the German generals at that time, have noted that the fall offensive did not aim to achieve a decisive success against the French army. What they have been unwilling to recognize, although Hitler explicitly stated it in the directive, is that the offensive did *not* aim to overthrow the Allied position on the continent but was aimed solely at *"the successful prosecution of the air and sea war against England* [my emphasis]."[84] Given the weak state of the German navy, it is clear that Hitler's strategy was relying on the Luftwaffe to knock the British out of the war. It is also worth noting the stress that Directive No. 6 gave to protecting the Ruhr from Allied air attacks.

Interestingly, the Luftwaffe's chief of staff for intelligence, "Beppo" Schmid, proposed in late November that the Reich rely on an exclusive air strategy to knock Great Britain out of the war. The Wehrmacht, he suggested, should carry out no operations against the French, but rather the entire Luftwaffe, with whatever help the navy could provide, should concentrate on attacking England's imports. Such a strategy should emphasize attacks on English ports and docks, and Schmid suggested that "should the enemy resort to terror measures, for example to attack our towns in western Germany, here again similar operations could be carried out with even greater effect, due to the greater density of population of London and the big industrial cities."[85] Hitler did not buy Schmid's strategic plan entirely, although elements of it remained in the OKW's directive of November 29. The OKW suggested that an attack on British imports would not occur until the army had either defeated the Allied armies in the field or until Germany had seized the coast opposite Britain.[86]

The great fall campaign never took place. Nevertheless, Hitler does not seem to have abandoned the initial conception until January 1940 when an aircraft carrying the plans crashed in Belgium. The weather that winter, one of the worst in memory, resulted in repeated post-ponements until the January accident. The inordinate squabbling be-tween Hitler and his generals that had begun in October continued into March, but Hitler, with the help of the young turks in the army and the ambitions of the commander in chief of Army Group A, forced the OKH to alter its plans (drawn up to meet Hitler's strategic con-ceptions in October) and to mount a massive armored thrust through the Ardennes. The new strategy aimed, not at creating the basis for an air and naval offensive against Britain, but rather at the overthrow of the Allied position on the continent. As late as mid-March the new strategy was meeting serious opposition in the army's high command.[87] The argumentation from October 1939 through March 1940 under-lines the fact that neither Hitler nor his generals had a clear conception of how Germany would escape the serious strategic difficulties into which the attack on Poland had landed the Reich. The initial response to that difficulty, the so-called Halder plan with the Low Countries and Northern France as its target, indicates two major factors in Ger-man strategy that historians have ignored. First, it was a serious con-ception molded to meet Hitler's economic and political difficulties.

Second, that very strategy relied on the Luftwaffe as an independent war-winning force. If we today correctly estimate that it was not, we should not allow ourselves to be deceived into believing that the Germans at that time did not regard it as such.

THE GERMAN ARMY AND THE PHONY WAR

The considerable opposition within the army that Hitler met in his demands for an immediate offensive against the West resulted less from doubts over the strategic conception than from worries over the general state of the army. On the surface the Polish campaign of September 1939 had been a smashing success. In less than a month the Wehrmacht had completely shattered an army of forty divisions and over one million men. Two-thirds of Poland had fallen into German hands. In every respect this campaign appeared to be an outstanding triumph. Yet, the OKH judged the operational success as insufficient and inadequate. In its view the troops had *not* met the high standards that the high command and general staff expected.

Historians have tended to explain the German victories in the first years of the war as the result of operational and strategic factors. What they have generally overlooked are the doctrinal, training, and organizational elements that contributed to these victories: in other words, they have rarely addressed the issue of German military competence. Nothing better indicates why the Wehrmacht was so superior to its opponents than the reassesment through which the army went after the Polish campaign. This reappraisal involved a two-faceted process. First of all, the high command closely examined the lessons of Poland and their application to doctrine and training. Second, the army established a training program beginning in October and ending in April 1940 that brought the army's reserve and Landwehr units, all varying widely in composition, background, and training, up to the standards of the regular army. What was of key importance in this process was that the German army in its "lessons learned analysis" did *not* use its studies to support *existing* doctrine. Rather it used its after-action reports to improve doctrine and military standards throughout the army.

The critical element in the German evaluation process was the system of after-action reports. Nearly all military organizations use similar systems, but German reporting methods were unique because they worked. Unlike many armies where the reporting system is distorted by what commanders wish to hear, the German system was both highly critical and honest within tactical and operational spheres. The higher the headquarters, the more demanding and dissatisfied were commanders with operational performances.[88] The Anschluss was a particularly good example of this process, for, as we have seen, military operations in March 1938 indicated serious deficiencies throughout the army. This willingness to criticize itself was to be a major factor in the German army's high level of competence throughout the Second World War.

This institutional insistence on critical analysis enabled the army consistently to upgrade performance levels. A Twelfth Army report on the Polish campaign stressed not only the value of the training that its officers and NCOs had received but the close connection between that training and the experiences gained in the occupation of the Sudetenland and subsequently of Prague during the previous year.[89] Similarly, an after-action report by the 6th Panzer Division on the 1940 campaign emphasized the role that the Polish campaign had played in improving armor doctrine.[90] At the conclusion of the Polish campaign the OKH pointed out that it was "in the interest of the whole army to collect as soon as possible the combat experiences in both the tactical and technical spheres," to disseminate these experiences widely among the troops, and to use them as the basis for training the replacement army.[91] The Germans were to do precisely that over the next seven months all too well. The training program was, over the winter of 1939-1940, to turn the army into one of the finest instruments of war in history.

Above all, German training based on the Polish campaign aimed to inculcate an aggressive spirit into those preparing for the coming push in the west. In a circular to Army Group B at the end of April 1940 Bock was still expressing doubts as to whether his troops and commanders had reached the proper level of offensive spirit: "In many exercises recently, particularly at the battalion and regimental level, an inclination to caution and circumspection has appeared. Therein lies the danger that on one side German leadership will pass up opportunities to seize favorable situations . . . while on the other hand the enemy will be allowed time to recognize our intention. . . . Once a commander has decided to attack, so must everything that he orders be established that the eyes, heart, and senses of the troops are directed to the front."[92] Bock's fears were exaggerated. By spring 1940, the German army had reached throughout its units, whether they be regular, reserve, panzer, or line infantry, a state of combat readiness that was far superior to that of its opponents. Moreover, the regular and reserve infantry divisions would play a crucial role in making possible the devastating victory. The brilliant Manstein plan, based on an armored thrust through the supposedly impassable Ardennes, has quite rightly received much attention from historians. However, Bock's Army Group B played an equally vital role in the victory. At the initiation of the offensive, Bock's forces, consisting nearly entirely of infantry divisions, fixed Allied attention on Northern Belgium and Holland. Then, once the nature of the German breakthrough in the Ardennes had become clear, the hammering pressure of Bock's infantry advance made it impossible for Allied forces to disengage to meet the terrible threat in the south.

In every respect the seven month period between the collapse of Poland and the invasion of Western Europe was of vital importance in bringing the Wehrmacht up to a uniformly high level of performance. Not only had the panzer and motorized forces significantly improved their standards and capabilities, but the infantry, reserve as well as regular, was prepared to play a decisive if unheralded role in the spring victory. In no fashion could the German army have performed at the same level of capability in fall 1939.

ALLIED STRATEGY

As the above discussion of the German economy indicates, the Allied strategic approach to the Second World War had a solid basis. It rested on the belief that the Germans faced serious difficulties in the economic sector, especially with the supply of raw materials. As the beginning of this chapter has pointed out, Allied leaders failed, however, to aim at the "maximum interruption of supplies of . . . goods in all cases where it was practicable" in the evolution of their prewar diplomacy and military planning.[93] This same unwillingness to address the difficult questions in terms of their grand strategy would now characterize Allied performance in the first months of the war. There were three specific areas where the Allies could undertake military operations that to one extent or another would affect the German economy: the western front, the Mediterranean, and Scandinavia. Unfortunately, the Allies were unwilling to exert military pressure of any kind. Confronted by the war that they had for so long dreaded, they apparently hoped that the German economy and war machine would exhaust themselves without a great clash of armies.

We have already discussed the military and diplomatic policies that led to strategic bankruptcy in the Mediterranean even before the outbreak of war. By allowing the Italians to escape into what Mussolini euphemistically termed "nonbelligerence" the Allies insured that Italy and the Mediterranean would serve as a conduit for German imports and that at the worst possible moment for the Allied cause the Italians would join the Third Reich. The fact that the Allies could not clamp down on Mediterranean trade with full vigor led General Maxime Weygand to admit in the fall that the blockade of the Balkans was "entirely ineffective. Everything was going through."[94]

Symptomatic of the Allied failure to address the problems raised by their strategic concept was the question of Scandinavian ore, particularly the exportation of high-grade Swedish ore through Narvik. The continued movement of Swedish iron ore from Narvik was of critical importance to the continued functioning and well-being of German weapons production. Unfortunately, discussions at the War Cabinet level and between interested parties within the British committee system again obscured the real issues and resulted in such a late decision to mine the Norwegian leads that the mining only served to provide the Germans with justification for an invasion of Norway that was already well underway.

As early as September 4, the Chiefs of Staff had directed their attention toward Norway. They suggested that the Allies should exert all possible political and economic pressure to halt shipment of Swedish ore through Narvik. They then admitted that should Germany undertake aerial reprisals by bombarding Norwegian cities there was nothing that they could do, since they were unwilling to bomb German airfields.[95] On September 19, Churchill, back in the Cabinet as First Lord of the Admiralty, first broached the subject of Norwegian neutrality when he pointed out the importance of the ore trade. He argued that if Allied political pressure on the Norwegians did not shut down such trade, then "he would . . . propose the remedy adopted in the last war, namely the laying of mines inside Norwegian territorial waters."[96] At the end of September Churchill again returned to the subject. In explanation as to why he was not urging a strong course yet, he pointed out that the Norwegians had temporarily shut Narvik down. If the supplies again started moving then he would ask for stronger measures.[97]

In the War Cabinet of October 4, the minister of economic warfare, R. H. Cross provided Churchill with strong evidence to support his argument. Cross pointed out that the Swedes would have to expand facilities massively at Lulea to ship all the ore through Swedish ports in the ice-free season. He suggested that if the Germans were limited to Swedish ports alone, their imports of Scandinavian ore would fall one-third to one-fourth from prewar totals. Finally, Cross noted that the Ministry of Economic Warfare doubted whether Germany held substantial reserves of iron ore.[98]

The subject of the ore trade lay dormant until November 19, when Churchill proposed that the navy lay a great mine barrage across the North Sea. Although he did not mention the ore trade directly, Churchill suggested that Britain include Norwegian territorial waters within the barrage.[99] Churchill's proposal met strong Foreign Office opposition. Halifax argued that Churchill's historical analogy was incorrect: the Allies had not mined the Norwegian leads in the First World War. Instead, after a great deal of military and diplomatic pressure from the Allies, the Norwegians had mined their own territorial waters in order to complete the Northern mine barrage. They had taken this action only in September 1918 when it was clear that Germany faced military catastrophe on the western front and could not retaliate.[100]

The two positions came into open conflict in the War Cabinet at the end of November. Churchill argued strongly for a mine barrage across the North Sea even if it did not include Norwegian territorial waters. Halifax raised the same objections that he had expressed in his Foreign Office paper. The Cabinet wavered and only decided to begin preparations for an extensive mine field. Churchill then attacked the issue head on and asked the Cabinet to allow the navy to mine Norwegian territorial waters, thus forcing German ore ships onto the high seas. The first lord obviously wanted to break the German ore trade immediately. He again met strong opposition from Halifax. The foreign secretary foresaw a whole host of problems: such an action would violate Norwegian neutrality; it would antagonize Scandinavian public opinion; and it might force the Germans to retaliate. Again the Cabinet delayed decision and asked for a series of papers from the Chiefs of Staff, and the Ministry of Economic Warfare.[101]

The Russian invasion of Finland at the end of November and the ensuing crisis in Scandinavia distracted Cabinet attention from the ore question until mid-December. For the time being British attention largely centered on possible western reaction to a combined Russo-German assault on Scandinavia.

Churchill seized the spotlight in mid-December when he proposed that since German submarines were attacking and sinking British ships in Norwegian territorial waters, Royal Navy destroyers should enter Norwegian waters and seize German ore ships in retaliation. Hoare supported Churchill with the observation that Britain had a great deal of goodwill in Scandinavia and thus such a move would receive widespread understanding. Halifax demurred. He asked for further study and underlined his belief that such a move would have a bad effect on the neutrals and might even jeopardize the chartering of neutral ships.[102] On the next day, December 16, Churchill presented a paper arguing that the stoppage of Norwegian ore supplies would "rank as a major offensive operation of war. No other measure is open to us for many months to come which gives so good a chance of abridging the waste and destruction of the conflict."[103]

On December 18, the Ministry of Economic Warfare finally produced its paper on the effect of a stoppage of Narvik's ore trade on the German war economy. On the whole, the paper was a carefully worded appraisal of the situation. Unfortunately, it also contained an argument that distorted the fundamental issue and eventually sidetracked the argument until too late. The Ministry of Economic Warfare first suggested that, although they had no definite proof, they felt that a stoppage of ore shipments from Narvik, given normal ice conditions in the Baltic, "would be likely to cause by next spring such a substantial curtailment of German steel production as to have an extremely serious repercussion on German industrial output." At this point the argument began to go haywire. The Ministry suggested that, although a closure of the Narvik route could have a serious impact on Germany, only the closure of Lulea and the Swedish ports would lead to decisive results. In addition the paper argued that interference in Norwegian territorial waters might cause an adverse reaction in Denmark and a cutting off of "bacon" imports from that country. Of great importance to future arguments over British-Scandinavian strategy were the figures presented in this paper. The Ministry argued that closure of Narvik would decrease German imports by only one million tons and somewhat illogically suggested that since Germany had already lost "nine million tons of iron ore imports a further one million would have no lasting effect."[104] The figures were, of course, completely wrong. As Raeder admitted to Hitler, the stoppage of Narvik trade would cause a drop of two and a half to three and a half million tons of imported ore per year.[105]

Now in the last half of December the Cabinet and its dissenting advisers hammered out Allied strategy toward Scandinavia. On December 20, the Chiefs of Staff entered the argument with a carefully worded paper. They argued that the question of establishing a mine barrier to stop the ore trade had now become embroiled in the larger question of Germany's entire ore trade with Scandinavia and Britain's general policy toward that region with regard to Russia as well as Germany. Generally they supported the mining operation but warned that the Western Powers might well not be able to reply to a German invasion of Scandinavia. The chiefs also quoted the Ministry of Economic Warfare as stating that closure of Narvik would be no more than an acute embarrassment to Germany.[106] Once again the arguments accumulated for inaction. At the same time that the chiefs presented their paper, Halifax came forward with a strongly worded argument against mining the leads. He quoted the Ministry of Economic Warfare and asked his colleagues whether this could create a sufficiently critical economic crisis in Germany to justify the diplomatic disadvantages, especially considering the probable reaction among neutrals.

On December 22 the War Cabinet again thrashed out the issues. Churchill continued to urge that Britain encourage both Sweden and Norway to help Finland and that the Allies guarantee them against a possible German reaction. Meanwhile he felt that Britain should not only mine Norwegian territorial waters but use her naval power directly to end the Norwegian ore trade; if Germany intervened in Scandinavia, so much the better. Halifax, however, remained unconvinced and seriously doubted whether Norway and Sweden would allow British troops to land at Narvik and occupy the ore fields. Moreover, Halifax argued that to cut off the ore at that point would end the possibility of eventual cooperation with Norway and Sweden to end all the Scandinavian ore trade. Chamberlain fully agreed, and Chatfield, minister for the coordination of defense, feared that an Allied move would stimulate a German reaction and speed up the whole tempo of the war. Cross conceded that his ministry had no precise knowledge of German iron-ore stocks. If German stocks were high, then Narvik would have no impact. Still he did admit that there was intelligence that some iron works in Bohemia had shut down for lack of ore.[107]

On December 27, the War Cabinet met to wrestle with the twin issues of aiding Finland and halting the ore trade to Germany. Halifax argued against making a twofold communication to the Scandinavian governments that would 1) reassure them of Allied support against the possible consequences of aiding the Finns, and 2) "inform them that [the Western Powers] proposed to take certain measures to stop the supply of iron ore to Germany." Halifax argued that the Swedes might react most "unfavorably" to such a *démarche*. Chamberlain, however, disagreed and argued that both communications should be made. Churchill, throughout the arguments and discussion, clearly aimed at a total interruption of the Swedish ore traffic to Germany but considered that a long-term goal. Above all he wished immediate action on the Narvik shipments by a combination of mines and active naval intervention by British destroyers.[108] Churchill seems to have had a sense of direction and understanding of strategic realities that his colleagues lacked. Nevertheless, he was still an outsider and not yet in a position to dominate his colleagues.[109]

Two major papers that appeared on the last day of the year best summarize the opposing points of view. The Chiefs of Staff presented their arguments in favor of a major operation in early spring to help the Finns and, as a corollary, to seize the ore fields of northern Scandinavia. Such a move, they argued, would cut off all iron-ore exports from Scandinavia and would have a final decisive effect on the German war economy. They admitted that, since the major operation could not occur until spring, it was possible to carry out the mining operation as a preliminary step. "By doing so we should prevent the passage of from half to three-quarters million tons of iron ore to Germany." They then stressed that such an action "must . . . prejudice the subsequent execution of the major operation."[110] What is particularly noteworthy about this document is the casual use of figures: Ministry of Economic Warfare estimates of one million tons loss had arbitrarily been lowered by 25 to 50 percent. In a parallel paper the chiefs argued that with Scandinavian cooperation, the Western Powers could totally cut off Germany from the northern ore. Such a policy carried with it serious risks and a major change in Allied strategy, but the chiefs saw it as a viable, attractive course of action.[111]

These arguments received a devastating reply from Churchill. For the first time in the 1930s the British system possessed a strategic mind that could see the forest through the trees. Churchill began by stating that he was in full agreement with the larger argument of the chiefs. But he was afraid that the effect of their position would lead "to a purely negative conclusion, and nothing will be done." He then paraphrased the chiefs' arguments and pointed out their full weaknesses.

> The self-contained minor operation of stopping the ore from Narvik and at Oxelsund must not be tried because it would jeopardize the larger plan. The larger plan must not be attempted unless Sweden and Norway cooperate. Not merely must they not resist militarily or adopt a purely passive attitude, but they must actively cooperate. . . . But is there any prospect of Sweden and Norway actually cooperating with us of their own free will to bring about a series of operations which as is well set out in their [the COS] paper will (a) ruin the trade of their ironfield and the shipping which carries it. (b) involve them in a war with Germany. (c) expose the whole southern part of both countries to German invasion and occupation? Left to themselves they will certainly refuse, and, if pressed diplomatically, they will protest loudly to the world. Thus, the minor operation is knocked out for the sake of the bigger, and the bigger is only declared practicable upon conditions that will not occur.[112]

Churchill then argued that the operation of mining the Norwegian leads might well, in fact, create the conditions under which the larger project became practicable. If the Germans reacted violently to Allied mining of Norwegian territorial waters, they might invade southern Scandinavia. Such an operation would not only make possible an

Anglo-French response but would certainly cut off all Scandinavian ore to Germany for a substantial length of time.

The argument came to a head in early January. The British government now informed the Norwegians and the Swedes that it was contemplating taking military action to stop the movement of ore. Both governments replied by stating that any Allied action in Norwegian territorial waters was completely unacceptable. The unexpectedly strong reaction led the British to pull back and drop consideration of the whole mining project.[113] The basic reason for dropping the mining operation seems to have been the feeling that any naval action would preclude the chances of the larger operation. By mid-January, naval forces that had been preparing for mining Norwegian territorial waters had completely stood down.[114]

From this point, Allied policy toward Scandinavia pursued the will-o'-the-wisp of a major intervention across the Arctic to aid the Finns and coincidentally occupy the ore fields. Considering the harsh Scandinavian reaction to the mere suggestion of naval operations in Norwegian territorial waters, it should have been clear that the major project had no chance. It is not the purpose of this work to examine further the tortuous discussion that took place over the winter. In a strategic sense the early January decision to postpone the mining project ended whatever chance there might have been to put pressure on the German steel industry and war economy. One final point, however, should be made. British mining of the Norwegian leads and territorial waters in January would have made it impossible for the Germans to carry out much of *Weserübung*, especially those sections of the plan that involved movement of German troops to central and northern Norwegian ports by empty ore ships. A Norwegian campaign that began only with a German occupation of southern Norway would have been a very different affair than the disaster of April and May 1940.

MILITARY OPERATIONS: THE WEST

An analysis of the strategic situation on the western front in 1939 and western strategy presents complex problems. Some commentators have suggested that a significant opportunity existed in September 1939 for the Allies in the west, while operations in the east occupied the bulk of the Wehrmacht.[115] However, two major factors worked against such a possibility. The most obvious was the problem of Belgian neutrality.[116] Belgium refused any military cooperation before May 10, and the Allies, who ostensibly were defending the rights of small nations, could hardly violate her neutrality.[117] On the military side the French possessed neither the doctrine, training, nor leadership for an offensive through Belgium into the Rhineland. French operations in September 1939 revealed a high command that was overly cautious, dependent on artillery, and incapable of rapid or audacious moves.[118]

French military weakness was not the result of either the human material or weaponry.[119] Rather, the French army was weak because its high command refused to adapt to the conditions of modern war. It was not merely that the French did not recognize the value of armor or mechanized warfare, but that they allowed the basic building block of any military organization, small unit tactics, to degenerate into a formula of "bombard, advance, and occupy." On all levels they had fallen behind the Wehrmacht.

Complicating French strategy in September was the fact that Germany's western defenses had undergone significant improvement over the course of the last year. Moreover, the OKH was able to deploy strong forces on the western frontier at the same time that it concentrated overwhelming superiority against the Poles. As mentioned above, the Germans deployed thirty-five divisions in the west by September 7. Of that number, eleven were regular divisions, more than a match for the best divisions in the French army; the seven reserve and two border security units were equal to the average French formation; and the nine Landwehr and six training divisions were equivalent to Class B French divisions, like those that collapsed on the Meuse in May 1940.

The critical section for defense of the west lay on the First Army's sector between the Rhine and Moselle, an area that guarded the Saar and entrance into the Rhineland. On this frontier the Germans had constructed the Westwall. The low probability of an Allied offensive elsewhere also allowed the OKH to concentrate strong forces behind the fortifications on this critical front. Along this ninety-mile sector, the Germans deployed ten divisions by September 1.[120] Each division's front averaged fifteen kilometers, compared to the twenty-five or thirty kilometers that German divisions had guarded during the Munich crisis. Of the ten divisions assigned to the First Army, seven were

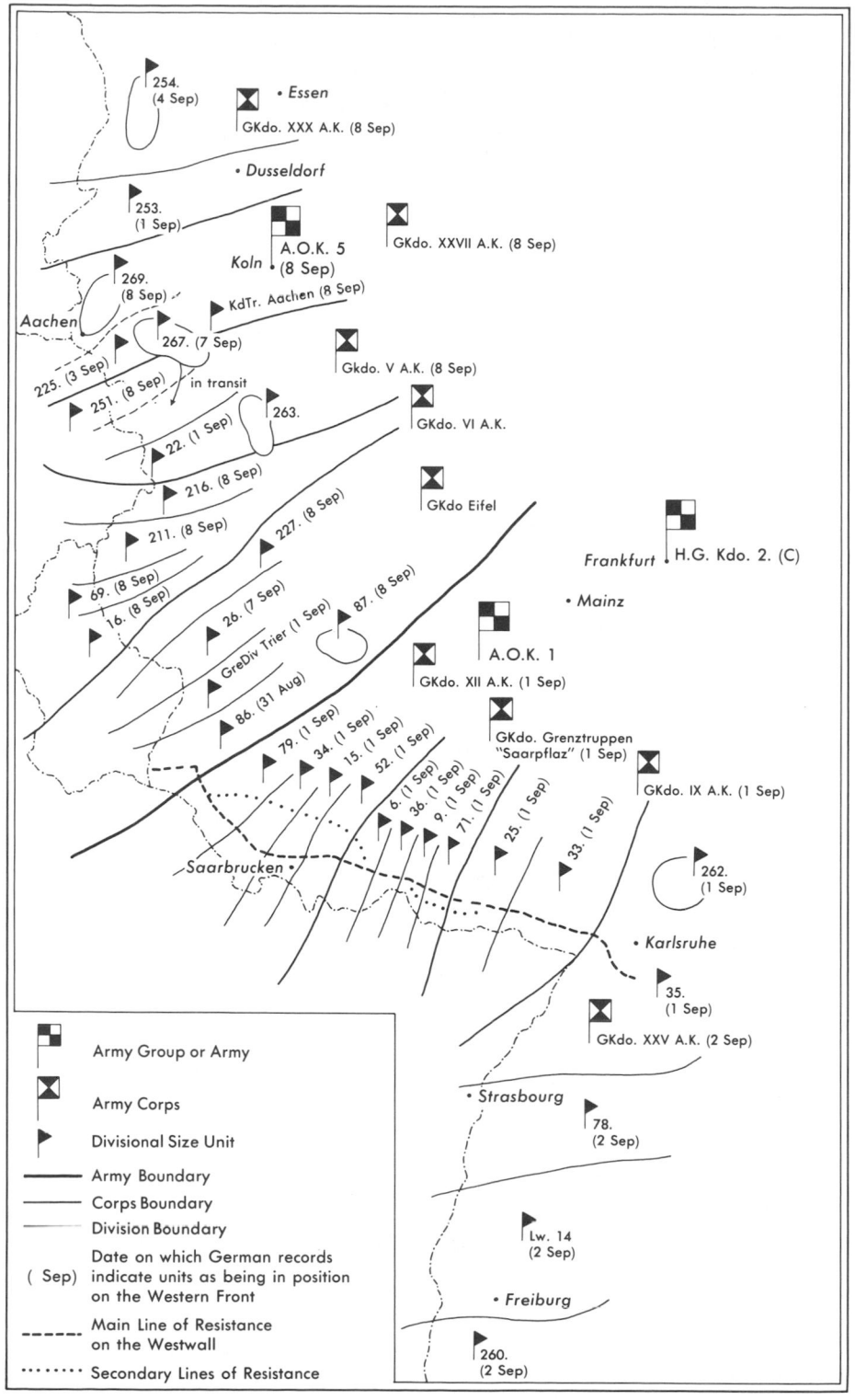

MAP XI *German Dispositions on the Western Front (September 1939)*

254.
(4 Sep)

• Essen

GKdo. XXX A.K. (8 Sep)

• Dusseldorf

253.
(1 Sep)

A.O.K. 5
(8 Sep)

Koln •

GKdo. XXVII A.K. (8 Sep)

269.
(8 Sep)

KdTr. Aachen (8 Sep)

Aachen

267. (7 Sep)

Gkdo. V A.K. (8 Sep)

225. (3 Sep)

251. (8 Sep)   in transit

263.

22. (1 Sep)

GKdo. VI A.K.

216. (8 Sep)

GKdo Eifel

211. (8 Sep)

227. (8 Sep)

H.G. Kdo. 2. (C)

Frankfurt •

69. (8 Sep)

16. (8 Sep)

26. (7 Sep)

87. (8 Sep)

• Mainz

GreDiv Trier (1 Sep)

86. (31 Aug)

A.O.K. 1

GKdo. XII A.K. (1 Sep)

79. (1 Sep)

34. (1 Sep)

15. (1 Sep)

52. (1 Sep)

GKdo. Grenztruppen
"Saarpflaz" (1 Sep)

GKdo. IX A.K. (1 Sep)

6. (1 Sep)

36. (1 Sep)

9. (1 Sep)

71. (1 Sep)

25. (1 Sep)

33. (1 Sep)

262.
(1 Sep)

Saarbrucken •

• Karlsruhe

35.
(1 Sep)

GKdo. XXV A.K. (2 Sep)

• Strasbourg

78.
(2 Sep)

Lw. 14
(2 Sep)

• Freiburg

260.
(2 Sep)

Army Group or Army

Army Corps

Divisional Size Unit

Army Boundary

Corps Boundary

Division Boundary

(Sep) Date on which German records
indicate units as being in position
on the Western Front

Main Line of Resistance
on the Westwall

Secondary Lines of Resistance

regular units, and the remaining three were reserve divisions made up of those who had recently completed military service.[121] In addition, the First Army received three Landwehr divisions in the period from September 2 to 5. This assigned strength was sufficient to prevent a French breakthrough into the Rhineland for at least the period required to destroy Poland.

Another major change in Germany's strategic position from 1938 was the strengthening of the Westwall. At the end of September 1938 only 517 bunkers had stood completed in the west. By September 1939 the total had risen to 11,283.[122] By July 1939 Todt could report that his organization had completed the main line of resistance and would soon finish construction of rear-area positions.[123] In addition, troops assigned to the west throughout 1938 and 1939 had spent considerable time in working on field fortifications, bunkers, and mine fields. By 1939 the Westwall, especially along the First Army's front, had become a line of considerable depth and strength.

Elsewhere in the west, the Germans were not so strong because they doubted whether the West would violate the neutrality of the Low Countries.[124] Yet, the Germans had made contingency plans for a French thrust through Belgium, and the swift victory in the east allowed a rapid redeployment from east to west. As early as September 10, Brauchitsch assured Army Group C that the Polish situation was so favorable that within two days the OKH would release divisions for the western front.[125]

What did catch the Germans by surprise was the almost complete passivity displayed by the French in the west. The 15th Infantry Division stationed near Saarbrücken reported one quiet day after another. Typical of the notations in its war diary were comments such as "*Sonst ruhiger Tag/ Sehr ruhige Nacht und ausserordentlich ruhige Tage.*"[126] French propaganda claims of tactical successes against the Westwall were deliberate, conscious distortions of the actual military situation. In reality French troops barely managed to reach the outposts of the Westwall.[127] One German intelligence report accurately summed up the sorry performance by commenting that the French army had allowed Poland to be smashed, while undertaking no significant military action itself, despite the fact that it held large reserves behind the Maginot line.[128]

And it is this complete unwillingness to undertake *any* military action that is so inexcusable. Admittedly the French were unlikely to achieve a strategic victory in view of the German strengths discussed above. However, the French were certainly in a position to hit and hurt badly an important economic region of the Reich. The Saar lay immediately across the French frontier, and some of its industry even lay within the range of French heavy artillery. Those factories and mines that were not would soon have been, if the French made any gains. Given their strength, the French possessed the capability to batter the Saar, if not to seize the whole region.

Although such a success would not have represented a decisive military achievement, it would have had considerable economic and strategic impact. Not only was this region a significant center of heavy industry, but nearly 8 percent of German coal came from its mines.[129] The issue here is not whether such an offensive would have crippled German industry. Even the capture of the entire Saar would not have done that. Rather, a military campaign against the Saar would have increased the economic pressure on Germany and parenthetically have forced the Germans into major expenditures of ammunition. Both factors would also have increased the pressures on Hitler to launch the Wehrmacht before winter and to seek an immediate decision in the west.

The French high command, of course, launched no such campaign. In spite of Polish pressure that France honor her prewar pledges of aid, the French undertook no more than a demonstration in front of the Westwall.[130] In mid-September Gamelin replied to desperate Polish appeals that half of his regular divisions were in contact with the Wehrmacht but that his army faced an opponent well prepared for defensive warfare and did not possess the artillery to move the enemy. In the air, Gamelin continued, the French air force believed that they held much of the Luftwaffe in the west. Gamelin concluded that he had "therefore already fulfilled his promise to undertake the first French offensive within fifteen days of mobilization. It is impossible for me to do more."[131] At the same time that Gamelin passed this cynical and false report to the Poles he was telling the British that "he did not envisage casualties on a large scale. The object underlying the operation now in progress was to help Poland by distracting the attention of Germany. His offensive was confined to activities in 'no man's' land and he had no intention of throwing his army against the German main defenses."[132] Meanwhile, the factories and the mines of the Saar remained in full production almost within sight of the French armies.

CONCLUSION

An Allied strategic study of April 1940 summed up the results of the West's diplomatic and military inactivity most accurately. It noted: "Hence, the Reich appears to have suffered relatively little wear and tear during the first six months of war, and that mainly as a result of the allied blockade. Meanwhile, it has profited from the interval to perfect the degree of equipment of its land and air forces, to increase the officer strength and complete the training of its troops, and to add further divisions to those already in the field."[133] Yet, such a state of affairs and the coming disastrous blow of May 1940 were not inevitable. The consistent unwillingness of Allied statesmen, however, as well as generals to address their grand strategy in a consistent fashion maximized their enemy's potential and minimized their own considerable strengths. It was this state of mind above all else that made 1940 possible. Perhaps nothing better sums up the bitter futility of those condemned to the front lines in the "Phony War" than an RAF raid on Wilhelmshaven launched in December 1939. Twenty-four Wellingtons set out to attack the German fleet. Upon arrival at the target the British discovered one battleship, one heavy cruiser, one light cruiser, and five destroyers tied up at docks. The Wellingtons took photographs, "but as the ships were lying in close proximity to buildings, no attempt was made to bomb them." Ten Wellingtons did not come home.[134]

Wolfe, shortly before he took Quebec in 1759, commented that "war is an option of difficulties." Certainly Western leaders in August and September 1939 faced enormous problems, but their absolute unwillingness to take risks, to incur losses, and to think through their strategy led them to refuse every possibility of pressuring a Germany that faced serious economic and strategic troubles. By allowing Italy to escape into neutrality at the beginning of the war, not only did they deny themselves the chance to gain victories on the cheap, but they created a conduit for German imports. Their failure to mine the Norwegian leads until April 1940 permitted the Germans to import Scandinavian ores throughout the "Phony War" and then launch

Weserübung before the first mines had been laid in Norwegian waters. Finally, the failure to launch a serious offensive against the Saar in September allowed the Germans to use the region's mines and foundries.

Any one of the above actions by itself would not have affected the Germans decisively. But in combination Allied pressure might well have pushed Hitler into launching his western offensive in the fall. Such an offensive without a great armored thrust through the Ardennes had considerably less chance of success than the Manstein plan of May 1940. Moreover, a fall offensive would have denied the German army the six months of the "Phony War" that allowed it to put its house in order. When the Germans came west in spring 1940, they came with maximum power and effect. The results were catastrophic for everyone.

XI

Conclusion

Historians have, by and large, rendered their readers a distinct disservice. In analyzing military and diplomatic history they have tended to simplify and clarify the arguments and difficulties through which governments and bureaucracies muddle in any decision-making process. That very clarification of what to a soldier in war is usually a chaotic, terrifying experience and to a diplomat in peace, a set of confusing and disagreeable choices brings with it the danger of fundamentally distorting the reality within which decisions were and are made. Churchill in his great work on the First World War noted at the beginning:

> One rises from the study of the causes of the Great War with a prevailing sense of the defective control of individuals upon world fortunes. . . . The limited minds even of the ablest men, their disputed authority, the climate of opinion in which they dwell, their transient and partial contribution to the mighty problem, that problem itself so far beyond their compass, so vast in scale and detail, so changing in its aspects—all this must surely be considered. . . . Could we in England perhaps by some effort, by some sacrifice of our material interests, by some compulsive gesture, at once of friendship and command, have reconciled France and Germany and formed that grand association on which alone the peace and glory of Europe would be safe? I cannot tell. I only know that we tried our best to steer our country through the gathering dangers of the armed peace without bringing her to war or others to war, and when these efforts failed, we drove through the tempest without bringing her to destruction. [1]

Conclusion

The previous chapters have attempted to bring to the reader some sense of the full context within which the decisions of 1938 and 1939 were made. They cannot, however, capture the full difficulties of the choices that were made. One can only judge the effectiveness of national policies, strategies, and decision-making processes on the basis of their overall response to the challenges of the late 1930s rather than on their specific responses to individual instances or incidents. Historians have a tendency to judge individuals, governments, and bureaucracies on an incident-by-incident basis. And the very complexity of the decision-making process or the benefit of hindsight makes it easy to justify or to condemn specific cases or decisions. Unfortunately such an approach is not only unrealistic but distortive. Only by looking at patterns and by comparing one organization with another can historians assess with some degree of accuracy the performance of individuals or of bureaucracies. Thus, the Chamberlain government's performance falls not on a single incident like Munich but rather on its consistent inability through to its fall in May 1940 either to judge or to execute any effective strategic response to the German threat. Similarly, only when compared to the tactical and operational developments in Germany, does the French army's competence in the late 1930s appear most unsatisfactory.

The basic problem that any government must master in diplomacy and peace as well as in strategy and war is the estimation of others' intentions. What do one's opponents intend to do and how? Because that estimation is so difficult, the issue all too often devolves into "bean counting." Bureaucracies, and the staffs that make bureaucracies function (unimaginative, worried about prerogatives, and careful to protect their flanks and rear), tend to fix on the counting of numbers rather than on intentions in casting strategic evaluations. Yet even in "counting beans," bureaucracies exhibit a willful and natural ability to count the beans so as to fix the results in accordance with preconceived notions.[2]

Once one moves to the arena of estimating intentions, then statesmen and soldiers face the most intractable of problems. Even with the advantage of hindsight and documentary evidence, historians find it difficult to judge the intentions of historical actors. How much more difficult then is the problem of those who make policy in the real world, where one can see and read intentions only dimly and imperfectly? Diplomacy and strategy, like war, represent, in fact, options between difficult courses of action, none of which are very satisfactory; and the influences of outside factors such as public opinion, personal prejudices, and hostilities within a governing group may have as great an impact on the decision-making process as policy discussions.

The complexities of estimating the strategy of one's opponent comes out clearly in the Spartan assembly of the fifth century B.C. In debating whether or not to fight the Athenians, the Spartan king Archidamus warned his listeners:

> Spartans, in the course of my life I have taken part in many wars, and I can see among you people of the same age as I am. They and I have had experience and so are not likely to share in what may be a general enthusiasm for war, nor to think that war is a good thing or a safe thing. . . . When we are engaged with Peloponnesians and neighbors, the forces on both sides are of the same type, and we can strike rapidly where we wish to strike. With Athens it is different. Here we shall be engaged with people who live far off, people also who have the widest experience of the sea and who are extremely well equipped in all other directions, very wealthy both as individuals and as a state, with ships and cavalry, and hoplites, with a population bigger than that of any other place in Hellas, and then, too, with numbers of allies who pay tribute to them. How then can we irresponsibly start a war with such a people? What have we to rely upon if we rush into it prepared? Our navy? . . . Or are we relying on our wealth? . . . What sort of war, then, are we going to fight? If we can neither defeat them at sea nor take away from them the resources on which the navy depends, we shall do ourselves more harm than good. . . .[3]

To these clearsighted warnings, not against war but against war now, the Spartan ephor replied succinctly that Sparta must come to the help of her allies and "not . . . betray them to the Athenians."[4] The Spartan assembly, comprised of hoplites, then overwhelmingly shouted approval for immediate war and against the argument for strategic preparation. Lest the reader be misled on the strategic ambiguities, one must note that the strategic premise on which the ephor's position had rested (that the Athenians would come out from their walls and fight) came close to being realized. Only by refusing to allow the assembly to meet could the Athenian leader Pericles keep the Athenians within their city.[5]

The difficulty that statesmen and soldiers alike face is the fact that we live in a world of action and reaction. The Spartan king was correct and the ephor wrong because the Athenians reacted in an unexpected manner to the Spartan invasion (at least in the eyes of most Spartans). By so doing they undermined the basis of Spartan strategic policy. Similarly in the Europe of the 1930s it proved exceedingly difficult, and quite naturally so, to predict actions or reactions. On the basis of events in 1938, Hitler had every reason in August 1939, since he had isolated Poland even more completely than Czechoslovakia the year before, to expect surrender rather than war from Britain and France. What he failed to see was that his actions had altered national attitudes and political perceptions in the body politic of the Western democracies. Thus, surrender, no matter how attractive philosophically for those controlling Anglo-French policy, was no longer an alternative. Unfortunately, bad statesmanship often results from an inability to see the realities of the action-reaction world in which we live; rather it believes that we inhabit a mechanistic universe in which our opponents react in a predictable manner. The Schlieffen plan perhaps best exemplifies that tendency in military planning.[6]

The difficulty in estimating an enemy's intentions lies not so much in predicting his initial reaction to events such as a declaration of war but rather in judging a whole series of responses in which weather, chance, fear, opportunity, changes in leadership or public opinion all may serve to drive him in very different directions from what one expects. In diplomacy or strategic planning in peacetime, all of the above factors (except obviously those directly influencing battlefield conditions) have a similar impact that contributes to the *general* unpredictability of human affairs. Carl von Clausewitz has been justly famous for his sense of the symbiotic relationship between military force, politics, and diplomacy (certainly a major theme in his work).[7] Clausewitz's concept of friction, closely tied to military operations, is a particularly useful tool in examining the problem of judging intentions. Clausewitz argued that due to the interaction of thousands of tiny incidents, all tending to retard, even the simplest task in war involving thousands of men becomes exceedingly difficult to perform.[8]

Similarly, in peacetime there are thousands of small impediments to the process of judging and evaluating enemy intentions. If statesmen and soldiers have a hard time in evaluating the quantitative side, then how much more difficult the task of evaluating intentions. The evidence is usually available, but it is invariably buried beneath a mountain of irrelevant information. How exceedingly easy it is for the strategic evaluation mechanisms to misinterpret or to select out what statesmen and generals do not wish to hear. Even good estimates are easily sabotaged or discounted when bureaucrats in the chain of command attack irrelevancies. Only by having the very rare individual at the center, able to evaluate and to drive what bureaucracies so unwillingly judge, can governments arrive at a more accurate picture of enemy intentions. Thus, without a driving strategic force at the center, the West in 1939, even though it had decided on an active anti-German foreign policy, found it difficult to get its bureaucracies to agree on any specific measures. Granting guarantees regardless of strategic realities is not policy. When, however, the time came to make the serious decisions to manipulate the strategic reality, frictions in the decision-making processes proved too great to overcome. Consequently, only the most negative of decisions—the declaration of war and the imposition of a blockade—were made.

There is a larger issue here. Twentieth-century historical analyses have tended to regard military organizations as peculiarly incompetent. In the index of Lloyd George's memoirs there is a revealing entry. Under "military mind," one finds, "narrowness of, 3051; stubbornness of, not peculiar to America, 3055; does not seem to understand arithmetic, 3077; its attitude in July 1918, represented by Sir Henry Wilson's fantastic memorandum of 25/7/18, 3109; obsessed with North-West Frontier of India, 3119; impossibility of trusting, 3124; regards thinking as a form of mutiny, 3422."[9] David Lloyd George's attitude toward the military finds more than sufficient supporting evidence in the disasters at Loos, the Somme, Paschendaele, Verdun, and Gallipoli. Yet, the underlying assumption presents difficulties; it rests on a belief that decisions by civil bureaucracies are, for the most part, more intelligent, judicious, and farseeing than those by the military, that, in other words, competence underlies most aspects of human affairs. Thus, the military institutions responsible for disasters such as the Somme do not really reflect the innate competence of the human race.[10] This author, however, finds little evidence in the behavior of civil or industrial bureaucracies to indicate that competence is any more prevalent on the civilian side than on the military side of society. In fact, shortsightedness, close-mindedness, and institutional rigidity seem as endemic to the civilian societies of the twentieth century that have produced the Great Depression, fifty straight years of planned agricultural disaster in the Soviet Union, and the "great leap forward" as to our century's military bureaucracies. The only real difference is that it is more difficult to hide the bloody disasters of military history.

If we accept, then, incompetence as the basis of human behavior, the performance of those facing Hitler in the late 1930s is perhaps less surprising, though no more excusable. Those who molded the response to Hitler acted no more effectively than those responding to the depression or to the wreckage of the First World War. The results in terms of the disasters of 1939 through 1945 were catastrophic. And after all, those who led Britain throughout the 1930s argued that they were particularly competent to manage the ship of state. The results belie their claims.

In the European world of the 1930s, however, Hitler moved with extraordinary effectiveness. Combining the qualities of a "true believer" with those of a brilliant tactical opportunist,[11] Hitler shattered the European diplomatic balance in his first years in power. Even as Germany was only just realizing her program of massive rearmament, Hitler destroyed what was left of the Treaty of Versailles, announced the creation of the Luftwaffe, and remilitarized the Rhineland. The years from 1933 to 1936 saw Hitler at the height of his capabilities. Yet his success carried with it the seeds of disaster. More and more, Hitler viewed the world as reacting to his will rather than to his ploys and stratagems, and as time passed, Hitler became less concerned with outmaneuvering his opponents than with forcing the world to fit his preconceived notions.

Thus, the period from 1936 to 1939 saw a less effective Hitler. The economic problems of rearmament proved unresponsive to the führer's will and caused Hitler to take risks in the international arena. And the scale and ease of the first great success (the Anschluss) led Hitler to embark on a course that nearly ended the adventure before it had begun. The Czech crisis very nearly precipitated war at a time when Germany had few prospects of winning, and the invasion of Poland in 1939 landed the Reich in a war for which it was not prepared. That the Germans squirmed out of their strategic difficulties temporarily in 1940 only made the results in 1944 and 1945 all the more terrible for their nation.

The problem was, in part, endemic to the German strategic system. In fact, "system" is an entirely inappropriate term; there was no system at all. As in the First World War the Germans proved remarkably skilled at doctrine, training, operations, and tactics. When it came to strategy, however, they were quite literally at sea. For all their vaunted organizational abilities, the German military under Hitler could not put together a workable high-command structure, much less a body governing overall strategy. Given Göring's position and naval obduracy, Blomberg and Reichenau had scant prospect for success in their efforts to make the War Ministry such a body, and Hitler, of course, had no intention of allowing such a body to exist; it would only have served to tie his hands. But one must emphasize that it was the army above all that opposed a decision-making body equivalent to the British Chiefs of Staff.[12] The result was an almost complete abdication of responsibility in the strategic sphere to Hitler—a state of affairs thoroughly in accordance with the führer's wishes.

Despite its protestations of having pride of place in strategic matters, the army exhibited little competence in strategy. Fritsch's failure to respond to the fact that the army's rearmament program would bankrupt the German state by 1939 speaks volumes on the strategic incompetence of the army's leadership.[13] Beck, the chief of staff, did a better job at sizing up the risks in 1938. But his memoranda, like those of Heye and Guse of the naval staff, would be *personal* studies—not studies reflecting the broad consensus of the officer corps or even the general staff. There was in reality no means of bringing such consensus forward or even to arrive at one.

This state of affairs undoubtedly reflected past historical and geographic influences. Perhaps the catastrophe of Jena-Auerstadt, which had in one afternoon pitched Frederick the Great's kingdom from the top ranks of European powers to the possibility of complete annihilation, perhaps the geography of Prussia and Germany, open to invasion from east and west, or perhaps the conflicts between Moltke and Bismarck had produced in the German military mind an overemphasis on tactics and operations and an underemphasis on strategy.

On the other hand, the simple geographic placement that has allowed British and American generals to face continental defeats as less catastrophic and that perhaps has forced Anglo-American generals to think of logistics and strategy before undertaking any operation may explain the peculiarly different competencies of those nations as opposed to the Germans. Whatever the reasons, the Germans fought the war of 1939-1940 (in fact the war in general) very much on the basis of an *ad hoc* strategy. The lack of realistic, hard-headed appraisal of risks, strengths, weaknesses, and economic factors in German strategic directives is striking when one compares British appreciations with whatever German ones come to mind, whether they be Hitler's or Beck's (others by operational commanders like Manstein or Guderian do not even deserve consideration). Thus, Germany in 1939 "clanked obstinately, recklessly, awkwardly towards the crater"[14] with only the barest outline of a possible strategy and the idle hope that Britain and France would not honor their obligations. That hope was not realized, and, relying on their tactical and operational competence, the Germans kept doubling the stakes until the game bankrupted them forever.

Even now, forty years after the German invasion of Western Europe in the spring of 1940, it is difficult to escape the feeling that the Wehrmacht enjoyed massive superiority over its opponents. Within a space of five weeks Holland, Belgium, and Luxembourg fell; the British beat an ignominious retreat from Dunkirk; and France collapsed. In a peripheral campaign the Germans seized Denmark and Norway despite British naval superiority.

Yet the Germans took immense risks to gain these victories. They did not possess greater strength in land armaments and were definitely inferior in naval forces. They held a clear advantage only in the air, and even that lead was tenuous, as the Battle of Britain would show. The real weakness in the Reich's strategic position lay in the economic sphere. The great western offensive was a one-shot affair: success, and Germany would acquire the economic base to fight a long war; failure, and the war would be over. Historians have for the most part interested themselves in the tactical and operational factors that led to the catastrophe. Unfortunately, they have failed to ask the crucial question in terms of grand strategy; how and why were the Germans allowed to husband their strength for this great throw of the dice?

As this study has suggested, Germany's strategic and economic base was most narrow for the grandiose dreams of European conquest toward which her leader drove. Given the nature of those dreams it was inevitable that a European war would occur. Nevertheless, the timing as to when and in what fashion the other powers would take up that challenge was beyond Hitler's control. As he announced to his cohorts shortly after taking power, if France had any statesmen, she would wage a preventive war immediately. The Polish statesman, Marshal Pilsudski, apparently did think in such terms. But there was no one in France, and certainly no one in England, with the ruthlessness to "wage a war now to prevent one in the future."

Yet if Hitler managed to escape the initial period of great weakness, at no time in the thirties was he able to build a decisive military lead over his opponents. The führer's strategic problem was how to break out from Germany's narrow economic base to gain the resources required to fight a great war. In terms of resources, Germany was not, in the late thirties, prepared to fight a lengthy war. Hitler realized that Germany did not have time to rearm in depth and could not wait until the completion of her armament programs. He must move when German strength had reached its maximum advantage over her possible opponents. Economic difficulties in 1937, combined with the pressures of the Fritsch-Blomberg crisis, led to the Anschluss, perhaps earlier than Hitler had foreseen. The ease of that triumph and the failure of the West to react in any fashion encouraged Hitler to move against Czechoslovakia. Hitler's anger at the Czech mobilization in May, however, almost led to a misstep. Western pusillanimity served to convince Hitler that he could get away with a limited war against Czechoslovakia. Thus, in 1938 he almost pushed Germany into a war for which she was militarily, economically, and strategically unprepared.

The West did not fight, however, despite its favorable situation. Admittedly, military counsel had consistently advised against any armed confrontation with the dictator powers. But when the crunch came in September 1938, many of the premises on which military planners had based their gloomy prognostications proved wrong. Japan's reluctance to add to the burdens of the China War made it unlikely that she would intervene in a European war. And also important at the end of September was a growing recognition that the Germans themselves viewed their strategic situation even more pessimistically than did the West. The decision not to force a military confrontation, then, was not based on fear that Britain would lose. Rather it rested on a fear of war and its consequences, even if Britain won. Two fundamental misconceptions contributed to this attitude. The first was a refusal to recognize the stability of society itself and the ability of industrialized countries to withstand the economic and military strains of war. The second, and perhaps decisive, misconception was a complete unwillingness to face up to the nature of the Nazi regime. Few of Britain's political leaders recognized that the Nazi regime had aims that were so far-reaching that compromise with such a regime was impossible. Thus, British statesmen felt that if Germany achieved an Anschluss with Austria and secured other "legitimate" claims in Eastern Europe, she would be satiated. The British never foresaw that their concessions might, and indeed did, create a situation in which Germany was the dominant power on the continent and which furthermore would allow the Germans to take the first steps toward escaping their economic and strategic limitations.

There would have been difficulties in following a harder course toward Germany. Whatever their political convictions, few in Britain recognized the necessity of a major rearmament effort. It is also doubtful whether many Englishmen would willingly have followed a hard line against Germany without overwhelming evidence that Hitler was a mortal danger to Britain. Nevertheless, the Chamberlain government refused to embark on a rearmament effort until *after* most of their countrymen had become convinced of its necessity. Moreover, Chamberlain pursued an appeasement policy up until the outbreak of the war. It is perhaps possible to excuse individual strategic and diplomatic decisions of the British government in the period from 1937 to 1939. But the Chamberlain government's overall record in the period is unpardonably dismal. The prime minister and his advisers made the wrong choice on almost every strategic and diplomatic question that they faced. That was the real failure of the Chamberlain government.

Since the war an historical school has developed that argues that Chamberlain's surrender at Munich saved Britain from military destruction and allowed her time to prepare for the Battle of Britain. There is no basis for such an argument. Even if Britain possessed no defense against a "strategic" bombing offensive in 1938, the Luftwaffe was not in a position to launch such an offensive. The weaknesses in the support branches as well as shortages of fuel and munitions would have made it impossible for the Germans to sustain a bombing offensive. In addition, the range and capabilities of German aircraft required that the Channel coast from Cherbourg to the North Sea be in German hands before they could launch air attacks on the British Isles. In other respects the German military situation was desperate. The German economy was strained to the breaking point. The Wehrmacht possessed sufficient strength to destroy Czechoslovakia, but it had neither the economic base nor the reserve strength to gain strategic victories in either the east or the west. The German navy could not have protected the ore trade with Norway and Sweden, much less have launched a major amphibious operation against Scandinavia. Even if the Allies did not have the will or military competence to have fully exploited Germany's weaknesses, the defeat of the Third Reich would have been inevitable. Germany just did not possess the strength to seize in 1938 the economic base that she acquired in spring 1940.

Chamberlain's approach to the Czech crisis reveals the fundamental faults in British diplomatic and strategic policy. As late as September 8, Halifax assured the Cabinet that the Czech fortifications lay outside Sudeten German districts. The fact that until mid-September no one even questioned the implications of the peaceful surrender of Czechoslovakia with her armaments and armament industries indicates an appalling lack of strategic perspective. If British military policy were based on a "worse case" analysis, Chamberlain founded British diplomatic policy on a "best case" analysis of Germany's aims. The combination was calamitous.

The French role in the disaster of 1938 is perhaps less obvious but no less important; the responsibility lies perhaps as far back as those who molded France's strategic and diplomatic responses to the victory of 1918. Certainly, direct responsibility must begin with the "Popular Front" government of Leon Blum that, as with so much of the Left in the 1930s (outside of the Soviet Union), saw the Fascist danger primarily in terms of an internal manifestation, while feeling sure that revolutionary enthusiasm could make up for weaknesses that existed in France's military forces. Unfortunately, whatever French social needs were in 1936 (and they were undoubtedly many), France faced a terrible danger on her northern frontier, and that growing danger could only be addressed by the substantial allocation of national resources to defense. The failure of the French air force in May 1940, as suggested in the third chapter, was as much due to the government's failure to rearm as to any other single factor. The aircraft industry and its products were antiquated because the government failed to provide the financial support for contracts until late 1938. In the procurement of modern weapons systems one does not simply turn on a spigot; one turns on the spigot and waits one to two years.

The French politicians, of course, and the generals who controlled the nation and its military forces in 1938 and 1939 deserve their share of the blame. Unwilling to take risks, unimaginative and unresponsive to a changing world, even by the normal standards of humanity, they waited and hoped 1) that the British would persuade the Germans to put off *"der Tag"* and 2) that the war would occur anywhere else but in northern France. When offered the chance to smash the Italians in the Mediterranean while the Germans were busy in Poland, they, as did the British, found every possible excuse for inaction. On the nature of the German regime, the French were undoubtedly more realistic in estimating the purposes and goals toward which the Germans were driving. Their overestimation of German military power, however, was on the same scale of magnitude as that of the British and even more corrosive to their willingness to take action.

The West wasted the period between Munich and the German occupation of Prague in March 1939. The Chamberlain government refused to change its rearmament policies, and only at the end of February did the prime minister finally recognize that Britain must have at least a respectable regular army to support France. Chamberlain hoped that Munich would set a precedent for a general settlement of European differences. The futility of such hopes reflects the fundamental conflict between British and German foreign policies. Hitler aimed at gaining domination over Europe, while the British hoped to channel German demands within limited boundaries—boundaries to which Hitler had no intention of agreeing. The French had few illusions as to the permanency of the Munich settlement or to the good faith of the dictators. They did find the surrender of Czechoslovakia, however, a particularly useful tool to force a fundamental reassessment of British strategic policy. And that reassessment, although it did not fully satisfy France's strategic needs, did force the British to commit an expeditionary force to the continent. Strategic planners on both sides recognized that although that commitment was only an opening wedge, it was an important one nevertheless.

The Nazi occupation of Prague in March 1939 was the logical outcome of Munich. In a diplomatic sense it caused Western attitudes, particularly public opinion, to harden drastically. Although the occupation considerably limited Germany's diplomatic freedom of maneuver (and Britain's as well), the logic of Hitler's aims and Germany's economic difficulties led directly to it. Munich was initially largely a diplomatic triumph; Germany made few of the economic and financial gains that had marked the Anschluss. Given the cost of the extravagant programs of summer 1938 the Germans were once again almost bankrupt. The major cutbacks in rearmament programs in the winter were an indication of how serious things had become. The seizure of Czechoslovakia with its economic, financial, and military resources was an obvious escape route from these difficulties.

The diplomatic and military policies of the West, and of Great Britain in particular, during the months following the German seizure of Prague now set the stage for the Second World War. Although Nazi Germany was fully responsible for the outbreak of the war, British behavior determined the exact circumstances under which war occurred. If war was inevitable, and considering Hitler's policies and long-term goals, it certainly was, British misconceptions and mistakes insured that war would occur under the worst possible conditions for the Western Powers.

In the last half of March 1939 the Chamberlain Cabinet feared that war was at hand. It panicked and decided that it could deter the Germans by guaranteeing the independence of Poland. While undertaking this momentous step, it showed no inclination to pursue an agreement with the Soviet Union. When the British and French distributed guarantees throughout Eastern Europe in April 1939, they made little effort to exact mutual obligations, and thus failed to encourage whatever tendencies might have existed to form an Eastern European bloc. The Polish guarantee gave Stalin an excellent bargaining position. He could now force the opposing sides to bid for his services, and the Germans had more to offer. In effect, the British guarantee to Poland had ended the isolation of the Soviet Union, and Stalin was to play an exceedingly clever game. Its success or failure would rest on how well the British, and even more the French, could resist the German tide when it came west. Thus, the failure of the Anglo-French armies in the west in 1940 was almost as great a strategic defeat for the Soviet Union as it was for France.

As a result of the Nazi-Soviet Non-Aggression Pact, Britain and France faced Germany alone. The direct cause was the amateurism of British strategic policies, but there were deeper causes. Throughout the interwar period British leaders refused to recognize that war was not only a real possibility but at times the only option. Thus, when public opinion forced the government to react to the German threat, Chamberlain's response was diplomatic, not strategic. In the circumstances after the occupation of Prague, only the most cool-headed diplomatic and strategic planning would have had effect. It would have been difficult to achieve an alliance with the Soviet Union and impossible to tie Russia *and* the Eastern European states together. The only conceivable method of reaching agreement with Russia was through a policy of keeping British options open. Considering the political atmosphere in Britain—with a general election approaching in the fall—such a policy of equivocation would have been most difficult. The public demanded immediate and drastic action to stop the Germans. Moreover, there might have been considerable problems even had the Allied governments reached accommodation with the Soviet Union. Might not such an agreement have forced Poland and Rumania into Germany's arms? The real condemnation of Chamberlain's Russian policy was not its failure but rather its inability to see how important an agreement with Russia was. The French were quite properly appalled at the prospect of losing Russia. They understood far better than Chamberlain and his advisors the political and strategic realities. Nevertheless, as so often throughout the 1930s, they followed in the wake of British policy, willing at times to argue, but never to fight for command. In 1939, perhaps too satisfied with having finally received firm guarantees and promises of troop reinforcements, the French allowed the British to determine Allied policy in Eastern Europe.

But the most disastrous shortcoming in Allied policy over the course of 1939 lay in its failure to implement fully the strategy upon which Western planners had agreed. This failure reflected not only the general ignorance of strategic affairs by political leaders but also the complete unwillingness of the military to think through its strategy. The result was that, despite a most serious economic situation, the Germans managed to escape the consequences of their strategic predicament, maximize and organize their forces for one great strike, and destroy their opponents on land in Western Europe.

The Allies made their greatest strategic mistake in allowing the Italians to slip into a posture of "nonbelligerence." For once, Chamberlain intuited correctly that the sooner the Italians were drawn into a conflict, the greater would be the economic and military strain on the Axis. But the Chiefs of Staff, by overestimating Italian military capabilities, dissuaded the Cabinet from its initial stand. Thus, for specious reasons, the West allowed Italy to husband her strength until that moment when Britain and France were stretched to the limit. The failure of the French to attack the Saar and the British unwillingness to cut the Scandinavian ore trade completed the collapse of Allied strategy.

Adolf Hitler, surveying the European strategic situation in the late summer of 1939, had seemingly every reason for satisfaction. His armies and air forces were now at last approaching a real state of readiness. His policies had in the past six months succeeded in tactically, operationally, strategically, and diplomatically isolating Poland in Eastern Europe. For a relatively cheap price the Soviet Union promised benevolent neutrality. Britain and France had no means available to bring direct military support to the Poles, and the indirect pressures available offered no quick strategic avenues to success. Yet, if the German strategic situation appeared satisfactory, appearances hid extraordinary weaknesses and difficulties. Above all, Germany's economy had few prospects of supporting the war effort over the long haul unless the Wehrmacht could rapidly expand the Reich's access to European raw materials. Doubts within the military in 1938 had led directly to the crisis of confidence in September, and doubts in fall 1939 were strong enough to cause at least some disturbance between the regime and its generals. In 1939 the German economy proved even more susceptible to blockade than it had in the First World War, and some materials, such as petroleum, were never throughout the Second World War available in satisfactory supply. However, by 1939 all shreds of its independent judgment had been lost and the Generalität had no real quarrel with Hitler's strategy. The quarrel was only over the operational decision as to when the campaign in the west would begin. Hitler had no clear strategic idea now that he had created the mess of a major European war except to strike in the west as soon as possible. And luck, bad weather, and the failure of the Allies to apply any pressure led to the postponement of battle until the spring.

The great defeat came in May-June 1940. In every respect it should have been avoided. But the diplomatic and strategic policies of the West, especially of Great Britain, the delusions of a British government firmly convinced that wars were something twentieth-century statesmen did not consider, and the strategic advice of a military that saw every situation in the darkest light led to Dunkirk and defeat in France. The responsibility of Chamberlain, Halifax, Hoare, Daladier, and Bonnet for the disaster of 1940 was clear almost from the start of the Second World War. But the military planners and leaders of Great Britain and France, the Chatfields, the Slessors, the Newalls, the Gorts, the Gamelins, and the Weygands bear an equal share of responsibility. At every turn in the long road from the Abyssinian crisis to the beginning of the Second World War, they had preached caution, seen dangers where none existed, prophesied doom, and agreed to the abandonment of every position. Largely because of their self-fulfilling prophecies Britain and France faced Germany alone in May 1940.

Abbreviations

ADAP   *Akten zur deutschen auswärtigen Politik*
AHB   Air Historical Branch
BA/MA   Bundesarchiv/Militärarchiv
BEF   British Expeditionary Force
CID   Committee on Imperial Defense
CIGS   Chief of the Imperial General Staff
COS   Chiefs of Staff
DBFP   *Documents on British Foreign Policy*
DCOS   Deputy Chiefs of Staff
DDF   *Documents Diplomatiques Français*
DRC   Defense Requirements Committee
FO   Foreign Office
FRUS   *Foreign Relations of the United States*
g.Kdo. geheime Kommandosache
GKdo   Generalkommando
HgKdo   Heeresgruppenkommando
IMT   International Military Tribunal
JP   Joint Planning [Committee]
JPC   Joint Planning Committee
JRUSI   *Journal of the Royal United Services Institute*
NARS   National Archives and Record Service
ObdM   Oberbefehlshaber der Kriegsmarine
OKH   Oberkommando des Heeres
OKM   Oberkommando der Kriegsmarine
OKW   Oberkommando der Wehrmacht

Abbreviations

PRO	Public Record Office
SEHR	*Scandinavian Economic History Review*
SIS	Secret Intelligence Service
TMWC	*Trial of Major War Criminals*
VfZG	*Vierteljahrshefte für Zeitgeschichte*

Notes

I. Germany: The Strategic Problem

1. "Aufzeichnung Liebmann," *Vierteljahrshefte für Zeitgeschichte* 2, no. 4 (October 1954).

2. Alan Bullock, *Hitler, A Study in Tyranny* (New York, 1964), pp. 314-315.

3. This helps to explain the inadequacies in the analyses of the German war economy and strategy contained in works by such Anglo-Saxon historians as Burton Klein, *Germany's Economic Preparations for War* (Cambridge, Mass., 1959), Alan Milward, *The German Economy at War* (London, 1965), and to a lesser extent Berenice Carroll, *Design for Total War* (The Hague, 1968).

4. Oberkommando des Heeres, *Der Weltkrieg, 1914 bis 1918*, Vol. XIV (Berlin, 1944), p. 41.

5. For a graphic description of this breakdown even in first-line infantry units see the entry for March 28 in Rudolf Binding, *A Fatalist at War* (London, 1929).

6. Institut für Weltwirtschaft an der Universität Kiel, "Die Kohlenversorgung Europas durch Grossdeutschland unter den gegenwärtigen kriegswirtschaftlichen Gesichtspunkten," October 1939, National Archives and Records Service (NARS) T-84/195/1560466.

7. Ibid., pp. 3-4, 8-12, 22-24.

8. Der Generalbevollmächtigte für die Kriegswirtschaft, letter to the Reichsverkehrsminister, 20.12.38., NARS T-77/539/1712852.

9. J. J. Jäger, *Die wirtschaftliche Abhängigkeit des Dritten Reiches vom Ausland* (Berlin, 1969), pp. 303-304.

10. Reichskredit-Gesellschaft, April 1938, "Treibstoffwirtschaft in der Welt und in Deutschland," pp. 34, 38, NARS T-84/51/1332658.

11. Abschrift einer Aufstellung der Überwachungsstelle für Mineralöl vom

3.5.38., "Deutschlands Mineralölbilanz nach In- und Auslandsaufkommen in den Jahren 1928-1937 in 1000 T," p. 2, NARS T-77/282/1107267.

12. Speech by Korvettenkapitän Haensel, 4.3.39., während des Kriegsspieles des Marinekommandoamtes in Oberhof, p. 13, NARS T-1022/2821/PG49089.

13. Institut für Weltwirtschaft an der Universität Kiel, Februar 1940, "Versorgung Grossdeutschlands und Kontinentaleuropas mit Mineralölerzeugnissen während der gegenwärtigen kriegerischen Verwicklungen," p. 4, NARS T-84/72/1358247.

14. OKW Economic Staff, "Die Arbeiten des Wi Rü Amtes an der Mineralöl—Versorgung," p. 37, NARS T-77/282/1107267.

15. Reichswirtschaftsministerium, 1943, "Tätigkeitsbericht: Buna Erzeugung," NARS T-71/109/611976.

16. Institut für Weltwirtschaft, "Die Eisenerzversorgung Grossdeutschlands während der gegenwärtigen kriegerischen Verwicklungen," December 1939, pp. 2-3, NARS T-84/195/1560527.

17. Wehrwirtschafts—Inspektor VI, 2.4.38., Nr. 206/38, "Wehrwirtschaftliche Übungsreise 1938," NARS T-77/539/1713054.

18. Jäger, *Die wirtschaftliche Abhängigkeit des Dritten Reiches*, p. 73.

19. IMT, *TMWC*, XXXVI, Doc 028EC, p. 123. For the Swedish iron ore question see the following: Rolf Karlborn, "Sweden's Iron Ore Exports to Germany, 1933-1944," *Scandinavian Economic History Review* (SEHR) 13, no. 1 (1965), and "Swedish Iron Ore Exports to Germany, A Reply," *SEHR* 16 (1968); A. S. Milward, "Could Sweden Have Stopped the Second World War?," *SEHR* 15 (1967); and for the most reasoned discussion: J. J. Jäger, "Sweden's Iron Ore Exports to Germany, 1933-1944," *SEHR* 15 (1967).

20. Reichsstelle für Wirtschaftsausbau, "Sofortmassnahmen im Mob-Fall auf Grund der heutigen Versorgungslage auf den Rohstoffgebieten, 3. Sachgebiet, Eisen und Stahl, 1938," p. 42, NARS T-71/108/611495.

21. Reichsamt für wehrwirtschaftliche Planung, März 1939, "Die rohstoffwirtschaftliche Bedeutung des Südostraumes für die deutsche Wehrwirtschaft," p. 23, NARS T-84/80.

22. Jäger, *Die wirtschaftliche Abhängigkeit des Dritten Reiches*, p. 89.

23. Ibid., pp. 81, 286.

24. OKW, Berlin, 11.10.38., Wehrwirtschaftsstab, "Wehrwirtschaftliche Bedeutung des sudetendeutschen Gebietes," NARS T-77/657/185753; Reichsamt für wehrwirtschaftliche Planung, März 1939, "Die rohstoffwirtschaftliche Bedeutung des Südostraumes für die deutsche Wehrwirtschaft," NARS T-84/80.

25. Vortrag des Oberst Gautier, Wehrmachtsakademie, 7.2.38., p. 19a, NARS T-84/169/1537319.

26. The Kiev and Leningrad thrusts of 1941 and the Caucasus strategy of 1942 spring immediately to mind. For the direct effect of fuel shortages on German naval strategy see: Wilhelm Meier-Dörnberg, *Ölversorgung der Kriegsmarine, 1935 bis 1945* (Freiburg, 1973).

27. Klein, *Germany's Economic Preparations for War*, pp. 19-21, 51, 79.

28. Ibid., p. 21.

29. Bundesarchiv/Militärarchiv (BA/MA), M 31/PG34162, B.Nr. 7127/38 OKM, Berlin, 25.5.38., Betr: "Schwierigkeiten in der Arbeiterfrage."

30. Klein, *Germany's Economic Preparations for War*, p. 213.

31. Jäger, *Die wirtschaftliche Abhängigkeit des Dritten Reiches*, p. 303.

32. A. Hillgruber, ed., *Staatsmänner und Diplomaten bei Hitler*, Vol. II (Frankfurt am Main, 1970), pp. 100-101.

33. For a fuller discussion of these problems see: Hans-Erich Volkmann, "Aussenhandel und Aufrüstung in Deutschland, 1933 bis 1939," in *Wirtschaft und Rüstung am Vorabend des Zweiten Weltkrieges*, edited by Friedrich Forstmeier and Hans-Erich Volkmann (Dusseldorf, 1975), p. 85.

34. Ibid., p. 89.

35. Ibid., p. 96.

36. Dieter Petzina, *Autarkiepolitik im Dritten Reich* (Stuttgart, 1968), p. 103.

37. Report by General Thomas, OKW Economic Staff: "Stand der wirtschaftlichen Lage," 1.4.37., NARS T-1022/2238/PG33525.

38. Lecture by Admiral Raeder, 1.9.37., NARS T-1022/2106/PG33579; Der Oberbefehlshaber der Kriegsmarine an den Herrn Reichskriegsminister, 25.10.37., NARS T-1022/2106/PG33579a.

39. OKW, "Stand der wirtschaftlichen Lage, 1.5.38," NARS T-1022/2957/PG48902.

40. IMT, *TMWC*, XXXII, Doc 3575PS, p. 413.

41. Ibid., Doc 1301PS.

42. J. Dülffer, *Weimar, Hitler und die Marine: Reichspolitik und Flottenbau, 1920-1933* (Dusseldorf, 1973), p. 504.

43. Volkmann, "Aussenhandel und Aufrüstung in Deutschland, 1933 bis 1939," p. 108.

44. Report by General Thomas, OKW Economic Staff, "Stand der wirtschaftlichen Lage, 1.10.37.," NARS T-1022/2238/PG33525; see also "Stand der wirtschaftlichen Lage, 1.2.37.," NARS T-1022/2238/PG33525.

45. Report by General Thomas, OKW Economic Staff, "Stand der wirtschaftlichen Lage, 1.7.37.," NARS T-1022/2238/PG33525.

46. Volkmann, "Aussenhandel und Aufrüstung in Deutschland, 1933 bis 1939," p. 88.

47. D. C. Watt, "Anglo-German Negotiations on the Eve of the Second

World War," *Journal of the Royal United Services Institute (JRUSI)* (May 1958), p. 202.

48. Gerhard Förster, *Totaler Krieg und Blitzkrieg* (Berlin, 1967), p. 101.

49. Reichswirtschaftsminister, Berlin, 10.8.40., Betr: "Sicherung von Ausfuhrfragen," NARS T-71/118/621477.

50. Volkmann, "Aussenhandel und Aufrüstung in Deutschland, 1933 bis 1939," p. 91.

51. For the best discussion of Hitler's long-range goals see: E. Jäckel, *Hitlers Weltanschauung* (Tübingen, 1969); and Klaus Hildebrand, *Deutsche Aussenpolitik, 1933-1945* (Stuttgart, 1970).

52. For an outstanding discussion of German foreign policy see either: Hans-Adolf Jacobsen, *Nationalsozialistische Aussenpolitik* (Frankfurt am Main, 1968), or Gerhard Weinberg, *The Foreign Policy of Hitler's Germany, 1933-1936* (Chicago, 1970).

53. Klein, *Germany's Economic Preparations for War*, p. 21.

54. See particularly Tom Lilley et al., *Problems of Accelerating Aircraft Production during World War II* (Boston, 1947), p. 5.

55. Anja E. Bagel-Bohlan, *Hitlers industrielle Kriegsvorbereitungen, 1936-1939* (Koblenz, 1975), pp. 11, 106-107.

56. Carroll, *Design for Total War*, p. 73.

57. Bagel-Bohlan, *Hitlers industrielle Kriegsvorbereitungen, 1936-1939*, p. 13.

58. Ibid., pp. 33-34.

59. See, in particular, Klein, *Germany's Economic Preparations for War*.

60. Wilhelm Treue, "Hitlers Denkschrift zum Vierjahresplan, 1936," *Vierteljahrshefte für Zeitgeschichte* 3, no. 2 (1955), p. 184.

61. Reichsstelle für Wirtschaftsausbau, Berlin, 12.7.38., "Wirtschaftlicher neuer Erzeugungsplan vom 12. Juli 1938," NARS T-71/109/611678.

62. Reichsstelle für Wirtschaftsausbau, Berlin, 30.6.38., "Der beschleunigte Plan," NARS T-71/110/613239.

63. Dr. C. Krauch, Berlin, 19.8.38., "Bericht über die veranlassten Massnahmen zur Durchführung des wirtschaftlichen neuen Erzeugungsplanes für die Zeit 1.8.-15.8.38." NARS T-71/110/612645.

64. Dr. C. Krauch, Berlin, 8.9.38., "Bericht über den Fortschritt der Arbeiten in der Zeit vom 15. Aug. bis 1. Sep. 1938 auf dem Sachgebiet des neuen wehrwirtschaftlichen Erzeugungsplanes," NARS T-71/110/612632; Berlin, 7.10.38., "Die zeitige Zementversorgung des Schnellplanes," NARS T-71/110/612615.

65. Reichsstelle für Wirtschaftsausbau, Berlin, 17.8.39., "Schnellplan vom 13.8.38. für die Erzeugung von Pulver, Sprengstoffen und chemischen Kampfstoffen einschliesslich der Vorprodukte," NARS T-71/110/613208.

66. Reichsstelle für Wirtschaftsausbau, Berlin, 7.1.39., "Verzögerung im Schnellplan vom 13.8.38. durch verringerte Stahlzuteilung," NARS T-71/110/613255.

67. OKW Vortragsnotiz: Wa A Nr. 1120/39, Wa Stan Ia, Betr: "Mob—Nachschuberzeugung an Waffen und Munition (Vergleich mit der Weltkriegshöchstleistung), 31.8.39.," NARS T-78/175/6113516.

68. Reichsstelle für Wirtschaftsausbau, 17.8.39., "Schnellplan vom 13.8.38. für die Erzeugung von Pulver, Sprengstoffen und chemischen Kampfstoffen einschliesslich der Vorprodukte," NARS T-71/110/613208.

69. "Bericht des Herrn Professor Dr. C. Krauch über die Lage auf dem Arbeitsgebiet der Chemie in der Sitzung des Generalrates am 24.6.41.," NARS T-84/217/1586749.

70. Charles W. Sydnor, Jr., *Soldiers of Destruction* (Princeton, 1977), pp. 345-346.

71. For a new and groundbreaking look at the issues involved in German rearmament, one should consult Wilhelm Deist's *The Wehrmacht and German Rearmament* (London, 1981) and that author's discussion in part III of Wilhelm Deist, Manfred Messerschmidt, Hans-Erich Volkmann, and Wolfram Wette, *Das Deutsche Reich und der Zweite Weltkrieg*, Vol. I, *Ursachen und Voraussetzungen der deutschen Kriegspolitik* (Stuttgart, 1979). For a work that discusses the intent of Hitler's foreign policy but none of the substantive issues involved in the rearmament process, Germany's economic difficulties, and the Reich's strategic situation, one can consult Gerhard Weinberg's *The Foreign Policy of Hitler's Germany*, Vol II, 1937-1939 (Chicago, 1980).

72. See in particular the testimony of Hitler's chief military adjutant, Friedrich Hossbach, in *Zwischen Wehrmacht und Hitler*, 1934-1938 (Hannover, 1949), p. 39.

73. Michael Geyer, *Aufrüstung oder Sicherheit, Die Reichswehr in der Krise der Machtpolitik*, 1924-1936 (Wiesbaden, 1980), p. 192ff.

74. For a more thorough discussion of these failings see my work on the defeat of the Luftwaffe: *Strategy for Defeat, The Luftwaffe 1933-1945* (Montgomery, 1983), chaps. II and III.

75. Horst Boog, "Higher Command and Leadership in the German Luftwaffe, 1935-1945," in *Air Power and Warfare*, edited by Alfred F. Hurley and Robert C. Ehrhart (Washington, D.C., 1979), p. 129.

76. The author would like to stress that no matter how much he might be impressed by the level of competence displayed by the German army in the Second World War, he has nothing but distaste for the results of this competence.

77. For those who believe that the size of the German army was instrumental in its learning the lessons of the First World War and in preparing

for the next, Robert Paxton's *Parades and Politics at Vichy* (Princeton, 1966) should prove most instructive.

78. For a fuller discussion of these points see: Williamson Murray, "The Change in The European Balance of Power, 1938-1939," Ph.D. dissertation, Yale University, 1975, chap. I.

79. Reichswehrministerium, Chef der Heeresleitung, Betr: "Harzübung, 8.1.22.," NARS T-79/65/000622.

80. See particularly the excellent discussion in Jehuda Wallach, *Das Dogma der Vernichtungsschlacht* (Frankfurt am Main, 1967), p. 342.

81. Dr. Erich Wagner, "Gedanken über den Wert von Kriegserinnerung und Kriegserfahrung," *Militärwissenschaftliche Rundschau*, no. 2 (1937), p. 232. Rommel also makes this claim in his papers. See Erwin Rommel, *The Rommel Papers*, edited by B. H. Liddell Hart (New York, 1953), p. 516.

82. Hossbach, *Zwischen Wehrmacht und Hitler, 1934-1938*, p. 39.

83. Telford Taylor, *The March of Conquest* (New York, 1958), pp. 17, 181. One must note that the terms "panzer" and "armored" are synonymous.

84. Erich von Manstein, *Aus einem Soldatenleben, 1887-1939* (Bonn, 1958), pp. 241-242.

85. For a suggestion that this was a possibility see Zygmunt J. Gasiorowski, "Did Pilsudski Attempt to Initiate a Preventive War?" *Journal of Modern History* 27 (June 1965).

86. Manstein, *Aus einem Soldatenleben*, p. 241.

87. R. O'Neill, "Doctrine and Training in the German Army," in *The Theory and Practice of War*, edited by Michael Howard (New York, 1966), p. 157.

88. Deist, *The Wehrmacht and German Rearmament*, pp. 42-43.

89. For Guderian's prewar criticism of the light-division concept, see: Heinz Guderian, "Schnelle Truppen einst und jetzt," *Militärwissenschaftliche Rundschau*, no. 2 (1939), p. 241; and for combat substantiation of the criticism: 7. Pz. Division (2. Leichte Division), Gera, 19.10.39., Ia Nr. 393/39, Betr: "Erfahrungen bei den Operationen im Osten," NARS T-315/436/000480.

90. For a comparison of how the Germans and the British viewed these attacks see: 7. Abteilung des Generalstabes des Heeres, "Die Entwicklung der deutschen Infanterie im Weltkriege, 1914-1918," *Militärwissenschaftliche Rundschau* (1938), pp. 399-400; and "F.S.B.," "Modern Warfare—Mobile or Missile?" *JRUSI* (November 1939), p. 742.

91. BA/MA, W 10-1/9, Oberstleutnant Matzky, "Kritische Untersuchung der Lehren von Douhet, Hart [sic], Fuller, und Seeckt," Wehrmachtsakademie, Nr. 90/35, Berlin, November 1935, p. 44.

92. Heinz Guderian, *Panzer Leader* (London, 1952), pp. 20-22. The Brit-

ish field manual to which Guderian refers is probably Broad's pamphlet "Mechanized and Armored Formations," which a certain Capt. Stuart sold to the Germans (K. Macksey, *Tank Warfare* [London, 1971], pp. 85-86).

93. Among other important items see: Reichswehrministerium, Berlin, 10.11.26., "Darstellung neuzeitlicher Kampfwagen," NARS T-79/62/000789; Reichswehrministerium, "England: Die Manöver mit motorisierten Truppen, September, 1929," NARS T-79/30/000983; and Der Chef des Truppenamts, Dez. 1934, "England: Manöver des Panzerverbandes, 18. bis 21.9.34.," NARS T-79/16/000790.

94. Public Record Office (PRO) CAB 16/112, DRC 31, 9.10.35., p. 271.

95. Guderian, *Panzer Leader*, appendix XXIV.

96. Guderian, "Schnelle Truppen einst und jetzt," p. 241; Kommando der Panzertruppen, Ia op. Nr. 4300, Berlin, 10.11.36., "Bemerkungen des kommandierenden Generals der Panzertruppen im Jahre 1936 und Hinweise für die Ausbildung 1936-1937," NARS T-79/30/000913.

97. Kommando der Panzertruppen, Ia Nr. 3770/37, Berlin, 15.11.37., "Besichtigungsbemerkungen des kommandierenden Generals des Kommandos der Panzertruppen im Jahre 1937," NARS T-79/30/000937.

98. M. Plettenberg, *Guderian: Hintergründe des deutschen Schicksals, 1918-1945* (Dusseldorf, 1950), p. 14.

99. For further elaboration on this point see my article, "The German Response to Victory in Poland: A Case Study in Professionalism," *Armed Forces and Society* (Winter 1981).

100. See particularly: Klein, *Germany's Economic Preparations for War*; Milward, *The German Economy at War*; and Carroll, *Design for Total War*.

101. Dennis Richards, *The Royal Air Force, 1939-1945*, Vol. I (London, 1953), p. 29. For others who have held this view see: Asher Lee, *The German Air Force* (New York, 1946), pp. 16-17; Herbert M. Mason, Jr., *The Rise of the Luftwaffe* (New York, 1973), pp. 213-215; Peter Calvocoressi and Guy Wint, *Total War* (London, 1972), p. 492; Basil Collier, *The Defense of the United Kingdom* (London, 1957), p. 121; surprisingly, Telford Taylor, *The Breaking Wave* (New York, 1967), p. 83; and Sir Charles Webster and Noble Frankland, *The Strategic Air Offensive Against Germany*, Vol. I, *Preparation* (London, 1961), p. 125. For a groundbreaking look at the Luftwaffe see Wilhelm Deist, Manfred Messerschmidt, Hans-Erich Volkmann, Wolfram Wette, *Das Deutsche Reich und der Zweite Weltkrieg*, Vol. I, *Ursachen und Voraussetzungen der deutschen Kriegspolitik* (Stuttgart, 1979) and Klaus A. Maier, Horst Rohde, Bernd Stegemann, and Hans Umbreit, *Das Deutsche Reich und der Zweite Weltkrieg*, Vol. II, *Die Errichtung der Hegemonie auf dem europäischen Kontinent* (Stuttgart, 1979). Deist's volume, *The Wehrmacht and German Rearmament* (chap. 4) is also excellent on the place of

the Luftwaffe in German rearmament. Also see chap. I in my *Strategy for Defeat, The Luftwaffe 1933-1945* (Montgomery, 1983) and my article "The Luftwaffe Before the Second World War: A Mission, A Strategy?" *Journal of Strategic Studies* (September 1981).

102. Deist et al., *Das Deutsche Reich und der Zweite Weltkrieg*, Vol. I, pp. 480-481.

103. Bernard Heimann and Joachim Schunke, "Eine geheime Denkschrift zur Luftkriegskonzeption Hitler-Deutschlands vom Mai 1933," *Zeitschrift für Militärgeschichte* 3 (1964), pp. 72-86.

104. For a full and excellent discussion of the industrial and engineering problems faced by the Luftwaffe see Edward L. Homze, *Arming the Luftwaffe, The Reich Air Ministry and the German Aircraft Industry, 1919-1939* (Lincoln, 1976), pp. 40-41.

105. Deist et al., *Das Deutsche Reich und der Zweite Weltkrieg*, Vol. I, pp. 478-479.

106. Homze, *Arming the Luftwaffe*, p. 60.

107. See in particular Wever's lecture to the Air War College, 1.11.35., "Vortrag des Generalmajors Wever bei Eröffnung der Luftkriegsakademie und Lufttechnischen Akademie in Berlin-Gatow am 1. November 1935," *Die Luftwaffe* (1936).

108. "Die Luftkriegführung," Berlin, 1935; copy made available to me by Oberstleutnant Klaus Maier of the Militägeschichtliches Forschungsamt, Freiburg, Federal Republic of Germany.

109. Heimann and Schunke, "Eine geheime Denkschrift zur Luftkriegskonzeption Hitler-Deutschlands vom Mai 1933," pp. 72-86.

110. Air Ministry, *The Rise and Fall of the German Air Force (1933-1945)* (London, 1948), p. 42.

111. See in particular the articles dealing with air power in the prestigious journal of the Kriegsministerium, *Militärwissenschaftliche Rundschau*, from its inception in 1936 through to the outbreak of war. The following articles, Oberst (E) Frhr v. Bulow, "Die Grundlagen neuzeitlicher Luftstreitkräfte," (1936); Major Bartz, "Kriegsflugzeuge, ihre Aufgaben und Leistung," (1936); and particularly Major Herhudt von Rohden, "Betrachtungen über Luftkrieg," (1937) are of particular interest.

112. See in particular Karl-Heinz Völker, *Die deutsche Luftwaffe, 1933-1939: Aufbau, Führung und Rüstung der Luftwaffe sowie die Entwicklung der deutschen Luftkriegstheorie* (Stuttgart, 1967) and H. Schliephake, *The Birth of the Luftwaffe* (Chicago, 1971), pp. 38-39. For further amplification on the failure to have a heavy bomber in the later 1930s see Edward L. Homze's excellent piece, "The Luftwaffe's Failure to Develop a Heavy Bomber Before World War II," *Aerospace Historian* (March 1977).

113. For the surprisingly low capacity levels of the German munitions industry in the thirties see "Bericht des Herrn Professor Dr. C. Krauch über die Lage auf dem Arbeitsgebiet der Chemie in der Sitzung des Generalrates am 24.6.41.," NARS, T-84/217/1586749.

114. Deist et al., *Das Deutsche Reich und der Zweite Weltkrieg*, Vol. I, p. 490.

115. Homze, *Arming the Luftwaffe*, pp. 167-168.

116. Conversation with Generalmajor a.D. Hans W. Asmus, Baden Baden, November 7 and 8, 1980 and letter from General Asmus, February 6, 1981.

117. Air Ministry, *The Rise and Fall of the German Air Force*, pp. 16-17.

118. Lehren aus dem Feldzug in Spanien, Einsatz von Schlachtfliegern, aus einer Studie der 8. Abt. des Generalstabes aus dem Jahre 1944; Hans Hennig Freiherr von Beust, "Die deutsche Luftwaffe im spanischen Krieg," 2.10.56., p. 162, Albert Simpson Historical Research Center, Maxwell Air Force Base, Karlsruhe Collection K 113.302.

119. Oberst Jaenecke, "Lehren des spanischen Bürgerkrieges," *Jahrbuch des deutschen Heeres*, 1938 (Leipzig, 1939).

120. Maier et al., *Das Deutsche Reich und der Zweite Weltkrieg*, Vol. II, p. 53.

121. David Irving, *The Rise and Fall of the Luftwaffe, The Life of Field Marshal Erhard Milch* (Boston, 1973), p. 68.

122. International Military Tribunal, *Trial of Major War Criminals*, Vol. XXXVIII, December 140-R.

123. Deist et al., *Das Deutsche Reich und der Zweite Weltkrieg*, Vol. I, pp. 478-479.

124. For an examination of this point the reader is urged to consult Horst Boog's excellent article "Higher Command and Leadership in the German Luftwaffe, 1935-1945," in *Air Power and Warfare*, edited by Col. Alfred F. Hurley and Maj. Robert C. Ehrhardt (Washington, D.C., 1979).

125. One of the surprising elements in the widespread willingness to accept the legend that the Luftwaffe was the "hand maiden" of the army is the fact that Göring never got on with the army. Thus, it seems totally in contradiction with what we know of his personality that he would accept a role that subordinated *his* air force to the army in overall German strategy. Readers who would like a further example of the Luftwaffe's emphasis on waging an independent, "strategic" air war should consult: Chef des Organisationsstabes der Luftwaffe, "Organisationsstudie 1950," NARS T-971/36/0002.

126. See particularly: V. R. Berghahn, *Germany and the Approach of War in 1914* (London, 1973); and *Der Tirpitz Plan: Genesis und Verfall einer innenpolitischen Krisenstrategie unter Wilhelm II* (Wiesbaden, 1971).

127. Unterhaltung, Gen. Stabschef dL und Gen. Stabschef dM, 24.11.38.,

NARS T-1022/2033/PG33046; Ibid., 4.5.38., 20.5.38., NARS T-1022/2048/ PG33272; see also Admiral Guse's comment at the second meeting of the planning committee, BA/MA, II L7/1, OKM A Chef 1615/38, g. Kdos., 27.9.38.

128. Friedrich Ruge, *Sea Warfare, 1939-1945* (London, 1957), p. 27; Michael Salewski, *Die deutsche Seekriegsleitung* (Frankfurt am Main, 1970), p. 43.

129. Salewski, *Die deutsche Seekriegsleitung*, p. 29.

130. BA/MA II M 17/1, Admiral u. Flottenchef Carls, Tender *Hela*, September 1938, "Stellungnahme zur Entwurfstudie: Seekriegführung gegen England."

131. OKM, Berlin, 17.2.38., Vortragsnotiz, NARS T-1022/2033/PG33045; and the Göring-Raeder correspondence on the subject of who was to control the naval air force in NARS T-1022/2033/PG33044.

132. BA/MA M 31/PG34162, Planstudie der Operationsabteilung über den weiteren U-boot-Ausbau.

133. BA/MA II M 17/2, Ob.d.M., Nr. 1992, 17.10.38., "Seekriegführung gegen England und die sich daraus ergebenden Forderungen für die strate-gische Zielsetzung und den Aufbau der Kriegsmarine."

134. BA/MA M 31/PG34 58, Marine Kriegsakademie, Winterarbeit Kptlt. Haack, 1938/1939, "Welche Wege kann die Seestrategie Englands in einem Krieg gegen Deutschland einschlagen und welche strategischen und opera-tiven Möglichkeiten ergeben sich daraus für die deutsche Seekriegführung?"; see also: BA/MA M 31/PG34162, 1. Skl., "Grundsätze für den Einsatz der U-boote"; and Salewski, *Die deutsche Seekriegsleitung*, pp. 25, 47.

135. BA/MA M 17/1, Admiral u. Flottenchef Carls, Tender *Hela*, Sep-tember 1938, "Stellungnahme zur Entwurfstudie: Seekriegführung gegen England."

136. F. H. Hinsley, *Command of the Sea* (London, 1949), p. 37.

137. OKM, Berlin, 3.9.39., "Gedanken des Oberbefehlshabers der Kriegs-marine zum Kriegsausbruch," NARS T-1022/2238/PG33525.

138. Maier et al., *Das Deutsche Reich und der Zweite Weltkrieg*, Vol. II, pp. 221-224.

139. Erich Raeder, *Struggle for the Sea* (London, 1952), p. 331.

140. F. H. Hinsley in his recent book on British intelligence rehashes all the old myths about the Germans creating a "Blitzkrieg" strategy. He argues among other things that the German economy possessed the capacity to expand greatly production in the prewar period, but that it was constrained by Hitler's strategy, etc. See F. H. Hinsley, *British Intelligence in the Second World War*, Vol. I (London, 1979), chap. I.

Notes

II. Britain

1. Arthur Marwick, *The Deluge, British Society and the First World War* (New York, 1970).

2. For a discussion of the assumption underlying British defense and foreign policies during the interwar period see: Correlli Barnett, *The Collapse of British Power* (London, 1972).

3. For an exhaustive discussion of the 1931 crisis see: Christopher Thorne, *The Limits of Foreign Policy, The West, the League and the Far Eastern Crisis of 1931-1933* (New York, 1973). For an examination of Britain's policies in Asia see: C. Bradford Lee, *Britain and the Sino-Japanese War* (Stanford, Cal., 1973).

4. In particular see: Henry Pownall, *The Diaries of Lt. General Sir Henry Pownall*, Vol. I, edited by Brian Bond (London, 1972).

5. See Arthur Marder, "The Royal Navy and the Italo-Ethiopian Crisis of 1935-1936," *American Historical Review* (June 1970).

6. PRO CAB 23/90A Cab 49 (37), Meeting of the Cabinet, 22.9.37., p. 373.

7. PRO CAB 23/87 Cab 5 (37), Meeting of the Cabinet, 3.2.37., p. 155A.

8. PRO CAB 24/259, CP (36), 12.2.36.

9. Sir John Slessor, *The Central Blue* (New York, 1957), pp. 160-161.

10. See Table I-5.

11. It is worth noting that the combination of executive and legislative powers in the hands of the prime minister as well as the punctilious structure of the committee system makes the British documents a joy to work with.

12. In fact this committee would play a role all out of proportion to the relatively junior rank of its members. In nearly every case the Joint Planning Committee would write the reports that the Chiefs of Staff would tender as their advice to the CID and Cabinet. For the most thorough description of the British military system before the war see: Norman Gibbs, *Grand Strategy*, Vol. I (London, 1977).

13. G. C. Peden, *British Rearmament and the Treasury, 1932-1939* (Edinburgh, 1973), p. 68.

14. Stephen Roskill, *Hankey*, Vol. III (London, 1974), p. 419.

15. PRO FO 371/22922, C 1545/281/17, Minute by Sir Robert Vansittart, 10.2.38., criticizing CP 40 (39), "Staff Conversations with France and Belgium."

16. PRO CAB 16/109, 14 Nov. 1933, 1st Meeting of the D.R.C.

17. CAB 24/247, CP 64 (34), 5.3.34. It is worth noting the modest nature of the committee's recommendations. They recommended an increase of no more than £15½ million per year in the defense budget.

18. Robert Paul Shay, Jr., *British Rearmament in the Thirties* (Princeton, 1977), p. 44.

19. David O. Kieft, *Belgium's Return to Neutrality* (Oxford, 1972), pp. 164-166.

20. L. S. Amery, *My Political Life*, Vol. III, *The Unforgiving Years* (London, 1955), p. 292.

21. Martin Gilbert, *The Roots of Appeasement* (London, 1966), p. 21.

22. PRO PREM 1/276, Chamberlain to Halifax.

23. Martin Gilbert and Richard Gott, *The Appeasers* (New York, 1967), p. 52.

24. For an outstanding discussion of the role of war in liberal thought see: Michael Howard, *War and the Liberal Conscience* (New Brunswick, N. J., 1978). The refurbishment of Chamberlain's reputation by so many recent historians is an indication of the fact that many liberal historians have come to understand that Chamberlain basically possessed a liberal Weltanschauung.

25. PRO CAB 23/88, Cab 20 (37), 5.5.37. The two recent works that have extensively investigated the process of rearmament in Great Britian, Peden's *British Rearmament and the Treasury* and Shay's *British Rearmament in the Thirties*, to a considerable extent underestimate Chamberlain's role.

26. See especially: PRO CAB 23/99, Cab 29 (39), Meeting of the Cabinet, 23.5.39., pp. 232-233; CAB 23/100 Cab 36 (39), Meeting of the Cabinet, 5.7.39. As a member of the liberal Cabinet in 1914 Simon almost resigned over the issue of war. In 1916 he resigned from the Cabinet with the introduction of conscription and went to France where he served as a staff officer in the RAF.

27. For a more favorable view of Inskip see: Shay, *British Rearmament in the Thirties*, pp. 138-140, 266-267, 283-284.

28. The documentary evidence is almost too overwhelming to cite. One might consult PRO CAB 21/585, C 2777/1941/18, 29.4.38., for a Henderson dispatch on the limited aims of German foreign policy. This dispatch was circulated to the Cabinet. See also: Cab 21/949, C 2829/1360/18, 10.3.39., Nevile Henderson to Halifax: "Report on Events in Germany During 1938." For an excellent study of Henderson see Felix Gilbert, "Two British Ambassadors: Perth and Henderson," *The Diplomats*, 1919-1939, Vol. II, edited by Gordon Craig and Felix Gilbert (New York, 1966).

29. L. B. Namier, *In the Nazi Era* (New York, 1952) p. 162.

30. Ibid., p. 163.

31. PRO CAB 23/94, Cab 32 (38), Meeting of the Cabinet, 13.7.38., p. 134.

32. *Documents on British Foreign Policy (DBFP)*, 3rd. Ser., Vol. II, Doc 590, 6.8.38., letter from Henderson to Halifax.

33. There is good reason to believe that the Italians were following anti-British policies before the outbreak of the Abyssinian crisis. See the Foreign Office file on Italian activities in Malta in late 1934 and early 1935. PRO FO 371/19535.

34. PRO CAB 21/509, Paper by Maurice Hankey, 18.1.37.; *Hast* and *Rast* were not capitalized in the original by Hankey.

35. PRO CAB 53/9, COS 245th Meeting, 25.7.38., COS Sub-Committee, p. 195.

36. PRO CAB 54/3, DCOS 24, December 1936, Deputy COS Sub-Committee: "Appreciation of the Situation in the Event of War with Germany," (Discussion of COS 513 [JP]).

37. See PRO CAB 53/8, COS/227th Meeting, 19.1.38., COS Sub-Committee, Minutes, Annex: Memorandum by the CNS; CAB 23/90A, CAB 46 (37), Meeting of the Cabinet, 8.12.37.; CAB 53/51, CP 30 (36), 7.2.36., Cabinet, CID, Defense Coordination paper written by Hankey; CAB 16/181 DP (P) 2nd Meeting, 11.5.37., "New Naval Construction," CID, Defense Plans (Policy) Sub-Committee; CAB 16/183A, DP (P) 48, 19.4.39., CID, "The Dispatch of the Fleet to the Far East in the Event of War Against Japan," Memorandum by the DCNS.

38. From the beginning of the Abyssinian crisis the COS and particularly the naval staff under Chatfield gave inflated estimates of Italian military power: See: PRO CAB 53/26, COS 421 (JP), 19.12.35., COS Sub-Committee, "Defense in the Eastern Mediterranean and the Middle East: Report by the Joint Planning Sub-Committee."

39. See Williamson Murray, "The Change in the European Balance of Power, 1938-1939" Ph.D. dissertation, Yale University, 1975, pp. 74-77.

40. PRO CAB 55/8, JP 155, 12.10.36., Joint Planning Sub-Committee, "Appreciation of the Situation in the Event of War against Germany in 1939"; CAB 24/27, 1921/B, 22.4.38., CID, "The German Army: Its Present Strength and Possible Rate of Expansion in Peace and War."

41. Compare the figures for French army strength given in CAB 53/37, COS 698 (Revise), COS Sub-Committee, 28.3.38., "Military Implications of German Aggression against Czechoslovakia"; and CAB 53/40, COS 747 (JP), 15.7.38., COS Sub-Committee, "Appreciation of the Situation in the Event of War against Germany in April 1939: Joint Planning Sub-Committee Appreciation" with the estimate in CAB 55/16, JP 407, 15.5.39., Joint Planning Sub-Committee, "Staff Conversations with Poland."

42. PRO CAB 23/100, Cab 36 (39), Conclusions of a Meeting of the Cabinet, 5.7.39., p. 122.

43. PRO CAB 53/41, COS 765 (Revise), COS Sub-Committee, 4.10.38., "Appreciation of the Situation in the Event of War against Germany."

44. PRO CAB 53/37, COS 698 (Revise), COS Sub-Committee, "Military Implications of German Aggression against Czechoslovakia," p. 149; see also: CAB 53/40, COS 747 (JP), 15.7.38., COS Sub-Committee, "Appreciation of the Situation in the Event of War against Germany in April 1939: Joint Planning Committee Appreciation," p. 40.

45. PRO CAB 53/8, COS/227th Meeting, 19.1.38., COS Sub-Committee, p. 276.

46. PRO FO 371/22915, C 1503/30/17, Minute by Vansittart, 11.2.39.

47. PRO CAB 23/90A, Cab 46 (37), Meeting of the Cabinet, 8.12.37., pp. 265-66; See also CAB 53/8, COS 227th Meeting, 19.1.38., COS Sub-Committee, Minutes, "Memorandum by CNS" p. 294.

48. PRO CAB 53/8, COS/227th Meeting, COS Sub-Committee: Annex, "Memorandum by the Chief of Naval Staff," p. 288.

49. PRO FO 371/21592, Joint Intelligence Center, 16.11.38.

50. PRO FO 371/21593, C 362/36/17, 31.1.38., Eden to Chamberlain; see also CAB 23/92, Cab 5 (38), Meeting of the Cabinet, 16.1.38., p. 135.

51. PRO CAB 16/182, DP (P) 13, 25.11.37., CID, "Strength of the RAF and Air Defense," by Anthony Eden, p. 109.

52. See particularly PRO CAB 24/268, CP 58 (37), 11.2.37., "The Preparedness of War of Great Britain in Relation to Certain Other Powers by May 1937," COS Sub-Committee; and CAB 24/273, CP 283 (37), 19.11.37., "Comparison of the Strength of Great Britain with that of Certain Other Nations as at January 1938," p. 141.

53. PRO CAB 21/587, Circular Telegram to the Governments of Canada, Australia, New Zealand, Union of South Africa, Eire, 28.9.38.

54. PRO CAB 23/83, CAB 3 (36), Meeting of the Cabinet, 29.1.36., p. 43.

55. PRO CAB 53/6, COS/195th Meeting, 15.2.37., COS Sub-Committee, Minutes: Discussion of the Paper "Review of Imperial Defense," COS 553 (JP), pp. 250-251.

56. PRO CAB 54/1, DCOS/11th Meeting, 24.11.36., DCOS Sub-Committee.

57. PRO CAB 53/6, COS/195th Meeting, 5.2.37., COS Sub-Committee, Minutes, p. 250.

58. PRO CAB 55/9, JP 193, 15.1.37., Joint Planning Committee, "Imperial Conference Annex," p. 8.

59. PRO CAB 53/41, COS 766, 16.9.38., COS Sub-Committee, "Appreciation of the Situation in the Event of War against Germany," Minute by the Minister for the Coordination of Defense, p. 101. The military did not consider this question voluntarily.

60. See the outstanding Yale dissertation by Nicholas Rostow, "Towards

Alliance: Thesis and Antithesis in Anglo-French Relations, 1934-1936," Ph.D. dissertation, Yale University, December 1979.

61. Henry Pelling, *Britain and the Second World War* (London, 1970), p. 87.

62. Lord Avon, *The Reckoning* (Boston, 1965), p. 123. I would like to thank Nicholas Rostow for pointing out these quotations and their significance to me.

63. As an example of British insensitivity to French feelings see Chamberlain's reply in December 1938 in the House of Commons that Great Britain had no obligation to come to the aid of France if she were attacked by Italy; PRO FO 371/21593, C 15385, 15505/13/17.

64. See the excellent discussion in Rostow, "Towards Alliance," pp. 136-138.

65. For the best secondary work on this subject see Michael Howard, *The Continental Commitment* (London, 1972).

66. PRO CAB 16/181, DP (P) 1st Meeting, 19.4.37., CID, Defense Plans (Policy) Sub-Committee, p. 2.

67. Ibid., p. 4; see also PRO CAB 21/575, 15.10.37., "French and German Maneuvers," Note by Field Marshal Sir C. Deverell; and CAB 23/93, Cab 21 (38), Meeting of the Cabinet, 27.4.38., p. 201.

68. PRO CAB 53/8, COS/228th Meeting, 28.1.38., COS Sub-Committee, p. 297.

69. PRO FO 371/21597, C 842/38/17, CID Paper 1395-B, 4.2.38., "Cable Communications between the United Kingdom and France."

70. PRO FO 371/21597, C 1459/38/17, CID, "Extract from the minutes of the 310th Meeting held on February 17, 1938."

71. PRO FO 371/21593, C 362/36/17, "Minutes on the Subject of Anglo-French Staff Conversations, January 21-27, 1938."

72. PRO CAB 4/27, CID Paper 1394-B, 4.2.38.; CAB 53/36, COS 680, COS Sub-Committee, 4.2.38.; see also CAB 29/159, AFC 3, "Anglo-French Staff Conversations, 1939, Summarized History of Staff Conversations," 24.3.39.

73. PRO CAB 23/93, Cab 18 (38), Meeting of the Cabinet, 6.4.38., p. 111.

74. PRO CAB 23/93, Cab 19 (38), Meeting of the Cabinet, 13.4.38., p. 152.

75. PRO FO 800/309, Letter from Halifax to Chamberlain, 14.4.38.

76. PRO CAB 23/93, Cab 21 (38), Meeting of the Cabinet, 27.4.38., p. 196.

77. PRO CAB 21/544, Letter from Hankey to Chamberlain, 28.4.38. There is a certain obtuseness to Hankey's comment because an extension of the Maginot line carried with it the implication that the French were writing

the Belgians off—an action that would have been disastrous for British interests in the Low Countries.

78. PRO FO 371/21595, C 4050/36/17, Cab 21 (38), Meeting of the Cabinet, 27.4.38.

79. PRO FO 371/21595, C 7006/36/17, CP 153 (38), 1.7.38., "Anglo-French Conversations: Annex II, Naval Staff Conversations."

80. Ibid., Minute by Mr. Strang.

81. PRO CAB 23/90A, Cab 49 (37), Meeting of the Cabinet, 22.12.37., p. 371. As early as 1935 Lord Chatfield argued that because Germany had caused the least harm to British interests she might be detached from the lists of Britain's enemies. CAB 16/112, DRC/25th Meeting, 12.11.35., CID, Defense Requirements Sub-Committee, p. 196.

82. PRO CAB 23/90A, Cab 46 (37), Meeting of the Cabinet, 8.12.37., pp. 266-267.

83. Peden, *British Rearmament and the Treasury*, p. 69.

84. Quoted in N. Thompson, *The Anti-Appeasers* (Oxford, 1971), pp. 156-157.

85. PRO CAB 53/8, COS/227th Meeting, 19.1.38., COS Sub-Committee, Minutes, p. 275.

86. PRO CAB 24/270, CP 165 (37), "Defense Expenditures," 25.6.37., p. 271.

87. Ibid., p. 271 and CAB 23/89, Cab 33 (37), Meeting of the Cabinet, 29.7.37., p. 128.

88. See Peden, *British Rearmament and the Treasury*, and Shay, *British Rearmament in the Thirties*.

89. It should be noted that in February 1939 Chamberlain would agree to a continental commitment, but only most unwillingly and only after great pressure from within and without the Cabinet.

90. Peden, *British Rearmament and the Treasury*, p. 97.

91. Ibid., p. 100.

92. This is not to say that the Canadian and U.S. navies would not play an important role, but the Royal Navy would carry the bulk of the struggle from September 3, 1939 through May 7, 1945.

93. Stephen Roskill, *Naval Policy Between the Wars*, Vol. I, *The Period of Anglo-American Antagonism, 1919-1929* (New York, 1969), p. 533.

94. For a fuller listing of naval strength see: Murray, "The Change in the European Balance of Power," pp. 91-93.

95. Leslie Jones, *Shipbuilding in Britain* (Cardiff, 1957), p. 125.

96. PRO CAB 24/283, CP 38 (39), 14.2.39., "Statement Relating to Defense," February 1939, (Cmd. 5944), p. 99.

97. Stephen Roskill, *The White Ensign* (Annapolis, 1960), pp. 24-25.

98. F. H. Hinsley, *Command of the Sea* (London, 1949), pp. 32-33.

99. C.B.A. Behrens, *Merchant Shipping and the Demands of War* (London, 1955), pp. 22, 39.

100. Roskill, *Naval Policy Between the Wars*, Vol. I, p. 539.

101. Russell Grenfell, "Our Naval Needs," *Journal of the Royal United Services Institute (JRUSI)* (August 1939), p. 495.

102. PRO CAB 23/82, Cab 33 (35), Meeting of the Cabinet, 19.6.35., p. 5.

103. PRO CAB 4/26, 1318-B, 24.3.37., CID, "Defense Against Submarine Attack," p. 5.

104. Ibid., p. 39.

105. PRO CAB 47/12, ATB (EPG), 10th Meeting, 11.11.38., CID, Advisory Committee on Trade Questions in Time of War Sub-Committee.

106. Russell Grenfell, *Sea Power in the Next War* (London, 1938), pp. 60-61.

107. Roskill, *Naval Policy Between the Wars* Vol. I, pp. 346, 536-537.

108. D. Macintyre, *The Battle of the Atlantic* (London, 1965), pp. 25-26.

109. Grenfell, "Our Naval Needs," p. 493.

110. Ibid., pp. 494-495.

111. Even with the experience of the Second World War not all air-power advocates were convinced that aircraft carriers were a useful weapon. See Slessor, *The Central Blue*, p. 192.

112. Arthur Hezlet, *Aircraft and Seapower* (London, 1970), p. 112.

113. Ibid., p. 80.

114. Roskill, *Naval Policy Between the Wars*, Vol. I, pp. 393-394.

115. R. K. Kemp, *Key to Victory* (Boston, 1958), p. 27.

116. Roskill, *The White Ensign*, p. 29.

117. Grenfell, *Sea Power in the Next War*, p. 66.

118. In particular the Royal Navy would prove most adaptable in its use of intelligence. In particular see: Patrick Beesley, *Very Special Intelligence* (Garden City, N.Y., 1978).

119. Barry D. Powers, *Strategy Without Slide Rule, British Air Strategy, 1914-1939* (London, 1976), p. 100.

120. Supreme War Council, Annex to procès-verbal, Third Session 1-A. Aviation Committee. Remarks by the British representative for the Third Session of the Inter-Allied Aviation Committee held at Versailles, 21st and 22nd July 1918. Trenchard Papers, RAF Staff College, Bracknell.

121. Air Ministry, "Results of Air Raids on Germany Carried Out by British Aircraft, January 1st-September 30th 1918," D.A.I., No. 5 (A.11B, October 1918), Trenchard Papers, RAF Staff College, Bracknell, D-4.

122. Powers, *Strategy Without Slide Rule*, pp. 163-164.

123. Arthur Harris claims never to have heard of Douhet before the Second World War, and Sir John Slessor admits in his memoirs that not only had he never read Douhet but also had never heard of him before the war. Interview with Arthur T. Harris, RAF Staff College Library, Bracknell; Sir John Slessor, *The Central Blue* (London, 1956), p. 41.

124. Sir Charles Webster and Noble Frankland, *The Strategic Air Offensive Against Germany*, 1939-1945, Vol. IV, *Annexes and Appendices* (London, 1961) appendix I, minutes of a conference held in the room of the Chief of the Air Staff, Air Ministry, on 19th July 1923.

125. PRO, AIR 20/40, Air Staff Memorandum No. 11A., March 1924.

126. Ibid.

127. Sir John Slessor, *Air Power and Armies* (London, 1936), pp. 15, 65, 68, 80, 214-215.

128. Guy Hartcup, *The Challenge of War* (London, 1967), p. 126.

129. See particularly the report of Mr. Butt to RAF Bomber Command, "Examination of Night Photographs, 15 August 1941," in Webster and Frankland, *The Strategic Air Offensive Against Germany*, p. 205.

130. PRO CAB 53/40, COS 747 (JP), 15.7.38., CID, COS Sub-Committee, "Appreciation of the Situation in the Event of War Against Germany in April 1939," p. 47.

131. Slessor, *The Central Blue*, pp. 203-205.

132. PRO CAB 21/902, Letter from Sir Warren Fischer to Neville Chamberlain, 1.10.38., p. 4.

133. See in particular the discussion in the COS Committee over this issue in PRO CAB 53/7, COS/198th Meeting, 18.2.37., CID, COS Committee Minutes, p. 31.

134. PRO AIR 2/2964, Headquarters, Fighter Command, RAF Stanmore, 25.6.38.

135. See in particular: Francis K. Mason, *Battle Over Britain* (Garden City, N. Y., 1969), pp. 82-83.

136 John Connell, *Wavell, Scholar and Soldier* (New York, 1964), p. 204.

137. PRO CAB 21/903, 18.11.39., "Bomber Support for the Army," memorandum by the Air Staff; see also the letter from Admiral Lord Chatfield to Chamberlain, 15.11.39., on the air force arguments against the provision of special units for the close support of the army.

138. Major General Evans, "The First Armored Division in France," *Army Quarterly* (May 1943), pp. 57-58.

139. PRO CAB 53/40, COS 747 (JP), 15.7.38, CID, COS Sub-Committee, "Appreciation of the Situation in the Event of War Against Germany in April 1939," Joint Planning Committee Appreciation.

140. See the discussion of the air war in North Africa by Air Chief Marshal Lord Tedder, *With Prejudice* (London, 1966).

141. See in particular: PRO CAB 55/2, JP/127th Meeting, 3.12.36., CID, Joint Planning Committee of the COS Committee, p. 5; see also the argument between Admiral Lord Chatfield and Ellington on the provision of aircraft to protect trade routes: CAB 53/6, COS/190th Meeting, 21.12.36., CID, COS Sub-Committee, Minutes, pp. 240-43; and finally PRO CAB 53/8, COS/221st Meeting, 4.11.37., CID COS Sub-Committee, Minutes, p. 12.

142. In particular see chap. 2 of my dissertation, "The Change in the European Balance of Power, 1938-1939."

143. PRO CAB 24/276, CP 94(38), "Staff Conversations with France and Belgium, Annex II," CID, Extract from Draft Minutes of the 319th Meeting, 11.4.38., p. 157.

144. PRO CAB 63/14, Letter from Sir A. Robinson to Sir Thomas Inskip, Minister for the Coordination of Defense, 19.10.36.

145. Critics of army slowness in developing tanks, such as Liddell Hart and Fuller, failed to take into account the real difficulties that the army faced in the 1920s.

146. Howard, *The Continental Commitment*, p. 32.

147. J.F.C. Fuller, "Gold Medal Essay," *JRUSI* (May 1920).

148. B. H. Liddell Hart, *Paris, or the Future of War* (London, 1925). For a brilliant analysis of Liddell Hart's thought that is critical as well as sympathetic see: Brian Bond, *Liddell Hart, A Study of his Military Thought* (New Brunswick, N.J., 1977).

149. For a fuller discussion see: Murray, "Change in the European Balance of Power," chap. 2.

150. Liddell Hart, *The Tanks*, Vol. I (London, 1959), pp. 292-294.

151. Liddell Hart, *Memoirs*, Vol. I (London, 1965), pp. 249-252.

152. Howard, *The Continental Commitment*, p. 32.

153. Liddell Hart, *The Defense of Britain* (London, 1939), pp. 44-45.

154. Liddell Hart, *Memoirs*, Vol. I, p. 227.

155. PRO CAB 23/88, Cab 20 (37), Meeting of the Cabinet, 5.5.37., p. 180.

156. Kieft, *Belgium's Return to Neutrality*, p. 157.

157. By the end of 1938 the British had begun to wake up to political reality: see particularly: PRO CAB 52/43, COS 811, 19.12.38., COS Sub-Committee, "The State of Preparedness of the Army in Relation to the Present International Situation," Memorandum by the CIGS, p. 39; CAB 53/44, COS 850 (JP), 28.2.39., COS Sub-Committee, "Staff Conversations with the French: Report by the Joint Planning Sub-Committee," p. 218; FO 371/22915, C 1503/30/17, COS 833, "The Strategic Position of France in a European War."

158. PRO CAB 24/275, CP 72 (38), 19.3.38., CID, "The Organization of the Army for its Role in War"; CAB 24/273, CP 316 (37), 17.12.37., "Defense Expenditure in Future Years," Interim Report by the Minister for the Coordination of Defense.

159. PRO CAB 53/43, COS 811, 19.12.38., COS Sub-Committee, "The State of Preparedness of the Army in Relation to the Present Situation," Memorandum by the CIGS, p. 42.

160. PRO CAB 2/7, CID, Minutes of the 308th Meeting held on January 27, 1938, p. 5.

161. B. H. Liddell Hart, *When Britain Goes to War* (London, 1935), p. 275.

162. PRO CAB 21/510, COS 811, 19.12.38., COS Sub-Committee, "The State of Preparedness of the Army in Relation to the Present International Situation," p.8.

163. PRO CAB 2/7, CID, Minutes of the 313th Meeting held on March 17, 1938.

164. See Murray, "Change in the European Balance of Power," pp. 47-51.

165. PRO CAB 54/4, DCOS 64, 8.2.38., DCOS Sub-Committee, "The Establishment of a Special Striking Force for Amphibious Operations," Letter from the DCAS to the Dep. Sec. CID.

166. PRO CAB 54/2, DCOS/30th Meeting, 15.11.38., DCOS Sub-Committee, p. 4.

167. PRO CAB 53/10, COS/268th Meeting, 18.1.39., p. 83.

168. Barnett, *The Collapse of British Power*, pp. 497-99, 502-503, 581.

169. Michael Howard, "The Liddell Hart Memoirs," *JRUSI* (February 1966), p. 61.

170. PRO CAB 24/269, CP 115 (37), 23.4.37., "The Organization, Armament, and Equipment of the Army," Memorandum by the Secretary of State for War, p. 138.

171. Liddell Hart, *Memoirs*, Vol. II, p. 88.

172. "Infantry and Tanks in the Spanish Civil War," *JRUSI* (February 1939), p. 99.

173. Capt. J. M. Lind, "Mobile Warfare in the West—a Myth," *JRUSI* (April 1940), p. 265.

174. B. H. Liddell Hart, *Europe in Arms* (London, 1937), pp. 234-235.

175. Howard, "The Liddell Hart Memoirs," p. 60.

176. Evans, "The First Armored Division in France," pp. 56-57.

177. Liddell Hart, *Memoirs*, Vol. I, p. 101.

178. B. H. Liddell Hart, *Deterrent or Defense* (New York, 1960), p. 186.

179. PRO FO 371/22915, C 1503/30/17, COS 833, "The Strategic Position of France in a European War," late 1938.

180. F. H. Hinsley, *British Intelligence in the Second World War*, Vol. I (London, 1979), p. 113.

181. Except perhaps for the decision to build fighters rather than bombers, and even here the Chamberlain government made its decision on the basis that fighters were cheaper than bombers rather than on any belief in the strategic utility of Fighter Command.

III. THE REST OF EUROPE

1. Winston Churchill, *The Gathering Storm* (Boston, 1948), p. 6.

2. *Documents diplomatiques français* (*DDF*), 2nd Ser., Vol. I, Doc 334, "Réunion chez le général Gamelin," 8.3.36.; Doc 525, "Note du général Gamelin," 28.3.36. Gamelin, however, told his government that the French army was barely equal in strength to the Wehrmacht. It seems likely that this estimate was manufactured as an excuse for inaction.

3. André Beaufre, "Liddell Hart and the French Army," in *The Theory and Practice of War*, edited by Michael Howard (New York, 1966), pp. 133-134; André Beaufre, *1940, The Fall of France* (New York, 1968).

4. For an excellent study of French diplomacy see Anthony Adamthwaite's, *France and the Coming of the Second World War, 1936-1939* (London, 1977). For a less successful review of the military response see Robert J. Young, *In Command of France, French Foreign Policy and Military Planning* (Cambridge, Mass., 1978). Young's study argues that the debacle of 1940 cannot be attributed to the incompetence of Gamelin and the French army. Such a position does not hold up under close analysis, largely because Young's understanding of the basic doctrinal issues that came out of the First World War is faulty. Moreover, his book shows little understanding of what was going on in the other armies of Europe, particularly the German. Thus, studied in isolation, the French army appears as an institution facing insurmountable difficulties, but when compared to other European military institutions, other than the Italian army, its faults are glaring.

5. After the war many historians saw Chamberlain as a weak figure. He was, of course, anything but weak, and no matter what one may think of his policies it is clear that he provided strong, forceful leadership to the British government.

6. Adamthwaite, *France and the Coming of the Second World War*, p. 28. For an excellent discussion of the weaknesses of the French political system see chap. VII of Adamthwaite's work.

7. See Table I-5.

8. Adamthwaite, *France and the Coming of the Second World War*, p. 169.

9. Col. A. Goutard, *The Battle of France* (London, 1958), p. 25.

10. See in particular: F. Gauché, *Le Deuxième Bureau au travail* (Paris, 1953). Gauché, even with the evidence available at the time that he wrote his memoirs, consistently overestimated German strength in the 1930s.

11. For different views that argue that there was not much wrong with French doctrine see: Young, *In Command of France* and Jeffrey A. Gunsburg, *Divided and Conquered, The French High Command and the Defeat of the West, 1940* (Westport, Conn., 1979).

12. Eugène Carrias, *La Pensée militaire française* (Paris, 1963), p. 318.

13. Beaufre, *1940, The Fall of France*, p. 157.

14. Young in his *In Command of France* paints an excessively gloomy picture of France's economic and financial resources. Compared to the Germans the French had relatively few problems. See Young, *In Command of France*, chap. I.

15. *DDF*, 2nd Ser., Vol. I, Doc 525, "Note du général Gamelin," 28.3.36.

16. See R.H.S. Stolfi, "Equipment for Victory in France in 1940," *History* (February 1970), pp. 18-19. Stolfi argues that it was an excellent piece of generalship that placed virtually the whole of the mechanized strength of the French army "in the path of the German advance." It was of course utter folly because there were no reserves left to meet the German breakthrough.

17. See particularly: 1. A.O.K., "Wir halten—Wir stürmen: Beton und Stahl: Kampf und Sieg der 1. Armee im Westwall und Maginot Linie," pp. 22-26, NARS T-312/1/750002.

18. Général Narcisse Chauvineau, *Une invasion, est-elle encore possible?* (Paris, 1940), p. 122.

19. PRO CAB 21/554, C 8758/122/17, Sir E. Phipps (Paris) to Mr. Eden, 22.12.37., Enclosure: Conversation between Col. F. Beaumont-Nesbitt, military attaché and General Billotte.

20. Günther Blumentritt, *Zwischen freiem Operationsplan und ständigen Befestigungen* (Foreign Military Studies, U.S. Army Europe, Historical Division, B-652, 1947), pp. 25-26.

21. Quoted in Philip Bankwitz, *Maxime Weygand and Civil-Military Relations in Modern France* (Cambridge, Mass., 1967), p. 126.

22. Quoted in Paul-Marie de la Gorce, *The French Army* (New York, 1963), p. 271.

23. Robert J. Young, "Preparation for Defeat," *Journal of European Studies* (June 1972), p. 170.

24. See Stolfi, "Equipment for Victory in France in 1940," p. 19.

25. Raymond Serreau, "L'évolution de l'armée blindée en Allemagne de 1935 à 1945," *Revue historique de l'armée* 6 (1950), pp. 68-70. There is a useful series of comparative tables on French and German tanks in Guy Chapman's, *Why France Fell* (New York, 1968), pp. 345-347.

26. See the quotation of a speech by General Estienne given at Brussels May 7, 1921 in Major Eddy Bauer, *La guerre des blindés* (Paris, 1947), pp. 19-20. See also the following article: General Jean Estienne, "Les forces matérielles à la guerre," *Revue de Paris* 1 (1922), pp. 225-238.

27. Beaufre, *1940, The Fall of France*, p. 157.

28. See the excellent dicussion of this in Bankwitz, *Maxime Weygand and Civil-Military Relations in Modern France*, pp. 152-155.

29. Alexander Werth, *The Twilight of France, 1933-1940* (London, 1942), p. 44.

30. *DDF*, 2nd Ser., Vol. I, Doc 82, 18.1.36., "Note de l'État-major de l'Armée pour le Haut-Comité militaire."

31. Assemblée Nationale, *Rapport au nom de la commission chargée d'enquêter sur les événements survenus en France de 1933 à 1945*, II (Paris, 1947). "Séance du Conseil de la Guerre tenue le 15 décembre 1937 sous la présidence de M. Daladier," p. 183.

32. Ibid., "Séance du Conseil supérieur de la Guerre, tenue le 2 décembre 1938 sous la présidence du général Gamelin."

33. Kenneth Macksey, *Tank Warfare* (London, 1971), p. 104.

34. Stolfi, "Equipment for Victory in France in 1940," pp. 11-12. The light cavalry divisions were cavalry divisions in name only. They were a mix of armored and motorized divisions similar to the German light division.

35. Beaufre, *1940, The Fall of France*, p. 43.

36. Ibid., p. 47.

37. OKH, Beurteilung franz. Führer, NARS T-314/373/000907.

38. Marc Bloch, *Strange Defeat* (New York, 1968), p. 30.

39. Beaufre, *1940, The Fall of France*, p. 19.

40. Bloch, *Strange Defeat*, pp. 36, 37, 45.

41. PRO FO 371/23017, C 5178/54/18, CID, DP (P) 44, COS 843, 20.2.39., "European Appreciation: Report by the Chiefs of Staff Sub-Committee on the European Situation, 1939-1940"; Admiral Paul Auphan, *The French Navy in World War II* (Annapolis, 1959), pp. 389-390; and Francis E. McMurtrie, ed., *Jane's Fighting Ships, 1939* (London, 1939), p. 175.

42. Auphan, *The French Navy in World War II*, p. 87.

43. PRO CAB 4/24, 1195 B, 8.10.35, CID, "French Air Force—Present Position in Regard to Expansion and Reequipment," p. 21.

44. PRO FO 371/21596, C 10163/36/17, Wing Cmdr. Goddard, Air Ministry to Mr. Mallet, Foreign Office.

45. The following discussion of Luftwaffe losses in the western campaign is based on the Luftwaffe loss tables drawn up by the quartermaster general: BA/MA, RL 2 III/1025, gen. Qu Abt. (IIIA), "Front-Flugzeug-Verluste," 1940 and on AHB, Translation VII/83, "German Aircraft Losses, September

1939-December 1940." For a fuller discussion of these issues see chap. II of my work: *Strategy for Defeat, The Luftwaffe 1933-1945.*

46. Enzo Angelucci and Paolo Matricardi, *World War II Airplanes* (Chicago, 1977), pp. 29, 39, 125, 251, 263.

47. See in particular: Patrice Buffotot and Jacques Ogier, "L'armée de l'air française dans la campagne de France (10 mai-25 juin 1940)," *Revue historique des Armées* 2, no. 3, pp. 88-117.

48. See the interesting article by J. Curry, "Hawk 75 in French Service," *American Aviation Historical Society Journal* 2, no. 1.

49. *DDF*, 2nd Ser., Vol. VII, Doc 325, 8.12.37., "Procès-verbal de la séance du Comité permanent de la Défense nationale du 8 décembre 1937 tenue au ministère de la Guerre sous la présidence de M. Edouard Daladier."

50. PRO CAB 23/89, Cab 35 (37), Meeting of the Cabinet, 29.9.37., p. 215.

51. PRO CAB 21/575, 15.10.37., "French and German Maneuvers," Note by Field Marshall Sir Charles Deverell on his visit to Europe.

52. See the last section of chap. III of my work *Strategy for Defeat.*

53. Young in his article, "The Strategic Dream: French Air Doctrine in the Inter-War Period, 1919-1939," *Journal of Current History* 9, no. 4 (October 1974), p. 62, argues that the key element in the weakness of the French air force in the late 1930s lay in its failure to evolve a coherent "strategic" bombing doctrine. Although arguments over doctrine contributed to its unpreparedness at the outbreak of war, it is surely an exaggeration to imply that had the French emphasized "strategic" bombing in the early 1930s they could have possessed such a capability at the end of the decade.

54. Ibid.

55. See chap. II of my work *Strategy for Defeat.*

56. What is surprising given the availability of documentary material and the general incompetence exhibited by Italian military forces in the Second World War is the willingness of current scholars to attribute capabilities to the Italians solely on the basis of exaggerated prewar estimates: Among others see: Young, *In Command of France*, p. 138.

57. Report by General Thomas, OKW Economic Staff, "Stand der wirtschaftlichen Lage," 1.7.37., NARS T-1022/2238/PG33525.

58. Militärattaché Rom, 12.4.37., Halbjahresbericht für die Zeit vom 1.10.36.-31.3.37., Anlage 1 zu Bericht Nr. 15/37 vom 12. April 1937, p. 1, NARS T-78/364/6326064.

59. ADAP, Series D, Vol. VI, Doc 459, "Ciano an Ribbentrop," 31.5.39.

60. Conversations between the chiefs of staff of the OKM and the OKL on 4.5.38., report dated 20.5.38., NARS T-1022/2048/PG33272.

61. Anlage 10, W.S. Ab Nr 959/38, 13.4.38., pp. 9-29, NARS T-77/959/

1712888; and speech by Korvettenkapitän Haensel, 4.3.39., während des Kriegsspieles des Marinekommandoamtes in Oberhof, NARS T-1022/2821/PG49089.

62. Study in Oberst Dr. Hedler of Wi Rü Amt Stab, "Mineralöl und die Versorgungslage im Kriege," 31.8.41., p. 77, NARS T-77/438/1301640.

63. ObdM, Berlin, 26.4.38., An das OKW, Betr: "Unterlagen für die Wünsche der Kriegsmarine für die Zusammenarbeit mit der italienischen Wehrmacht im Frieden und im Falle eines Krieges bei dem Italien zumindesten wohlwollend neutral ist," NARS T-1022/2130/PG33316.

64. Marineattaché Rom, 2.2.40., An OKM/MAH, B. Nr 386/40, Betrifft: "Militärische Betrachtungen zur Lage in Italien," NARS T-1022/2519/PG45170.

65. MacGregor Knox, *Mussolini Unleashed* (London, 1982), p. 31.

66. For a refutation of the legend that there was a period in the 1920s during which a "good" Mussolini cooperated in the maintenance of the European order see: Alan Cassals, *Mussolini's Early Diplomacy* (Princeton, 1970).

67. Knox, *Mussolini Unleashed*, pp. 38-39.

68. Ibid., pp. 3-4.

69. Ibid., pp. 7-8, 16-18.

70. Bernard MacGregor Knox, "1940. Italy's 'Parallel War,' " Yale University, Ph.D. dissertation, 1976, p. 27.

71. For a general discussion of the Italian disaster in Greece see: Mario Cervi, *The Hollow Legions* (New York, 1971); and Knox, *Mussolini Unleashed*, chaps. 5 and 6.

72. General Enno von Rintelen, *Italian-German Cooperation, Oct. 1936-Nov. 1940* (Foreign Military Studies, U.S. Army Europe, B-495, 1947), p.3; General Enno von Rintelen, *Mussolini als Bundesgenosse* (Stuttgart, 1951), pp. 21-24.

73. Militärattaché Rom, 12.4.37., Anlage 1 zu Bericht Nr. 15/37 vom 12.4.37., Betr: "Halbjahresbericht für die Zeit vom 1.10.36.-31.3.37.," p. 12, NARS T-78/364/6326064; 20.10.37., Nr. 175/37 Anlage 1 zu Bericht Nr. 37 vom 22.10.37., Betr: "Halbjahresbericht für die Zeit vom 1.4.-30.9.37.," pp. 8-9, NARS T-78/364/6325717.

74. Militärattaché Rom, 8.4.37., Nr. 36/37 Betr: "Italienische Auffassung über die Niederlage bei Guadalajara," NARS T-73/364/6326099.

75. Knox, *Mussolini Unleashed*, p. 28.

76. Amt Ausland Abwehr, Ag Ausland Nr. 438/44, Ausl. 1 (D 3), An W F St/VO Ag Ausland, Betr: "Italienische Denkschrift aus militärischen Akten Rom, 20.2.44.," German translation of a report by an unnamed Italian general, NARS T-1022/2501/PG45026.

77. Rintelen, *Mussolini als Bundesgenosse*, p. 66.

78. Amt Ausland Abwehr, Ag Ausland Nr. 438/44, Ausl. 1 (D 3), An W F St/VO Ag Ausland, Betr: "Italienische Denkschrift aus militärischen Akten Rom, 20.2.44.," NARS T-1022/2501/PG45026.

79. Capitano di Vascello G. Fioravanzo, German translation of his work, p. 10, NARS T-1022/3016/PG48834.

80. Rintelen, *Mussolini als Bundesgenosse*, p. 55.

81. Militärattaché Rom, Conversation with General Pariani, 5.5.39., Abschrift, NARS T-1022/2130/PG33316.

82. Marineattaché Rom, Bericht Nr. G 1464, 16.5.40., Betr: "Rede des italienischen Unterstaatssekretärs für die Marine," NARS T-1022/2537/PG145923.

83. Knox, *Mussolini Unleashed*, p. 26.

84. Eugene Dollman, *The Interpreter* (London, 1967), p. 122.

85. Heinz Heggenreiner, *Kämpfe vor Eintreffen der deutschen Truppen unter Marschall Graziani* (Foreign Military Studies, U.S. Army Europe, D-216, 1947), pp. 5-9.

86. Knox, *Mussolini Unleashed*, p. 30.

87. Hans Meier-Welcker, "Zur deutsch-italienischen Militärpolitik und Beurteilung der italienischen Wehrmacht vor dem Zweiten Weltkrieg," *Militärgeschichtliche Mitteilungen*, 1/70, p. 65; Galeazzo Ciano, *Ciano's Diary, 1937-1938* (London, 1952), p. 185.

88. OKM, Berlin, 16.6.39., 3. Abteilung, SKL, NARS T-1022/3015/PG48833.

89. Knox, *Mussolini Unleashed*, p. 21.

90. Ibid., p. 26.

91. Marineattaché Rom, 16.6.37., G 71, An OKM, NARS T-1022/3015/PG48832.

92. Marineattaché Rom, "Schlussbetrachtung, 26.7.-28.7.38.," NARS T-1022/2007/PG33745.

93. Marineattaché Rom, Anlage 8 zur Schlussbetrachtung, 26.7.-28.7.38., NARS T-1022/2007/PG33745.

94. Knox, *Mussolini Unleashed*, p. 20.

95. Marineattaché Rom, 17.3.38., Nr. G 457, Bericht G 450, An OKM, AA, Betr: "Kammerdebatte Marinehaushalt," NARS T-1022/3015/PG48833; see also R. J. Minney, ed., *The Private Papers of Hore Belisha* (London, 1960), p. 115.

96. Knox, *Mussolini Unleashed*, pp. 24-25.

97. Aldo Fraccaroli, "The Italian Navy in the Last War," *JRUSI* (1948), p. 440.

98. The fact that no part of the Mediterranean was out of range of shore-based aircraft made it much more difficult to wage a submarine war.

99. Marineattaché Rom, 16.7.37., G 71, An OKM, Betr: "Besuch des Reichskriegsministers," NARS T-1022/3015/PG48832.

100. Marineattaché Rom, 4.8.39., Kapitänleutnant Oehrn, NARS T-1022/2007/PG33745.

101. Ufficio Storico delle Marina Militare, *Le Marina Italiana nella Seconda Guerra Mondiale*, Vol. XXI (Rome, 1972), p. 82.

102. Friedrichshafen meeting between Raeder and Cavagnari, 21.6.39., NARS T-1022/3016/PG33746.

103. Marineattaché Rom, 7.7.39., B.NR. 1419, An OKM, Betr: "Äusserungen des italienischen Admirals Sansonetti in kleinem Kreise," NARS T-1022/2519/PG45170; see also Galeazzo Ciano, *The Ciano Diaries, 1939-1943* (New York, 1946), pp. 95-96.

104. Verbindungsstab beim Admiralstab der kgl. ital. Marine, 10.7.40., Militärischer Bericht Nr. 2., "Operation der italienischen Kriegsmarine zur Überführung eines wichtigen Transportes nach Libyen (Bengasi)," p. 17, NARS T-1022/1773/PG32211; for further intelligence reports on the battle see: Marineattaché Rom, 12.7.40., an das OKM und OKW, Betr: "Italienisches Seegefecht am 9.7. im ionischen Meer," NARS T-1022/2537/PG45923.

105. Ibid., "Operation der italienischen Kriegsmarine," p. 17.

106. Luftattaché Rom, 8.12.38., B. Nr. 133/38, Anlage 1 z. L-Ber. Nr. 39/38, Rom-Berlin, 13.12.38., "Die luftstrategische Lage Italiens im Herbst 1938," p. 6, NARS T-1022/1892/PG32937. Sicily and Sardinia had only four air bases by the end of 1938.

107. Ibid., p. 1.

108. Intelligence Report, 9.3.39., Gen St d Lw, NARS T-1022/1892/PG32937.

109. Marineattaché Rom, 16.6.37., G 71, An OKM, Betr: "Besuch des Reichskriegsministers," pp. 11-12, NARS T-1022/3015/PG48832.

110. Marineattaché Rom, 14.7.38., Nr. 193/38, Anlage 1 zu Bericht Nr. 20/38 vom 15.7.38., Betr: "Bericht über den Besuch General Parianis beim Ob.d.L.," pp. 1-2, NARS T-1022/365/6326706.

111. Luftattaché Rom, 8.12.38., B.Nr. 133/38, Anlage 1 zu L-Ber. Nr. 39/38, Rom-Berlin, 13.12.38., "Die luftstrategische Lage Italiens im Herbst 1938," NARS T-1022/1892/PG32937.

112. Ciano, *The Ciano Diaries, 1939-1943*, p. 147.

113. Further complicating the Polish attitude toward Czechoslovakia was the fact the Czechs had refused to transship French arms supplies across their territory in 1920 when Poland faced defeat from an invading Bolshevik army.

114. Emanuel Moravec, *The Strategic Importance of Czechoslovakia for Western Europe* (Prague, 1936), pp. 40-41.

115. These new divisions did not receive regular division numbers but

because of a lack of parliamentary approval were designated by the names of their commanders.

116. OKH, Generalstab des Heeres, December 1938, NARS T-78/301/6252026. The total cannot be calculated because many reservists formed fortress regiments and other specialized units that did not fit into a divisional structure.

117. OKH, 1.9.38., "Kurze Angaben über den derzeitigen Stand der tschechoslowakischen Kriegswehrmacht," NARS T-79/314/000764.

118. Arbeitsstab Leeb, Merkblatt, "Gliederung für die Ausstattung und Kampfführung einer schnellen Division," p. 1, NARS T-79/24/000260.

119. Ibid., pp. 2-3.

120. OKH, Generalstab des Heeres, December 1938, NARS T-78/301/625031.

121. The Germans felt that the Czech fortifications were so similar to French fortifications that they used photographs of Czech fortresses to illustrate intelligence reports on the Maginot line. OKH, "Der französische Landesbefestigungs-Stand vom 15.3.40.," NARS T-79/16/836-951.

122. OKH, Generalstab des Heeres, December 1938, NARS T-78/301/6252031. For a detailed examination of Czech fortifications in 1938 see: Jonathan Zorach, "Czechoslovakia's Fortifications, Their Development and Role in the 1938 Munich Crisis," *Militärgeschichtliche Mitteilungen* 2/76.

123. NARS T-79/314/00784.

124. OKH, Generalstab des Heeres, December 1938, NARS T-78/301/6252034.

125. PRO FO 371/21770, C 9606/4786/18, Mr. Newton (Prague) to Halifax, Enclosure by the military attaché, 6.9.38.

126. *DBFP*, 3rd Ser., Vol. I, Docs 120 and 129, March 29, 1938 and April 6. Reports by the military attaché.

127. PRO FO 371/21770, C 9606/4786/18, Newton to Halifax, Enclosure by the military attaché, 6.9.38.

128. Ibid., see also *DBFP*, 3rd Ser., Vol. II, Doc 1148, Newton to Halifax, 27.9.38.; see also the interesting personal account: Brigadier H.C.T. Stronge, "The Czechoslovak Army and the Munich Crisis: A Personal Memorandum," in *War and Society*, Vol. I (London, 1975).

129. Hubert Ripka, *Munich, Before and After* (London, 1939), p. 83.

130. For the best analysis of Polish policy see: Anna M. Cienciala, *Poland and the Western Powers, 1938-1939* (Toronto, 1968).

131. PRO CAB 53/50, COS 927, 15.6.39., COS Sub-Committee, "Anglo-Polish Staff Conversations, 1939," Report by the United Kingdom Delegation, p. 144.

132. OKH, Gen St des H., 15.12.37., "Zusammenstellung der wichtigsten

Veränderungen in den fremdländischen Heeren im Jahre 1937," NARS T-79/314/000979.

133. PRO CAB 53/50, COS 927, 15.6.39., COS Sub-Committee, "Anglo-Polish Staff Conversations, 1939," Report by United Kingdom Delegation, pp. 139, 144.

134. Ibid., p. 144.

135. PRO CAB 53/48, COS 881 (JP), April 1939, COS Sub-Committee, "Anglo-French Conversations: Military Implications of the new Situation in Europe."

136. B. H. Liddell Hart, *The Red Army* (New York, 1956), p. 140; and John Erickson, *The Soviet High Command* (London, 1962), p. 585.

137. Erickson, *The Soviet High Command*, p. 351.

138. John Erickson, *The Road to Stalingrad* (New York, 1975), p. 5.

139. For the twisted rationale behind the purges see: Robert Conquest, *The Great Terror, Stalin's Purges of the Thirties* (London, 1968); and Adam B. Ulam, *Stalin, The Man and his Era* (New York, 1973).

140. See G.E.R. Gedye, *Betrayal in Central Europe: Austria and Czechoslovakia: The Fallen Bastions* (New York, 1939), p. 378, for one of the early arguments about the contribution of the Great Purge to the efficiency of the Red Army.

141. Liddell Hart, *The Red Army*, p. 69.

142. *DBFP*, 3rd Ser., Vol. I, Doc 355, Col. Firebrace to Mr. Vereker, 30.5.38.

143. Erickson, *The Road to Stalingrad*, p. 26.

144. PRO CAB 53/48, COS 887, 24.4.39., COS Sub-Committee, "Military Value of Russia: Report," p. 146; CAB 24/286, CP 108 (39), 10.5.39., "Balance of Strategic Value in War as Between Spain as an Enemy and Russia as an Ally," p. 93; CAB 27/624, FP (36), 43rd Meeting, 19.4.39., Cabinet, Committee on Foreign Policy, pp. 295-296.

145. Albert Kesselring, *A Soldier's Record* (New York, 1953), p. 90.

146. PRO CAB 53/48, COS 887, 24.4.39., COS Sub-Committee, "Military Value of Russia: Report," p. 146.

IV. THE LINE OF DEPARTURE:
EUROPEAN BACKGROUND TO THE ANSCHLUSS

1. Martin Gilbert, *Winston S. Churchill*, Vol. V, 1922-1939 (London, 1976), p. 927.

2. *ADAP*, Series D, I, Doc 19, "Niederschrift über die Besprechung in der Reichskanzlei am 5. November 1937 von 16,15-20,30 Uhr," 10.11.37.

3. For the best account in English on German foreign policy during this

period consult Gerhard Weinberg's work: *The Foreign Policy of Hitler's Germany, 1933-1936* (Chicago, 1970).

4. So, one might add, did Winston Churchill. For a full account of Churchill's opposition to Nazism from the earliest days consult Gilbert, *Winston Churchill*, Vol. V.

5. This of course represented the minimum. For a fuller discussion of Hitler's grandiose visions see Klaus Hildebrand, *Deutsche Aussenpolitik, 1933-1945* (Stuttgart, 1970) and E. Jäckel, *Hitlers Weltanschauung* (Tübingen, 1969).

6. For a fuller discussion of the Rhineland crisis see James Thomas Emmerson, *The Rhineland Crisis* (London, 1977).

7. For discussions of the Anglo-German Naval Agreement see: Stephen Roskill, *Naval Policy between the Wars*, Vol. II (London, 1976); D. C. Watt, "The Anglo-German Naval Agreement of 1935: An Interim Judgment," *Journal of Modern History* 28, no. 2 (1956); and Robert Ingrim, *Hitlers glücklichster Tag: Am 18. Juni 1935* (Stuttgart, 1962).

8. For the long-range German attitude toward the Naval Agreement see Weinberg, *The Foreign Policy of Hitler's Germany*, p. 216.

9. See Arthur Marder, "The Royal Navy and the Italo-Ethiopian Crisis of 1935-1936," *American Historical Review* 75, no. 5 (1970).

10. See Weinberg, *The Foreign Policy of Hitler's Germany*, pp. 284-299.

11. Ibid., p. 298.

12. *New Statesman* (August 22, 1936).

13. Alexander Werth, *The Twilight of France, 1933-1940* (New York, 1942), p. 44.

14. Harold MacMillan, *Winds of Change* (New York, 1966), pp. 497-498.

15. Bernard MacGregor Knox, "1940. Italy's 'Parallel War,' " Ph.D. dissertation, Yale University, 1976, p. 23.

16. See the operational ready rates for the Luftwaffe, 1937-1940, in Air Historical Branch, London, G. 302694/AR/9/51/50.

17. Lecture by Admiral Raeder, 1.9.37., NARS T-1022/2106/PG33579; letter from Raeder to Göring, 25.10.37., NARS T-1022/2106/PG33579a.

18. Letter from Blomberg to Göring, 3.9.37., NARS T-1022/2106/PG33579.

19. Report by General Thomas, OKW Economic Staff, "Stand der wirtschaftlichen Lage, 1.2.37.," NARS T-1022/2238/PG33525.

20. See A.J.P. Taylor, *The Origins of the Second World War* (London, 1961) for a very different interpretation of Hitler's intentions.

21. Gordon Brook-Shepherd, *The Anschluss* (Philadelphia, 1963), pp. 11-12.

22. For the Hossbach memorandum see: *ADAP*, Series D, I, Doc 19,

"Niederschrift über die Besprechung in der Reichskanzlei am 5. November 1937 von 16,15-20,30 Uhr," 10.11.37.

23. For the most striking work on Hitler's world view see: Jäckel, *Hitlers Weltanschauung*. For Hitler as an opportunist with long-range goals see: Alan Bullock, "Hitler and the Origins of the Second World War," in *European Diplomacy Between Two Wars*, edited by Hans W. Gatzke (Chicago, 1972). For other important studies of Hitler's foreign policy see: H. Trevor-Roper, "Hitlers Kriegsziele," *Vierteljahrshefte für Zeitgeschichte* (1960); Klaus Hildebrand, *Vom Reich zum Weltreich* (Munich, 1969), and *Deutsche Aussenpolitik, 1933-1945* (Stuttgart, 1970); Axel Kuhn, *Hitlers aussenpolitisches Programm* (Stuttgart, 1970); Andreas Hillgruber, "England's Place in Hitler's Plans for World Dominion," *Journal of Contemporary History* 9, no. 1 (January 1974).

24. *ADAP*, Series D, VII, Doc 192, "Aufzeichnung ohne Unterschrift," 22.8.39.

25. IMT, *TMWC*, XXXIV, Doc 175c, p. 734.

26. See Harold Deutsch, *Hitler and his Generals* (Minneapolis, 1974), pp. 78-85.

27. Gerhard Engel, *Heeresadjutant bei Hitler, 1938-1945*, edited by Hildegard von Kotze (Stuttgart, 1975), p. 20.

28. For the most thorough discussions of the Fritsch-Blomberg crisis see Deutsch, *Hitler and his Generals*; Jost Dülffer, "Überlegungen von Kriegsmarine und Heer zur Wehrmachtsspitzengliederung und Führung der Wehrmacht im Krieg im Februar-März 1938," *Militärgeschichtliche Mitteilungen*, 1/71; Klaus-Jürgen Müller, *Das Heer und Hitler* (Stuttgart, 1969); and R. J. O'Neill, *The German Army and Nazi Party* (London, 1966).

29. Deutsch, *Hitler and his Generals*, pp. 251-252.

30. It is worth noting that although some historians have seen this as an extraordinary decision, it was not. After all, Daladier held the positions of premier and defense minister throughout his time in office as did Winston Churchill.

31. Deutsch, *Hitler and his Generals*, pp. 221-222, 227-228.

32. For the most complete discussion of the purge and the movement in military ranks see: Telford Taylor, *Munich* (Garden City, N.Y., 1979), pp. 324-327.

33. Taylor dates the meeting as February 5 and Deutsch, as February 4. Taylor, *Munich*, p. 327; Deutsch, *Hitler and his Generals*, pp. 263-264.

34. 10. Division, Ia, 3.2.38., "Kommandeursbesprechung in Nürnberg am 7.2.38." NARS T-79/221/000115.

35. Deutsch, *Hitler and his Generals*, pp. 216-218.

36. Ibid., p. 401.

---

37. IMT, *TMWC*, XXVIII, Doc 1780-PS, Jodl Diary entry for January 31, 1938.

38. *ADAP*, Series D, I, Doc 294, "Protokoll über die Besprechung vom 12. Februar 1938."

39. In the accord of July 11, 1936, the Germans promised not to interfere in the internal affairs of Austria, and Austria agreed to mold her policy around the principle that she was a "German state." *ADAP*, Series D, I, Doc 152, "Das Deutsch-Österreichische Abkommen vom 11. Juli 1936."

40. Telford Taylor, *Sword and Swastika, Generals and Nazis in the Third Reich* (New York, 1952), p. 180.

41. Erich von Manstein, *Aus einem Soldatenleben, 1887-1939* (Bonn, 1958), p. 322.

42. Ibid., pp. 320-325.

43. Deutsch, *Hitler and his Generals*, pp. 341-343; and Wilhelm Deist, Manfred Messerschmidt, Hans-Erich Volkmann, and Wolfram Wette, *Das Deutsche Reich und der Zweite Weltkrieg*, Vol. I, *Ursachen und Voraussetzungen der deutschen Kriegspolitik* (Stuttgart, 1979), p. 636.

44. J. Dülffer, "Weisungen an die Wehrmacht 1938/1939 als Ausdruck ihrer Gleichschaltung," *Wehrwissenschaftliche Rundschau* (November/December 1968), p. 654.

45. Taylor, *Sword and Swastika*, p. 181.

46. IMT, *TMWC*, XX, p. 604.

47. Heeresgruppenkommando 3., Ia Nr. 400/38, 18.7.38., "Der Einsatz der 8. Armee im März 1938 zur Wiedervereinigung Österreichs mit dem deutschen Reich," pp. 1-2, NARS T-79/14/000447.

48. Ibid., p. 3.

49. Ibid., p. 3.

50. Generalkommando XIII A.K., Ib Nr 1500/38 geh. Kdos., Nürnberg, 6.5.38., "Erfahrungsbericht über den Einsatz Österreich, März/April 1938," pp. 1-5, NARS T-314/525/00319.

51. Heeresgruppenkommando 3., Ia Nr. 400/38, 18.7.38., "Der Einsatz der 8. Armee im März 1938 zur Wiedervereinigung Österreichs mit dem deutschen Reich," p. 3, NARS T-79/14/447; see also 27. Div., Augsburg, 21.4.38., "Erfahrungsbericht," p. 15, NARS T-79/14/000575.

52. 27. Div., Augsburg, 21.4.38., "Erfahrungsbericht," p. 38, NARS T-79/14/000575.

53. 7. Div., München, 29.4.38., Betr.: "Erfahrungen grundsätzlicher Art," NARS T-79/14/000694.

54. Generalkommando XIII A.K., Ib Nr 1500/38, "Erfahrungsbericht über den Einsatz Österreich, März/April 1938," Nürnberg, 6.5.38., p. 37, NARS T-314/525/000319.

55. Wehrsatzinspektion Nürnberg, 26.4.38., "Erfahrungen beim Einsatz Österreich," p. 9, NARS T-79/275/000001.

56. 7. Div., München, 29.4.38., NARS T-79/15/000227.

57. Stab. Geb. Jäg, Regt 100, Bad Reichenhall, 8.4.38., "Erfahrungen bei der Probemobilmachung," pp. 2-3, NARS T-79/14/000671.

58. Landwehr Kommandeur, München, 22.4.38., "Erfahrungsbericht über den Einsatz Österreich," pp. 9-13, NARS T-79/253/000071.

59. Ibid., p. 32.

60. Generalkommando XIII A.K., lb Nr 1500/38, Nürnberg, 6.5.38., "Erfahrungsbericht über den Einsatz Österreich, März/April 1938, Anlage 3, Landwehr Inf. Rgt. 119, 21.3.38.," p. 4, NARS T-314/525/000319.

61. Wehrsatzinspektion Nürnberg, "Erfahrungen beim 'Einsatz Österreich,' " p. 17, NARS T-79/275/000001.

62. Generalkommando XIII A.K., Ib Nr 1500/38, Nürnberg, 6.5.38., "Erfahrungsbericht über den Einsatz Österreich, März/April 1938," p. 12, NARS T-314/525/000319.

63. Ibid., p. 10.

64. 27. Div., Augsburg, 21.4.38., "Erfahrungsbericht," NARS T-79/14/000575.

65. I/AR 608 Landsberg 11.4.38., "Erfahrungsbericht," p. 43, NARS T-79/14/000516.

66. 7. Div., München, 29.4.38., NARS T-79/15/000516.

67. Wehrsatzinspektion Nürnberg: Erfahrungen beim "Einsatz Österreich," 26.4.38., NARS T-79/275/000001; see also Generalkommando XIII A.K., Nürnberg, 20.4.38., Betr.: "Mob. Erfahrungen," p. 10, NARS T-79/223/000509.

68. Generalkommando XIII A.K., Ib Nr 1500/38, Nürnberg, 6.5.38., "Erfahrungsbericht über den Einsatz Österreich, März/April 1938," p. 58, NARS T-314/525/000319.

69. Heeresgruppenkommando 3., Ia Nr. 400/38, 18.7.38., "Der Einsatz der 8. Armee im März 1938 zur Wiedervereinigung Österreichs mit dem deutschen Reich," pp. 11-12, NARS T-79/14/000447.

70. Generalkommando XIII A.K., Ib Nr 1500/38, "Erfahrungsbericht über den Einsatz Österreich, März/April 1938," p. 59, NARS T-314/525/000319.

71. Heeresgruppenkommando 3., Ia Nr. 400/38, 18.7.38., "Der Einsatz der 8. Armee im März 1938 zur Wiedervereinigung Österreichs mit dem deutschen Reich," p. 12, NARS T-79/14/000447.

72. Ibid., pp. 26-27.

73. *DBFP*, 3rd Ser., Vol. I, Doc 37, 11.3.38., Henderson to Halifax.

74. G.E.R. Gedye, *Betrayal in Central Europe* (New York, 1939), p. 304.

75. Heinz Guderian, *Panzer Leader* (London, 1952), pp. 36-37.

76. Adolf Hitler, *Hitler's Secret Conversations, 1941-1944* (New York, 1961), p. 207.

77. Generalkommando XIII A.K., Ib Nr 1500/38, Nürnberg, 6.5.38., "Erfahrungsbericht über den Einsatz Österreich, März/April 1938, Anlage 5, Auszug aus den Erfahrungen des I./Panzer Regiment 25," NARS T-79/204/001076.

78. 7. Div., München, 29.4.38., "Kurze Darstellung der Ereignisse (Einsatz Österreich)," p. 14, NARS T-79/15/000022.

79. Heeresgruppenkommando 3., Ia Nr. 400/38, 18.7.38., "Der Einsatz der 8. Armee im März 1938 zur Wiedervereinigung Österreichs mit dem deutschen Reich," p. 21, NARS T-79/14/000447.

80. Generalkommando XIII A.K., Ib Nr 1500/38, Nürnberg, 6.5.38., "Erfahrungsbericht über den Einsatz Österreich, März/April 1938," p. 62, NARS T-314/525/000319.

81. 27. Div., Augsburg, 21.4.38., "Erfahrungsbericht," p. 36, NARS T-79/14/000575.

82. 7. Div., München, 29.4.38., "Erfahrungen grundsätzlicher Art," NARS T-79/16/000696.

83. Generalkommando XIII A. K., Nürnberg, 6.5.38., Ib Nr. 1500/38, "Erfahrungsbericht über den Einsatz Österreich, März/April 1938," p. 11, NARS T-79/274/000899.

84. 1. Gebirgs Div., München, 19.4.38., "Auszug aus dem K.T.B. der 1. Gebirgs Div. 'Einsatz Österreich' 10.3.38-2.4.38.," p. 5, NARS T-79/15/000242.

85. Armeeoberkommando 8., Wien, 18.3.38., "Armeetagesbefehl Nr. 5," NARS T-79/15/000380.

86. Generalkommando XIII A.K., Ib Nr 1500/38, Nürnberg, 6.5.38., "Erfahrungsbericht über den Einsatz Österreich, März/April 1938," p. 54, NARS T-314/525/000319.

87. Der kommandierende General des VII. Armeekorps, Nr. 2918/38, München, 19.4.38., Betr: "Erfahrungen aus 'Einsatz Österreich' hier: Ausführung von Befehlen," NARS T-79/15/000225. General Schobert obviously did not know much about military history, because General François displayed anything but unconditional obedience during the battle.

88. Heeresgruppenkommando 3., Ia Nr. 400/38 g.Kdos., 18.7.38., "Der Einsatz der 8. Armee im März 1938 zur Wiedervereinigung Österreichs mit dem deutschen Reich," p. 22, NARS T-79/14/000447.

89. Ibid., pp. 17-20.

90. Knox, "1940. Italy's 'Parallel War,' " p. 64.

91. Deist et al., *Das Deutsche Reich und der Zweite Weltkrieg*, Vol. I (Stuttgart, 1979), p. 325.

92. Ibid., p. 325.

93. W. Sorgel, *Metallindustrie und Nationalsozialismus* (Frankfurt am Main, 1965), p. 68.

94. Norbert Schausberger, "Die Bedeutung Österreichs für die deutsche Rüstung während des Zweiten Weltkrieges," *Militärgeschichtliche Mitteilungen*, 1/72, pp. 60, 62, 81.

95. Deist et al., *Das Deutsche Reich und der Zweite Weltkrieg*, Vol. I, pp. 323-324.

96. OKW, W. Stab W WI, Nr. 1005/38, April 1938, "Wehrwirtschaftliche Bedeutung der Eingliederung Österreichs," pp. 2a, 12b, 13, 18, NARS T-77/657/1856817.

97. Heeresgruppenkommando 3., Ia Nr. 400/38, 18.7.38., "Der Einsatz der 8. Armee im März 1938 zur Wiedervereinigung Österreichs mit dem deutschen Reich," p. 21, NARS T-79/14/000447.

98. *DBFP*, 3rd Ser., Vol. I, Doc 111, 23.3.38., Henderson to Halifax, Enclosure by Colonel Mason-MacFarlane.

99. General von Leeb's manuscript diary, made available by Georg Meyer, MGFA, Freiburg.

100. Guderian, *Panzer Leader*, p. 38.

101. Taylor, *Munich*, p. 373.

102. Erich von Manstein, *Aus einem Soldatenleben*, p. 314.

103. Generalkommando XIII A.K. Ib Nr 1500/38, Nürnberg, 6.5.38., "Erfahrungsbericht über den Einsatz Österreich März/April 1938," p. 106, NARS T-314/525/000319.

104. Taylor, *Munich*, p. 577.

105. Knox, "1940. Italy's 'Parallel War,' " p. 62.

V. FROM AUSTRIA TO CZECHOSLOVAKIA

1. PRO CAB 23/92, Cab 6 (38), Meeting of the Cabinet, 19.2.38, p. 183.

2. PRO CAB 23/92, Cab 10 (38), Meeting of the Cabinet, 2.3.38, p. 291.

3. *DDF*, 2nd Ser., Vol. VIII, Doc 304, Annexe, 2.3.38.

4. Anthony Adamthwaite, *France and the Coming of the Second World War, 1936-1939* (London, 1977), p. 80.

5. Ibid., p. 84.

6. PRO CAB 23/92, Cab 12 (38), Meeting of the Cabinet, 12.3.38, pp. 349-350.

7. PRO CAB 27/623, FP (36) 25th Meeting, Meeting of the Foreign Policy Committee, 15.3.38.

8. PRO CAB 53/36, COS 697, 16.3.38, CID, COS Sub-Committee, "Situation in the Event of War Against Germany," p. 104.

9. This should not suggest that they would have produced a more optimistic report had they possessed greater freedom. However, it does indicate that the credit for this gloomy report must be shared by the government as well as by the military.

10. PRO CAB 53/37, COS 698 (Revise) (also see paper DP [P] 22), CID, COS Sub-Committee, "Military Implications of German Aggression against Czechoslovakia," 28.3.38, pp. 145-146.

11. Ibid., p. 146.

12. Ibid., p. 147.

13. Ibid., pp. 150-151.

14. Ibid., p. 151.

15. Ibid., appendix I, p. 153.

16. Ibid., p. 152.

17. Ibid., p. 150.

18. PRO CAB 27/623, FP (36)/26th Meeting, 18.3.38., Cabinet, Committee on Foreign Policy, p. 167.

19. PRO CAB 27/263, FP (36)/27th Meeting, Cabinet Committee on Foreign Policy, 21.3.38.

20. PRO CAB 23/93, Cab 15 (38), Meeting of the Cabinet, 22.3.38., p. 30ff. It is probably on the final comment in the quotation that Gerhard Weinberg bases his strange assertion that "Chamberlain and Halifax at first favored a British commitment," but the documentary sources clearly indicate that they were being disingenuous. See Gerhard Weinberg, *The Foreign Policy of Hitler's Germany*, Vol. II, *Starting World War II*, *1937-1939* (Chicago, 1980), p. 347.

21. See among others PRO CAB 23/93, Cab 21 (38), Meeting of the Cabinet, 27.4.38; and *DBFP*, 3rd Ser., Vol. I, Doc 106, 22.3.38., Halifax to Phipps.

22. *DDF*, 2nd Ser., Vol. VIII, Doc 127, 8.2.38., Note du Secrétariat général du Conseil supérieur de la Défense nationale, "Les données actuelles du problème militaire française."

23. General Maurice Gamelin, *Servir*, Vol. II (Paris, 1947), p. 347.

24. Assemblée Nationale, *Rapport au nom de la commission chargée d'e-quêter sur les évenéments survenus en France de 1933 à 1945*, Vol. I, p. 45.

25. *DDF*, 2nd Ser., Vol. VIII, Doc 331, 7.3.38., M. Daladier, Ministre de la Défense nationale et de la Guerre, au Général Jamet, Secrétaire Général du Conseil supérieur de la Défense nationale, Annexe, "Note sur nos alliés éventuels en cas de conflit et demandes de collaboration à leur adresser."

26. Ibid., Doc 303, Bulletin de Renseignements de l'état-major de l'Armée, 2ᵉ Bureau, 2.3.38., "Les forces militaires polonaises."

27. Ibid., Doc 432, Note du Chef d'Etat-major général de la Défense

nationale et de l'Armée, "Sur les conséquences de la réalisation de l'Anschluss," 14.3.38.

28. Ibid., Doc 446, Procès-verbal, Comité permanent de la Défense nationale, "Séance du 15 mars 1938 tenue sous la présidence de M. Edouard Daladier, ministre de la Défense nationale et de la Guerre, vice-président du Conseil."

29. Ibid., Vol. IX, Doc 121, 6.4.38, Note du Vice-Président du Conseil supérieur de la Guerre, "Relative aux possibilités de l'axe Rome-Berlin."

30. Gerhard Weinberg makes much too much of the supposed willingness of the British government to open staff talks with the French; the documentary evidence suggests overwhelming reluctance on the part of the British (see above, Chapter II). Weinberg, *The Foreign Policy of Hitler's Germany*, Vol. II, pp. 349 and 357.

31. PRO CAB 23/92, Cab 12 (38), Meeting of the Cabinet, 12.3.38., p. 350.

32. PRO CAB 27/623, FP (36) 26th Meeting, 18.3.38., Cabinet: Committee on Foreign Policy, p. 167.

33. PRO FO 800/269, Letter from Cadogan to Henderson, 22.4.38.

34. PRO CAB 27/623, FP (36), 26th Meeting, 18.3.38., Cabinet Committee on Foreign Policy, p. 164.

35. PRO FO 800/313, Letter from Henderson to Halifax, 7.4.38. In May Henderson wrote: "Yet even when I try to imagine that which I feel in my heart to be inevitable and evolutional is neither, and when I think in terms of British interests only, regardless of right or wrong, I still feel that however repugnant, dangerous, and troublesome the result may be or may seem likely to be, the truest British interest is to come down on the side of the highest moral principles. And the only lastingly right moral principle is self-determination. The British Empire is built upon it and we cannot deny it without incalculable prejudice to something which is of infinitely greater importance to the world than apprehensions of the German menace." FO 800/314, p. 49, Henderson to Halifax, 12.5.38.

36. See: PRO FO 371/21715, C 2801/1941/18, Phipps to Halifax, 5.4.38.; FO 800/311, p. 6, Letter from Phipps to Alexander Cadogan, 22.3.38.

37. See particularly PRO FO 800/311, p. 27, Letter from Phipps to Halifax, 11.4.38.

38. PRO FO 371/21595, C 4050/36/17, Cab 21 (38), Meeting of the Cabinet, 27.4.38.

39. PRO CAB 23/93, Cab 22 (38), Meeting of the Cabinet, 4.5.38., p. 235.

40. See particularly PRO FO 371/21719, C 4426/1941/18, Letter to Mr. Somerset Maxwell, conservative M.P. from King's Lynn, from his constituents, 4.5.38.

41. See D. C. Watt, "Der Einfluss der Dominions auf die Britische Aussenpolitik vor München, 1938," *Vierteljahrshefte für Zeitgeschichte* 8 (1960).

42. *DBFP*, 3rd Ser., Vol. I, Doc 164, "Record of Anglo-French Conversations, held at No. 10 Downing Street, on April 28 and 29, 1938."

43. Telford Taylor, *Munich* (Garden City, N.Y., 1979), p. 510.

44. PRO FO 371/21718, C 4213/1941/18, Mr. Newton (Prague) to Halifax, 9.5.38.

45. For what the French told the Czechs see *DDF*, 2nd Ser., Vol. IX, Doc 296, 7.5.38., Lacroix (Prague) to Bonnet.

46. PRO CAB 24/277, CP 127 (38), 24.5.38., "British Influence in Central and South East Europe, Memorandum by the Secretary of State for Foreign Affairs," p. 69.

47. PRO CAB 27/623, FP (36) 30th Meeting, 1.6.38., Cabinet Committee on Foreign Policy, p. 285.

48. Manfred Messerschmidt in his chapter on German military and diplomatic policy after the Anschluss in *Das Deutsche Reich und der Zweite Weltkrieg*, Vol. I, argues that the western reaction to the Anschluss "strengthened Hitler's underestimation of England (p. 638)." This is somewhat unfair, for Hitler's evaluation of Britain and her leaders was very close to the mark. He was only wrong in his failure to believe that Chamberlain would go to war for principle and ignore entirely strategic factors.

49. Letter from the OKW, Abteilung L, Berlin, 28.3.38., NARS T-1022/2048/PG33627.

50. *ADAP*, Series D, Vol. II, Doc 133, 22.4.38., "Aufzeichnung des Majors im Generalstab Schmundt: Grundlage zur Studie Grün."

51. Der Chef des Oberkommandos der Wehrmacht, 20.5.38., L Ia Nr 38/38, g.Kdos., Chefsache, "Entwurf für die neue Weisung 'Grun.' " NARS T-77/1510/000270.

52. Deist et al., *Das Deutsche Reich und der Zweite Weltkrieg*, Vol. I (Stuttgart, 1979), p. 641.

53. On May 16 Hitler asked the OKW staff how many German divisions would be immediately available upon mobilization to march against Czechoslovakia. OKW, Oberstleutnant Zeitzler an Major Schmundt, 16.5.38., NARS T-77/1510/000265-6. The answer was 12.

54. PRO CAB 23/93, Cab 25 (38), Meeting of the Cabinet, 22.5.38., Appendix II: Telegram sent to Sir E. Phipps, 22.5.38.

55. *DBFP*, 3rd Ser., Vol. I, Doc 349, 26-27.5.38, "Notes by Mr. Strang on Conversations with Members of His Majesty's Legation at Prague."

56. *ADAP*, Series D, II, Doc 210, 26.5.38., "Der Botschafter in Paris an das Auswärtige Amt."

57. PRO CAB 23/94, Cab 35 (39), Meeting of the Cabinet, 27.7.38.

58. The British were particularly worried that the press both in Czecho-

slovakia and in the West would unduly upset the Germans; see PRO FO 371/21770, C 5213/4815/18, Circular telegram to the Dominions: Nr. 148, 31. 5. 38.

59. *ADAP*, Series D, Vol. II, Doc 221, 30.5.38., "Der Oberste Befehlshaber der Wehrmacht an die Oberbefehlshaber des Heeres, der Marine und der Luftwaffe, Weisung für Plan Grün;" General Alfred Jodl, *The Jodl Diaries with Annotations by General der Artillerie a.D. Walter Warlimont*, Vol. I (Foreign Military Studies, U.S. Army Europe, P-215), 4.1.37-29.9.38 and 23.8.39-25.8.39, p. 186.

60. IMT, *TMWC*, XXV, Doc 388-PS, Pt. 8, pp. 431-432.

61. BA/MA, M 31, PG 34162, 24.5.38., OKM, Zu B. Nr 7127A.

62. *ADAP*, Series D, Vol. II, Doc 221, 30.5.38., "Der Oberste Befehlshaber der Wehrmacht an die Oberbefehlshaber des Heeres, der Marine und der Luftwaffe, Weisung für Plan 'Grün.' "

63. Der Chef des Oberkommandos der Wehrmacht, 20.5.38., L Ia Nr. 38/38, "Entwurf für die neue Weisung Grün; Der Oberste Befehlshaber der Wehrmacht," 30.5.38., OKW 42/38, LI "Zweifrontenkrieg mit Schwerpunkt Südost (Aufmarsch 'Grün')." NARS T-77/1510/000270.

64. The following discussion is based on Beck memoranda available in the Beck Nachlass, BA/MA, N 28/3,4.

65. See below, chap. VII, for my analysis of the actual strategic situation at the time of Munich.

66. BA/MA, N 28/3, Beck Nachlass: "Betrachtungen zur gegenwärtigen mil. politischen Lage, 5.5.38."

67. BA/MA, N 28/3, Beck Nachlass: "Bemerkungen zu den Ausführungen des Führers am 28.5.38.," 29.5.38.

68. For a statement of this view see: Wolfgang Schumann and Gerhart Hass, eds., *Deutschland im Zweiten Weltkrieg*, Vol. I, *Vorbereitung, Entfesselung und Verlauf des Krieges bis zum 22. Juni 1941* (Berlin, 1974), p. 121.

69. OKW, LIaH, Berlin, 9.6.38., "Kurze Übersicht über die Bewaffnung des tschech. Heeres"; Lla, "Fragen des Führers vom 9.6.38.," NARS T-77/1510/000260.

70. See particularly PRO FO 371/21769, C 5771/4786/18, Minute by Sir Robert Vansittart, and Halifax to Henderson, 15.6.38.; see also *DBFP*, 3rd Ser., I, Doc 393, 10.6.38., and Doc 400, 12.6.38.

71. OKH, Generalstab des Heeres, Az. 3n, 12. Abt. I, Nr 30/38, 1.12.38., Betr: "Auswertung der Spannungszeit über das Verhalten der Armeen Osteuropas in der Spannungszeit 1938," NARS T-78/301/6252034. See also PRO FO 371/21770, C 8373/4786/18, Col. van Cutsem, War Office to F. K. Roberts, 16.8.38. for Czech army strength over the course of the summer.

72. IMT, *TMWC*, XXV, Doc 388-PS, pp. 451-456.

73. OKH,Generalstab d. Heeres, 4. Abteilung, Nr. 1141/38, 10. Abt. Nr. 680/38 g. (Iva), Berlin, 20.5.38, NARS T-79/268/000754.

74. "Berichte des ehemaligen stellvertretenden Chefs des Wehrmachtführungsstabes, General der Artillerie Warlimont," 24.9.45., NARS T-84/271/ 1009; see also comment in BA/MA, N 28/4. Beck Nachlass, Der Chef des Generalstabes des Heeres, An den Herrn Oberbefehlshaber des Heeres, 15.7.38., p. 5.

75. Der ObdH, Berlin, 9.7.38., An den Herrn ObdH der Heeresgruppe 2., p. 3, NARS T-311/42/7052113.

76. Ulrich von Hassell, *The von Hassell Diaries, 1938-1944* (New York, 1947), p. 6. Harold Deutsch in his book *Hitler and his Generals* (Minneapolis, 1974), pp. 220-30, is particularly good on why Brauchitsch was so weak in his dealings with Hitler.

77. BA/MA, N 28/4, Beck Nachlass, Der Chef des Generalstabes des Heeres, An den Herrn Oberbefehlshaber des Heeres, 15.7.38.

78. BA/MA, K 10-2/6, Captain Heye, "Beurteilung der Lage Deutschland-Tschechei, Juli 1938."

79. BA/MA, K 10-2/6, Admiral Guse 17/7 (38).

80. BA/MA, N 28/3, Beck Nachlass, "Nachtrag am 19.7.38."

81. Wolfgang Foerster, *Generaloberst Ludwig Beck* (Munich, 1953), pp. 138-140.

82. Taylor, *Munich*, p. 693.

83. Telford Taylor, *Sword and Swastika, Generals and Nazis in the Third Reich* (New York, 1952), p. 199.

84. Taylor, *Munich*, p. 695.

85. Klaus-Jürgen Müller, *Armee, Politik und Gesellschaft in Deutschland, 1933-1945* (Paderborn, 1979), pp. 96-99.

86. ADAP, Series D, Vol. II, Doc 259, 20.6.38., "Aufzeichnung aus dem Auswärtigen Amt, 8.6.38. an R.M. v. Ribbentrop gegeben"; see also Ernst von Weizsäcker, *Papiere, 1933-1950*, edited by Leonidas Hill (Frankfurt am Main, 1974).

87. For other Weizsäcker memoranda see: Ibid., Doc 304, 21.7.38., "Aufzeichnung des Staatssekretärs"; Doc 374, 19.8.38., "Aufzeichnung aus dem Auswärtigen Amt"; and Doc 409, 30.8.38., "Aufzeichnung des Staatssekretärs."

88. ADAP, Series D, II, Doc 332, "Runderlass des Reichsaussenministers," 3.8.38.

89. In September-October 1930, Beck had defended two of his lieutenants on trial at Ulm for distributing pro-Nazi propaganda in their regiment.

90. Gerhard Engel, *Heeresadjutant bei Hitler, 1938-1945*, edited by Hildegard von Kotze (Stuttgart, 1975), p. 24.

91. Ibid., pp. 25-26. Hitler was quite correct regarding the armament of the Pzkw IV.

92. Ibid., footnote 50, p. 27.

93. Ibid., pp. 27-28.

94. Ibid., p. 28.

95. Foerster, *Generaloberst Ludwig Beck*, p. 141.

96. Manstein claims in his memoirs the meeting lasted two hours; Jodl in his diary states it lasted three. The Jodl figure is most probably correct.

97. Erich von Manstein, *Aus einem Soldatenleben, 1887-1939* (Bonn, 1958), pp. 337-338.

98. Jodl, *The Jodl Diaries*, entry for 10.8.38., p. 206.

99. IMT, *TMWC*, XXV, Doc 388-PS, pp. 460-462.

100. The British government had clear evidence Beck had resigned as early as September 5. Nevertheless, the Chamberlain government minimized reports of internal troubles in Germany. Had the news become public, the British government would have had a more difficult time in maintaining the fiction of overwhelming German strength. See: *DBFP*, 3rd Ser., Vol. II, Doc 775, p. 242, Letter from G. Warner (Berne) to Halifax, 5.9.38.; and Doc IV, Appendix, p. 689, Letter from Mr. S. Stevenson to Strang, 8.9.38.

101. Engel, *Heeresadjutant bei Hitler*, pp. 24, 35.

102. BA/MA, 28/3 Beck Denkschrift, 29.5.38.

103. Deist et al., *Das Deutsche Reich und der Zweite Weltkrieg*, Vol. I, p. 645.

104. *ADAP*, Series D, Vol. II, Doc 145.

105. PRO CAP 27/627, FP (36) 66, 28.6.38., Cabinet Committee on Foreign Policy: "The Objection to Holding a Plebiscite in the Sudeten Areas of Czechoslovakia," p. 85. Feelers made to the Prague embassy on the possibility of a plebiscite met a negative reaction. *DBFP*, 3rd Ser., Vol. I, Doc 349, "Notes by Mr. Strang on Conversations with members of His Majesty's Legation at Prague, 26-27.5.38."

106. PRO FO 371/21723, C 5235/1941/18, Halifax conversation with Masaryk, 1.6.38.

107. PRO FO 371/21788, C 6039/1941/18, Halifax to Phipps, 9.6.38.

108. PRO FO 371/21725, C 6061/1941/18, FP (36) 31st Mtg., Cabinet Committee on Foreign Policy, 16.6.38.

109. PRO FO 371/21729, C 7404/1941/18, Henderson letter to Strang, 20.7.38.

110. *DBFP*, 3rd Ser., Vol. I, Doc 531, 21.7.38., Newton to Halifax.

111. PRO CAB 23/94, Cab 35 (38), Meeting of the Cabinet, 27.7.38., p. 220.

112. See in particular, *ADAP*, Vol. II, Doc 107, 28.3.38., "Vortragsnotiz

über meine Besprechung mit dem Führer der Sudetendeutschen Partei, Konrad Henlein und seinem Stellvertreter Karl Hermann Frank."

113. PRO CAB 23/93, Cab 27 (38), Meeting of the Cabinet, 1.6.38., p. 378.

114. PRO CAB 21/586, Letter from Mr. H. M. Howard to Inskip, 10.6.38.

115. PRO FO 371/21698, C 8881/307/18, Henderson to Sargent, 12.8.38.

116. PRO CAB 53/40, COS 747 (JP), 15.7.38., COS Committee, "Appreciation of the Situation in the Event of War Against Germany in April 1939," Joint Planning Committee Appreciation, p. 43; CAB 4/28, 1449-B, 21.7.38., CID, "The German Army: Its Present Strength and Possible Rate of Expansion in Peace and War." The Joint Planning Committee appreciation appears as CAB 53/40, COS 755, CID, COS Committee, "Appreciation in the Event of War Against Germany in April, 1939."

117. PRO CAB 64/19, Henderson to Halifax, Berlin Telegram No. 310, 18.7.38.

118. PRO FO 371/21731, C 8189/1941/18, Report by Lord Lloyd, 3.8.38.

119. PRO CAB 64/19, Letter from Ismay to Inskip, 4.8.38.

120. PRO CAB 64/19, C 7891/65/18, Henderson to Halifax, Enclosure by the military attaché, 4.8.38.; Major von Mellenthin of the OKH attaché group emphasized to Col. Mason-MacFarlane that "the work now in progress on the western defenses and also other military measures now being taken were necessitated by the fact that Germany had so much lee-way to make up and had so little time to do it." (FO 371/21733, C 8911/1941/18, Enclosure by the military attaché, 26.8.38).

121. PRO FO 371/21732, C 8595/1941/18, Report by the military attaché in Germany, 21.8.38.

122. PRO FO 371/21729, C 7614/1941/18, Memorandum by Vansittart for Chamberlain and Halifax (seen by both) 25.7.38.; and Vansittart's minutes FO 371/21736, C 9608/1941/18, 25.8.38; FO 371/21729, C 7512/1941/18, 18.7.38; FO 800/314, p. 41, 10.8.38; and particularly FO 371/21735, C 9377/1941/18, 30.8.38.

123. PRO FO 800/328, Letter from R. A. Butler to Halifax, 30.7.38.

124. PRO FO 371/21723, C 5518/1941/12, Letter from Henderson to Cadogan, 8.6.38.

125. PRO CAB 23/94, Cab 32 (38), Meeting of the Cabinet, 13.7.38., p. 137.

126. This was the key period in the development of the opposition within Germany to the Nazi regime and the period in which some leading Germans came to the conclusion that the Nazi regime would have to be overthrown to avoid a catastrophe. See Bernd-Jürgen Wendt, *München 1938: England zwischen Hitler und Preussen* (Frankfurt, 1965) for an excellent study of the English view of the German opposition.

---

127. *DBFP*, 3rd Ser., Vol. II, Doc 659, 21.8.38., Henderson to Halifax.

128. PRO FO 371/21731, C 8391/1941/18, Henderson to Halifax, 16.8.38. A number of writers have confused Major Ewald von Kleist-Schmenzin with the future field marshal, General Ewald von Kleist. Among others who have made this mistake see: Roger Parkinson, *Peace for Our Time* (London, 1971), pp. 13-14; *DDF*, 2nd Ser., Vol. X, footnote 4, p. 688; William Shirer, *The Rise and Fall of the Third Reich* (New York, 1960), pp. 373, 380-381, 557; and, surprisingly, Telford Taylor, *Munich*, p. 1065.

129. *DBFP*, 3rd Ser., Vol. II (ii), pp. 686-687. Churchill may also have had some impact on the prime minister's disquiet. On August 20 he wrote to Halifax about his meeting with von Kleist-Schmenzin: "Kleist was also very emphatic that all the generals were convinced that they could not possibly fight for more than three months and that defeat was certain." PRO FO 800/309, p. 241, Letter from Churchill to Halifax, 20.8.38.

130. This meeting was not characterized as a full Cabinet meeting and thus received no "Cab" designation. However, Chamberlain, Simon, Hoare, De La Warr, Inskip, Hore-Belisha, Colville, Morrison, Maugham, Halifax, MacDonald, Duff Cooper, Wood, Stanley, Stanhope, Brown, and Winterton were present. Henderson also attended: PRO CAB 23/94, Notes on a Meeting of Ministers, 30.8.38.

131. Ibid., pp. 286-288.

132. Ibid., pp. 289-291.

133. Ibid., p. 293.

134. Ibid., pp. 294-296.

135. Ibid., pp. 297-306.

136. Ibid., pp. 303-317.

137. See the excellent discussion in Adamthwaite, *France and the Coming of the Second World War*, p. 193.

138. *DDF*, 2nd Ser., Vol. X, Doc 97, 26.6.38., François-Poncet to Bonnet.

139. Ibid., Doc 131, 1.7.38., "Compte rendu d'un entretien du général Le Rond avec le chancelier Hitler."

140. Ibid., Doc 113, 11.6.38., François-Poncet to Bonnet.

141. Ibid., Doc 312, 1.8.38., François-Poncet to Bonnet.

142. Ibid., Doc 238, 20.7.38., "Note du ministre des Affaires étrangères sur sa conversation du 20 juillet avec M. Osusky."

143. ADAP, Series D, Vol. II, Doc 422, 2.9.38., "Der Botschafter in Paris an das Auswärtige Amt."

144. PRO FO 371/21600, C 12854/55/17, Phipps to Halifax, "Events in France: Report During Third Quarter of 1938," 22.10.38.

145. Anna M. Cienciala, *Poland and the Western Powers, 1938-1939* (Toronto, 1968), p. 77.

146. *DDF*, 2nd Ser., Vol. X, Doc 12, 10.6.38., "Le général Musse, attaché militaire de France à Varsovie à M. Daladier."

147. Ibid., Doc 340, 8.8.38., "Note du Département, Hongrie-Petite Entente."

148. Taylor, *Munich*, p. 521.

149. *DDF*, 2nd Ser., Vol. X, Doc 370, 12.8.38., François-Poncet to Bonnet.

150. Taylor, *Munich*, p. 524.

151. For a full account from the French side see ibid., Doc 401, 18.8.38., François-Poncet to Bonnet; Doc 429, 21.8.38., François-Poncet to Bonnet; and Doc 444, 23.8.38., "Compte rendu du général chef d'état-major de l'Armée de l'Air." Jean-Baptiste Duroselle in his *La Décadence, 1932-1939* (Paris, 1979), p. 341ff. gives a most superficial account of Vuillemin's visit with little effort to discuss the actual air situation.

152. See particularly: Paul Stehlin, *Témoignage pour l'histoire* (Paris, 1964), pp. 86-91.

153. *DDF*, 2nd Ser., Vol. X, Doc 458, 25.8.38., "2ᵉ Bureau de l'État-major de l'Armée."

154. Taylor, *Munich*, p. 664.

VI. Munich: The Diplomatic Crisis

1. See particularly: PRO FO 371/21740, C 10664/1941/18, Halifax to Chamberlain (at Godesberg), 23.9.38.

2. Lord Strang, *Home and Abroad* (London, 1953), p. 134.

3. PRO FO 371/21581, C 9259/5589/21, Minute by F. K. Roberts on a dispatch from Prague.

4. PRO FO 371/21770, C 9101/4786/18, Newton to Halifax, 2.9.38.

5. Ibid., Minutes by Roberts, 5.9.38., and Halifax, 8.9.38.

6. *DBFP*, 3rd Ser., Vol. II, Doc 814, 9.9.38.

7. PRO FO 371/21782, C 9741/9726/18, Minute by Mr. Strang on a conversation between the German naval attaché and Admiral Troup, DNI (underlined in text), 10.9.38.

8. PRO CAB 23/95, Cab 37 (38), Meeting of the Cabinet, 12.9.38., pp. 8-10.

9. PRO CAB 23/95, Cab 37 (38), Meeting of the Cabinet, 12.9.38., pp. 10-21.

10. *DDF*, 2nd Ser., Vol. XI, Doc 22, 6.9.38., François-Poncet to Bonnet.

11. Ibid., footnote 1, p. 34.

12. Ibid., Doc 27, 6.9.38., General Ronondeau, military attaché in Berlin to General Dentz, vice-chief of the general staff.

13. Ibid., Doc 38, 7.9.38., François-Poncet to Bonnet.

14. PRO FO 800/311, 31.10.38., Letter from Phipps to Halifax, p. 120.

15. *DDF*, 2nd Ser., Vol. XI, footnote 1, p. 30. The report obviously referred to the blowup between Adam and Hitler in late August.

16. Ibid., Doc 40, 7.9.38., "2ᵉ Bureau de l'état-major de l'Armée."

17. Ibid., Doc 54, 8.9.38., François-Poncet to Bonnet, Appendix by M. Aris.

18. *DBFP*, 3rd Ser., Vol II, Doc 874, 14.9.38., Phipps to Halifax.

19. PRO FO 371/21737, C 9704/1941/18, Phipps to Halifax, 13.9.38.

20. PRO FO 371/21596, C 9944/36/17, Phipps to Halifax, 16.9.38.

21. PRO CAB 24/279, CP 206 (38), p. 52, Col. Fraser to Phipps, 23.9.38.

22. Anthony Adamthwaite, *France and the Coming of the Second World War, 1936-1939* (London, 1977), p. 210.

23. See in particular *DDF*, 2nd Ser., Vol. XI, Doc 65., 9.9.38., "Note du Chef d'État-major général de la Défense nationale," and Doc 195, 17.9.38., "Note du Directeur politique."

24. PRO FO 371/21771, C 9749/4815/18, Circular B to the Dominions, No. 218, 10.9.38.

25. *DBFP*, 3rd Ser., Vol. II, Doc 814, 9.9.38., Halifax to Phipps.

26. *ADAP*, Series D, Vol. II, Doc 502, 16.9.38., "Der Geschäftsträger in Prag an das Auswärtige Amt"; and Doc 513, 17.9.38., "Der Geschäftsträger in Prag an das Auswärtige Amt."

27. PRO CAB 23/95, Cab 38 (38), Meeting of the Cabinet, 14.9.38., pp. 34-43.

28. Ibid., pp. 55-56.

29. See Cabinet Paper CP 199, 14.9.38. (CAB 24/278). This had only minor changes from COS paper 764 (JP), 13.9.38., (CAB 53/41), which the Joint Planning Committee wrote. The Chiefs of Staff produced their own version of the report, COS 765 (Revise) (CAB 53/41), 4.10.38., which differs from the other versions only in minor respects. Just to make sure that no one missed the point the Defense Policy Committee released this paper to its members on the same date as DP (P) 32, (CAB 16/138A).

30. PRO CAB 27/646, CS (38), 16.9.38., Cabinet: Situation in Czechoslovakia: Note of a Meeting of Ministers.

31. PRO CAB 23/95, Cab 39 (38), Meeting of the Cabinet, 17.9.38., p. 64ff.

32. Ibid., p. 95.

33. Sargent commented to Cadogan: "I see it is suggested in the newspapers that we should offer to guarantee a 'reconstituted Czechoslovakia' on the ground that by such an offer we might be able to induce the Czech government to agree to the cession of the Sudeten area. I hope that if such an idea is

being seriously considered no decision will be taken without careful reflection as to the ulterior consequences of such a guarantee by us. I cannot help feeling that, even if it served our immediate purposes in obtaining a peaceful settlement of the present crisis, we should be laying up for ourselves a terrible humiliation in the not distant future when we might be called upon to implement a guarantee now given." PRO FO 371/21739, C 10322/1941/18, Memorandum by Sargent to Cadogan, 18.9.38.

34. *DBFP*, 3rd Ser., Vol. II, Doc 928, "Record of Anglo-French Conversations held at Number 10 Downing Street on 18.9.38."

35. PRO FO 371/21782, C 9983/9572/18, Newton to Halifax, 17.9.38.

36. See particularly David Vital, "Czechoslovakia and the Powers, September 1938," in *European Diplomacy Between Two Wars* (1919-1939), edited by Hans W. Gatzke (Chicago, 1972) for an excellent dicussion on why the Czechs agreed to the German demands and refused to stand alone.

37. PRO FO 371/21770, C 10119/4786/18, Newton to Halifax, 19.9.38.

38. PRO CAB 23/95, Cab 41 (38), Meeting of the Cabinet, 21.9.38., p. 163.

39. PRO CAB 27/646, CS (38) 7, Cabinet: Situation in Czechoslovakia, Notes of a Meeting of Ministers.

40. PRO FO 371/21740, C 10664/1941/18, Telegram dispatched to the prime minister while he was at Godesberg.

41. *DBFP*, 3rd Ser., Vol. II, Docs 550, 562, 573, 585, 584.

42. PRO FO 371/21770, C 10411/4786/18, Minute by Vansittart, 23.9.38.

43. General Alfred Jodl, *The Jodl Diaries with Annotations by General der Artillerie a.D. Walter Warlimont*, Vol. I (Foreign Military Studies, U.S. Army Europe, P-215), entry for 8.9.38.

44. Ibid., 13.9.38.

45. PRO FO 371/21675, C 6386/132/18, Paris Embassy to Central Department, 27.6.38.

46. *DBFP*, 3rd Ser., Vol. II, Doc 714, 31.8.38., Sir G. Ogilvie Forbes (Berlin) to Halifax.

47. See *DBFP*, 3rd Ser., Vol. II, Doc 775, 5.9.38., G. Warner to Halifax; and Doc IV, Appendix, 8.9.38., Mr. S. Stevenson to Strang.

48. See the next chapter for a full discussion of the military aspects of the Czech crisis.

49. A.J.P. Taylor, *Origins of the Second World War* (London, 1961), p. 171ff.

50. See the next chapter for a full discussion of German military planning in September 1938.

51. *ADAP*, Series D, Vol. II, 21.9.38., "Aufzeichnung des Legationsrats Erich Kordt."

52. IMT,*TMWC*, XXVI, Doc 798 PS, p. 338. See Engel, *Heeresadjutant bei Hitler*, p. 58, for a slightly different phrasing of the same statement.

53. Peter Bor, *Gespräche mit Halder* (Wiesbaden, 1950). For the most thorough study of German resistance see Peter Hoffmann, *Widerstand, Staatsstreich, Attentat* (Munich, 1969).

54. Gerhard Ritter, *The German Resistance* (London, 1958), p. 103; see also M. Farber du Faur, *Macht und Ohnmacht* (Stuttgart, 1953).

55. Gert Buchheit, *Der deutsche Geheimdienst* (Munich, 1966), p. 147.

56. Heidemarie Gräfin Schall-Riacour, *Aufstand und Gehorsam* (Wiesbaden, 1972), p. 248.

57. See particularly a fascinating series of essays written by soldiers of an Austrian mountain division about their attitudes during the Czech crisis in T-314, Roll 1638.

58. Gkdo. XIII A. K. Nr 5800/38, Ib Nürnberg, 15.11.38., "Erfahrungsbericht 'Einsatz Sudetendeutschland,' " p. 158, NARS T-314/525/000537; 7. Div. München, 15.11.38., "Erfahrungsbericht über Aufstellung und Einsatz der 7. Div. beim Einmarsch in die Tsch.," NARS T-79/47/000250. For the attitude of one of Weizsäcker's sons see: Ernst von Weizsäcker, *Weizsäcker-Papiere, 1933-1950*, edited by Leonidas Hill (Frankfurt am Main, 1974), entry for 30.9.38.

59. PRO CAB 27/646, CS (38) 13, 24.9.38., Cabinet: "Situation in Czechoslovakia, Notes on a meeting of Ministers, 3:30 P.M.," p. 91.

60. PRO CAB 23/95, Cab 42 (38), Meeting of the Cabinet, 24.9.38., p. 178.

61. Ibid., pp. 179-180.

62. Alexander Cadogan, *The Diaries of Sir Alexander Cadogan, 1938-1945* (New York, 1972), pp. 102-105.

63. The eight ministers who desired to oppose Germany were: Lord Halifax, foreign secretary; Leslie Hore-Belisha, secretary of state for war; Walter Elliot, minister of health; Viscount Hailsham, lord president of the council; Earl De La Warr, lord privy seal; Alfred Duff Cooper, first lord of the Admiralty; Oliver Stanley, president of the Board of Trade; and Earl Winterton, chancellor of the duchy of Lancaster. The four who were still doubtful: Thomas Inskip, minister for the coordination of defense; William S. Morrison, minister of agriculture and fisheries; Samuel Hoare, home secretary; and Kingsley Wood, secretary of state for air. The ministers who supported the prime minister without reservation were: Lord Maugham, lord chancellor; Marquess of Zetland, secretary of state for India; Sir John Simon, chancellor of the exchequer; John Colville, secretary of state for Scotland; Edward L. Burgen, minister of transport; Malcolm MacDonald, secretary of state for colonies; Earl Stanhope, president of the Board of Education; and Ernest Brown, minister of labor.

64. B. H. Liddell Hart, *Memoirs*, Vol. II (London, 1965), pp. 164-170. The *Times* no longer printed his articles although he was their military correspondent.

65. PRO CAB 23/95, Cab 43 (38), Meeting of the Cabinet, 25.9.38., p. 195ff.

66. PRO CAB 23/95, Cab 42 (38), Meeting of the Cabinet, 24.9.38., p. 187.

67. PRO CAB 23/95, Cab 43 (38), Meeting of the Cabinet, 25.9.38.

68. *Foreign Relations of the United States, 1938, General*, Vol. I, p. 652, "The Ambassador in the United Kingdom (Kennedy) to Secretary of State." The ministers mentioned by Stanley were: definitely Stanley, Duff Cooper, Winterton, De La Warr, probably Hore-Belisha, and possibly Morrison and Elliot.

69. PRO CAB 23/95, Cab 43 (38), Meeting of the Cabinet, 25.9.38., p. 227.

70. *DBFP*, 3rd Ser., Vol. II, Doc 1093, "Record of Anglo-French Conversations held at Number 10 Downing Street, 25.9.38."

71. PRO CAB 23/95, Cab 44 (38), Meeting of the Cabinet, 25.9.38., 11:30 P.M., p. 239.

72. PRO FO 371/21659, C 14471/42/18, Secret Intelligence Service, 18.9.38. The Secret Intelligence Service (better known by its military designation MI 6) held responsibility for foreign espionage. From 1921 on it was under the Foreign Office and was funded from the Foreign Office's secret vote. Unfortunately, when the British archives were opened up in the early 1970s, the intelligence documents remained closed and only a few documents (including this one) slipped through the PRO document review process. Therefore, it is difficult to gain a clear picture of what the SIS was recommending in its intelligence estimates to the services and the Cabinet. This document does suggest a thoroughgoing pessimism supporting the inclinations of those wishing to avoid war. One must note that the SIS remained underfunded throughout the interwar period and at least on the basis of this document does not appear to have possessed any of the fiendish cleverness attributed to it by the Germans. Its position in the arguments over British policy in the late 1930s would seem to have been considerably less important than that of the Joint Planning Committee of the Chiefs of Staff.

73. PRO CAB 55/13, JP 315, 23.9.38., Joint Planning Committee, "The Czechoslovak Crisis," p. 4. This paper appeared on the same day in slightly altered form under the Chiefs of Staff's signatures. CAB 16/183A, DP (P) 33. (COS 770).

74. PRO CAB 53/13, JP 317, 24.9.38., Joint Planning Committee, "The Czechoslovak Crisis."

75. PRO CAB 53/41, COS 773, COS Committee, "The Czechoslovak

Crisis," 24.9.38. The emphasis is mine. It is interesting to note that the Chiefs of Staff were still preparing to issue the gloomy forecast of the Joint Planning Committee (COS 764 [JP]) as their own paper.

76. PRO CAB 53/41, COS 766, COS Committee, "Appreciation of the Situation in the Event of War against Germany: Minute by the Minister for the Coordination of Defense," p. 10. Keith Middlemas claims in his *Diplomacy of Illusion* (London, 1972), p. 330, that the Joint Planning Committee had prepared a first draft on September 13 and references CAB 53/41, COS 766. CAB 53/41, COS 766 is dated 16.9.38. and is only a request from Inskip to the chiefs for a report on the effect of allowing Germany to absorb Czechoslovakia. The chiefs did not have time to comply with this request, although the Ismay paper mentioned at the end of the above paragraph was perhaps a start. All Joint Planning Committee papers in the Chiefs of Staff series are followed by the initials (JP). The only paper completed on the 13th is COS 764 (JP). This became the basis for CP 199, 14.9.38. (CAB 24/278), and COS 765 (Revise), 4.10.38. (CAB 53/41). It had nothing to do with what would happen if Germany seized Czechoslovakia without a struggle.

77. PRO CAB 21/544, "Note on the Question of Whether it would be to our Military Advantage to Fight Germany now or to Postpone the Issue," by General Ismay, 20.9.38. The distribution list indicates that only Edward Bridges, the Cabinet Secretary, Sir Horace Wilson, and Sir Thomas Inskip saw this report. No further action on the question was taken. Ismay modified this assessment after the war. In his memoirs he writes: "There are those who say that we would have done far better to fight in 1938, rather than postpone the struggle until 1939. There are others who say that the year's breathing space saved us. It seems to me that, from the purely military point of view it would have paid us to go to war in 1938." General Lord Ismay, *The Memoirs of General Lord Ismay* (New York, 1960), pp. 92-93.

78. For descriptions of Gamelin's conversations with the British see: PRO CAB 21/595, 26.9.38., "Notes on a meeting held at about 11 a.m. on the 26th of September to obtain the views of General Gamelin on the military aspects of the Czech crisis"; FO 371/21782, C 10722/10722/18; Foreign Office memorandum: Mr. Crestwell, "Notes on a Conversation with General Gamelin and British Ministers." For the French side see *DDF*, 2nd Ser., Vol. XI, Doc 376, 26.9.38., "Compte Rendu des Conversations techniques du Général Gamelin au Cabinet Office 26 septembre 1938." The British minutes are more complete.

79. *DDF*, 2nd Ser., Vol. XI, Doc 377, 26.9.38., Vuillemin to Guy La Chambre, air minister.

80. Ibid., Doc 378, 26.9.38., Note by Chief of Naval Staff, "Au sujet de la politique française de défense nationale."

81. PRO FO 371/21740, C 10670/1941/18, CP 211 (18), Letter from Jan Masaryk to Halifax, 25.9.38.

82. The *Times* (September 28, 1938).

83. *DBFP*, 3rd Ser., Vol. II, Doc 843, 12.9.38., Halifax to Phipps.

84. *DDF*, 2nd Ser., Vol. XI, Doc 376, 26.9.38., "Compte Rendu des Conversations techniques du Général Gamelin au Cabinet Office 26 septembre 1938."

85. Ibid., Doc 379, 26.9.38., "Note du Ministre."

86. Adamthwaite, *France and the Coming of the Second World War*, p. 219.

87. PRO FO 371/21770, C 10759/4786/18, From the military attaché Berlin for the War Office, 26.9.38.

88. PRO FO 371/21770, C 10908/4786/18, Newton to Halifax, 27.9.38. It is worth noting that Gerhard Weinberg in *The Foreign Policy of Hitler's Germany*, Vol. II, *Starting World War II*, 1937-39 (Chicago, 1980), p. 362 implies that the British military attaché in Czechoslovakia gave a gloomy picture of Czechoslovakia's strategic situation. This is misleading, for the attaché's reports, though realistic and uncompromising, clearly suggested that the Czechs could put up a good fight.

89. PRO CAB 21/550, Czechoslovakia: Diary of Events, 27.9.38., p. 40.

90. PRO CAB 23/95, Cab 46 (38), Meeting of the Cabinet, 27.9.38., 9:30 P.M., p. 261.

91. D. C. Watt argues that the dominions, because of their desire not to get involved in European affairs and in particular in another war, were a strong restraining force on British foreign policy. See particularly: D. C. Watt, *Personalities and Policies* (London, 1965), and "Der Einfluss der Dominions auf die britische Aussenpolitik vor München 1938."

92. PRO FO 371/21777, C 11226/5302/18, From high commissioner South Africa, 29.9.38.; FO 371/21740, C 10622/1941/18, Henderson to Halifax, 25.9.38. The South Africans were not planning to leave Berlin if war broke out.

93. Keith Middlemas, *Diplomacy of Illusion* (London, 1972), p. 327.

94. PRO CAB 21/550, Czechoslovakia: Diary of Events, September 27.

95. PRO FO 371/21777, C 10972/5302/18, Message from the high commissioner in Australia, 27.9.38.

96. PRO FO 371/21777, C 11112/5302/18, Message from the high commissioner in Canada, 28.9.38.

97. Adamthwaite, *France and the Coming of the Second World War*, p. 220.

98. Weizsäcker, *Weizsäcker-Papiere*, entry 9.10.38.

99. David Irving, *The War Path* (New York, 1978), p. 147.

100. William L. Shirer, *Berlin Diary* (New York, 1941), pp. 142-143.

101. Winston Churchill, *The Gathering Storm* (London, 1948), pp. 327-328.

VII. Munich: The Military Confrontation

1. The best work of scholarship on the military aspects of the Czech crisis is David Vital, "Czechoslovakia and the Powers," *Journal of Current History* (October 1966). Other works that criticize the Munich Agreement are: Telford Taylor, *Sword and Swastika* (New York, 1952); Christopher Thorne, *The Approach of War, 1938-1939* (London, 1967); The Royal Institute of International Affairs, *Survey of International Affairs, 1938*, Vol. III (London, 1953); Radomir Luža, *The Transfer of the Sudeten Germans* (New York, 1962); L. B. Namier, "Munich Survey: A Summing-Up," *The Listener* (December 2, 1948); L. B. Namier, *Europe in Decay* (Gloucester, 1963); L. B. Namier, *Diplomatic Prelude* (London, 1948); Hubert Ripka, *Munich, Before and After* (London, 1939); J. W. Wheeler-Bennett, *Munich, Prologue to Tragedy* (New York, 1948); Winston Churchill, *The Gathering Storm* (London, 1948); Ian Colvin, *The Chamberlain Cabinet* (London, 1971); Martin Gilbert and Richard Gott, *The Appeasers* (New York, 1967); Lord Vansittart, "A Morally Indefensible Agreement," *The Listener* (November 4, 1948); Peter Bor, *Gespräche mit Halder* (Wiesbaden, 1950); Wolfgang Foerster, *Generaloberst Ludwig Beck*; B. H. Liddell Hart, *The German Generals Talk* (New York, 1958); Erich von Manstein, *Aus einem Soldatenleben, 1887-1939* (Bonn, 1958); Heidemarie Gräfin Schall-Riacour, *Aufstand und Gehorsam* (Wiesbaden, 1972); J. W. Wheeler-Bennett, *The Nemesis of Power* (New York, 1964); Correlli Barnett, *The Collapse of British Power* (London, 1972); B. H. Liddell Hart, *Memoirs*, Vol. II (London, 1965). See also Telford Taylor, *Munich* (Garden City, N.Y., 1979), and my article "Munich, 1938: The Military Confrontation," *The Journal of Strategic Studies* (December 1979).

2. Among those who support the thesis that Munich saved Great Britain from military defeat are: Keith Eubank, *Munich* (Norman, Okla., 1963); Keith Eubank, "The Role of Czechoslovakia in the Origins of the Second World War," in *Czechoslovakia, Past and Present*, edited by Miloslav Rechcigl (The Hague, 1968); William E. Scott, "Neville Chamberlain and Munich: Two Aspects of Power," in *The Responsibility of Power*, edited by Fritz Stern (New York, 1967); Basil Collier, *History of the Second World War* (London, 1965); Keith Robbins, *Munich* (London, 1968); Lawrence Thompson, *The Greatest Treason* (New York, 1968); Sir John Slessor, *The Central Blue* (London, 1956); Air Marshal Sholto Douglas, *Combat and Command* (New York, 1966); Viscount Simon, *Retrospect* (London, 1952); Sir Nevile

Henderson, *Failure of a Mission, 1937-1939* (London, 1940); F. S. Northedge, *Freedom and Necessity in British Foreign Policy* (London, 1972); and
Stephen Roskill, *Hankey*, Vol. III (London, 1974).

3. PRO FO 800/309, Pt. IV, Letter from Henderson to Cadogan, 4.9.38.

4. PRO CAB 23/95, Cab 39 (38), Meeting of the Cabinet, 17.9.38., pp.
98-99.

5. PRO CAB 53/41, COS 773, COS Committee, "The Czechoslovakia
Crisis," 24.9.38.

6. Williamson Murray, "The Change in the European Balance of Power,"
Ph.D. dissertation, Yale University, 1975, chap. 5.

7. One additional armored division was formed in late summer 1938 but
had only begun training.

8. Taylor, *Sword and Swastika*, p. 262; Burkhard Mueller-Hillebrand in
his book *Das Heer, 1933-1945*, Vol. I (Darmstadt, 1954), p. 61, gives the
following totals: 34 infantry divisions, 4 motorized infantry divisions, 2 mountain divisions, 4 panzer divisions, 1 light division, 1 light motorized brigade,
1 cavalry brigade, and 1 mountain brigade. These figures are wrong. There
were only 3 panzer divisions combat ready in the fall of 1938. In addition,
the operational orders for the invasion of Czechoslovakia indicate the presence
of 3 mountain divisions and 3 light divisions.

9. IX Army Corps an Arbeitsstab Leeb, 13.9.38., NARS T-79/24/000635.

10. Guy Chapman, *Why France Fell* (New York, 1968), p. 347. Over the
summer of 1938 Hitler expressed considerable anger over the armament of
the Pzkw IV, but because production was about to begin it was impossible
to change the cannon. Gerhard Engel, *Heeresadjutant bei Hitler 1938-1943*,
edited by Hildegard von Kotze (Stuttgart, 1975), p. 25.

11. Heinz Guderian, *Panzer Leader* (London, 1952), p. 472.

12. *Trial of War Criminals*, Vol. X, *Case 12, U.S. vs. von Leeb et al.*,
p. 860.

13. Siegfried Westphal, *The German Army in the West* (London, 1951),
p. 36.

14. *Trial of War Criminals*, Vol. X, *Case 12, U.S. vs. von Leeb et al.*,
p. 529.

15. Gkdo. XIII A.K., Nr. 5800/38, Nürnberg, 15.11.38., "Erfahrungsbericht 'Einsatz Sudetendeutschland,' " NARS T-314/525/000537.

16. Mueller-Hillebrand, *Das Heer*, Vol. I, p. 63; Walter Bernhardt, *Die
deutsche Aufrüstung, 1934-1939* (Frankfurt am Main, 1969), p. 92.

17. Ibid., p. 61.

18. Gkdo. XIII A.K., Nr 5800/38, 15.11.38., "Erfahrungsbericht 'Einsatz
Sudetendeutschland,' " p. 15, NARS T-314/525/000537.

19. Gkdo. XIII A.K., "Erfahrungsbericht über Einsatz und Bereitstellung
an der Westgrenze," 15.11.38., NARS T-79/209.

20. ObdH, 8.7.38., NARS T-79/64/000116.

21. Rheinhard Gehlen, *The Service* (New York, 1972), p. 25.

22. Siegfried Westphal, *The German Army in the West* (London, 1951), pp. 69-70.

23. Manstein, *Aus einem Soldatenleben*, p. 334.

24. Walter Bernhardt, *Die deutsche Aufrüstung, 1934-1939* (Frankfurt am Main, 1969), p. 117.

25. Murray, "The Change in the European Balance of Power," pp. 148-153.

26. Bernhardt, *Die deutsche Aufrüstung*, pp. 96-97.

27. Engel, *Heeresadjutant bei Hitler*, p. 25.

28. See H. A. Jacobsen, "Motorisierungsprobleme im Winter 1939/1940," *Wehrwissenschaftliche Rundschau* (September 1956).

29. BA/MA, K 10-2/5, OKW, Berlin, 27.9.38., W F A/L, Nr. 2305/38, signed by Keitel.

30. 10. Abteilung, 3.8.38., Ia Nr. 58/38. Betr: Reise des Führers nach dem Westen 27.-29.8.38., NARS T-78/300/6251364.

31. BA/MA, K 10-2/5, OKW, 27.9.38., W F A/L, Nr. 2305/38, II.

32. Gkdo. XIII A.K., Nr. 5800/38, Nürnberg, 15.11.38., "Erfahrungsbericht 'Einsatz Sudetendeutschland,' " NARS T-314/525/000537.

33. Ibid., pp. 7-11.

34. 7. Div., München, 15.11.38., "Erfahrungsbericht über Aufstellung und Einsatz der 7. Div. beim Einmarsch in die Tsch.," NARS T-79/47/000250.

35. Gkdo. XIII A.K., Nr. 5800/38, Nürnberg, 15.11.38., "Erfahrungsbericht 'Einsatz Sudetendeutschland,' " NARS T-314/525/000537.

36. 25th Panzer Regiment to the Commanding General IX A.K., September 1938, NARS T-79/24/000705.

37. 7. Div., 15.11.38., "Erfahrungsbericht über Aufstellung und Einsatz der 7. Div. beim Einmarsch in die Tsch.," NARS T-79/47/000250.

38. Übungs-Division, XIII A. K., 20.10.38., Betr: "Erfahrungsbericht über die Aufstellung, den Einsatz, und die Auflösung der Übungs-Division, XIII A.K.," NARS T-79/224/000316.

39. PRO FO 371/21715, C 2805/1941/18, 6.4.38., Newton to Halifax, Enclosure by Lt. Col. Stronge, military attaché.

40. PRO FO 371/21578, C 2322/2322/12, Report by the miltiary attaché in Czechoslovakia, 29.3.38. For the military attaché's views after the war see Brigadier H.C.T. Stronge, "The Czechoslovak Army and the Munich Crisis: A Personal Memorandum" in *War and Society*, Vol. I (London, 1975); for a more detailed and less favorable description of the Czech fortification system see: Jonathan Zorach, "Czechoslovakia's Fortifications. Their Development

and Role in the 1938 Munich Crisis," in *Militärgeschichtliche Mitteilungen*, 2/76.

41. OKH, Generalstab des Heeres, Az. 3n. 12. Abt. I Nr. 30/38, 1.12.38., Betr: "Auswertung der Spannungszeit, Erfahrungen über das Verhalten der Armeen Osteuropas in der Spannungszeit 1938," NARS T-78/301/6252027.

42. PRO FO 371/21769, C 7690/4786/18, "Tour of the Silesian frontier by the assistant military attaché," 22.7.38.; see also C 7691/4786/18, Report on Czech fortifications by the military attaché, 26.7.38.

43. OKH, 1.9.38., "Kurze Angaben über den derzeitigen Stand der tschechoslowakischen Kriegswehrmacht," p. 15, NARS T-79/314/000764.

44. KTB GKdo. VII/Ia während des Einsatz Böhmen, NARS T-79/16/000353.

45. KTB für Heeresgruppenkommando Arbeitsstab Leeb, NARS T-79/16/000475.

46. Arbeitsstab Leeb, "Erfahrungsbericht," 15.10.38., NARS T-79/16/000941.

47. Generalkommando XIII A.K., Nr. 5800/38, Nürnberg, 15.11.38., "Erfahrungsbericht 'Einsatz Sudetendeutschland,' " NARS T-314/525/000537, pp. 71-72. Interestingly the comment that the corps with its artillery and well-trained troops would have needed only one day to break through the Czech defenses has a large question mark in the margin.

48. *ADAP*, Series D, Vol. II, Doc 424, 4.9.38. "Aufzeichnung des Majors im Generalstab Schmundt," "Besprechung vom 3. September 1938 auf dem Berghof."

49. 18.9.38., Breakdown of armies and their assigned divisions, NARS T-77/1510/000345-46.

50. *ADAP*, Series D, Vol. II, Doc 424, 4.9.38. "Aufzeichnung des Majors im Generalstab Schmundt," "Besprechung vom 3. September 1938 auf dem Berghof."

51. Engel, *Heeresadjutant bei Hitler*, p. 36.

52. *ADAP*, Series D, Vol. II, Doc 448, 9.-10.9.38. "Aufzeichung des Majors im Generalstab Schmundt."

53. Engel, *Heeresadjutant bei Hitler*, pp. 36-37.

54. Luža, *The Transfer of the Sudeten Germans*, footnote 176, p. 148.

55. OKH, Generalstab des Heeres, Az. 3n. 12. Abt. 1 Nr. 30/38, 1.12.38., Betr: "Auswertung der Spannungszeit, Erfahrungen über das Verhalten der Armeen Osteuropas in der Spannungszeit 1938," NARS T-78/301/6252027.

56. *DBFP*, 3rd Ser., Vol II, Doc 794, Enclosure by the military attaché, 3.9.38.

57. Murray, "The Change in the European Balance of Power," p. 224.

58. OKH, Generalstab des Heeres, Az. 3n. Abt. 1 Nr. 30/38, 1.12.38.,

Betr: "Auswertung der Spannungszeit, Erfahrungen über das Verhalten der Armeen Osteuropas in der Spannungszeit 1938," NARS T-78/301/6252027.

59. See KTB Arbeitsstab Leeb, NARS T-79/16/000396; and KTB GKdo. VII/ Ia während des Einsatz Böhmen, NARS T-79/16/000342.

60. On October 1 a major front moved through Czechoslovakia. It covered most of the region in dense clouds and rain. On October 2 the front moved out and weather improved, but there remained locally heavy showers. On October 3, in the morning, the weather was clear except for heavy fog along rivers and in the mountain valleys. In the evening, however, another front moved through and the weather deteriorated—especially over Bohemia where heavy rain fell. October 4 saw morning fog over many areas and rain over much of Czechoslovakia by the afternoon. Only on October 5 did the weather break so that relatively good flying conditions prevailed over all of Czechoslovakia for most of the day. BA/MA RL 7/164, Der kommandierende General und Befehlshaber der Luftwaffengruppe 3., Ia Nr. 7829/38, 1.12.38., "Erfahrungsbericht über die Spannungszeit 1938 'Fall Grün,' " This after-action report contains complete weather maps for Czechoslovakia for three periods each day from 1 October through 5 October 1938.

61. Murray, "The Change in the European Balance of Power," p. 456.

62. BA/MA RL 7/164, Der kommandierende General und Befehlshaber der Luftwaffengruppe 3., Ia Nr. 7829/38, 1.12.38. "Erfahrungsbericht über die Spannungszeit 1938 'Fall Grün,' Teil III."

63. BA/MA RL 7/1, Der kommandierende General und Befehlshaber der Luftwaffengruppe 1., Ia Nr. 197/38, 11.7.38., Betr: "Planstudie 'Grün' 1938."

64. BA/MA RL 7/67, "Planstudie 1938, Hauptteil II, Teil A, Aufmarsch und Kampfanweisung 'Fall Grün' zu Lw. Gruppenkommando 3., Führungsabteilung, Az Plst 38/Ia op, Nr. 525/38, 20.7.38."

65. Ulrich von Hassell, *The von Hassell Diaries, 1938-1944* (Garden City, N.Y., 1947), p. 9.

66. Hans B. Gisevius, *Bis zum bittern Ende* (Zurich, 1946), p. 303.

67. PRO FO 371/21676/132/18, Sir R. Campbell (Belgrade) to Halifax, 5.12.38. It is worth noting that the German general staff exercise of June 1938 suggested that the German forces attacking Czechoslovakia would succeed in achieving a final decision over Czech forces by the eleventh day and that within seven days the OKH could begin to pull troops out of combat for transfer to the west. Klaus-Jürgen Müller, *Armee, Politik und Gesellschaft in Deutschland, 1933-1945* (Paderborn, 1979), p. 98.

68. Anna M. Cienciala, *Poland and the Western Powers, 1938-1939* (Toronto, 1968), p. 54.

69. DDF, 2nd Ser., Vol. XI, Doc 275, 21.9.38., Le général Musse, attaché militaire de France à Varsovie, à M. Daladier.

70. *Trial of War Criminals*, Vol. X, *Case 12, U.S. vs. von Leeb et al.*, p. 511.

71. ADAP, Series D, Vol. II, Doc 409, 30.8.38., "Aufzeichnung des Staatssekretärs."

72. PRO FO 371/21697, C 8225/267/18, Mr. Norton (Warsaw), "Incidents in the Polish Corridor," 9.8.38.; C 8921/267/18, Norton "Anti-German riots in western Poland," 27.8.38. PRO FO 371/21805, C 9503/220/55, Kennard to Sargent, 7.9.38.

73. *DBFP*, 3rd Ser., Vol. II, Doc 829, 10.9.38., Kennard (Warsaw) to Halifax.

74. PRO CAB 21/586 C 9661/5302/18, Halifax to Kennard, 13.9.38., "Circulated to the Cabinet by the Direction of the Secretary of State for Foreign Affairs."

75. PRO FO 371/21782 C 10722/10722/18, Foreign Office memorandum, Mr. Creswell, 26.9.38.

76. *Foreign Relations of the United States, 1938*, Vol. I, *General*, "The Ambassador in France (Bullitt) to the Secretary of State," 26.9.38.

77. PRO FO 371/21766, C 9648/5302/18, Kennard to Halifax, 10.9.38.

78. PRO FO 371/21808, C 11992/2168/55, Letter from Kennard to Halifax, 5.10.38.

79. See Andrew Rothstein, *The Munich Conspiracy* (London, 1958); also V. Kral, "Die Tschechoslowakei und München," *Zeitschrift für Geschichtswissenschaft* 7, no. 1 (1959).

80. Lord Vansittart, "A Morally Indefensible Agreement," *The Listener* (November 1948), pp. 676-677.

81. *Documents Relating to the Eve of the Second World War*, Vol. I (Moscow, 1949), p. 204.

82. This is not a moral judgment but a factual statement. Those who deride the Soviet Union's intentions in 1938 are by and large the same ones who defend Chamberlain's refusal to support the Czechs.

83. The sorry Russian performance against the Finns hardly argues that the Russians were militarily prepared to fight in a major European war in 1938. For the influence of the purges on British strategic thinking see particularly: CAB 53/38, COS 716, CID, COS Sub-Committee, 26.4.38., "Situation in the Event of War against Germany," p. 77; see also *DBFP*, 3rd Ser., Vol. I, Doc 148, 18.4.38., Moscow to London, report by Col. Firebrace; CAB 24/268, CP 58 (37), 11.2.37., "The Preparedness for War of Great Britain in Relation to Certain other Powers by May 1937."

84. George Lambert in the post-Anschluss debate. Hansard, *Parliamentary Debates*, 5th Ser., Vol. 333, *House of Commons Official Report* (London, 1938), Col. 1435, 24.3.38.

85. For the most detailed account of the effect of the purges on the Soviet Army see John Erickson, *The Road to Stalingrad* (New York, 1975), pp. 1-49. See also B. H. Liddell Hart, *The Red Army* (New York, 1956), p. 69 and John Erikson, *The Soviet High Command* (London, 1962).

86. PRO FO 371/21766, C 9648/5302/18, Kennard to Halifax, 10.9.38. and FO 371/21808, C 11992/2168/55, Letter from Kennard to Halifax, 5.10.38.

87. Ferdinand Friedensburg, "Die sowjetischen Kriegslieferungen an das Hitlerreich," *Vierteljahrshefte für Wirtschaftsforschung*, 1962; see also Institut für Weltwirtschaft an der Universität Kiel, "Der kriegswirtschaftliche Beitrag Osteuropas für das deutsche Reich, 1936-44," pp. 16-17, NARS T-84/72.

88. W. Ru. A. Stab., Oct. 1938, "Seitens des Auslands im Sep. 1938 getroffene Massnahmen," pp. 1-3.

89. ADAP, Series D, Vol. II, Doc. 402, 29.8.38., Budapest to Berlin.

90. The Germans never had sufficient resources to begin major fortification work along the Belgian and Luxembourg borders. Some field works were constructed there in 1938 and 1939.

91. 10. Abteilung, 23.7.38., Nr. 34/38, (Ia), An O.Qu.I, p. 1, NARS T-78/300/000257.

92. OKH, 2. Abt. (IIIc), Gen St. d. H., Nr. 32/38, 13.8.38., NARS T-78/300/000284.

93. 10. Abteilung, 23.7.38., Nr. 34/38 (Ia), An O.Qu.I, pp. 1-2, NARS T-78/300/000257.

94. Ibid., p.2.

95. Günther Blumentritt, *Zwischen freiem Operationsplan und ständigen Befestigungen* (B-652, Foreign Military Studies, Historical Division, U.S. Army Europe, 1947), pp. 30-32.

96. Wilhelm Keitel, *The Memoirs of Field Marshal Keitel* (New York, 1964), p. 72.

97. Blumentritt, *Zwischen freiem Operationsplan und ständigen Befestigungen*, p. 32.

98. Festung-Pionierstab, Saarbrücken, 27.9.38., An: Festungsinspektion VI, NARS T-311/123/7166285.

99. Festungsnachschubstelle Wiesbaden: "Der Westwall: Übersicht des Gesamtbedarfs an Baustoffen," NARS T-311/125/7168842.

100. See particularly the amusing complaint of Oberbaurat Hartwieg, Oberbauleiter der Oberbauleitung Trier I zu Grenzkommandantur Trier, 26.9.38., about the treatment that he had received from an artillery captain while inspecting fortification work, NARS T-311/122/7166182.

101. Heeresgruppenkommando 2., General Adam, 13.8.38., NARS T-311/123/7166357.

102. Heeresgruppenkommando 2., Ia L Nr. 2290/38, 25.10.38., An: OKH

Genst. d.H. 10. Abt., "Sicherung des Nachschubes und der Arbeitskräfte für den weiteren Ausbau West," NARS T-311/123/7166668.

103. Inspektion der Westbefestigungen Wiesbaden, 21.11.38., "Vorschlag für die festungsmässige Verstärkung der Westbefestigungen," NARS T-311/124/7167400.

104. Entwurf: Beurteilung der Lage, Juli 1938, HgKdo 2., pp. 7-9, NARS T-311/42/7052121.

105. Ibid., pp. 7-9.

106. Ibid., see also Heeresgruppenkommando 2., 17.8.38., An OKH, Betr: Aufmarschanweisung, signed by General Adam, NARS T-311/42/7052197.

107. Jodl, *The Jodl Diaries with Annotations by General der Artillerie a.D. Walter Warlimont*, entry for 10.8.38., p. 206.

108. 10. Abteilung, Ia Nr 50/38, 3.9.38., Betr: "Reise des Führers nach dem Westen 27.-29.8.38.," NARS T-78/300/000364.

109. Paul-Marie de la Gorce, *The French Army* (New York, 1963), p. 270.

110. There are two British accounts of this meeting, PRO CAB 21/595, 26.9.38., "Notes on a Meeting held at about 11 a.m. on the 26th of September to obtain the views of General Gamelin on the military aspects of the Czech crisis"; and PRO FO 371/21782, C 10722/10722/18 Foreign Office memorandum: Mr. Creswell, "Notes on Conversation with General Gamelin and British Ministers." The latter is mentioned in a footnote in the *DBFP*, 3rd Ser., II, p. 575, which correctly implies that Gamelin talked on both sides of the issue. For the French account see *DDF*, 2nd Ser., Vol. XI, Doc 376, 26.9.38., "Compte Rendu des conversations techniques du Général Gamelin au Cabinet Office, 26 septembre 1938." For an examination of the less than sterling performance of the French military during the crisis see: R. J. Young, "Le Haut Commandement Français au moment de Munich," *Revue D'Histoire Moderne et Contemporaine* (January-March 1977).

111. PRO CAB 24/279, CP 206 (38), Col. Fraser to Phipps, 23.9.38., p. 52.

112. Ibid., p. 52.

113. PRO CAB 53/41, COS 764, CID, COS Sub-Committee, 12.9.38., "German Aggression against Czechoslovakia: French Military Plans," p. 71.

114. PRO CAB 27/646, CS (38) 15, 27.9.38., Cabinet: The Situation in Czechoslovakia: Notes on a Meeting of Ministers.

115. BA/MA II 171/1, Abteilung Marinenachrichtendienst A III, 23.3.38.; 1. Seekriegsleitung, "Übersicht über Bereitschaftsgrade der Seestreitkräfte für die Monate August bis Oktober (1938)," NARS T-1022/2036/PG33987.

116. Michael Salewski, *Die deutsche Seekriegsleitung, 1933-1945* (Frankfurt am Main, 1970), pp. 15-16.

117. BA/MA M 31/PG34162, 1. Seekriegsleitung B. Nr. 1174/38, 3.5.38.; see also BA/MA M 31/PG34162, Flotte Kdo. 490 A Iv 10.6.38., Pt. III.

118. BA/MA II M 17/1 Admiral u. Flottenchef Carls, g.Kdos., Tender *Hela* Sep 1938, Stellungnahme zur "Entwurfstudie Seekriegführung gegen England."

119. BA/MA M 517/PG38626, Marine Gruppenkommando Ost, Studie: Ostseekriegführung, late 1938, p. 1.

120. BA/MA M 31/PG34162, Flottenkommando B. Nr. 490 A g.Kdos., 10.6.38., An OKM: Betr: "Grundsätzliche Fragen der Ostseekriegführung."

121. Erfahrungsbericht Gruppenkommando Ost, 19.11.38., NARS T-1022/2648/PG39874.

122. Gruppenkommando Ost, Abschnitt A zum Mob. Übung, 1938, NARS T-1022/2762/PG 39875.

123. BA/MA M 31/PG34162, Der Kriegsmarine Ergebnisse: Operative Überlegung 1937/1938, Kriegführung in der Ostsee.

124. PRO CAB 24/273, C.P. 283 (37), 29.11.37., p. 141.

125. Chef des Nachschubsamts, Nr. 3365/g.Kdos., 3.11.38., Milch Collection, Imperial War Museum, Reel 55, Vol. 57.

126. William R. Emerson, "Operation Pointblank," Harmon Memorial Lectures, no. 4 (Colorado Springs, 1962), p. 41.

127. Sholto Douglas, *Combat and Command*, p. 355.

128. Slessor, *The Central Blue*, p. 208. Slessor had a special reason to take this line because as a member of the Joint Planning Committee he had a major share of the responsibility for the military advice that the Chiefs of Staff tendered to the government and Cabinet.

129. L.E.O. Charlton, C. T. Garrett, and Lt. Cmdr. R. Fletcher, *The Air Defense of Great Britain* (London, 1937), pp. 170-171.

130. Sir Charles Webster and Noble Frankland, *The Strategic Air Offensive against Germany*, Vol. I, *Preparation* (London, 1961), p. 79.

131. Slessor, *The Central Blue*, p. 223.

132. Basil Collier, *The Defense of the United Kingdom* (London, 1957), p. 65.

133. PRO CAB 24/279, CP 218 (38), 25.10.38., "Relative Air Strengths and Proposals for the Improvement of this Country's Position," p. 131.

134. Air Ministry, Air Historical Branch, Translations, Vol. VII, G. 302694/AR/9/51/50.

135. PRO CAB 3/8, p. 2, 301-A, 14.11.38., CID, "Review of Precautionary Measures (Civil Defense) Taken During the Czech Crisis, September 1938," Appendix III, Review by the War Office.

136. Karlheinz Kens and Heinz J. Nowarra, *Die deutschen Flugzeuge, 1933-1945* (Munich, 1964), pp. 15, 416.

137. Richard Suchenwirth, *The Development of the German Air Force, 1919-1939* (New York, 1969), p. 97.

138. BA/MA RL 2 11/115, Der Reichsminister der Luftfahrt und Oberbefehlshaber der Luftwaffe, Luftwaffenführungsstab, Az. 89a Nr. 3400/38, 1. Abt. III, 4, 1.12.38., Leistungstabelle der deutschen Kriegsflugzeuge.

139. Milch Collection, Imperial War Museum, Reel 55, Vol. 57, 3.6.38., "Vorläufiges Flugzeug—Beschaffungs Programm."

140. Letter from the Reichsminister der Luftfahrt und Oberbefehlshaber der Luftwaffe, 10.8.38., NARS T-79/24/000606.

141. Air Historical Branch, Air Ministry, Vol. VII, Translation: Luftwaffe Strength and Serviceability Statistics. G. 302694/AR/9/51/50.

142. BA/MA RL 7/164, Der kommandierende General und Befehlshaber der Luftwaffengruppe 3., 1.12.38., "Erfahrungsbericht über die Spannungszeit 1938: Einsatzbereitschaft der Fliegerverbände (personell)."

143. Ibid., Pt. II.

144. Milch Collection, Imperial War Museum, Reel 55, Vol. 57, Der Chef des Nachschubamts, Nr. 3365/38, 3.11.38.; Anlage L.E. 2. Nr. 15.222/ 38 g.Kdos., "Erfahrungsbericht über die Spannungszeit," p. 3270.

145. L. W. Gr.Kdo. 2., Führungsabteilung, Nr. 210/38, g.Kdos., Chefs., 22.9.38., Betr: "Planstudie 'Fall Blau' " quoted in Suchenwirth, *Hans Jeschonnek*, pp. 39-40. "Fall Blau" was the code name given to Luftwaffe preparations for air attacks on Great Britain.

146. PRO CAB 21/595, 26.9.38., "Notes on a meeting held at about 11 a.m. on 26.9.38. to obtain the views of General Gamelin on the military aspects of the Czech crisis."

147. BA/MA RL 7/64 Planstudie 1938, Hauptteil III Aufmarsch und Kampfanweisung "Fall Rot" zu Lw. Gruppenkommando 3., Az Plst. 38/Ia op, Nr. 450/38 2.6.38.

148. L.W. Gr.Kdo. 2., Führungsabteilung, Nr. 210/38, g.Kdos., Chefs., 22.9.38., Betr: "Planstudie 'Fall Blau,' " quoted in Richard Suchenwirth, *Hans Jeschonnek*, pp. 39-40.

149. Vortragsnotiz über Besprechung mit Ia des Befehlshabers der Luftwaffengruppe Braunschweig, 25.8.38., NARS T-1022/2307/34562.

150. Karl Gundelach, "Gedanken über die Führung eines Luftkrieges gegen England bei der Luftflotte 2. in den Jahren 1938/1939," *Wehrwissenschaftliche Rundschau* (January 1960), p. 35.

151. BA/MA RL 2 II/24, OKL Chef. 1. Abt., 22.11.39., "Luftkriegführung gegen England."

152. L.W. Gr.Kdo. 2., Führungsabteilung, Nr. 210/38 g.Kdos, Chefs., 22.9.38., Betr: "Planstudie 'Fall Blau,' " quoted by Suchenwirth, *Hans Jeschonnek*, pp. 39-40.

153. BA/MA RL 7/42, RL 7/43, Luftflottenkommando 2., Führungsab-teilung, Nr. 7093/39, 13.5.39., "Schlussbesprechung des Planspieles 1939."

154. Ob.d.L., Generalstab, L. Abt., Nr. 5095/39, 22.5.39., "Operative Zielsetzung für die Luftwaffe im Fall eines Krieges gegen England im Jahre 1939," quoted in Suchenwirth, *Hans Jeschonnek*, pp. 40-41.

155. See particularly BA/MA RL 7/50, IW/38, "Die Wetterberatung im Englandfall," IW 23/39 g. Vortrag Planspiels 10-14.5.39., "Die Organisation des Reichswetterdienstes"; BA/MA RL II/101 Luftwaffengruppenkommando 2., 6.12.38., Führung Abt/IW B. Nr. 129/38 g.Kdos., Betr: "Wetterberatung im Falle 'Blau.' " During the war the Germans were partly able to cover this gap by submarine reports and long-range flights with specially equipped Ju 88s and Condors. In 1938 there were not sufficient submarines and the long-range aircraft were not yet available.

156. BA/MA RL 2 II/101, "Zusammenhänge zwischen Meteorologie und Taktik," Vortrag: General der Flieger Kesselring, Chef der Luftflotte 1, 1.3.39.

157. Air Historical Branch, Air Ministry, AHB 6 No. VII/153, "German Air Force Policy during the Second World War, A Review by Oberst Bernd von Brauchitsch," p. 3.

158. Gundelach, "Gedanken über die Führung eines Luftkrieges gegen England bei der Luftflotte 2. in den Jahren 1938/1939," p. 35.

159. PRO FO 371/21776, C 9506/5302/18, Charles (Rome) to Halifax, 9.9.38.

160. PRO FO 371/21776, C 10203/5302/18, Foreign Office Minute by Mr. Strang: "Following conversations passed along by Belgian Embassy London: 'Conversation between Belgian Ambassador in Rome and Count Ciano.' "

161. PRO FO 371/21777 C 10802/5302/18, Perth (Rome) to Halifax, 26.9.38.

162. PRO FO 371/21743, C 11016/1941/18, Perth to Halifax, 29.9.38.

163. See particularly: PRO FO 371/21782, C 10068/9572/18, Charles to Halifax, 18.9.38.; CAB 21/550, "Czechoslovakia, Diary of Events," p. 31, 25.9.38.; PRO FO 371/21777, C 10795/5302/18, Perth to Halifax, 26.9.38.; PRO FO 371/21777, C 10613/5302/18, Perth to Halifax, 24.9.38.

164. Galeazzo Ciano, *Ciano's Diary*, 1937-1938 (London, 1952), entry for 25.9.38., p. 161.

165. For a full discussion of the problem of Italy in British strategy see: Williamson Murray, "The Role of Italy in British Strategy 1938-1939," *JRUSI* (September 1979).

166. Murray, "The Change in the European Balance of Power," chap. 5.

167. PRO FO 371/21596, C 10082/36/17, Conversation of the military attaché (Paris) with Col. Petibon, 17.9.38.

168. Marine Attaché, Rom, g.Kdos., Italien Land Mobilmassnahmen, June 1938-August 1938. Conversation late August with unidentified Italian general officer. NARS T-1022/2524/PG45212.

169. Marine Attaché, Rom, 10.11.38., An das OKW, Betr: "Rückblick auf die militärische Einstellung des italienischen Volkes zu einem Kriege um die Tschechoslowakei," NARS T-1022/3016/PG48834.

170. PRO CAB 55/13, JP 305, CID Joint Planning Committee, 19.8.38., "The number of divisions that Italian industry might maintain in the field."

171. PRO CAB 53/9, COS/252 Meeting, CID, COS Committee, 23.9.38., p. 249.

172. FDR Library, PSF 46 Message from Lord Halifax, 26.9.38.

173. See particularly ADAP, Series D, Vol. IV, Doc 534, 29.10.38., "Aufzeichnung ohne Unterschrift"; Doc 535, 1.11.38., "Der Botschafter in Tokio an das Auswärtige Amt."

174. C. Bradford Lee, *Britain and the Sino-Japanese War* (Stanford, Cal., 1973), p. 221.

175. PRO FO 371/22185, F 8912/152/23, Campbell (Paris) to Halifax, 18.8.38.

176. PRO FO 371/22185, F 9887/152/23, Craigie (Tokyo) to Halifax, 15.9.38.

177. PRO Adm 1/9588, "Japanese Navy and Naval Air Service: Annual Report for 1938," Pt. II, p.12.

178. FDR Library, PSF 3, Vol. I, Telegram from Grew, "The Attitude of Japan with Regard to the Present Crisis," 6.10.38. See also the Grew dispatch in *FRUS*, 1938, Vol. III, p. 298.

179. Quoted in Wilhelm Deist et al., *Das Deutsche Reich und der Zweite Weltkrieg*, Vol. I (Stuttgart, 1979), p. 329. Original source cited: IMT, *TMWC*, Vol. XXVII, p. 163.

180. Dieter Petzina, *Autarkiepolitik im Dritten Reich* (Stuttgart, 1968), pp. 126-127.

181. Dr. C. Krauch, Berlin, 19.8.38., "Bericht über die veranlassten Massnahmen zur Durchführung des wirtschaftlichen neuen Erzeugungsplanes für die Zeit 1.8.-15.8.38.," NARS T-71/110/612645.

182. Dr. C. Krauch, Berlin, 8.9.38., "Bericht über den Fortschritt der Arbeiten in der Zeit vom 15. Aug. bis 1. Sep. 1938 auf dem Sachgebiet des neuen wehrwirtschaftlichen Erzeugungsplanes," NARS T-71/110/612632; Letter, Berlin, 7.10.38., "Die zeitige Zementversorgung des Schnellplanes," NARS T-71/110/612615.

183. Reichsstelle für Wirtschaftsausbau, Berlin, 17.8.39., "Schnellplan vom 13.8.38., für die Erzeugung von Pulver, Sprengstoffen und chemischen Kampfstoffen einschliesslich der Vorprodukte," NARS T-71/110/613208.

184. Festungsnachschubstelle Wiesbaden, "Der Westwall: Übersicht des Gesamtbedarfs an Baustoffen," NARS T-311/125/7168840.

185. Report by General Thomas, OKW Economic Staff, "Stand der wirtschaftlichen Lage, 1.9.38.," NARS T-1022/2238/PG33525; and Reichswirtschaftsministerium, "Tätigkeitsberichte: Buna Erzeugung," p. 3, NARS T-71/109/611976.

186. Georg Thomas, *Geschichte der deutschen Wehr- und Rüstungswirtschaft, 1918-1943/45* (Boppard am Rhein, 1966), p. 130.

187. Report by General Thomas, OKW Economic Staff: "Stand der wirtschaftlichen Lage," 1.4.37., NARS T-1022/2238/PG33525; Petzina, *Autarkiepolitik im Dritten Reich*, p. 103. Moreover, there was the problem of a critical lack of capacity in the machine tools and heavy engineering sectors. Thus, there was some question of how much increased steel production could have helped armaments production. Steel was one, albeit an important one, among many elements necessary for rearmament.

188. Berlin, 13.10.38., "Sitzung des kleinen Generalrates vom 13. Okt.," p. 3, NARS T-77/657/1856947.

189. For a more complete discussion of the petroleum problem see: Murray, "The Change in the European Balance of Power," pp. 128-136.

190. OKW Economic Staff, "Die Arbeiten des Wi Rü Amtes an der Mineralölversorgung," probably sometime in 1944, NARS T-77/282.

191. D. Eickholz, *Geschichte der deutschen Kriegswirtschaft, 1939-1945* (Berlin, 1969), p. 23.

192. "Bericht des Herrn Professor C. Krauch über die Lage auf dem Arbeitsgebiet der Chemie in der Sitzung des Generalrates am 24.6.41.", NARS T-84/217.

193. Reichswirtschaftsministerium, "Tätigkeitsbericht: Buna Erzeugung," 1943, NARS T-71/109.

194. See Murray, "The Change in the European Balance of Power," pp. 137-148.

195. Reichsstelle für Wirtschaftsausbau, Berlin, 7.1.39., "Verzögerung im Schnellplan vom 13.8.38. durch verringerte Stahlzuteilung," NARS T-71/110; OKW Vortragsnotiz: Wa A Nr. 1120/39, Wa Stab Ia, "Mob.—Nachschuberzeugung an Waffen und Munition (Vergleich mit der Weltkriegshöchstleistung), 31.8.39., NARS T-78/175.

196. W. Rü. IV, "Wehrwirtschaftliche Erfahrungen im Jahre 1938," 4.11.38., NARS T-77/657.

197. Timothy W. Mason, "Innere Krise und Angriffskrieg, 1938/1939," in *Wirtschaft und Rüstung am Vorabend des Zweiten Weltkrieges*, edited by Friedrich Forstmeier and Hans-Erich Volkmann (Dusseldorf, 1975), pp. 167-169.

198. Reichsverteidigungsausschuss, 15.12.38., NARS T-1022/3048/PG33272.

199. IMT, *TMWC*, Vol. XXXII, Doc 3575PS, p. 413.

200. "Sitzung des kleinen Generalrates vom 13.10.38," NARS T-84/146.

201. Ibid., "32. Sitzung des Generalrates vom 28.10.38"; for more on the difficulties with railroads see: BA/MA RL 7/257, Luftkreisintendant Dr. Ronde, 19.12.38., "Vermerk über die Intendanten—Besprechung in Berlin am 15., 16., und 17.12.38."

202. Lecture by Dr. Peters of Wi Rü Amt, "Wehrwirtschaft des Auslands," 15.5.39., pp. 10-11, NARS T-73/185/3397601; lecture by Chef W. Stab., 28.3.39., NARS T-77/657/1857396.

203. W. Rü. A. Stab., Okt. 1938, "Seitens des Auslands im Sep. 1938 getroffene Massnahmen," pp. 1-3, NARS T-77/657/1857008.

204. Ibid., pp. 20-25.

205. Sit, Rep. no. 1, 5.9.38., OKM, 3. Abt. Skl, NARS T-1022/1780/PG32538.

206. W. Rü A. Stab., October 1938, "Seitens des Auslands im Sep. 1938 getroffene Massnahmen," pp. 1-3, NARS T-77/657/1857008.

207. Institut für Weltwirtschaft an der Universität Kiel, "Die Versorgung Grossdeutschlands und Kontinentaleuropas mit Mineralölerzeugnissen während der gegenwärtigen kriegerischen Verwicklungen," Februar 1940, NARS T-84/72/135827; see also speech by Korvettenkapitän Haensel, 4.3.39., während des Kriegsspieles des Marinekommandoamtes in Oberhof, p. 33, NARS T-1022/2821/PG49089.

208. OKM, 3. SKL, 2.8.38, NARS T-1022/2307/PG34562.

VIII. THE AFTERMATH OF MUNICH

1. "Die Wirtschaftsstruktur der neuen Tschecho-Slowakei," 16.12.38., NARS T-84/266/1597310; OKW, An 31/10/32 W Stb W Wi Iv, 11.10.38., "Wirtschaftliche Bedeutung des sudetendeutschen Gebietes," NARS T-77/657/185 753; BA/MA, M 1539/PG49156, "Die Stellung der alten Tschecho-Slowakei in der Weltwirtschaft."

2. Quoted in J. Griffen, *Lost Liberty* (London, 1938), p. 177.

3. PRO FO 371/21768, C 12254/4770/18, Palairet (Bucharest) to Halifax, 7.10.38.

4. PRO FO 371/21676, C 14810/132/18, Nigel Law to Sargent, 29.11.38.

5. PRO FO 371/21805, C 12726/220/55, Minute by R. L. Spreaight on dispatch from Kennard, 19.10.38.

6. PRO FO 371/21808, C 11992/2168/55, Minute by I. Mallett on Kennard dispatch.

7. ADAP, Series D, IV, Doc 81, 21.10.38., "Weisung des Führers und Obersten Befehlshabers der Wehrmacht"; Doc 137, 23.11.38., "Aufzeichnung des Leiters der Politischen Abteilung," and Doc 152, 17.12.38., "Weisung des Chefs des Oberkommandos der Wehrmacht."

8. WFA Chef, "Der Führer und oberste Befehlshaber der Wehrmacht," 19.10.38., NARS T-77/775/5500269.

9. For the reaction of German soldiers see the essays written by soldiers in a mountain division on the Czech crisis, NARS T-314/1638/367ff.; see also Heeresdienststelle 6, 1.11.38., An g.Kdo. XIII A.K., Erfahrungsbericht.

10. PRO FO 371/22966, C 2639/15/18, PRO FO Minute, Mr. Hadow, 27.2.39., "Report by Major Joubert, South African Staff Corps."

11. Francis L. Loewenheim, *Peace or Appeasement?* (Boston, 1965), p. 69.

12. PRO FO 371/21658, C 12816/42/18, Ogilvie-Forbes to Halifax, 21.10.38.; see also C 12395/42/18, Henderson to Halifax, 13.10.38.; C 12288/42/18, Henderson to Strang, 10.10.38.

13. Wilhelm Treue, "Rede Hitlers vor der deutschen Presse (10 November 1938)," VfZG, pp. 175-191.

14. ADAP, Series D, Vol. V, Doc 272, 1.16.39., "Aufzeichnung des vortragenden Legationsrats Hewel."

15. Wilhelm Deist et al., *Das Deutsche Reich und der Zweite Weltkrieg*, Vol. I (Stuttgart, 1979), p. 329.

16. Reichsverteidigungsausschuss, 15.12.38., NARS T-1022/2048/PG33272.

17. IMT, TMWC, Doc 3575PS, p. 413.

18. Ibid., Doc 1301PS.

19. Jost Dülffer, *Weimar, Hitler, und die Marine: Reichspolitik und Flottenbau, 1920-1939* (Dusseldorf, 1973), p. 504.

20. Deist et al., *Das Deutsche Reich und der Zweite Weltkrieg*, Vol. I, pp. 331-332. Quoted from *Anatomie des Krieges*, edited by Dietrich Eichholtz and Wolfgang Schumann (Berlin, 1969), p. 204.

21. PRO FO 800/314, p. 186; and PRO FO 371/21659, C 14471/42/18, Minute by Gwatkin, 27.10.38.

22. See PRO CAB 23/95, Cab 47 (38), Meeting of the Cabinet, 30.9.38.; Lord Strang, *At Home and Abroad* (London, 1956), p. 148; and PRO FO 371/21658, C 11535/42/18, Berlin embassy to Central Desk, 1.10.38.

23. PRO PREM 1/266A, p. 23, Letter from Stanley to Chamberlain, 3.10.38.

24. Hansard, *Parliamentary Debates*, 5th Ser., Vol. 339, Cols. 50-67.

25. Ibid., Cols. 29-40.

26. Ibid., Col. 203.

27. It has now become the fashion among English historians to attack

Churchill for his failures and to ignore his strengths. But when all is said and done Churchill was right in 1938 and 1939 about the dangers that Britain faced and about the nature of the Nazi regime. Churchill's failure to influence British policy in this period is a reflection, not on him, but on those who were in control of the British government. For a gratuitous and unfair slight to Churchill see Stephen Roskill, *Hankey*, Vol. III, 1931-1963 (London, 1974), pp. 302, 386. For the leading work in this genre see Robert Rhode James, *Churchill: A Study in Failure*, 1900-1939 (New York, 1970).

28. Hansard, *Parliamentary Debates*, 5th Ser., Vol. 339, Col. 304.

29. Vansittart commented on Henderson's performance: "In my opinion the proceedings of the international commission have been scandalous. Sir N. Henderson's principle is always to give the Germans everything: He never made an attempt to get a compromise between 1910 and 1918 [population breakdown of nationalities] *as instructed.* He simply reproduced Godesberg, after we had flattered ourselves publicly on having got away from it—a source of great political embarrassment to us though not to him. And over 3/4 of a million Czechs are now apparently to be under German rule." PRO FO 371/ 21783, C 11616/11169/18, Note by Vansittart, 11.10.38. Months later Henderson would turn red with embarrassment when reminded of the commission. R. Coulondre, *De Staline à Hitler* (Paris, 1950), p. 172.

30. PRO FO 800/328, p. 169, Letter from Halifax to Chamberlain, 11.10.38.

31. David Irving, *The War Path, Hitler's Germany 1933-1939* (New York, 1978), p. 156.

32. Hansard, *Parliamentary Debates*, 5th Ser., Vol. 339, Cols. 49-50.

33. PRO PREM 1/330, p. 43. Note from Wilson to Chamberlain: "Points made by Sir Nevile Henderson," 20.10.38.

34. Hansard, *Parliamentary Debates*, 5th Ser., Vol. 339, Cols. 49-50.

35. PRO CAB 23/95, Cab 48 (38), Meeting of the Cabinet, 3.10.38., p. 304.

36. PRO CAB 24/279, CP 234 (38), 21.10.38., "Defense Preparations: Forecast."

37. PRO CAB 23/96, Cab 50 (38), Meeting of the Cabinet, 26.10.38., pp. 59-60.

38. PRO CAB 27/648, D (38), 2nd Meeting, 28.10.38., Cabinet: Committee on Defense Programs and Their Acceleration: Minutes, pp. 9-11.

39. PRO CAB 27/648, D (38), 3rd Meeting, 31.10.38., Cabinet: Committee on Defense Programs and Their Acceleration: Minutes, pp. 2-3.

40. PRO CAB 27/648, D (38), 4th Meeting, 1.11.38., Cabinet: Committee on Defense Programs and Their Acceleration: Minutes, p. 4.

41. PRO CAB 27/648, D (38), 7, 2.11.38., Cabinet: Committee on Defense Programs and Their Acceleration, Note by the Secretary setting out

conclusions. Gerhard Weinberg in his *Foreign Policy of Hitler's Germany*, Vol. II, *Starting World War II* (Chicago, 1980), p. 522, entirely distorts the effort that the British were making by implying that a "press on" mentality existed in London with regards to rearmament.

42. PRO CAB 23/96, Cab 53 (38), Meeting of the Cabinet, 7.11.38., pp. 155-164.

43. PRO CAB 23/96, Cab 53 (38), Meeting of the Cabinet, 7.11.38., Conclusions, pp. 168-171. Even the suggestion to lay down additional escort vessels worried Chamberlain as to the effect it might have in Germany.

44. See particularly: PRO CAB/143, DPR 285, 14.10.38., CID, 24th Progress Report: "Week Ending 1.10.38."; DPR 291, 14.12.38., 25th Progress Report; DPR 297, 26th Progress Report; PRO CAB 16/144, DPR 305, 27th Progress Report, 18.4.39.; and DPR 312, 28th Progress Report, 14.6.39.

45. PRO CAB 27/648, D (38), 3, Cabinet: Committee on Defense Programs and Their Acceleration, "The Role of the Army in Light of the Czechoslovakian Crisis," Memorandum by the Secretary of State for War, October, 1938.

46. PRO CAB 27/648, D (38), 4th Meeting, 1.11.38., Cabinet: Committee on Defense Programs and Acceleration, p. 3. Robert Shay argues that by the fall of 1938 the Treasury's rationing of the services had collapsed. This is surely an overstatement. Although the Treasury may well have been fighting a rearguard action, it still was able to severely limit defense spending. For the other interpretation see: Robert Paul Shay Jr., *British Rearmament in the Thirties* (Princeton, 1977), pp. 228-239.

47. PRO FO 371/21600, C 14025/55/17, Phipps to Halifax, 16.11.38. When all French documents are finally open to historians our understanding of French policy will undoubtedly undergo a radical revision. The strains of coalition government, military planning, and the effect of British lack of support will go far to expanding our knowledge of what happened. For a start in this direction see: Susan B. Butterworth, "Daladier and the Munich Crisis: A Reappraisal," *Journal of Current History* 9, no. 3 (July 1974).

48. Anthony Adamthwaite, *France and the Coming of the Second World War, 1936-1939* (London, 1977), p. 266.

49. Ibid., p. 267.

50. PRO FO 371/21600, C 12637/55/17, Minute by Sargent, 22.10.38.

51. See in particular PRO FO 371/21592, C 14067/13/17, Letter from the military attaché (Paris) to the War Office, 18.10.38.

52. PRO FO 371/21592, C 14138/13/17, Minute by Sargent, 16.11.38.

53. PRO CAB 27/648 D (38) 3, Cabinet: Committee on Defense Programs and Their Acceleration, "The Role of the Army in the Light of the Czechoslovakian Crisis," Enclosure 1, p. 16.

---

54. *DBFP*, 3rd Ser., Vol. III, Doc 325, "Record of Anglo-French Conversations at the Quai d'Orsay on November 24, 1938"; see also PRO FO 371/21593, C 15399/13/17, "Meeting with Dominion Representatives," 1.12.38. The latter account of the meeting indicates, which the Foreign Office account does not, that the French raised the effect of the loss of the Czech divisions at the start of the conversations.

55. See among others: PRO CAB 2/8, CID, Minutes of the 241st Meeting held on Dec. 15, 1938, p. 94; PRO FO 371/21597, C 15175/36/17, Note by F. K. Roberts, 7.12.38.; and ibid., Minute by Vansittart, 21.12.38.

56. PRO FO 371/21593, C 15630/13/17, 12.12.38.; for the reaction in France see PRO FO 371/21593, C 15385/13/17, Phipps to Halifax, 13.12.38.

57. I would like to thank Brian Sullivan of Columbia University for making available to me a draft of his dissertation, from which this aspect of the Mediterranean confrontation is drawn.

58. PRO FO 371/21593, C 15682/13/17, Phipps to Halifax, 19.12.38.

59. PRO CAB 23/97, Cab 2 (39), Meeting of the Cabinet, 25.1.39., p. 56. See also Chamberlain's remark on February 1; PRO CAB 23/97, Cab 3 (39), Meeting of the Cabinet, 1.2.39., p. 112.

60. PRO CAB 53/10, COS/268th Meeting, 18.1.39., CID, Chiefs of Staff Committee, Minutes, p. 80.

61. PRO CAB 53/43, COS 811, 19.12.38., CID, Chiefs of Staff Sub-Committee, "The State of Preparedness of the Army in Relation to the Present International Situation," Memorandum by the Chief of the Imperial General Staff, p. 46.

62. PRO CAB 53/43, COS 825, 16.1.39., CID, Chiefs of Staff Sub-Committee, "The Strategic Position of France in a European War," pp. 179-182.

63. PRO FO 371/22915, Foreign Office Minute, 12.1.39. (Answered by COS 833.)

64. PRO CAB 27/627, FP 9 (36) 74, Cabinet: Committee on Foreign Policy, "Possible German Intentions," 19.1.38.

65. PRO CAB 23/97, Cab 2 (39), Meeting of the Cabinet, 25.1.39. It is not clear who was responsible for all these rumors. A possible explanation may be that the *Abwehr* and Canaris and Lt. Col. Hans Oster, having seen the British almost totally ignore the accurate intelligence that they had been fed over the summer of 1938, decided to wake them up by a stronger dose of medicine. For the various rumors see particularly: PRO FO 371/22957, C 356/13/18, Counsel General Munich, "Call up of reservists in Munich on the same scale as during the Czech crisis," 10.1.39.; C 398/13/18, Ogilvie-Forbes to Halifax, Mason MacFarlane: "Much military activity of a preparatory nature in Progress," 11.1.39.; PRO FO 371/22961, C 602/15/18, Sir R. Cleves (Belgium) to Halifax, "Belgian belief the Germans were preparing

to move against Holland," 13.3.39.; C 603/15/18, Phipps to Halifax, 13.1.39. See PRO FO 371/22957 and PRO FO 371/22958 for more rumors of German military activities, mobilizations, and future aggressive plans. See also PRO CAB 27/627, 19.1.39. Memorandum by Halifax for the Foreign Policy Committee.

66. PRO CAB 23/97, Cab 3 (39), Meeting of the Cabinet, 1.2.39., p. 117.

67. PRO FO 371/22962, C 1098/15/18, FP (36), 35th Meeting, Committee on Foreign Policy, 23.1.39.

68. PRO CAB 23/97, Cab 5 (39), Meeting of the Cabinet, 2.2.39., p. 174.

69. PRO CAB 24/282, CP 23 (39), 27.1.39., CID, "Supply Organization in Time of War: Extract from the Draft Minutes of the 345th Meeting of the Committee of Imperial Defense, Held on 26.1.39.," p. 205.

70. PRO FO 371/22922, DP (P) 47, CID, "Strategic Position of France in Relation to the Role of the British Army in War," Note by the Secretary of State for Foreign Affairs on Report (COS 833) by the COS Sub-Committee.

71. PRO CAB 23/97, Cab 8 (39), Meeting of the Cabinet, 22.2.39., p. 306.

72. PRO CAB 23/96, Cab 53 (38), Meeting of the Cabinet, 7.11.38., p. 136.

73. Anti-Semitism was not entirely absent from the attitudes of some British statesmen. In the summer of 1938 Henderson in a conversation with Dirksen had accused the Jews, the communists, and the intelligentsia of wanting a preventive war. He then urged Dirksen that the treatment of the Jews be regularized in an orderly and systematic manner. PRO FO 371/21658, C 8049/42/18, Henderson to Halifax, 5.8.38. Weinberg in his *Foreign Policy of Hitler's Germany*, Vol. II, p. 522, is far too kind to the British on their reaction to the November pogrom.

74. PRO FO 371/21658, C 14396/42/18, FP (36) 32nd Meeting, 14.11.38. It is difficult to see exactly what Chamberlain was getting at. Colonial concessions to the Germans had been discussed several times in Cabinet meetings but no agreement had been reached among British politicians and diplomats, nor had detailed planning been undertaken.

75. PRO FO 371/21701,C 15228/528/18, Kirkpatrick (Berlin): "Herr Hitler's Word," 7.12.38.

76. PRO CAB 27/624, FP (36) 32 Meeting, 14.11.38., Cabinet: Committee on Foreign Policy.

77. PRO FO 371/22962, C 1143/15/18, Ogilvie-Forbes to Halifax, 27.1.39.

78. PRO FO 371/22988, C 2013/16/17, Henderson to Halifax, "Interview with von Ribbentrop," 16.2.39.

79. *DBFP*, 3rd Ser., Vol. IV, Doc 118, 18.2.39., Henderson to Halifax.

80. PRO FO 800/270, p. 18, Letter from Henderson to the King, 22.2.39. On the same day Henderson wrote Halifax that he felt confident of the prospects of peace were it not for that section of the British press inspired by the Jews and the intelligentsia who hated Hitler and the Nazis. PRO FO 800/315, p. 24, Henderson to Halifax, 22.2.39.

81. PRO FO 800/315, Letter from Henderson to Chamberlain, 23.2.39.

82. *DBFP*, 3rd Ser., Vol. IV, DOC 162, 28.2.39., Henderson to Halifax.

83. PRO FO 800/294, p. 27, Letter from Henderson to Halifax, 9.3.39.

84. PRO FO 371/22965, C 2139/15/18, Minute by Vansittart, 22.2.39.

85. PRO FO 800/294, p. 28, Memorandum by Alexander Cadogan, 26.2.39.

86. PRO FO 800/294, p. 31, Letter from Cadogan to Henderson, 13.3.39.

87. Ibid., Vansittart minute, 8.3.39.

88. Adamthwaite, *France and the Coming of the Second World War*, p. 271.

IX. The Reaction to Prague: Diplomatic Prelude

1. *DBFP*, 3rd Ser., Vol. IV, Appendix I, viii, p. 595, 15.3.39., Henderson to Halifax.

2. PRO CAB 23/98, Cab 11 (39), Meeting of the Cabinet, 15.3.39., pp. 7-8.

3. Ibid., pp. 9-13.

4. Ibid., p. 15.

5. Hansard, *Parliamentary Debates*, 5th Ser., Vol. 345, House of Commons (London, 1939), Cols. 437-440. Chamberlain was referring to Inskip.

6. Ibid., Col. 615.

7. See PRO FO 371/23061, C 379/3356/18, Minute by Sir R. Vansittart, and PRO FO 371/23060, C 3434/3356/18, Knox to Halifax, 18.3.39. See also: C. A. Macartney, *October Fifteenth*, Vol. I (Edinburgh, 1957), pp. 340-341.

8. See among other reports: *DBFP*, 3rd Ser., Vol. IV, Doc 298, Minute by Sargent, 16.3.39.; Doc 395, 17.3.39., Halifax to Sir R. Hoare (Bucharest); Doc 390, 17.7.39., Halifax to Kennard (Warsaw); Doc 428, 19.3.39., Halifax to Hoare; and PRO FO 371/23061, C 3615/3356/18, Hoare to Halifax, 20.3.39.

9. It is hard to see how Chatfield came to this conclusion. After all Germany had controlled Rumania from 1916 on and that had not allowed her to escape the effects of the blockade in 1917-1918. Chamberlain had made several major changes in his Cabinet in late February 1939. Among the foremost had been the replacement of Inskip by Chatfield. This change reflected not only a growing popular disenchantment with Inskip but an even

greater public dissatisfaction with the government's defense policies. Inskip's removal represented a useful distraction to public pressures.

10. PRO CAB 23/98, Cab 12 (39), Meeting of the Cabinet, 18.3.39., pp. 42-58.

11. Ibid., Cab 13 (39), Meeting of the Cabinet, 20.3.39., p. 81.

12. Ibid., Cab 12 (39), Meeting of the Cabinet, 18.3.39., p. 52.

13. PRO FO 371/22958, C 3954/13/18, Brigadier F. Beaumont-Nesbitt to Strang, 24.3.38.

14. PRO FO 371/23061, C 4042/3356/18, Ogilvie-Forbes to Halifax, 25.3.39. The change, especially in Mason-MacFarlane's attitude, is noteworthy. The explanation undoubtedly lies in the fact that MacFarlane had become convinced that war with Germany was now inevitable.

15. PRO CAB 23/98, Cab 12 (39), Meeting of the Cabinet, 18.3.39., p. 52.

16. For the best discussion of the unlikelihood of an agreement between the West and the Soviet Union see Adam Ulam, *Expansion and Coexistence* (New York, 1971), pp. 266-279.

17. *DBFP*, 3rd Ser., Vol. IV, Doc 459, 21.3.39., Kennard to Halifax. See also PRO FO 371/23061, C 3727/3356/18, Kennard to Halifax, 21.3.39.; and PRO FO 371/23061, C 3849/3356/18, Mr. Snow (Helsingfors to Halifax, 22.3.39.).

18. PRO FO 371/23061, C 3735/3356/18, Conversation between Sargent and M. Cambon, 20.3.39.

19. *DBFP*, 3rd Ser., Vol. IV, Doc 458.

20. PRO CAB 23/98, Cab 14 (39), Meeting of the Cabinet, 22.3.39.

21. PRO FO 371/22968, FP (36), 38th meeting, Cabinet: Committee on Foreign Policy, 27.3.39.

22. *DBFP*, 3rd Ser., Vol. IV, Doc 538, 27.3.39., Halifax to Kennard and Hoare. Halifax used almost exactly the same words in describing to the Cabinet why the Four-Power Declaration had not worked. (CAB 23/98, Cab 15 (39) Meeting of the Cabinet, 29.3.39.)

23. PRO FO 371/22968, FP (36), 38th meeting, Cabinet: Committee on Foreign Policy, 27.3.39., pp. 2-4.

24. Included in the annex of the March 30 Cabinet meeting was a report by the Chiefs of Staff. The deputy director of military intelligence did not think that Germany intended to go beyond demands on Danzig or that the Poles would fight for Danzig. "There is in fact no evidence that either the Germans or Italians intend to make any major move." PRO CAB 23/98, Cab 16 (38), Meeting of the Cabinet, 30.3.39., p. 183, Annex B, Report by the Chiefs of Staff Committee to the minister for the coordination of defense.

25. PRO CAB 23/98, Cab 16 (39), Meeting of the Cabinet, 30.3.39., p. 156.

26. Ibid., p. 160. Later in the meeting Chamberlain repeated this point, p. 169.

27. It is interesting that here from the first the Chiefs of Staff considered the question of the consequences of allowing Germany to absorb Poland— something they had never done in regard to Czechoslovakia.

28. PRO CAB 23/98, Cab 16 (39), Meeting of the Cabinet, 30.3.39., p. 163. All of this makes strange reading when compared to the chief's assessment of the military situation the previous year.

29. PRO CAB 23/98, Cab 17 (39), Meeting of the Cabinet, 31.3.39., p. 187. Halifax added later in the meeting that any question in Parliament as to why the guarantee made no mention of Russia could be answered by saying "that the present was only an interim arrangement and that the inclusion of Russia was a matter which it was intended to deal with in the discussions next week."

30. Ibid., p. 195.

31. Winston Churchill, *The Gathering Storm* (London, 1948), p. 347.

32. Wilhelm Deist et al., *Das Deutsche Reich und der Zweite Weltkrieg*, Vol. I (Stuttgart, 1979), p. 333.

33. Ibid., pp. 333-334.

34. Walter Hummelberger, "Die Rüstungsindustrie der Tschechoslowakei, 1933 bis 1939," in *Wirtschaft und Rüstung am Vorabend des Zweiten Weltkrieges*, edited by Friedrich Forstmeier and Hans-Erich Volkmann (Dusseldorf, 1975), p. 318.

35. Deist et al., *Das Deutsche Reich und der Zweite Weltkrieg*, Vol. I, p. 334.

36. OKH, 5.4.39., Betr: "Abtransport tschechischen Kriegsmaterials," NARS T-79/93/412.

37. Quoted in Jon Kimche, *The Unfought Battle* (New York, 1968), p. 29.

38. Deist et al., *Das Deutsche Reich und der Zweite Weltkrieg*, Vol I, p. 332.

39. Correlli Barnett in *The Collapse of British Power* (London, 1972), p. 556, claims that the occupation of Prague increased German strength by forty divisions.

40. See particularly the following for German use of Czech arms: ADAP, Series D, Vol. VI, Doc 659, 12.7.39., "Das auswärtige Amt an den Chef des Oberkommandos der Wehrmacht"; Doc 703, 22.7.39., "Aufzeichnung des Leiters der wirtschaftspolitischen Abteilung."

41. Waffen SS Erfahrungsberichte on Czech weapons during the French campaign were particularly enthusiastic; see NARS, T-175/104/2626133ff.

42. Col. Merglen, "Les Chars Tcheques dans l'Armée de Hitler," *Revue Historique de L'Armée* 21, no. 2 (1965).

43. IMT, *TMWC*, XXXVI, Doc 028EC.

44. OKH, 18.11.39., Am: 81, 82, 83, 88 Divisions, setting forth training program, NARS T-315/1150/472.

45. *ADAP*, Series D, Vol. VII, Doc 192, 22.8.39., "Aufzeichnung ohne Unterschrift."

46. For these feelers and the Polish response see: *ADAP*, Series D, Vol. V, Doc 81, 24.10.38., "Aufzeichnung des Legationsrats Hewel"; Doc 101, 19.11.38., "Aufzeichnung des Reichsaussenministers"; Doc 119, 5.1.39., "Aufzeichnung des Gesandten Schmidt"; Doc 120, 9.1.39., "Aufzeichnung des Reichsaussenministers"; and Doc 126, 1.2.39., "Aufzeichnung des Reichsaussenministers."

47. Ibid., Doc 119, 5.1.39., Aufzeichnung des Gesandten Schmidt."

48. *ADAP*, Series D, Vol. VI, Doc 61, 21.3.39., "Aufzeichnung des Reichsaussenministers."

49. Alan Bullock, *Hitler, A Study in Tyranny* (London, 1964), p. 437.

50. *ADAP*, Series D, Vol. VI, Doc 103, 27.3.39., "Der Staatssekretär an die Botschaft in Warschau."

51. Ibid., Vol. VI, Doc 118, 29.3.39., "Der Botschafter in Warschau an das Auswärtige Amt"; *Polish White Book*, Doc 64, 29.3.39.

52. Bullock, *Hitler, A Study in Tyranny*, p. 445. The Abwehr was the German military intelligence organization, originally part of the War Ministry, but after establishment of the OKW, part of that organization.

53. *ADAP*, Series D, Vol. VI, Doc 149, 3.4.39., "Weisung des Chefs des Oberkommandos der Wehrmacht."

54. PRO CAB 24/287, CP 149 (39), "Note on the Financial Situation," 3.7.39.

55. PRO CAB 27/657, DP (39), 1st Meeting, 20.3.39., Cabinet: "Committee on Defense Programs and their Acceleration."

56. PRO CAB 16/209, SAC/4th Meeting, CID, Strategic Appreciations Sub-Committee, p. 75.

57. PRO PREM 1/296, Letter from Simon to Chatfield, 17.4.39.

58. PRO CAB 23/100, Cab 36 (39), Meeting of the Cabinet, 5.7.39., pp. 108-128.

59. PRO CAB 23/98, Cab 15 (39), Meeting of the Cabinet, 29.3.39., p. 133.

60. PRO CAB 29/160, AFC (J) 3rd Meeting, Anglo-French Staff Conversations, 1939, Minutes of the 3rd Meeting, 30.3.39., p. 12.

61. PRO CAB 53/47, COS 876, CID, Chiefs of Staff Committee, "Staff Conversations with France: Report on Stage 1: Part II," p. 110.

62. PRO CAB 23/98, Cab 21 (39), Meeting of the Cabinet, 19.4.39., p. 346.

63. PRO CAB 23/99, Cab 22 (39), Meeting of the Cabinet, 24.4.39., p.

6. Chamberlain's reluctance to organize a conscripted army was not only due to personal inclination but to domestic pressure. The Labour party remained steadfast in its opposition to conscription in any form, and the Cardinal Archbishop of Ireland issued "a solemn declaration that the application of conscription to Mother Ireland would be disastrous and . . . invited the prayers of the faithful that this calamity might be averted." CAB 23/99, Cab 25 (39), Meeting of the Cabinet, 1.5.39., p. 104.

64. ADAP, Series D, Vol. VI, Doc 729, 27.7.39., "Aufzeichnung des vortragenden Legationsrats Schnurre"; Doc 736, 29.7.39., "Der Staatssekretär an den Botschafter in Moskau"; Doc 744, 31.7.39., "Der Staatssekretär an die Botschaft in Moskau." An alliance with the West to protect Poland would automatically involve war against Germany after the Germans launched their attack on Poland.

65. PRO CAB 53/47, COS 871 (JP), 28.3.39., CID, Chiefs of Staff Committee: "Military Implications of an Anglo-French Guarantee to Poland and Rumania," p. 17. Robert Manne in his article, "The British Decision for Alliance with Russia, May 1939," *Journal of Contemporary History* 9, no. 3 (July 1974), argues that throughout the spring of 1939 the chiefs recommended that the government seek an agreement with the Soviet Union rather than with Poland. This is an overstatement. Manne argues that on March 18 the chiefs recommended alliance with Russia over Poland. Basically they urged this because of Russia's deterrent value on Japan, not because of her military strength in Europe. Moreover, the many military papers produced by the various strategic committees consistently pointed out Russian military weakness.

66. *DBFP*, 3rd Ser., Vol. IV, Doc 183, 6.3.39., Seeds to Halifax.

67. PRO CAB 53/10, COS/283rd Meeting, 18.3.39.

68. PRO CAB 23/98, Cab 18 (39), Meeting of the Cabinet, 5.4.39., pp. 207-212.

69. Ibid., pp. 213-214.

70. PRO CAB 23/98, Notes of a Conference of Ministers, 8.4.38., pp. 242-243.

71. PRO CAB 16/209, SAC/5th Meeting, CID, Strategic Appreciations Sub-Committee, 11.4.39.

72. See particularly, PRO CAB 23/98, Cab 20 (39), Meeting of the Cabinet, 13.4.39., pp. 286-297. For an excellent study of France's role in the guarantees to Balkan countries see: C. A. MacDonald, "Britain, France and the April Crisis of 1939," *European Studies Review* 2, no. 2 (April 1972).

73. See particularly Butler's minute on the success of Britain's tough diplomacy: PRO FO 371/22970, C 5864/15/18, Foreign Office minute, Mr. Butler, 19.4.39.

74. The words "offensive diplomacy" are Butler's in the above-referenced minute.

75. PRO CAB 53/49, COS 914, CID, Chiefs of Staff Committee, "Conversations with France (AFC 25)," Anglo-French Staff Conversations, 1939, Report on Stage II, Annex I, p. 226, April 1939.

76. PRO FO 371/22969, C 5460/15/18, Memorandum by Sir Alexander Cadogan, 19.4.39., on a dispatch by Seeds to Halifax.

77. PRO CAB 27/624, FP (36) 43rd Meeting, 19.4.39., Cabinet: Committee on Foreign Policy.

78. See particularly: *DBFP*, 3rd Ser., Vol. V, Doc 241, 20.4.39., "Letter from Phipps to Sargent"; Doc 252, 21.4.39., "Minute by Strang."

79. Anthony Adamthwaite, *France and the Coming of the Second World War* (London, 1977), p. 311.

80. Robert J. Young, *In Command of France* (Cambridge, Mass., 1978), p. 236.

81. PRO CAB 27/624, FP (36) 43rd Meeting, 19.4.39., Cabinet: Committee on Foreign Policy, p. 203.

82. PRO CAB 53/48, COS 887, 24.4.39., CID, Chiefs of Staff Committee, "Military Value of Russia: Report."

83. Ibid.

84. PRO CAB 27/624 FP (36) 44th Meeting, 25.4.39., Cabinet: Committee on Foreign Policy, p. 319.

85. PRO CAB 23/99, Cab 24 (39), Meeting of the Cabinet, 26.4.39., pp. 57-61. See also Gafencu's comment to the British Minister, Mr. R. Clive, in Brussels, 21.4.39., FO 371/23064, C 5749/5356/18.

86. PRO CAB 23/99, Cab 26 (39), Meeting of the Cabinet, 3.5.39., pp. 128-130.

87. For MacDonald's worries see: PRO CAB 27/624, FP (36) 44th Meeting, 25.4.39., Cabinet: Committee on Foreign Policy, p. 319; and PRO CAB 23/99, Cab 26 (39), Meeting of the Cabinet, 3.5.39., pp. 128-130.

88. PRO CAB 23/99, Cab 29 (39), Meeting of the Cabinet, 3.5.39., pp. 128-130.

89. PRO CAB 24/286, CP 108 (39), 10.5.39., "Balance of Strategical Value in War as between Spain as an Enemy and Russia as an Ally: Report by the Chiefs of Staff Committee," pp. 95-96.

90. PRO CAB 27/625, FP (36), 47th Meeting, 16.5.39., Cabinet: Committee on Foreign Policy.

91. *DBFP*, 3rd Ser., Vol. V, Doc 3413, 8.5.39., Henderson to Halifax, footnote 2.

92. PRO CAB 27/625, FP (36), 47th Meeting, 16.5.39., Cabinet: Committee on Foreign Policy.

93. PRO CAB 23/99, Cab 30 (39), Meeting of the Cabinet, 24.5.39.

94. PRO CAB 27/625, FP (36), 50th Meeting, 9.6.39., Cabinet: Committee on Foreign Policy, p. 109.

95. For these reports see: PRO FO 371/22972, C 6733/15/18, Mr. Gasoigne (Budapest) to Halifax, 6.5.39.; PRO FO 371/22973, C 6735/15/18, Henderson to Halifax, 8.5.39.; PRO FO 371/22972, C 7457/15/18, Henderson to Halifax, 18.5.39.; PRO FO 371/ 22973, C 7827/15/18, Account by Mr. Kirkpatrick on Conversation with M. Cambon, 26.5.39.; PRO FO 371/22973, C 8924/15/18, Foreign Office minute, Mr. Ridsdale, 16.6.39.; *DBFP*, 3rd Ser., Vol. VI, Appendix I, i, Letter from Henderson to Cadogan, 13.6.39.

96. PRO CAB 23/100, Cab 38 (39), Meeting of the Cabinet, 19.7.39., p. 186.

97. PRO CAB 23/100, Cab 41 (39), Meeting of the Cabinet, 22.8.39., p. 320.

98. Heinz Guderian, *Panzer Leader* (London, 1952), pp. 63-64.

99. PRO CAB 27/625, FP (36), 48th Meeting: Cabinet Committee on Foreign Policy, 19.5.39., p. 67.

100. PRO CAB 23/99, Cab 26 (39), Meeting of the Cabinet, 3.5.39., pp. 117-118.

101. *DBFP*, 3rd Ser., Vol. V, Doc 542, 17.5.39., Henderson to Halifax.

102. PRO CAB 24/286, CP 115 (39), 19.5.39., "Negotiations with Russia, draft Memorandum: Meeting of the Committee of Foreign Policy," p. 275.

103. *DBFP*, 3rd Ser., Vol. V, Doc 570, 20.5.39., "Extract from Record of Conversation between the Secretary of State and MM. Daladier and Bonnet at the Ministry of War, in Paris."

104. PRO CAB 27/625, FP (36), 51st Meeting, 13.6.39., Cabinet Committee on Foreign Policy, p. 138.

105. ADAP, Series D, Vol. VI, Doc 716, 24.7.39., "Vermerk über die Unterredung mit Sir Horace Wilson am 18.7., 3:15 Uhr bis 4:30 Uhr Nachmittags und am 21.7. von 13:00 Uhr bis 13:30 Uhr, mit Sir Joseph Ball am 20.7. 17:30 Uhr bis 19:30 Uhr und mit Mr. Hudson am 20.7. 17:30 Uhr bis 18:30 Uhr Nachmittags (Alle Unterredungen erfolgten auf Aufforderung der englischen Herrn mit Wissen des Botschafters von Dirksen)." See also Hudson's account of his discussions with Wohlthat in *DBFP*, 3rd Ser., Vol. V, Doc 370, 20.7.39., "Record of a Conversation between Mr. R. S. Hudson and Dr. Wohlthat."

106. PRO FO 371/22990,C 10359/16/18, Henderson to Halifax, 24.7.39. How exactly the word got out to the British Press is uncertain. Nevertheless, the tone of the leaks (encouraging maximum outrage in Germany as well as in Britain with the suggestion that the Reich could be bought) suggests that

someone high in the Foreign Office either tolerated or cooperated in getting the word out. There is an interesting minute for Halifax by Vansittart (PRO FO 371/22990, C 10533/16/18) urging that no investigation be made into the matter of how the press had found out. The possibility is that either Vansittart had talked or (more likely) that he knew who had tipped off the press.

107. PRO CAB 23/100, Cab 43 (39), Meeting of the Cabinet, 26.8.39., p. 377.

108. PRO CAB 23/100, Cab 47 (39), Meeting of the Cabinet, 1.9.39., p. 443.

X. Grand Strategy and the War's Beginning

1. PRO CAB 47/14, A.T.B. 181, "Plan for Economic Warfare Against Germany," 22.7.38.

2. PRO CAB 53/44, COS 831 (JP), 26.1.39., CID, Chiefs of Staff Committee, "European Appreciation, 1939-1940, Joint Planning Committee Draft," p. 157, Pt. III, "Broad Strategic Policy on the Conduct of War."

3. How Italy could possibly maintain her Mediterranean and Black Sea trade in the face of overwhelming Allied naval superiority was not discussed.

4. PRO FO 371/23017, C 5178/54/18 DP (P), 44 (COS 843), "European Appreciation: Report by the Chiefs of Staff Sub-Committee," CID, Chiefs of Staff Committee, 20.2.39.

5. PRO CAB 29/160, AFC (J), 8 Anglo-French Staff Conversations, 1939, "The Broad Strategic Problem," 28.3.39.

6. PRO FO 371/22958, C 4760/3/18, Ogilvie-Forbes to Mr. Strang, 29.3.39.

7. PRO CAB 29/159, AFC 16, 22.4.39., Anglo-French Staff Conversations, United Kingdom Delegation, Annex I, p. 73; see also PRO CAB 53/48, COS 881 (JP), CID, Chiefs of Staff Committee, "Anglo-French Staff Conversations, 1939," "Military Implications of the New Situation in Europe, Annex I, Economic Note: The German and Italian Situation," p. 351.

8. PRO CAB 47/14, A.T.B. 181, "Plan for Economic Warfare Against Germany," 22.7.38.

9. PRO CAB 47/15, ATB (EPB) 61/DM (39) 31, Cabinet: Defense Preparedness Committee: "Plans for Economic Warfare against Germany and Italy," p. 4, "Effects of Italy Entering the War."

10. ObdM, Berlin, 26.4.38., An das OKW, Betr: "Unterlagen für die Wünsche der Kriegsmarine für die Zusammenarbeit mit der italienischen Wehrmacht im Frieden und im Falle eines Krieges, bei dem Italien zumindesten wohlwollend neutral ist," NARS T-1022/2130/PG33316.

11. Marineattaché Rom, B. Nr 386/40, "Militärische Betrachtungen zur Lage in Italien," 2.2.40., NARS T-1022/2519/PG 45170.

12. PRO CAB 16/209, SAC/1st Meeting, 1.3.39., CID, Strategic Appreciations Sub-Committee, p. 12.

13. PRO CAB 53/3, JP/243rd Meeting, 20.3.39., CID, Joint Planning Sub-Committee, p. 2.

14. PRO CAB 55/15, JP 382, COS, Joint Planning Sub-Committee: "Allied Plans Against Italy," 27.3.39.

15. PRO CAB 55/15, JP 388, 28.3.39., CID, Joint Planning Sub-Committee, "Military Implications of an Anglo-French Guarantee to Poland and Rumania," p. 12 (also listed in CAB 53/47, COS 871 (JP), 28.3.39., p. 25).

16. PRO CAB 29/160, AFC (J) 28, 3.4.39., Anglo-French Staff Conversations, 1939: "German and Italian attacks against France," p. 121.

17. PRO CAB 53/48, COS 900, 5.5.39., CID, Chiefs of Staff Committee, "Joint Franco-British Action in the Event of Germany Adopting a Strictly Defensive Attitude in the West while Attacking Poland, Italy Possibly Being Neutral," Annex: "Extract from the Minutes of the Anglo-French Conversations Held on 3rd May 1939," p. 246.

18. PRO CAB 55/16, JP 406, 5.5.39., CID, Joint Planning Committee, p. 3.

19. PRO CAB 53/50, COS 916, 30.5.39., CID, Chiefs of Staff Committee: "The Consequences of the Possible Neutrality of Italy."

20. Oliver Warner, *Admiral of the Fleet, Cunningham of Hyndhope* (Cleveland, 1967), p. 92.

21. PRO CAB 27/625, FP (36), 52nd Meeting, 19.6.39., Cabinet: Committee on Foreign Policy, p. 146.

22. PRO CAB 2/8, CID Minutes of the 360th Meeting held on 22.6.39., p. 232.

23. PRO CAB 55/18, JP 470, 12.7.39., CID, Joint Planning Committee: "The attitude of Italy in war and the problem of Anglo-French support to Poland," p. 3. See also PRO CAB 53/52, COS 942 (JP), 12.7.39., for the same report.

24. PRO CAB 53/51, COS 939 (Revise), CID, Chiefs of Staff Committee: "The attitude of Italy in war and the problem of Anglo-French support to Poland," p. 200.

25. PRO CAB 2/9, CID, Minutes of the 368th meeting held on July 24, 1939, p. 74.

26. PRO CAB 53/11 COS/309th meeting, 19.7.39., CID, Chiefs of Staff Minutes, p. 170; PRO CAB 2/9, CID, Minutes of the 368th meeting held on July 24, 1939, p. 74.

27. "Réunion du Conseil Suprême Interallié qui s'est tenu à Brighton,"

22.9.39. Fondation Nationale des Sciences Politiques. See also Fonds Daladiers No. 5, "Note pour le conseil des ministres," 20.9.39.

28. PRO CAB 53/11, COS/312th meeting, CID, Chiefs of Staff Committee, Minutes, 24.8.39.

29. PRO CAB 53/54, COS 965, 24.8.39., CID, Chiefs of Staff Committee: "Attitude of Italy in War."

30. PRO CAB 27/662, DM (39) 21, Cabinet: Defense Preparedness Committee: "Plan for Economic Warfare Against Italy and Germany," 1.9.39., p. 4.

31. PRO FO 371/23818, R 6901/399/22, Foreign Office minute by J. Nichols, 29.8.39.

32. For the best discussions of this see: MacGregor Knox, *Mussolini Unleashed* (London, 1982), pp. 42-43, 46; and Christopher Thorne, *The Approach of War* (London, 1967), pp. 168-169.

33. PRO FO 371/22976, C 11813/15/18, Lorraine (Rome) to Halifax, 23.8.39.

34. See Halifax's comments to the Cabinet in the meeting on 22.8.39. PRO CAB 23/100, Cab 41 (39), 22.8.39.

35. D. C. Watt in the introduction to Lawrence R. Pratt, *East of Malta, West of Suez* (London, 1975), p. 10.

36. For a fuller discussion of German planning and the conduct of operations in the Polish Campaign see: Robert M. Kennedy, *The German Campaign in Poland, 1939* (Washington, 1956); and Klaus A. Maier, Horst Rohde, Bernd Stegemann, and Hans Umbreit, *Das Deutsche Reich und der Zweite Weltkrieg*, Vol. II, *Die Errichtung der Hegemonie auf dem Europäischen Kontinent* (Stuttgart, 1979), Pt. 3.

37. Kennedy, *The German Campaign in Poland*, p. 62.

38. Maier et al., *Das Deutsche Reich und der Zweite Weltkrieg*, Vol. II, p. 93.

39. Ibid., p. 103.

40. Kennedy, *The German Campaign in Poland*, p. 77.

41. Maier et al., *Das Deutsche Reich und der Zweite Weltkrieg*, Vol. II, pp. 101-102.

42. B. H. Liddell Hart, *History of the Second World War* (London, 1970), pp. 27-28.

43. Kennedy, *The German Campaign in Poland*, pp. 51-52.

44. Maier et al., *Das Deutsche Reich und der Zweite Weltkrieg*, Vol. II, pp. 108-110.

45. Kennedy, *The German Campaign in Poland*, p. 84.

46. Maier et al., *Das Deutsche Reich und der Zweite Weltkrieg*, Vol. II, p. 117.

47. For a description of the German victory along the Bzura see: Rolf Elbe, *Die Schlacht an der Bzura im September 1939 aus deutscher und polnischer Sicht* (Freiburg, 1975).

48. Maier et al., *Das Deutsche Reich und der Zweite Weltkrieg*, Vol. II, p. 133.

49. IMT, *TMWC*, Vol. XXVI, Doc 798 PS, pp. 342-343.

50. Schlesisches Institut für Wirtschafts-und Konjunkturforschung," Zahlen des deutschen Aussenhandels seit Kriegsbeginn," August 1940, pp. 2-7, NARS T-84/195/1560551.

51. Bericht des Herrn Professor Dr. C. Krauch über die Lage auf dem Arbeitsgebiet der Chemie in der Sitzung des Generalrates am 24.6.41., "Treibstoff-Vorräte," NARS T-84/217/1586749.

52. Study by Oberst Dr. Hedler of Wi Rü Amt Stab, "Mineralöl und die Versorgunglage im Krieg," 31.8.41., p. 100, NARS T-44/438/1301640.

53. Maier et al., *Das Deutsche Reich und der Zweite Weltkrieg*, Vol. II, p. 267.

54. A. Hillgruber, *Hitler, König Carol und Marshall Antonescu: Die deutsch-rumänischen Beziehungen, 1938-1944* (Wiesbaden, 1954), pp. 67-68.

55. See in particular CAB 65/1 WM (39), War Cab 16 (39), 15.9.39.; and CAB 66/3 WP (39) 134, 20.11.39., "German Oil Supplies."

56. Study by Oberst Dr. Hedler of Wi Rü Amt Stab, "Mineralöl und die Versorgungslage im Kriege," 31.8.41., pp. 72-76, NARS T-77/438/1301640.

57. Schlesisches Institut für Wirtschafts-und Konjunkturforschung, Zahlen zur Entwicklung des deutschen Aussenhandels seit Kriegsbeginn," August 1940, Tab. XII, NARS T-84/195/1560551.

58. Institut für Weltwirtschaft an der Universität Kiel, Februar 1940, "Versorgung Grossdeutschlands und Kontinentaleuropas mit Mineralölerzeugnissen während der gegenwärtigen kriegerischen Verwicklungen," p. 3, NARS T-84/72/1358247.

59. Study by Oberst Dr. Hedler of Wi Rü Amt Stab, "Mineralöl und die Versorgungslage im Kriege," 31.8.41., p. 87, NARS T-77/438/1301640.

60. IMT, *TMWC*, Vol. XXXVI, Doc 028EC, p. 123, Speech by General Thomas to members of the Foreign Office; see also BA/MA M 31/PG 34162, 1 Abt SKL A Ia, 551/38, Berlin, 3.5.38.

61. Maier et al., *Das Deutsche Reich und der Zweite Weltkrieg*, Vol. II, pp. 194-196.

62. Williamson Murray, "Change in the European Balance of Power," Ph.D. dissertation, Yale University, 1975, p. 162.

63. Jäger, *Die wirtschaftliche Abhängigkeit des Dritten Reiches*, p. 89.

64. For the best discussion of the metals situation see Jäger, *Die wirtschaftliche Abhängigkeit des dritten Reiches.*

65. Ferdinand Friedenburg, "Die sowjetischen Kriegslieferungen an das Hitlerreich," in *Vierteljahrshefte für Wirtschaftsforschung*, 1962, p. 331.

66. Institut für Weltwirtschaft an der Universität Kiel, "Der kriegswirtschaftliche Beitrag Osteuropas für das deutsche Reich 1936-1944," pp. 16-17, NARS T-84/72/1358661; see also Schlesisches Institut für Wirtschafts- und Konjunkturforschung, "Zahlen des deutschen Aussenhandels seit Kriegsbeginn," p. 7, NARS T-84/195/1560551.

67. Reichswirtschaftsminister, 15.5.40., Betr: "Ausfuhr nach Übersee auf dem Wege über Siberien-Japan," NARS T-71/118/621462; and Institut für Weltwirtschaft an der Universität Kiel, "Der kriegswirtschaftliche Beitrag Osteuropas für das deutsche Reich, 1936-1944," pp. 20-21, NARS T-84/72/1358661.

68. Institut für Weltwirtschaft an der Universität Kiel, Februar 1940, "Versorgung Grossdeutschlands und Kontinentaleuropas mit Mineralölerzeugnissen während der gegenwärtigen kriegerischen Verwicklungen," p. 3, NARS T-84/72/1358247. Study by Oberst Dr. Hedler of Wi Rü Amt Stab, "Mineralöl und die Versorgungslage im Kriege," 31.8.41., p. 87, NARS T-77/438/1301640.

69. Reichsstelle für Wirtschaftsausbau, 17.8.39., "Schnellplan vom 13.8.38. für die Erzeugung von Pulver, Sprengstoffen und chemischen Kampfstoffen einschliesslich der Vorprodukte," NARS T-71/110/613208.

70. See "Bericht des Herrn Professor Dr. C. Krauch über die Lage auf dem Arbeitsgebiet der Chemie in der Sitzung des Generalrates am 24.6.41.," NARS T-84/217/1586749.

71. "Bericht des Herrn Professor Dr. C. Krauch über die Lage auf dem Arbeitsgebiet der Chemie in der Sitzung des Generalrates am 24.6.41.," NARS T-84/217.

72. Reichswirtschaftsministerium, 1943, "Tätigkeitsbericht: Buna Erzeugung," NARS T-71/109/611976.

73. Institut für Weltwirtschaft, "Die Eisenversorgung Grossdeutschlands während der gegenwärtigen kriegerischen Verwicklungen," December 1939, pp. 7-10, NARS T-84/195/1560527.

74. Jäger, *Die wirtschaftliche Abhängigkeit des Dritten Reiches*, pp. 174-175.

75. OKW files: "Denkschrift und Richtlinien über die Führung des Krieges im Westen," Berlin, 9.10.39., NARS T-77/775.

76. See in particular Harold C. Deutsch, *The Conspiracy against Hitler in the Twilight War* (Minneapolis, 1968).

77. It is worth noting that Allied actions in Norwegian territorial waters in February alarmed Hitler to such an extent that he ordered that preparations be made for the occupation of Scandinavia. This was a reflection of worries over the continued importation of Swedish ore.

---

78. BA/MA, RL 7/42, RL 7/43, Luftflottenkommando 2., Führungsab-teilung, Nr. 7093/39, 13.5.39., "Schlussbesprechung des Planspieles 1939."

79. Maier et al., *Das Deutsche Reich und der Zweite Weltkrieg*, Vol. II, pp. 63-64.

80. David Irving, *The War Path, Hitler's Germany, 1933-1939* (New York, 1978), p. 225; for further discussion of this visit see David Irving, *The Rise and Fall of the Luftwaffe* (Boston, 1973), pp. 73-74.

81. ADAP, Series D, Vol. VII, Doc 192, 22.8.39.

82. "The Luftwaffe in Poland," a study produced by the German Historical Branch (8th Abteilung), 11.7.44., Air Historical Branch Translation No. VII/33.

83. H. R. Trevor-Roper, ed., *Blitzkrieg to Defeat, Hitler's War Directives* (New York, 1965), Directive No. 6 for the Conduct of the War, 9.10.39., p. 13.

84. Ibid.

85. "Proposal for the Conduct of Air War against Britain," made by General Schmid of the German Air Force Operations Staff (intelligence), 22.11.39., AHB, Translation No. VII/30.

86. Trevor-Roper, *Blitzkrieg to Defeat*, Directive No. 9, Instructions for Warfare against the Economy of the Enemy, 29.11.39., p. 18.

87. See in particular Guderian's description of the major argument in the March conference between himself on one side and Generals Halder and Busch on the other. Heinz Guderian, *Panzer Leader* (London, 1952), pp. 90-92. For more complete accounts of the arguments within the German high command over the proper strategy for the coming campaign see: Telford Taylor, *The March of Conquest* (New York, 1958); Alistair Horne, *To Lose a Battle, France 1940* (London, 1969); and Hans-Adolf Jacobsen, *Fall Gelb. Der Kampf um den deutschen Operationsplan zur Westoffensive 1940* (Wiesbaden, 1957).

88. Among others see in particular: Heeresgruppenkommando 3., 18.7.38., "Der Einsatz der 8. Armee im März 1938 zur Wiedervereiningung Österreichs mit dem deutschen Reich," NARS T-79/14/447; and Generalkommando XIII A.K., "Erfahrungsbericht über den Einsatz Österreichs März/April 1938," 6.5.38., NARS T-314/525/000319. German experience reached back before the Anschluss. Von Thoma underlined that nothing new had been learned in Poland that had not already been indicated in Spain. Panzer Regiment 3, 20.1.40., "Erfahrungen aus dem poln. Feldzug," NARS T-78/379/6344436.

89. Armeeoberkommando 12, Betr.: Erfahrungsbericht, 25.10.39., NARS T-315/671/000890. For a detailed examination of what the German army was able to do over the next six months, see my article in *Armed Forces and Society*, "German Response to Victory in Poland: A Case Study in Professionalism" (Winter 1981).

90. 6 Pz Div., 18:7.40., "Erfahrungsbericht der 6 Pz. Div., Feldzug Frankreich," NARS T-311/49/7061274.

91. OKH, Berlin, Okt 7, 1939, Betr: "Erfahrungsbericht bei den Operationen im Osten," NARS T-315/435/00491.

92. Heeresgruppe B, Ia Nr. 2211/40, 28.4.40., "Bemerkungen zu den Truppenübungen im Frühjahr, 1940," NARS T-312/752/8396741.

93. PRO CAB 47/14, A.T.B. 181, "Plan for Economic Warfare Against Germany," 22.7.38.

94. PRO CAB 66/4 WP (39) 159, 13.12.39., "The Balkan Problem."

95. PRO CAB 66/1 WP (39) 5, 4.9.39., "Norwegian Neutrality."

96. PRO CAB 65/1 WM (39), War Cabinet 20 (39), 19.9.39.

97. PRO CAB 66/2 WP (39) 57, "Norway and Sweden."

98. PRO CAB 65/1 WM (39), War Cabinet 37 (39), 4.10.39.

99. PRO CAB 66/3 WP (39) 136, 19.11.39., "Northern Barrage."

100. PRO CAB 66/3 WP (39) 143, 28.11.39., "The Northern Barrage; Memorandum by the Secretary of State for Foreign Affairs."

101. PRO CAB 65/2 WM (39), War Cabinet 99 (39), 30.11.39.

102. PRO CAB 65/2 WM (39), War Cabinet 116 (39), 15.12.39.

103. PRO CAB 66/4 WP (39) 162, 16.12.39., "Norway-Iron Ore Traffic," W.S.C.

104. PRO CAB 67/3 WP (G39) 153, 18.12.39., "Stoppage of Iron Ore from Narvik."

105. J.R.M. Butler, *Grand Strategy*, Vol. II, *September 1939- June 1941* (London, 1957), p. 92.

106. PRO CAB 66/4 WP (39) 169, 20.12.39., "Stoppage of the Export of Swedish Iron Ore to Germany," Report by the Chiefs of Staff Committee.

107. PRO CAB 65/4 WM (39), 122nd Conclusion, 22.12.39.

108. PRO CAB 65/4 WM (39), 123rd Conclusion, Minute 1, Confidential Annex, 27.12.39.

109. Sir Llewellyn Woodward, *British Foreign Policy in the Second World War*, Vol. I (London, 1970), p. 58.

110. PRO CAB 66/4 WP (39) 180, 31.12.39., "Stoppage of the Export of Iron Ore to Germany; Balance of Advantages between the Major and Minor Projects," Chiefs of Staff.

111. PRO CAB 66/4 WP (39) 179, 1.12.39., "Military Importance of a Policy Aimed at Stopping the Export of Swedish Iron Ore to Germany," Chiefs of Staff.

112. PRO CAB 66/4 WP (40) 3, 31.12.39., "Swedish Iron Ore," W.S.C.

113. Woodward, *British Foreign Policy in the Second World War*, Vol. I, p. 62.

114. PRO CAB 66/5 WP (40) 23, 16.1.40., "Scandinavian Plans and Preparations," Chiefs of Staff.

115. See: Nicholas Bethell, *The War Hitler Won, September 1939* (London, 1975); and Jon Kimche, *The Unfought Battle* (London, 1967).

116. For the origins of Belgium's neutrality see David O. Kieft, *Belgium's Return to Neutrality* (Oxford, 1972). For the role of Belgium during the first months of the war see: Brian Bond, *France and Belgium, 1939-1940* (London, 1975).

117. Not to mention the fact that Britain had entered the First World War because of Germany's violation of Belgium's neutrality.

118. OKH 27.9.39., "Stimmung im französischen Heer," NARS T-312/1652; A.O.K. 1, Erfahrungsberichte, 14.9.39., NARS T-311/125; and OKH, 20.9.39., "Beobachtungen über Kampfverfahren und Kampfwert der französischen Truppe und Verhalten der eigenen Truppe bei Kampfhandlungen im Westen bis zum 16.9.39.," NARS T-312/1652.

119. On the subject of French military equipment see: R.H.S. Stolfi, "Equipment for Victory in France in 1940," *Journal of European Studies* (June 1972).

120. This left twenty-five divisions for deployment elsewhere in the west.

121. A.O.K.1,"Wir halten—wir stürmen: Beton und Stahl: Kampf und Sieg der 1. Armee im Westwall und Maginot Linie," pp. 2-3, NARS T-312/1/7500002.

122. Festungsnachschubstelle Wiesbaden, "Der Westwall: Übersicht des Gesamtbedarfs an Baustoffen," NARS T-311/125/7168842.

123. Fritz Todt, Berlin, 25.7.39., An General Witzleben, Hg.Kdo. 2., NARS T-311/124/7167796.

124. Franz Halder, *Kriegstagebuch, annotations by Generalmajor R. von Collenberg*, Foreign Military Studies, U.S. Army Europe, P-217, p. 1.

125. H.Gr.C, Gespräch mit Generaloberst von Brauchitsch, 10.9.39./12:15 Uhr, NARS T-311/38.

126. Kriegstagebuch, 15 I.D., NARS T-315/660.

127. 1. A.O.K., "Wir halten—Wir stürmen: Beton und Stahl: Kampf und Sieg der 1. Armee im Westwall und Maginot Linie," NARS T-312/1/7500002.

128. "Beurteilung der Lage an der Westfront, Stand: 25.9.39.," NARS T-77/1423.

129. Institut für Weltwirtschaft an der Universität Kiel, "Die Kohlenversorgung Europas durch Grossdeutschland unter den gegenwärtigen kriegswirtschaftlichen Gesichtspunkten," October 1939, pp. 103, NARS T-84/195/1560466.

130. The Poles deserved better. As we now know, Polish intelligence would play a major role in the cracking of the German enigma encoding machines—a contribution of perhaps decisive importance in the winning of the Second World War. See Ronald Lewin, *Ultra Goes to War* (New York, 1978), chap. 1.

131. OKH Genst.d.H., Abt. Fremde Heere West, 18.7.40. "Auswertung

von franz. Beutematerial," "Der Oberbefehlshaber Gamelin an Oberst Fyda, polnischer Militär-Attaché in Paris," September 1939, NARS T-311/234/43.

132. PRO CAB 66/1 WP (39) 38, Record of the First War Council, 19.9.39., p. 4.

133. PRO CAB 85/16, M.R. (J) (40) (s) 2, 11.4.40., Allied Military Committee, "The Major Strategy of the War, Note by the French Delegation."

134. PRO CAB 66/4 WP (40) 1, 1.1.40., "Air Operations and Intelligence."

XI. CONCLUSION

1. Winston Churchill, *The World Crisis* (Toronto, 1931), p. 6.

2. The most glaring example of this occurred in the Chiefs of Staff's evaluation of comparative naval strength available in 1938. By counting the three German "pocket battleships" as battleships, one German battle cruiser that would not be combat-ready until 1939, and two Italian battleships undergoing major modification in dockyard while not including three British ships undergoing a similar refit, the COS were able to distort considerably the naval balance of power. See PRO CAB 53/37, COS 698 (Revise), CID, COS Sub-Committee, "Military Implications of German Aggression against Czechoslovakia," 28.3.38, Appendix I, p. 153.

3. Thucydides, *History of the Peloponnesian War*, translated by Rex Warner (Harmondsworth, 1976), pp. 82-83.

4. Ibid., p. 86.

5. Ibid., pp. 138-139.

6. In fairness to Schlieffen the real irony of the 1914 campaign is the fact that the French came perilously close to playing the role assigned to them by Schlieffen.

7. Carl von Clausewitz, *On War* (Princeton, 1976), p. 87.

8. Ibid., p. 119.

9. David Lloyd George, *Memoirs*, Vol. VI (London, 1936), p. 3497.

10. For a social-science attempt to argue this point see particularly: Norman Dixon, *On The Psychology of Military Incompetence* (London, 1976).

11. This is not the place to cite the extensive literature on Hitler's goals and aims. This author accepts Alan Bullock's "Hitler and the Origins of the Second World War" as authoritative.

12. See in particular the letter of 21.7.38., from Manstein to Beck in BA/MA, N 28/3, in which at the height of the Czech crisis Manstein spends much of the time arguing why the OKH rather than OKW must control strategy.

13. See Wilhelm Deist, *The Wehrmacht and German Rearmament* (London, 1981), pp. 48-51.

14. Churchill, *The World Crisis*, p. 6.

Bibliographical Essay

Because of the breadth of this work, this essay could not possibly cover all the source and secondary material. Rather, I intend it as a guide to the most significant works in the period covered by this study and to the archives and source material that I have found the most useful.

UNPUBLISHED PRIMARY SOURCE MATERIAL

The extent of the unpublished documentary material available in the archives on the military and diplomatic history of the late 1930s is staggering. The most complete materials are in England, and most of these have become available to scholars with the change to the thirty-year rule. The organization of the British government, with its concentration of both legislative and executive branches within Parliament and the Cabinet, and the bureaucratic framework within which the British system functioned gives a detailed picture of the choices that Britain faced, the process of decision making, and the execution of policy. The minutes of meetings at all levels of government reflect the strains, arguments, and internal crises.

A few words of caution are in order. The very extent of this material can mislead. Concentration upon one particular level of the bureaucracy can distort the actual course of events. The documents are persuasive and at times overwhelming. The military documents in particular are all framed in the "worst case" analysis and do not necessarily reflect the actual military situation.

Within these records the Cabinet minutes (CAB 23 Series and CAB 65 Series) are the most important body of papers. They provide a detailed week-by-week, and in crisis situations, day-by-day account of Cabinet discussions on diplomatic, strategic, and domestic policy. They indicate, as can no other source, the stress and conflict at the highest levels of government. The Cabinet papers (CAB 24 Series and CAB 66 Series) contain the most important departmental papers presented to the ministers for evaluation of critical issues. Supplementing Cabinet minutes are minutes that during the Czech crisis record informal meetings of ministers—some attended by the prime minister (CAB 27 Series).

Of the Cabinet committees dealing with strategic questions, the two most relevant were the Foreign Policy Committee and the Committee of Imperial Defense with its subcommittees. Although relatively new, the Foreign Policy Committee (CAB 27 Series) played an important role in determining foreign policy. Both committee minutes (very important) and papers (not as important) exist.

The papers and minutes of the Committee of Imperial Defense (CAB 2 Series) are critical to an understanding of Great Britain's foreign and strategic policies. Underneath the committee were a group of subcommittees, all important in defense and strategic decision making. The minutes and memoranda of the Chiefs of Staff Committee, the most important of these subcommittees (CAB 53 Series), are essential to an understanding of British defense policy, and the minutes and papers of the Joint Planning Committee (CAB 55 Series) are almost as important, as many of the Planning Committee papers formed the basis for Chiefs of Staff reports. The Deputy Chiefs of Staff Sub-Committee records (CAB 54 Series) are not as important, but the committee was active in important areas of military policy such as combined operations.

During Baldwin's last years, the Defense Requirements Sub-Committee (CAB 16 Series) assumed great importance. Under Chamberlain it was less significant. Other CID subcommittees of interest are: the Colonial Defense Sub-Committee (CAB 5 Series); the Air Defense Coordination of Active and Passive Measures Sub-Committee (CAB 13 Series); the Middle East Sub-Committee (CAB 51 Series); the Strategic Appreciations Sub-Committee (CAB 16 Series); and the Defense Policy Sub-Committee (CAB 16 Series). Two special Cabinet committees are noteworthy: the Committee on Defense Programs and Their Acceleration, established after Munich; and the Committee on Defense Programs and Their Acceleration (CAB 16 Series), convened after Prague to speed rearmament.

The next most important body of material is available in Foreign Office files. The Public Record Office maintains a complete index of every item in these files. The FO 371 series contains incoming as well as outgoing messages, letters, correspondence with other departments, intelligence surveys, minutes by Foreign Office personnel, and so forth. The internal minutes reveal attitudes and currents within the ministry. The private files of such diplomats as Halifax, Vansittart, and Cadogan (FO 800 Series) exist outside of the regular Foreign Office files and are also useful.

Other departmental files are also of importance. The Treasury, War Office, Admiralty, and Royal Air Force collections delineate departmental policies. The official papers of the prime minister (PREM Series) contain some significant letters the prime minister received, but as a whole, this collection is spotty. Some British records are not yet open. Intelligence files are closed and will remain so in the foreseeable future. The files of the Secret Intelligence Service, the various branches of military intelligence, and the Industrial Intelligence Service would all be invaluable. Some of this material has slipped through and is available in Foreign Office files. It gives only a glimpse, but a crucial one.

Unpublished German documentation is as extensive as the British but is more uneven. Some time periods receive adequate coverage, whereas others have little documentation. The National Archives of the United States possess an immense body of material on microfilm. Guides to the microfilms are detailed and useful. Coverage of the OKW and OKH for this period is incomplete. There is important material from the economic ministry, the Four Year Plan, and the economics staff of the OKW. Material on the western military districts is extensive. Unfortunately there is not much material in either the National Archives or in West Germany from the Saxon and Silesian military districts. Moreover, although the Eighth Army drew up a complete after-action report on the Anschluss, no comparable document exists in western archives for the projected invasion of Czechoslovakia. Such material may exist in East German archives, to which I was refused access.

In the National Archives there is excellent coverage on the development of panzer tactics during the interwar period. Intelligence material is a valuable source on the strengths and capabilities of Eastern European armies. The Germans were well informed on all important developments in foreign armies. The attention paid to the development of armor in Britain is a case in point. The Tambach collection of naval documents is also available in Washington, although in abridged form. Although many naval files were filmed, some important files were not. Thus, the microfilmed Tambach material must be supplemented by material from the Bundesarchiv/Militärarchiv in Freiburg. Naval files in Freiburg contain important staff studies relating to the strategic situation in summer 1938.

The National Archives has little microfilmed material on the air force. In London, some of Milch's papers are available on microfilm at the Imperial War Museum, and the Air Historical Section of the Air Ministry has some information on crew training and maintenance during the period from 1938 to 1942. The Bundesarchiv/Militärarchiv in Freiburg is the single most important source for German military history. The collections of private papers, especially those of Beck, are invaluable.

Bibliographical Essay

There is adequate coverage of the Luftwaffe. Documents dealing with maintenance and supply, when supplemented by material in the British Air Ministry and the Milch collection, give a complete picture of this important aspect of Luftwaffe capabilities.

There are also important dispatches from the various German military attachés assigned to Italy in the late 1930s and early period of the war. This material is available both on microfilm in Washington and in Freiburg. It details the Italian military unpreparedness and German doubts as to their ally's usefulness.

Unpublished Studies

At the end of the Second World War the Western Allies captured most of the important German generals. The American army and air force hired many of these officers to write a series of studies on their wartime experiences. Although most of these studies deal with military operations during the war, they contain some important material on the prewar period. These studies are available in the National Archives. Among the more important are: Hermann Plocher, "The German Air Force in the Spanish Civil War," (Air Force Study 150); Günther Blumentritt, "Zwischen freiem Operationsplan und ständigen Befestigungen," (Foreign Military Studies, B-652, Historical Division, U.S. Army Europe, 1947); Enno von Rintelen, "Italian-German Cooperation, October 1936-November 1940," (Foreign Military Studies, B-495, 1947); Heinz Heggenreiner, "Kämpfe vor Eintreffen der deutschen Truppen unter Marschall Graziani," (Foreign Military Studies, D-216, 1947); Günther Blumentritt, "Abhängigkeit des militärischen Operationsplanes von Politik und Wirtschaft," (Foreign Military Studies, B-654, 1947); Heinz Guderian, "Spitzenvertretung der Panzertruppen in der obersten Führung des Heeres, 1938-1945," (Foreign Military Studies, P-041, 1948); Heinz Heggenreiner, "Deutsch-italienische Zusammenarbeit in italienisch Nord Afrika," (Foreign Military Studies, D-217, 1947). Two in this series deserve special note: Alfred Jodl, "The Jodl Diaries with Annotations by General der Artillerie a.D. Walter Warlimont," (Foreign Military Studies, P-215); and Franz Halder, "Kriegstagebuch with annotations by Generalmajor R. von Collenberg," (Foreign Military Studies, P-217). In spite of the titles, both are in German. They provide an excellent commentary along with diary entries.

Several air force studies have been published: among them are Richard Suchenwirth, *The Development of the German Air Force, 1919-1939* (New York, 1968); Paul D. Deichmann, *German Air Force Operations in Support of the Army* (New York, 1968).

461

Bibliographical Essay

PUBLISHED DOCUMENTARY SOURCES

Published diplomatic and other collections are an important source. There are, however, significant differences from nation to nation, not only in approach but in philosophy. Thus, the *Documents on British Foreign Policy* consist exclusively of documents drawn from Foreign Office files, whereas the German and French diplomatic series contain important military documents. The *Documents on British Foreign Policy* are still an important guide to British diplomacy but are now a supplement rather than the basic source.

The German diplomatic documents, *Akten zur deutschen auswärtigen Politik*, are a key guide to German foreign policy. They are amplified by the various other collections available on the Third Reich, especially those published by the International Military Tribunal: *Trial of Major War Criminals* (Nürnberg, 1947-1949); and *Trials of the War Criminals Before the Nurnberg Military Tribunals* (Washington, D.C., n.d.).

The French published material is spottier. The series of French diplomatic documents, *Documents diplomatiques français*, now goes through Munich and contains critical strategic surveys by the French military as well as the diplomatic documents. The records of the parliamentary commission established to investigate the 1940 disaster, *Les événements survenus en France de 1933 à 1945: Temoignages et documents recueillis par la Commission d'Enquête Parlementaire* (Paris, 1947-1954) are still of great importance for French military history between the wars.

The American diplomatic documents, *Foreign Relations of the United States*, contain important reports by the American ambassadors about European events in the late 1930s. Other documentary collections of use are: Václav Král, ed., *Das Abkommen von München 1938: Tschechoslowakische diplomatische Dokumente, 1937-1939* (Prague, 1968); Václav Král, ed., *Die Deutschen in der Tschechoslowakei* (Prague, 1964); Fritz Berber, ed., *Europäische Politik, 1933-1938, im Spiegel der Prager Akten* (Essen, 1942); Karl-Heinz Völker, ed., *Dokumente und Dokumentarfotos zur Geschichte der deutschen Luftwaffe* (Stuttgart, 1968); and *Documents and Materials Relating to the Eve of the Second World War*, 2 vols. (Moscow, 1948).

MEMOIRS AND BIOGRAPHICAL SOURCES

As with the documents, the most extensive memoir and biographical material is available on Britain. On the broader aspects of the crisis in the late 1930s, Winston Churchill, *The Gathering Storm* (London, 1948) is a persuasive and brilliantly written indictment of appeasement. Anthony Eden, *Facing the Dictators* (London, 1962) is still useful, although the author presents himself in rather too favorable a light. Leopold Amery, *The Unforgiving Years* (London, 1955) is an outstanding attack on the whole course of the national government from 1931 to 1940 by the man who played a major role in finally bringing it down. Hugh Dalton, *The Fateful Years* (London, 1957) is the best work from the Labour party's point of view. Other works of note are: Alfred Duff Cooper, *Old Men Forget* (London, 1953); Harold Nicolson, *Diaries and Letters* (London, 1960); and Harold Macmillan, *Winds of Change* (New York, 1966). Works that are mostly forgettable by men who held important positions are: Clement Attlee, *As It Happened* (London, 1954); Earl of Halifax, *Fullness of Days* (New York, 1957); Nevile Henderson, *Failure of a Mission* (London, 1940); Nevile Henderson, *Water under the Bridges* (London, 1945); Viscount Simon, *Retrospect* (London, 1952); Viscount Templewood, *Nine Troubled Years* (London, 1954).

On the diplomatic side two important diaries have been published in the seventies: Alexander Cadogan, *The Diaries of Sir Alexander Cadogan*, edited by David Dilkes (New York, 1971); and Oliver Harvey, *The Diplomatic Diaries of Oliver Harvey*, edited by John Harvey (London, 1970). Lord Strang, *Home and Abroad* (London, 1956) also contains useful information but is more limited.

The biographies of important officials are available in increasing numbers. The best in this genre and a convincing reply to the critics of Winston Churchill is Martin Gilbert, *Winston Churchill*, Vol. V, *1922-1939* (London, 1976). Unfortunately most of the remaining biographies are panagyrics rather than serious historical works. Both of the important biographies of Chamberlain, Keith Feiling, *The Life of Neville Chamberlain* (London, 1947), and Ian Macleod, *Neville Chamberlain* (London, 1961) are too favorable to their subject. Keith Middlemas' and John Bernes' *Baldwin, A Biography* (London, 1969) is too long. Stephen Roskill's *Hankey*, Vol. III, *1931-1963* (London, 1974) is important because of the author's extensive use of the Hankey papers and his skill in utilizing records in the Public Record Office. Nevertheless, Roskill's handling of the military situation in the late thirties leaves much to be desired.

On the military side B. H. Liddell Hart, *Memoirs*, 2 vols. (London, 1965) are a gold mine of information on the interwar happenings within the army, the development of modern tactics, and the inability of the Chamberlain government, as well as the author's own newspaper, the *Times*, to perceive the realities of the European situation. But one must use Liddell Hart's *Memoirs* with caution because the author does not always present the whole story, and his persuasiveness can be misleading. J.F.C. Fuller, *The Army in My Time* (London, 1935) is more tendentious but interesting on Fuller's estrangement from the army. An important and useful source on the army is Henry Pownall, *The Diaries of Lt. General Sir Henry Pownall*, Vol. I, edited by Brian Bond (London, 1972). Sir John Slessor, *The Central Blue* (New York, 1957) is the best air force memoir of the period by the man who was chief of plans in the Air Ministry and a member of the Joint Planning Committee in the late 1930s. Admiral of the fleet, Viscount Cunningham of Hyndhope, *A Sailor's Odyssey* (New York, 1951) is the best naval memoir. Other important military sources are: R. J. Minney, *The Private Papers of Hore-Belisha* (London, 1960); Edward Spears, *Assignment to Catastrophe* (London, 1954); Lord Ismay, *The Memoirs of General Lord Ismay* (New York, 1960); R. Macleod and A. Kelley, eds., *The Ironside Diaries, 1937-1940* (London, 1963); Sholto Douglas, *Combat and Command* (New York, 1966); Lord Tedder, *With Prejudice* (London, 1966).

Brian Bond's *Liddell Hart, A Study of his Military Thought* (New Brunswick, N.J., 1977) is a superlative study of the strengths and weaknesses of that great military journalist. Anthony J. Trythall's, *'Boney' Fuller, The Intellectual General, 1878-1966* (London, 1977) is excellent. K. J. Mackesy's *Armored Crusader* (London, 1967) is a good biography of the British tank pioneer, Sir Percy Hobart, and gives an excellent picture of resistance to change in the British army. Two other biographies of note are: John Connell, *Wavell, Scholar and Soldier* (New York, 1964); and Basil Collier, *Leader of the Few* (London, 1961).

The German memoir sources on the diplomatic side are a good deal less satisfactory. Ernst von Weizsäcker, *Memoirs* (London, 1951); Herbert von Dirksen, *Moskau, Tokio, London* (Stuttgart, 1949); *The Ribbentrop Memoirs* (London, 1954) are disappointing. Ernst von Weizsäcker, *Papiere, 1933-1950*, edited by Leonidas Hill (Frankfurt am Main, 1974) has recently been published and contains interesting material from Weizsäcker's diary. The Ciano Diaries, Count Galeazzo Ciano, *Ciano's Diary, 1937-1938* (London, 1952) and *The Ciano Diaries, 1939-1943* (New York, 1946), are an important source on German-Italian relations and Axis cooperation; nevertheless, they should be used with caution, as Ciano apparently worked over his entries while minister to the Vatican.

The German memoir sources on military events are more comprehensive, but most have the major failing that they deal with the war in detail and only in passing briefly discuss the prewar events. Erich von Manstein, *Aus einem Soldatenleben, 1887-1939* (Bonn, 1958), despite a rather narrow point of view, has excellent material on the development of the German army's rearmament program under Fritsch and Beck, on the Anschluss, and on the Czech crisis. Friedrich Hossbach, *Zwischen Wehrmacht und Hitler* (Hannover, 1949) is also an important source on rearmament and invaluable on the relations between Hitler, Blomberg, and the army. Hossbach is also important for the Fritsch-Blomberg crisis. Heinz Guderian, *Panzer Leader*

(New York, 1952), has some important observations on the development of German armor, but, considering his role, discussion of the prewar period is disppointing. Leo Frhr. Geyr von Schweppenberg's *Erinnerungen eines Militärattachés, London 1933/1937* (Stuttgart, 1949) is more the account of his social triumph as the first German military attaché in London since 1914 than of his role in passing British ideas on armored tactics back to Berlin. Memoirs that deal with the high command are: Walter Warlimont, *Im Hauptquartier der deutschen Wehrmacht, 1939-1945* (Bonn, 1966) and Bernhard Lossberg, *Im Wehrmachtführungsstab* (Hamburg, 1958). Other memoirs of some use are Siegfried Westphal, *The German Army in the West* (London, 1951); F. W. von Mellenthin, *Panzer Battles* (New York, 1956); Adolf Heusinger, *Befehl im Widerstreit* (Tubingen, 1950). There are two particularly important diaries: Gerhard Engel, *Heeresadjutant bei Hitler, 1938-1943*, edited by Hildegard von Kotze (Stuttgart, 1975), and Helmut Groscurth, *Tagebücher eines Abwehroffiziers, 1938-1940*, edited by Harold Deutsch and Helmut Krausnik (Stuttgart, 1969).

There are several important biographical works on the military, Wolfgang Foerster, *Generaloberst Ludwig Beck* (Munich, 1938) is useful, and Gert Buchheit, *Ludwig Beck* (Munich, 1964) is a more complete historical study. The most recent work on Beck, Klaus-Jürgen Müller, *General Ludwig Beck, Studien und Dokumente zur-politisch-militärischen Vorstellungswelt und Tätigkeit des Generalstabschefs des deutschen Heeres 1933-1938* (Boppard am Rhein, 1980), is by far and away the best, for it strips away the mythology that has grown up around Beck and places him within the real framework of events in the 1930s. The two works on Halder, Peter Bor, *Gespräche mit Halder* (Wiesbaden, 1950), and Heidemarie Gräfin Schall-Riacour, *Aufstand und Gehorsam* (Wiesbaden, 1972), are too uncritical of their subject matter.

Memoirs of the German air force and navy are less satisfactory. Most mention the prewar period only in passing. A few that have some significance are: Cajus Bekker, *The Luftwaffe War Diaries* (Garden City, N.Y., 1968); Adolf Galland, *The First and the Last* (New York, 1954); Albert Kesselring, *A Soldier's Record* (New York, 1953); Karl Dönitz, *10 Jahre und 20 Tage* (Frankfurt, 1963); Karl Dönitz, *Mein wechselvolles Leben* (Göttingen, 1968); and Erich Raeder, *Mein Leben* (Tubingen, 1957).

French memoirs have been of great importance only because French archives have remained closed until recently. In most respects they are disappointing. Robert Coulondre, *De Staline à Hitler* (Paris, 1950) is the best of the French diplomatic memoirs. The British documents indicate that François-Poncet, *The Fateful Years* (New York, 1949) was not completely honest or open. Georges Bonnet, *Défense de la paix* (Geneva, 1946-1947) is an exercise in dishonesty. On the army side André Beaufre, *Memoires, 1920-*

1945 (Paris, 1969) is excellent. F. Gauche, *Le Deuxième Bureau au travail* (Paris, 1953) ignores all the evidence available when written. Maurice Gamelin, *Servir*, II, *Le Prologue du drame*, in spite of efforts to cover over the author's responsibility, is revealingly ignorant of modern warfare. Maurice Weygand, *Memoires: Mirages et realité* (Paris, 1957) and *Memoires: Rappelé au service* (Paris, 1950) are both useful. G. Warner, *Pierre Laval and the Eclipse of France* (New York, 1968) and Philip Bankwitz, *Maxime Weygand and Civil-Military Relations in Modern France* (Cambridge, Mass., 1966) are both invaluable biographies that go beyond their subjects to provide a broad picture of the weaknesses that led to 1940.

The memoir material on Eastern Europe is spotty. The best on Polish policy are Count Jan Szembeck, *Journal, 1933-1939* (Paris, 1952) and Jozef Lipski, *Papers and Memoirs* (New York, 1968). Col. Jósef Beck, *Dernier rapport* (Paris, 1946) is disappointing. Grigore Gafencu, *The Last Days of Europe* (London, 1947) is interesting but unreliable. Emmanuel Moravec, *Das Ende der Benesch Republik* (Prague, 1941) is fascinating and in some respects revealing. G.E.R. Gedye, *Betrayal in Central Europe* (New York, 1939); Joan and Jonathan Griffen, *Lost Liberty* (London, 1939); and Sydney Morrell, *I Saw the Crucifixion* (London, 1939) are interesting eye-witness accounts of the fall of Austria and Czechoslovakia. Dr. Hubert Ripka, *Munich, Before and After* (London, 1939) is a forthright and persuasive account of why the British and French should have fought alongside of the Czechs in 1938.

SECONDARY WORKS

Britain

The opening of nearly all the official records for the 1930s has made much of the earlier diplomatic and military history of the period outdated. Substantial work based on this material has now been published and varies widely in quality. The best use of the British documents has been made by authors who have concentrated on specific issues. Peter Dennis, *Decision by Default, Peacetime Conscription and British Defense, 1919-1939* (London, 1972) is an excellent study of the issue of conscription in Great Britain during the interwar period. Michael Howard, *The Continental Commitment* (London, 1972) is equally good on the British attitude toward the problem of a continental strategy. The most ambitious work on British foreign and strategic policy is Correlli Barnett, *The Collapse of British Power* (London, 1972). Keith Middlemas, *The Diplomacy of Illusion* (London, 1972) has some use in the study of Britain's strategic policy and its role in appeasement. Unfortunately, there are sloppy mistakes that detract from the work. Less useful because they are simple rephrasings of Cabinet or other committee minutes are: Ian Colvin, *The Chamberlain Cabinet* (New York, 1971); and Roger Parkinson, *Peace in our Time* (London, 1971). Peter Ludlow's masterful article, "The Unwinding of Appeasement" in *Das 'Andere' Deutschland im Zweiten Weltkrieg*, edited by L. Kettenacker (Stuttgart, 1977), explodes the historical myth that appeasement ended in March 1939 and indicates that it was alive well into the first months of the Second World War.

Two works have devoted considerable effort to a study of the Treasury's role in the rearmament process: G. C. Peden, *British Rearmament and the Treasury, 1932-1939* (Edinburgh, 1979); and Robert Paul Shay, Jr., *British Rearmament in the Thirties* (Princeton, 1977). Of the two works the Peden book is the most balanced, but both works suffer from too great a diet of Treasury arguments. Lawrence R. Pratt, *East of Malta, West of Suez* (London, 1975) adequately covers British Mediterranean policy but fails to place the issues in perspective. Norman Gibbs, *Grand Strategy*, Vol. I (London, 1977) is a careful examination of the development of defense policy within the bureaucratic structure. Unfortunately, Professor Gibbs rarely moves outside of the purely military sphere to address some of the larger issues. J.R.M. Butler, *Grand Strategy*, Vol. II, *September 1939-June 1941* (London, 1957) has been reissued with citations from documentary sources.

The best general work on the diplomatic crisis of 1938 and 1939 is Christopher Thorne, *The Approach of War, 1938-1939* (London, 1967), which sets the standard against which the diplomatic histories of the period must be evaluated. The best general work on British diplomacy is W. N. Medlicott, *British Foreign Policy since Versailles* (New York, 1968). F. S. Northedge, *The Troubled Giant: Britain among the Great Powers, 1916-1939* (London, 1968) is much denser and has some questionable assumptions. F. S. Northedge, *Freedom and Necessity in British Foreign Policy* (London, 1972) adds nothing to his earlier work. Arnold Wolfers, *Britain and France Between the Wars* (New York, 1940) reads astonishingly well considering that it was written immediately after the outbreak of the war. C. L. Mowat, *Britain Between the Wars, 1918-1940* (Chicago, 1955) provides a useful background to British foreign policy in the interwar period. Sir Llewellyn Woodward's *British Foreign Policy in the Second World War*, Vol. I (London, 1970) is a balanced, accurate study of British diplomacy in the opening year of the war. Michael Howard's *War and the Liberal Conscience* (New Brunswick, N.J., 1978) is a brilliant essay, analyzing those liberal misconceptions on the relationship between war and human society. It is basic to an understanding of how and why appeasement failed. D. C. Watt's *Too Serious a Business* (Berkeley, 1975) is interesting at times but dead wrong on many critical issues. Watt's *Person-*

alities and Policies (London, 1965) contains a collection of useful and important essays on British foreign policy. On British-Russian relations between the wars Gottfried Niedhart, *Grossbritannien und die Sowjetunion* (Munich, 1972) makes some use of Cabinet material, but, because Niedhart has not used CID and COS material, the key strategic questions and the influence of military factors on British policy are mentioned only in passing. Bernd-Jürgen Wendt, *Appeasement, 1938, Wirtschaftliche Rezession und Mitteleuropa* (Frankfurt, 1966) and *Economic Appeasement* (Dusseldorf, 1971) are important works on an aspect of appeasement that some historians have ignored. Still, the fact that these studies were written without the full use of the material now available in the Public Record Office detracts from their overall usefulness. Dieter Aigner, *Das Ringen um England: Das deutschbritische Verhältnis: Die öffentliche Meinung, 1933-1939* (Munich, 1969) is massive rather than perceptive.

There are a series of important works on appeasement written before the records opened up that are still worth consulting. Martin Gilbert and Richard Gott, *The Appeasers* (Boston, 1963) remains a standard work. Martin Gilbert, *The Roots of Appeasement* (New York, 1966) is less satisfactory, and Margaret George, *The Warped Vision, British Foreign Policy, 1933-1939* (Pittsburgh, 1967) is even less so. William R. Rock, *Appeasement on Trial* (New York, 1966) deals with the policy of appeasement and its critics. Neville Thompson, *The Anti-Appeasers* (Oxford, 1971) studies the opponents of appeasement in the ranks of the Conservative party. Other works that deal with British appeasement are: Peter Lundgren, *Die englische Appeasement-Politik bis zum Münchener Abkommen* (Berlin, 1968); R. Kieser, *Englands Appeasement-Politik und der Aufstieg des Dritten Reiches im Spiegel der britischen Presse, 1933-1939* (Winterthur, 1964); and Günter Holzweissig, *Das Deutschlandbild der britischen Presse im Jahre 1935* (Hamburg, 1967). John F. Naylor, *Labour's International Policy* (London, 1969) covers the Labour party's less than glorious waffling. K. W. Watkins, *Britain Divided* (London, 1963) is an excellent discussion of the Spanish Civil War's effect on the British political scene. Three books worth consulting for a discussion of British society in the 1930s are Robert Graves and Alan Hodge, *The Long Weekend: A Social History of Great Britain, 1918-1939* (New York, 1941); A. L. Rowse, *All Souls and Appeasement* (London, 1961); and Malcolm Muggeridge, *The Thirties* (London, 1939). L. B. Namier's *Europe in Decay* (New York, 1950) and *In the Nazi Era* (New York, 1952) still make delightful reading.

Useful for the study of British military history is Robin Higham, *A Guide to the Sources of British Military History* (Berkeley, 1971). The British army has been the subject of numerous works dealing with the interwar period. The best, fairest, and most thorough appraisal is Brian Bond's *British Military*

Policy between Two World Wars (Oxford, 1980). It not only places the proper emphasis on failings within the army but examines and underlines the outside influences and factors beyond the army's control that contributed so much to its weakness in 1940. Jay Luvaas, *The Education of an Army* (Chicago, 1964) remains an excellent work. Robin Higham's two works, *Armed Forces in Peacetime* (Hamden, Conn., 1962) and *The Military Intellectuals in Britain, 1918-1939* (New Brunswick, N.J., 1965), are helpful. David Divine, *The Blunted Sword* (London, 1964) is an unbridled and at times justified attack on the British military establishment. Divine's book also contains some astounding quotations. B. H. Liddell Hart's *The Royal Tank Regiment* (London, 1959), along with his *Memoirs*, is the most authoritative work on the development of the British armor. J.F.C. Fuller's *On Future Warfare* (London, 1928) and *The Army in My Time* (London, 1935) are interesting for Fuller's views. B. H. Liddell Hart's contemporary works, *The British Way in Warfare* (London, 1932); *Europe in Arms* (London, 1937); *The Defense of Britain* (London, 1939); and *Dynamic Defense* (London, 1940) are all important and, except for the last, had an important impact on Chamberlain's strategic policies. Any student of British military history in the interwar period must consult the following journals: *Journal of the Royal United Services Institute,* and *The Army Quarterly.*

The Royal Air Force is less well covered. The official history of bomber command, Sir Charles Webster and Noble Frankland, *The Strategic Bombing Offensive Against Germany, 1939-1945* (London, 1961), is official history as it should be written. The outcries of rage on both sides of the Atlantic that greeted its publication indicate its excellence. Guy Hartcup, *The Challenge of War* (London, 1967) is an excellent study of science and war. The best work on the Battle of Britain is F. K. Mason, *The Battle over Britain* (Garden City, N.Y., 1969). Derek Wood and Derek Dempster, *The Narrow Margin: The Battle of Britain and the Rise of Air Power, 1930-1940* (London, 1961) is outdated. Contemporary works that are worth consulting are: J. C. Slessor, *Air Power and Armies* (London, 1936); L.E.O. Charlton, *War from the Air* (London, 1935); L.E.O. Charlton, G. T. Garrett and Lt. Cmdr. R. Fletcher, *The Air Defense of Britain* (London, 1937); L.E.O. Charlton, *The Menace of the Clouds* (London, 1937); and Jonathan Griffin, *Glass Houses and Modern War* (London, 1938).

The best work on the navy in the interwar period is Stephen Roskill, *Naval Policy Between the Wars,* Vol. I, *1919-1929* (New York, 1969), and Vol. II, *1930-1939* (London, 1976). Other useful works by Roskill are: *White Ensign* (Annapolis, 1960); and *The War at Sea,* I (London, 1954). F. H. Hinsley, *Command of the Sea* (London, 1947) is somewhat dated, but has some interesting observations. Leslie Jones, *Shipbuilding in Britain* (Cardiff, 1947) and J. R. Parkinson, *The Economics of Shipbuilding in the United Kingdom* (Cambridge, 1970) are important on the state of the shipbuilding industry in Great Britain and the implications for the coming battle of the Atlantic. C.B.A. Behrens, *Merchant Shipping and the Demands of War* (London, 1955) is important on the problems of merchant shipping in wartime. Contemporary works that are still of use: Russell Grenfell, *Sea Power in the Next War* (London, 1938); and Sir H. W. Richmond, *Statesmen and Seapower* (Oxford, 1946).

Three recent works on intelligence are F. H. Hinsley, *British Intelligence in the Second World War*, Vol. I (London, 1979); Patrick Beesley, *Very Special Intelligence* (Garden City, N.Y., 1978); and Ronald Lewin, *Ultra Goes to War* (London, 1978).

Germany

Since the appearance of A.J.P. Taylor's *Origins of the Second World War* (London, 1961), it seems that Mr. Taylor no longer fully subscribes to the theories he advanced in that work and has defended so strongly in the past. He has written: "Hitler was not an ordinary politician, drifting from one problem to the next. He had a powerful, though untutored mind that thought in long-range and systematic terms. Underlying all his policies and strategy was a single aim: to make Germany a world power." A.J.P. Taylor, "Hitler as Strategist," *War Monthly*, no. 1 (April 1974). Adolf Hitler, the historical figure, has undergone careful examination. The major work on the compatibility of Hitler's long-range aims and his tactical skills is Alan Bullock's "Hitler and the Origins of the Second World War," in *European Diplomacy Between Two Wars*, 1919-1939, edited by Hans W. Gatzke (Chicago, 1972). The most fluent and thoughtful work on Hitler's foreign policy is Klaus Hildebrand, *Deutsche Aussenpolitik*, 1933-1945 (Stuttgart, 1970). E. Jäckel, *Hitlers Weltanschauung* (Tubingen, 1969) is valuable on the growth of Hitler's philosophy and outlook on the world. Other important works on German foreign policy are: Gerhard Weinberg, *The Foreign Policy of Hitler's Germany*, 1933-1936 (Chicago, 1970); Klaus Hildebrand, *Vom Reich zum Weltreich* (Munich, 1969); Hans-Adolf Jacobsen, *Nationalsozialistische Aussenpolitik*, 1933-1938 (Frankfurt, 1968); Andreas Hillgruber, "England's Place in Hitler's Plans for World Dominion," *Journal of Contemporary History* 9, no. 1 (January 1974); Axel Kuhn, *Hitlers aussenpolitisches Programm* (Stuttgart, 1970); and H. Trevor-Roper, "Hitlers Kriegsziele," *Vierteljahrshefte für Zeitgeschichte* (1970). Gaines Post, *The Civil-Military Fabric of Weimar Foreign Policy* is a useful work on foreign policy and strategic planning in Weimar Germany. Also useful on Hitler's prewar military plans is E. M. Robertson,

Hitler's Pre-War Policy and Military Plans, 1933-1939 (New York, 1963). Unfortunately, Gerhard Weinberg's second volume, *The Foreign Policy of Hitler's Germany, Starting World War II, 1937-1939* (Chicago, 1980) is considerably weaker than his first. Although Professor Weinberg presents an enormous amount of material underlining the mendaciousness of Nazi foreign policy, his work discusses little of the strategic and military background to European diplomacy in the late 1930s. Moreover, his discussion of British policy often distorts Chamberlain's diplomatic and strategic response and attempts to present the British prime minister in as favorable a light as possible.

The best of the works on the German economy is Berenice Carroll, *Design for Total War: Arms and Economics in the Third Reich* (The Hague, 1968). Two other works which have major faults are: Burton H. Klein, *Germany's Economic Preparations for War* (Cambridge, Mass., 1959); and Alan Milward, *The German Economy at War* (London, 1965). T. W. Mason, "Some Origins of the Second World War," *Past and Present* (December 1964) is an outstanding review of some of the major faults in Taylor's *Origins of the Second World War* and Klein's *Germany's Economic Preparations for War.* Mason's recent article, "Innere Krise und Angriffskrieg, 1938/1939," edited by Friedrich Forstmeier and Hans-Erich Volkmann in *Wirtschaft und Rüstung am Vorabend des Zweiten Weltkrieges* (Düsseldorf, 1975) is an important work on the prewar economy and the difficulties within the Nazi economic system. The best work on an individual sector of the German economy is J. J. Jäger, *Die wirtschaftliche Abhängigkeit des Dritten Reiches vom Ausland* (Berlin, 1969). Anja E. Bagel-Bohlan, *Hitlers industrielle Kriegsvorbereitungen, 1936-1939* (Koblenz, 1975) is a useful short study. Also useful are: Dieter Petzina, *Autarkiepolitik im Dritten Reich* (Stuttgart, 1968); Wilhelm Treue, "Hitlers Denkschrift zum Vierjahresplan, 1936," *Vierteljahrshefte für Zeitgeschichte* 3, no. 2 (1955); Georg Thomas, *Geschichte der deutschen Wehr- und Rüstungswirtschaft, 1918-1943/45* (Boppard am Rhein, 1966); and Andreas Hillgruber, *Hitler, König Carol, und Marschall Antonescu: Die Deutsch-rumänischen Beziehungen, 1938-1944* (Wiesbaden, 1954). Gerhard Weinberg, *Germany and the Soviet Union, 1939-1941* (Leiden, 1954) is still excellent on the German-Soviet negotiations over the summer of 1939.

The German military services have received extensive attention, and the army has received the bulk of this scrutiny. The first two volumes of the West German official history of the Second World War have appeared. The first volume, Wilhelm Deist, Manfred Messerschmidt, Hans-Erich Volkmann, and Wolfram Wette, *Das Deutsche Reich und der Zweite Weltkrieg,* Vol. I, *Ursachen und Voraussetzungen der deutschen Kriegspolitik* (Stuttgart, 1979), is a model for scholarly standards and objectivity. It addresses all the major questions. The second volume is less important: Klaus A. Maier, Horst Rohde,

Bernd Stegemann, and Hans Umbreit, *Das Deutsche Reich und der Zweite Weltkrieg*, Vol. II, *Die Errichtung der Hegemonie auf dem Europäischen Kontinent* (Stuttgart, 1979). The East German study, Wolfgang Schumann and Gerhart Hass, eds., *Deutschland im Zweiten Weltkrieg*, Vol. I, *Vorbereitung, Entfesselung und Verlauf des Krieges bis zum 22. Juni 1941* (Berlin, 1974), is thoroughly unsatisfactory. The three best works on the Nazis and the army are Klaus-Jürgen Müller, *Das Heer und Hitler* (Stuttgart, 1966); Robert J. O'Neill, *The German Army and Nazi Party* (London, 1966); and Manfred Messerschmidt, *Die Wehrmacht im NS-Staat* (Hamburg, 1969). The O'Neill book suffers because the last chapters covering the period from the Fritsch-Blomberg crisis to the outbreak of war appear to have been added as a publisher's afterthought. Other useful works on party-army relations are: Harold Deutsch, *Hitler and His Generals* (Minneapolis, 1974); Klaus-Jürgen Müller, *Armee, Politik und Gesellschaft in Deutschland, 1933-1945* (Paderborn, 1979); Telford Taylor, *Sword and Swastika* (New York, 1952); and John Wheeler-Bennett, *The Nemesis of Power* (New York, 1964). Two important articles on an aspect of this subject are by Jost Dülffer, "Weisungen an die Wehrmacht 1938/1939 als Ausdruck ihrer Gleichschaltung," *Wehrwissenschaftliche Rundschau* (November/December 1968); and "Überlegung von Kriegsmarine und Heer zur Wehrmachtspitzengliederung und zur Führung der Wehrmacht im Krieg im Februar-März 1938," *Militärgeschichtliche Mitteilungen*, 1/71. On German rearmament two works are worth noting: Walter Bernhardt, *Die deutsche Aufrüstung, 1934-1939* (Frankfurt, 1969); and Gerhard Meinck, *Hitler und die deutsche Aufrüstung, 1933-1937* (Wiesbaden, 1959). Hansgeorg Model, *Der deutsche Generalstabsoffizier* (Frankfurt, 1968) is an excellent study on why the German staff system produced such outstanding officers. Hans-Adolf Jacobsen, "Motorisierungsprobleme im Winter, 1939-1940," *Wehrwissenschaftliche Rundschau* (September 1956) is an important article on the motorization of the German army. B. H. Liddell Hart, *The German Generals Talk* (New York, 1958) deals mostly with the war but has some useful material on the prewar period.

Jehuda Wallach, *Das Dogma der Vernichtungsschlacht* (Frankfurt, 1967), is one of the most comprehensive and thoughtful studies on the development of German strategic thought. Another important, though less useful, work is Gerhard Förster, *Totaler Krieg und Blitzkrieg* (Berlin, 1967). Robert J. O'Neill, "Doctrine and Training in the German Army," edited by Michael Howard in *The Theory and Practice of War* (New York, 1966) is a starting point on tactical developments during the interwar period. On the formation of the Wehrmacht during the rearmament period see: Georg Tessin, *Formationsgeschichte der Wehrmacht, 1933/1939* (Boppard am Rhein, 1959); and Burkhard Mueller-Hillebrand, *Das Heer, 1933-1945*, I (Darmstadt, 1954). Rolf

Elbe, *Die Schlacht an der Bzura im September 1939 aus deutscher und polnischer Sicht* (Freiburg, 1973), recounts the early combat experience of the Wehrmacht. Charles W. Sydnor, Jr., *Soldiers of Destruction* (Princeton, 1977) is not only an outstanding unit history but once and for all ends the legend that the Waffen SS were soldiers just like the others. My article, "German Response to Victory in Poland: A Case Study in Professionalism," *Armed Forces and Society* (Winter 1981) is also worth consulting on why the German army was to prove so effective in the 1940 campaign. Contemporary works that should be consulted are: Erwin Rommel, *Infantrie Greift an* (Berlin, 1939); Erich Wagner, "Gedanken über den Wert von Kriegserinnerung und Kriegserfahrung," *Militärwissenschaftliche Rundschau*, no. 2 (1937); Heinz Guderian, "Schnelle Truppen einst und jetzt," *Militärwissenschaftliche Rundschau*, no. 2 (1939). Any student of the German army in the interwar period must consult the *Militärgeschichtliche Mitteilungen* and the contemporary journals, *Militärwochenblatt* and *Militärwissenschaftliche Rundschau*.

There are two key works on the German navy, Michael Salewski, *Die deutsche Seekriegsleitung, 1935-1945* (Frankfurt, 1970) and Jost Dülffer, *Weimar, Hitler, und die Marine: Reichspolitik und Flottenbau, 1920-1939* (Dusseldorf, 1973). Both give a clear picture of weaknesses in the German navy in political as well as the tactical spheres. Michael Salewski, "Marineleitung und politische Führung, 1931-1935," *Militärgeschichtliche Mitteilungen*, 2/71 is also worth consulting. Carl A. Gemzell, *Raeder, Hitler und Skandinavien, Der Kampf für einen maritimen Operationsplan* (Lund, 1965) is a pioneering study on the navy's planning and urging for a strike at Norway and Denmark. Paul W. Zieb, *Logistische Probleme der Kriegsmarine* (Neckargemünd, 1961) is an interesting work on the technical problems of naval warfare. Wilhelm Meier-Dörnberg, *Ölversorgung der Kriegsmarine, 1935 bis 1945* (Freiburg, 1973) delineates the impact of fuel shortages on German naval strategy. P. K. Lundeberg, "The German Naval Critique of the U-boat campaign," *Military Affairs* 27 (1963) is an important study on the German submarine campaign. Of considerably less use are: Friedrich Ruge, *Sea Warfare, 1939-1945* (London, 1957); Arthur Marthiessen, *Hitler and His Admirals* (London, 1948); and Edward von der Porter, *The German Navy in World War II* (New York, 1969).

The best work on the Luftwaffe in the 1930s is Karl Heinz Völker, *Die deutsche Luftwaffe* (Stuttgart, 1967). Karl Gundelach, "Gedanken über die Führung eines Luftkrieges gegen England bei der Luftflotte 2. in den Jahren 1938/1939," *Wehrwissenschaftliche Rundschau* (January 1960) is an important work on Luftwaffe planning or lack of planning—mostly the latter—for an attack on Great Britain. The British Air Ministry's study, *The Rise and Fall of the German Air Force, 1933-1945*, pamphlet no. 248 (London, 1948) remains a useful source. Karlheinz Kens and Heinz Nowarra, *Die deutschen Flugzeuge, 1933-1945* (Munich, 1964) and Roy Wagner and Heinz Nowarra, *German Combat Planes* (Garden City, N.Y., 1970) have useful technical statistics on German aircraft types and the capabilities of different models.

Outstanding, pioneering works on Fascist Italy's contribution are Bernard MacGregor Knox's brilliant dissertation: "1940. Italy's 'Parallel War,' Part I, From Non-Belligerence to the Collapse of France," Yale University, 1976, and his even more carefully thought out book, *Mussolini Unleashed* (London, 1982). Hans Meier-Welcker, "Zur deutsch-italienischen Militärpolitik und Beurteilung der italienischen Wehrmacht vor dem Zweiten Weltkrieg," *Militärgeschichtliche Mitteilungen*, 1/70 is excellent on German-Italian military relations. See also Enno von Rintelen, *Mussolini als Bundesgenosse* (Stuttgart, 1951).

France

The opening of French archives has resulted in some important works as well as several unsatisfactory ones. Anthony Adamthwaite, *France and the Coming of the Second World War, 1936-1939* (London, 1977) is generally excellent. Jean-Baptiste Duroselle, *La Décadence, 1932-1939* Paris, 1979) is more superficial. Alexander Werth, *The Twilight of France, 1938- 1940* (New York, 1942) is still interesting. Susan Butterworth's "Daladier and the Munich Crisis: A Reappraisal," *Journal of Contemporary History* vol. 9, no. 3 (July 1974) is a new start in re-evaluating Daladier's role. G. Warner, *Pierre Laval and the Eclipse of France* (New York, 1968) is the best work on French politics in the 1930s. David O. Kieft, *Belgium's Return to Neutrality* (Oxford, 1972) is excellent on the internal and external factors that led to Belgian neutrality. The French military side has been covered in more detail, especially the catastrophic defeat of 1940. We have, however, gone about as far as we can, given the availability of documents. Alistair Horne, *To Lose a Battle* (Boston, 1969), despite some needless slips into slang, is an exciting and gripping account of the destruction of the French army in 1940. André Beaufre, *1940,The Fall of France* (New York, 1968) is excellent, and Marc Bloch, *Strange Defeat* (New York, 1968) remains a classic description of the fall of France. Less important but still useful are Guy Chapman, *Why France Fell* (New York, 1968); and Col. A. Goutard, *The Battle of France* (London, 1958). A new work, Jeffery Gunsburg, *Divided and Conquered, The French High Command and the Defeat of the West, 1940* (Westport, Conn., 1979) argues that the French deserve little of the blame for 1940; it was all the fault of the Belgians and the British. The work will undoubtedly receive an enthusiastic reception in France. Philip Bankwitz's *Maxime Weygand and Civil-Military Relations in Modern France* (Cambridge, Mass., 1967) and "Maxime Weygand and the Fall of France: A Study of Civil-Military Relations," *Journal of Modern History* (September 1959) are outstanding discussions not only of Weygand's role in the interwar period, but of developments, both political and military, within the army during this period. The bibliography in Bankwitz's book is outstanding. Far less satisfactory is Robert J. Young's *In Command of France, French Foreign Policy and Military Planning* (Cambridge, Mass., 1978). A number of articles have appeared in the 1970s that present a useful picture of French doctrine: R.H.S. Stolfi, "Equipment for Victory in France in 1940," *History* (February 1970); R. J. Young, "Preparations for Defeat," *Journal of European Studies* (June 1972); and less important because of its serious misreading of air history, R. J. Young, "The Strategic Dream: French Air Doctrine in the Interwar Period, 1919-1939," *Journal of Contemporary History* (October 1974).

Eugene Carrias, *La pensée militaire française* (Paris, 1963) is excellent. Also useful are Eddy Bauer, *La guerre des blindés* (Paris, 1947) and Paul-Marie de la Gorce, *The French Army* (New York, 1963). On the Maginot line, see André Pretelat, *La destin tragique de la Ligne Maginot* (Paris, 1950). Contemporary works that are of definite interest: Jean Estienne, "Les forces matérielles à la guerre," *Revue de Paris* 29 (January 15, 1922); Charles de Gaulle, *Vers l'armée de métier* (Paris, 1934); Narcisse Chauvineau, *Une invasion, est-elle encore possible?* (Paris, 1940); and Maxime Weygand, "L'armée d'aujourd'hui," *Revue des deux mondes* 46 (May 1968). On the French air force see Paul Stehlin, *Témoignage pour l'histoire* (Paris, 1964). On the French navy see Paul Auphan, *The French Navy in World War II* (Annapolis, 1959).

Eastern Europe

The best work on general Russian foreign policy is Adam Ulam, *Expansion and Coexistence: History of Soviet Foreign Policy, 1917-1967* (New York, 1971). Max Beloff, *The Foreign Policy of Soviet Russia, 1929-1941*, 2 vols. (London, 1947, 1949) is also of use. One of the better works on an individual Eastern European nation is Anna M. Cienciala, *Poland and the Western Powers, 1938-1939* (Toronto, 1968). J. B. Hoptner, *Yugoslavia in Crisis, 1934-1941* (New York, 1962) is of use but has some major weak points. C. A. Macartney, *October Fifteenth, A History of Modern Hungary*, Vol. I, 1929-1941 (Edinburgh, 1956) is an excellent history and contains a detailed analysis of the role of Rumania and Hungary, in precipitating the British guarantees after the German occupation of Prague. C. A. Macartney and

A. W. Palmer, *Independent Eastern Europe* (London, 1962) is an excellent survey of Eastern Europe between the wars. On the military side of the Eastern European situation John Erickson's *The Road to Stalingrad* (New York, 1975) lays out the full impact of the purges on the Red Army. His earlier work, *The Soviet High Command* (London, 1962) is still useful. B. H. Liddell Hart, ed., *The Red Army* (New York, 1956) is uneven in quality but has some good essays on the Russian army. Rudolf Kiszling, *Die militärischen Vereinbarungen der kleinen Entente* (Munich, 1959) has some fascinating material on the military cooperation and plans of the members of the "Little Entente." Leonard Mosley, *On Borrowed Time* (New York, 1969) has an interesting criticism of British strategic policy in supporting the Polish government but, because it was written before the Cabinet material became available, is outdated. Jon Kimche, *The Unfought Battle* (New York, 1968) and Nicholas Bethell, *The War Hitler Won* (London, 1972) misinterpret the military information and the strategic situation of 1939. Jonathan Zorach's "Czechoslovakia's Fortifications, Their Development and Role in the 1938 Munich Crisis," *Militärgeschichtliche Mitteilungen*, 2/76, is interesting but limited in focus.

THE 1938-1939 CRISIS

The welter of works that deal with the European diplomatic and military crisis of the late 1930s is too extensive to hope to cover in an essay of this nature. Thus, I will mention only the most significant works dealing with the major aspects of the crisis in Europe in the late 1930s. As already noted, Christopher Thorne, *The Approach of War, 1938-1939* (London, 1967) covers the diplomatic developments in the critical years in concise and incisive fashion. The three basic works on the Anschluss are Ulrich Eichstädt, *Von Dolfuss zu Hitler* (Wiesbaden, 1955); Jürgen Gehl, *Austria, Germany and the Anschluss* (London, 1963); Gordon Brook–Shepherd, *The Anschluss* (Philadelphia, 1963). Telford Taylor's *Munich* (Garden City, N.Y., 1979) maintains the high scholarly standards of his earlier works in German military history. J. W. Brügel, *Tschechen und Deutsche, 1918-1938* (Munich, 1967) provides an excellent background to the Czech crisis of 1938. Jörg K. Hoensch, *Geschichte der tschechoslowakischen Republik, 1918-1965* (Stuttgart, 1966) is useful. Radomir Luza, *The Transfer of the Sudeten Germans* (New York, 1962) mostly covers wartime and postwar Czech-German relations but has some interesting material on the prewar period. Elizabeth Wiskemann, *Czechs and Germans* (London, 1938) is dated. Alice Teichova, *An Economic Background to Munich: International Business and Czechoslovakia, 1918-1938* (London, 1973) is interesting but narrow in scope. Still good on the diplomatic aspects of the crisis are Boris Celovsky, *Das Münchener Abkommen von 1938* (Stuttgart, 1958), and R.G.D. Laffan, *The Crisis over Czechoslovakia*, Vol. II, *Royal Institute of International Affairs, Survey of International Affairs, 1938* (London, 1951). On the military aspects of the crisis, The Royal Institute of International Affairs, *Survey of International Affairs, 1938*, Vol. III (London, 1953) is still worth consulting. Francis L. Loewenheim, *Peace or Appeasement?* (Boston, 1965) is a useful collection of documents and articles on the Czech crisis. Gerhard Weinberg, "Germany and Czechoslovakia, 1933-1945," in *Czechoslovakia, Past and Present*, edited by Miloslav Rechcigl (The Hague, 1968) provides an excellent background to the crisis. David Vital, "Czechoslovakia and the Powers, September, 1938," in *European Diplomacy Between Two Wars, 1919-1939*, edited by Hans Gatzke (Chicago, 1972) is important on the military situation in fall 1938. Leonidas Hill, "Three Crises, 1938-1939," *Journal of Contemporary History* 3 (January 1968) is useful.

Helmuth Rönnefarth, *Die Sudetenkrise in der internationalen Politik* (Wiesbaden, 1961) is unashamedly pro-German and anti-Czech. John Wheeler–Bennet, *Munich, Prologue to Tragedy* (New York, 1948) has some useful information but is now outdated. Works that support Chamberlain's surrender at Munich on the basis of Britain's supposedly desperate military situation are: Keith Eubank's *Munich* (Norman, 1963) and "The Role of Czechoslovakia in the Origins of the Second World War," in *Czechoslovakia, Past and Present*, edited by Miloslav Rechcigl (The Hague, 1968); Keith Robbins, *Munich* (London, 1968); and Lawrence Thompson, *The Greatest Treason* (New York, 1968). More temperate is William E. Scott, "Neville Chamberlain and Munich: Two Aspects of Power," in *The Responsibility of Power*, edited by Fritz Stern (New York, 1967). Scott argues that, although Chamberlain saved Great Britain from disaster at Munich, the year that was gained was disastrously misused, and the West lost the armaments race. Works that support Chamberlain's Munich surrender but that are not wholly concerned with the crisis are Basil Collier, *History of the Second World War* (London, 1965); F. S. Northedge, *Freedom and Necessity in British Foreign Policy* (London, 1972). Another work on the Munich crisis worth consulting is: Gordon Craig, "High Tide of Appeasement, The Road to Munich, 1937-1938," *Political Science Quarterly* 65 (1950).

Bernd-Jürgen Wendt, *München, 1938, England Zwischen Hitler und Preussen* (Frankfurt, 1965) is perhaps the best work on why the English refused to listen to the warnings of the opposition groups within Germany. Even though the Cabinet papers were not yet open when this study was written, Wendt's conclusions have largely held up. Donald N. Lammers, *Explaining Munich: The Search for Motive in British Policy* (Stanford, Cal., 1966) is an excellent study on why the anticommunist explanation for appeasement is not satisfactory. Andrew Rothstein, *The Munich Conspiracy* (London, 1938) and Vaclav Kral, "Die Tschechoslowakei und München," *Zeitschrift für Geschichtswissenschaft* 7 (1959) present the Marxist interpretation.

The most thorough study on the German resistance movement is Peter Hoffman, *Widerstand, Staatsstreich, Attentat* (Munich, 1969). Other important works that cover the German resistance during this period are Gert Buchheit, *Der deutsche Geheimdienst* (Munich, 1966) and Gerhard Ritter, *The German Resistance* (London, 1958).

Studies that deal with the May crisis of 1938 are Henderson Braddick, *Germany, Czechoslovakia, and the 'Grand Alliance' in the May Crisis, 1938* (Denver, 1968); William V. Wallace, "The Making of the May Crisis of 1938," *Slavonic and Eastern European Review* (June 1963); D. C. Watt, "The May Crisis of 1938: A Rejoinder to Mr. Wallace," *Slavonic and Eastern European Review* (July 1966); and Gerhard Weinberg, "The May Crisis of 1938," *Journal of Modern History* (September 1957).

On the military aspects of the Munich crisis Brigadier H.C.T. Stronge, "The Czechoslovak Army and the Munich Crisis: A Personal Memorandum" in *War and Society*, Vol. I (London, 1975), and Jonathan Zorach, "Czechoslovakia's Fortifications: Their Development and Role in the 1938 Munich Crisis," in *Militärgeschichtliche Mitteilungen*, 2/76, are both worth consulting on the military situation of Czechoslovakia in September 1938. Other articles of significance on the Munich affair are: Bernadotte E. Schmitt, "Munich," *Journal of Modern History* 25 (1953); Eduard Táborský, The Triumph and Disaster of Eduard Beneš," *Foreign Affairs* 36 (1957-1958); Eduard Táborský, "Beneš and the Soviets," *Foreign Affairs* 22 (1949); F. Vnuk, "Munich and the Soviet Union," *Journal of Central European Affairs* 21 (October 1961); William V. Wallace, "The Foreign Policy of President Beneš in the Approach to Munich," *Slavonic and Eastern European Review* 39 (1960); Sir Charles Webster, "Munich Reconsidered," *International Affairs* 37, no. 2 (April 1961); Gerhard Weinberg, "Secret Hitler-Beneš Negotiations, 1936-1937," *Journal of Central European Affairs* (September 1957).

Contemporary articles that are of interest are: Hamilton F. Armstrong, "Armistice at Munich," *Foreign Affairs* (January 1939); Arnold J. Toynbee, "A Turning Point in History," *Foreign Affairs* (January 1939); Hubert Ripka, "Czechoslovakia: The Key to the Danube Basin," *Slavonic Review* 17 (1938); Major B. T. Reynolds, "An 'Observing Officer' in Czechoslovakia during the Crisis," *JRUSI* (February 1939). On the post-Munich fallout for Czechoslovakia George Kennan, *From Prague after Munich* (Princeton, 1968), and Theodore Prachazka, "The Delineation of Czechoslovak-German Frontiers after Munich," *Journal of Central European Affairs* 21 (July 1961) are both useful.

Index

Library of Congress Cataloging in Publication Data

Murray, Williamson.
The change in the European balance of power, 1938-1939.

Bibliography: p.   Includes index.
1. Europe—Politics and goverment—1918-1945.
2. Munich Four-Power Agreement (1938).
3. World War, 1939-1945—Causes.
4. Balance of power. I. Title.
D727.M87 1984   940.5'2   83-43085
ISBN 0-691-05413-4 / 0-691-10161-2 (pbk.)

Williamson Murray is Associate Professor of History and
Director of the Military History and Strategic Studies Program
at Ohio State University and has served as
Visiting Professor of Military History at West Point.